ETHNIC STRATIFICATION

ETHNIC STRATIFICATION

A Comparative Approach

TAMOTSU SHIBUTANI
and KIAN M. KWAN

with contributions by
ROBERT H. BILLIGMEIER

THE MACMILLAN COMPANY, NEW YORK
COLLIER–MACMILLAN LIMITED, LONDON

Preface

In a world beset with so much misunderstanding and animosity among ethnic groups a study of the perplexing question of "color" requires no special justification. It must be stated at the outset, however, that this is not a book on "race relations" as a social problem. No ameliorative procedures are proposed; instead, our objective is a better understanding of these phenomena through a comparative study of the contact of peoples throughout the world and in different periods of history. On the basis of a preliminary survey we have attempted to sketch the outlines of a comprehensive theory of inter-ethnic contacts, a set of generalizations that enable us to look at diverse and seemingly unrelated episodes as manifestations of the same recurrent processes. The tragedies that occur have been considered; when these events are viewed in broad perspective, they are no less distressing, but they take on a different significance.

Considerable interest has developed among social scientists in topics such as acculturation, conflict, marginal persons, prejudice, nationalistic movements, segregation, and social change in underdeveloped areas. An extensive literature by specialists in many fields has been accumulating, and we have tried to bring some of this material together into an orderly scheme. Since so few generalizations are well established, the formulation of a theory may appear premature; this is so. We felt, however, that it would be helpful to bring some kind of provisional order into this vast, chaotic field. A theoretical scheme will give direction to research by providing useful concepts and specific hypotheses. Anyone who has attempted a comparative study based upon published reports not originally prepared for this purpose has experienced the frustration that arises when the accounts become mute just at the point where some crucial proposition is to be tested. What falls short of ideal scientific procedure is not thereby useless, as long as its tentative character is clearly understood.

During the early history of any science theory is not adequately supported by evidence. Although the generalizations in this book are not contradicted by any of the data known to the authors, they cannot be regarded as tested. The only attempt at verification made thus far is by *simple enumeration*—the collection of confirmatory cases and a diligent search for negative cases. Although on occasion the results of experimental studies have been cited, most of the data presented are only illustrative. In spite of the uncertainty, however, we have formulated the propositions explicitly, for they cannot otherwise be tested. In a very real sense, then, this book is more a statement of a point of view than a report of research findings. We have attempted to chart a field of study, and many more years of data collection and testing lie ahead. As more facts become known, this theory will no doubt be revised and eventually displaced.

Since ethnic identity lies at the core of the self-conception of so many people, it is not surprising that this subject matter is explosive. Some persons, including many social scientists, find it difficult to contemplate the question dispassionately. The field is filled with misinformation. In spite of overwhelming scientific evidence on the decisive importance of culture, for example, many learned historians dwell at length on the ancestral "stock" of various leaders, as if this had some bearing on their psychological attributes. They are too sophisticated to use the word "race," but the concept is still there. Furthermore, social scientists often take sides in political controversies, and this colors their work. Nationalists insist that all minority peoples should be assimilated; those who advocate cultural pluralism, however, view individuals who assimilate as traitors who are guilty of "self-hatred." Proponents of segregation dismiss anyone who is not convinced of "natural" differences between ethnic groups as hypocrites. To liberal reformers, on the other hand, anyone who even suggests that ethnic groups are different is clearly "prejudiced." It should be emphasized that these are all *political* positions, and those involved in conflict often regard failure to condemn an opponent as an indication of approval. Many social scientists devote considerable effort to supporting or refuting such positions, and they sometimes evaluate generalizations on the basis of desirability rather than evidence. Some intellectuals favoring cultural pluralism, for example, deny that integration is almost invariably the end product of the contact of peoples, in spite of the vast body of historical evidence showing that exceptions are rare. But the task of social scientists is to describe and explain regularities in human behavior and to evaluate generalizations solely in terms of evidence. This means that from time to time it will become necessary to accept propositions that are discomforting, perhaps even repulsive. The authors do not claim complete personal or moral detachment; we believe this to be impossible for human beings. We are convinced, however, that inquiries are more likely to be fruitful when made as dispassionately as possible. Every attempt should be made to regard social processes as the activities of well-meaning human beings, to avoid condemnation, and to guard against the use of intellectual tools as weapons.

This book is addressed to the general reader as well as to undergraduate students in sociology. Although technical terms are defined as they are introduced, some previous training in sociology—at least an introductory course—is presupposed. Any attempt to treat varied events in so many historical contexts as manifestations of a limited number of processes entails working at a high level of abstraction. This means that some oversimplification is inevitable. This shortcoming, it is hoped, can be balanced by the broad perspective gained from such an approach. Furthermore, in any comparative study within the scope of a single volume it is necessary to sacrifice depth for breadth. It would be desirable, therefore, that this book be read in conjunction with several longitudinal case studies. An intimate familiarity with the details of concrete instances of inter-ethnic contact will greatly facilitate the comprehension of principles. Fortunately a large number of descriptive studies is available, and a short annotated list of such accounts has been appended.

Proper names have been the source of special problems. In designating an ethnic group we have tried to use the name preferred by the people themselves. Unfortunately, this has not always been feasible, and we have had to rely on terms in more common usage. We realize that some of these terms are regarded in some circles as epithets. Although the term "native" has no derogatory connotation in most of the world, some persons in former European colonies find it offensive. Furthermore, many of the popular designations are inaccurate. Most "white men" do not have a white complexion, and many "Europeans" in Africa and Asia have never been in Europe. Circumlocutions that would be more accurate are cumbersome, and in a book in which it is necessary to make repeated reference to various ethnic groups some means of easy designation is necessary. It should be understood that in using the terms we have chosen, no derogation is intended. For geographical reference we have adopted the place names in use at the time of the event in question. Thus, what happened in Java in the nineteenth century is recorded as having taken place in the Dutch East Indies rather than in Indonesia. This procedure is necessitated by the fact that the boundaries of current geographical units do not coincide with those of the past.

In a book dealing with thousands of facts documentation becomes a serious problem. Sources must be cited in a field in which there is so much controversy, but we have tried to keep the number of footnotes down to reasonable proportions. Historical facts that are generally accepted, as well as items easily checked in an almanac or encyclopedia, have not been documented. Unless otherwise specified, all references to events that have occurred since World War II have been taken from *The New York Times*. On the other hand, special care has been taken to cite the sources of unusual or controversial matters.

Although the position developed in this book differs in several important respects from that of Robert E. Park, there can be little doubt that we have been heavily influenced by him and his many students—notably, Herbert Blumer, E. Franklin Frazier, Everett C. Hughes, and Louis Wirth. We have tried to build on the basis of their pioneering efforts. The manuscript has benefited from the criticisms and comments of Walter Buckley, Charles J. Erasmus, and Andrée and Gideon Sjoberg, and we are most grateful to them. As is so often the case, we are deeply indebted to our respective wives for the understanding forbearance that made early completion of this project possible.

Tamotsu Shibutani
Kian M. Kwan

September, 1963

contact ——→ competition → accommodation → assimilat

Contents

Part II

DIFFERENTIATING PROCESSES

Part III

SUSTAINING PROCESSES

Part IV

DISJUNCTIVE PROCESSES

Part V

INTEGRATIVE PROCESSES

CONCLUSION

Introduction

CHAPTER 1

The Problem

of Ethnic Differences

On the morning of May 29, 1953, two weary but grinning men thumped one another on the back in joy, for by reaching the summit of Mount Everest they had fulfilled the age-old dream of mountaineers. As they descended, they received the enthusiastic accolades of their colleagues. News of their victory preceded them to the frontier settlements in Nepal, and they were greeted with wild acclaim. Shortly, however, the heroes found themselves in the midst of a bewildering maelstrom, as questions were raised that struck them as irrelevant. Who had set foot on the summit first? Was it a *white* man or a man of *color?* One widespread rumor was that Tenzing, after reaching the top, had hauled up the exhausted Hillary on a rope. The announcement in London that Hillary but not Tenzing would be knighted added to the resentment, and some tactless remarks by the expedition leader about Tenzing's lack of technical knowledge infuriated the proud Nepalese. Fingers were pointed in anger, and in the end even the principals parted in ill will.

This pathetic postscript to one of the most courageous accomplishments of our time is symptomatic of one of the basic concerns of men in the twentieth century and discloses the kinds of categories in terms of which they perceive and evaluate human experiences. Inherited differences among men have long been noticed, but rarely have they assumed the importance they have today. Skin color has become a symbol around which men can be rallied with remarkable ease. Of course, there are other types of cleavages in our society—differences in religious faith, in class, and in national loyalty. But ours is an era in which ethnic differences appear to be assuming greater prominence. Even events unrelated to ethnic identity tend to be interpreted in terms of it. Some have charged, for example, that the atomic bomb was dropped on Japan rather than on Germany because the Japanese were not white, although there is no evidence such considerations even arose among the officials involved in the decision to use the weapon. The importance of understanding inter-ethnic contacts is obvious. How can this subject matter best be studied?

Ethnic Differences and World Politics

The various migrations of peoples across our planet are an important part of history, for they have much to do with the distribution of ethnic groups and social institutions in the world today. These movements create nations, determine the extension of languages and laws, bring wealth to some regions and leave others neglected, and define the routes of commerce. How else can one account for the fact that there are so many similar surnames among Filipinos and Cubans, that Singhalese, spoken in southern Ceylon, is related to Icelandic, or that there are so many "bush" Negroes in Jamaica with Irish names such as Burke, Collins, Kennedy, McCormick, and O'Hare? The distribution of peoples in Europe today rests largely upon the migrations during the declining years of the Roman Empire. The disturbances apparently started in Mongolia, and they had their repercussions westward. In 377 A.D., the Goths were driven across the Danube River into Rome, and there followed a period of widespread unrest from the Caspian Sea to the Atlantic. During this period the Goths, Vandals, Swabians, Burgundians, Franks, Saxons, and Lombards settled in various parts of the disintegrating empire; their descendants still inhabit these areas.[1] Neither the customs of the Basques in the Pyrenees nor the culture evolving in the United States today can be explained apart from such movements.

A great many different things happen on the frontiers of inter-ethnic contact, but what so often attracts attention is the misunderstandings and conflicts. No profound knowledge of history is needed to know something of the injustices perpetrated against strangers who appeared to be of a different breed; the record of colonization is one replete with exploitation. In the United States the settlement of the Western frontier, often depicted in such romantic terms in fiction and in motion pictures, involved the mass slaughter and virtual extermination of various Indian tribes. Even the British colonization of India, one of the more humane cases of military occupation, is full of incidents British historians would like to overlook. In many cases subjugated peoples have enjoyed material advantages as a result of the contact, but they have invariably dwelled upon the indignities. Sometimes people in minority groups have rebelled openly, but in many cases they have had to take out their resentments in disguised form. Equality of opportunity, the right to control their own destinies, the possibility of living with dignity and self-respect—these demands have been made frequently by oppressed peoples.

In all ages there have been compassionate men who have demanded fair play. Invidious distinctions and the exploitation of fellow human beings have long been attacked on humanitarian grounds. Especially among Christians, clergymen and idealists have taken stands against practices such as slavery, even when some of them believed that there were innate differences among men that made some inferior to others. Americans have been especially disturbed over the treatment of Negroes in this country because it is so obviously inconsistent with our avowed democratic faith.[2] What is called "race relations" has long been a problem of concern to moralists and reformers, who have struggled to bring actual practices into line with avowed ideals.

What is happening on the various frontiers of inter-ethnic con-

[1] Cf. James Bryce, "The Migration of the Races of Man Considered Historically," *Annual Report of the Smithsonian Institution, 1893* (Washington, D.C.: Government Printing Office, 1894), pp. 567–88.

[2] Cf. Gunnar Myrdal, *An American Dilemma* (New York: Harper, 1944), pp. 3–80.

tact today is much like what has happened in the past, but recent political developments are forcing many Americans to view these events from a different perspective, one in which the emphasis is placed on expediency rather than on morality. At the turn of the century much of the globe was under European domination. Virtually all of Africa, Southeast Asia, and Oceania had been divided into colonies, and although Australia, Latin America, and the United States enjoyed their political independence, European culture also prevailed in these areas. The ideology of the "white man's burden" was widely accepted, and most Europeans assumed that their ascendancy was to be explained in terms of their innate superiority. Even professional sociologists were inclined to regard the lower status of minority peoples as a manifestation of their natural inferiority.[3] This order was so well established that there seemed to be no possibility of its ever being changed. Everywhere the white man ruled, and others were subservient.

With the development of nationalism various ethnic minorities in Europe and the Middle East became restive and began to call for their independence. A variety of political movements emerged: spokesmen demanded reforms, and terrorists harassed government forces. Some revolutionaries sought the aid of foreign powers, in some cases the traditional foes of their rulers. Some of the smaller minority groups sought protection of their rights through international guarantees. Concentrations of Christians and Jews in the Middle East, for example, were protected by the governments of France and Great Britain. Although such arrangements improved the lot of some of the people, they also aroused the wrath of their neighbors, who looked upon these minorities as potential traitors in time of war. In many cases a policy of repression followed. The massacres in which the Armenian population in Turkey was almost exterminated occurred when the Turks became convinced that these people were the domestic allies of various Christian powers plotting to destroy the Ottoman Empire.[4]

During World War I considerable attention was focused upon minority groups. Various labor and other "liberal" organizations in

[3] Cf. E. Franklin Frazier, "Sociological Theory and Race Relations," *American Sociological Review,* XII (1947), 265–71.

[4] Cf. Max H. Boehm, "National Minorities," *Encyclopedia of the Social Sciences,* Vol. X, pp. 518–25; and Albert H. Hourani, *Minorities in the Arab World* (London: Oxford University Press, 1947).

France, Great Britain, and the United States called for the right of each ethnic group to form its own government. Even before American entry into the war President Wilson had become an outspoken champion of the principle of self-determination, and this ideal was incorporated into the war aims of the Allied Powers. Under the provisions of the Treaties of Versailles and of St. Germaine numerous plebiscites were held, and although the minorities whose interests conflicted with those of the victors were not always given an opportunity to express their views, many areas were ceded, and boundary disputes of long standing were settled. New countries, such as Czechoslovakia and Yugoslavia, emerged, and massive population transfers were arranged in the Balkans in an attempt to create ethnically homogeneous nations.[5] Soviet Russia early announced its support of the principle, although the newly-founded regime did not always follow it in the treatment of its own minorities. Furthermore, although the principle of self-determination was applied only to European minorities, others could not help but learn of it.

The mistreatment of ethnic minorities reached its peak in the persecution of the Jews in Nazi Germany. The Nazi leaders contended that German superiority was inherited through the genes. They blamed most of the difficulties in the country upon the presence of Jews in their midst and advocated a program for the "purification" of German "blood." With the passage of the Nuremberg Laws in 1935, marriage and even extramarital sex relations between Germans and Jews were prohibited. Jews were excluded from restaurants and other public places; they were forced to sell their holdings; they were often not protected from mob violence. Before the downfall of the Third Reich what was termed the "final solution of the Jewish problem" resulted in a program of extermination unique in the annals of human massacres. An estimated 6 million Jews perished in the concentration camps.[6] For those who are not Jewish these may only be statistics, but the reading of accounts such as Anne Frank's *Diary of a Young Girl* can help one begin to appreciate the magnitude of the tragedy.

During World War II the various combatants found it necessary

[5] Cf. C. A. Macartney, *National States and National Minorities* (London: Oxford University Press, 1934).

[6] Cf. Paul Hilberg, *The Destruction of the European Jew* (Chicago: Quadrangle Books, 1961); and Gerald Reitlinger, *The Final Solution* (New York: A. S. Barnes, 1961).

to minimize ethnic differences in their populations in the interests of national unity. The Japanese faced a shortage of manpower, and they stressed the importance of harmony among the Ainu, Koreans, and Japanese; as a consequence many Koreans fought valiantly for the Japanese Empire. In the conquered areas of Southeast Asia they launched the slogan "Asia for the Asiatics," and postwar events attest to its effectiveness even though the Japanese made themselves extremely unpopular. The Russians also emphasized the common interests of their many ethnic groups, and Americans were reminded repeatedly that their country was made up of the descendants of immigrants from all over the world. There was considerable embarrassment when Negro soldiers were forced to use segregated facilities in the South, and anti-Semitic rumors were condemned as enemy-inspired. The extreme racist policy of Nazi Germany made the task of Allied publicists much simpler, for those who made invidious distinctions could be accused of sympathizing with the enemy. Some went so far as to insist that the mere recognition of ethnic differences was akin to treason.

Since the end of World War II the international scene has degenerated into a struggle of rival ideologies. Two major powers have emerged, and the entire globe has been transformed into an arena in which they compete for popular support. Because of the population explosion resulting from the availability of better medical care, well over half the world will probably consist of men of "color," and these people may well hold the balance of power in the cold war. Both the Communists and the supporters of the West have declared themselves in favor of equality; each points with pride to the ease with which different ethnic groups get along at home and publicizes the disturbances in areas controlled by the opposition. Those who are held responsible for any incident that attracts unfavorable publicity are accused of feeding enemy propaganda, and a marked solicitousness is being shown for the well-being of people who in the recent past had been objects of scorn. The whole question of ethnic identity has become a pawn in the contest of ideologies.

The situation is complicated by the fact that a succession of technological developments is breaking down the walls of isolation everywhere. The industrialization of the so-called "underdeveloped areas" is disrupting conventional patterns and creating dislocated minorities, as well as new elite groups. At the same time, the entire world is being converted into a single economic system. Ease of transportation is also facilitating the contact of different peoples. But more than anything else the development of the media of mass communication—radio, newspapers, magazines, books, television, and the motion pictures—have broken down the walls of provincialism, and people in hitherto isolated communities are getting a glimpse of the world beyond their local horizons. The entire civilized world is being transformed into a potential universe of discourse. People who neither look alike nor think alike are being brought together in transactions of all kinds, direct and vicarious. This at once arouses curiosity about strangers and tends to make people sensitive to slights that imply inferiority. News circulates quickly, and on many issues public opinion is formed on a global basis. But the development of efficient communication also facilitates propaganda: even the most trivial incident may be blown up into a *cause célèbre* that can do irreparable damage to the prestige of a powerful nation.

The democratic nations are being challenged at a time of decided disadvantage, for minority groups throughout the world are rebelling against European domination. The Communists are thus far enjoying the initiative, because they are attacking highly unpopular interests and institutions—the brutalities of colonialism, the property rights of village usurers, the exploitative policies of feudal landowners, the indignities of militarism and clericalism, the corruption of inefficient puppet governments. When supporting the old order, we appear to be in favor of retaining poverty, disease, and ignorance, and we sometimes fail to appreciate the extent to which the "white man" has become a symbol for a rejected way of life. This rising tide of hostility is, of course, a transitory phenomenon—a reaction against the European conquests of the past five centuries. Had the cold war been waged during the century after the death of Mohammed, after the Arabs had overrun much of the Eastern Hemisphere, or on the heels of the conquests of Tamerlane's Tartar horsemen, the resentment would no doubt have been focussed elsewhere. Communist China apparently enjoys an advantage simply because the Chinese are not regarded as "white," even though their skin pigmentation does not differ markedly from that of most Europeans.

The people in many ethnic minorities appear to realize that they hold the key to the balance of power. There is growing self-consciousness and pride among those who had once been subjugated, and this is being manifested in the countless nationalistic movements developing throughout the world. The rebellion of the Mau Mau in Kenya, the expulsion of the Dutch from Indonesia, the struggle against the French in Indo-China and in Algeria—all are a part of this tendency. In many parts of Africa common hatred of the white man is the only rallying cry that can unite tribes that had been fighting one another for centuries. American Negroes, who had long been subservient, are now assuming a militant stance; they are fighting back and are demanding immediate reforms. In fact, some ethnic minorities are adopting a racist position of their own.[7] This may result in much unnecessary strife, for the negotiation of reasonable settlements is made more difficult when the leaders are angry men more concerned with vengeance than with justice.

Thus for many Americans the problem of "race relations" is assuming a new significance. Whereas these injustices had once been the concern of members of underprivileged minorities and the reformers who championed their cause, these matters have now been transformed into a political problem of importance even to those who never see anyone different from themselves. In a world that seems perpetually on the brink of disaster, the problem of "color" has become one of the most sensitive of issues. There is a dawning realization that the fate of millions of men and women, perhaps for many centuries to come, may hinge upon the ability of one side or other to meet this age-old problem. What was once regarded as a matter of hurt feelings, conscience, and personal conviction has now become a question of winning the support of strange peoples throughout the world. Of course, humanitarian considerations are still present; there are always men who fight for moral principles, but they are now being joined by others whose concern is primarily practical.

For the first time in human history the extermination of the species is a distinct possibility, and many Americans are searching, sometimes in desperation, for ways to improve the situation. A prodigious effort is now being made to minimize the difficulties arising out of inter-ethnic contacts within our borders. There are hundreds of organizations—civic, fraternal, and religious—each doing what it can toward this end. But the participants are often ambiguous about their specific objectives, and there are numerous disagreements among

[7] Cf. Louis E. Lomax, *The Reluctant African* (New York: Harper, 1960).

them. A variety of programs have been attempted: changing minds through education or propaganda, exposing people to new experiences by providing opportunities for friendly contacts, terminating objectionable practices through litigation. In spite of the sincerity and conscientiousness of those involved in this work, the actual effectiveness of their efforts is still in doubt. Indeed, in some cases those who are trying to put out conflagrations do not know whether the hoses they are using are filled with water or with gasoline.[8] With a growing appreciation of the dangers involved in this delicate situation, more and more people are becoming concerned with the possibilities of instituting reforms that will enable us to present a stronger case for the democratic way of life.

Value Judgments and Social Research

Those who believe that social problems can best be met through intelligent planning are in increasing numbers turning to social scientists for help. Administrators in school systems that are being desegregated, executives and foremen in factories employing a mixed labor force, policemen and probation officers in areas marked by inter-ethnic tension, social workers who deal with minority populations— all need some explanatory scheme that would enable them to interpret events and to understand the situations in which they are involved. Colonial administrators at various levels, who must maintain order and at the same time implement the policies of the mother country, also seek reliable knowledge. At the same time, men with vested interests in perpetuating a system of exploitation are also turning to social scientists in the hopes of finding more effective ways of protecting their ascendance. In spite of this increased demand for generalizations about the contact of peoples, what social scientists have been able to produce thus far has proved disappointing.[9]

The literature relevant to this area of inquiry is quite extensive, however, for a concern over ethnic differences played an important part in the early history of social theory. As explorers and colonists brought back reports of strange people and their odd customs, there

[8] Louis Wirth, "Research in Racial and Cultural Relations," *Proceedings of the American Philosophical Society*, XCII (1948), 381–86.

[9] Cf. Hans L. Zetterberg, *Social Theory and Social Practice* (New York: The Bedminster Press, 1962).

arose among European scholars considerable interest in the significance of such diversity. The task of accounting for what appeared to
be differential rates of development became one of the central problems in the philosophy of history. Two writers who attracted widespread attention by their extreme views were Arthur de Gobineau
and Houston S. Chamberlain, who explained the growth of civilization in terms of innate superiority and advocated racial purity as a
defense against decadence. Views such as these resulted in serious
controversies and subsequently elicited from John Stuart Mill the
remark: "Of all vulgar modes of escaping from the consideration of
the effect of social and moral influences on the human mind, the
most vulgar is that of attributing the diversities of conduct and character to inherent natural differences." In more recent times Arnold
Toynbee and Frederick J. Teggart have contended that it is in the
encounters among ethnic groups that occasions are provided for sudden spurts in the development of culture. Work along similar lines
was done by some of the forerunners of political science. Walter
Bagehot wrote that nations were the product of the contact of peoples, and Ludwig Gumplowicz and Gustav Ratzenhofer accounted
for social stratification and the formation of government in terms of
the conquest and subjugation of peoples. Although much of this work
was speculative, many of the key hypotheses developed by these
writers are still seriously entertained today.

Sociologists have made substantial contributions in this field. In
the United States there has been much interest in immigration, and a
number of studies were made of the manner in which these newcomers and their children have found their way into American life.
Pioneering work was done by W. I. Thomas and Robert E. Park, and
their many students have produced several fine monographs on the
social worlds of various ethnic minorities. Park is one of the few
scholars who have attempted to formulate a comprehensive theory of
inter-ethnic contacts; in fact, his general theory of society appears
to have been developed through investigations in this area.[10] There is
also a large body of literature on Negroes; indeed, one of the most
extensive sociological investigations ever conducted was the study
of Negro life by a team of sociologists under the direction of Gunnar

[10] Robert E. Park, *Race and Culture*, ed. E. C. Hughes, *et al.* (Glencoe, Ill.;
The Free Press, 1950). Cf. Robert E. Park and E. W. Burgess, *Introduction to
the Science of Sociology* (Chicago: University of Chicago Press, 1924).

Myrdal, reported in *An American Dilemma* and its companion volumes. Since World War II there has been a copious outpouring of descriptive and experimental studies on almost every phase of inter-ethnic contacts. Students of social stratification have also taken an interest. Although they are agreed that ethnic identity has something to do with a person's standing in his community, they are disagreed on how to fit their observations into their theoretical schemes. One prominent approach stresses the similarities between the color line in the South and the caste system of India and then delineates class differences within each ethnic group. Sociologists in Europe have also conducted a number of studies, especially of social structures in colonial areas. This material is rich and varied, but much of it is descriptive.

Anthropologists have contributed several types of data. Specialists in anthropometry have developed precise techniques for measuring physical attributes such as the pigmentation of the skin, the texture and color of hair, and the shape of the eyes, nose, skull, and body. These measurements, when used in conjunction with archaeological findings, have been found useful for making inferences about unrecorded migrations in the distant past, but the categories used by anthropologists do not coincide with the "races" recognized in popular discourse. As a result of their detailed studies of traits inherited biologically and those learned from participation in an organized society, anthropologists have long been in the forefront of the assault upon popular misconceptions about the inheritance of mental characteristics. In addition, ethnographers have provided a number of studies on the social organization of various minority groups. They have also studied the fate of tribal people coming into contact with industrial civilization, and these materials dovetail nicely with studies by sociologists of social changes in urban settings. Studies of acculturation, the selective adoption of the culture traits of another group, are increasing in number and in sophistication. Although theoretical work has not been extensive, these studies provide a rich source of data on inter-ethnic contacts all over the world.[11]

During the past few decades an increasing number of psychologists and psychiatrists have concerned themselves with "race preju-

---

[11] Cf. Charles J. Erasmus, *Man Takes Control* (Minneapolis: University of Minnesota Press, 1961); and George M. Foster, *Traditional Cultures and the Impact of Technological Change* (New York: Harper, 1962).

dice," the stubborn and seemingly unreasonable attitudes frequently adopted by people who encounter outsiders. A variety of scales have been developed to measure such attitudes, and thousands of inquiries have been made on how they develop, how they are related to overt behavior, and how they are transformed. There have also been many attempts to delineate some of the typical personality traits of individuals who appear to be more intensely prejudiced than others, and the monumental study by Adorno and his associates, *The Authoritarian Personality*, has provided some provocative leads. Although it has been shown that hostility toward ethnic minorities is more frequently found among those suffering from certain personality disorders, the relevance of this finding to other observations has not yet been established.

There are several other sources from which data may be drawn for the systematic study of inter-ethnic contacts. Demographers studying population growth are investigating the relation between certain types of family structure and differences in reproduction rates. Economists gathering materials on the industrialization of underdeveloped areas are showing how old institutions and elite groups are being replaced by the new. Students of linguistics are gathering data on the formation of dialects on the frontiers of contact, thereby getting a glimpse of how new languages come into existence. Finally, there is available the vast reservoir of historical records. Although sociology originally developed out of the philosophy of history, thus far historical data have barely been tapped.

Much valuable material has been gathered, and many of the facts are interesting, but facts become significant only insofar as they are relevant to general principles. Scientific knowledge consists of a set of interrelated *generalizations* that have been tested empirically. The attempt by Suchman and his associates to summarize the existing knowledge in the social sciences pertinent to the desegregation of schools in the South provides an indication of the strength and weakness of what is available. Most of the generalizations are plausible but untested, and they do not fit together into a coherent scheme.[12] Several theories of limited scope have been formulated, but no comprehensive theory of inter-ethnic contacts has been developed to tie together what must otherwise remain fragmentary and unrelated.

[12] Edward A. Suchman, John P. Dean, and Robin M. Williams, *Desegregation: Some Propositions and Research Suggestions* (New York: Anti-Defamation League of B'nai B'rith, 1958).

But the compilation of reliable knowledge is a painstaking process, and many fear that the patient may die while the research is still under way. In view of the urgency of the problems with which they are confronted, administrators and reformers cannot afford to wait for satisfactory results. They are forced to rely upon "rule of thumb" judgments and to hope for the best; for this reason efforts to improve "race relations" have been of a trial-and-error character, and many programs have been marked by a conspicuous lack of success. Most of these failures do not stem from lack of sincerity or effort; they are the result of inadequate understanding.

Ironically, one of the major barriers to a better comprehension of these phenomena is the indignation of the investigators. Social scientists are human beings, and their emotional reactions to the injustices they see make difficult the cultivation of a detached standpoint. Men who are angry often look for a responsible agent to blame, and this search for culprits often vitiates research. There was a time when other obnoxious phenomena were explained in terms of malevolence; earthquakes and diseases have been attributed to the machinations of personal enemies. Other scientists seem to have overcome the animistic approach, but it still persists in the social sciences. When difficulties are perceived in moral terms, there is a tendency to explain events by imputing vicious motives to those who are held responsible. Furthermore, moral indignation often blinds the student to many facts that would otherwise be obvious. All too often deeds regarded as reprehensible are assumed to be fundamentally different from those that are approved, and the moral dichotomy often prevents one from recognizing that both may be manifestations of the same social process. John Dewey once wrote that the greatest single obstacle to the development of the social sciences was the tendency to approach human problems in terms of moral blame and approbation, and in no field is this more true than in the study of inter-ethnic contacts.[13]

One of the major controversies among intellectuals today is the place of values in scientific research. Although this is an old issue among philosophers, it has assumed particular importance since the explosion of thermonuclear devices has demonstrated the destructive purposes for which knowledge could be used. There have been many heated arguments, and two of the questions being debated are rele-

[13] Cf. John Dewey, *Logic: The Theory of Inquiry* (New York: Henry Holt, 1938), pp. 494-95.

vant to the study of inter-ethnic contacts. One centers on the question of objectivity. Some have argued that values have no place in scientific work. They contend that problems should be selected in a rational manner by locating gaps in the existing body of knowledge and that observations should be made objectively from an impersonal standpoint. On the other hand, others have pointed that all human beings have values, and that to the extent that scientists are human they cannot be completely objective. Recent research on perception suggests that objectivity in observation may be impossible. What any person perceives depends upon the expectations he projects toward the object, and these are formed through participation in organized groups.[14] Objectivity is even more difficult for the social scientist than it is for biologists and physical scientists. One contention, for example, is that a person who is studying segregation is a part of the society in which it occurs. Therefore, he is for it or against it; he is not likely to be indifferent.[15]

There can be little doubt that research problems are usually chosen in terms of value judgments, even though the scientist himself may not be aware of it. The conscientious efforts of microbiologists who are investigating a crippling disease are based upon its being evaluated as undesirable. Economists study business cycles because they dislike depressions, and physicists study nuclear fission in the hopes that inexpensive power can be found to convert the world into a better place to live. Even though the choice of problems rests upon value judgments, however, the investigation itself must be carried out as dispassionately as possible *in order to* solve the problem effectively. That absolute objectivity is not possible does not mean that an investigator should allow his personal preferences to govern his work. A scientist cannot afford to turn his back on facts simply because he does not like them. Many of the facts in inter-ethnic contacts are not pleasant to contemplate, but the student must try to maintain a position of ethical neutrality.[16]

This difficulty is compounded because the problem of "race relations" is one that is defined in a "common sense" universe of discourse.

[14] Cf. Hadley Cantril, *The "Why" of Man's Experience* (New York: Macmillan, 1950); and Kurt Riezler, *Physics and Reality* (New Haven: Yale University Press, 1940).

[15] Nathan W. Ackerman and Marie Jahoda, *Anti-Semitism and Emotional Disorder* (New York: Harper, 1950), pp. 1–2.

[16] Cf. Max Weber, *Methodology of the Social Sciences*, trans. Edward A. Shils and Henry A. Finch (Glencoe, Ill.: The Free Press, 1949).

We encounter at the outset a number of semantic difficulties arising from the uncritical adoption of popular terms, for popular categories, unlike scientific concepts, are not clearly defined. They are not necessarily inaccurate, but they tend to be vague, and in many cases they also contain irrelevant associations and implicit value judgments. Different individuals use the same term in somewhat different ways, and although their meanings may be close enough for purposes of ordinary conversation, difficulties arise when precision is required. For example, everyone feels intuitively that he knows what "happiness" is, but very few can provide an exact definition. Furthermore, value judgments slip in without being noticed; most people assume that happiness is desirable, and the possibility that a particular euphoric state is unattainable except at great cost to one's health may not even occur to them. Terms such as "race," "prejudice," and "discrimination" all refer to popular categories; they are all vague and laden with value judgments. Before a more systematic analysis can be made, a more neutral and technical vocabulary, in which more explicit references can be made, will have to be substituted. An entomologist uses Latin names for genus and species not to confuse the uninitiated, but to make possible designations more precise than "big blue bugs" and "small red bugs." A similar reconceptualization and translation must be made in this field of inquiry.

Two terms that are commonly used in discussions of inter-ethnic contacts are "prejudice" and "discrimination." Although these words may be satisfactory for daily discourse, their use hinders systematic research. In a democratic society both "prejudice" and "discrimination" are condemned on moral grounds. But the making of distinctions of some kind is an essential part of all social life; for example, a gentleman rises when a woman approaches his dinner table, but he may not rise for another man. This is differential treatment, but very few people are likely to find it objectionable. In the American South a white person may decline an invitation to sit down to dinner with a Negro. He would acknowledge making a distinction, but he would insist that he is not discriminating against the Negro, for he does not believe that he is doing anything wrong; he is merely conforming to a custom.[17] "Prejudice" designates an attitude of which the speaker disapproves. When a person avows a prejudice, he is saying that he

17 Percy Black and Ruth D. Atkins, "Conformity versus Prejudice as Exemplified in White-Negro Relations in the South," *Journal of Psychology,* XXX (1950), 109–21.

holds views he cannot justify. Thus, he may feel uncomfortable whenever he encounters a woman who outranks him, although he believes that for competent women not to be promoted would be unfair. The two terms have diverse meanings because different people disapprove of different things; our failure to appreciate whale blubber would no doubt strike many Eskimos as a stupid prejudice. Until these concepts are clearly identified, generalizations cannot be formulated and tested.

Furthermore, the value judgments implied in these concepts result in the formulation of problems in moral terms. Since both words refer to behavior that is condemned, the question naturally follows: What is *wrong* with a person who is prejudiced? Hypotheses also tend to be couched in a vocabulary indicating disapproval. An argument often advanced is that people who are prejudiced are sadistic, unintelligent, or mentally ill, and although it is emotionally gratifying to insist that the people of whom we disapprove are defective or deranged, such accusations do not provide satisfactory explanations of the behavior patterns we want to understand.

Some scholars have raised the question of whether there can be an emotionally neutral vocabulary to refer to human affairs. Jeremy Bentham made a diligent but unsuccessful search for such a vocabulary, and many are inclined to doubt that such a thing is possible. Human speech takes form from its use by cooperating individuals to coordinate their respective efforts. As an adjunct of action it contains many elements of exhortation and threat to guide and elicit desired responses. Thus, most words have good or bad connotations.[18] Nonetheless, we can still avoid such emotion-laden terms as "prejudice" to minimize the temptation to use one's study as a political weapon.

Among those who take an extreme position in this controversy are social scientists who engage in what is frankly labelled as "action research." The objective of such enterprises is not the formulation and testing of generalizations but such practical ends as the admission of some underprivileged family into a housing project or the reduction of tension in some neighborhood. Since the aim is practical, the participants often become more concerned with political tactics than with the truth or falsity of propositions. Although this is not necessarily the case, what often passes for knowledge in such studies con-

---

[18] Cf. Kenneth Burke, *Permanence and Change* (Los Altos, Calif.: Hermes Publications, 1955), pp. 175–78, 188–94.

sists of rationalizations to justify a particular program of action. While social scientists cannot be condemned for being eager to fight injustices, these activities are not likely to produce the kind of accurate generalizations that will enable us to understand the things men do. Effective remedial action must be based upon accurate knowledge, and demonstrated knowledge can be developed only through more objective inquiry. Many studies of inter-ethnic contacts that have been carried out with commendable intentions are in the long run self-defeating. By distracting the attention of social scientists they are hindering the development of the kind of reliable knowledge that may eventually make some kind of effective reform possible. The recognition that social scientists are human beings who cannot avoid value judgments should not be a license to transform research into a moral crusade.[19]

The second pertinent question in the controversy over values is the moral responsibility of scientists for the use made of their work. The successful development of more adequate knowledge will not automatically solve social problems. Knowledge is a source of power, for it facilitates control—a person who understands how something works can manipulate some of the conditions so that the course of events can be redirected to his benefit. But knowledge is ethically neutral. In itself it is neither good nor bad, and it can be used in many ways. Although it is generally used to implement the values accepted in a society, in our pluralistic world men are not always agreed on what ought to be done. Generalizations about inter-ethnic contacts might be used to facilitate exploitation as well as to further the welfare of mankind. Colonial governments may use the generalizations to devise more effective techniques of suppression, just as social reformers may use them to implement their values. Precisely because of the possibilities of exploitation the problem of the development of knowledge cannot be separated from considerations of political power and moral standards.

As human beings all social scientists have value commitments of some sort. Some are very conservative in their outlook; others entertain quite radical beliefs. The fruits of their research possibly may be used to implement policies to which they are unalterably opposed, but all that scientists can do is to provide some of the tools with which

---

[19] Cf. Bruno Bettelheim, "The Victim's Image of the Anti-Semite: The Danger of Stereotyping the Adversary," *Commentary*, **V** (1948), 173-79.

men shape their destiny. We cannot declare a moratorium upon attempts to gain a better comprehension of the world until absolute safeguards have been instituted. There is little doubt that many of the difficulties we now face will be eliminated with increased understanding, and ways may even be found for settling disputes without resorting to violence. The potential utility of a better comprehension of the contact of peoples is too great. Students of human society who favor democratic values can only proceed on the faith that in the long run most men prefer peace to strife and justice to exploitation.

The Comparative Study of Stratification

The aim of social scientists who study the contact of peoples is the formulation of generalizations that can be tested through empirical evidence. But a number of scholars, impressed by the uniqueness of each historical situation, question whether a scientific study of such phenomena is possible. Some historians have argued that while superficial similarities may be noted, these statements are not comparable to the generalizations of the natural sciences, for there are too many exceptions. They argue, furthermore, that such generalizations fail to take into account the distinctive qualities of each event and that in human life what happens at a particular place and time cannot be explained adequately without taking these unique features into account. They insist, therefore, that the further accumulation of accurate descriptions is all that can be expected. The desirability of such studies cannot be denied, for they provide excellent data.

But scientific inquiry rests upon the assumption that there are regularities in the occurrences of nature—that things happen over and over in a sufficiently similar manner to permit the operations to be described in abstract terms. Although there are no two instances of inter-ethnic contact that are exactly alike, an examination of cases throughout the world reveals remarkable resemblances. Segregation is not peculiar to South Africa; it is found at some phase in the history of almost all inter-ethnic contacts. Myths about the alleged dangers of miscegenation are not only widespread, but opposition to intermarriage is usually justified in the same terms. Over and over we find the disintegration of underprivileged minorities into bickering factions as soon as the more ambitious become able to better their lot. Many historical occurrences display sufficient similarity to warrant our treating them as representatives of a class of events. All this suggests that generalizations about the contact of peoples can be formulated. Once such general principles have been established, they may be used to interpret any particular situation.[20]

For example, assimilation is a phenomenon found in all cases of inter-ethnic contacts in which one group does not exterminate the other. In the United States one need only review the history of various immigrant groups—the Irish, the Poles, the Jews, the Italians, the Chinese, the Mexicans—to see the regularity with which many of them have become incorporated into the mainstream of American life. Sociologists have long recognized that assimilation is a mental process, involving a drastic change of perspectives. An immigrant becomes assimilated to the extent that he sees himself from the standpoint of Americans in general. When the transformation is under way, the individual suffers from intense feelings of inferiority. Until he becomes accepted by his new associates and fully integrated, he is forced to live simultaneously in two social worlds and is plagued by doubts and pangs of guilt. Several questions arise. What are the conditions under which people in ethnic minorities become sensitized to the views of outsiders? What is the character of the process through which perspectives are altered? How is the transformation related to the accessibility of communication channels, the individual's position in his primary group, or the criteria of success in his social world? A comparison of the American materials with other records—the experiences of African migrants in Johannesburg, the Jews in Germany a generation after their "emancipation," the Maoris in New Zealand after the termination of their struggle with the English settlers, and the victorious Manchus after their conquest of China —reveals that patterns of human experience, though infinitely varied, repeat themselves over and over in diverse cultural contexts.

Although the approach developed by Park and his students has many shortcomings, it provides an excellent point of departure for an attempt to construct a comprehensive theory of ethnic stratification. The work done thus far suggests that the most promising route is one that is *historical* and *comparative*. Data may be drawn from historical and ethnographic records of the contacts of peoples

[20] Cf. Park and Burgess, *op. cit.*, pp. 1–63; and Frederick J. Teggart, *Theory and Processes of History* (Berkeley: University of California Press, 1941), pp. 141–67.

throughout the world during the past 5,000 years. Such an approach would enable us to minimize the dangers of provincialism, of becoming so narrow in our outlook as to mistake as a generic process something peculiar to a particular place and time. This type of comparative analysis will even facilitate the understanding of a single case, for one can isolate at once the unique features from the general ones. Of course, this does not rule out other kinds of inquiries; data can be drawn from any source, but we shall be in a better position to review these findings in their proper perspective.

Before this comparative analysis of historical data can be made we must establish some of the categories in terms of which events may be classified and examined. Our task in this regard is facilitated by the fact that sociologists have long been concerned with the study of such phenomena and have already developed an extensive vocabulary for dealing with them. We may therefore begin by adopting standard sociological terminology, making subsequent modifications or additions as the need arises. Thus the semantic problem mentioned earlier can be met at least in part by arranging the materials in terms of sociological rather than popular concepts. This reconceptualization will result in an approach considerably different from the usual treatment of "race relations" in much of the social science literature. Several topics formerly thought to be essential to an understanding of the subject will be omitted, and other materials that are rarely included will occupy a central position in the discussion.

A program of research of the kind just outlined, if it is to be carried out systematically, would require the cooperative efforts of hundreds of scholars for a considerable period of time. Indeed, it could never be completed. As life conditions change, new patterns of social interaction evolve. As new perspectives develop, events of the past are reinterpreted, and historical accounts are rewritten to stress events previously overlooked. Satisfactory results will not soon become available, and all we can hope for at present is a preliminary statement indicating the kinds of generalizations to be considered. The hypotheses presented in this book are drawn primarily from sociological theory, although propositions have also been borrowed from the writings of anthropologists, economists, philosophers, political scientists, psychologists, and psychiatrists. These generalizations, of course, cannot be accepted as demonstrated truths; they are as yet only plausible hypotheses to be examined in the light of available evidence. But we should not be discouraged by the inadequacy of our understanding of this subject matter. All fields of inquiry have had seemingly unpromising beginnings. At first, investigators use the language of daily discourse, ask ordinary questions, and formulate answers that sound reasonable even to the untrained layman. Then, with the successive correction of errors, the work becomes progressively more reliable, and more precise and less obvious knowledge is obtained.

This program of study requires the extensive reading of history and ethnography as well as some familiarity with all of the social sciences. An American who is concerned primarily with the difficulties facing him today may very well wonder whether the expenditure of so much effort is really necessary. Precisely because we want to understand what is happening in this country, it is desirable for us to get outside of it, since by seeing things in a broader perspective we can gain a far better comprehension of ourselves. When reviewing events that occurred in central Asia several hundred years ago, we do not feel personally involved; therefore, we do not feel guilty and are less defensive, and this often enables us to see rather obvious factors that might otherwise remain repressed.

The objective of this book, then, is the presentation of a conceptual scheme for the study of inter-ethnic contacts. Attention will be centered upon the kinds of distinctions men make on the basis of traits believed to be inherited. This is what is commonly called the "color line," which, as we shall see, is one of the several forms of social stratification. Although we shall not be able to present the results of a systematic comparative analysis, sufficient data will be provided to give an indication of what can be done. This book, then, is more a statement of a program than a summary of research findings.

Summary and Conclusion

Although inter-ethnic contacts have long been marked by exploitation, the indignities take on a new significance because of recent political developments. Whereas the grievances had once been of concern primarily to moralists and reformers, they are now becoming matters of vital concern to everyone. Practical men searching for rational solutions to the difficulties confronting them are turning to social scientists for a better understanding of these phenomena, but the latter have not yet been able to provide satisfactory explanations. One of the major barriers in the way of developing more reliable knowledge has been the moral indignation of some investigators, which has blinded them to many facts. Additional difficulties of a semantic nature arise from their uncritical adoption of popular concepts with their implicit value judgments. One procedure that might facilitate the institution of more dispassionate inquiries is the comparative analysis of historical data.

Maintaining a position of ethical neutrality does not mean that a student of inter-ethnic contacts is without feeling nor that he is indifferent to injustices. On the contrary, precisely because he does care, he wants to develop more effective knowledge. As Francis Bacon once pointed out, a man who would control nature must first learn to obey nature's laws. Furthermore, this does not mean that a student of the social sciences in his capacity as a private citizen should not protest what he finds objectionable. But when he assumes the role of an investigator, he must strive for Olympian detachment and concentrate upon finding accurate answers to intelligently formulated questions. By maintaining a clear distinction between these two social roles he can most effectively contribute to the implementation of his values.

PART I

Identity and Status

CHAPTER 2

Ethnic Identity
and Social Stratification

In *Gentleman's Agreement*, an imaginative novel by Laura Hobson, a writer tells some of his acquaintances he is Jewish and is astonished at the sudden change in the way in which he and his family are treated. Neither the man nor his son had changed—in appearance nor in conduct. As soon as they are labelled as "Jews," however, they are subjected to a number of humiliating experiences; he is denied admission to places where he had been welcomed before, and his son is taunted as a "stinky kike." Many Jews can testify from their own experiences that this actually happens; the unusual situation described in the novel points clearly to what is otherwise difficult to see—that how a person is treated does not depend so much upon *what he is* as upon the *manner in which he is defined*.

What is it that is ordinarily called the "color line"? Whether one is looking at anti-semitism in Germany, "Jim Crow" practices in the American South, or *apartheid* in South Africa, the one outstanding feature is the distinction made among different kinds of people. Some

[27]

individuals are forced to use separate facilities, not allowed to join exclusive clubs, not permitted to marry outside their group, and required to defer to others. There is no objection to a person in an underprivileged group being married, as long as he marries someone of his own kind. There is no objection to his seeking adequate housing, as long as he does so in areas reserved for his type. There is no objection to his bettering himself by getting a more lucrative job, as long as he remains in fields deemed appropriate for able men of his sort. There is no objection to his children getting the best education they can, as long as they get the type of education believed appropriate for their kind in schools especially established for them. People become upset only when there is a violation of their sense of propriety; the discomforts and protests arise when someone is seen doing something he has no *right* to do. Objections arise when something happens to violate one's conception of the manner in which social relations are supposed to be ordered.

An examination of the situations to which the term "color line" is applied suggests that it is an invisible wall, consisting of a set of common understandings concerning proper conduct. Objections that someone is acting improperly imply a set of norms as to what constitute his rights *vis à vis* other people. There are unwritten rules—and sometimes written ones as well—as to what is appropriate for people of each sort. Therefore, in studying the color line we are concerned with the manner in which human beings are classified and evaluated in a community; in short, we must focus upon the study of *identification* and *social status*. The study of the color line requires an investigation of various forms of social stratification, the ranking of people within a community.

Systems of Social Stratification

Although human communities are not designed according to plan, they are nonetheless organized. There are accepted procedures for earning a living, allocating rights and privileges, incorporating new members into groups, minimizing competition and conflict, and enforcing such regulations. Men are able to cooperate in a variety of transactions in spite of their individual differences and to carry on in an orderly manner because they share common understandings concerning the proper things to do under given circumstances. These shared understandings, fixed in custom and law, are called *conventional norms*, and the totality of these norms constitutes *social structure*—the established patterns of concerted action. The manner in which human beings are classified and ranked is an important part of the structure of any community.

Human beings are classified in all communities. If nothing else, they are distinguished from one another in terms of age, sex, and natural ability. Children, unless they happen to be of royal birth, are not as important as their elders and do not have the same prerogatives. In most societies women are assigned to subordinate positions, and persons of exceptional talent are given additional responsibilities. But beyond this the criteria in terms of which classifications occur differ from one society to another. In some, men are classified in terms of the work they do; in others, they are classified in terms of the history of their families; in still others, they are classified in terms of their religious beliefs. Furthermore, in virtually all communities, regardless of ideologies about equality, the various categories of human beings are placed into some kind of hierarchical order, some being rated as superior to others. Thus, each person may be classified in several ways, but the most important criteria are those that determine his status in the community. Some people enjoy certain rights, immunities, and prestige, and are given special responsibilities by virtue of being classified in a certain way.

When they speak of *social stratification*, sociologists are referring to the ranking of *categories* of people, not the ranking of individuals. Some persons live in comfort while others endure deprivation, not because of their age, sex, or personal qualities, but because of their *social status*. Status refers to one's standing in his community; it consists of a complex network of claims and obligations. In a stratified society the positions are ranked in a hierarchical order, although the basis of differentiation varies from one community to another. In the study of social stratification, then, our interest centers upon the unequal access to goods, services, and pleasures, and those conventional norms concerning what kind of people are to enjoy what is coveted and what kind of people are to be deprived. These strata tend to persist from generation to generation.[1]

[1] Cf. Kurt B. Mayer, *Class and Society* (New York: Doubleday, 1955); Everett C. and Helen M. Hughes, *Where Peoples Meet* (Glencoe, Ill.: The Free Press, 1952), pp. 100–15; and Reinhard Bendix and Seymour M. Lipset (eds.), *Class, Status, and Power* (Glencoe, Ill.: The Free Press, 1953).

Since there are many possible criteria for classification, there are several types of social stratification. One system with which most Americans are familiar—from novels and motion pictures—is the class system that developed in England from the time of the Industrial Revolution. Although the system has changed considerably since the end of World War II, class lines are even today more readily discernible than they are in the United States. In the privileged classes—with their titled aristocracy, their *rentiers*, and others of great wealth—there was a way of life marked by country estates, titles, a distinctive style of speech, and a complex set of customs. The boys attended such public schools as Eton or Harrow and matriculated to Oxford or Cambridge, where they studied the classics rather than more modern subjects. Great stress was placed upon "breeding," and while some had not been born into these circles, the way of life was one that could not easily be acquired in a short time. On the bottom of the scale were the working classes, those engaged in manual labor or routine unskilled work. They are often depicted in stereotyped form, with their Cockney accent, informal modes of dress, and coarse manners. Between these strata came the middle classes—the public servants, the businessmen and managers, the professional people, the independent farmers, the shopkeepers, and the traders. These people also developed a distinct style of life, one that stressed respectability, with a large proportion of their limited income going to the education of their children and for domestic help. The English people were class conscious; most of them recognized and acknowledged superiority and inferiority, associated largely with others of their station in life, and took pride in knowing their "place" and conforming to the expectations of their equals as well as those above and below.[2]

A quite different pattern of ranking is the caste system of India, one of the oldest and most complex forms of social stratification in the world. There are four major strata (*varnas*): the Brahman (priest), the Kshatriya (warrior), the Vaishya (merchant), and the Sudra (servant, laborer, or peasant). Each of these is divided into subcastes, called the *jatis*. No one knows just how many *jatis* there are, but in 1901, when the last attempt was made to count them in the Indian census, there were over 2,300—some with only a few members and

---

[2] Cf. Roy Lewis and Angus Maude, *The English Middle Classes* (London: Phoenix House, 1949).

others with millions. The *jatis* are further subdivided into local units, and these are the most important for social control. Each local unit is like a brotherhood: each has a caste name in terms of which the members can identify themselves, and each has a distinctive way of life. Although there are some exceptions, in most cases each caste has a traditional vocation, and this calling is regarded as its sacred duty. Membership in a caste is hereditary and for life. Since each caste is supposed to be strictly endogamous—that is, the members must marry among themselves—there is no possibility of altering one's inherited rank. Each caste has norms governing its relationships with other castes, rules concerning physical contacts, association on intimate terms, dining together, and eating food prepared by outsiders. There are rituals of purification for those who inadvertently violate these rules. Each local unit has its own government and enforces its own regulations. Since social mobility from one caste to another is impossible, the ambitious can improve their lot only by raising the standing of the entire caste. Brahmans periodically reevaluate the various units, and the prestige of the caste in any locality is closely guarded. At the bottom of the social scale—even below the Sudra—are the outcastes, the "untouchables." These people are traditionally the sweepers, scavengers, tanners, and latrine cleaners. Membership in this category is also hereditary, children being born defiled. The entire system is supported by custom and law and reinforced through a religious ideology. Each person is believed to have all eternity to work out his salvation, and those who perform their duties well in this life are assured of being reincarnated in a more favorable position. During the period of British rule Europeans were superimposed above the entire system. Since India won her independence in 1947, many attempts have been made to modify this rigid system. The new constitution gives rights even to the outcastes; their lot is improving, for their votes are now eagerly sought by politicians. With increasing urbanization and industrialization the caste system is changing somewhat. Especially in large cities, where people are too busy to make such distinctions, Hindus of all castes are beginning to eat in the same restaurants, go to the same movies, and rub shoulders on buses. But in the village communities the same old patterns persist.[3]

[3] Cf. Kingsley Davis, *The Population of India and Pakistan* (Princeton: Princeton University Press, 1951), pp. 162–76; and Govind S. Ghurye, *Caste and Class in India* (Bombay: Popular Book Depot, 1950).

The color line is another form of social stratification, and one of its clearest manifestations is to be found in the Union of South Africa, where the population is divided into categories defined exclusively in terms of ancestry. Approximately 60 per cent of the "Europeans" are descended from the Dutch settlers of three centuries ago and the rest from more recent English colonists. Persons of African ancestry are called "Natives," whether they be Basuto, Bechuana, Zulu, or of some other group. The "Asiatics" are mostly from India, although there are some Chinese and Malayans. The "Coloured" consist of people of acknowledged mixed ancestry, mostly offspring of European and Native unions. Even before the Nationalist Party came to power in 1948, a rigid pattern of separation had been instituted. Approximately half of the Natives lived in *reserves*, areas set aside for them to continue their tribal life. The rest tried to improve their lot by working for Europeans. A large number were farm laborers; others lived in *compounds* operated by gold or diamond mines. Some lived in *locations*, segregated districts in cities, or they were confined to servants' *quarters* in the rear of European homes. They were not free to come and go as they pleased but were required to carry passes; anyone caught without a pass was subject to prosecution as a vagrant. The Natives were limited to the most menial occupations and were not permitted to vote. The Coloureds held a somewhat more favorable position. They could own property, and in Cape Province, if they met certain qualifications, they could exercise the right of franchise. The rules concerning residence were not so rigid for them, and they were able to aspire for more respectable occupations. While the property rights of the Asiatics were restricted, they also enjoyed a more favorable position than the Natives.

Since 1948, however, *apartheid* has become official policy. This represents an effort to magnify ethnic differences and to establish institutions that will preserve the "racial purity" and way of life of the Afrikaners—South Africans of Dutch ancestry. It not only reinforces the patterns of restriction sponsored by previous governments but calls for more complete segregation and the separate development of different ethnic groups. The Asiatics and the Coloureds have been deprived of advantages they once had, and there has been a tightening of the registration and pass laws. Since membership in ethnic categories is hereditary, under these laws there is no possibility of altering one's status. Resistance by the various minority groups has only made the Afrikaners more rigid and determined.[4]

In the United States today one's social status depends upon his position in two coexisting systems of social stratification: class and ethnic. Class position depends to a large extent upon the occupation and income of the head of the household. Where a person lives, the kinds of people with whom he associates on an intimate basis, the kind of education his children receive—all rest largely upon the manner in which he earns a living. Although social mobility may not be as prevalent as we would like to believe, the son of a poor man can attain high rank; the "self-made man" is not uncommon in American life. But Americans are also classified in terms of ethnic identity. The descendants of European immigrants are called "American," a heterogeneous category encompassing the most amazing variety of people. Those who are known to have at least one African ancestor are classified as "Negro," regardless of their appearance or culture. Other common ethnic categories include "Indian," "Jew," "Mexican," and "Oriental." There are marked regional variations in the importance of each of these categories. A Jew encounters many barriers in the large cities of the East and Midwest that he does not meet elsewhere; in the Southwest Mexicans are singled out for differential treatment; and in the South being a Negro is an overriding consideration in determining status to a far greater extent than is true elsewhere in the country. Ethnic identity, in most cases, cannot be changed, but people in minority groups can improve their lot through economic advancement. However, one's ethnic identity, in those areas in which it makes a difference, places a *ceiling* upon the extent to which he can rise.[5]

In any system of social stratification the people in the highest stratum, by interacting primarily among themselves, develop a characteristic style of life. They generally inhabit the most desirable areas in the community—either by tradition or, if the economy is a competitive one, by being the only people who can afford to pay so much for land. In these exclusive areas they have intimate and ex-

[4] Cf. Eugene P. Dvorin, *Racial Separation in South Africa* (Chicago: University of Chicago Press, 1952); and James G. Leyburn, "Urban Natives in South Africa," *American Sociological Review*, IX (1944), 495–502.

[5] Cf. St. Clair Drake and Horace R. Cayton, *Black Metropolis* (New York: Harcourt, Brace, 1945), pp. 214–311.

clusive social access to one another. They are often immune from prosecution for deeds that might result in others' being incarcerated for years; their word of honor is respected in situations in which the testimony of others is not; they are exempted from many burdensome tasks. They have higher incomes, more comfort, and time for diversions of all kinds. In this context they develop a way of living that is not easy to imitate: a mode of speech, consumption patterns, a refined knowledge of the arts, a sophisticated taste in clothing, leisure pursuits, an involved etiquette. Those in privileged groups are usually conscious of their advantages; they enforce conventional norms among themselves, and they teach their children the mode of conduct deemed proper for people in their station. In many cases there is a feeling of *noblesse oblige*, the philosophy that it is the responsibility of those in high positions not to abuse their privileges and to look out for the welfare of those who are less fortunate. These characteristics set these people farther apart from the others; they facilitate making invidious distinctions and add to a sense of exclusiveness.

Those who enjoy high standing are addressed with deference, with ritualized salutations and honorifics. They enjoy precedence in order, and others acquiesce to their having such advantages. But strange as it seems, those who attain high social status are not always accorded greater prestige. For example, in the area along the western end of the Great Wall of China, where Mongols and Chinese have been in contact for centuries, the less privileged Chinese have been the ones who enjoyed higher prestige. Although the boundary shifted back and forth, the Mongols more often held the upper hand, and the Chinese farmers lived at their mercy. Even under Manchu rule the Mongols were granted a number of special privileges to minimize chances of their participation in a rebellion. But the Chinese still regarded the Mongols as an inferior people, and as individual Mongols adopted Chinese customs and approximated the Chinese way of life, they were viewed with more respect. When intermarriage occurred, it was usually between Chinese men and Mongol women.[6] The *evaluation* of an ethnic category in a community, then, is not to be confused with the objective advantages or disadvantages it has in relation to

[6] Owen Lattimore, "Chinese Colonization in Inner Mongolia," *Pioneer Settlement: Cooperative Studies by 26 Authors* (New York: American Geographical Society, 1932), p. 297.

the other categories. Men are not honored because of their inherent characteristics, but only when they are believed to be worthy of honor. What is held to be desirable or excellent varies from community to community, and while people who occupy the highest position are usually the most respected, this is not necessarily the case.[7]

Those who occupy the lowest stratum do not always identify with one another; when they do, however, they also develop a distinctive style of life. The underprivileged in a system of ethnic stratification are usually referred to as *minority groups*. They are not minorities in a numerical sense; especially in colonial areas, the underprivileged natives far outnumber their conquerors. For example, according to the *Statistical Abstract of the Netherlands East Indies*, in 1940 the Europeans represented less than 0.5 per cent of the entire population of the Dutch East Indies but accounted for almost 65 per cent of the total income subject to taxation; the foreign Asiatics made up 2 per cent of the population and made about 25 per cent of the money; and the native Indonesians, who constituted 97.5 per cent of the population, acquired only 13 per cent of the assessable income.[8] Furthermore, ethnic groups are not necessarily minorities; with the exception of a few marginal individuals everyone belongs in some ethnic category—even those who enjoy the highest status. A minority group consists of people of low standing—people who receive unequal treatment and who therefore come to regard themselves as objects of discrimination. They are usually held in low esteem and are often forced to assume roles that make it difficult for them to maintain their self-respect. Not surprisingly, people in the lower classes, outcastes, and ethnic minorities often develop a typical defensive mentality.[9]

In most communities there are people who fall between the highest and the lowest ranks. Most Americans cannot conceive of a society in which the middle ranks are unimportant or nonexistent, for in the United States middle-class people are not only the most numerous but play a significant part in the governing of their respective communities. In Latin America, however, the middle classes are

[7] Cf. Hans Speier, "Honor and Social Structure," *Social Research*, II (1935), 74–97.
[8] Erich H. Jacoby, *Agrarian Unrest in Southeast Asia* (New York: Columbia University Press, 1949), p. 63.
[9] Cf. Louis Wirth, *Community Life and Social Policy*, ed. E. W. Marvick and A. J. Reiss (Chicago: University of Chicago Press, 1956), pp. 237–60.

small and not especially influential. In India there are a large number of merchant and trading castes, whose members are able to lead a respectable and satisfactory life, though not having all of the advantages of the Brahmans. In ethnic stratification too there may be categories standing between the dominant and minority groups. When much of Southeast Asia was under European domination, Chinese and Indian traders and usurers occupied a position between the natives and the colonists. But there are communities in which there is a huge gap in status gradations; the ethnic groups in contact are so different in appearance and culture that they lead separate existences; in such cases it is virtually impossible for anyone to cross the chasm.

What is so important about social status is that each person's life chances depend upon the manner in which he is classified. Each individual finds his niche in life partly by luck and mostly through his personal attributes—those particular skills and qualities that make him what he is. He gets a job, wins honors and recognition, finds a place to live, and attracts a mate—all by utilizing the equipment with which he happens to be endowed. Especially in industrial societies each is encouraged to do the best he can, but his efforts are circumscribed by his status. Some people go through life without doing a day of work; others spend virtually all their time in perpetual drudgery. Even the most able members of minority groups are often limited to subordinate positions.

Social status depends to a large extent upon family connections. Most of the people in each stratum are from families that have occupied the same relative positions through several generations. Even in a class society in which social mobility is encouraged, membership in each rank tends to remain fairly stable. People are born into positions with advantages and disadvantages; the possession of goods, the knowledge of magic formulae, or the chance to get a superior education are often inherited. Several students of class differences have pointed to the importance of the family in lending stability to this type of stratification. Families often come to the aid of those members who are unable to maintain the proper style of life, and those who advance to higher status often discover that their family background constitutes an obstacle to full acceptance in the new circles.[10] In ethnic stratification most people find it difficult to escape their origins,

[10] Cf. Walter Buckley, "Social Stratification and the Functional Theory of Social Differentiation," *American Sociological Review*, XXIII (1958), 369–75.

for they bear with them visible evidence of their ancestry. To be sure, there are some exceptional individuals who are able to overcome all handicaps and to win eminence and respect, but such individuals are rare. Those who avow an egalitarian ideology feel that a person should not be condemned for life when he had no way of choosing his ancestors.

Although systems of ranking may appear to be imposed upon a community by those who benefit from them, in many cases the institutional arrangements are supported even by those who appear to be victims of exploitation. In well-established systems of stratification members of minority groups publicly acknowledge the superiority of persons of higher status and participate in the enforcement of norms that an outside observer might regard as unfair. Mothers in underprivileged groups teach their children to know their "place"; they discourage excessive ambition and train their offspring to live decent and happy lives within the bounds of their station. All stable systems of social stratification rest upon *consensus;* the conventional norms governing the rights and duties of those in each category are taken for granted. Much of what is called "discrimination" is not a manifestation of individual sentiments; certain individuals are accorded differential treatment because they are thought to have different rights.[11] A color line is something existing in the presuppositions of men.

Of course, there are contexts in which the domination of the privileged may be challenged, a situation becoming increasingly common in the twentieth century. When people in minority groups no longer accept their lot in life, the course of events depends largely upon relative *power.* Since those of higher rank usually control superior economic resources, means of violence, and communication channels, they can usually force others to submit and thus insure their ascendancy for a time. But the capacity for coercion is not always in the hands of those who enjoy the greatest advantages or prestige. Much of the resentment against the Chinese in Southeast Asia and against the Jews in Europe and America arises from these minority groups' possessing economic power not commensurate with their standing in the community. Power, then, plays a decisive part in inter-ethnic contacts in the absence of consensus—either when the color line is developing or when it is breaking down. When a social

[11] Cf. Michael P. Banton, *White and Coloured* (New Brunswick, N.J.: Rutgers University Press, 1960), pp. 39-51, 92-113.

system is well established, a display of power by the privileged is not only unnecessary but often appears uncouth. In the study of ethnic stratification, therefore, we must distinguish among (a) *social status*, the standing of a category of people as defined by objective advantages and disadvantages, (b) the prevailing subjective *evaluation* of a category in the community, and (c) the *power* of a given stratum to enforce its demands.[12] In a stable community privilege, prestige, and power tend to go together, but this is not the case when a society is undergoing change.

Ethnic Identity and Social Control

Much of the life of any person is spent in the company of other people; human beings make up the most important part of his environment. What is of decisive importance is that *human beings interact not so much in terms of what they actually are but in terms of the conceptions that they form of themselves and of one another.*[13] As they participate together in group transactions of all kinds, each person tries to anticipate what the others are likely to do, and these expectations facilitate their making cooperative adjustments to each other. To anticipate what someone is likely to do, one must make inferences about his intentions. Successful coordination requires that each participant form certain assumptions about the others; without these presuppositions one has no basis for making the necessary inferences about the probable contributions of his associates.

The conduct of people whom we know intimately is relatively easy to anticipate. We know our friends and acquaintances as distinct personalities, and we are familiar with their idiosyncracies and interests. The better we know someone, the more likely we are to make correct inferences about his intentions; for this reason we feel more secure among those we know well. The vast majority of the people with whom we come into contact in the course of a day, however, we do not know on an intimate basis. This is especially true

---

[12] Although this distinction is similar to the one made by Weber in this discussion of class, status, and power, there is a difference in terminology. Weber used the term "status" to designate the evaluation of a category. Cf. Max Weber, *Essays in Sociology*, trans. & ed. Hans H. Gerth and C. Wright Mills (New York: Oxford University Press, 1946), pp. 180–95.

[13] Cf. Harry S. Sullivan, *The Interpersonal Theory of Psychiatry*, ed. Helen S. Perry and Mary L. Gawel (New York: W. W. Norton, 1953), pp. 117–22, 167–68, 198–219, 236–38.

in large urban communities. Interacting with strangers also requires our being prepared, and one way of making inferences about their motives is through classification. We place people into categories— spinster, policeman, conscientious objector, travelling salesman. We make assumptions about the kinds of interests people in such categories are likely to have in the situation and get ready to deal with them in the appropriate manner. The assumptions made about the category are in some cases unfair to the particular individual; a salesman may be judged unfairly when selfish motives are imputed to him. This procedure, however, seems to be unavoidable in any large community. Except in a small village one cannot possibly treat each individual he encounters as a unique human being, for he has neither the time nor the opportunity to acquire all the pertinent details. In such contexts as these, ethnic categories assume importance.

One of the most common ways in which human beings are classified is in terms of what in daily discourse is called "race." This popular concept is not to be confused with the technical term used by scientists. Anthropologists and geneticists speak of race to refer to a population sharing characteristics known to be inherited genetically. These specialists insist that the major biological types into which mankind is often divided—Caucasoid, Mongoloid, and Negroid— are only convenient statistical categories and that no clear lines of demarcation can be drawn. Ironically, the actual, measurable hereditary differences among human beings are often of little consequence in the affairs of men. People who are genetically alike do not necessarily identify with one another; sometimes they form separate groups and act as if they were different. The differences that are *believed* to exist are what are important.[14]

Long ago W. I. Thomas wrote that what men do depends upon their *definition of the situation*, and one of the most persistent and pervasive popular beliefs is in the special significance of genetic ties. Various modes of thought and action are believed to be inherited from one's ancestors, and blood is regarded as the medium through which these hereditary qualities are transmitted. Expressions like "royal blood" and "flesh and blood" point to the mystical quality attributed to such connections. People who believe they are so related assume that they are alike, that they can understand one another

[14] Robert Redfield, "What We Do Know About Race," *Scientific Monthly*, LVII (1943), 193–201.

in ways others cannot. They feel obligated to act in a special manner toward those who are "blood" relatives. Even when such definitions are demonstrated scientifically to be in error, if the person remains unconvinced, his behavior will continue to rest upon his own version of reality.[15] Today scientists and scholars generally agree that popular beliefs about race are superstitious survivals of an unenlightened past. Modern studies in embryology show that blood is in no way connected with the transmission of hereditary traits. In fact, there is no passage of blood from mother to child, and in many cases members of the same family belong to different blood groups.[16] So long as people continue to believe that categories of human beings who occupy different positions in their status system are genetically different, however, they will continue to act as if this were the case. Even scholars who are familiar with the evidence from anthropological and genetic research sometimes feel intuitively that "blood is thicker than water."

Since our interest centers upon behavior patterns that are predicated upon popular concepts, we must recognize and label them. To avoid confusion with the scientific concept of race we shall use another term altogether. Some social scientists have tried to overcome this difficulty by substituting the expression "race, religion, and national origin," but this is both clumsy and inaccurate. What is needed is a technical term to designate the popular distinctions without accepting the false beliefs upon which they rest. Ideally suited for this purpose is the term *ethnic*, which corresponds roughly to what German scholars mean by *Volk*; the term is used by anthropologists to refer to a "people." An ethnic group consists of people who conceive of themselves as being of a kind. They are united by emotional bonds and concerned with the preservation of their type. With very few exceptions they speak the same language, or their speech is at least intelligible to each other, and they share a common cultural heritage. Since those who form such units are usually endogamous, they tend to look alike. Far more important, however, is their *belief* that they

---

[15] William I. Thomas and Florian Znaniecki, *The Polish Peasant in Europe and America* (New York: Alfred A. Knopf, 1927), Vol. II, pp. 1846–49.

[16] Cf. Theodosius Dobzhansky, "The Genetic Nature of the Differences Among Men," in Stow Persons (ed.), *Evolutionary Thought in America* (New Haven: Yale University Press, 1950), pp. 86–155; Leslie C. Dunn and T. Dobzhansky, *Heredity, Race, and Society* (New York: New American Library, 1952); and M. F. Ashley Montagu, "The Myth of Blood," *Psychiatry*, **VI** (1943), 15–19.

are of common descent, a belief usually supported by myths or a partly fictitious history. A people do not necessarily constitute a nation; although men who regard themselves as being of a kind tend to move in that direction, they are not necessarily united under a single government.[17] In common parlance, when one speaks of a "French race," a "Jewish race," or a "Turkish race," the word "race" is being used in this manner.

The manner in which a person identifies himself, regardless of the accuracy of his beliefs, is a matter of crucial importance, for what he does or does not do depends largely upon his conception of himself.[18] A man who regards himself as an inferior object is apologetic about thrusting himself into the company of others, hesitant about pushing his demands, and defers to the judgment of others; his brother, who regards himself as brilliant, acts in quite different ways in the same contexts. When a person classifies himself within some ethnic category, he assumes that he is endowed with those attributes in terms of which the category is defined. Even if he himself does not feel the endowed traits, he often believes he should. Many Americans born of immigrant parents believe, for example, that they should know something about the "old country"; many of them even send their own children to a foreign language school to learn what to the youngsters is an alien tongue, believing that it would be shameful for the children not to know something about their forebears and their traditions. A man who learns for the first time in middle age that his parents were Jews who had become assimilated into the Gentile community may suddenly feel obligated to find out something about the history of the Jews. Even if he does not reach this point, he would certainly be more offended by anti-Semitic remarks than he had been in the past. There is no change in his biological make-up, but his behavior patterns are somewhat altered by virtue of his new identification. This mystical belief in the importance of biological ties persists even in the face of extensive evidence that cultural characteristics are unrelated to heredity.

People who are placed into an ethnic category by outsiders do not always acknowledge being alike. In colonial Africa, for example,

[17] Cf. E. K. Francis, "The Nature of the Ethnic Group," *American Journal of Sociology*, **LII** (1947), 393–400.

[18] Cf. Nelson N. Foote, "Identification as the Basis for a Theory of Motivation," *American Sociological Review*, **XVI** (1951), 14–21; and Anselm L. Strauss, *Mirrors and Masks: The Search for Identity* (Glencoe, Ill.: The Free Press, 1959).

all natives were treated alike, but they certainly did not conceive of themselves as being of a kind. They had deeply-rooted tribal affiliations, and conflicts among their ancestors reached back far beyond the arrival of the first white man. When those who are classified together do conceive of themselves as being alike, however, there develops among them a "consciousness of kind," which plays a decisive part in their lives. This feeling of unity arises from a perception of resemblances among themselves and differences from outsiders. Any readily visible means of identification—similarity of physical attributes, distinctive modes of dress, or a common language—certainly facilitates the development of such awareness.[19]

The internal cohesiveness of a group and its ability to act as a unit in competition with other groups depends to a large extent upon the degree to which the members are aware of their identity. This conviction that they are fundamentally alike enables people in some ethnic categories to become cohesive groups and to engage in effective concerted action. Men more easily believe they are alike when they think they are descended from the same ancestors. Inherited attributes in themselves may not be important, for consciousness of kind may rest more upon a common culture. But what is presumed to be inherited is of decisive importance.[20]

Consciousness of kind involves some sort of sympathetic identification with others in the same category. The assumption is that the inner experiences and emotional reactions of people like oneself would be similar to one's own. There are varying degrees of understanding and intimacy that characterize all relationships among human beings, and sociologists use the concept of *social distance* to designate this variable. Social distance does not refer to linear distance but to the subjective sense of nearness felt to certain individuals. The concept is based upon popular usage. We refer to a particular mother and child as being "close" to each other and to someone who maintains his reserve at all times as being a "distant" person. When social distance is low, people can enter imaginatively into one another's minds and share their experiences; they are able to sympathize with one another's pains, joys, sorrows, hopes, and fears. Those who feel close to each other are more relaxed and tend to be less defensive,

[19] Cf. Franklin H. Giddings, *Inductive Sociology* (New York: Macmillan, 1901), pp. 91–110.

[20] Park, *op. cit.*, pp. 81–116. Cf. Ernst M. Manasse, "Max Weber on Race," *Social Research*, **XIV** (1947), 191–221.

for each feels that he can understand those around him. He feels "at home," that he "belongs" in this company. This kind of intimacy may be blocked by self-consciousness. When social distance is high, the other individual is seen as a representative of a different category. We feel apprehensive before a creature unlike ourselves, for we are not sure of what he will do. Even after long acquaintance there remains a residue of uncertainty—a vague apprehension, especially if the stranger maintains his reserve. In speaking of social distance, then, we are referring to the psychological barriers that facilitate or deter easy, spontaneous interaction.[21] Of course, not all people placed in the same ethnic category can relax in one another's company, but they can more easily do so when they can assume a fundamental similarity.

Those who develop consciousness of kind also become convinced that outsiders are basically different from themselves. This is a matter of decisive importance, for if outsiders are different kinds of creatures, obviously they should be treated differently. The contrast shows up most clearly in moral codes. All human beings recognize and usually live up to moral obligations to the people with whom they identify. One is expected to deal honestly with others of his kind; should he fail to do so, he is regarded as a despicable individual. When a person fails to honor the claims of someone with whom he identifies, he can readily anticipate the other's chagrin; therefore, he is struck by pangs of guilt. But there is no similar sense of obligation to outsiders. They may be treated decently, just as any human being might be, but this is more often a gift than an obligation. In some cases, one may even take pride in his ability to deceive and exploit strangers. Tourists often encounter "friendly natives" who manage to separate them from their money through all kinds of guile. Victimizing an outsider in this manner seldom arouses guilt feelings.

For a person who identifies with an ethnic category, its history provides a backdrop before which to review his own conduct. The history of any group consists of those collective memories shared by its members of the glorious deeds of their forebears, of their unfair persecution, and of the decisive events that resulted in its present situation. This historical past often includes fictitious accounts, but the way in which the history of a group is remembered is far more important than what it has actually been. Those who identify can conceive of themselves as a part of something larger than themselves,

21 Cf. Park, *op. cit.*, pp. 256–60.

something of far greater importance. For example, many an American Jew, including those who were not ardent supporters of Zionism, have come away from a visit to Israel with a different perspective. Visiting the places they had read about in the Old Testament, they are reminded of the words of the prophets and of the centuries of suffering during the diaspora. They feel themselves a part of this panorama of history, an enormous transaction stretched out over centuries in which destiny is on their side. They feel an inner sense of pride at being Jews. A person who sees himself as a participant in such a magnificent scheme is able to view his own life, his misfortunes and his progress, in a new light.

Most important, the other people with whom one identifies become his most important reference group. In the drama of life, as on the stage, each person performs for some kind of *audience*. There are certain individuals whose opinions are most important, and a *reference group* consists of those people whose perspective is used as the frame of reference in perceiving the world.[22] When there is consciousness of kind, one's quest for recognition is confined largely within the group; the ethnic group becomes an effective agency of social control. For example, a Mexican *bracero* working in the United States daydreams of the reactions of his friends and relatives in his village in Mexico, of the joys they will share upon his return, and of the tales he will relate of his adventures. He cares little of the opinions of the "Gringo" with whom he must deal while north of the border, and their disapproval would hardly prevent him from purchasing gifts that he thinks will be appreciated at home. Thus, people who locate themselves within an ethnic category feel obligated to conform to the culture of their group, to pursue its values, and to show the other members that they are decent human beings. A man's conception of himself is subject to the confirmation of other people, especially of those who are like himself. The extent to which a person feels constrained to comply depends upon the degree to which he identifies; the more intense his identification, the more likely he will act exclusively for a limited audience.

Since lines of demarcation between peoples can be drawn on the basis of any criterion believed to be inherited, popular classifications vary considerably from one area to another. Most Americans are

[22] T. Shibutani, *Society and Personality* (Englewood Cliffs, N.J.: Prentice–Hall, 1961), pp. 249–80.

accustomed to thinking in terms of categories such as "Negro" and "White"; we take it for granted that these are the natural divisions of mankind and that facial characteristics and skin color are reliable criteria everywhere. But in communities of the Middle East skin color is relatively unimportant; pigmentation is not a good index for differentiating among Arabs, Armenians, Assyrians, Bedouins, Jews, Kurds, and Turks. Language, religious observances, and food habits are some of the bases of a more positive identification. People who may actually have very few ancestors in common may develop a consciousness of kind; this is especially likely in situations in which there is another category of even more different people who stand in contrast to them. This was the case for American settlers facing hostile Indians; the pioneers were descended from various ethnic groups in Europe who had fought one another for centuries, but they readily united as "white men" to fight against "red men." Even a superficial knowledge of history and genetics reveals that all American Negroes are not descended from the same set of ancestors. Many Negroes have more forebears from Europe than from Africa, as is apparent from their numerous Caucasoid features. All this suggests that real physical or cultural differences between different ethnic categories are not nearly as important as the fact that the people in a community *think* they are different. Classifications of human beings are matters of social usage.

A dramatic illustration of the different ways in which similar human beings can be classified is provided by the sharp contrast between the areas north and south of the Rio Grande River. The entire Western Hemisphere was inhabited by Indians until the sixteenth century, when Europeans crossed uncharted seas to penetrate the wilderness for economic gain, overcame and dispossessed the Indians, imported slaves from Africa, developed national consciousness, and established independent republics. There were, of course, some differences. The area that is now the United States and Canada was settled largely by Protestants from northern Europe, most of whom had intentions of building permanent homes. The settlers came in large numbers, encountered empty country sparsely inhabited by nomads, and as the competition for land became intense, virtually exterminated the Indians. In contrast, Latin America was settled by Catholics from southern Europe, who were accompanied by priests intent upon converting the Indians to Christianity. The Spaniards did not come in such large numbers; they encountered established agricultural people who were numerically superior and subjugated them. There has been far greater intermingling in Latin America, although the people in Argentina, Chile, Costa Rica, Santo Domingo, and Uruguay are still predominantly European in culture and appearance.[23]

In contrast to the United States, "Negro" is not a significant ethnic category in much of Latin America. In Mexico, from the sixteenth to the eighteenth century, the population was stratified into the Gachupine (European-born Spaniard), Criollo (Mexican of Spanish ancestry), Mestizo (mixed ancestry), and Indio (Indian). Although these distinctions were outlawed in 1820, when Mexican independence was achieved, the last three categories still persist. Some 135,000 African slaves were brought into Mexico, but they have disappeared into the general population. The Mestizo dominate Mexican life today, especially in the cities, where European culture prevails. But Mexico is predominantly a country of villages, and here the culture of the Indian prevails. Although some sensitivity exists about darker skin color, Indio is a category primarily defined in terms of a way of life. An Indio is a person who speaks an Indian language, wears *huaraches* (sandals) and Indian costume, lives in a *jacal* (hut), maintains low standards of sanitation, and has little knowledge of the outside world. It is estimated that there are approximately 5 million people whose outlook is Indian. Although a person of dark complexion is looked down upon only if he lives like an Indian, he cannot easily escape this category. Thus, north of the Rio Grande, people who are culturally alike are separated on the basis of physical appearance, and south of the river people who are more alike physically are distinguished on the basis of cultural differences.[24]

Ethnic categories are significant bases for stratification because people believe them to be the natural divisions of mankind. Since the lines of demarcation are so arbitrary, the question arises whether ethnic groups are subjective or objective phenomena. There has been considerable controversy over the same question among students of

[23] Cf. Ralph L. Beals, "Social Stratification in Latin America," *American Journal of Sociology*, LVIII (1953), 327–39; and Ernest H. Gruening, *Mexico and Its Heritage* (New York: Century, 1928), p. 3.

[24] Cf. Clarence H. Haring, *The Spanish Empire in America* (New York: Oxford University Press, 1947), pp. 213–21, 260–61; Frank Tannenbaum, *Mexico: The Struggle for Peace and Bread* (New York: Alfred A. Knopf, 1950), pp. 9–19; and Nathan L. Whetten, *Rural Mexico* (Chicago: University of Chicago Press, 1948), pp. 50–63, 355–71.

class stratification.[25] Ethnic categories are subjective in that they exist only in the minds of men, but they are *not* subjective in the sense that a person can imagine himself to be whatever he wishes. The categories are objective in that they are well-established beliefs held in common by a great many people, and they are objective in that they exist independently of the desires of any particular individual. The classification of people in any community is a matter of consensus, and as far as any given individual is concerned, it is a part of the external world to which he must adjust.

Thus, *an ethnic group consists of those who conceive of themselves as being alike by virtue of their common ancestry, real or fictitious, and who are so regarded by others.*[26] The utility of this definition can be seen in considering the Jews. The Jews are often called a "race," but the variety of physical characteristics found among them reveals that they are thoroughly mixed in ancestry. Studies show that Jews resemble in appearance the people among whom they have settled, and this is brought out clearly by the bewildering diversity of cultural and physical traits found among the immigrants to Israel, all of whom claim to be Jews.[27] Jews are also regarded as a religious group; but there are many schisms within Judaism, and many Jews are atheists. The Jews, then, are people who conceive of themselves as descendants of common ancestors and are so identified by others. Those who live in segregated colonies tend to develop common cultural characteristics; special values and a distinctive outlook develop and are manifested in behavior patterns that are sometimes mistaken for inherited traits. But Jewish colonies are scattered throughout the world, and in each a somewhat different culture has developed. Furthermore, many Jews are assimilated into the life of the larger communities of which they are a part and are physically and culturally indistinguishable from Gentiles.[28] If they

[25] Cf. Richard Centers, *The Psychology of Social Classes* (Princeton: Princeton University Press, 1949), pp. 26–29; and Seymour M. Lipset and Reinhard Bendix, "Social Status and Social Structure," *British Journal of Sociology*, II (1951), 150–58.

[26] Cf. Hughes and Hughes, *op. cit.*, pp. 100–29.

[27] Maurice Fishberg, *The Jews: A Study of Race and Environment* (New York: Scribner's, 1911), pp. 21–178; Raphael Patai, *Israel Between East and West* (Philadelphia: Jewish Publication Society of America, 1953); and Harry L. Shapiro, *The Jewish People: A Biological History* (Paris: UNESCO, 1960).

[28] Cf. Joseph Bram, "The Social Identity of the Jews," *Transactions of the New York Academy of Science*, VI (1944), 194–99; and Louis Wirth, *The Ghetto* (Chicago: University of Chicago Press, 1928), pp. 63–96.

are questioned about it, they would acknowledge that some of their forebears had been classified as Jews. Some people become conscious of themselves as Jews only when they encounter anti-Semitism. Unless outsiders continue to insist that such people are Jews, they would probably disappear into the surrounding population—as so many have in the past centuries. What is crucial, then, is the manner in which a person is identified.

The expectations with which human beings approach one another rest upon the manner in which they classify each other. Rights and obligations depend upon identification. The manner in which categories affect conduct is revealed in the hostility of many people toward a wealthy woman who treats her pet dog with more consideration than she does people she encounters on the street. But if someone is a stranger to her, why should she be concerned with his welfare? The dog is unquestionably a source of considerable gratification to her, and her concern with it is quite understandable. But most people would expect the woman to sacrifice her pet to save the life of another human being. Why? Would such an expectation be reasonable if human beings did not identify with one another as a kind, in contrast to dogs and other animals? In the same manner ethnic identity enters into a multitude of transactions. In the study of ethnic stratification we are concerned with the typical forms of social interaction among people who are conscious of differences that they believe they have inherited.

Variations in Ethnic Stratification

All systems of ethnic stratification have certain properties in common: human beings are divided into categories in terms of their presumed ancestry, and the categories are placed into a hierarchical order. But there are many local variations, for the social structure of each community is the product of its peculiar history. When dealing with phenomena that are so complex and seemingly so irregular, one fruitful point of departure is the identification of some of the dimensions along which the variations occur.

Systems of ethnic stratification differ in complexity and in the magnitude of the distinctions made. In some communities there is a high degree of specialization and a multiplicity of gradations. The social system is so complicated that a large number of positions are delineated, and there are complex procedures through which various individuals are channeled into each. The extent of the social distance maintained between the strata also varies. In some communities the distinctions are obvious; in others, the differences are quite subtle and only intuitively felt. In some cases the differences are openly manifested only in crisis situations. Sometimes one ethnic group is acknowledged by everyone to be dominant, all others being clearly subordinate, but in other cases the minorities are regarded as only slightly inferior.

A second dimension along which variations can be found is the degree of clarity of the distinction between categories, the extent to which the groups in contact actually differ from one another— physically and culturally. Early in the history of the contact of two or more ethnic groups the contrast is usually very great. In colonial areas, for example, the conqueror and conquered are so different in appearance that there is no doubt of who belongs to which category. After prolonged contact, however, the differences usually become negligible or nonexistent. Even after people become indistinguishable, however, they may continue to conceive of themselves as different and maintain the traditional patterns of separation. The Irish and the English cannot be distinguished in terms of physical characteristics, nor can the Flemish from the Walloon in Belgium. Even anthropologists have difficulty in distinguishing among the Chinese, the Japanese, and the Koreans. Even though the people in such ethnic groups look alike, they do not think nor act alike.

There are also varying degrees of similarity in the cultures of groups in contact. Again, the differences are most noticeable during the early phases of contact, but they may remain different for centuries. In European colonial expansion the white man not only dressed differently, ate different food, used a highly mechanized technology, and killed with firearms, but he also brought in strange conceptions of government, a different orientation toward God, and even some peculiar ideas about race. The most profound differences among peoples are probably cultural, for those who are culturally different do not perceive their common environment in the same manner. Cultural differences are differences in presuppositions, and men are usually not even aware of the things that they take for granted. But when people live side by side for a long period of time, they usually learn to appreciate something of one another's perspectives and become more and more alike. It would be difficult to find any group in the United States that is culturally more American than the Negroes. Even when people share a common culture, however, they may remain convinced of their differences and retain their conventional social distance.

Whatever differences that do exist play an important part in the preservation of the color line. Sociologists speak of readily discernible differences as the "visibility" of minority groups. Whenever underprivileged people attempt to improve their lot, the extent to which they succeed often depends upon the degree to which they no longer stand out. Cultural traits can be altered through effort, although this is usually much more difficult than most people realize. Where physical differences are negligible or are considered unimportant, a person may in some societies alter his ethnic identity by acquiring a new culture. A French-Canadian can learn to speak fluent English, give up his Catholic faith, and change his name. In Latin America an Indian can raise his status by giving up his native costume, learning Spanish, and altering some of his living habits. In all such cases, of course, the person would have to move to another community, preferably to a large city, where the details of his genealogy are not likely to become known. But when one carries a visible stigma that cannot be removed, such as skin color, he is confronted by an insuperable obstacle. What makes men so preoccupied with inherited attributes is that they may become highly visible symbols that cannot be escaped or changed.

A third dimension is the degree of social solidarity that develops in the strata. There may be considerable variation in the extent to which the groups involved in a stratified social system attain consciousness of kind. Usually the group that is numerically smaller—a colony of immigrants in a large country or a colonial elite outnumbered by natives—is more conscious of itself. An ethnic group that is widely dispersed—as the Gypsies or the Jews—may be acutely conscious of itself in one situation and not in another; consciousness of kind is often accentuated by external hostility. There are cases in which people who are placed in an ethnic category may refuse to identify with one another, making all kinds of distinctions among themselves, as in the case of the Indians on the American frontier. In some cases there are specific organizations to promote group interests; in other cases the categories remain unorganized. Such differences are important, for the capacity of any category of people to mobilize for collective action depends upon their sense of identity. There can be no revolt as long as people of minority status distrust one another. Similarly, there can be no concerted defense of a system of stratification if those occupying positions of privilege despise one another and are unwilling to sacrifice for their common good. This suggests that in speaking of ethnic groups the term "group" is being used loosely, for there are many cases in which people who make up an ethnic category do not constitute a *group* in the sociological sense. Those so labelled may possess certain common characteristics, in contrast to other people, but they are not likely to engage in concerted action unless they develop consciousness of kind.

Another important dimension is the extent to which social mobility is possible. *Social mobility* refers to a change of status, as in the advancement of a boy born in an underprivileged category to a position of eminence. Movement from one position to another is usually through personal achievement or failure and sometimes through marriage. Since there are bound to be gifted and ambitious people in underprivileged strata and incompetent people in the privileged, tensions inevitably will arise unless some provisions exist for adjusting the disproportion in rewards. Hence, the ease with which mobility can occur is to some extent a measure of the flexibility of a system. But in ethnic stratification upward social mobility is usually more difficult than in class stratification. A successful person may acquire the culture of the dominant group, but he may still carry with him the physical marks of his ancestry. In some cases there are special procedures for the provisional acceptance—as "exceptions"—of individuals who have unusual talent. The barriers are partially relaxed, and a few individuals are able to gain some measure of self-respect, but the status of others in the minority group remains unchanged.

In most systems of ethnic stratification social mobility is difficult; in some, it is almost impossible. In Egypt during the Hellenic era ethnic categories were defined in terms of cultural differences that could not easily be acquired in a single generation. A Greek was a person whose speech was intelligible to other Greeks, and "barbarians" were jabberers. While there were some feelings of common origin in the fourth and fifth century B.C., the recognized differences were not impassable chasms; the Greeks claimed superiority and were granted certain privileges, but the category was not absolutely closed to those who had non-Greek ancestors in the distant past.[29] On the other hand, there are societies in which barriers to social mobility are almost impenetrable. Until the end of World War II the Japanese government maintained a system of registration in which the genealogy of each individual was open to public inspection. Thus, even after living in Japan for several generations, Koreans who had become physically and culturally indistinguishable could not marry into a Japanese family without revealing their ancestry. An even more rigid system of registration and control is now in operation in the Union of South Africa.

Since the significant differences among ethnic groups are thought to be inherited, people who wish to preserve the color line obviously would be opposed to offspring of mixed parentage, legitimate or illegitimate. But whenever people in different ethnic groups come together, some miscegenation almost invariably takes place. Sometimes the offspring are placed in the minority category, as in the United States; sometimes they are acknowledged by parents of the dominant group, as in Brazil; and sometimes they are put into a new category, as in the case of Eurasians in the cities of Asia. To minimize such problems the prohibition of intermarriage is a barrier that is found almost everywhere, but the intensity of the opposition varies from a rigid prohibition to mild disapproval. In Mexico, for example, there may be some hesitation about marrying a person of darker skin, but there is no serious opposition to such matches if the principals insist.

Although all systems of ethnic stratification rest upon popular beliefs about inherited traits, there are differences in the extent to which strict biological lineage is emphasized in the ideology used to support and justify the practices. This constitutes a fifth important dimension. In some cases, as in South Africa or in Japan, "blood" is a final and irrevocable criterion. The dominant group believes that those who have inherited the proper genes are destined to rule. But there are other communities in which such views are ridiculed or condemned. Sometimes there are only vague feelings of common origin and responsibility, especially in periods of great danger, but

[29] Simon Davis, *Race Relations in Ancient Egypt* (New York: Philosophical Library, 1952), pp. 1–2. Cf. Theodore J. Haarhoff, *The Stranger at the Gate* (Boston: Beacon Press, 1951), pp. 51–59.

otherwise little attention is paid to ancestry as such. In Brazil the national ideology is one that places a high value upon mixture, although in actual practice there is considerable sensitivity about skin color. In New Zealand much publicity is given to the amicable relations between the Maori and the European settlers; many distinctions are actually made, but the people who make them are forced to assume a defensive stance. Among Americans who are not in any of the more visible minorities, ancestry is for most purposes an irrelevant consideration.

Most important of all, systems of ethnic stratification vary considerably in the extent to which they are institutionalized. When they are well established, the common understandings defining the categories and their relative standing are taken for granted; no one questions their propriety. When physical and cultural differences are obvious, there is little doubt about where the lines of demarcation are to be drawn. Marginal individuals, such as the children of mixed parentage and persons of exceptional ability, have their special "places." The traditional practices are not only accepted by all parties as morally justified; they are upheld even by those who suffer from them. Before the Civil War in the United States, for example, many of the slaves in the South not only accepted their treatment but felt ill at ease in the presence of a Yankee who did not observe the color line. When confronted by people who did not know the proper way to address them, the slaves did not know just what to expect.[30] In a stable society minority peoples acknowledge their inferiority, accept the grounds upon which the dominant group claims ascendancy, and are resigned to their fate as subordinate participants in a moral order.

When a system of ethnic stratification is undergoing change, however, there is no such consensus. There are many disagreements concerning the proper classification of people. Is a Sudeten German a German or a Czech? Is there a difference between a Mexican and a Spanish-American? Those who have studied ethnic differentiation in Bangkok, Thailand, point out, for example, that the cleavages are more analytic distinctions introduced by observers than deeply-felt divisions which the residents make in ordering their lives. Although the people would not necessarily disagree with such a picture of their

[30] Cf. Bertram W. Doyle, *The Etiquette of Race Relations in the South* (Chicago: University of Chicago Press, 1937), pp. 68–80.

society, the lines of demarcation suggest a structure that is more rigid than the situation warrants.[31] Sometimes the lines become so blurred that legal definition becomes necessary. In Nazi Germany the Jews had become so much like other Germans that they could not be set apart; to decide which persons would be subject to restrictive legislation, therefore, the category had to be defined in the Nuremberg Laws. When a system is undergoing change, there is considerable public discussion of ranking procedures, and some people openly flout conventions. What individuals admit in public is sometimes a flat contradiction of what they practice in private. Minority groups, especially those that are becoming assimilated to the way of life of their rulers, disagree with the low estimate placed upon them, feel resentful, and make various efforts to raise their status. They are frequently joined by reformers of the dominant group who champion their cause. In a changing society people interact on the basis of different assumptions; therefore, there is bound to be some misunderstanding and tension.

Summary and Conclusion

What is commonly called "race relations" does not consist of relationships among men who are genetically different. The study of this subject matter has been rendered especially difficult by a number of irrelevant associations, especially the emphasis upon skin color. A more fruitful inquiry may be launched by recognizing that the color line is one of several forms of social stratification. In every community there are conventional understandings concerning the divisions of mankind, and there are customary procedures governing their social interaction. What is important is that under certain conditions the people who are classified together come to conceive of themselves as being of a kind, and this mutual identification places them under special obligations to one another. Our subject matter consists of the recurrent patterns of interaction among men who believe they are fundamentally different by virtue of heredity. These beliefs have been repeatedly demonstrated by scientists to be false, but men act on the basis of their own interpretations of reality.

[31] Cf. G. W. Skinner, *Leadership and Power in the Chinese Community of Thailand* (Ithaca, N.Y.: Cornell University Press, 1958), p. 19; and Lauriston Sharp *et al.*, *Handbook of Thailand* (New Haven: Human Relations Area Files, 1956), p. 162.

One important implication of approaching the subject matter in this manner is that the community as a whole, rather than an ethnic group, becomes the basic unit of analysis. Much attention has been directed to the study of the culture of minority groups; these studies are valuable as such, but there cannot be a minority group unless there is also a dominant group. Both are involved in a common social system, and what happens in each cannot be understood satisfactorily apart from this involvement. Furthermore, there are often more than two ethnic groups on a given frontier of contact, all of them interlocked in a common system; they must be studied together. To be sure, the boundaries of a community are sometimes difficult to ascertain. It may consist of a single village, a section of a country, or a large part of a continent—depending upon the range of effective communication. Furthermore, the boundaries of a community must be defined historically as well as geographically; there are areas and periods of common life. What must be emphasized is that all of the ethnic groups inhabiting a common territory participate in a common economic system and are parts of the same system of social stratification. In most cases the people who are involved in a common social system are also ruled by the same government, but there are occasions when a color line crosses national frontiers.

CHAPTER 3

The Symbols of

Ethnic Differentiation

Differences among human beings have always been a source of fascination. The arrival of a stranger whose hair is of an unusual color, the birth of a child with fully developed teeth, or the presence of someone who stutters is the source of excitement and comment. People speculate over the differences among various categories of men—aristocrat and peasant, imaginative artist and practical man of affairs, male and female. There is similar interest in the differences between ethnic groups. Those who advocate segregation or immigration restrictions often emphasize their differences, and they are sometimes surprised to find that their foes are very much like themselves. Reformers of "liberal" persuasion frequently insist that all men are alike, and upon coming into contact with the people whose cause they champion, many of them are shocked to discover that they are in fact quite different. In some respects men all over the world are alike; in other respects those who are participants in a given social group are alike; and in still other respects each human

[56]

being is unique. In what respects are those in an ethnic category alike?

The lines of demarcation between ethnic categories are matters of customary usage, but in most cases noticeable physical differences seem to be involved. Indeed, these patterns of social interaction are designated as "race relations" because of the frequency with which the lines coincide with visible distinctions. This leads to an important question: how are inherited physical attributes related to ethnic categories? What is the significance of skin pigmentation and other attributes inherited from one's ancestors? What are some of the basic differences among people in diverse ethnic categories, and what is the connection between hereditary traits and these differences?

The Cultural Attributes of Ethnic Groups

What makes differences among human beings important is that men who are not alike sometimes must deal with one another; indeed, they may find themselves thrust into situations in which they are mutually interdependent. Men are able to engage in concerted action because they share common understandings concerning the responsibilities of each participant, and the coordination of diverse contributions becomes possible only when each person is able to anticipate to some extent what the others are likely to do and can make the necessary adjustments. But men who do not think alike encounter difficulties. Even when each acts in good faith, harmful things are done inadvertently, misunderstandings arise, feelings are hurt, and the common enterprise ends in failure. Ethnic categories differ significantly only to the extent that the members define situations differently and behave differently. Ethnic groups do not always differ in this respect, but when they do, the differences that are important are cultural.

Culture, according to Redfield, consists of those conventional understandings, manifest in act and artifact, that characterize particular groups.[1] Among the people in each group there are common understandings concerning the meaning of various objects and the proper ways in which they are to be handled. There are shared values—conceptions of what is beautiful or ugly, good or bad, desirable or undesirable. There are numerous norms of conduct—how various

[1] Robert Redfield, *The Folk Culture of Yucatan* (Chicago: University of Chicago Press, 1941), p. 132.

categories of people are to be approached and what may or may not be done with reference to them. Culture consists of the assumptions with which people in a particular group approach their world, assumptions that are learned by each new generation while participating in organized transactions. Because they have similar orientations toward their environment, men who share a common culture develop similar behavior patterns. Each social group develops a unique culture, a set of presuppositions that evolve in a succession of collective adjustments to the historical situations in which the people find themselves.

These conventional norms, which provide the basis for individual and collective action, are sustained and creatively reaffirmed from day to day in the social interaction of the individuals in the group. In their daily lives men are continually bolstering and supporting one another's perspectives. Each person watches the reactions of other people to his efforts, and to the extent that they respond in the expected manner, he is able to continue with the assurance that what he is doing is not improper. By responding in expected ways, then, the others are supporting his outlook. When things happen according to custom, they are to some extent predictable, and when events are predictable, each person can anticipate what is likely to happen and confidently make the appropriate adjustments. If for any reason someone does the unexpected, the situation is no longer adequately defined. Other people become puzzled at this strange behavior, and concerted action temporarily breaks down. To the extent that an individual acts as he is supposed to act, his conformity reinforces the existing norms. Cultural patterns, then, are built up and perpetuated in social interaction.[2]

Unique cultures are the product of communication. To the extent that there is differential association in a community, diverse perspectives develop. In any stratified society most people tend to associate primarily with others of their own kind, and their relationships with outsiders are largely utilitarian or exploitative. There may be varying degrees of social distance: for example, the use of different languages presents a formidable barrier. Even when such linguistic barriers are overcome, distance is maintained as long as social inter-

---

[2] Park, *op. cit.*, pp. 36–52; and Edward Sapir, *Selected Writings in Language, Culture, and Personality*, ed. D. G. Mandelbaum (Berkeley: University of California Press, 1949), pp. 104–09, 308–31.

course remains formal and polite. People on both sides maintain their reserve, do not act spontaneously, and do not get "close" to outsiders. A common feeling among American Jews, for example, is that while many of the "Goyim" are very nice, they are "cold." Thus, the extent to which a distinctive culture develops among people in a given ethnic category depends upon the degree of their social isolation from others. The formation of a characteristic point of view is facilitated when physical separation makes communication difficult—as in the long isolation of feudal Japan. An ethnic minority that is segregated into a ghetto also develops a culture of its own, for all meaningful and trustworthy contacts are with others who are similarly confined. When members of an ethnic category are becoming assimilated in large numbers, however, there are many who no longer participate actively in the group. Under these circumstances a number who are still identified with the group develop quite different patterns of thought and action. People in a given ethnic category are culturally distinct, then, *only to the extent that they participate together in exclusive communication channels.*

Language is an essential part of culture and at the same time the instrument through which other aspects of culture are organized. To the extent that members of different ethnic groups speak different languages, they develop separate perspectives. People who live in the same community may experience identical events quite differently, if they are oriented toward their environment with different vocabularies.

Those with dissimilar perspectives define the same situation differently, responding selectively to diverse aspects of their environment. Especially revealing is the ingenious experiment by Bagby comparing Mexican and American subjects. He set up ten pairs of slides to be viewed through a stereoscope. On one side he mounted pictures of objects familiar to most Mexicans—such as a matador, a dark-haired girl, a peon. On the other side he mounted a similar picture of objects familiar to most Americans—such as a baseball player, a blonde girl, a farmer. The corresponding photographs resembled one another in contour, texture, and the distribution of light and shadows. Although there were a few exceptions, most of the Americans saw only what was already familiar to them, and most of the Mexicans likewise saw only the scenes placed in their own culture. Thus, the selection and interpretation of sensory cues rest to a surprising extent upon the presuppositions formed while participating in organized groups.[3] People from different cultural backgrounds approach their environment with unlike expectations and respond to different perceptual cues. Even when there is no discrepancy in perception, interpretations often vary. Mexican and American spectators of a bullfight would probably agree that the matador had killed the bull; but while the Mexicans are acclaiming the brave matador and voting him the ears of the animal, some of the Americans may become so ill as to vomit. Since the same act can have so many different meanings, there are numerous possibilities for misunderstanding.

Many cultural differences, especially during the early phases of inter-ethnic contact, are obvious. When a group with a technology based upon electronics, atomic energy, and automation encounters a people with a simple handicraft and food-gathering economy, there is little doubt that they are different. Among the customs that frequently attract notice are differences in food habits, procedures for disposing of the dead, and the regulation of sex relations. For example, in Kansu, a province in central China, a number of clearly delineated ethnic groups have been living together for many centuries: the Chinese, the Moslem descendants of Arab mercenaries who entered the area in the eighth century, the Tibetans, the Mongols, and several smaller groups who are remnants of the various invaders who had overrun the area. Although the Moslems speak Chinese and have acquired a number of other Chinese cultural traits, they remain separate and retain their identity. There is the religious difference, of course, but there is also a major conflict in diet. The Chinese eat pork as one of their chief meats, but the Moslems abhor it, believing pigs to be unclean. Strong feelings are also aroused by burial customs. The Chinese bury their dead in coffins; since the Moslems refuse to use coffins, the Chinese look upon them as savages, who bury their loved ones like dogs.[4] Customs concerning sex and marriage are often misinterpreted. When European adventurers and

[3] James W. Bagby, "A Cross-Cultural Study of Perceptual Predominance in Binocular Rivalry," *Journal of Abnormal and Social Psychology*, LIV (1957), 331–34. Cf. A. Irving Hallowell, "Cultural Factors in the Structuralization of Perception," in John H. Rohrer and Muzafer Sherif (eds.), *Social Psychology at the Crossroads* (New York: Harper, 1951), pp. 164–95.

[4] Robert B. Ekvall, *Cultural Relations on the Kansu–Tibetan Border* (Chicago: University of Chicago Press, 1939), pp. 22–23.

traders first came upon the Marquesas Islands in the South Seas, they were surprised to find natives who were attractive by European standards and whose sex life appeared completely uninhibited. Sexual intercourse was frequently witnessed by children, and regular participation began even before puberty. Considerable emphasis was placed upon erotic attraction, and many women took open pride in the number of men they could satisfy in a single evening. Strict incest taboos and other norms were not even noticed, and the reputation of the islands for licentiousness spread quickly. There was little appreciation of the cultural context in which these activities occurred.[5]

But there are many cultural differences that are not so readily discernible. Each culture is a distinctive way of looking at the universe—a *Weltanschauung*. Each group has a cosmology or a religious outlook, a set of beliefs about the nature of man and his place in the universe. Americans often fail to recognize that their scientific outlook is but one of many possible world views; what is natural to us is not so apparent to those who do not share our perspective. In each group there is a distinct set of values, which follow logically from the world view, and differences in values are among the most important sources of misunderstanding between ethnic groups. Values are preferences, which in many instances are only intuitively felt; one becomes familiar with the assumptions underlying conduct largely through a long period of participation in a group. Since values are usually taken for granted, no one bothers to state them explicitly or to explain them.[6] Thus, outsiders often witness behavior that strikes them as repulsive because they do not understand the assumptions upon which it rests. They may conclude that a person is a monster, for his responses appear to be inhuman. Furthermore, many deeply ingrained tendencies, though learned, are much like inborn reflexes. The very spontaneity of such responses further reinforces the belief that people in other ethnic groups are of another species.

One of the most important aspects of the culture of any group is its vocabulary of motives. Much of what a man does depends upon his intentions, and in each culture a somewhat different set of inten-

---

[5] Ralph Linton, "Marquesan Culture," in Abram Kardiner, *The Individual and His Society* (New York: Columbia University Press, 1939), pp. 137–96.

[6] Cf. Florence R. Kluckhohn and Fred L. Strodtbeck, *Variations in Value Orientations* (Evanston, Ill.: Row, Peterson, 1961); and Ralph B. Perry, *General Theory of Values* (New York: Longmans, Green, 1926).

tions is regarded as the natural ground of conduct. Popular beliefs about the "reasons" for various acts differ from group to group; furthermore, there are different words to designate them, and each group has a distinct vocabulary. In the United States today individualistic, hedonistic, and pecuniary motives are generally regarded as the plausible bases of action, and most of us have difficulty realizing that such intentions have not always and everywhere been recognized as plausible. If someone says that he did something in order to make money or to have a good time, his statement is usually accepted as true, even by those who disapprove of his deed. Most of us are inclined to question the sincerity of those who avow religious motives; yet many devout groups take for granted that man's conduct is a manifestation of divine will.[7] Men form judgments of one another by evaluating their conduct, and this usually involves an imputation of motives. We judge others by projecting our own inner experiences to them. Thus, people who do not share the same vocabulary of motives are not likely to understand one another.

All this suggests that the manner in which a person appraises the conduct of others depends upon his conception of human nature. For example, those who believe that all men are basically egoistical can avow and impute only selfish motives, and if someone acts generously, he is thought to have an ulterior motive. Extreme egocentrism is apparently a personality trait, and rigidly self-centered individuals are to be found in all societies. But there are cultural differences in the extent to which individualistic values are emphasized. For example, in a study of values McClelland and his associates compared a matched sample of German and American students and found that the Americans scored significantly higher on participation in group activities and in the extent to which they were guided by group opinion. The Germans reported a greater number of individualistic outside activities and subscribed to statements picturing the individual as being independent of other people. Americans conceived of their obligation to society in terms of participation in groups, but Germans regarded their obligation to society in terms of adhering to a set of impersonal standards—an abstract code above selfish considerations. The authors suggest that what outsiders regard as

[7] Cf. C. Wright Mills, "Situated Actions and Vocabularies of Motive," *American Sociological Review*, V (1940), 904-13.

authoritarianism in Germany may consist of conformity to an abstract code of honor rather than a desire to dominate others.[8]

Thus, each group has different conceptions of the life goals that it thinks are worth pursuing. In some groups in the United States great emphasis is placed upon personal success. Whether one is an artist, a craftsman, a businessman, or an entertainer, he is expected to work hard and to advance as far as he can in his field. Those who fail to make conscientious efforts are viewed with disdain. Some measure of aggressiveness is expected, and sometimes even success at the expense of others is tolerated as inevitable. In other groups emphasis is placed upon the enjoyment of life. For example, many Americans regard Mexican peasants as lazy, although those who know Mexicans well agree that they work very hard on tasks that are important to them. The Mexican milieu has long been overlaid with expectations of sudden injury, violence, or death; the history of Mexico is dotted with a succession of earthquakes, epidemics, and internal strife. Fatalism and indifference may appear irresponsible to outsiders; but when one cannot tell what tomorrow may bring, each person must live for the here and now. From such a perspective those who are constantly struggling to get ahead are seen as pathetic people, foolishly depriving themselves of pleasures and wasting their lives.[9] In still other groups great stress is placed upon personal honor. There are diverse conceptions of what is honorable as well as differences in the extent to which an individual is expected to sacrifice to perserve honor. There are groups in which men are expected to die rather than face disgrace; elsewhere such drastic demands are seen as indicative of mental aberrations.[10]

The importance of cultural differences is revealed in the case of American Jews. Even superficial observation reveals that the Jews have provided a disproportionate share of great artists, composers, writers, scientists, and professional men, and systematic studies confirm this general impression. When compared with other ethnic

[8] David C. McClelland, J. F. Sturr, R. H. Knapp, and H. W. Wendt, "Obligations to Self and Society in the United States and Germany," *Journal of Abnormal and Social Psychology*, LVI (1958), 245–55.

[9] Cf. Lyle Saunders, *Cultural Difference and Medical Care* (New York: Russell Sage Foundation, 1954), pp. 104–40; and Tannenbaum, *op. cit.*, pp. 16–19.

[10] Cf. Hsien Chin Hu, "The Chinese Concepts of 'Face'," *American Anthropologist*, XLVI (1944), 45–64; and George F. Jones, *Honor in German Literature* (Chapel Hill: University of North Carolina Press, 1959).

minorities, the Jews have been characterized by a high rate of upward social mobility.[11] Since all American minorities have been similarly handicapped and have been given roughly the same opportunities for a free education, how is this difference to be explained? In New Haven a team of scholars made a comparative study of two immigrant groups—Jews from eastern Europe and southern Italians. Boys in the two categories were asked what kind of occupational aspirations their parents had for them. While lofty goals were imputed to parents in both groups, the Italian boys indicated that their parents would be satisfied even if they had to settle for less. In contrast, Jewish boys were under the impression their parents would be sorely disappointed if they did not achieve their high aims. Thus, most of the Jewish boys felt themselves under considerably more pressure to succeed.[12]

Several observers have suggested that the culture that developed in the Jewish communities of eastern Europe emphasized values favorable to success in the United States.[13] One value that seems to be related to upward mobility is stress upon the individual's responsibility for his own fate. Among Jews there is a belief that the world is orderly and subject to rational control; therefore, each person should make plans to control his own destiny; many Jews feel that a person can make some of his own "breaks." Judaism is an intensely individualistic religion, and Jewish tradition stresses the possibility of the individual's rationally mastering his world.

On the other hand, Italians are more fatalistic and believe that the individual has little control over his life situation. They feel that all human beings have limitations and that there is not much point in striving for perfection. One should do whatever he can and then count on the sacrament of absolution. Italians emphasize closeness of family ties and are unhappy about their sons' going away to seek advancement elsewhere. Furthermore, in contrast to the Jews, there is a tendency toward assuming collective responsi-

[11] Edward P. Hutchinson, *Immigrants and their Children, 1850–1950* (New York: John Wiley, 1956), pp. 180, 189–90, 253–54.

[12] Fred L. Strodtbeck, Margaret R. McDonald, and Bernard C. Rosen, "Evaluation of Occupations: A Reflection of Jewish and Italian Mobility Differences," *American Sociological Review,* **XXII** (1957), 546–53.

[13] Nathan Hurvitz, "Sources of Middle Class Values of American Jews," *Social Forces,* **XXXVII** (1958), 117–23. Cf. Mark Zborowski and Elizabeth Herzog, *Life Is with People* (New York: International Universities Press, 1953).

bility and credit.[14] Similar results were reported by Rosen, who studied mother-son pairs of a number of ethnic groups in 62 communities in the northeastern states. Questions were raised about achievement and independence—training the child to do things well and to do them on his own. Rosen found that Jewish children are expected to develop self-reliance at a younger age than all others. Jewish parents expect and reward achievement even among very young children; they teach their youngsters to outdo others and to succeed on their own ability. Rosen's data also show that southern Italians attach less importance to independence and achievement.[15]

Another conspicuous value in Jewish communities is respect for learning. In many other ethnic groups in the United States intellectual interests are regarded as effeminate, but Jewish boys are encouraged to study. Those without intellectual interests are chided and compared unfavorably to others who aspire to become rabbis. Whereas many other American children are expected to go to work as soon as they are old enough to contribute to the financial support of the family, Jewish parents are honored for making sacrifices to enable their sons to pursue higher education and specialized training. Learning gives an individual prestige, authority, and a chance for a better marriage. The attitude of Italian immigrants toward education provides a sharp contrast. In Italy educated men were in another class, entirely apart from peasant life. Italians feel that to acquire property and thereby gain some measure of security is the primary goal. Among Jews a wealthy man without some learning is regarded as vulgar. Most Jews are unimpressed by physical prowess, but an Italian manual worker never has to be ashamed of his strength. These contrasting values throw considerable light on the different mobility rates found in the two categories of immigrants.[16]

The values emphasized in many Jewish communities point to possibilities of misinterpreting motives and to some of the possible sources of anti-Semitism in Europe and in the United States. People brought up in contexts in which individualism has been stressed tend

[14] Fred L. Strodtbeck, "Family Interaction, Values, and Achievement," in David C. McClelland *et al.*, *Talent and Society* (Princeton: D. van Nostrand, 1958), pp. 135–94.

[15] Bernard C. Rosen, "Race, Ethnicity, and the Achievement Syndrome," *American Sociological Review* **XXIV** (1959), 47–60.

[16] Strodtbeck, *op. cit.*

to become impatient with those nurtured on the importance of team-
work. To some Jews Gentile associates appear sanctimonious and
hypocritical. In business, artistic, and professional circles Jews are
frequently accused of being excessively ambitious, of showing a
callous disregard for the interests of their colleagues, of sacrificing
everything to get ahead. But men who are striving for advancement
are only responding to the demands of their reference group. The
expectations that are imputed to their parents, relatives, and friends
constitute pressures to succeed, even in the face of the hostility and
suspicion of the Gentile world. Most of the charges made by anti-
Semitic people are ridiculous, but some of the accusations may arise
from an inability to understand the cultural contexts in which some
Jews perform.

It should be emphasized that a great many Americans who
conceive of themselves as Jews do *not* share these values. Only those
who participate in Jewish communities and have access to its communication channels are likely to develop these attributes. That a
great many Jews do not share these values is revealed by the reaction
of the Sabras, Jews born and reared in Israel, to some of the characteristics of the "diaspora Jew." Some of the young Israelis have been
so hostile that they have been accused of anti-Semitism.[17]

To the extent that people who believe they have common
ancestors communicate effectively among themselves they develop
a distinct culture. Although some reformers insist that there are no
differences between ethnic groups, this belief is false. But the important differences are in culture rather than physique, for cultural
differences result in misunderstandings, frustrations, and conflict.
Obviously, then, the central feature of the popular concept of "race"
is the confusion of two distinct processes through which behavior
patterns are formed: (a) what is learned as a participant of an organized society and (b) what is acquired through genetic transmission. The popular conception rests on the belief that interests and
habits are inherited. If someone gesticulates a great deal, for example,
it is explained on the grounds that his grandmother was French. For
this reason children of intermarriage are sometimes condemned as
"mongrel"; people assume that the mixture of incompatible tendencies would produce an inferior creature that is full of contradictions.

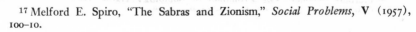

[17] Melford E. Spiro, "The Sabras and Zionism," *Social Problems*, V (1957),
100–10.

This is not a peculiarity of our times; even in the distant past observers have been inclined to attribute similarity of customs to a similarity of ancestry.[18] Scientists have long scoffed at the absurdity of these beliefs; a child born of Swedish parents who is abandoned in the Philippines would grow up speaking Tagalog and would behave much like his Filipino neighbors. Anthropologists in particular have denied vehemently that there is any evidence of differences in mentality corresponding to differences in physical characteristics.[19] This confusion of biological and cultural traits gives rise to most of the problems of "race relations."

Hereditary Traits as Status Symbols

In all transactions that occur outside of one's circle of personal acquaintances effective participation becomes difficult unless there is some way of identifying the other people involved. Common understandings concerning one another's status are essential for the smooth coordination of activities. Therefore, conventional symbols of all kinds are used to divide people into readily recognized categories. Any visible mark will serve. These symbols designate position, not the ability of the particular individual who bears them. As Spencer pointed out in his discussion of ceremonial institutions, they are ways of controlling social intercourse.[20]

Status symbols play an important part in all systems of social stratification. A status symbol is any readily visible mark or mode of conduct that serves as an indicator of one's standing in the community. The marks chosen for this purpose are a matter of common usage; hence, they vary from community to community. Among the symbols familiar to us are the uniforms, insignia, and salutes of soldiers and policemen; they would not be able to exercise authority without them. In some juvenile gangs the "duckbill' haircut serves the same purpose as heavy horned-rimmed glasses, beard, beret, and sandals do in other circles. In a class society those in positions of privilege

18 Cf. Kenneth E. Bock, "Cultural Differences and Race," *Commentary*, **XXIII** (1957), 179–86.
19 Cf. Dunn and Dobzhansky, *op. cit.*; and Otto Klineberg, *Race Differences* (New York: Harper, 1935).
20 Herbert Spencer, *The Principles of Sociology* (New York: D. Appleton, 1897), Vol. II, pp. 3–232. Cf. Erving Goffman, "Symbols of Class Status," *British Journal of Sociology*, **II** (1951), 294–304.

often develop indicators of high status, such as assuming residence in the more desirable sections of a city, emphasizing tastes and manners others have no time to cultivate, or engaging in what Veblen called "conspicuous consumption," the purchasing of things they do not need just to let others know that they can afford to do so. The display of such symbols is important, for the manner in which a person is treated among strangers depends in large part upon the category into which he is placed. Once classified, a person is addressed as if he had certain traits, whatever the characteristics may be that are attributed to the category—a violent temper, favors for those who ingratiate themselves, or an unsavory interest in pretty girls.

In communities in which people are stratified along ethnic lines skin pigmentation and other physical features provide an important basis for making distinctions. To the extent that people in a given ethnic category share a common culture, these marks can be accurate indicators of what to expect in dealing with them. To the extent that individuals in a group are becoming assimilated, however, the marks become less and less effective indices of expected patterns of thought and action. Members of each ethnic group use these symbols to locate others with whom they can identify; those in minority groups are usually much more sensitive than others to these marks.

Since ethnic categories are believed to consist of people who are alike by virtue of common ancestry, hereditary marks such as hair and skin color quite naturally become the symbols of identification. In the United States we take into account a number of attributes; these include the shape of the nose, hair texture, the thickness of the lips, eye color, stature, and the shape of the head. Such features are usually combined into patterns; there are stereotyped beliefs concerning the appearance of each category, and certain individuals are pointed out as being typical. This selection of features in terms of which people are differentiated is arbitrary and conventional. Human beings could just as easily be classified by the size of their ears, the slant of their eyebrows, or the size of their feet. These attributes are also inherited, but they are regarded as irrelevant in our society. In using inherited traits as status symbols, we are immeasurably aided by the models we have in our minds. We use these conceptions of how different categories of people are supposed to look as standards against which individuals are measured. In each society ethnic groups are identified in terms of what Park called their "racial uniform." [21] It is indeed ironic that differences that are biologically so superficial have assumed such importance as criteria for distinguishing among groups.

The marks used for differentiating ethnic groups vary from one community to another. In some places the most obvious differences are in stature. Body build varies considerably: limbs may be long or short; some people have a broad pelvis with a pronounced lumbar curve, while others are tall and have sloping shoulders, and still others have a heavy torso and short legs. In Burundi about 85 per cent of the population consists of the Bahutu, who are of medium height and much like other Bantu-speaking peoples of central Africa. Most of the Bahutu are farmers, and prior to their rebellion in 1959, they occupied the middle stratum in the stratification system. The tall Watusi, who are primarily herders, were at one time believed to be inherently superior and until the uprising enjoyed a position of privilege. At the bottom of the social scale were the Twa Pygmies, who are primarily potters and hunters; they constituted a pariah group. All three groups speak a Bantu language, share a similar theory of racial differences, and are subject to the commands of the same king. Although there are other differences among these ethnic categories, the most conspicuous criterion is height. The mean height of the rural Watusi is 69.5 inches, and the urban Watusi average 69 inches. The average height of the rural Bahutu is 65.9 inches; of the urban Bahutu, 65.4 inches. The Twa Pygmies average only 61 inches. Although there has been some mixing, the groups are ordinarily endogamous, and the lines have been maintained for a long time.[22]

In some communities people become highly sensitized to facial characteristics. The face is admirably suited for the purpose of identification; the various features are undeniably inherited, and they fit together into recognizable configurations. There may be marked differences in head form, those in one group having narrow heads and the other having round heads. Eyes vary in color, in shape, in slant, and in size in proportion to the rest of the face; some people,

[21] Park, *op. cit.*, pp. 159–60. Cf. Melvin Tumin, *Caste in a Peasant Society* (Princeton: Princeton University Press, 1952), pp. 59–62.

[22] Ethel M. Albert, "Socio-Political Organization and Receptivity to Change," *Southwestern Journal of Anthropology*, XVI (1960), 46–74.

especially in Asia, have epicanthic folds. The nose varies considerably in shape and size. Some noses are relatively long; others are short and flat. Some have a high bridge, and others have none. The profile may be concave or convex; the tip of the nose may be thick or pointed. Even after a long period of contact, when clearcut differences have vanished, some people still examine faces with care to make inferences about an individual's ancestry.

Physical types—the distinctive configurations of hereditary traits—are the product of isolation and inbreeding.[23] Where there is differential association, as is the case in most instances of inter-ethnic contact, there is likely to be endogamy, and the prominent characteristics of each group tend to be reproduced. Even when there are contacts with outsiders, as long as social distance is maintained, the chances of people getting to know one another well enough to intermarry are minimized. Clandestine affairs and the exploitation of the women of minority groups result in some mixtures, but there are usually a number of barriers that make miscegenation on a large scale difficult. Not until social distance is reduced and people begin to identify on a different basis does miscegenation become commonplace.

Since a distinctive culture is also the product of isolation, there is a possibility that physical differences will correspond to cultural differences. But this is true only in communities in which segregation is rigidly maintained. People who live together in the same community usually learn about one another's culture long before large-scale intermarriage takes place. Thus, the coincidence of physical and cultural traits is usually found only in the earlier phases of inter-ethnic contact.

Although hereditary marks are only symbols that sometimes indicate the cultural characteristics of those who bear them, people in many ethnic groups regard both the marks and their distinctive modes of thought and conduct as inherited. There is much confusion about this matter, and the confusion is often compounded when the symbol itself is evaluated. If invidious distinctions are made on the basis of hereditary marks, it is natural that people in minority groups would become concerned with the symbols themselves. They sometimes develop strong feelings of inadequacy over the color of their skin, the texture of their hair, the size of their nose, or the shortness of

[23] Cf. Dunn and Dobzhansky, *op. cit.*

their legs. These marks become objects of strong sentiments, and in time they come to assume meanings all their own.

In the world today there seems to be more concern over pigmentation of the skin than over any other hereditary trait. In diverse contexts darkness of complexion seems to have a similar meaning. Common linguistic usage in English reveals the negative evaluation placed upon the color black. "Black magic" designates malevolence; a "black letter day" is an unlucky one; a "blacklist" contains suspects or those deserving censure; "blackmail" is extortion; a "black lie" is mendacity at its worst; a "black sheep" is a misfit. Each time such expressions are used the connotation is reinforced.[24] Even among people who resent the domination of white men and profess to oppose their "prejudices," darkness sometimes implies inferiority. In India there are perceptible differences in color among the various castes, the higher castes being lighter. Many a Hindu takes pride in his color; he regards himself as the bearer of superior "blood" than those who are darker. Mothers sometimes reproach daughters with darker complexions that they will never marry.[25] There is a similar sensitivity to skin color among American Negroes. Numerous studies show that they make all kinds of distinctions among themselves, placing a lower estimate upon those whose appearance is clearly Negroid.[26]

Of course, there is no necessary connection between dark complexion and inferiority. This widespread tie is only the consequence of the European conquests of the past five centuries and the establishment of lightly pigmented people in positions of prestige. In Greek art, literature, and mythology there are many descriptions of Negroes, and all indications are that they were viewed with respect. Their contributions to astrology were highly regarded. Their military prowess was respected, and many Negro warriors were hired as mercenaries.[27] In the Middle East the Arabs who ruled during the Umayyad Caliphate called themselves the "swarthy people," with a

[24] Simon Podair, "Language and Prejudice Toward Negroes," *Phylon*, **XVII** (1956), 390–94.

[25] Cf. Nirad C. Chaudhuri, *The Autobiography of an Unknown Indian* (New York: Macmillan, 1951), pp. 51–57, 118–24, 365–81.

[26] W. Lloyd Warner, Buford H. Junker, and Walter A. Adams, *Color and Human Nature* (Washington, D.C.: American Council of Education, 1941); and Myrdal, *op. cit.*, pp. 695–700.

[27] Frank M. Snowden, "The Negro in Ancient Greece," *American Anthropologist*, **L** (1948), 31–44.

connotation of superiority, in contrast to the "ruddy people," their Persian and Turkish subjects.[28] It has been suggested that the Portuguese colonists in the Western Hemisphere mixed more freely with Indians and Negroes because they did not have the same attitude toward darkness as the settlers from northern Europe. Since the Moors had dominated the Iberian peninsula for a long time, darkness of skin color had a different significance.[29] Darkness obviously does not imply inferiority among Africans who are not in constant contact with Europeans. Both Stanley and Livingstone reported that the paleness of Europeans struck many Africans as repulsive, and both indicated a sense of shame over their own lightness, which appeared ghastly in contrast to the rich black and bronze around them.[30]

It would be difficult to find an area in which there is more preoccupation with skin color than in the islands of the Caribbean, where there is no legal segregation and where the people profess an ideology in which ethnic differences are minimized. Puerto Ricans often take pride in absence of "color prejudice," but there is evidence that many avoid those who are darker than themselves.[31] Haiti is often called a Negro republic, but the elite group is still noticeably lighter, and approximation of European standards is valued as a mark of refinement. Although dark skin color is not an absolute barrier, candidates for upward mobility find lightness a great asset.[32] Sensitivity to color probably reaches its height in Jamaica. Although the distribution of physical types in Jamaica is not too different from the rest of the Caribbean, the most refined distinctions are made among the numerous shades from the very light to the very dark. "Colour" is evaluated not only in terms of actual skin color, but also in terms of hair formation and facial features; it is assessed by the nearness of an individual to European standards. People are highly sensitized to appearance because it makes such a difference in their life chances—

[28] Arnold J. Toynbee, *A Study of History* (London: Oxford University Press, 1934), Vol. I, p. 226.

[29] Cf. Donald Pierson, *The Negroes in Brazil* (Chicago: University of Chicago Press, 1942), pp. 116–17, 326–29.

[30] William I. Thomas, *Primitive Behavior* (New York: McGraw-Hill, 1937), pp. 30–31.

[31] Cf. Maxine W. Gordon, "Race Patterns and Prejudice in Puerto Rico," *American Sociological Review*, XIV (1949), 294–301; and Melvin M. Tumin and Arnold S. Feldman, *Social Class and Social Change in Puerto Rico* (Princeton: Princeton University Press, 1961), pp. 227–46.

[32] John Lobb, "Caste and Class in Haiti," *American Journal of Sociology*, XLVI (1940), 23–34.

the range of jobs for which one is eligible, the possibilities of a desirable marriage, and the opportunities for advancement for their children. The meaning of color is a legacy of the slavery days, when being light meant to be free. The early mulattoes were acutely aware of what their fate would be if they were identified with the slaves, and they went out of their way to show contempt for the "blacks" and to emulate the "whites." The mulattoes refused to do "nigger's work"; when they were granted some privileges, they guarded them jealously.[33]

The social status of a Jamaican depends not only on skin color but also on the respectability of his family, his occupation, the type of marriage he contracts, and his wealth. But appearance is related to all of the other criteria. Upward mobility is referred to as an attempt to "advance colour." A child with a fair complexion may marry well and abandon his parents and siblings. This is accepted by those who have been left behind for the sake of the grandchildren he will have, who will presumably enjoy a better fate. Successful men try to marry women who are lighter than themselves so that their children will have more advantages. Such a marriage also enhances the prestige of the man; it is said that "he has lifted his colour." The pinnacle of success is marriage to a white woman; although this is almost impossible in Jamaica, some have managed to find brides in England. The same principle applies in the choice of a mistress. Thus, by judicious selection of a mate a deliberate effort is made to alter the traits of one's progeny—to correct his "faults." [34] Where people believe that a change of hereditary traits is the only way to improve their lot, there is no other way.

The preoccupation with symbols rather than the meanings they represent is also revealed in the variety of cosmetic and surgical techniques used to alter undesirable hereditary traits. Although social scientists may be able to demonstrate that the fate of ethnic minorities stems more from false beliefs and customary procedures than from hereditary marks, the underprivileged only know that they are deprived of so many opportunities they crave because of the marks, and they blame these traits for their misfortunes. In most cases

[33] Fernando Henriques, "Colour Values in Jamaican Society," *British Journal of Sociology*, II (1951), 115–21; and Eric E. Williams, *The Negro in the Caribbean* (Washington, D.C.: Associates in Negro Folk Education, 1942), pp. 57–69.
[34] Fernando Henriques, *Jamaica: Land of Wood and Water* (London: MacGibbon & Kee, 1957), pp. 92–109, 127–41.

not very much can be done, but even the slightest "improvement" is thought to be beneficial. Among Negroes, hair-straightening has become a big business, and beauty parlors also feature "tonics" and "packs" for whitening the skin.[35] In areas in which anti-Semitism is prevalent, Jews with prominent noses feel extremely self-conscious, and some resort to plastic surgery.[36] Japanese who are familiar with European standards of beauty are often self-conscious about the smallness of their eyes. Since the surgery required to alter the epicanthic fold is relatively simple, a number undergo the operation each year. The pain and expense involved in all these treatments represent the efforts of unhappy people to improve their lot by attacking what they believe to be the source of their troubles.

Hereditary attributes are important, then, not because of their physiological relevance but because they constitute such obvious marks of distinction and can therefore be connected to taboos and other mystical conceptions. Inherited traits make a difference in social conduct *only* when people become conscious of them and use them as the basis for identification.

Auxiliary Symbols of Ethnic Identity

In areas where ethnic groups have been in contact for a long time, physical differentiation becomes progressively more difficult; various auxiliary symbols of ethnic identity must then be used in conjunction with the hereditary traits. Under some circumstances these secondary symbols may completely supersede the hereditary marks, so that people who are genetically different are placed together into a single category.

Naming customs vary considerably from culture to culture, but hereditary family names were used in China as early as 2852 B.C. Although the ancient Greeks had no surnames, the practice of deriving one's name from his father became widespread in England after the Norman conquest, and patronymical suffixes are now found in all European languages.[37] In much of the world today the surname is

---

[35] *Ibid.*, pp. 128–29.

[36] Frances C. MacGregor *et al., Facial Deformities and Plastic Surgery* (Springfield, Ill.: Charles C. Thomas, 1953), pp. 39–52.

[37] Cf. Gustav Fransson, *Middle English Surnames of Occupation, 1100–1350* (Lund, Sweden: C. W. K. Gleerup, 1935), pp. 33–41; and Elsdon C. Smith, *The Story of Our Names* (New York: Harper, 1950), pp. 27–43, 124–64.

used as one of the symbols of ethnic identity. In various parts of Latin America one of the major differences between a Mestizo and an Indio is that the former is likely to have a Spanish surname, while the latter is likely to have an Indian name. In Yucatan, for example, no matter how dark a man's complexion may be, if he has a Spanish surname, he conceives of himself as a superior human being and is treated as such.[38] As might be expected in a nation of immigrants, there are by far a greater variety of surnames in the United States than in any other country, and many people are placed in ethnic categories primarily by name. Even though the American population has become so mixed that names are no longer an effective index, many still examine them as a possible clue to identity. There are still some social circles, as among executives of large corporations, where a foreign name is unacceptable. To the extent that names serve as the bases for making distinctions and fixing responsibilities, they help to bring order into social relationships.

Because children usually learn the mother tongue of their parents, language may also serve as a symbol of ethnic identity. Although there is no evidence to support it, there is a widespread belief that the capacity to speak a given language is inherited—it seems natural for a Bohemian to speak Czech. Speech is not only spontaneous, but most adults are unable to enunciate many of the sounds that occur in languages they did not learn as children. Apparently infants throughout the world are able to produce a wide range of sounds, but as they grow older they learn to articulate skillfully the limited number of sounds in their own language and lose the ability to make others.[39] Thus, even immigrants who learn to speak the language of their adopted land fluently can usually be identified by their accent. In some countries special dialects develop in isolated areas, and a person who is familiar with them can sometimes locate the place of birth of an individual merely by listening to him speak. A study of dialectical differences in Khalapur, a village in northern India, showed a significant relationship to status. The greatest difference found was between the untouchables and the castes. These differences were not the product of geographical isolation, because people of the same stratum

[38] Robert Redfield, "Race and Class in Yucatan," *Cooperation in Research* (Washington, D.C.: Publication of the Carnegie Institution, 1938), pp. 511–32.
[39] Cf. M. M. Lewis, *Infant Speech* (New York: Harcourt, Brace, 1936), pp. 55–142.

who lived in different areas spoke the same dialect. This suggests that people who associate with one another on an informal basis tend to speak alike.[40] Such linguistic differences serve as status symbols in a variety of contexts. In the United States a Southerner who migrates to other regions sometimes finds that his drawl places him into the category of "hillbilly," an object of contempt.[41] In Mexico the use of an Indian language is an important criterion for identifying an Indio.

Bodily gestures of all kinds are also used as identification symbols. To study the extent to which bodily gestures become standardized in different cultures, Efron compared Jewish immigrants from Lithuania and Poland, immigrants from southern Italy, and the American-educated children in both groups. Collecting his data through extensive observations, sketches, and motion pictures, he devised a complex procedure for coding each movement; the two immigrant groups could be distinguished quite easily, for each was characterized by a traditional pattern of gesticulation.[42] Gestures of this type are apparently acquired intuitively, and most people are not aware of the extent to which they use them. They are generally more useful to those within a given ethnic group who are trying to locate a fellow member, for outsiders rarely develop sufficient familiarity with such subtle behavior patterns. Jews frequently contend that they can recognize another Jew, even if the latter is a complete stranger; they can "feel" it. Such intuitive recognition, to the extent that it actually occurs, may rest upon the detection of conventional gestures.

In some communities religion may serve as a useful index of ethnic identity. This is especially true where there are sharp differences in overt behavior—in rituals and in dietary practices. Although religion is not inherited, the beliefs and practices are learned early in life, usually from one's parents. In the Middle East religion is the most important basis for differentiation. The Moslems in Khalapur, who constitute about 10 per cent of the population, are not part of the caste system. They are rated somewhere between the lower

---

[40] John J. Gumperz, "Dialect Difference and Social Stratification in a North Indian Village," *American Anthropologist*, LX (1958), 668–82.

[41] Lewis M. Killian, "The Adjustment of Southern White Migrants to Northern Urban Norms," *Social Forces*, XXXII (1953), 66–69.

[42] David Efron, *Gesture and Environment* (New York: King's Crown Press, 1941).

middle *jatis* and the untouchables. Although they are integrated into the regular neighborhood patterns of borrowing implements and social intercourse, some Hindus feel that they should be denied use of the village wells.[43]

There are a variety of other cultural traits that may serve as status symbols. After centuries of inter-ethnic contacts the African city of Timbuctoo has a polyglot population. The various ethnic groups—among them Arab, Songhoi, and Tuareg—can be distinguished primarily in terms of sartorial and tonsorial differences. These marks are not easily altered. Models are so well established that an individual whose language and manners do not match his external appearance would seem ludicrous.[44] In southern Mexico and Guatemala, where hereditary traits are not reliable symbols, the Ladino and the Indio are also distinguished by the clothing they wear. The former wear European clothing, and the latter wear peon costumes. On special occasions the Indio may also wear garments of European design, but they never wear neckties or shoes.[45] In Tibetan villages being invaded by Chinese settlers, the latter can be identified by the wearing of trousers. Tibetans wear long coats and regard trousers as superfluous, but the Chinese view such dress as indecent. When the villages are undergoing change, especially when they are becoming more Chinese, the wearing of trousers becomes a mark of high status, and it is even adopted by some of the Tibetans.[46]

Whenever rulers find it necessary to make distinctions among people who are otherwise indistinguishable, artificial symbols are used. Soon after the spread of Islam, Christians and Jews living under the caliphs were required to dress in ways that would make them easy to recognize. The practices varied, but in many locales they wore girdles. In some parts of Spain Jews were required to dress in yellow and were not allowed to wear turbans.[47] In 1215, Pope Innocent III ordered that all Jews and Moslems be required to wear badges on their outermost garment, ostensibly to prevent intermarriage and

[43] Gumperz, *op. cit.*

[44] Horace Miner, *The Primitive City of Timbuctoo* (Princeton: Princeton University Press, 1953), pp. 19–31.

[45] John Gillin, "Race Relations Without Conflict: A Guatemalan Town," *American Journal of Sociology,* LIII (1948), 337–43; Redfield, "Race and Class in Yucatan," *op. cit.*; and Tumin, *op. cit.*, pp. 59–70.

[46] Ekvall, *op. cit.*, pp. 43–45.

[47] Arthur S. Tritton, *The Caliphs and Their Non-Muslim Subjects* (London: Oxford University Press, 1930), pp. 115–26.

concubinage. The size, shape, and color of the badge was left to the discretion of local authorities. In England the badges were yellow; in Austria Jews were forced to wear different clothing as well.[48] This practice was revived in Nazi Germany, where Jews again had to wear yellow badges. After the Manchu conquest of China the new rulers decreed that any person found wearing clothes of Chinese design, retaining Chinese coiffure, or binding the feet of their female children would be severely punished. Thus, from 1644 Chinese men were forced to wear Manchu dress and a queue—the "pigtail"—as a symbol of their submission to Manchu rule. This practice was continued until the 1911 revolution.[49] Through such symbols barriers may be perpetuated between ethnic groups that have been in contact so long that they have no other differentiating marks.

Like hereditary marks these symbols may become so closely associated with ethnic identity that they are confused with what they represent. Those who disagree on questions of ethnic identity become embroiled in controversies over the symbols. Distinctive names are revered by some and hated by others. In countries such as the United States, where upward mobility is relatively easy, name-changing is a fairly common practice. Although some people alter their names only for convenience, others make changes in hopes of becoming eligible for jobs and homes that are not open to "foreigners." Many Jews have found that they could "pass" for Gentiles by changing their name and moving to a new community. But this practice is strongly condemned by those who want to preserve the identity of the group.[50]

Controversies also arise over the use of language. Children of immigrants are often sensitive about the foreign accent of the older generation and become upset when their parents speak in public in a foreign tongue. In some communities the right of a minority group to use its own language may become a key political issue. During the latter part of the nineteenth century, when the Hungarian government launched its program to institute cultural uniformity within its borders, it encountered resistance from the Rumanian peasants. When

---

48 Israel Abrahams, *Jewish Life in the Middle Ages* (New York: Meridian Books, 1958), pp. 291–306; and Ulysse L. L. Robert, *Les signes d'infamie au moyen age* (Paris: Honoré Champion, 1891), pp. 6–113.

49 Herbert A. Giles, *China and the Manchus* (London: Cambridge University Press, 1912), pp. 20–28.

50 Cf. Louis Adamic, *What's Your Name?* (New York: Harper, 1942).

the government stopped subsidizing schools that did not give instruction in Hungarian, some of the poorer Rumanian schools became bankrupt. In 1879 a new law was passed requiring all elementary school teachers to have a knowledge of the national tongue. The use of Rumanian was finally prohibited, even for public notices, such as danger warnings. But most Rumanians held firm and retained their ethnic identity.[51] In India, where there are 12 major languages, each spoken by at least 5 million people, serious linguistic problems threaten national unity. When independence from British rule had been achieved, there were widespread demands for the establishment of states on a linguistic basis, and an attempt is being made to carry out such a policy. Some Indians fight for the right to speak their own language from fear that others will attain unfair advantages; for most people, however, there is a vague apprehension that their cultural heritage would be lost once another language becomes official.[52]

In communities in which the language of the dominant group is well established, minority groups often set up their own schools. In the United States children in a number of ethnic minorities attend foreign language schools on weekends and after regular school hours.[53] Before World War II, when the Thai government closed the Chinese language schools, some parents sent their children to China or to Malaya. In British Borneo in 1949, the Chinese Chamber of Commerce levied a tax of its own on all Chinese cargo in order to obtain funds for the local language schools. This is not an unusual practice among the Chinese in Southeast Asia.[54] Thus, some parents in minority groups are willing even to undergo the pain of being separated from their children to assure the perpetuation of the ethnic group.

In some communities religious conversion is a prerequisite for a person in a minority group who wishes to raise his status. Under such circumstances some of the ambitious avail themselves of the oppor-

[51] R. W. Seton-Watson, *A History of the Roumanians* (London: Cambridge University Press, 1934), pp. 405–09. Cf. Leon Dominian, *The Frontiers of Language and Nationality in Europe* (New York: Henry Holt, 1917), pp. 154–73.

[52] Cf. D. K. Hingorani, "The Role of Language in the Development of National Consciousness in India," *Publications of the Modern Language Association of America*, **LXXII** (April 1957), 32–37.

[53] Cf. W. Lloyd Warner and Leo Srole, *The Social Systems of American Ethnic Groups* (New Haven: Yale University Press, 1945), pp. 220–53.

[54] Victor Purcell, *The Chinese in Southeast Asia* (London: Oxford University Press, 1951), pp. 185, 432.

tunity as a matter of expediency. To those who do not hold their religious beliefs seriously, learning the rituals of another religion is not a great sacrifice. In Kansu, where the Moslems rebelled against Chinese rule approximately every 30 years, raiders attacked Chinese villages, capturing women for wives and proselyting for their religion. Faced with the alternative of conversion or death, many Chinese accepted the new faith. In this way the Moslem group managed to replenish its otherwise declining population.[55] Genuine conversions are rare occurrences; they usually involve serious disturbances in interpersonal relations over a long period of time, the lowering of one's level of self-esteem, a period of torment from a sense of worthlessness, and the sudden grasp of a new outlook that enables one to form a new self-conception. This type of conversion cannot be expected to take place on a large scale.

The external uniform through which people are identified varies from community to community; what is emphasized in each locale is a matter of customary usage. But people often place an estimate upon the symbols. To those who value their cultural heritage and identify strongly with a group, some of the identification symbols become sacred objects; nothing is more sinful than giving up one's language or mode of dress, especially if the group is attacked or ridiculed because of it. To people in minority groups who wish to become assimilated, however, these symbols become barriers that are held responsible for retarding their advancement. Unlike hereditary marks the auxiliary symbols can be changed, and those who wish to escape a despised category do make changes whenever an opportunity arises. Some of the most intense conflicts that occur within ethnic minorities arise over this issue, and few people realize that they are fighting over symbols that stand for vague and often erroneous beliefs.

Summary and Conclusion

Differences among human beings are important insofar as they make concerted action difficult or impossible. To the extent that important differences exist among ethnic groups, they are cultural. Cultures are the product of communication; hence, to the extent that an ethnic group is isolated from others, it develops a distinctive culture. As long as ethnic groups are endogamous, hereditary marks serve as

[55] Ekvall, *op. cit.*, pp. 20–23.

useful symbols of identification, for they also develop through isolation and inbreeding. When people have been in contact for a long time, however, they become more and more alike—both culturally and physically. If under these circumstances people in different ethnic categories still conceive of themselves as being different, other symbols of identity are used. Characteristics that are believed to be related to ancestry—such as names, language, religion, or other prominent and readily visible cultural traits—are used as indices of each category.

The arbitrary character of the connection between these symbols and what they represent is shown by the variations from one community to another. What is regarded as a basic criterion in one community is ignored as irrelevant in another; any visible symbol can serve as the basis for drawing lines of demarcation. That there is no *necessary* connection between hereditary marks and ethnic identity is revealed in those cases in which physical traits become unreliable indices. Then, other marks take their place and in some cases completely supersede them. But the fact that these criteria are arbitrary does not mean that they can be changed easily; they are well established in each community and supported by a high degree of consensus.

We are now in a position to compare the popular approach to "race relations" to the theory being developed in this book. Ordinarily "race relations" is thought to involve the interaction of people of different races, people who have inherited different tendencies to act. Actually, problems such as segregation and lynching arise from misunderstandings among people who are culturally different. Because these acquired differences are erroneously believed to be inherited, hereditary marks are used as symbols for identifying the people in each category. This means that what is commonly called "race relations" is essentially a *psychological* problem, not one of genetics. If hereditary traits were actually at the root of the difficulties, the only solution would be either intermarriage on a large scale or extermination of the undesirable people. The tragedy of Nazi Germany and the pathetic sacrifices being made in Jamaica are cases to the point. Most inherited traits cannot be changed, but the beliefs of men can be altered. The problem confronting mankind in the twentieth century is one of identification rather than one of amalgamation.

CHAPTER 4

Popular Conceptions
of Ethnic Identity

In a frequently cited essay William James wrote of a "certain blindness" in human beings, a blindness to the feelings of people different from themselves. Each person is so preoccupied with his own life, so convinced of the importance of his own duties, so absorbed with his own vital interests, that he is unable to comprehend the concerns of those in different walks of life. During a journey through the mountains of North Carolina he was repelled by the squalor around the cabins which he thought spoiled the natural beauty of the area. When he was told by one of the inhabitants that the people there could not be happy unless they were hard at work clearing the land, however, he suddenly realized how meaningless academic life at Harvard would be to these mountaineers. He then understood that an observer can only see what is on the outside, and from his standpoint many of the things that other people do appear absurd. Were he able to see the activity from the standpoint of the observed, however, his experiences would be so different that he could readily comprehend their

[82]

pleasures. Spectators are almost sure not to appreciate fully the joys of active participants.[1]

In inter-ethnic contacts people generally see one another from the outside. Even when they approach one another without malice, men are often blind to the meaning of life to members of other ethnic groups. Hence, they form all kinds of judgments about one another that are not only inaccurate but make mutual understanding more difficult.

Probably the most widespread explanation of this phenomenon is "race prejudice." Some contend that people have an irrational attitude toward minority groups and that this is the "cause" of practices like segregation. Reformers intent upon altering such arrangements have therefore devoted considerable time to the study of prejudice and have tried to develop techniques for eliminating it. But social psychologists have been unable to ascertain just what prejudice is. There seems to be general agreement that human beings develop persistent orientations toward various objects—thunderstorms, television, snakes, aristocrats, as well as ethnic categories—and that the orientation of each individual toward such objects tends to be a bit different. Some poets regard thunderstorms romantically, as outbursts of nature's emotional tensions; others are only frightened by them. Some people treasure their television sets as the source of countless pleasures and edification; others dismiss them as "idiot boxes." It appears that *some* of the orientations of this sort are condemned as prejudices but that most of them are not. The central problem of this chapter is to ascertain the characteristics of the stable orientations that individuals develop toward ethnic categories, whether they are condemned or not.

Ethnic Stereotypes as Popular Concepts

All men live in a symbolic environment, a substitute world in which objects and events fall into an orderly scheme. Life is much too complicated for any individual to respond to each item he encounters in terms of its distinctive characteristics. Each object is unique, but there is rarely time enough to examine it with care before handling it. Hence, objects and events must be classified, and

---

[1] William James, *Talks to Teachers on Psychology and to Students on Some of Life's Ideals* (New York: Henry Holt, 1912), pp. 229–42. Re: P-O.

men act as if all items in each category have the same characteristics. For example, no two chairs in the world are alike, but we assume that all chairs have certain common attributes and sit with
confidence even upon a chair that we have never before encountered.
To facilitate reference to these categories, each is given a label; words
are names that designate categories. Much of the environment in
which human beings make their way, then, consists of objects that
are classified and labelled.

The use of such symbols helps to organize experiences; sensory
cues of all kinds—light waves, sound waves, pressures—tend to be
ordered in terms of meanings that are designated by linguistic symbols. For the most part we do not see and then define; we define and
then see. We are selectively responsive to those cues that confirm our
expectations; we tend to see things in patterns that have already been
organized. Thus, the environment as men experience it is not a direct recording of their sensations but a reconstruction of what they
see, hear, and feel into a variety of conventional meanings. Furthermore, each person lives in a small part of the world and knows only
a few people in it, but he often becomes concerned with events that
he cannot observe directly. His conceptions of these objects must be
pieced together from what others report and from what he can
imagine. The ability to classify events and to manipulate symbols
obviously simplifies the task of living; men are able to conceive of
their complex and ever-changing world as if it were relatively stable,
orderly, and to some extent predictable. The symbolic environment
is not a mere reproduction of the external world; it is a reconstruction
of it in terms of group interests and the available linguistic categories.[2]

No two things in the world are exactly alike. Different modes
of natural existence shade off into each other, but classifications
are essential for planned and coordinated action. Classifications are
usually based upon the most general resemblances among unique
objects; hence, they always imply overlooking some qualities and
placing selective emphasis upon others. Any conspicuous property

[2] Cf. Susanne K. Langer, *Philosophy in a New Key* (Cambridge: Harvard University Press, 1942); Alfred R. Lindesmith and Anselm L. Strauss, *Social Psychology* (New York: Dryden Press, 1956), pp. 45–130; and Walter Lippmann,
Public Opinion (New York: Harcourt, Brace, 1922), pp. 79–156.

can be used as the basis for establishing a category. If different items look more or less alike, this alone facilitates placing them together. Unlike the classifications used by scientists, which are precisely defined, popular categories often rest upon criteria that are not made clear, and the boundaries between them are in many cases not sharply defined. In some cases the categories overlap. Objects may be classified together on the basis of a superficial likeness. Sometimes things happen to coexist, and for convenience they may be placed together. Sometimes things are classified together because someone has an interest in creating a likeness. Systems of classification persist as long as they are useful, and some categories continue to be used even when they are known to be inaccurate.

Human beings not only classify objects and events; they categorize people—themselves as well as others. Participation in coordinated action requires some knowledge about one's associates. While we can take the roles of those we know intimately with relative ease, we must place strangers into categories and work on the assumption that everyone in a given category is alike. Our relations with strangers depend largely upon superficial cues provided by dress, coiffure, facial expression, and vocabulary. Human beings are generally classified into *social types,* and they are approached or avoided on the basis of their classification. Social types of all kinds are recognized and used daily—beatnik, spinster, playboy, Texan, professional man. The alleged characteristics of those in each category are matters over which there is considerable consensus, and they are frequently acknowledged by the people themselves. Social types, like other popular concepts, make it possible for men to organize their world—to anticipate more effectively what the people they encounter are likely to do. Although they are not entirely accurate, their existence facilitates concerted action. Each group has its own repertoire of social types.

Social types are abstractions. They are constructed by selecting and putting together some of the more conspicuous traits that are supposed to characterize a category of people. Thus, we ordinarily think of college professors in terms of esoteric interests, extensive vocabularies, absent-mindedness through preoccupation with specialized work, and kindliness in their relations with students. Although social types are gross oversimplifications, they are not necessarily distortions. Specific cases can be shown not to fit the pattern in all details, but to prove the beliefs are entirely false is difficult.[3] What is called "common sense" consists of a set of beliefs many of which cannot be justified on rational grounds, and social types are among the popular concepts making up these world views.

A group normally supports its social types. The models often serve as the basis for recruiting, training, and controlling people who perform various tasks. Men place themselves as well as others into social types, and they then try to live up to group expectations. Social types are models that guide positively by imitation and negatively by avoidance. Once an individual has typed himself in a certain way, he struggles to cultivate the tastes and skills deemed appropriate for the sort of person he wants to be. He rejects suggestions and associations that are inconsistent with the type and seeks out those that tend to support it. For example, a person appointed to a professorship sometimes feels obliged to purchase tweed clothing and to use uncommon words in his discourse. Much of what is called a "front" or an "affectation" is a struggle to achieve a type that is out of line with one's actual capacities. The manner in which a person classifies himself, then, is an important part of his conception of himself.[4]

Ethnic stereotypes are social types. People in a well-established ethnic group develop a distinctive culture, and outsiders pick out conspicuous traits and exaggerate them to construct a shorthand depiction of them. Thus, Wirth contends that the Jews are a social type, to the extent that they are identifiable at all, a category of people who can be identified in terms of cultural traits that developed during centuries of segregation.[5] In a pioneering study published in 1933, Katz and Braly reported the consistency with which American college students characterized various ethnic groups and nationalities. Jews were described as intelligent, ambitious, industrious, shrewd, mercenary, and grasping. The Irish were thought to be quick-tempered, pugnacious, witty, honest, and very religious. Negroes were regarded as ignorant, superstitious, lazy, happy-go-lucky, ostentatious, and musical.[6] They are also believed to have a special liking

[3] Roger Brown, *Words and Things* (Glencoe, Ill.: The Free Press, 1958), pp. 363–71. Cf. Otto Klineberg, *Tensions Affecting International Understanding* (New York: Social Science Research Council, 1950), pp. 118–23.

[4] Orrin E. Klapp, *Heroes, Villains and Fools* (Englewood Cliffs, N. J.: Prentice-Hall, 1962), pp. 1–24.

[5] Wirth, *The Ghetto, op. cit.*, pp. 63–74.

[6] Daniel Katz and Kenneth W. Braly, "Racial Stereotypes of 100 College Students," *Journal of Abnormal and Social Psychology*, XXXIII (1933), 280–90.

for chicken and watermelon and a tendency to fight with razors. Such traits are often thought to be inherited. A comparative study of ethnic categories conducted by UNESCO in 1952 revealed the extent to which various groups are similarly characterized in different parts of the world.[7] Thus, members of different ethnic groups interact on the basis of the conceptions they form of one another. Stereotypes may not be accurate, but they represent the ways in which people see each other.

Since ethnic stereotypes are formed through selection and exaggeration, an individual fitting one exactly would be difficult to find. When such categories become conventional, however, they are no longer arbitrary, no matter how inaccurate they may be. They become group definitions, and they are supported by collective sanctions. An individual may disagree with them, but unless he works with conventional meanings, others will not understand him. Thus, the lines of demarcation between ethnic categories are drawn by common consent. The characteristics attributed to each category are established in popular beliefs, and the symbols of identification in terms of which individuals are located in each type are also matters of convention. The meanings of ethnic categories are learned by participating in an organized society, and they are constantly reinforced in social interaction.

That men tend to perceive one another in terms of such abstract concepts has been demonstrated in empirical studies. Once conventional meanings have become well established, already organized responses are set off by the symbols of the category, such as physical appearance. The subjects of a study by Secord and his associates consisted of 58 white students in Atlanta, Georgia. They were given an attitude test to ascertain the extent of their antipathy toward Negroes and were then shown photographs of 15 people, arranged on a continuum from a person with obvious Negroid features to one with obvious Caucasoid features. The students were asked to rate the physical and psychological characteristics of the individual in each picture. As they were shown photographs of people progressively more Caucasoid in appearance, stereotyped conceptions did not change correspondingly in small increments. Anyone who was identified as a Negro was characterized as having all the Negro attributes.

[7] William Buchanan and Hadley Cantril, *How Nations See Each Other: A Study in Public Opinion* (Urbana: University of Illinois Press, 1953).

Furthermore, subjects with strong antipathies toward Negroes tended to exaggerate the stereotype.[8] Thus, once a human being is classified, even on the basis of dubious cues, he is regarded as having the traits common to that category. Riddleberger and Motz showed pictures of the same four Negroes in two sets of situations—one stereotyped and one not. They found that their subjects did not even notice that the same four individuals were involved in different settings. When the Negroes were perceived in the stereotyped situations, judgments tended to be unfavorable.[9]

People frequently conceive of themselves in terms of such stereotypes, although they do not acknowledge all of the negative traits attributed to them by others. Kusunoki found that the Japanese viewed themselves much as others did but that they disavowed traits such as treachery.[10] In northwestern Manchuria the Tungus criticized the Cossacks because of thefts that occurred among them, something unknown among themselves, and the Cossacks praised Tungus honesty. But the Cossacks, whose violence tended to be premeditated, criticized the Tungus for their random violence when intoxicated, and the latter deplored this weakness on their part.[11] Bayton found that Negro college students characterized Negroes in much the same manner as others did, except that they denied being ignorant, stupid, slovenly, or dirty.[12] Among themselves American Jews often refer to an individual who happens to resemble the stereotype as a "typical Jew." They also tell jokes among themselves that would be pointless unless one took for granted the stereotyped conception. Within each ethnic group, however, all kinds of subcategories are recognized. Thus, the college students Bayton questioned distinguished between the "typical Negro" and "Negro college

---

[8] Paul F. Secord, William Bevan, and Brenda Katz, "The Negro Stereotype and Perceptual Accentuation," *Journal of Abnormal and Social Psychology*, **LIII** (1956), 78–83.

[9] Alice B. Riddleberger and Annabelle B. Motz, "Prejudice and Perception," *American Journal of Sociology* **LXII** (1957), 498–503.

[10] K. Kusunoki, "Mental Characteristics of the Japanese Race as Seen by Japanese and American Students," *Japanese Journal of Applied Psychology*, **IV** (1936), 232–37.

[11] Ethel J. Lindgren, "An Example of Culture Contact Without Conflict," *American Anthropologist*, **XL** (1938), 605–21.

[12] James A. Bayton, "Racial Stereotypes of Negro College Students," *Journal of Abnormal and Social Psychology*, **XXXVI** (1941), 97–102. Cf. Guy B. Johnson, "Stereotype of the American Negro," in Otto Klineberg (ed.), *Characteristics of the American Negro* (New York: Harper, 1944), pp. 5–10.

students"; the latter were intelligent and progressive. Social types that develop within each ethnic group are rarely known to outsiders.[13]

Ethnic stereotypes vary along several dimensions—among them degree of clarity, degree of complexity, extent to which people are consciously aware of them, degree of stability, extent to which they enjoy consensus, and manner in which they are evaluated. Some stereotypes are clearly organized patterns; others are vague, fragmentary impressions. For example, when people in the Middle East were asked to characterize the Irish, several admitted frankly that they knew nothing about them. There was much variation in the answers that were given, a few mentioning such traits as being religious and militaristic.[14] Some stereotypes are simple in that there are a limited set of organized responses. Most Americans have heard of the "stingy" Scotchman, but no other traits are regularly attributed to this category. On the other hand, the stereotype of the Negro in the South is very complex. There are a wide variety of reactions, depending upon the context in which Negroes are encountered. Nor is the stereotype entirely negative; Negroes are often credited with being shrewd judges of human nature and by some with being loyal and devoted friends of white people.[15] Men vary in their awareness of their orientations toward objects. Consciousness is generally more acute in crisis situations; at other times awareness tends to wane. For example, during the depression LaPiere interviewed people in Fresno, California, about Armenians and found acute concern over the presence of this alien group, which was charged with being dishonest and deceitful. Even responsible officials whose own records contradicted their charges insisted that the Armenians were a financial burden to the community and were always getting into trouble with the law.[16] Since that time there has been progressively less concern with Armenians, and by now most people in the area hardly notice them.

Ethnic stereotypes also vary in stability. Some are transformed

[13] Cf. Samuel M. Strong, "Social Types in a Minority Group," *American Journal of Sociology*, **XLVIII** (1943), 563–73.

[14] Terry Prothro, "Cross-Cultural Patterns of National Stereotypes," *Journal of Social Psychology*, **XL** (1954), 53–59.

[15] Johnson, *op. cit.*, pp. 3–22.

[16] Richard T. LaPiere, "Type-Rationalizations of Group Antipathy," *Social Forces*, **XV** (1936), 232–37.

almost as quickly as they are formed. Once they become firmly established, however, they tend to persist. Since stereotypes do not actually describe individuals accurately, attempts are frequently made to correct the erroneous beliefs. However, such corrective efforts are usually in vain. For centuries after their invasion, Huns were feared by the various peoples of central Europe. Their marauding raids were recalled with terror, and they were pictured as savage brutes who drank human blood. During the fifteenth and sixteenth centuries, when Magyar troops served as the "shield of Europe and Christianity" against the Turks, they were temporarily redefined as fine cavalrymen. By the end of the eighteenth century, however, they were again viewed as savage, unreliable, and tyrannical. Their revolutionary uprising in 1848 aroused considerable sympathy, but their love of freedom was romanticized as the passionate demand of "natural" man.[17] After World War II Gilbert repeated the Katz-Braly study on a new generation of American students, and he found little change in conceptions of the various categories other than the Germans and the Japanese.[18] Social workers, reformers, and colonial administrators who struggle for years in behalf of a minority group are often unable to establish close ties with any but a handful of assimilated leaders, who themselves have a stereotyped conception of their group; in many cases, their compassion for a people appears to rest upon a stereotype. The fact that so many of these categories are not sensitive to contradictory evidence is the reason they are called "stereotypes," like the metal plates cast in composing rooms by printers.

Since an actor's intention cannot always be ascertained by observing the overt deed alone, the same act can be interpreted in several different ways. For this reason ethnic stereotypes are reinforced no matter what the principals may actually do. Perception is always selective: we perceive only those things that are relevant to our interests, and we tend to notice only those cues that confirm our expectations. Once stereotypes are learned, people are perceived in terms of them. The more firmly established the expectations, the more easily they are confirmed.[19] Contradictory evidence usually does not

[17] A. N. J. den Hollander, "As Others See Us: A Preliminary Study into Group Images," *Syntheses*, **VI** (1947–48), 223–25.

[18] G. M. Gilbert, "Stereotype Persistence and Change Among College Students," *Journal of Abnormal and Social Psychology*, **XLVI** (1951), 245–54.

[19] Cf. Leo Postman, "Toward a General Theory of Cognition," in Rohrer and Sherif, *op. cit.*, pp. 242–72.

alter the concept. In many cases contradictory evidence is not even noticed. In some cases the factual validity of such evidence is denied. In other cases incompatible instances are rendered harmless by conceiving of them apart from the category. Thus, an intelligent Negro is seen as a "professor" or as a "friend" and not as a Negro. Incompatible evidence is segregated and not considered in testing the stereotype. Riddleberger and Motz found that people with antipathies against Negroes saw the situations that were not stereotyped as accidental meetings.[20] When exceptional individuals appear who cannot be ignored, the evidence is often dismissed with expressions such as "the exception proves the rule." There is a constant reaffirmation of the world view of the group through trite expressions, shibboleths, and clichés.[21] Stereotypes persist even in communities in which there are no representatives of the category present. In an isolated village in Guatemala, where there were no Jews, Siegel found that the Indians believed that all Jews had horns and tails and that they were the evil men who had killed Christ. These views were constantly reaffirmed not only in informal talk but also in annual religious festivals, in which Jews were portrayed on the stage according to this model.[22]

The use of ethnic stereotypes involves more than a mere classification of human beings. The meaning of any object is the way in which one is disposed to act toward it. Since the items in each category are assumed to have certain attributes, men are prepared to respond in appropriate ways upon meeting representatives of the class. Upon encountering a tiger loose on the street, most people would run for cover. Although that particular tiger might be quite tame, they are not likely to remain on the scene long enough to find out. Thus, categorization implies a program of action. When a man thinks he knows what kind of human being he is dealing with, he imputes the appropriate motives to him and makes the necessary adjustments. Just as a man exercises special caution when confronted at a busy intersection by a woman driver, so he is prepared to act in special ways in dealing with members of other ethnic groups. When involved in a financial transaction with a Jewish merchant, some

---

[20] Riddleberger and Motz, op. cit. Cf. Eunice Cooper and Marie Jahoda, "Evasion of Propaganda," Journal of Psychology, XXIII (1947), 15–25.

[21] Maurice N. Richter, "The Conceptual Mechanism of Stereotyping," American Sociological Review XXI (1956), 568–71. Cf. Gustav Ichheiser, "Misunderstandings in Human Relations," American Journal of Sociology, LV (1949), No. 2, Part 2.

[22] Morris Siegel, "Horns, Tails, and Easter Sport," Social Forces, XX (1942), 382–86.

people take special care. Similarly, a man trying to make friends with an American Negro may invite him to a dinner of chicken and watermelon. This is the way in which the categories in use in each group organize the conduct of its members. Men approach their environment with the assumptions they have learned—about the characteristics of various physical objects, sequences of events, and types of people. This enables them to anticipate to some extent what is likely to happen and to get ready to meet the situation. Men interact in terms of the assumptions they form of each other, and ethnic stereotypes are among the popular beliefs that underlie concerted action.

Such dispositions to act are given overt expression, however, only if they happen to be consistent with the requirements of conventional roles. To understand the significance of stereotypes we must distinguish among (a) meanings of objects, (b) the definition of the situation, (c) inner dispositions to act, and (d) overt conduct.[23] The kind of inner impulse that is elicited depends upon the definition of the situation. Even those who have unfavorable stereotypes do not automatically react with hostility upon coming into contact. A person who is quite content with his Japanese gardener might be aroused to violence if the man tried to purchase the house next door, but this sense of outrage arises only if there is a violation of his sense of propriety. The definition of each situation might be regarded as a conclusion, one that is reached by combining what is perceived with premises about the key objects involved. The manner in which each situation is defined, then, depends upon the fund of meanings an individual brings to bear upon it. A man who believes that all Negroes have designs on white women would define as threatening a situation in which a swarthy man is standing beside a white woman, when others not sharing such meanings would not even take notice. White people from the South who visit Northern cities are continually upset by situations that the natives take for granted. But there is little they can do about it because overt behavior is subject to social control. In most instances what a man actually does depends upon his conventional role. He does what a person of his position in that community is expected to do, and this sometimes requires the suppression of his personal feelings. Just as a police officer is bound to enforce the law even when he would personally prefer to do something else, each person acts overtly in terms of the expecta-

[23] Cf. Shibutani, *op. cit.*, pp. 31–138, 179–280.

tions he imputes to the people around him. If his inner dispositions happen to coincide with conventional expectations, he can act freely. If not, he must inhibit his desires. Men are not free to attack those they dislike, nor even to insult those who displease them. "Discrimination" is often said to be "caused" by "prejudice." At first blush this sounds reasonable, but the statement is not true. Patterns of segregation can be enforced only when there is consensus over the meanings of ethnic categories and when men are agreed that separation should be maintained.

Ethnic stereotypes vary in the extent to which they enjoy consensus. In a stable society meanings are well established, but in a changing society consensus breaks down. The same categories have different meanings to different individuals; hence, the same situation may be defined in diverse ways. Europeans in South Africa are by no means agreed on what to do about the natives: Pettigrew found that those born in Africa were significantly more hostile than the others, supporters of the Nationalist Party were more ardent supporters of segregation, and Afrikaans-speaking persons were more hostile than the English-speaking.[24]

In such contexts inner dispositions cannot always be expressed in overt action; the deeds may not be sanctioned by part of the group. If one is confronted by a man he considers dangerous, he experiences an impulse to flee. But adults are not free to run in panic whenever they are frightened, especially in situations others do not regard as dangerous. If one observes someone he regards as inferior demanding equal status, he becomes resentful and wants to chide and scold him. But if others disagree with his definition of the situation, he cannot indulge his impulses. This means that in changing societies there may be considerable discrepancy between inner dispositions to act and overt conduct. A man may become involved in a commercial transaction with people he dislikes; if it is a profitable one, his associates would not tolerate disagreeable incidents. Thus emotional reactions are aroused, tensions develop, and explosive violence sometimes breaks out.

In changing societies, then, the appropriate treatment of various ethnic groups is in question, and the inner dispositions triggered by stereotyped conceptions are manifested primarily in situations in

---

[24] Thomas F. Pettigrew, "Personality and Sociocultural Factors in Intergroup Attitudes," *Journal of Conflict Resolution*, II (1958), 29-42.

which choices are permitted or where action is not subject to social control. There are numerous contexts in which individuals are able to act in terms of their personal preferences. In the United States most people feel they have the right to choose their associates, to marry whom they desire, to work where they wish, and to live among neighbors of their liking. Those who find certain ethnic groups obnoxious can avoid them. They also have the right to choose their careers, and they can avoid those that are likely to bring them into contact with people who make them feel uncomfortable. Such private dispositions may also be manifested in crisis situations, where the usual requirements of conventional roles break down. A man may struggle to save a white child while allowing his Negro playmate to drown. The most common way in which personal preferences are expressed is in the *style* of one's act. People often find that they must do what is required of them in their conventional roles, but the manner in which they perform gives some indication of their personal feelings. Duties can be performed with enthusiasm or in a perfunctory fashion: all customers may be served in a restaurant, but a waitress may address them curtly or with deference. In situations of this kind charges are often made of "race prejudice," which are difficult to prove precisely because the inner experiences and intentions of others cannot be ascertained without their cooperation.

Recurrent Evaluations of Ethnic Categories

There are very few emotionally neutral objects. Most of them— including ethnic categories—are evaluated in some manner. Objects that have been the source of gratification are prized or coveted; objects that have been the source of frustration are hated and attacked when possible; objects that have been the source of pain are avoided; objects that are readily controlled are regarded as unimportant and sometimes viewed in contempt. Since most preferences are learned as members of an organized society, each person has value orientations toward many objects he has never encountered directly; he learns of them through communication. Of course, individual experiences may alter some of these evaluations. On the whole, however, conventional values are constantly reaffirmed in the regularized responses of other people. Should one individual's estimate vary from those of people around him, he is likely to encounter all kinds of difficulties.

The manner in which the people in one ethnic group consistently treat those in another depends largely upon the estimate that is placed upon it. Some of the ways in which ethnic categories are evaluated are commonly called "prejudice." Unfortunately, most studies of "prejudice" either measure it on a unidimensional scale—for or against someone—or rank various categories of people by order of preference.[25] Because of this careless usage necessary distinctions are seldom made, and arguments frequently arise over what "prejudice" *really* is. In the United States, for example, Negroes are usually regarded as inferior people, but Jews are seldom so evaluated. This suggests that a negative orientation toward Negroes may be quite different from anti-Semitism. This gross oversimplification in studies of "prejudice" has been recognized by some scholars, and a start has been made toward a more effective approach.[26]

The entire problem can be seen in a broader perspective by considering several different ways in which alien groups may be evaluated. Each ethnic stereotype is unique. Each ethnic group develops a distinct set of cultural and physical characteristics in the course of its history, and some of these traits are included in the manner in which they are depicted. However, certain ways in which ethnic categories are evaluated are recurrent; typical orientations are found over and over in a wide variety of historical contexts. In daily discourse we speak of "condescension," "paternalism," "*nouveau riche* mentality," "antipathy," or "friendly cooperation" in characterizing relations between groups. These terms suggest that in spite of the unique features of each instance of contact, certain kinds of orientations develop with sufficient regularity to be recognized and named. *Recurrent ways of evaluating ethnic categories apparently depend upon the relative positions of the groups in a system of stratification.* There are only a limited number of relationships that can exist.

[25] Cf. John Harding et al., "Prejudice and Ethnic Relations," in G. Lindzey (ed.), *Handbook of Social Psychology* (Cambridge, Mass.: Addison-Wesley Publishing Co., 1954), Vol. II, pp. 1025-27.

[26] Cf. Pierre L. van den Berghe, "The Dynamics of Racial Prejudice," *Social Forces*, XXXVII (1958), 138-41; Bruno Bettelheim and Morris Janowitz, *Dynamics of Prejudice* (New York: Harper, 1950); and Gustav Ichheiser, "Fear of Violence and Fear of Fraud," *Sociometry*, VII (1944), 376-83.

Groups may be stratified, coordinated, or in opposition. In each context typical orientations develop. The evaluation of social types depends, then, upon the context in which the people interact.[27]

Much of the behavior condemned as "race discrimination" is based on the evaluation of members of ethnic minorities as *inferior objects*. This type of estimate develops in clearly stratified societies in which members of the dominant group occupy most of the desirable positions and others perform most of the menial tasks. The most widely-accepted stereotype of the Negro in the United States is of this type. In the European colonies in Africa the natives were usually seen as lacking in self-control, discipline, and foresight. Their thoughts were believed to be concentrated on events of the moment, with little apprehension for the future or grief for the past. They were people with the virtues and defects of attractive children; once their confidence was won, they would defer without question and without envy to those who were older and wiser.[28] In New Zealand many Europeans look upon the Maori as unreliable, improvident, happy-go-lucky individuals with no ambition but to sit in the sun, to become intoxicated, and to live off the government. These traits are regarded as inherently Polynesian, part of the general moral and intellectual inferiority of all colored peoples.[29] When a stratified society is well established, people do not even bother to discuss their relative worth; they take for granted that members of minority groups are childlike—emotional, irrational, and incapable of heavy responsibilities. But the characterization is not entirely negative; such people are also seen as warm, friendly, and considerate.

This orientation is manifested in a definite pattern of responses. If an inferior person is seen to be in trouble, the tendency is to go to his aid. If he works hard in a menial position, one expresses approval and offers rewards. But if he claims equal status, there is at first contemptuous laughter and then outrage if he persists. If he is caught se-

[27] Clarence E. Glick, "Social Roles and Types in Race Relations," in A. W. Lind (ed.), *Race Relations in World Perspective* (Honolulu: University of Hawaii Press, 1955), pp. 239–62. Cf. Herbert Blumer, "Race Prejudice as a Sense of Group Position," in J. Masuoka and P. Valien (eds.), *Race Relations: Problems and Theory* (Chapel Hill: University of North Carolina Press, 1961), pp. 217–27.

[28] Frederick D. Lugard, *The Dual Mandate in British Tropical Africa* (London: W. Blackwood & Sons, 1923), pp. 69–72, 400–01. Cf. Hortense Powdermaker, *Copper Town: Changing Africa* (New York: Harper & Row, 1962), pp. 69–86.

[29] David P. Ausubel, *Maori Youth* (Wellington, N. Z.: Price Milburn, 1961), pp. 43–44.

ducing a woman of the dominant group, both he and the woman are subjected to severe punishment, almost as if the relationship were incestuous. If he is placed in a position of power, there is great fear, as if an undisciplined child had been handed a loaded shotgun. Inferior people are expected to behave like children—to be docile, respectful, and obedient. As long as they behave in this manner, they are rarely addressed with hostility; the most common approach is one of condescension. Members of the dominant group feel responsible for looking after the well-being of those who are less fortunate, and some of them go to considerable sacrifice to live up to their obligations. The ideal government is seen as a benevolent despotism. Thus, a common complaint in Java and Malaya was that the colonial officials coddled the people and treated them like children; in Burma the Burmese were treated like naughty children.[30]

This type of orientation is by no means restricted to those who are in dominant groups. Groups that had once been powerful often continue to look upon themselves as superior people. Thus, the Chinese and the Indians looked upon European colonists with disdain; they conceived of themselves as part of an ancient civilization, temporarily inconvenienced by barbarians. In central Asia the Chinese found it difficult to conceive of the Mongols as rational human beings; they were especially fearful of Mongols when the latter became violent.[31] The Chinese who migrated to Southeast Asia developed a similar view of the various peoples they encountered. In Indonesia they found the natives inferior in ability, intelligence, and energy. The Peranakan, offspring of Chinese fathers and Indonesian mothers, were assumed to be less capable because of their "blood." [32] In Thailand the natives were viewed as indolent; the women were morally loose and the officials corrupt.[33] In some Jewish circles the stereotype of the "Goyim" is that they are anti-Semitic by nature and people of not much intellectual capacity, even if they are educated. They are incapable of love. Their family life is strained; hence, their children can leave home without any pangs. Furthermore, they are

[30] John S. Furnivall, *Colonial Policy and Practice* (London: Cambridge University Press, 1948), p. 424.

[31] Owen Lattimore's introduction to Ma Ho-t'ien, *Chinese Agent in Mongolia*, trans. John de Francis (Baltimore: Johns Hopkins Press, 1949).

[32] Donald E. Willmott, *The Chinese of Semarang* (Ithaca, N. Y.: Cornell University Press, 1960), pp. 94–97, 103–16.

[33] Richard J. Coughlin, *Double Identity: The Chinese in Modern Thailand* (London: Oxford University Press, 1960), pp. 83–85.

incapable of appreciating voluptuousness or sensuality.[34] Many European intellectuals who have become refugees in the United States look upon Americans as childlike people of good will who are to be tolerated but hardly to be taken seriously.

Although the traits assigned to inferior objects are not entirely negative, the more favorable ones—physical strength, virility, courage, endurance—are often seen as part of their subhuman nature. During the Crusades some Arabs admired the courage and daring of the Franks; this bravery, however, was seen as being of the kind displayed by animals and hence less virtuous than similar deeds in their own group.[35] Negroes in central Brazil were credited by others with ability to do hard work, but this, too, was regarded as a manifestation of animal-like capacity for exertion.[36] Some of the Jews imprisoned in Nazi concentration camps developed similar conceptions of the SS guards. They were regarded as anti-Semitic individuals of inferior intelligence, little education, and low standing in the German community. They were physically powerful and bloodthirsty, but they were not human; they were beasts. Hence, the prisoners were terrified, and they did not attack the SS men even when they had nothing to lose, knowing that they were going to die.[37]

In many dominant groups there is widespread interest in the sexual prowess of their subject peoples. Thus, the natives in South Africa were regarded as moved to wild, unrestrained gratification. The men were thought to be more virile and potent than white men, and the women were thought to have more "abandon." [38] In the United States lower-class Negroes in the South apparently enjoy a higher degree of sexual freedom than most middle-class Americans. Although these folkways have been condemned by middle-class Negroes, they have been the subject of considerable curiosity among white people. Popular beliefs about the size of Negro genital organs

[34] Wayne Clark, "Portrait of the Mythical Gentile," *Commentary*, **VII** (1949), 546–49.

[35] Usamah Ibn-Munqidh, *An Arab-Syrian Gentleman and Warrior in the Period of the Crusades*, trans. Philip K. Hitti (New York: Columbia University Press, 1929), p. 161.

[36] Marvin Harris, "Race Relations in Minas Velhas," in Charles Wagley (ed.), *Race and Class in Rural Brazil* (New York: Columbia University Press, 1952), pp. 51–56.

[37] Bettelheim, *op. cit.*

[38] Ian D. MacCrone, *Race Attitudes in South Africa* (New York: Oxford University Press, 1937), pp. 298–302.

are widespread, and they are entertained even among prostitutes, who sometimes seek out Negro procurers in their quest for special thrills.[39]

Well-established categories of this kind may become symbols of anything base, to be viewed in contempt or disgust. Epithets designating such groups are used in name-calling, even in situations in which ethnic identity is irrelevant. For example, American children often add incentive to their races by yelling that the "last one there is a nigger baby," and the resulting concern over being called a "nigger" is generally enough to elicit maximum effort. When an object is regarded as disgusting, there is a tendency to avoid contact or identification; such symbolic usage, therefore, reaffirms the conventional meaning.

Groups occupying privileged positions usually conceive of themselves as *valuable objects*, and in many cases they are so regarded by others. Members of the dominant group assume that they are more capable than other people, and they feel that others would be pleased to be like them. Among the traits commonly avowed by those who regard themselves as superior are intelligence, strength, self-control, honesty, benevolence, and tolerance. Of course, some members of elite groups are conscious of their foibles as well. As George Orwell points out in his famous essay, "Shooting the Elephant," those in positions of privilege sometimes undergo considerable discomfort in order to live up to the expectations of their subjects.

Members of ethnic minorities are often reluctant to admit openly that their rulers are superior people. However, they approach members of the dominant group with respect and deference; their acts are predicated upon the assumption that the others are valuable objects. If a superior person is being attacked by someone, they would be shocked at the audacity of the assailant and would do what they could to assist the victim. If he seduces a woman of an inferior group, it is resented by the group but shrugged off as inevitable; if he is in a position of power, this is accepted as natural. If a superior person insists upon equality of status, there is considerable discomfort; there is a feeling that something is not right, and in many cases suspicions

[39] John Dollard, *Caste and Class in a Southern Town* (New York: Doubleday, 1957), pp. 158–72, 364–89, 393–400; and Harold Greenwald, *The Call Girl* (New York: Ballantine Books, 1958), pp. 136–37.

arise of some ulterior motive. The silent assumptions underlying such contacts are revealed when a member of the dominant group is seen in a lowly position. When a white woman is observed performing a menial task, for example, members of minorities frequently comment that it is a shame that someone with so many advantages should be doing something so commonplace. They do not see her merely as an ordinary human being but as a valuable object. If she happens to be attractive, that she should be doing such work seems especially wasteful. Thus, people in positions of privilege are expected to live up to high standards, and those who look up to them express disappointment at failures in situations in which one of their own number would be excused. This commonplace reaction presupposes an overevaluation by virtue of classification. Although this orientation is rarely condemned as "prejudice," it is nonetheless a stable way of approaching another ethnic category.

When there is opposition between ethnic groups, each stands in the way of the other's aspirations, and they tend to regard one another as *frustrating objects*. Subjugated peoples who have not yet accepted the conquest develop great resentment against their rulers. When the Japanese dominated Korea, they pointed with pride to the bridges and hospitals they had built and thought that the Koreans were grateful for the "progress"; the Koreans, however, referred to their rulers as *wai nom*—"evil little men." Upwardly mobile people who find a barrier beyond which they cannot rise develop deep hostility against the dominant group; thus, white men are hated throughout the world today by ascending minorities. A study made just before Ghana became independent revealed that Africans were ambivalent toward the Europeans in their midst. They conceded the superiority of white men on many points—cleanliness, technical skills, intelligence, punctuality. But these people were also seen as opposed to African advancement and unwilling to acknowledge the equality of educated Africans. The frustrations and disappointments of ex-servicemen and the general revulsion against colonial rule exploded in the anti-white riots of 1948.[40]

Many American Negroes look upon the white man as their traditional enemy. That this hatred is based upon frustration is revealed by the fact that the more successful Negroes have a far less hostile

[40] Gustav Jahoda, *White Man* (London: Oxford University Press, 1961), pp. 26–43, 61–75, 82–87.

conception. Lower-class Negroes are inclined to blame more of their woes upon white people.[41] In urban settings throughout the world direct competition for jobs tends to intensify mutual antagonism. In such situations, in which there is no clearcut division of labor along ethnic lines, periodic outbursts of violence occur. Hostility may also develop from other forms of rivalry. A study of the attitudes of American soldiers in France, Germany, and England soon after World War II revealed that many Americans had a more favorable view of their former enemies than they did of their allies. They did not have to compete with Germans as they did with the others for girls, souvenirs, and alcohol.[42]

Opponents are often respected in a way that inferior objects are not; thus, many subject peoples agree that white men are intelligent and efficient. But frustrating objects are more often characterized as hypocritical, unjust, ruthless, selfish, cold, cruel, inhuman, arrogant, exploiting, and deceitful. The orientation is revealed by a characteristic pattern of responses. If a person regarded as a frustrating object is seen being attacked by someone else, there is a disposition to sit back to enjoy the show. If anything, one might go to the aid of the assailant or at least keep watch for him while he inflicts damage. If he is seen seducing a woman of one's own group, there is deep resentment, and hostility is directed against both the woman and the seducer. If he is in a position of power, this may be accepted and yet resented as unjust; there are thoughts of vengeance and dreams of a time when the power structure will have been altered. If he insists that he is of equal status, there is agreement but immediate suspicion of ulterior motives. If he is seen in a menial position, there is glee and contemptuous laughter. Even if it is not thought to be quite appropriate, it is seen as a fate deserved by those who try to exploit others. Frustrating objects may be respected, but they often become the target of virulent hatred and aggression.

When opposition between groups is heightened—either in intense rivalry or open conflict—the adversaries regard one another as

[41] Tilman C. Cothran, "Negro Conceptions of White People," *American Journal of Sociology*, **LVI** (1951), 458–67; Mozell C. Hill, "Basic Racial Attitudes Toward Whites in the Oklahoma All-Negro Community," *ibid.*, **XLIX** (1944), 519–23; and Frank R. Westie and David H. Howard, "Social Status Differentials and the Race Attitude of Negroes," *American Sociological Review*, **XIX** (1954), 584–91.

[42] Daniel Glaser, "The Sentiments of American Soldiers Abroad Toward Europeans," *American Journal of Sociology*, **LI** (1946), 433–38.

dangerous objec   ch realizes that the success of the opponent
may mean inconvenience, frustration, or even death. People who are
convinced that their vital interests are in danger act with self-right-
eousness; much of the viciousness found in the history of inter-ethnic
contacts is based upon such evaluations of the other group. Minority
groups that are economically more successful than others tend to be
feared both by the dominant group and by other minorities. The
stereotype of the Jew in recent times in Europe and in the United
States has been that of a dangerous rival. Jews are regarded as ambitious and aggressive, intelligent, unusually adept and underhanded
in financial transactions, clannish, and always grasping for power
and control. Similarly, in Australia the Jews are not regarded as inferior people. They are characterized as ambitious, exploitative, and
primarily loyal to other Jews. More objection was raised to the immigration of Jews to Australia than to the admission of any other
group except Negroes.[43] Similar charges have been levelled against
the Chinese in Southeast Asia. In 1878, fear of Chinese encroachments
led to the enactment in Australia of the Chinese Immigration Restriction Act.[44]

Dangerous objects are regarded as aggressive and cunning, and
they are usually approached with a defensive stance. In all conflict
situations perception becomes more selective, and combatants become more sensitized to those attributes of their opponents that
would support and justify their own aggressive impulses. They are
usually characterized as immoral, crafty, treacherous, brutal, cruel,
arrogant, clannish, greedy, corrupt, and exploiting. More than 50
years after the Turkish massacres a group of Armenian students in
Lebanon were asked to describe the Turks; 85 per cent saw them
as criminals.[45]

The stance is manifested in a typical pattern of responses. If a
person regarded as a dangerous object is seen being attacked by another party, the tendency is to cheer and lend encouragement to
the assailant. If he is seen seducing a woman of one's own group,
there is outrage and concern for the woman. If he is in a position
of power, there is fear of exploitation. His claiming equality of status

[43] Oscar A. Oeser and S. B. Hammond, *Social Structure and Personality in a
City* (New York: Macmillan, 1954), pp. 51–65, 92–110.
[44] Wilfrid D. Borrie, *Italians and Germans in Australia* (Melbourne, Australia:
F. W. Cheshire, 1954), pp. 5, 211.
[45] Prothro, *op. cit.*

would evoke little interest. If he occupies a menial position, there is contemptuous laughter, but protective measures are taken to see that damage is not done. Allport and Kramer found that anti-Semitic people tend to be able to identify Jews more accurately from photographs, suggesting that they are more highly sensitized to identification symbols that would help locate their enemies. Since this study was based on the assumption that Jews and Gentiles could be distinguished by appearance alone, the finding has become the center of considerable controversy.[46]

Frustrating and dangerous objects may become symbols toward which aggressive tendencies developed elsewhere may be displaced. The Jews have long been such a symbol. In times past they have been identified with the devil and assigned traits that others rejected in themselves.[47] In many parts of the world today Jews have become the symbol of preoccupation with money and cunning business acumen. For example, King Rama VI of Thailand labelled the Chinese as "Jews of the East" and denounced their stranglehold on the economy.[48] Ichheiser suggests that the Jew is seen primarily as a swindler. In an organized society in which brute force is checked, fear of being swindled may be greater than fear of violence because it is intangible and a disguised form of coercion.[49] According to the theory of displaced hostility, derived from psychoanalysis, the virulent hatred in anti-Semitism is not developed in actual contact with Jews. The aggressive tendencies are formed and nurtured elsewhere, perhaps in unsatisfactory interpersonal relations within the family, and then are displaced upon a convenient scapegoat.[50] That such displacements can occur was demonstrated in an experiment by Miller and Bugelski; when boys in a summer camp were deliberately subjected to a frustrating experience by the camp management, their

---

[46] Gordon W. Allport and B. M. Kramer, "Some Roots of Prejudice," *Journal of Psychology*, XXII (1946), 9–39. Cf. Leo Goodman, "Quantitative Methods for the Study of Identifiability," *American Journal of Sociology*, LXV (1959), 246–57.

[47] Otto Fenichel, "Elements of a Psychoanalytic Theory of Anti-Semitism," in E. Simmel (ed.), *Anti-Semitism: A Social Disease* (New York: International Universities Press, 1946), pp. 11–32. Cf. David Riesman, "The Politics of Persecution," *Public Opinion Quarterly*, VI (1942), 41–56; and Maurice Samuels, *The Great Hatred* (New York: Alfred A. Knopf, 1941).

[48] Purcell, *op. cit.*, pp. 154–55.

[49] Ichheiser, "Fear of Violence and Fear of Fraud," *op. cit.*

[50] John Dollard *et al.*, *Frustration and Aggression* (New Haven: Yale University Press, 1939). Cf. Ackerman and Jahoda, *op. cit.*, pp. 56–61; and Leonard Berkowitz, *Aggression: A Social Psychological Analysis* (New York: McGraw-Hill, 1962), pp. 132–64.

hostility against Japanese and Mexicans increased.[51] Further support for the hypothesis comes from a study of World War II veterans by Bettelheim and Janowitz; they found that hostility against various ethnic minorities tended to be concentrated among those who were unsuccessful.[52] Once an ethnic group become a symbol for hated objects, all kinds of rationalizations develop to justify the aggression directed against it.

There are many situations in which members of different ethnic groups find it mutually advantageous to trade or to cooperate on other matters of joint interest. When they become consciously aware of their interdependence, they evaluate one another as *useful objects*. Although this is often overlooked by students of prejudice, there are many cases of friendly cooperation in which a typical orientation develops among the participants. They approach one another with special consideration, overlooking those attributes that they find distasteful, and they are very careful not to alienate their friends. Useful objects are generally characterized as friendly, intelligent, strong, trustworthy, hard-working, benevolent, and courageous. The orientation is manifested in a typical pattern of responses. If a person regarded as a useful object is seen being attacked by someone else, one goes to his assistance and tries to drive off the assailant. If he is caught seducing a woman in one's own group, one shrugs the matter off tolerantly; in some instances an attractive woman may even be offered for bait. If he is in a position of power, there may be some apprehension, since he is different, but one continues to cooperate. If he claims equality, this is agreed to with cordiality. If he occupies a menial position, one may try to help him achieve something better.

Sometimes members of different ethnic groups live together in the same community without becoming too involved in transactions that affect their vital interests. This is especially true when there are only a few representatives of the category present. In such instances the outsiders may be viewed as *esoteric objects*. The fact that they are different is recognized, but they are approached with curiosity, friendliness, and tolerance. Some individuals may even develop a special fascination for the strangers.

If the manner in which ethnic categories are evaluated depends

[51] N. E. Miller and R. Bugelski, "Minor Studies in Aggression," *Journal of Psychology*, XXV (1948), 437–42.
[52] Bettelheim and Janowitz, *op. cit.*, pp. 42–61.

upon the relative positions of groups in a system of stratification, one implication is that the estimate placed upon a group would change as its status is altered. This means that the same ethnic group —with the same cultural attributes—may be evaluated in quite different ways in different historical contexts. Since Jews occupy somewhat different positions in different parts of the world, they have been characterized in diverse ways. Because anti-Semitism refers to hostility against the same ethnic group, it is often thought to be a unitary phenomenon; actually it has taken many forms. In medieval Europe Jews were believed to have tails and a special odor, which disappeared at the moment of their conversion to Christianity. They were generally regarded as unclean and were forbidden to bathe in rivers. Since people endowed with such physical features could be capable of the most horrible deeds, such as sacrificing Christian children and using their blood in Passover rites, they were greatly feared. When the Bubonic plague swept through Europe in the fourteenth century, Jews were accused of poisoning the wells and in many cases were burned as sorcerers.[53] Few people today would claim that Jews are unsanitary or malodorous. Some Europeans are more concerned with the alleged machinations of Jewish "international bankers," and some Americans accuse them of being too ambitious and aggressive. Very likely, as the status of Negroes rises in the American class structure, they will cease to be viewed as inferior objects and will increasingly be regarded as dangerous. If this happens, many of the traits currently assigned to Jews—aggressiveness, clannishness, unfairness—may be attributed to Negroes.

When inter-ethnic contacts are extended over a long period of time, the stereotype of a group may become a composite concept, and its evaluation may become ambivalent. During the Spanish rule of the Philippines the Chinese were regarded with mixed feelings. Economically they were seen as useful objects, and as in other parts of Southeast Asia where the natives were believed to be indolent, they were welcomed as industrious workers. Once they became well established, however, they were redefined as dangerous objects. They were resented as shrewd and grasping and were accused of draining away the silver subsidies which the Spaniards had received from Mexico and Peru. Morally the Chinese were regarded as inferior

---

[53] Louis Golding, *The Jewish Problem* (Middlesex, England: Penguin Books, 1938), pp. 58–70; and Justus F. C. Hecker, *The Epidemics of the Middle Ages*, trans. B. G. Babington (London: Trübner, 1859), pp. 38–43.

objects—corrupt and given to all kinds of superstitions and vices. Although there were occasional uprisings in their large colony in Manila, the Chinese were in the main submissive and seldom posed a serious threat to established authority. Thus, in spite of their misgivings, the officials never enforced the laws restricting Chinese immigration as vigorously as they opposed the Japanese, whose ambition and aggressive spirit they feared.[54]

Evaluations of ethnic categories are conventional meanings and are supported by group sanctions. In a stable society such estimates are taken for granted, and individuals who do not comply are punished. In a changing society, however, there are individual variations. Misunderstandings arise because each person reacts somewhat differently. There is much hesitation, and impulses are suppressed. In addition, there is likely to be more ambivalence. Those who participate in more than one reference group are likely to learn somewhat different evaluations of each ethnic category.

Evaluations of ethnic categories are learned and reinforced in social contexts. We may learn that one is dirty and upon contact react with loathing; we may learn that another is dangerous and automatically assume a defensive stance; we may learn that another is childlike and prepare to enjoy him in a patronizing way. Such meanings become structured in this manner as a result of past episodes and communication. Many of them are learned as by-products of other activities, often activities having nothing to do with ethnic identity. Unlike the subjects taught by teachers or by parents, many meanings are learned informally in contexts that are soon forgotten.[55] Hence, from time to time each person experiences impulses to act that he cannot understand nor justify. Upon coming into contact with members of an ethnic group he may experience a strong aversion; he can think of no reason for it but cannot "help it." Similarly, some people feel a compelling fascination for a group. Thus some meanings appear irrational.

Many of the statements made about ethnic categories are actually rationalizations after the fact. A man feels uncomfortable in the presence of someone but can see no rational grounds for his reaction. If pressed for reasons, he may say that the person is dirty

---

[54] William L. Schurz, *Manila Galleon* (New York: E. P. Dutton, 1939), pp. 63–128. Cf. Purcell, *op. cit.*, pp. 455–56, 663–67.

[55] Cf. Chester Alexander, "Antipathy and Human Behavior," *American Journal of Sociology*, LI (1946), 288–92.

or smells bad. Actually he has reacted to an abstract concept, which has been evaluated negatively, and then rationalized his conduct. Thus, conclusive proof that most Negroes are neither dirty nor immoral would not make such an individual less apprehensive about a Negro family's moving in next door. He may even tell himself that his conduct is stupid, but he does not feel any less uncomfortable.

The Personal Equation in Ethnocentrism

In his classic study of folkways Sumner pointed out that all people are necessarily *ethnocentric* in that they use the values of their own group as standards for judging everyone else. To the extent that any group is isolated, it develops a distinctive way of viewing the universe. The conventional ways of doing things in one's own group appear right and natural. Thus, all people refer to themselves as "men" and see others as something less than human —as "barbarians," "frogs," or "gooks." Outsiders living in adjacent territories are often referred to with epithets—"raw eaters," "uncircumcised," "idolators," or "eater of snakes." When viewed in terms of one's own standards, outsiders invariably seem strange— perverse, comical, or even immoral.[56] Each group regards its own women as irresistible and assumes that all other men covet them. In American fiction, for example, the beautiful white heroine is pursued by savages, Arabian sheiks, King Kong, and even creatures from outer space. During the Boxer uprising in China, when the foreign settlement in Peking was besieged by Chinese revolutionaries, European and American troops forgot their other differences and struggled together against great odds to protect white women from a "fate worse than death." [57]

Europeans and Americans have dominated most of the world for several centuries; hence, they conceive of themselves as valuable objects and assume that other people appreciate them as such. For this reason they are often surprised to learn how some other people actually do see them. In *Dead Man in the Silver Market* Menen gives a charming account of the reaction of his grandmother, a high-caste

---

[56] William G. Sumner, *Folkways* (Boston: Ginn, 1906) pp. 13–15. Cf. George P. Murdock, "Ethnocentrism," *Encyclopedia of the Social Sciences*, Vol. V, pp. 613–14.

[57] Cf. Smedley D. Butler, "Dame Rumor: The Biggest Liar in the World," *American Magazine*, CXI (June 1931), 24–26, 155–56; and Peter Fleming, *The Siege at Peking* (New York: Harper, 1959).

Hindu, to the English. She had never met any Englishmen but knew all about them; they were tall, fair, given to strong drink, and had conquered her country. Her chief complaint was that they were so dirty; they did not take the minimum of two baths a day, as all decent people should. She was not surprised that the English ate ham or beef; after all, the outcastes who cleaned her latrines ate anything. But their way of eating went beyond the pale of human decency. In her house each person ate separately, preferably in a secluded corner. The thought that human beings could sit opposite each other and watch one another thrust food into their mouths, masticate, and swallow it left her horrified.[58] Americans need only think of the stereotype of the "Gringo" in Latin America to realize that their ways are not appreciated everywhere. Humphrey found that educated Mexicans who had not been in the United States saw Americans as overactive, puritanical Babbitts, with more money than "culture," buying respect but lacking in urbanity. The wealth and power of the country was acknowledged, but it was seen as a nation of crass materialists—much like the Roman Empire on the edge of catastrophe. Americans were seen as superior in technology but inferior in poetry, philosophy, and a feeling for art and music. The forthrightness and bluntness that characterizes many Americans was seen as an indication of a lack of courtesy and an insensitivity to the feelings of others. The sexual morality of American women was thought to border on that of the prostitute.[59]

Although anthropologists and others who have read and traveled widely may succeed in overcoming part of their ethnocentrism, it is difficult even for them. A scholar may recognize that values are relative and accept intellectually the fact that a man who is about to murder someone is only performing his duty, but the whole episode is still likely to leave him shaken. Once a perspective is well established, it interferes with its own revision; a way of seeing is also a way of not seeing. When a pattern of expectancy has been established, it is readily confirmed with a minimum of sensory cues. People develop an intuitive sense of what appropriately goes with what, and they tend to see things in these terms. There is a closed

[58] Aubrey Menen, *Dead Man in the Silver Market* (New York: Scribner's, 1953), pp. 24–29.
[59] Norman D. Humphrey, "Ethnic Images and Stereotypes of Mexicans and Americans," *American Journal of Economics and Sociology* XIV (1955), 305–13.

circle: those who use a given perspective set up the standards in terms of which its adequacy is judged. This means that people develop a "trained incapacity" for seeing things that are inconsistent with their beliefs, things that may be perfectly obvious to anyone else.[60] The inability to see contradictory evidence plays an important part in all forms of social stratification. Upper-class people are often unable to understand the discontent of the poor; many sincerely believe that the impoverished were born indolent and that they enjoy living in poverty.

Because of ethnocentrism people in different ethnic groups frequently fail to comprehend one another's intentions and deeds. Misunderstandings arise especially in areas regarded as sacred. The violation of sacred values arouses emotional reactions; sometimes people are so repulsed by what they see that they feel nauseated, and this makes them even more convinced that the outsiders are of a different breed. In every group there are conventional norms governing interpersonal relations—ways of showing affection and loyalties. The inability to understand these norms often results in misinterpretations. In the Dutch East Indies, for example, the Chinese concluded that the Dutch did not possess any of the cardinal virtues. They allowed husbands and wives to separate and remarry and even permitted a widow to go live with another man before her husband had been dead for a month. Furthermore, the Dutch seemingly made no distinctions of rank among themselves, and men and women mingled together. They were obviously devoid of any sense of propriety.[61] In each culture there are understandings about modesty; a decent person is expected to cover certain parts of his body, and there are times and places for defecation, urination, belching, or flatulence. Thus, Americans who visit France are often shocked by the sidewalk urinals, for some of them provide a shield hardly more than four feet in height. Since members of different ethnic groups have different conceptions of personal honor, people sometimes insult one another inadvertently. The German adventurer Siemel recounts that his brother was stalked through the Matto Grosso by a Brazilian he had thrashed in an argument. Neither of the Siemels realized until much later that being beaten with fists was the most humiliating thing that could happen to a Brazilian;

[60] Cf. Burke, *op. cit.*, pp. 5–79.
[61] Purcell, *op. cit.*, p. 481.

the latter would have preferred to be killed. Hence, he pursued relentlessly a man who only thought to spare him from serious injury.[62]

Thus, what is decisive about "race relations" is not that people are genetically different but that they approach one another with dissimilar perspectives. The basic differences between ethnic groups, if there are any at all, are in mentality. The fact that men start with different premises accentuates other, more visible differences. For this reason most of the phenomena occurring in inter-ethnic contacts are also found in the associations of other kinds of groups whose perspectives differ. When folk or rural people come into contact with sophisticated urbanites, similar misunderstandings arise. In areas of the world that are now undergoing industrialization, people are being brought into contact with a new way of life through the media of mass communication. Although in many cases there are relatively few actual contacts with outsiders, many of the phenomena described in this book occur. The development of a new mentality is more important than the presence of people with a different set of ancestors.

As long as people remain completely ethnocentric, they will continue to perceive one another in stereotyped terms. But close and frequent contacts across the color line provide many opportunities for seeing contradictory evidence. Since stereotypes are abstract concepts, there are very few human beings that will actually fit them, and even those who appear to have some of the more conspicuous traits will upon closer examination prove to have many other characteristics that do not fit. The more one meets members of other ethnic categories, the more exceptions he finds. In fact, the better one gets to know anyone, the more he is seen as a distinct personality that does not fit into any social type. Thus, in a small midwestern rural community Brookover and Holland found that the people shared unfavorable stereotypes of Negroes and Jews but that they did not act in terms of them in their associations with the individual Negroes and Jews who lived there. They were known as distinct individuals and were treated as such.[63] After close per-

---

[62] Sasha Siemel, *Tigrero* (New York, Prentice-Hall, 1953).
[63] Wilbur Brookover and John B. Holland, "An Inquiry into the Meaning of Minority Group Attitude Expressions," *American Sociological Review,* XVII (1952), 196–202.

sonal contacts with members of other ethnic groups, some individuals revise their estimates, but others do not. In the antebellum South masters and household slaves lived in constant association throughout their lives. Some became very close personal friends, but others remained strangers to the end.

Developing an appreciation of a perspective other than one's own is apparently a difficult thing to do, and individuals differ considerably in their ability to assume a relativistic standpoint. Some are able to accept the fact that other people have different standards of conduct, and they learn to tolerate things that they themselves find distasteful. Others, however, find it painful to admit that their outlook is not absolute; they find it disquieting to question what they had previously taken for granted. They are apparently unable to perceive accurately behavior that contradicts their expectations, and in many cases they may even project their own characteristics to others to make what they see more meaningful.[64]

In situations in which the color line is undergoing change, there are many occasions in which members of different ethnic groups come into close and frequent contact. Since there is no consensus on what is to be done, there are more opportunities for acting on the basis of one's personal preferences. In such contexts individuals vary considerably in the extent to which they maintain social distance from people whom they regard as different from themselves. Consciousness of status differences interferes with the establishment of intimacy. Distinctions of all kinds call for manifestations of deference—obeisance, condescension, ceremonies. Such rituals reinforce personal reserve as well as stereotyped conceptions.

Since Park suggested the metaphor in 1924, many studies have documented the phenomenon of social distance. An attitude scale was devised by Bogardus. He asked each subject if he would be willing to admit members of a given ethnic group to kinship by marriage, to his club as a personal chum, to the same street as a neighbor, to employment in the same occupation, to citizenship in his country, to his country only as a visitor, or would insist upon their total exclusion. On the basis of the replies Bogardus was able to compute a numerical score indicating the degree of closeness

[64] Cf. Frederick W. Koenig and Morton B. King, "Cognitive Simplicity and Prejudice," *Social Forces*, **XL** (1962), 220–22; and Milton Rokeach, *The Open and Closed Mind* (New York: Basic Books, 1960).

between each subject and each ethnic category.[65] Since that time the scale has undergone several modifications, but the basic rationale has remained unchanged. Hundreds of studies have been conducted with it throughout the world, revealing extensive regional and individual variations. Some individuals are willing to admit members of other ethnic groups into the intimacy of their own family; they approve of intermarriage. Others are unwilling to go that far but are willing to accept outsiders as co-workers or neighbors. They maintain their reserve, but they try to be friendly in their contacts. Still others are unwilling to work or live with strangers but are willing to have them live in the same town—as long as they remain away from them. As a matter of principle they defend the rights of these people to livelihood and decent treatment before the law. Still others are not willing to have them in the same community; they would be happier if all "foreigners" went to live in other countries. Some may even support repressive measures against them. In a changing society, such as we have in the United States today, there are many shades of opinion on almost all issues, and definitions of ethnic categories vary.

Some individuals treat members of each ethnic group differently. They have somewhat different conceptions of each, and they act accordingly—favoring some and opposing or avoiding others. Thus, Bettelheim and Janowitz found that the orientation of most of their subjects toward Negroes was quite different from that toward Jews. Other individuals, however, treat all alien peoples alike—in most cases unfavorably. In the study reported in *The Authoritarian Personality*, Adorno and his associates found that those who were hostile toward one ethnic minority were likely to be against all others. This confirmed the results of an earlier study by Murphy and Likert, who found high correlations in social distance toward 21 different ethnic groups.[66] Hartley subsequently questioned his subjects concerning 35 ethnic categories, including three fictitious ones—Danireans, Pireneans, and Wallonians—and found that those who were hostile to one were likely to be against all the others, including those that did not even exist.[67]

[65] Emory S. Bogardus, "Measuring Social Distance," *Journal of Applied Sociology*, **IX** (1925), 299–308.

[66] Gardner Murphy and Rensis Likert, *Public Opinion and the Individual* (New York: Harper, 1938).

[67] Eugene L. Hartley, *Problems in Prejudice* (New York: King's Crown Press, 1946).

This suggests that some individuals are rigid in their perception of outsiders and have particular difficulty in getting outside their ethnocentric perspectives. The central thesis of *The Authoritarian Personality* was that political, economic, and social convictions form a broad and coherent pattern—a "mentality"—and that this pattern is a manifestation of underlying tendencies in an individual's personality. Using a wide variety of research techniques—questionnaires, attitude scales, clinical interviews, projective tests—the team of psychologists questioned large numbers of college students as well as members of the armed forces, of unions, of fraternal organizations, and of various voluntary associations. They found consistently high intercorrelations between certain personality traits: inability to see anything except in terms of egocentric interests, intensity and venom in hostility toward other people, and numerous beliefs, such as political conservatism and unfavorable views of ethnic minorities. They developed a simplified device—called the F-scale—which provided a relatively easy way of measuring this mentality. In comparing those with very high scores on the F-scale with those with very low scores, they found that the most clearcut differentiation between them was yielded by the manner in which the subjects evaluated themselves. Those with high scores—designated as "authoritarian personalities"— are not able to face unacceptable tendencies within themselves and cannot integrate them into their conscious self-image. Hence, there is a tendency to project them to others; other people are seen as hostile and threatening. There are attempts to compensate for a low level of self-esteem through a compulsive drive for success and power, and there is much concern over the opinions of others and an excessive preoccupation with social status. One of the major characteristics of such individuals is rigidity—a tendency to maintain a simple, firm, stereotyped cognitive structure. The authors contended that this type of person is the product of conditional affection from parents who are rigid disciplinarians overly concerned with matters of status.[68] Following this study an extensive body of literature has developed concerning the characteristics of the "prejudiced man." [69]

Because of the scope and significance of the study there have been many elaborations and critiques, and it has been the center of

---

[68] T. W. Adorno, Else Frenkel-Brunswik, Daniel J. Levinson, and R. Nevitt Sanford, *The Authoritarian Personality* (New York: Harper, 1950).

[69] Cf. Gordon W. Allport, *The Nature of Prejudice* (Cambridge, Mass.: Addison-Wesley Publishing Co., 1954), pp. 395–457.

considerable controversy. The methods have been subjected to careful review, and many attempts have been made to recheck the findings.[70] A number of studies have confirmed the findings or have developed hypotheses consistent with them. Ackerman and Jahoda studied people undergoing psychoanalytic therapy and found that certain types of people tended to displace their hostility upon Jews.[71] Bettelheim and Janowitz found that hostility against minority groups was found more often among men who were embittered, who felt deprived, who rejected various institutions. They found that intolerant men not only worked with stereotyped conceptions but tended to avoid reality testing.[72] On the other hand, there have been contradictory findings. In South Africa Pettigrew found that almost 70 per cent of his European subjects held stereotyped conceptions of the natives but that their F-scale scores did not differ significantly from those of Americans who were less rigid.[73] Furthermore, in a comparative study of American subjects in the North and South, he found considerably more hostility toward Negroes in the South but no significant regional differences in scores on the F-scale.[74] Although ethnic stratification cannot be explained adequately in terms of personality variables, there seems to be little doubt that some individuals have greater difficulty in accepting members of other ethnic groups. Psychiatrists have long pointed out that certain types of people are more readily disposed to hostility; they see their world as a threatening place and find it necessary constantly to defend themselves. If such individuals happen to be in positions of power and influence, they could wield disproportionate influence upon the course of events.

Summary and Conclusion

The manner in which people are treated depends upon the way

[70] Cf. Richard Christie and Marie Jahoda (eds.), *Studies in the Scope and Method of the Authoritarian Personality* (Glencoe, Ill.: The Free Press, 1954).

[71] Ackerman and Jahoda, *op. cit.*

[72] Bettelheim and Janowitz, *op. cit.*, pp. 32–47, 62–140. Cf. Jack and Jeanne Block, "An Investigation of the Relationship Between Intolerance of Ambiguity and Ethnocentrism," *Journal of Personality*, **XIX** (1951), 303–11.

[73] Pettigrew, *op. cit.*

[74] Thomas F. Pettigrew, "Regional Differences in Anti-Negro Prejudice," *Journal of Abnormal and Social Psychology*, **LIX** (1959), 28–36. Cf. Edwin H. Rhyne, "Racial Prejudice and Personality Scales: An Alternative Approach," *Social Forces*, **XLI** (1962), 44–53.

in which they are classified and evaluated. Men interact in terms of the assumptions they form about each other, and ethnic stereotypes are among the popular concepts underlying concerted action. Typical evaluations of ethnic categories depend upon the relative positions of groups in a system of stratification. Ethnic categories and their evaluations are group definitions. In a stable society these meanings enjoy a high degree of consensus; in a changing society, however, the estimates vary. Opportunities arise for individuals to act in terms of their personal preferences, and they differ considerably in their ability to understand the behavior of those with different cultural backgrounds. The fact that some individuals seem almost incapable of noticing evidence that contradicts their stereotyped conceptions has led to the study of personality types that may be rigidly ethnocentric.

If an individual discloses an attitude that is not approved by those around him and finds that he cannot readily alter his stance, he is commonly described as prejudiced. This popular concept is useful in daily discourse for designating those attitudes of which the speaker happens to disapprove. For purposes of sociological analysis, however, its reference is much too imprecise. Several types of orientations have been described in this chapter, and only some of them are called "prejudice"—by those who happen to disapprove of them. Other orientations, which constitute the same type of behavior, tend to be overlooked, for they are not singled out for condemnation. What is commonly called "race prejudice" is not a unitary phenomenon; the same term is used to refer to a variety of activities. We cannot formulate and test generalizations without agreement over what it is that is being designated by the concepts; since the word "prejudice" has different meanings for different sociologists, we would do better to abandon it in sociology. The subjective orientations of the participants in ethnic stratification are important, but they must be studied through concepts that are more neutral.

CHAPTER 5

Recurrent Patterns
of Transformation

Viewed in broad historical perspective the story of mankind consists of a succession of contacts of ethnic groups, their conflicts, their accommodations to one another, and their eventual fusion into new ethnic groups. When the newly formed groups come into contact with still other ethnic groups, each similarly formed, the cycle appears to start all over again. Such transactions have occurred over and over, and the question arises: can we generalize about them? Most sociologists are committed to the position that fruitful generalizations about group activities can be constructed, and much of their time is devoted to the formulation and testing of such propositions.

We may begin by agreeing with historians that every situation of inter-ethnic contact is unique. The culture of the groups involved vary, and the peculiar circumstances under which they meet are not likely to be repeated; each system of ethnic stratification has its distinctive characteristics. In spite of this diversity in historical contexts, however, certain types of events are repeated, and our attention will be focused upon the uniformities found in the behavior of men under stated conditions. All generalizations are abstractions; they necessarily omit some things and emphasize others. There is no science in which the "laws" constitute a carbon copy of reality, and sociologists likewise are concerned only with describing regularities. An examination of concrete cases of inter-ethnic contacts shows that almost every conceivable type of social interaction has been involved, and the quest for generalizations is rendered difficult by these extensive variations. Our first query, then, is: how can descriptive data best be ordered for the formulation and testing of generalizations about ethnic stratification?

The Incorporation of Immigrants

Historical and ethnographic accounts provide a mass of data, and one useful way of organizing these materials was proposed by Park in his "race relations cycle." Park believed that inter-ethnic contacts everywhere resulted in competition and conflict between the groups and that out of this arose new forms of association. The developmental sequence he provided is one that is familiar to most Americans. It begins with the arrival of immigrants in a well-established community. Since the newcomers cannot compete for jobs on an equal basis, they are relegated to the bottom of the social ladder. But their descendants get an education, move upward, and eventually are assimilated into the general population. Park regarded this cycle as the *natural history* of the contact of peoples. When a biologist speaks of a natural history, he is referring to the stages of development through which some plant or animal grows. Similarly, a sociologist developing a natural history would collect, compare, and classify historical facts to isolate a *typical* pattern of development, one that would hold irrespective of time or place. According to Park, the cycle everywhere repeats itself, and it is progressive and irreversible. Custom regulations, immigration restrictions, and segregation may slow it down and may even halt it altogether for a time, but its direction cannot be changed or reversed.[1] We shall begin by reviewing Park's cycle, particularly as it applies to the successive waves of immigrants into the United States. This will enable us to see how natural histories illuminate bodies of historical data and at

[1] Park, *op. cit.*, pp. 138-51.

the same time provide a useful overview of the contact of peoples to serve as the basis for the more detailed discussions to follow.

The first stage in the cycle is the establishment of *contact* between two or more ethnic groups, and this is the result of migration. The United States is a nation of immigrants. For more than two centuries it has been the common man's utopia, and from 1815 to 1914 more than 35 million people came here from Europe. Those who had been impoverished by changes in agricultural system, overpopulation, or disasters, as well as victims of religious persecution, war, or revolution, came in search of new opportunities. The immigrants provided much needed labor for the rapidly expanding economy, and most of them were welcomed. There was no thought of conquest on the part of the newcomers. In some cases they did not even regard their move as permanent, and they were sometimes called "birds of passage," since they desired only to make their fortunes and to return "home." From 1830 to 1860 most of the immigrants were from the British Isles. From 1860 to 1890 the majority came from the Rhine Valley, the English midlands, Scandinavia, the Baltic provinces, Poland, and Austria. From 1890 to 1914 the bulk of the immigrants were drawn from the Mediterranean region—from Italy, the Balkans, and the Near East.[2] Prior to the abolition of the slave trade there was also a steady flow of Africans to the Southern states. The Pacific Coast and the Southwest attracted a large number of immigrants from China, Japan, and Mexico. The most recent mass migration has been from Puerto Rico. Although some believe that the people who arrived before 1776 were fundamentally different from those who followed, there was actually no difference in the motives, problems, and difficulties faced by all of these people, except for the African slaves.

Contact is followed by *competition*, especially for land and for jobs. With the exception of some skilled artisans and professional men, the immigrants started as unskilled agricultural or industrial workers. Because of their newness and lack of familiarity with the culture, especially the language, they could not compete on equal terms. They had to accept whatever work was available, and these were often the jobs that better-established people were unwilling to do. Even if these were not desirable jobs in the eyes of their new

---

[2] Marcus L. Hansen, *The Atlantic Migration, 1607–1860* (New York: Harper, 1961).

countrymen, many immigrants found the tasks easy and the pay high in comparison to what they had received at home; thus they were happy with their work and pleased their employers by their enthusiasm and conscientious performance. The kind of work that no one else wants usually carries the lowest status; therefore immigrants were often the target of scorn. In some cases, when competition was intensified, it turned into conflict.

The outcome of competition and conflict is *accommodation*, the establishment of relatively stable patterns of concerted action. Conflict in particular is disagreeable, and some kind of *modus vivendi* is worked out. The working arrangements by which members of different ethnic groups are able to approach one another with fixed expectations constitute a system of ethnic stratification. The competition for jobs results in the distribution of ethnic groups into different kinds of work. Thus, in New England during the interwar years, there was a disproportionately large number of French-Canadians working in cotton and woolen mills, Poles in iron foundries, Italians in heavy road and ditch-digging jobs, Greeks in restaurants, and Chinese in laundries. Banks and brokerages were operated by the "Yankees" of the older families.[3] Once such an ethnic division of labor becomes a set pattern, it is used to demonstrate that certain kinds of people are naturally suited for certain kinds of work. Thus, competition results in the formation of a new economic structure, which in turn becomes the basis for a new political order. What starts as the struggle for existence terminates in the struggle for status—for recognition and prestige—within a political and moral order.

The competition for space results in the formation of segregated ethnic islands, each of which develops a distinctive culture. Members of each minority group tend to congregate in areas where they can speak their own language and follow their own customs. Many such colonies were formed in the United States—Harlem in New York, Little Sicily in Chicago, and Chinatown in San Francisco. In competing for a place to live, the immigrants were at a disadvantage. They did not have sufficient income to afford anything better than substandard housing in the slums. Furthermore, they were sometimes the target of hostility and were not permitted to live in the

[3] Elin L. Anderson, *We Americans* (Cambridge: Harvard University Press, 1937), pp. 51–77.

more desirable areas. In addition, many immigrants wanted to be among people with whom they identified—among whom they could relax and from whom they could count on sympathetic support.[4] Once such colonies are established, people of a given ethnic group tend to gravitate to them.

The fourth stage in the cycle is _assimilation_. Members of minority groups acquire the culture of the dominant group and in time are absorbed into the general population. Here Park was speaking more of the sharing of common perspectives than of intermarriage and amalgamation, although the latter phenomena usually follow. This transition is by no means an easy one. In most minority groups in the United States assimilation did not occur with the immigrants themselves but with their children and grandchildren. During the transitional period the ethnic colonies became disorganized; the incidence of crime, delinquency, and dependency was high. This resulted in part from the breakdown of social control. As the children acquired standards of conduct and aspirations different from those of their parents, they no longer respected them enough to comply with their demands. Furthermore, these people lived in areas that had attracted those engaging in illicit activities—criminals, prostitutes, drug addicts, hoboes, and thrill seekers. The youngsters grew up in areas in which deviant values were emphasized. Thus, one ethnic group after another became the object of police vigilance.

After a period of sustained contact, however, cultural differences between ethnic groups progressively diminish. Friendships inevitably cut across the color line and undermine segregation. As increasing numbers in minority groups become assimilated, intermarriages become more common, and this results eventually in the formation of a new physical type. After several more generations most traces of the immigration disappear. Thus, the final stage of the cycle is the occupation of the territory by people who share a common culture and identify with each other as being of a kind.

 This pattern of temporary segregation and upward mobility characterizes virtually all immigrant groups in the United States. Although the immigrants almost invariably started at the bottom of the

---

[4] Robert E. Park, Ernest W. Burgess, and Roderick D. McKenzie, _The City_ (Chicago: University of Chicago Press, 1925). Cf. Walter Firey, "Sentiments and Symbolism as Ecological Variables," _American Sociological Review_, X (1945), 140–48; and Maurice R. Stein, _The Eclipse of Community_ (Princeton: Princeton University Press, 1960), pp. 13–46.

economic scale, they soon began to move upward because of their habits of thrift and their willingness to do hard work. If this did not occur in the first generation, it generally happened in the second. The more ambitious families moved into better neighborhoods as soon as possible. But assimilation is basically a psychological transformation. When a person of Irish ancestry no longer conceives of himself as an Irishman but as an American, he is well on his way. He sees himself, his parents, and other people from the same perspective as other Americans. When this happens on a large scale in any minority group, the only barrier to the disappearance of ethnic islands is opposition from the outside. Thus far, immigrants from areas other than Europe have encountered more resistance, but even these barriers seem to be breaking down.

Thus, in the United States a succession of ethnic groups have gone through roughly the same cycle, and some others are still on the way. The descendants of Irish, Scotch, English, Scandinavian, and German immigrants have long been assimilated. Italians and Greeks are well on their way, although some sense of ethnic identity still remains. Chinese, Japanese, and Mexicans are still segregated to some extent, while Negroes and Puerto Ricans face serious problems. A glance at the history of any low-status occupation will show that the positions have been filled by representatives of a succession of ethnic groups, each as it stood near the bottom of the social scale. A review of prominent boxers in the United States from 1909 to 1948 reveals that they were at first mostly Irish and Jewish, then Italian, and lately predominantly Negro.[5] The tribulations of a Norwegian family in San Francisco, so movingly portrayed in Kathryn Forbes' *Mama's Bank Account*, have been repeated over and over among the Poles, the Chinese, and the Jews. The disappearing Irish-Americans depicted in the novels of James T. Farrell pursued careers now being enacted by Puerto Ricans, Mexicans, and Negroes.

Although this pattern of development is most readily discernible in the United States, it can also be observed elsewhere. Similar sequences apparently took place among the Jews who migrated to various German cities in the eighteenth and nineteenth centuries, the Koreans who migrated to Japan, and the European refugees who

[5] S. Kirson Weinberg and Henry Arond, "The Occupational Culture of the Boxer," *American Journal of Sociology*, LVII (1952), 460–69.

settled in Australia after World War II. Since the establishment of modern Israel, Jewish refugees from all over the world have arrived, found themselves surrounded by strange people who also called themselves Jews, and formed a pluralistic society. But their children, the Sabras, are developing a new culture quite different from those of their parents.[6]

Because of the influence of Park and his students the "race relations cycle" has been widely used by sociologists. Although this developmental sequence is found in a great many cases, many difficulties arise when an attempt is made to apply it everywhere. Because there are so many exceptions other sociologists have proposed revisions.[7] Actually, a review of the data reveals that there are at least three other natural histories that can be found with considerable frequency.

Patterns of Conquest and Domination

In the second type of cycle a large number of colonists move into a relatively undeveloped area with the intention of establishing a permanent settlement. Where necessary, they displace the native population. In most cases such settlements develop in areas with geographical conditions similar to those in the homeland. The westward movement of American pioneers was a migration of this kind, as was the movement of European settlers to Australia, New Zealand, and South Africa.[8]

Initial contacts are generally friendly. As increasing numbers of immigrants encroach on native territory, however, competition turns into conflict. The resolution of the difficulties is a matter of relative power. If the invaders are expelled, contact is terminated at this point, except for a small number of stragglers and traders who are eventually incorporated into the native population. If the invaders win, however, the entire pattern of life in the area is transformed.

[6] S. N. Eisenstadt, *The Absorption of Immigrants* (Glencoe, Ill.: The Free Press, 1955).

[7] Cf. W. O. Brown, "Culture Contact and Race Conflict," in E. B. Reuter (ed.), *Race and Culture Contacts* (New York: McGraw-Hill, 1934), pp. 34–37; E. K. Francis, "Variables in the Formation of So-Called Minority Groups," *American Journal of Sociology*, LX (1954), 6–14; Glick, *op. cit.*; and Stanley Lieberson, "A Societal Theory of Race and Ethnic Relations," *American Sociological Review*, XXVI (1961), 902–10.

[8] Cf. René Maunier, *The Sociology of Colonies*, trans. E. O. Lorimer (London: Routledge & Kegan Paul, 1949), Vol. I, pp. 75–85; and A. Grenfell Price, *White Settlers and Native Peoples* (Melbourne, Australia: Georgian House, 1950).

On the American frontier the early contacts were friendly. Since the Indians had no conception of private ownership of land, they at first had no objections to Europeans settling in their midst. When they realized that their own subsistence was threatened, however, serious difficulties broke out. For a time the United States government purchased land west of the Mississippi and exchanged it for land east of the river. One by one the tribes moved, and by 1842 there were only a few Indians left east of the Mississippi, but the whole vast area to the west was "Indian territory."

The intrusion of a new ethnic group, even if it is peaceful, disrupts the way of life that had previously developed in the area. The new group not only increases the total population relative to the available natural resources but also brings in new techniques for exploiting the resources. The introduction of superior agricultural methods, firearms, and the horse changed the way of life of the Indians. Ancient customs that were out of line with the new circumstances died. Many Indians found it easier to trade pelts for manufactured goods than to make their own utensils and weapons. This required specialization in hunting, however, and it ruined their means of subsistence. The native population is sometimes reduced through depopulation. In some cases the food supply becomes limited; the American pioneers decimated the buffalo herds of the Plains Indians. New diseases against which immunities had not been developed may cut the natives down; thus, the Missouri Indians became extinct from smallpox. In some cases depopulation may result from social disorganization. With the breakdown of the traditional order there is widespread vice and prostitution; venereal diseases and personal demoralization take their toll.

The natives generally make some attempt to resist the encroachments of the settlers, and intense conflict takes place. Although the term "genocide" is relatively new, the practice is not. When the settlers become convinced that their interests are incompatible with those of the natives, they may undertake a campaign of mass slaughter. As the enemy comes to be regarded as something less than human, identification with the victim is reduced to a minimum; the slaughter goes on until the losers are exterminated, expelled, or segregated. The British colonists in Tasmania viewed the natives as a degenerate "race." Some of them hunted the aborigines for sport or to provide meat for their dogs; they chained up the women, raped, and then killed them. When the natives retaliated, a full-scale war began. Finally, to stop the slaughter, the governor offered a bounty of £5 for every adult and £2 for every child captured alive. The colonists formed a cordon of 5,000 armed men, stretching from one end of the island to the other, to capture every native, but only two were caught. Later on, a man who had won the confidence of the Tasmanians persuaded them to give themselves up. The 203 survivors were segregated, and the last of them died in 1876.[9] Even when conflict does not go to such extremes, the native group is usually subjugated and set aside. The *apartheid* program of the Union of South Africa may be regarded as a delayed attempt at complete segregation. Public opinion in the rest of the world would not now tolerate mass slaughter, and at this stage even segregation cannot be accomplished without damaging the economy. But *apartheid*, if carried out, would result in a partial displacement of the native population.

Americans who are horrified by these cases should remember that the expansion of the Western frontier was not exactly amicable especially from the standpoint of the Indians. Not all the land west of the Mississippi was traded to Indians of the east. Missouri became a state in 1821, and when Texas was seized from Mexico, the Santa Fe trail was opened to the West. The discovery of a pass through the Rockies led to the establishment of the Oregon trail, and in 1837, when a depression drove the unemployed out of the Great Lakes area, many caravans began to enter Indian country. The gold rush in California led to another stream. The rivalry between the North and the South led to further encroachments on Indian territory; each side wanted settlers sympathetic to its cause to take over land to bring a new "slave" or "free" state into the Union. Before 1848 the United States government had treaties with the various Plains Indians permitting wagon trains to go through unmolested; these agreements stipulated that the wagons were to stay on the trails and that the pioneers were not to bother bisons nor to stop to farm. When these treaties were violated, fighting broke out. From 1864 to 1890 there were a series of uprisings of the Plains Indians. The mass slaughter of Indians apparently started on the Pacific Coast, where some tribes were almost exterminated. Whenever a white man was found dead, people assumed that an Indian had killed him; in retaliation all Indians in the

[9] Clive Turnbull, *Black War* (London: F. W. Cheshire, 1948).

vicinity—men, women, and children—were rounded up and killed. The Indians were called "bucks" and "squaws" and were regarded as half-beasts. Attempts to eliminate these "savages" went to the point of deliberately leaving clothing infected with smallpox in the woods where Indians were known to pass. One political party openly advocated their annihilation. By 1890 the Indians were subdued by superior military power, and the survivors were herded into reservations, where they became wards of the government.[10]

When war ends, one ethnic group is so reduced in number that it becomes insignificant. The few who remain are eventually absorbed into the general population and lose their identity. At this stage, when the minority group is no longer threatening, this cycle resembles that of the absorption of immigrants, except that the dominant group consists of the invaders. A large number of Indians are still living on reservations, but many are now attempting to resettle in the mainstream of American life. Although they have sometimes been treated as aliens on their own land, they are gradually becoming assimilated.[11]

Chinese colonial settlements have usually been more peaceful, but remnants of other ethnic groups have been absorbed into the Chinese population in the same manner. In Kansu the Chinese have long been displacing the Tibetans. Since one Tibetan male in three went into a monastery, there was generally a shortage of men. Prior to the Communist revolution many Chinese migrated, fleeing from overpopulation or from bandits. At first they adopted the Tibetan way of life; as their numbers increased, however, each village became more Chinese. The wearing of trousers became a symbol of high rank, as did the use of chopsticks and the installation of a *kang* (heated bed). Soon the people took on surnames, adopted carts, and buried their dead. In a few generations everyone in the area was Chinese.[12] A similar displacement took place on Formosa. With each change of dynasties in China, a new wave of settlers came from Kwantung and Fukien. The newcomers drove out the Dutch colonists and forced the natives to retreat into the mountains. By 1935 the aboriginal population made up only 4 per cent of the total, and most Formosans

[10] William C. MacLeod, *The American Indian Frontier* (New York: Alfred A. Knopf, 1928).

[11] Burt W. Aginsky, "The Interaction of Ethnic Groups: A Case Study of Indians and Whites," *American Sociological Review*, XIV (1949), 288-93.

[12] Ekvall, *op. cit.*

today are descendants of the Chinese settlers.[13] Other ethnic groups that have been displaced include the Hottentots in South Africa, the Ainus in Japan, and the Negritos of the Malay archipelago. Thus, the final stage in the cycle finds the area occupied by one ethnic group.

The third type of cycle is found in places where the climate is not thought suitable for settlement. Here colonies are established for profit. Where there are vast differences in technology and military power, a relatively small number of colonists can subjugate a large native population and hold the area as an economic complement to the mother country.[14] In most cases, especially after the Industrial Revolution, the economies have been based upon mines or plantations. The Dutch in the East Indies, the British in the West Indies, in India, and in central Africa, the French in Indo-China, and the Spanish and the Portuguese in much of Latin America established colonies of this nature.

Contacts in which economic interests are conspicuously involved are usually friendly in the beginning. Where only a few traders and explorers venture into a strange area, they are hardly in a position to begin asserting their superiority. Traders generally have little interest in the native culture, and no matter how objectionable the customs may appear, they make no effort to alter them. They are reluctant to do anything that might jeopardize their connections. As profitable enterprises are established, however, various governmental agencies take over to maintain order and to insure continuation. In the European colonies difficulties usually arose from the problem of recruiting an adequate labor supply. Since the temperature in these areas was high, the colonists themselves were reluctant to work. In some cases the natives were induced to work; where they proved to be reluctant, attempts were made at enslavement and forced labor. Where even this proved unsatisfactory, labor was imported from other parts of the world. Thus, Negroes were imported to the Americas because the Indians would not work; in South Africa Chinese and Indians were imported because the Negroes would not work. In time, new generations more accustomed to the new economic system provided a home-grown labor force.[15] The division of labor that develops in

[13] George W. Barclay, *Colonial Development and Population in Taiwan* (Princeton: Princeton University Press, 1954), pp. 4–5, 14–16.

[14] Cf. Albert G. Keller, *Colonization* (Boston: Ginn, 1908), pp. 3–78; and Maunier, *op. cit.*, Vol. I, pp. 8–20.

this manner provides the basis for accommodation. Systems of ethnic stratification formed in such contexts are generally inflexible; upward mobility for natives is almost impossible. Rigidity may arise from the dominant group's being so greatly outnumbered; its members try to protect their ascendancy by retaining exclusive control over the sources of power.

European colonization of this type has resulted in the breakdown of the native economy and of the indigenous culture. Systems of peasant proprietorship were replaced by the plantation economy. Those who had lived on a subsistence economy were gradually drawn into the larger system. When they could not produce enough on their farms to make a profit, they began to work for wages in the plantations and mines. In the labor force natives from a number of different tribes came into contact, and their ethnocentrism began to break down. Whereas each had originally thought of his tribe as the center of the universe and had accepted its values as absolute, he was now able to see that strangers had ways of doing things that might be superior. The questioning of sacred beliefs led to increasing sensitivity to new possibilities. In many cases the breakdown of ethnocentrism was accompanied by personal demoralization and maladjustment. With the increasing secularization of life, disorganization in many cases became widespread.[16] In the locations in Johannesburg crime and vice have become extremely difficult to control.

There was a typical sequence in the reactions of the natives who were in close contact with their European rulers. At first there was bewilderment; they saw little in the culture of the white man other than his material goods. Then, a new generation grew up that was scornful of the old ways; the young people tried to rise above these "superstitions." They copied the white man's ways, even when they did not understand them, and they tried to win acceptance. When these people were rejected, they were left dangling between the two social worlds; since their ethnocentrism had been broken, they could not go back to the traditional ways, but they were not really a part of the white man's world. As such marginal individuals increased in number, they often formed their own societies, culturally resembling

[15] Cf. Edgar T. Thompson, "Population Expansion and the Plantation System," *American Journal of Sociology*, XLI (1935), 314–26.

[16] Cf. Alexander H. Leighton and Robert J. Smith, "A Comparative Study of Social and Cultural Change," *Proceedings of the American Philosophical Society*, XCIX (1955), 79–88.

that of their rulers but with great resentment against them. Some of the rebuffed idealized native culture. They developed an intellectual interest in the indigenous arts, crafts, and folk literature.[17] Men thus disillusioned often became articulate leaders of the discontented masses, and they played an important role in politics.

The balance of power gradually changes. As an increasing proportion of natives become familiar with the culture of the dominant group, their shattered way of life is reorganized. They learn the new language and acquire many technical skills. Children of mixed parentage grow up with special advantages. As the natives assume an increasingly more important position in the economy, they acquire additional power. If the colonists accept the more successful into their own group, they may retain their hold for some time. In this way the ruling group is constantly replenished by talented people, while the minority group is deprived of potential leadership. In most cases, however, colonists are reluctant to extend privileges to successful natives, and they thereby create bitter and capable enemies. All kinds of political movements are begun. At first they win little support among the natives, but as mass discontent increases, the people eventually rally behind the militant leadership of marginal men. Most of the nationalistic movements in European colonies have been of this nature. There are demands for self-government and the abolition of special privileges. Whether or not there is a violent revolution depends upon the reaction of the colonists. When political protests are suppressed, explosive violence occurs. Thus, the Dutch were driven out of Indonesia, and the French were driven out of Vietnam. Men rarely abdicate power without a struggle, but it has happened, as in the dissolution of the British Empire.

If the revolutionary war is successful, descendants of the original colonists must accept native rule or leave. Many French *colons* left Algeria before it became an independent nation, and many other white people have departed from the rest of Africa. Sometimes, as in the case of Indonesia, they may be expelled to their mother country. The few who remain eventually become assimilated to the new way of life, and in time a relatively homogeneous group is left occupying the territory.

A fourth type of cycle is found in cases in which a highly re-

[17] Cf. A. P. Elkin, "The Reaction of Primitive Races to the White Man's Culture," *Hibbert Journal*, **XXXV** (1937), 537–45.

spected group is conquered by invaders with a simpler culture. The conquerors set up political rule, but they learn from their subjects. This happened during the "barbarian" invasions of Rome, and three of the dynasties of China were established by invaders. The first step in the collapse of empires is the gradual assimilation of people living on its borders. Many of them work for the empire and thereby learn something of its way of life. Women in these groups intermarry with soldiers and traders, and their children acquire the culture of the father's group. Long before the collapse of Roman rule people from the outlying provinces served as soldiers or were employed in administration. Many settled on Roman territory and played an important part in Roman political life. The penetration was for the most part peaceful, for the Germans valued Roman culture and tried to acquire it.[18] The Manchus who conquered China in 1644 and ruled it to 1911 were a comparatively small Tungus tribe on the northern frontier, but they did not come straight out of the steppes to the imperial throne. At first they settled on the border and became well acquainted with Chinese culture. Their leader was a lord in one of the feudal states used by the Ming dynasty to guard the frontier, and, having served as an interpreter in the colonial service, he knew the Chinese world from personal experience. By constantly intermarrying with their captives, the Manchus grew in size, and in time they became powerful enough to become contenders for the throne.[19]

When once-powerful empires collapse, political control passes on to outsiders. Since the minority group is highly respected, however, the rulers acquire the culture of their subjects and in the end are absorbed into the general population. The Ming dynasty in China collapsed from within. When disorders broke out, the Manchus at first tried to help restore order by curbing the corruption. When they finally seized control, they adopted the Chinese system of political rule—its bureaucracy, its civil service examinations, as well as its ideology that people support their ruler because of his virtues. They encouraged education and retained the scholar-gentry class in a privileged position. Although they retained some of their own social

[18] James Bryce, *The Holy Roman Empire* (New York: Schocken Books, 1961), pp. 14–33; and Alfons Dopsch, *The Economic and Social Foundations of European Civilization* (London: Kegan Paul, Trench, Trubner, 1937), pp. 48–131.

[19] Franz Michael, *The Origins of Manchu Rule in China* (Baltimore: Johns Hopkins University Press, 1942). Cf. Owen Lattimore, *Inner Asian Frontiers of China* (Boston: Beacon Press, 1962).

institutions, they called them by Chinese names. They explained their own customs by analogy to Chinese usages, and some even tried to prove the Chinese origin of the practices. Many were ashamed of being Manchu, and only their clan system prevented a more rapid absorption by the Chinese. Thus, they fulfilled the Confucian saying, "When the barbarian enters China, he becomes Chinese." [20] The collapse of the Roman Empire occurred in a similar manner; then the "barbarians" adopted the Roman language and customs and became lost in the population. When this happens, a single ethnic group occupies the territory.

There have been many other cases in which the descendants of successful invaders have been absorbed by their subjects. In central Asia nomadic Mongols and Chinese farmers were in conflict for many centuries. The nomads had the advantage, for they could leave their possessions and families at a safe distance; if they were defeated in battle, they did not lose everything. All the Chinese could do was to retire behind the Great Wall. Thus, tribes from the Mongolian plateau repeatedly conquered the Chinese, only to become Chinese—and then to be conquered by subsequent waves of Mongol invaders.[21] In what is now Nigeria the Fulani empire was established after a successful holy war launched by the sheik Othman dan Fodio. There had been a gradual infiltration of the Hausa kingdoms over several centuries, but the military conquest was not completed by the Moslems until 1802. Fulani imperial structure was loosely organized and highly decentralized. Toward the latter part of the nineteenth century local units became increasingly autonomous, and the rulers became assimilated to the way of life of their subjects. There was large-scale intermarriage, and the Fulani soon lost their distinguishing physical and cultural marks. The majority of the people in the area today speak only Hausa, although many continue to claim descent from the Fulani.[22]

The contact of peoples almost invariably results in the occupation of an area by a single ethnic group, but this may occur in several different ways. All four natural histories begin with migration and are terminated when the people identify with one another and share

[20] Michael, *op. cit.;* and Sergei M. Shirokogorov, *Social Organization of the Manchus* (Shanghai: Royal Asiatic Society, 1924).
[21] Lattimore, "Chinese Colonization in Inner Mongolia," *op. cit.,* pp. 288–93.
[22] James S. Coleman, *Nigeria: Background to Nationalism* (Berkeley: University of California Press, 1958), p. 21.

a common culture. These four cycles by no means exhaust all the possibilities, but they are the most common developmental sequences. All of the cycles take time, often several centuries, and the people who are involved in them see only part of the sequence. But historical records indicate that what is happening today has happened before a great many times.

Regularities in Inter-Ethnic Contacts

Although the color line may appear stable, even rigid, to those who feel they are being deprived of their rights, the illustrations given show that it is something that is constantly changing. When systems of ethnic stratification are examined in detail, even the more stable are found to be undergoing some kind of transformation as the individual participants adjust and readjust to one another's demands.[23] To be sure, some of the changes occur very slowly, but events cannot be understood outside of the changing context. Some of the difficulties faced by sociologists studying "race relations" have arisen from their looking at different phases of the various cycles; hence, their generalizations applied to some cases but not to others. Generalizations about events in the period of initial contact cannot be expected to apply to cases in which the groups have been living together for several centuries. This suggests that ethnic stratification should be viewed as an on-going *process* rather than as a *structure*—a "becoming" rather than a "being." This is not to say that color lines cannot be studied in terms of their organization. But even relatively stable structures are transitory states, phases somewhere between the establishment of contact and the formation of a new ethnic group.

Unfortunately, natural histories do not provide adequate generalizations. If the cycles were descriptions of invariant sequences of events, one could say that the natives in Portuguese Angola would inevitably develop nationalistic sentiments and eject their rulers in a revolutionary uprising. This may actually happen, but such a forecast could not be made with confidence. In the social sciences natural histories are of very limited value for anticipating what will happen. As many critics of cyclical theories of history have observed, these developmental sequences may stop anywhere; there are too many

[23] Cf. Harry J. Walker, "Changes in the Structure of Race Relations in the South," *American Sociological Review*, XIV (1949), 377–83.

truncated instances. For example, ethnic islands are generally transitory phenomena, followed by assimilation. But some groups, the Jews in Europe and the Middle East for example, have lived among aliens for many centuries.[24] Furthermore, some of the stages may be reversed. By World War II many Chinese in Java were well on their way to assimilation, but the trend was slowed by the hostility of Indonesians. Now that Communist China has emerged as a world power, there is some doubt as to whether these people will lose their identity.[25] Similarly, Negroes in the United States were becoming assimilated, being held back only by the opposition of other Americans. With the emergence of independent nations in Africa, however, there has been greater consciousness of kind. Bitter resentments have led to increasing support for political movements such as the Black Muslims, who advocate a separate existence.[26] Although the data reveal that the sequences are common, none of them is inevitable. There are too many cases in which unexpected events have "interfered" with the completion of a cycle.

Natural histories are crude empirical generalizations, describing rough sequences that are readily discernible. That the sequences are not inevitable does not make them useless, for they are very helpful in the initial ordering of vast bodies of data. The isolation of convenient stages of development provides a useful point of departure for more detailed analyses, as long as one understands at the outset that there is nothing inexorable about the series. No effort will be made in this book to support a cyclical theory of history.[27]

The natural histories enable us to see more easily that certain classes of phenomena are recurrent in the contact of peoples. Furthermore, they suggest ways in which these phenomena are related to one another. For example, conflict is not found in all cases of inter-ethnic contact, but it does occur in many. In the establishment of colonial settlements conflict comes early in the cycle, soon after the invasion gets under way. In the absorption of immigrants, however, it occurs

---

24 Cf. Amitai Etzioni, "The Ghetto—A Re-Evaluation," *Social Forces*, XXXVII (1959), 255–62; and Stanley A. Freed, "Suggested Type Societies in Acculturation Studies," *American Anthropologist*, LIX (1957), 55–68.

25 Cf. Willmott, *op. cit.*

26 Cf. C. Eric Lincoln, *The Black Muslims in America* (Boston: Beacon Press, 1961).

27 Cf. Filmer S. C. Northrop, *The Logic of the Sciences and the Humanities* (New York: Macmillan, 1947), pp. 35–76; and Teggart, *op. cit.*

after a well-established color line begins to break down. In exploitation colonies conflicts are found both at the very beginning and at the end, when there is a revolutionary uprising. Similarly, segregation is not found in all instances of inter-ethnic contact, but it is a frequent occurrence. Immigrants usually live in ethnic islands; in colonial settlements the surviving natives are herded into reservations; in exploitation colonies the rulers segregate themselves into elite colonies. Assimilation is also found in most cases of inter-ethnic contact. The absorption of immigrants occurs when the second and subsequent generations learn a new way of life. In colonial settlements the natives who are not exterminated eventually find their way into the general population. In exploitation colonies some of the second-generation natives become assimilated, and after the revolutionary uprising the remaining colonists become absorbed into the new nation. In the conquest of empires by invaders assimilation of the rulers begins early and continues throughout the cycle. Concepts such as conflict, segregation, and assimilation refer to *social processes*. They are recurrent patterns of social interaction extended over time, a complex of events that go on together. Each specific instance differs, but the transactions are characterized by certain fundamental attributes. The initial task with which we are confronted is the *description* of these processes. In considering such phenomena our first concern is with ascertaining *how these things happen*.

But conflict, segregation, and assimilation do not always take place. The second task with which we are confronted, therefore, is ascertaining the *conditions* under which these processes occur. Thus, we want to formulate generalizations concerning the characteristics of various social processes and the conditions under which they occur, regardless of where they happen to come in any natural history. In this way we shall propose a set of generalizations that will explain why (a) each natural history or (b) each specific instance of inter-ethnic contact develops as it does. If a cycle is truncated, we shall understand why things turned out that way. Thus, natural histories may be used as points of departure for the formulation of more abstract generalizations that have wider applicability and greater predictive power.

In the pursuit of answers to these questions the approach should be comparative—the examination of a large number of descriptions of specific cases of inter-ethnic contact to see what likenesses there are. Excellent beginnings in this direction have already been made.[28] However, the comparative analysis of historical and ethnographic data presents many difficulties, and historical narratives in particular must be handled with caution. For one thing, the original records are never complete; in brutal conflicts, for example, history can be written only by the survivors. Furthermore, selections are made from what is recorded; in their reconstructions, historians must choose from many sources. To make data intelligible historians often construct explanatory theories, and in many cases they are not aware of their biases. Thus, even the best historical studies may have serious shortcomings, and some of the accounts are useless for sociological research.[29] Of course, most historians are not trying to provide data for social scientists. In spite of all these difficulties, however, sociologists have no alternative. Most cases of inter-ethnic contact take place over several centuries. Since the events cannot be understood out of context, historical accounts must be consulted. We cannot possibly formulate and test generalizations about long-term social change without recourse to history.

One further preliminary comment should be made about the standpoint of this book. We shall be studying some of the ways in which human society changes. Are these changes to be explained in terms of material factors or in terms of transformations in mentality? We have already noted that what men do depends upon their definition of the situation. But changes in the objective world tend to make men selectively responsive to certain kinds of beliefs and dispose them to certain kinds of activities. We shall be concerned primarily with changes in mentality, but our attention will be focused upon the conditions under which typical modes of thought are likely to develop. In particular, emphasis will be placed upon the study of isolation and communication—the manner in which certain ways of thinking come to be shared by various segments of people in a community.

---

[28] Cf. Fred Eggan, "Social Anthropology and the Method of Controlled Comparison," *American Anthropologist*, LVI (1954), 743–63; and Charles Wagley and Marvin Harris, *Minorities in the New World* (New York: Columbia University Press, 1958).

[29] Cf. Franz Adler, "The Basic Difficulty of Historical Sociology," *Sociological Quarterly*, II (1961), 3–20; and Franz Boas, *Race, Language, and Culture* (New York: Macmillan, 1940), pp. 270–80.

Summary and Conclusion

Park's "race relations cycle" is a useful way of ordering data on the manner in which immigrants become incorporated into an already-established society. However, there are many exceptions. Colonial settlements are established after the massacre, expulsion, or segregation of the natives. When their number becomes too small to be threatening, the survivors are assimilated. Exploitation colonies are established after the subjugation of the natives. This often results in the disruption of their moral order, detribalization, and the eventual development of revolutionary movements. There have also been cases in which ethnic groups living on the border of a once-powerful empire seize control. The rulers have so much respect for the culture of their subjects that they eventually become assimilated to their way of life. The utility of such natural histories is limited; we would do better to develop abstract generalizations about the social processes involved.

The remainder of this book will deal with the important social processes found in the contact of peoples. The discussion has been organized around four major sets of processes. Although the order of presentation coincides roughly with the stages in Park's natural history, we want to emphasize that this is only a convenient way of arranging material. Part II on "differentiating processes" deals with the problem of how color lines come into existence. It describes the manner in which different ethnic groups come into contact, interact, and form stable status relations. Part III on "sustaining processes" is addressed to the problem of how color lines are reinforced in the face of pressures to change. Life conditions are always changing, but patterns of coordinated activity sometimes persist for many centuries. How is this possible? The remainder of the book deals with the problem of how color lines break down. In Part IV on "disjunctive processes" the various forms of inter-ethnic conflict are described, as well as the various ways in which differences may be resolved. Part V on "integrative processes" deals with the manner in which once-different peoples come to regard themselves as alike and thereby form a new ethnic group. The fact that this section is placed last in the book does not mean that all ethnic groups in contact necessarily become integrated.

PART II

Differentiating Processes

CHAPTER 6

Patterns of

Migration and Settlement

During the latter part of the nineteenth century social scientists and political apologists alike were strongly influenced by Darwin's theory of evolution. Students of social change, ethnocentric in spite of their learning, assumed that the society in which they lived was the most highly developed, placed societies least like their own at the bottom of the ladder, and contended that social evolution occurred on a unilinear scale from the most "primitive" to the most "advanced." The exploitation of alien peoples was sometimes justified in terms of the expression "the survival of the fittest." Some apologists argued that primitive men had not yet developed the capacity for civilized living and had to undergo a long period of tutelage before they would be ready. This enthusiastic misapplication of Darwin's ideas elicited a strong negative reaction and eventually resulted in the widespread rejection by social scientists of the entire approach. Since there is no necessary connection between Darwin's theory and the political uses to which some of it had been put, the wholesale rejection of evolutionary theory was a case of "throwing out the baby with the bath." To the student of human society it is still important in at least two ways: (a) if biotic phenomena are ignored, many aspects of social change become difficult to explain, and (b) the principle of *natural selection*—which need not be confined to organic processes—provides a powerful tool for the explication of a variety of social phenomena.

In the study of differentiating processes we are concerned with the problem of how color lines come into existence. How do human beings inhabiting the same territory become divided into separate ethnic categories in different ranks? Differentiating processes are usually found soon after the initial contact of alien groups. However, the realignment of people into separate ethnic categories may also occur after they have been in contact for some time, long after an initial accommodation had taken place. Under certain conditions, the already-established color line breaks down; people are reclassified, and a new system of stratification comes into existence. Asking how color lines develop is part of the question of how human communities get their organization. Since differences between ethnic groups are established and maintained through differential communication, the central problem is that of ascertaining some of the conditions under which one segment of the population becomes isolated from another segment.

We shall begin with a consideration of some biotic processes that are related to ethnic stratification. The relative number of people in each category is often a matter of considerable importance. The kinds of social institutions found in a community in which the dominant group is vastly outnumbered by its subjects are different from those in communities in which the minority groups constitute small enclaves in the general population. The geographical distribution of the various ethnic groups is also important. Although ethnic groups are not always segregated, their distribution in space is rarely a random matter. Since physical proximity facilitates the establishment of communication channels, absence of segregation results in the formation of a different type of color line. We can begin, then, by asking about the relative size of ethnic groups and how they come to be distributed geographically as they are.

Ecological Basis of Ethnic Stratification

All living creatures in a given habitat are involved in a common web of life, and each finds its niche through competition and natural selection. Living organisms dwell in mutual interdependence. The symbiotic associations of diverse plants set the basic structure of any habitat; through the food supply and the breeding places it makes available, it limits the type of animal population that can survive. The kind of ecological organization that develops in any area—the distribution of fauna and flora—is the product of the struggle for existence, the spontaneous cooperation and competition of all living creatures in that area. In this struggle some species enjoy an advantage over others by virtue of distinctive characteristics that happen to be well suited for survival in that particular environment. Those with favorable traits survive and reproduce; others do not live long enough to perpetuate their species. Thus, the organisms in each locale are closely adjusted to the peculiar conditions of their habitat. In certain altitudes of the Rocky Mountains, for example, there are a disproportionate number of aspen trees. An influenza epidemic represents the temporary dominance of certain viruses. The life conditions at a given time and place favor some species and not others, and those who happen to have the competitive advantages dominate the scene.

Equilibrium is maintained through the continuous adaptation of all living creatures in the habitat, and any disturbance in any part of this intricate balance necessitates adjustments on the part of all organisms. The pattern remains stable as long as life conditions remain unchanged. If anything happens to upset this balance, however, a change of climate, the exhaustion of certain resources, the overpopulation of a species, or an invasion by some alien species, the struggle is renewed and continues until a new equilibrium is reached. Adaptations may be genetic or somatic; somewhat modified species may develop that are better suited to the new circumstances, or there may be changes in form and activity within the limits set by genetic structure. Thus, each living organism has a place in the web of life, which is the product of natural selection. The biotic community is constantly in flux, and the problem of life is the maintenance of growing, multiplying forms in a restricted but ever-changing environment.

Scholars have long argued the question of whether human beings possess attributes that make them basically different from all other animals, and there have been numerous attempts to define the essential qualities of man. Whatever else men may be, they are living organisms. They have many attributes that set them off as a distinct species, but like all other living organisms men are inextricably implicated in the web of life. Whenever there are changes in life conditions, men are forced to make adjustments. The dominance of other species—jackrabbits in Australia or locusts in China—requires drastic adjustments for survival. The ways in which men relate themselves to each other in order to live in their habitats yields a description of the basic structure of a community. Although some sociologists have been inclined to dismiss the study of human ecology, those concerned with social change cannot ignore these processes.

Everywhere in nature, of which man is a part, there is a constant "struggle for existence." This does not mean that living creatures all hate one another, as some have misinterpreted Darwin's phrase. All organisms strive to preserve life, to pursue their interests, to reproduce; this requires coming to terms with extant environmental conditions. Where there are insufficient resources to support all of the population, there is *competition;* the parties *independently* strive for values that are in short supply. Each does his best with the resources at hand, and those who are unsuccessful are left out. The participants do not consciously single out their competitors, nor do they blame the others for their losses. In this sense competition is unconscious and impersonal. For example, if an unskilled worker loses his job and finds that he must move to another community to find work, he has been defeated in competition. This does not mean, however, that someone else had maliciously "bumped" him. Each person does his best to earn his livelihood, and those who have the least to offer find their services not wanted. Like all other living creatures, then, human beings compete for their niche.

This is the way in which the concept of competition is used in biology and in economics, and it is not to be confused with two other concepts that will be used in our study of inter-ethnic contacts. When the participants become conscious of their precarious position and are able to identify the opposition, competition is transformed into *rivalry.* When suitors compete for the hand of a maiden or politicians vie for public office, there is a realization that the success of the opponent would mean one's own failure. The struggle then becomes a conscious, deliberate attempt to outdo one's rival. Such contests, however, are carried out according to conventional norms, and the use of fraud and violence is discouraged or forbidden. When rivalry is intensified to the point where the parties become convinced that they cannot achieve their legitimate goals as long as the opponent stands in the way, the contest is transformed into *conflict.* Consciousness of the enemy and his moves is enhanced, and the primary goal of the participants becomes the neutralization or the destruction of the enemy.[1]

Natural selection operates in human society whether or not we are aware of the fact. Like all other creatures men must meet their sustenance needs and seek favorable conditions for reproduction, but the resources of a given area are often limited. The position one achieves in an economic system depends upon the traits he brings into the competition. Certain areas of a community are regarded as more valuable than others, and those with special assets win the right to live in the most desirable places. Suitable mates are also distributed through natural selection; even in societies in which marriages are arranged through conventional norms, the most desirable women tend to be selected by men of high rank. Each person finds his position in his community by competing with the particular skills and qualities that make him what he is. He attracts a mate, wins honors and recognition, gets a job, and finds a place to live—all by utilizing his distinctive traits. In the study of human ecology sociologists are interested in the arrangements that arise among human beings inhabiting a given territory by virtue of their being living organisms continually adapting to their environment. Interest centers upon the kinds of relationships that develop among men as the reaction of a population to its habitat.[2]

Competition among human beings has certain distinctive characteristics; for one thing men often compete in groups. Biologists

---

[1] Cf. Park and Burgess, *op. cit.,* pp. 504–662; and Quincy Wright, "The Nature of Conflict," *Western Political Quarterly,* IV (1951), 193–209.

[2] Cf. Robert E. Park, *Human Communities,* ed. E. C. Hughes, *et al.* (Glencoe, Ill.: The Free Press, 1952); Philip L. Wagner, *The Human Use of the Earth* (Glencoe, Ill.: The Free Press, 1960); and Wirth, *Community Life and Social Policy, op. cit.,* pp. 133–71.

have long known that the structure as well as the behavior of organisms is affected by their living together with other organisms as well as by the peculiarities of their habitat. All human beings live in groups. Probably the most important attribute of man is the capacity for linguistic communication, which enables him to interact with himself as well as with others. Because he can think and exchange experiences with others, man develops a culture, and this alters the character of his adjustments. Because men live in symbolic environments and act in terms of interpretations, their group affiliations and self-conceptions enter into their adjustments. Sociologists are concerned primarily with uniformities found in the organized activities of men in groups. Most of these patterns arise out of communication, but there are biotic and physical factors that must also be taken into account.

Men often compete with one another on a collective basis, as if they belonged to different species. Much of what happens in interethnic contacts can be understood better when seen in this light. A word of caution must be introduced at the outset, however, to avoid serious misinterpretations. Men in different ethnic groups sometimes compete *as if* they belonged to different species. Indeed, the concept of "race" suggests that human beings are divided into different species. This notion has been investigated thoroughly by biologists and rejected; by generally accepted standards all human beings are of the same genus and species. Their bodies are constructed in much the same manner; their basic biotic functions are alike; they can crossbreed. The differences are superficial. But many men *believe* that they are of different species, and they act on the basis of their definitions. They compete as units, cooperating with those with whom they identify. Inter-ethnic contacts are contacts among people who are conscious of differences that they believe are inherited. What is called the instinct of the "preservation of the species" in other animals seems to have a counterpart in men; those who identify on a "racial" basis act as if they were alike and make sacrifices in order that their kind can be perpetuated. Thus, competition among human beings is complicated by their sense of identity.[3]

Men compete not only for survival but also for cultural values.

---

[3] Cf. Roderick D. McKenzie, "Cultural and Racial Differences as Bases of Human Symbiosis," in Kimball Young (ed.), *Social Attitudes* (New York: Henry Holt, 1931), pp. 136–65.

Most human beings do not live at the margin of existence; among widely-sought values are income, deference, security, and mates. But what constitutes an appropriate income, the proper symbols of deference, sufficient safety, or a desirable mate is a matter of cultural definition. The struggle for existence among human beings, then, is something more than a struggle for livelihood. Most human needs are cultural rather than nutritional; conventional norms, religious beliefs, aesthetic ideals, ethical prescriptions—all shape the wants of men. Much of what happens in a competitive situation depends upon the values of the particular groups involved.

The tools with which men compete are also cultural. Technology represents the means of harnessing and using energy in the pursuit of values, and groups differ considerably in their level of technology. The way of life of a group depends upon the type of energy employed, for the energy available sets limitations to what people can do. Some groups rely exclusively on organic energy; food-gathering and food-raising societies use plants and animals as converters. Others exploit inorganic energy, natural forces such as the wind and water. Steam was the key to the Industrial Revolution, and since that time petroleum, electricity, the internal combustion engine, and atomic energy have provided other sources of power.[4] When the culture is simple, man's place in the biotic community resembles that of other animals, but every technological advance enhances his control over his habitat and raises his position in the scale of dominance. Unlike plants and other animals most men today are not directly dependent upon their environment; in many ways they create part of their environment. Thus, ecological processes become less compelling in proportion to technological level and economic organization. As technology increases, there is a decrease in dependence for food supply and other needs upon the seasonal cycles of plant and animal life.[5] Among human beings, then, survival depends upon the ability of a group to take advantage of the available resources.

Competition and natural selection as they occur among human beings are often mitigated by conventional norms. Men are bound by conscious rules—laws, customs, traditions—and even a fight to

[4] W. Fred Cottrell, *Energy and Society* (New York: McGraw-Hill, 1955). Cf. Harrison Brown, *The Challenge of Man's Future* (New York: Viking Press, 1954), pp. 149–86; and Wladimir S. and Emma S. Woytinsky, *World Population and Production* (New York: Twentieth Century Fund, 1953), pp. 924–83.

[5] Wagner, *op. cit.*, p. 22.

the death is usually carried out according to norms. Humanitarian ideals often inhibit full exploitation of competitive advantages, setting limits to the extent to which subject labor might be utilized and to the ways in which military power might be employed. The importance of ideals is not to be underestimated, for human conflict is rarely a bald struggle for survival.[6] Because of this some scholars have contended that human beings do not compete in the biological sense. Competition undoubtedly is somewhat complicated by the fact that men can think and make choices, but natural selection is found in human society nonetheless. As Dewey pointed out, the difference between man and other living creatures is not that selection ceases but that conscious foresight introduces additional alternatives from which choices might be made.[7] Natural selection among human beings is modified by conventional understandings, but the process is not altered in its basic character.

In other species dominance depends upon such considerations as food supply, light, temperature, moisture, and shelter; among human beings, however, it depends more upon the cultural attributes of the group. Dominance is established by the group that enjoys *competitive advantages,* and these are primarily cultural. Although superior military strength may bring temporary victory to others, in the long run the group with the more advanced technology, the higher literacy rate, and the more efficient political organization is likely to win ascendancy. With greater technical proficiency there is greater adaptive specialization, less dependency upon the immediate environment, and greater flexibility of adjustment—in short, more ability to adjust to varying circumstances. The long history of China provides an instructive illustration. Chinese civilization rested upon an intensive agricultural economy based upon irrigation, drainage, and transport by a widespread network of canals. All this made possible the production of a grain surplus, which provided the basis of political power. All invaders have been absorbed and assimilated to Chinese culture, but the converse is also true. Outside this natural area the thermodynamic superiority of Chinese culture was lost, and other

[6] Cf. Park, *Human Communities, op. cit.,* pp. 240–62; and Robert Redfield, *The Primitive World and Its Transformations* (Ithaca, N. Y.: Cornell University Press, 1953), pp. 139–65.

[7] John Dewey, *The Influence of Darwin on Philosophy* (New York: Henry Holt, 1910).

economic systems have proved more effective. Every attempt made by the Chinese, no matter how powerful at the time, to range too far beyond the northern frontier has resulted in the outlying Chinese taking to nomadic pastoralism, becoming tribalized, and eventually turning back on China as "barbarians." Successful Chinese expansion has always been toward the south rather than the north. Only with recent industrialization has the ancient ecological and cultural cleavage between the steppe and the farmland been obliterated.[8] *The group whose culture is best suited for the exploitation of the resources of a given environment tends to become dominant.*

The organization of a community, ecological and social, is the product of collective adjustments made by all parties to extant life conditions. However, among human beings some of the patterns that originally arise through competition may be perpetuated long after the ecological balance has actually changed. People become accustomed to an established order, and challenges are not made until much later, when further changes in life conditions make these arrangements intolerable.

There are three classes of ecological phenomena that are of special interest to students of inter-ethnic contacts. One is the distribution of various categories of people on land. Because of different potentialities for exploitation or enjoyment, certain areas in each community come to be coveted. Sometimes an equitable allocation of the terrain can be worked out, especially if the needs of the groups happen to be complementary. A nomadic group, for example, may be interested primarily in the highlands, where flocks can be grazed, while an agricultural people may want to remain on level ground near the water supply. Where there is not enough land for both, however, competition develops, and the losers are relegated to the badlands. The contention of human ecologists, then, is that at least in the beginning the kind of spatial patterns that develop in a given community are not so much a product of deliberate planning but of competition and natural selection.

Another is the type of economic system that develops in a com-

---

[8] Ch'ao-Ting Chi, "The Economic Basis of Unity and Division in Chinese History," *Pacific Affairs*, VII (1934), 386–94. Cf. Marshall D. Sahlins and Elman R. Service (eds.), *Evolution and Culture* (Ann Arbor: University of Michigan Press, 1960), pp. 69–92.

munity and the positions in it occupied by each group. The initial phase in the formation of an economy is largely an ecological process, for sustenance relations develop through competition. In most cases there is some kind of division of labor. In some, different ethnic groups are allocated different kinds of work. The position that a person occupies in the system depends upon his competitive advantages, and ethnic identity itself may be one of them. Although some economic systems are planned in advance and imposed upon a conquered area by those who have political power, in most instances the complex web of relationships develops without deliberate design. The formation of black markets in socialist economies provides an example of how sustenance relations may arise independently of planning.

The third ecological process of interest is the formation of physical types, the selective reproduction of human beings with given attributes. Although we become aware of this only under unusual circumstances, each person competes with everyone else in his age group of the same sex for the most desirable mate. Conventional norms place many potential partners out of range, but the eligible do compete. People who are defined as least desirable are less likely to reproduce, and some of their traits are likely to become extinct. Physical marks that become important as status symbols are sought after, and the preference for mates who will perpetuate these marks increases the likelihood that they will be reproduced. A genetic adaptation may take place; characteristics resulting from hereditary variation are perpetuated through natural selection. Thus, ethnic groups attain dominance through cultural characteristics and then reproduce those physical traits that happen to become its identification symbols.

The Relative Size of Ethnic Groups

All systems of ethnic stratification begin with some kind of migration; we shall therefore start with a brief consideration of spatial movements. There are many kinds of migrations; men move for many different reasons and under varying circumstances. Persecuted people wander about with no particular destination, looking for places where they can go unopposed; those with commerical interests try to establish colonies; conquerors try to extend their political influence; people in overpopulated areas sometimes participate in mass migrations to underdeveloped areas where labor is needed and appreciated.[9] The type of color line that develops in a community depends in part upon the relative number of people in each ethnic category, and this is the result of migration and of reproduction rates.

Any change in life conditions requires adjustment, and one way of coping with an unfavorable situation is to emigrate. The disequilibrium is sometimes biotic, as in the exhaustion of natural resources. People tend to leave areas with high population density, contracting economy, and declining demand for labor to go to sparsely settled places with an expanding economy. Nomadic and tribal movements in which ethnic groups move as units in search for subsistence constitute one type of migration in which biotic factors are prominently involved. In some cases the same areas are used alternately. Some Bedouins spend their winters in Yemen and their summers on the slopes of the Caucasus; their movements are not random but focused upon certain temporary centers of operation.[10] The foundations for the national configurations of modern Europe were laid by a complex series of tribal migrations beginning in the middle of the third century A.D. There were movements of Goths, Huns, Avars, and Turks to Byzantium and the Italian cities. In the tenth century the Magyars followed earlier invaders into Italy and Germany, marauding and seeking places for settlement. The victory of Otto the Great over the Magyar tribes in 955 checked their advance and forced them to remain in the Hungarian plains, which they had just seized from Slavic peoples.[11]

There are many migrations in which biotic considerations have been secondary, as in the departure of those persecuted for their political or religious beliefs. Flight has always been an important form of migration. Dissident parties move to preserve their way of life, even when there is no economic necessity for leaving. After their

[9] Cf. Wilfrid D. Borrie *et al.*, *The Cultural Integration of Immigrants* (Paris: UNESCO, 1959), pp. 17–88; Bryce, "The Migration of the Races of Men Considered Historically," *op. cit.*; William Petersen, *Population* (New York: Macmillan, 1961), pp. 592–621; and Walter F. Willcox (ed.), *International Migrations* (New York: National Bureau of Economic Research, 1931), Vol. II.

[10] Richard C. Thurnwald, "Nomads," *Encyclopedia of the Social Sciences*, Vol. XI, pp. 390–92. Cf. Carleton S. Coon, *Caravan: The Story of the Middle East* (New York: Henry Holt, 1951), pp. 191–225; and Lawrence Krader, "The Ecology of Nomadic Pastoralism," *International Social Science Journal*, XI (1959), 499–510.

[11] Seton-Watson, *op. cit.*, pp. 3–9.

conquest by the Turks, a continuous stream of Serbian and Croatian villagers moved from the plains to the less fertile mountain slopes where Turkish control was weak or absent. In 1691 alone, more than 30,000 left the Ottoman Empire. They were welcomed in Hungary, and as the population in the mountainous areas grew beyond their capacity to sustain it, the refugees were directed to other sparsely settled areas. After the defeat of Turkey by Austria in 1715, however, the harshness of Austrian rule and the efforts of Jesuits to force Orthodox Serbs to become Roman Catholics led many to seek refuge in Turkey.[12] Southeast Asia, especially the area that is now Vietnam, had long been a refuge for fugitive supporters of fallen Chinese dynasties. During the past century Chinese emigration has almost invariably shown a marked increase with every major political upheaval. After the Bolshevik revolution of 1917, refugee Russians fled to China and set up colonies in Sinkiang and Shanghai.[13] Modern Israel is a nation built by migrants pursuing a religious belief, in many cases moving from prosperous lands to this arid area. Furthermore, attempts to impose religious or political views upon others have resulted in many migrations. Among the most spectacular of these migrations are the spread of Islam and the Crusades of the middle ages. Historians have ample records of empire-building. Millions of men have died for the privilege of being identified with the grandeur of a powerful empire, and the conquests of the Greeks, the Mongols, the Romans, and the British have all left their mark in the distribution of ethnic groups in the world.

Colonization involves both the movement of people and the extension of political power, and the establishment of colonies is an ancient practice. Commercial colonies were founded by the ancient Aegians, Phoenicians, Greeks, and Chinese. These were largely trading posts, but they were manned by people from the motherland to insure regularity in economic transactions. In some instances, as with Carthage, the colony eventually became more powerful than the source. The practice became more common after the development of capitalism. As Henri Sée points out, the kind of economy stressing the accumulation of private wealth through individual initiative re-

---

[12] Jozo Tomasevich, *Peasants, Politics, and Economic Change in Yugoslavia* (Stanford, Calif.: Stanford University Press, 1955), pp. 36–37.

[13] Purcell, *op. cit.*, p. 220; Bruno Lasker, *Asia on the Move* (New York: Henry Holt, 1945), p. 105; Francis C. Jones, *Manchuria Since 1931* (London: Royal Institute of International Affairs, 1949), pp. 76–80.

quires continual expansion. Men are driven to seek new markets and fresh supplies of raw materials. By a fortuitous combination of circumstances the Europeans had at the time they "discovered" the rest of the world a culture well developed in navigational skills, military organization and refinement of lethal weapons, and commercial efficiency.[14] The distribution of ethnic groups in the world today is largely the product of the migrations of people from Europe since the sixteenth century, their proliferation, and their subjugation of other peoples.

The practice of sending settlers into a new area to establish and maintain political control is an old one. After the Roman conquest of Dacia, a province roughly equivalent to present-day Rumania, the Emperor Trajan brought in large numbers of colonists from all parts of the empire to secure a reliable local population. Care was taken to choose those who could contribute to the development of the gold, silver, and salt mines.[15] In the subsequent history of Europe a number of kings have encouraged settlers to take up permanent residence in frontier areas to strengthen defenses against marauding tribes. In the middle of the twelfth century, for example, the king of Hungary invited Germans into the valleys of Transylvania; these migrants prospered and managed to preserve their ethnic identity in the midst of a population that was predominantly Rumanian.[16] Although Manchuria was not essential for Japanese economic development, it was conquered in 1931 by the Japanese army as a step toward the establishment of Japanese hegemony in the Far East. Manchuria was wanted as a continental base in the event of war, and the plan was to colonize the area with Japanese farmers to provide a solid block of reservists to serve as auxiliaries to the army. At the same time the migration would relieve some of the overpopulation in Japan. Many large-scale colonization schemes were launched to make the move more attractive, and in 1936 the government approved a project that would bring 5 million Japanese into Manchuria over a period of 25 years. Although the plan fell short of this goal, the Japanese civilian

---

[14] Henri Sée, *Modern Capitalism: Its Origin and Evolution,* trans. Homer B. Vanderblue and Georges F. Doriot (New York: Adelphi, 1928), pp. 41–117. Cf. Melvin M. Knight, "Colonies," *Encyclopedia of the Social Sciences,* Vol. III, pp. 653–63; and Toynbee, *op. cit.,* Vol. VIII, pp. 110–11.

[15] Seton-Watson, *op. cit.,* pp. 2–3.

[16] Nicholas Iorga, *A History of Roumania* (London: T. Fisher Unwin, 1925), p. 48.

population in Manchuria grew from 240,000 in 1931 to 837,000 in 1939.[17]

Some colonies are established primarily for the exploitation of natural resources. This type of migration is usually organized by entrepreneurs looking for profits. The economy is usually organized around a single product—tobacco, rice, sugar-cane, cotton, diamonds, coal, oil, rubber. Production is not for subsistence; the product is mass-produced for a world market. There is no thought of diversification, even during depressions, and this tends to make the colonies more dependent upon the motherland for everything else. Since the formation of mineral resources is such a slow process, those who wish to use them must go where they can be found in abundant supply. Successful large-scale agriculture also depends upon environmental conditions, and those who want large profits must go where the resources can be exploited most effectively. Thus, many of these colonies are located in places where the geographical conditions differ greatly from those of the homeland; in such cases the colonists are predominantly male, youthful, and unmarried.[18] Characteristically the labor force does not participate in the profits. Even the great oil and wine latifundia of ancient Rome were manned by captured slaves, and the opening of a vein of silver ore near Athens during the time of Pericles marked the beginning of slavery in Attica.[19] In the more recent European colonies the natives have been hired as low-paid laborers. One of the most extreme cases of exploitation occurred in the Congo soon after it came under Belgian rule. King Leopold II made the land his private property and forced the natives to sell ivory and rubber to his monopolies. His overseers were given unlimited power over the natives, and their abuses were so severe that the matter finally became a political issue among outraged Europeans. The devastation of resources and epidemics of sleeping sickness reduced the population from an estimated 20 million in 1885 to only 9 million in 1900. The Congo was finally taken away from the king and annexed by the Belgian government in 1908.[20]

[17] F. C. Jones, *op. cit.*, pp. 14–15, 36, 81, 140–47, 167.

[18] Raymond Kennedy, "The Colonial Crisis and the Future," in Ralph Linton (ed.), *The Science of Man in the World Crisis* (New York: Columbia University Press, 1945), pp. 309–10. Cf. Keller, *loc. cit.*; and Edgar T. Thompson, "The Climatic Theory of the Plantation," *Agricultural History*, XV (1941), 49–60.

[19] Alfred E. Zimmern, *The Greek Commonwealth* (London: Oxford University Press, 1922), pp. 397–402.

[20] Harry H. Johnston, *A History of the Colonization of Africa by Alien Races* (Cambridge: Cambridge University Press, 1899), pp. 348–56.

Systems of ethnic stratification also develop from mass migrations from impoverished areas of people seeking better opportunities. When large numbers of men become dissatisfied with their lot, they communicate their discontent to one another and become sensitized to the possibilities of moving. Initially only the outcasts, alienated intellectuals, and adventurers leave. If they manage to make a satisfactory adjustment, the pioneers get word back to their relatives and friends. Soon accounts of their experiences are reported in the press and by word of mouth; through letters, rumors, and the testimony of the successful who return home, the destination comes to be visualized in idealized terms. Increasing numbers migrate, the earlier migrants often helping to finance the passage of those who follow. The unsettled conditions that made the Manchu conquest of China possible led to the early migration of Chinese into Manchuria. The movement continued even after 1776, when the emperor issued an edict against it. By 1850 Mukden had virtually become a Chinese city. The disorders of the Taiping rebellion resulted in even more migrations, and in 1878, when the official barrier was removed, the stream of Chinese moving northward became even greater. Early in the twentieth century more than 3 million Chinese migrated from Shantung to escape famine, extortion, terrorism, and overpopulation, and by 1930 an estimated 90 per cent of the population of Manchuria had become Chinese.[21] The population of the United States is also a product of such movements. In some parts of Sweden "America fever" became so intense that going to the new world became one of the accepted career patterns.[22] During the past 50 years there have been similar movements among Negroes in the rural South who have been migrating to urban centers of the North and the West.[23] What characterizes mass migrations is the convergence of decisions on the part of individual migrants. Each leaves his home voluntarily, but the movement takes on a cumulative character as friends and associates join one another in the venture.

When immigration does not provide the desired population, deliberate attempts may be made to import people. During the twelfth and thirteenth centuries the feudal princes and prelates in lower

[21] C. Walter Young, "Manchuria: A New Homeland of the Chinese," *Current History*, XXVIII (1928), 529–36; and F. C. Jones, *op. cit.*, pp. 8–9.

[22] Cf. John S. Lindberg, *The Background of Swedish Emigration to the United States* (Minneapolis: University of Minnesota Press, 1930).

[23] E. Franklin Frazier, *The Negro Family in the United States* (Chicago: University of Chicago Press, 1939), pp. 291–324.

Germany, finding that German peasants knew little of clearing swamps, imported Dutch and Flemish settlers to reclaim the land and transform their estates into productive farms.[24] Catherine the Great encouraged the colonization of foreigners to aid in the development of southern Russia. She and Alexander I were responsible for the founding of hundreds of colonies of German Lutherans, Mennonites, and other ethnic groups in the area of the Volga and the Black Sea.[25] Many subsequent migrations have gained impetus from the promotional efforts of entrepreneurs searching for a stable and reliable labor force. During the period of immense industrial expansion in the United States, a large labor force was needed, and immigration was deliberately induced by American employers, various middlemen, and steamship agents.[26] An interesting facet is that emigration from Europe developed at a time when the standard of living there was rising; increases in the number departing correlate not with depressed conditions there but with the business cycle in the receiving country.[27]

Thus, there are many kinds of migrations, and ethnic groups come together under a variety of circumstances. In spite of their cultural differences the initial contacts are often quite friendly. More often than not, there is considerable curiosity about the strangers, and the more adventurous go forth to establish contacts. Many groups practice ceremonial gift-giving, and this frequently facilitates the establishment of trade relations. Of course, alien cultural traits are often misinterpreted, but even these errors sometimes facilitate contact. In their initial contacts with Europeans the American Indians thought they were dealing with gods, and some of the peoples in Africa apparently submitted to European rule under a similar impression. The miraculous firearms, lavish personal supply of clothing, elaborate domestic equipment even for camping, technical wonder and variety in even trivial goods, unlimited wealth suggested by the supply of cotton cloth—all seemed so marvelous. The newcomers appeared to have complete mastery over the material world and

[24] James W. Thompson, "Dutch and Flemish Colonization in Medieval Germany," *American Journal of Sociology*, XXIV (1918), 159–86.

[25] David Rempel, *The Mennonite Colonies in New Russia* (unpublished Ph.D. dissertation, Stanford University, 1933).

[26] Maurice Davie, *World Immigration* (New York: Macmillan, 1936), pp. 96–98, 179–83.

[27] Harry Jerome, *Migration and Business Cycles* (New York: National Bureau of Economic Research, 1926).

even controlled life and death with their medicines and firearms.[28]

Even when the contacts are friendly, any invasion disturbs the pre-existing web of life. Whatever type of migration it may be, the arrival of a new group upsets the previous equilibrium. The balance of population to available resources is disrupted, and even those who never see the newcomers are affected. During the early nineteenth century large numbers of Chinese left the crowded lowlands of China and moved over the Great Wall into the semi-arid desert beyond to live among the nomadic Mongol herders. Since the land was not suited to agriculture, the Chinese farmers soon exhausted the soil and cut down the forests for lumber. The area became arid and full of dust storms, and especially in the region east of Kalgan the nomads were forced to move.[29] On the American frontier the coming of the white settlers altered the way of life of the Indians long before they were herded into reservations. Among the Sioux, for example, the buffalo had been used for food, for building tepees, for bedding, and for war shields; it had been a focal point in many ritual and social activities. When the buffalo was destroyed, the Sioux were not only deprived of food; their art and pride in workmanship were also destroyed.[30] There has been some controversy among scholars over the extent to which the introduction of the horse altered the pattern of Indian life. Some have argued that before the coming of the Spaniards the Plains Indians lived in small units, had no draft animals for extensive cultivation, and hunted afoot with bows and arrows. With the adoption of the horse, hunting and warfare became more efficient, and larger groupings became necessary for protection and labor. Others have argued, however, that the most profound change was psychological, that the horse widened the horizons of the Indians and enabled them to do more easily things they had always done.[31] In either case the relation of the Indians to their environment was drastically altered. As collective adjustments are made by all living

[28] Cf. Lucien Lévy-Bruhl, *Primitive Mentality*, trans. Lilian A. Clare (New York: Macmillan, 1923), pp. 352–83; and Aidan W. Southall, *Alur Society* (Cambridge: W. Heffer, 1956), p. 230.

[29] George B. Cressey, "Chinese Colonization in Mongolia," in *Pioneer Settlement, op. cit.*, pp. 273–87.

[30] Bernard Barber, "Acculturation and Messianic Movements," *American Sociological Review*, VI (1941), 664.

[31] Clark Wissler, "The Influence of the Horse in the Development of Plains Culture," *American Anthropologist*, XVI (1914), 1–25. Cf. Frank G. Roe, *The Indian and the Horse* (Norman: University of Oklahoma Press, 1955).

creatures to the changed conditions, a new equilibrium develops.

The numerical strength of each ethnic group in a community depends not only upon migration but also upon its rate of growth. Relative size can be of great importance, especially if the groups have approximately the same technological capacity. On the west coast of Colombia the Indians are gradually being displaced by Negroes whose ancestors first entered the area as slaves. They are not losing ground through warfare but through their inability to reproduce as quickly. The Negroes are tall and powerfully built in comparison to the Indians; they are apparently better adapted to the heat and less susceptible to the diseases introduced by the Europeans. Having associated with the Spaniards, the Negroes have the additional advantages of language and culture. As the Negro population increases, the Indians are being forced farther back into highlands that are not suited to their old way of life. This is making their survival even more difficult.[32] Thus, under some circumstances differential rates of increase can result in ecological succession. This may account for the occasional alarms sounded in some quarters over the rapid growth of unpopular ethnic groups.

When the birth rate is higher than the death rate, there is a natural increase in population; this may be augmented by immigration. However, the reproduction rate of a group does not depend solely upon capacity for procreation; much depends upon its culture. All human beings have a tremendous potentiality for increasing their numbers, but it is rarely realized. Contraception, infanticide, and abortion are widespread practices. Societies are likely to have high fertility if premarital intercourse is permitted, if the ideal age for marriage is low, if the proper family size is large, or if the kinship system stresses the perpetuation of lineage so that a marriage is regarded as incomplete until a son is born. On the other hand, placing a high value upon personal success and the acquisition of material goods may require the postponement of marriage and the practice of birth control; this is likely to result in lower fertility. In Tibet a high value is placed upon celibacy, and elsewhere there are other taboos that reduce the number of potential parents.[33]

When the web of life is broken by immigration, the rate of

[32] Robert C. Murphy, "Racial Succession in the Colombian Chocó," *Geographical Review*, XXIX (1939), 461-71.

[33] Frank Lorimer, *Culture and Human Fertility* (Paris: UNESCO, 1954), pp. 15-251.

growth of the original population may be altered. The sudden introduction of unfamiliar diseases and new weapons has resulted in depopulation in many of the areas conquered by Europeans. Ethnic
groups show a differential susceptibility to diseases; people who have
had long contact with a disease are believed to develop greater im-
munity to it. The estimated Indian population in Mexico at the time
of the Spanish conquest in 1521 was from 7 to 9 million; by 1800
there were only about 4.5 million left. This loss resulted partly from
war and forced labor but mostly from epidemics of smallpox, influenza, measles, typhoid, and typhus. Entire communities were wiped
out.[34] Within 150 years of the first visit of Europeans in Hawaii,
the native population dropped to one-tenth its original size, primarily
from the ravages of venereal diseases. The introduction of firearms
also added to the casualty rates in internal wars.[35] The initial contact
of the Maori of New Zealand with Europeans was similarly disastrous; the decline of Maori population from 1840 to 1890 was so
spectacular that many observers believed them to be a dying people.[36]
There was a similar decline of population in West Africa and the
Congo. The slave trade, with its consequent aggravation of interne-
cine warfare, and unfamiliar diseases took their toll. The trend did
not reverse itself until the middle of the nineteenth century, when
slavery was abolished.[37]

Depopulation following contact with alien groups may also result from social disorganization. In Oceania it is estimated that the
population of the islands dropped from 3 million in 1522 to 2 million
in 1939.[38] Several observers of this dramatic reduction have noted
that in addition to mortality from conflict and new diseases, there
was also a decline in fertility. After a study of several islands Pitt-
Rivers found all explanations of the widely observed depopulation
inadequate and contended that the most important reason for the
decline was psychological: the disinclination of the natives to bear

[34] Tannenbaum, op. cit., pp. 9–10; and John L. Phelan, The Hispanization of
the Philippines (Madison: University of Wisconsin Press, 1959), pp. 107–08, 156.
[35] Andrew W. Lind, An Island Community (Chicago: University of Chicago
Press, 1938), pp. 94–99.
[36] Ivan L. G. Sutherland (ed.), The Maori People Today (London: Oxford
University Press, 1940), pp. 9, 28, 229–30, 276; and Douglas L. Oliver, The Pacific
Islands (Cambridge: Harvard University Press, 1951), pp. 119–21.
[37] William M. Hailey, An African Survey (London: Oxford University Press,
1957), pp. 57, 552.
[38] Oliver, op. cit., p. 255.

children. Although he could cite no direct evidence, he pointed to the widespread social disorganization and insisted that there was a "loss of interest in life." [39] Although Pitt-Rivers' hypothesis has not been fully accepted, more recent studies show that the structure of family life was disturbed by the contacts. Furthermore, increased extramarital and other proscribed sex relations may have led to the use of abortion, contraceptive practices, and types of sexual activity less likely to produce live births. With estrangement between spouses there may have been less frequency of coitus. Recent observations in Africa also reveal that the disorganization of traditional cultural patterns has resulted in a similar avoidance of child-bearing.[40]

On the other hand, the introduction of a higher standard of living may result in a population explosion. According to the widely entertained theory of "demographic transition" industrialization raises the standard of living and lowers mortality; therefore, it results in a substantial increase in population. When peasant groups that had been reproducing to the limits of their way of life begin to participate in an industrial economy, higher income and better medical care reduces infant mortality. In India and Pakistan, for example, there has been a spectacular fall in mortality with a continuation of the high birth rate.[41] Even without industrialization the establishment of a stable order sometimes makes greater fertility possible. Once people become adjusted to the new conditions, the rate of increase turns upward again. In the area that is now Burundi, temporary accommodation to Watusi rule resulted in a rapid increase of the Bahutu. On Guam and the Marianas the Chamorro, hard-hit in their initial contact with Europeans, became converted to Catholicism, and their birth rate has risen.[42] Since World War II the introduction of more effective medical care throughout the world under the auspices of the United Nations has cut the death toll considerably; tuberculosis, malaria, intestinal parasites, and leprosy have been brought under better control. This has resulted in the recent population explosion, which has led to predictions of world overpopulation.

[39] George H. L. Pitt-Rivers, *The Clash of Culture and the Contact of Races* (London: George Routledge & Sons, 1927), pp. 142–233. Cf. William H. R. Rivers (ed.), *Essays on the Depopulation of Melanesia* (Cambridge: Cambridge University Press, 1922).

[40] Lorimer, *op. cit.*, pp. 115–50.

[41] Cf. Petersen, *op. cit.*, pp. 11–14, 307–503; and Kingsley Davis, "Institutional Patterns Favoring High Fertility in Underdeveloped Areas," *Eugenics Quarterly*, II (1955), 33–39.

[42] Lorimer, *op. cit.*, pp. 29–31, 134–39, 145–50; and Oliver, *op. cit.*, pp. 236–42.

The crisis occasioned by immigration initiates a period of rapid change during which competition is intensified. Sometimes the invader is hurled back or exterminated, and sometimes the newcomers gain dominance. The survivors of the struggle arrive at some kind of *modus vivendi* that enables them to live in the same area and somehow cooperate. A new equilibrium develops with a somewhat different pattern. The customary procedures that arise to provide a framework within which the people can continue to interact constitute what is commonly called the color line.

Patterns of Land Use and Occupancy

The geographic distribution of various groups within a community is an important aspect of ethnic stratification. Members of a small minority group may be scattered throughout an area. Sizable ethnic groups, however, are frequently segregated, although there is considerable variation in the patterns that develop and in the harshness with which the boundaries are enforced. All ethnic groups tend to congregate into natural areas, natural in the sense that they are not planned. The spatial distribution of people is seldom the product of deliberate design; after each migration new patterns of settlement develop through competition and natural selection. Once formed, each natural area develops its own universe of discourse, traditions, and standards of decency and propriety. The lines may then be enforced by custom and by law.

The distribution of ethnic groups within a community is related to the prevailing system of land use, the manner in which natural resources are allocated. Each method of converting energy requires a somewhat different use of land and other resources; hence, most migrations disturb the previously existing allocation. In Brazil and the United States, for example, the arrival of peasants from Europe and Asia resulted in the transformation of waste lands and swamps into fertile fields. Immigrants from barren soil were overjoyed to find rich virgin land and built agricultural empires. If the interests of the groups in contact happen to be complementary, they become interlocked in a common, more diversified economy. Throughout the world ethnic groups with different cultures, using different tools and utensils, have settled in the immediate neighborhood of each other. In the Sahara the Tuareg are camel herders, while the Berbers and other Africans have entirely different economies. Their huts and settlement patterns differ, but they coexist without conflict.[43] Once such patterns are established, the groups may retain their identity for centuries, each occupying territory that is defined in tradition and carrying out customary roles.

When the interests of the groups are incompatible, however, competition is intensified into rivalry or conflict. In New Zealand the Maori resisted the incursion of Europeans in a series of bloody wars; the Hawaiians defended their land by legislation and political bargaining.[44] In the end the victorious group imposes its system of land use upon the entire community, and the minority groups must adjust or leave. Even when the losers are not driven off the land, the introduction of new techniques of exploiting the resources often disrupts their culture. In many cases food, shelter, family ties, and social organization are inextricably bound up with particular ways of occupying and cultivating soil. Social bonds based on ancient systems of landholding collapse. Those who are unable to compete on equal terms are shunted into menial jobs and occupy the least desirable areas. They thereby become incorporated into the lower rungs of the new economy. In Kenya, for example, the European settlers seized the most fertile lands for their farming operations, and the natives were forced to farm elsewhere as best they could. Hunting and food-gathering activities were also curtailed in the choice areas, and many of the dispossessed were forced to work for the colonists to eke out a livelihood.[45] Thus, the resolution of the conflict results in the formation of a common system of land use.

There are several kinds of communities, and somewhat different patterns of land use and spatial segregation develop in each of them. Many cases of inter-ethnic contact occur in areas in which population density is low, as in agricultural settlements, small villages, and nomadic communities, and the formation of systems of ethnic stratification is somewhat circumscribed by the type of social contacts that take place. A distinctive mode of life develops in sparsely-settled areas where many people know one another on a personal basis. In

[43] Richard Thurnwald, *Economics in Primitive Communities* (London: Oxford University Press, 1932), pp. 26–27, 79–84.

[44] John B. Condliffe, *New Zealand in the Making* (London: George Allen & Unwin, 1959), pp. 28–31, 62–74; and Lind, *op. cit.,* p. 45.

[45] Louis S. B. Leakey, *Mau Mau and the Kikuyu* (London: Methuen, 1955). Cf. Thomas M. Franck, *Race and Nationalism: The Struggle for Power in Rhodesia-Nyasaland* (New York: Fordham University Press, 1960), pp. 64–86.

small communities social control is largely traditional; the societies are made up more of families than of individuals.[46] Contacts between ethnic groups tend to be friendly, and superficial associations such as those found in trade and bartering are relatively easy to establish. Since each group has a strong sense of mutual identification and solidarity, however, the barriers of social distance are not likely to be relaxed. In the contacts of nomadic groups with each other and with people in rural settlements, social distance is retained to the point where they can intermingle for centuries without altering their respective ways of life.

In this type of context conflicts frequently arise between agricultural people and those who depend primarily on pastoral or hunting pursuits. Farmers need to occupy land for fairly long periods, and they must have some assurance of keeping it under control until their crops have been harvested. Hunting, collecting, and pastoral economies require freedom of movement and extensive areas, for only superficial use is made of available plant life. Much of the struggle between the settlers and the Indians on the American frontier was a conflict between groups with different patterns of land use. In Canada this issue resulted in a series of disturbances culminating in the Riel rebellion of 1885. During the century after trappers and traders went in large numbers into the Canadian northwest, offspring of these frontiersmen and their Indian wives developed into an ethnic group—known as "half-breeds," *bois brulé*, or Méti. Although these people dressed like white men and spoke either French or English in addition to an Indian language, they lived apart in their own communities. After 1860 the westward movement of Canadian settlers led to demands that the territory be annexed by Canada, and fur trading and hunting were increasingly brought under legal control. The Méti claimed territorial rights by virtue of their Indian ancestry; they felt that the country was theirs and resented the intrusion. When they realized that their buffalo hunting and carefree way of life were coming to an end, they rebelled.[47]

Another type of community in which inter-ethnic contacts take place is the settlement that is the by-product of large-scale produc-

---

[46] Cf. Robert Redfield, "The Folk Society," *American Journal of Sociology*, LII (1947), 293–308.

[47] George F. G. Stanley, *The Birth of Western Canada: A History of the Riel Rebellions* (New York: Longmans, Green, 1936), pp. 3–11, 48–66.

tion: plantations and mines. These commercial enterprises require the concentration of a large and reliable labor force, whether the workers be slaves, immigrants, or migratory laborers. The pattern of land use is clearly defined; plantation boundaries are marked and guarded, and within the boundaries activities are coordinated to maximize the profits of the owners. Although plantations differ from medieval manors in that production is not diversified and self-sufficient, as social units they are much like the feudal communities. The labor force is cared for by a paternalistic regime. There are sharp and clearly defined differences of status, usually between a literate owner class and an illiterate working class, and the privileges and responsibilities of each rank are noticeably different. The workers are dependent upon the owners to the point where they cannot exercise initiative without great risk to themselves. The plantation is also a place in which minority groups become acculturated to the standards of their rulers. Sanitation standards are administered by the owners not only to maintain a reliable working force but also to protect their own health. Workers become acquainted with the language of the dominant group, and if their children are educated at all, it is often in the culture of their rulers. There is a tendency for plantations and mines to develop and perpetuate a rigid system of stratification. When more than one ethnic group is involved, the conflicting class interests tend to coincide with ethnic lines.

In most communities of this type each ethnic group is clearly segregated except during working hours. In spite of the separation, however, close contacts are inevitable among those who work together. The frequency with which a large population of mixed parentage develops in such communities suggests that illicit relations and the exploitation of minority-group women is commonplace.[48]

Another type of community is the city, which has a high population density and distinctive land use. Large cities have existed from the dawn of recorded history, and inter-ethnic contacts have been going on in them for many centuries. Roman artisans, merchants, and mining engineers often migrated beyond the confines of the empire; cities such as Constantinople, Alexandria, and Palermo received large numbers of immigrants and were known for the heterogeniety

---

[48] Cf. Gilberto Freyre, *The Masters and the Slaves* (New York: Alfred A. Knopf, 1946); and E. Franklin Frazier, *Race and Culture Contacts in the Modern World* (New York: Alfred A. Knopf, 1957), pp. 235–52.

of their population.[49] Since the Industrial Revolution there has been a spectacular growth of urban centers, for large-scale production requires a large labor force within commuting distance from the factories. In recent times growing cities have encroached upon the surrounding regions, and in some areas there is little countryside left. Cities have always played an important part in the history of interethnic contacts.

In industrial cities, especially in one that is growing rapidly, the segregation of ethnic groups develops through a selective process. People of low status settle in those areas where the rent is low and there is least opposition to their presence; those who can afford better housing usually live in mixed areas with the more successful members of other minority groups. In Great Britain approximately two-thirds of the colored population live in ethnic islands. The dockland areas have a heavier concentration of West Africans. The more ambitious, especially among the immigrants from the West Indies, strike out into districts with fewer minority peoples. In London the concentration is in Stepney.[50] In Kampala, Uganda, there is no zoning by ethnic groups, but most natives live in the "African area." African civil servants and professional men live in neighborhoods that are predominantly Asian or among Europeans.[51] Where the conquerors are greatly outnumbered, they establish their own enclaves. In Batavia during the colonial days of the Dutch East Indies, the administrators and traders lived in spacious villas in the most desirable areas; the Indonesian middle class and some Chinese lived in brick houses in more crowded areas; and throughout the city, wherever they were tolerated, there were kampongs for the lower-class Indonesians.[52] In Durban to a noticeable degree, different ethnic groups live in separate quarters. The distinctive character of each region of the city reflects the cultural life of the inhabitants as well as their economic

---

[49] Cf. Robert of Clari, *The Conquest of Constantinople*, trans. E. H. McNeal (New York: Columbia University Press, 1936), p. 105; and Gideon Sjoberg, *The Preindustrial City: Past and Present* (Glencoe, Ill.: The Free Press, 1960), pp. 25–79.

[50] Michael P. Banton, *The Coloured Quarter: Negro Immigrants in an English City* (London: Jonathan Cape, 1955), pp. 68–69, 104. Cf. Paul K. Hatt, "Spatial Patterns in a Polyethnic Area," *American Sociological Review*, X (1945), 352–56.

[51] Walter Elkan, *Migrants and Proletarians* (London: Oxford University Press, 1960), p. 17.

[52] Nathan Keyfitz, "The Ecology of Indonesian Cities," *American Journal of Sociology*, LXVI (1961), 348–54.

standing. The Europeans, having the highest average income, occupy the most desirable residential areas in terms of view of the sea, altitude, and accessibility to the center of the city.[53] The spatial distribution of ethnic groups develops through competition; the patterns develop as the members of each group settle in the best housing they can find.

Industrial cities frequently have a characteristic biotic pattern and psychological orientation. The population is made up largely of young people who migrate there from the surrounding countryside, spend most of their productive years there, and then retire elsewhere. The population of Livingstone, Northern Rhodesia, for example, shows an overloading in the age groups from 20 to 40, a preponderance of male over female, and the relative absence of older people of both sexes.[54] What is significant about very large cities is that the concentration of so many people into a limited area makes it impossible for anyone to know everyone else on a personal basis, and the anonymity results in the formation of a distinctive way of life. City-dwellers are in constant association with other people, but a large proportion of their contacts are with nodding acquaintances and strangers. Social relationships tend to be categorical, and people are identified in terms of the uniform they wear—ethnic or otherwise. Hence, the bonds of kinship, neighborliness, and friendship that arise from sharing numerous experiences do not enter into many transactions. City life is marked by a utilitarian accent. People tend to be highly rational and individualistic, and each goes about pursuing his own interests. Men often stand in a relationship of reciprocal utility toward one another; the pecuniary nexus often replaces personal preference as the basis for association. Where people use each other in the pursuit of their own ends, each person has to protect himself against exploitation; hence, urbanites tend to be more sophisticated and less idealistic. Timbuctoo, for example, is large enough so that the status of an individual is not known outside the immediate area in which he lives, and economic dealings with strangers are often ruthless. Outside the circle of his family and friends,

---

[53] Leo Kuper, Hilstan Watts, and Ronald Davies, *Durban: A Study in Racial Ecology* (New York: Columbia University Press, 1958), pp. 110–58. Cf. D. H. Reader, *The Black Man's Portion* (Cape Town: Oxford University Press, 1961), pp. 10–35.

[54] Merran McCulloch, *A Social Survey of the African Population of Livingstone* (Manchester, England: Manchester University Press, 1956), p. 15.

each person expects this kind of treatment and remains on guard.[55] When young people away from home live together in this type of atmosphere, there is a relaxation of traditional standards. This relative freedom from moral controls often facilitates the establishment of contacts across the color line.[56]

There is some kind of ethnic segregation in virtually all cities, and the formation of natural areas is easiest to see in the growing industrial city, where the distribution of peoples and institutions develops through competition on the open market. There are other cities, however, which are old, well-established, and not in an industrial economy. Many of these are collections of self-contained villages. Many of the old cities of Asia are as much political as economic centers; they constitute the point from which rulers control the numerous villages around it. Their location depends more upon the will of the prince than upon economic convenience. The location of institutions and peoples is traditional, although at times the internal arrangement is determined by decree. Religious and political institutions are usually found in the center of the city, along with the homes of the wealthy. The poorer people usually live on the periphery. There are special quarters for each ethnic group; in many cases they are virtually self-sufficient units with their own regulations.[57] In Timbuctoo, for example, there are four traditional quarters, with additional areas with bad reputations on the outskirts of the city. Although there is no clearcut segregation, a preponderance of people of a given class or ethnic group are found in each quarter. Furthermore, there are widely-held beliefs about the kind of people who supposedly dwell in each of these areas.[58] Social control is not as impersonal as it is in an industrial city, and the lines of demarcation between ethnic categories tend to be more stable.

In all types of communities the most desired areas belong to the ethnic group whose culture provides competitive advantages in that particular environment. In Swat, in northwestern Pakistan, the Pathan, sedentary farmers who speak an Iranian language, inhabit the valley. They are the most powerful group, but their territorial

---

[55] Miner, *op. cit.*, pp. 24-25, 245-46.

[56] Georg Simmel, *The Sociology of Georg Simmel*, trans. Kurt Wolff (Glencoe, Ill.: The Free Press, 1950), pp. 409-24; and Wirth, *Community Life and Social Policy, op. cit.*, pp. 110-32.

[57] Sjoberg, *op. cit.*, pp. 95-103, 133-37.

[58] Miner, *op. cit.*, pp. 32-47.

expansion is limited by their culture; they must remain at an altitude in which two crops can be raised each year. The Kohistani, who speak a Dardic language, have a two-fold economy, and they are not limited by this barrier. They plant on narrow terraces with irrigation and also keep herds; in season they leave their lands and go up as high as 14,000 feet. Since the size of their herd depends on the supply of winter fodder, they must have some fields. The Gujars, who are Gujiri-speaking nomadic herders, can survive on any part of the land, but they move about in small bands and do not have the military strength to challenge the others. Hence, they must carve out their niche from what is left by the others.[59] If the culture of a minority group is better suited to the environment, it may eventually displace the dominant group. In eastern Canada and in New England the French-Canadians have been spreading at the expense of the English-speaking Protestants. The French work on the soil and buy farms whenever they can, while the English farmers are too ambitious for their sons and find themselves without successors. Thus, their large-family farm system has enabled the French to compete successfully against the dominant group. Human beings compete with their sentiments and customs as well as with their technical skills and money.[60]

These ecological processes are sometimes complicated by political policies. In some European colonies, for example, there was a view that the colonial administration was responsible for opening up the resources not only for the homeland but also for the benefit of the indigenous people. In some British colonies there were laws prohibiting the sale or transfer of land from natives without the consent of the governor; these laws were designed to protect the native proprietor. When Great Britain assumed protection of Uganda in 1900, the crown took as its share about half of the territory, mostly uncultivated land. The cultivated area was considered the property of the native chiefs, and the colonial government maintained control over these aristocrats so that they could not sell freely. Various decrees favored small freehold tenure, and a system of peasant proprietorship developed. British policy in Nigeria also supported the

[59] Fredrik Barth, "Ecologic Relationship of Ethnic Groups in Swat, North Pakistan," *American Anthropologist*, LVIII (1956), 1079-89.

[60] Everett C. Hughes, *French Canada in Transition* (Chicago: University of Chicago Press, 1943), pp. 16-21.

indigenous form of land ownership. The effect was to keep out foreign capital and to prevent the growth of a European settler community.[61] Thus, individual members of the dominant group are not always free to exploit their advantages. Although ecological processes appear to be modified by law, it should be remembered that such laws are enforced by authorities of the dominant group.

Summary and Conclusion

Ethnic groups in contact occupy a common habitat, and those who live together become involved in a common existence. What happens to the people in one group cannot be explained independently of the activities of the others. All living organisms find their niche in the web of life through competition and natural selection, but human beings compete on the basis of group identity and with cultural tools. One product of the struggle for existence is the distribution of various categories of people in space, with the more desirable areas going to those who enjoy competitive advantages. Another product is the size of each of the groups, which depends upon migration and rates of growth. What is important is that the patterns that develop initially in competition subsequently become fixed in custom. Once an ethnic group establishes its ascendancy, it may enforce the patterns through law.

Reformers in the United States have tried to improve the lot of minority groups through "urban renewal" programs that consist largely of tearing down old buildings and putting up new ones. Much disappointment has been expressed in some circles when new slum areas with the same ethnic colonies reappear elsewhere in the city. As long as members of ethnic minorities are poor, they cannot afford to live in newly-built apartments; as long as they are culturally different, they feel uncomfortable in the midst of outsiders; as long as outsiders are hostile toward them, most would prefer to live where they will be left alone. Hence, they tend to congregate where they meet the least resistance. Those who fail to recognize that segregated areas arise through natural selection are bound to be disappointed in spite of their good intentions and conscientious efforts.

[61] Coleman, *op. cit.*, pp. 58–60. Cf. Thomas R. Adam, *Modern Colonialism: Institutions and Policies* (New York: Doubleday, 1955), p. 25.

CHAPTER 7

The Formation of
a Multi-Ethnic Economy

For three days in January 1949, Africans rioted in the streets of Durban, but much to everyone's surprise, their wrath was directed at Indians rather than Europeans. This becomes comprehensible only when we consider the position of the Indians in the community. Although South African society is one in which the Europeans are dominant and the Africans clearly subordinate, the outsiders with whom Africans are most likely to come into contact in their daily lives are the Asians who provide commercial and professional services. While the Europeans may be the primary enforcers of the color line, the Indians are the ones whom the Africans constantly encounter in their efforts to make their way in life. Ill will had developed from competition in retail trade and from high rentals charged by landlords in the slum areas. When tensions were ignited by a spark, the explosion was directed against the people who were directly experienced as "tormenters." No system of social stratification can be understood without some knowledge of the economy, for much of

[168]

the ordering of social life depends upon the kinds of relationships men enter into in the course of earning a livelihood.

In every community some kind of cooperative arrangement for feeding, clothing, and sheltering the populace develops, and there is usually some kind of division of labor that is of mutual benefit to all parties. Different people do different things, and their respective contributions fit together. The differentiation of tasks, at least by age and sex, is found even in the simplest economies. Where there is a specialization of tasks, a method of distributing goods develops, since no one can produce alone everything he needs for himself and his family. In all communities there are property rights of some sort, conventional understandings concerning who controls what object— sometimes including other human beings. In many communities people in different ethnic categories perform different tasks, have different property rights, and get unequal shares of the rewards. When ethnic groups come into contact, how do they become involved in a common economic system? How are the various tasks allocated? How is the evolving division of labor related to the emergence of a new system of ethnic stratification?

Patterns of Production and Distribution

Throughout the world ethnic groups occupying adjacent territories have established mutually profitable economic ties with their neighbors. There is archaeological evidence showing how old and widespread trade is, and trade routes were already established by the time history was first recorded.[1] There are many instances in which such transactions are carried on over a long period without significant changes in the cultures of the groups involved. An extreme example is the "silent trade," in which exchange is carried on regularly by people who neither see nor address one another; each side deposits goods at a customary spot and receives in return some other commodity that had been established by tradition as their equivalent. The practice is apparently very old, for it is described by Herodotus. The Carthaginians left their goods on a beach in Libya and returned to their ships to build fires; the natives saw the smoke and brought gold to the beach, not removing any of the goods until after the gold

[1] Cf. Melville J. Herskovits, *Economic Anthropology* (New York: Alfred A. Knopf, 1952), pp. 180–237.

had been accepted. If the Carthaginians felt that there was not enough gold, they returned to their ship and waited until more was brought. Similar practices have subsequently been reported from various parts of the world.[2]

Thus, ethnic groups with radically different cultures often enter into symbiotic relationships and become economically interdependent. Cases of peaceful contacts limited largely to bartering surpluses or making arrangements for the passage and lodging of caravans and travellers are also quite common. In central China the Mongols and the Chinese farmers have had such relationships for centuries. The Mongols, who were nomadic herders, exchanged milk, cheese, cattle, sheep, and wool for grain and other agricultural products, cloth, boots, and trinkets. During their off seasons the Mongols herded for a small fee the draft ponies and plow cattle of the Chinese.[3] Further to the west the Tibetan nomads lived too high in elevation for agriculture, and they had to trade for some of their food. Since the Tibetan farmers who lived closer to the pasture-lands seldom had surpluses, the nomads travelled farther to trade for grain with the Chinese-speaking Moslems. When the Moslem caravans travelled through Tibet, they stopped regularly with hosts with whom they had traded, and there were established procedures for the treatment of guests by the hosts.[4] All these groups have retained their respective identities and cultures. This suggests that in the many centuries of contact, each side has maintained social distance.

The coming of a new ethnic group into a community results in some kind of transformation of the economic system. When groups with different technological skills come into contact in a frontier community, there may be competition between them for the limited resources, resulting in open warfare. When the invader is a powerful conqueror, the old system may be smashed and replaced by a new one. Even when immigrants move into a well-established community and accept subordinate positions in an already-established industrial system, they alter it by swelling the labor force, raising the output, and providing a larger number of consumers. Thus, the old pattern

[2] P. J. Hamilton Grierson, *The Silent Trade* (Edinburgh: William Green & Sons, 1903), pp. 30–68; and Herskovits, *op. cit.*, pp. 36–37, 185–87.

[3] Lattimore, "Chinese Colonization in Inner Mongolia," *op. cit.*, p. 305.

[4] Ekvall, *op. cit.*

is necessarily altered; if nothing else happens, there are more people to feed. Where ethnic groups meet, new economic systems develop through competition and natural selection.

Since the sixteenth century the migration of Europeans has resulted in the gradual incorporation of the rest of the world into a common economy. Many of the inter-ethnic contacts of this period were by-products of the expansion of European capitalism. Various pressures—the growth of national states, the weakening of central church authority, the maritime discoveries—made feudalism an inadequate method of production in Europe. With the growth of commerce and industry the accumulation of capital became an important aim, and the concept of wealth as separated from goods developed. Capital consists not so much of land or the instruments of production but of transferable securities—sums invested to bring in interest. An essential characteristic of the capitalistic system is the mobility of capital—its ability to overcome time and distance. When manufacturing that had been in the hands of local tradesmen was given capital, it blossomed into corporations. Early capitalism was a dynamic, explosively potent system of production, and there appeared to be unlimited opportunities for the expansion of business enterprise.[5] The resulting combination was European capital and native labor, although sometimes the labor also had to be imported. Economic development in the colonies was encouraged in a limited way; the colonies were set up to serve as suppliers of needed materials and as markets for manufactured goods. This required the transformation of the native economy. Alien languages were introduced along with the technology and institutions of capitalism—the free market, the profit motive, private property, money, and the improvement of public health.[6] In the twentieth century the European monopoly was broken; in Asia and Oceania Chinese and Japanese entered the field as entrepreneurs. Since World War II the less exploitative United Nations technical assistance program and the "Point Four" plan of the United States have brought foreign investments into areas not yet industrialized. Indigenous economies are also being disrupted by

[5] Sée, op. cit.; and Werner Sombart, "Capitalism," Encyclopedia of the Social Sciences, Vol. III, pp. 195–208. Cf. John Strachey, The End of Empire (New York: Random House, 1960), pp. 98–124.

[6] Nicholas J. Spykman, "The Social Background of Asiatic Nationalism," American Journal of Sociology, XXXII (1926), 396–411.

the Communists, who have not introduced some of the capitalistic institutions.[7]

During the initial phases of industrialization there is a period of transition during which a dual economy develops. At the time of their conquest by the Dutch, the Javanese had an agricultural economy in which they produced for subsistence. In good years they did not even bother to cultivate all the land they owned, for they had no interest in building up a surplus they could neither eat nor preserve. There was some trading of surpluses, but this was on a barter basis. The European colonists brought in a money economy and introduced the plantation system, in which agricultural work was done for profit. For a while the natives remained aloof, and the traditional village economy continued to operate side by side with the plantations.[8] A similar case of coexistence can be found in Point Hope, a village of about 250 Eskimos in northwestern Alaska. The seasonal subsistence cycle had long been set by the arctic environment; because of the movements of the ice, animals had to be hunted in season—seals in the autumn and spring; polar bears in the winter; cod, crabs, and whales in the spring. Summer had traditionally been a period of inactivity, when many left the village to fish at nearby rivers. From about 1850, whaling vessels began stopping there, bringing in manufactured goods and weapons. Before long, much of the Eskimo material culture was abandoned, and manufactured furniture, flashlights, cooking utensils, and radios became commonplace. To purchase these objects money was earned from the sale of skins, summer employment, and in recent winters from unemployment compensation. When a radar station was constructed at Cape Lisburne in 1951, many joined the building trades. Since outside employment was largely restricted to the summer months, however, it dovetailed into the seasonal cycle, and the two economies operated simultaneously.[9]

---

[7] Cf. Joseph N. Froomkin, "The Migration of Capital, People, and Technology," in Harold F. Williamson and John A. Buttrick (eds.), *Economic Development: Principles and Patterns* (New York: Prentice-Hall, 1954), pp. 277–317; and Helen Constas, "The U.S.S.R.—From Charismatic Sect to Bureaucratic Society," *Administrative Science Quarterly*, VI (1961), 282–98.

[8] J. H. Boeke, *The Structure of Netherlands Indies Economy* (New York: Institute of Pacific Relations, 1942), pp. 8–13, 57–103.

[9] James W. van Stone, "A Successful Combination of Subsistence and Wage Economies on the Village Level," *Economic Development and Cultural Change*, VIII (1960), 174–91.

Even where there is peaceful coexistence in the beginning, however, minority groups are gradually drawn into the economy of
their rulers as their traditional system is destroyed. The strain of
sheep herded by the Mongols, for example, had been well suited to
their economy. It was hardy enough to withstand the bitter winters;
its coarse felt was ideal for Mongol tents; its meat was high in the fat
content needed for the winter diet; its skin made warm and durable
clothing. When the Japanese moved into Manchuria, however, they
decided that the wool had to be "improved" if Japanese industry was
to become independent of the Australian wool supply. The new
breeding program made the sheep less hardy and the products less
useful to the herders. The Mongol economy was ruined, and the
people became dependent upon Japanese imports.[10]

This process is facilitated by changes in the consumption patterns of minority groups; once people become accustomed to manufactured implements, medicines, weapons, and other objects that can
only be purchased with money, they are more easily drawn into the
new economy.[11] Toward the end of the nineteenth century the
"ethical policy" of bringing the benefits of "civilization" to the natives resulted in a stream of money going into the villages in the
Dutch East Indies. Once the Javanese had been shown the advantages
of products made in Europe, they searched for ways of getting
money besides selling surplus agricultural goods. The only alternative was labor in the plantations.[12] From 1830 on, travellers and
traders in Bechuanaland exchanged European goods for ivory and
ostrich feathers. After the discovery of Lake Ngami in 1849, more
Europeans came, and missionaries established stations with most
tribes. By starting schools and insisting upon "civilized" forms of
dress, they helped stimulate demand for manufactured wares. By
employing natives as servants and assistants, they also introduced the
practice of working for wages. After the discovery of diamonds at
Kimberley, more and more men were attracted to the diggings by
reports of the goods that could be earned there. The indigenous arts

[10] Owen Lattimore, "The Eclipse of Inner Mongolian Nationalism," *Journal
of the Royal Central Asian Society*, XXIII (1936), 421–22.

[11] Herskovits, *op. cit.*, pp. 269–97. Cf. Elizabeth E. Hoyt, "The Impact of a
Money Economy on Consumption Patterns," *Annals of the American Academy of
Political and Social Science*, CCCV (May 1956), 12–22; and Monica Hunter, *Re-
action to Conquest* (London: Oxford University Press, 1936), pp. 544–47.

[12] Boeke, *op. cit.*, pp. 59–67; and W. F. Wertheim, *Indonesian Society in Transition* (The Hague: W. van Hoeve, 1956), pp. 90–105.

and crafts disappeared, and the subsistence economy was replaced by a money economy. More and more status came to rest upon wealth; a man was judged by his house, clothing, and food.[13] Thus, the people in European colonies were drawn into the elaborate exchange system through which they were tied to the markets of the world.

The use of money is not restricted, of course, to the capitalistic system. Durable, portable tokens that symbolize stores of value had long been accepted as standards of deferred payment in West Africa and the Congo, in Melanesia and Micronesia, and among the Indians in the western part of North America. But the concept of money is alien to many peoples. In a capitalistic economy everything is made subservient to the acquisition of money and is evaluated in terms of utility. Human beings are seen as consumers or as part of the labor force; nature is seen as an instrument of production; and life itself is sometimes viewed as a commercial transaction.[14] Even after the utility of money as a medium of exchange is clearly understood, some groups still regard the accumulation of money beyond one's immediate needs as senseless. Thus, in areas in which a money economy is just developing, men often work only until they have accumulated enough to purchase what they want and to pay necessary taxes; they then quit. Hence, there is high labor turnover and low productivity. The evaluation of personal services in monetary terms is especially strange to many peoples. In medical care, for example, witch doctors and traditional healers had been paid in goods or deeds. A modern doctor, however, must be paid in money, for his medicine cabinet must periodically be refilled. Many people require time to get used to the idea of paying for such services with money rather than with gifts.[15]

Thus, the introduction of a money economy facilitates the break-up of traditional patterns. Subsistence agriculture is replaced by the cultivation of cash crops. As farmers begin to produce a surplus for sale, they become vulnerable to price fluctuations in the world market. In some regions the cultivation of cash crops has accelerated the process of soil erosion. In addition, the withdrawal of

[13] Isaac Schapera, *Migrant Labour and Tribal Life* (London: Oxford University Press, 1947), pp. 6–8, 121–25.

[14] Herskovits, *op. cit.*, pp. 238–68; and Sombart, *op. cit.*

[15] Cf. Buwei Y. Chao, *Autobiography of a Chinese Woman* (New York: John Day, 1947), p. 159.

large numbers of able-bodied men from family farms to work in plantations and factories leads to a deterioration in farm practices. When mining became a dominant industry in Northern Rhodesia, for example, the younger men left the kraal to work, and their absence affected the development of rural areas.[16] Furthermore, the introduction of money almost invariably results in widespread rural indebtedness. The peasants go to money lenders for loans, sometimes for productive purposes but often to finance religious or family observances or to purchase some desired object. In this way many lose possession of their land. In the Dutch East Indies the natives were drawn into plantation work largely through their debts.[17]

The concept of private property is also alien to many peoples. The idea is so commonplace to most Americans that we assume that there is some kind of necessary connection between an object and its owner. We fail to realize that property is a social institution, that the relationship between an object and its owner is defined by conventional understandings. These norms vary from culture to culture. Among the Aborigines in Australia, for example, vegetable and animal food were regarded as provided by supernatural agencies; all men had to do was to collect them. When the European settlers took up so much of their space that game became scarce, they simply speared the cattle and sheep instead of looking for kangaroos.[18]

Where individuals are able to pursue successful careers by acquiring money, clans and tribes tend to be replaced by the formation of family units consisting of a man, his wife, and their children. Traditional ties tend to be replaced by individualistic values; the bonds are corroded by the strong attraction of individual profit through outside activities. As new opportunities arise for accumulating wealth, there is a drift toward individualized landholding and wage employment. The traditional concept of landholding in Africa emphasized communal rights; after European colonization, however, this yielded first to the individualization of land rights and then to commerciali-

[16] Hailey, op. cit., pp. 486, 809, 823, 1316–17, 1386–87; and Lind, An Island Community, op. cit., pp. 40–41.

[17] Boeke, op. cit., pp. 59–67; Justus M. van der Kroef, "The Arabs in Indonesia," Middle East Journal, VII (1953), 311–17; and Wertheim, op. cit., pp. 89–104. Cf. C. K. Meek, Land Law and Custom in the Colonies (London: Oxford University Press, 1949), pp. 60–74.

[18] Ronald M. and Catherine Berndt, From Black to White in South Australia (Melbourne: F. W. Cheshire, 1951), pp. 26, 61.

zation, in which land was sold, mortgaged, or leased.[19] In 1847, when the king of Hawaii renounced his exclusive ownership of the land, the traditional system of landholding collapsed. Commoners were able to secure title to the land they actually occupied and used. Once the people grasped the idea of private property and individual title, however, they sold in increasing numbers to foreigners.[20] Similarly, when the Japanese developed sugar, copra, and other industries on their mandated islands in the Pacific after World War I, landholding changed from common to private ownership. As more and more natives responded to the call for wage labor, the chieftains lost much of their power and prestige.[21] Apart from the desire for manufactured goods, the principal stimulant to wage employment is that monetary wealth becomes the key to status and the criterion of success in the emerging social structure.

This suggests that the most significant change that occurs when an economic system is undergoing transformation is the acceptance of new beliefs and values by the people in minority groups. European peasants who migrated to American cities, African migrant workers in the compounds of Johannesburg, Javanese toiling on the Dutch plantations—all were exposed to new ideas that broke the "cake of custom" of their traditional order. New ideas disrupt social relationships that had hitherto appeared natural, and increasing numbers realize that some of the cumbersome restrictions of their culture are arbitrary. In the European colonies missionaries often played an important part in challenging the old moral order. They came in with set convictions about the "right" way to live—to work hard, to save money, to live in one's own house, to possess one's own goods, and not to belong to silly tribes.[22] Today men all over the world are committing themselves to the way of life of an industrial society—capitalistic or socialistic. The introduction of new technological devices into underdeveloped areas often has the same effect even when inter-

---

[19] Hailey, *op. cit.*, pp. 775, 802–05. Cf. Coleman, *op. cit.*, pp. 66–71; Herskovits, *op. cit.*, pp. 313–70; and Meek, *op. cit.*, pp. 3–27, 162–92.

[20] Lind, *An Island Community*, *op. cit.*, pp. 45–58.

[21] Tadao Yanaihara, *Pacific Islands Under Japanese Mandate* (London: Oxford University Press, 1940), pp. 29, 148–53, 223.

[22] Arthur H. Cole, "The Relation of Missionary Activity to Economic Development," *Economic Development and Cultural Change*, IX (1961), 120–27; and Park, *Race and Culture, op. cit.*, pp. 331–41.

ethnic contacts are not involved, for the effective use of these devices requires a new mode of thinking.[23]

Ethnic groups sharing a common habitat sooner or later become incorporated into a common economic system. There is some kind of allocation of tasks in each community, and the arduous duties are usually relegated to minority groups. Even where there are no laws prohibiting certain ethnic categories from given occupations, definite patterns can be found. In Malaya during the interwar years Malayans worked in rice plantations and Indians in rubber plantations; the labor in mines was provided mostly by Chinese; most Eurasians worked as clerks; and the Chinese operated much of the retail trade.[24] In the Ituri forest in the Congo basin Pygmies and their taller hosts live side by side. The Pygmies provide honey and meat and receive plantains in return. The relationship is interfamilial; the association between the Pygmy family and the host family is inherited on both sides from father to son. There is no bargaining, nor does anyone bother to keep an account. If one party feels that the other is not providing enough, he holds back on his next contribution. If the transactions become entirely unsatisfactory, the Pygmy family may leave to look for another host—a separation that is much like a divorce in our society.[25] As long as the various ethnic groups retain their identity and culture, they fit together into a colorful mosaic in a diversified society.[26]

The pattern of social relationships that eventually crystallizes into a color line often has its origin in the sustenance arrangements that develop in the community. Economic systems vary considerably in complexity. In an agricultural settlement at which nomadic groups make seasonal stops, for example, the division of labor is relatively simple. There may be a few shopkeepers, innkeepers, and craftsmen, but the major distinction is between the farmer and the herdsman. In an industrial city, however, there are thousands of occupations, and the stratification of a metropolitan population is very complex.

[23] Cf. Karl Polanyi, *The Great Transformation* (Boston: Beacon Press, 1957); and James S. Slotkin, *From Field to Factory* (Glencoe, Ill.: The Free Press, 1960), pp. 21–31.

[24] McKenzie, *op. cit.*

[25] Patrick Putnam, "The Pygmies of the Ituri Forest," in Carleton Coon (ed.), *A Reader in General Anthropology* (New York: Henry Holt, 1948), pp. 322–28.

[26] Cf. Coon, *Caravan, op. cit.*; J. S. Furnivall, *Netherlands India* (New York: Macmillan, 1944); Hughes and Hughes, *op. cit.*, pp. 51–60; Miner, *op. cit.*, pp. 52–71.

This suggests that the degree of specialization in a system of ethnic stratification is related to the complexity of the economy. The differentiation of roles necessary for carrying out sustenance activities tend to crystallize into a status order.

Since the economic system that develops generally serves the interests of the dominant group, it appears to be something that is imposed upon the community by force. Although this is sometimes the case, most systems of production and distribution develop as the various ethnic groups adjust and readjust to the new situation created by the contact. Although subsistence patterns were displaced by capitalism in the European colonies, the colonial economies were not the same as those in Europe. In each area adjustments were made to the peculiar combination of résources, skills, and manpower. Nor do conquerors invariably retain their own system of production. Where the economy of the vanquished is better suited to the environment, the invaders may work themselves into the existing system—as in the case of the conquerors of China. In each situation of contact, special needs arise, and those who are affected make an effort to meet these needs. Institutional arrangements involving parties from different ethnic groups evolve gradually, beginning in those areas in which there is some common interest. Those who perceive common interests begin to cooperate, at first tentatively, and then in time their expectations of one another become fixed. If the cooperation proves to be mutually profitable, other areas are explored. Economic contacts are relatively easy to establish even with strangers, for the advantages are usually immediate and tangible, and trade is impersonal. When ecological patterns are disrupted, then, adjustments are made by all parties to the exigencies of the situation. The procedures that prove fruitful are repeated until they become crystallized. The niche that each ethnic group wins in the new web of life depends largely upon the competitive advantages provided by its culture and leadership.[27]

The Organization of the Labor Force

In many communities there is sufficient labor available to meet the needs of the new productive system. Where the units of produc-

[27] Cf. Joseph A. Schumpeter, *Theory of Economic Development* (Cambridge: Harvard University Press, 1934), pp. 57–94.

tion are very large, however, as in the case of mines and plantations, getting and maintaining an adequate labor force sometimes becomes a major problem. The techniques used for the recruitment of labor have much to do with the formation of stratified societies.

One way of securing necessary labor is slavery. The practice of slavery varies considerably in form, but it is both ancient in origin and widespread in its geographic distribution. Men have been enslaved in many ways—through captivity in war, purchase abroad, bondage as a result of unpaid debts, or inheritance from slave parents. Slaves are not always exploited or mistreated, although there is little question of their servile position. In ancient Rome, for example, Greek slaves were used as teachers and entrusted with the care of children. There was slavery in Europe during the Middle Ages, although there was some agitation against the sale of Christians to Moslems and Jews. American Indians of the Northwest enslaved their prisoners. The captives performed menial tasks and were excluded from ceremonies. They were permitted to marry only among themselves, and their children inherited slave status. Sometimes they were given away as gifts. Although we tend to think of slaves and their owners as being in different ethnic groups, there have been many cases in which there were no marked ethnic differences. The Negro slaves who were first brought to the United States in the early seventeenth century were in many instances accorded the same treatment as the indentured white servants. Where there are ethnic differences between master and slave, however, possibilities of sympathetic identification are apparently minimized; thus, exploitation becomes less difficult.[28]

The growth of European influence after the sixteenth century was greatly facilitated by the slave trade. Efficient exploitation of the resources in the colonies usually required considerably more labor than the Europeans themselves could provide, and others had to be induced or forced to participate in the new economies. During the period of initial contact the colonists were often under the impression that an abundance of manpower was available, since they had been greeted by a large number of curious onlookers. Investments were often made on the basis of such impressions; then the colonists learned to their dismay that the natives were not willing to

[28] Bernhard J. Stern *et al.*, "Slavery," *Encyclopedia of the Social Sciences*, Vol. XIV, pp. 73–92.

work. In many cases the idea of working for money was incomprehensible to them. Their refusal to work created in the colonists the impression that the natives were indolent and lazy; that the same people toiled diligently on tasks that they themselves regarded as important was overlooked. Thus, the maritime discoveries opened up a new era in the history of slavery, for prosperity in the colonies depended upon large-scale production. The overseas export of slaves from Africa was inaugurated by the Portuguese in 1442, and the movement was supported by the Moslems, among whom slavery was sanctioned by religion and civil law. By 1712 Great Britain had secured a virtual monopoly over the slave trade on the west coast of Africa; in 1807, however, the British government declared the practice illegal, and foreign slave dealers rushed in to fill the vacuum. In 1885 each of the European powers signing the Berlin Act agreed to use all means at its disposal to put an end to slave traffic; this was ratified in 1892, and a campaign of suppression followed.[29]

Even where slavery was not clearly established, forced labor was used to protect investments. The *encomienda* system used by the Spanish conquerors in the Americas was much like slavery. A number of Indians, with or without the land they occupied, were assigned to a Spaniard, who was entitled to extract services from them. When the system was abolished toward the end of the colonial era, the Spaniards substituted other methods to retain Indians in peonage. They paid the tribute imposed on the Indians, supplied them with food and clothing, and lent them money for funerals and weddings; since the wages were so low, the longer the Indians worked, the more they were in debt. In the Philippines a similar tribute was imposed on all men from 18 to 60, and the entire population was apportioned into *encomiendas*. When this system died down, it was replaced by a labor draft known as the *polo*.[30] In the colonization of Africa roads and railways were essential, and in many cases the natives were forced or tricked into providing the labor. Some of the harshest practices developed where coercion was felt to be necessary to protect large investments, as in the case of the mines of South Africa. Since legal

[29] Coleman, *op. cit.*, pp. 40–41; Frazier, *Race and Culture Contacts in the Modern World*, *op. cit.*, pp. 110–26; and Hubert Herring, *A History of Latin America* (New York: Alfred A. Knopf, 1955), pp. 101–09.
[30] George M. McBride, "Peonage," *Encyclopedia of the Social Sciences*, Vol. XII, pp. 69–72; Phelan, *op. cit.*, pp. 93–100; and Lesley B. Simpson, *The Encomienda in New Spain* (Berkeley: University of California Press, 1950).

documents meant little to most Africans at that time, they did not feel any obligation to honor labor contracts under unpleasant conditions. They could not understand why Europeans became so upset over their quitting when they had earned all the money they needed. Therefore, guarded stockades were erected to compel men to remain at work for stipulated periods. Slavery was illegal, and the men were paid for their work, but this could hardly be regarded as voluntary labor.[31] To man plantations in the South Seas the "blackbirders" captured native chiefs and their families and held them as hostages until enough able-bodied followers had signed contracts committing them to work in some distant place. Some of the workers from Micronesia and Polynesia were taken as far away as Mexico and Peru.[32]

As opposition to slavery mounted throughout the world, native labor was recruited in many colonies by creating an artificial demand for money. The most effective method was taxation. Although the colonial governments often needed revenue, the taxation of Africans was designed primarily as a means of getting the natives to work in plantations, mines, public construction projects, and industrial undertakings. The Natal administration imposed a poll tax as early as 1849; the hut tax on natives not working for Europeans was raised in 1857 from 7 to 11 shillings a year. One of the major objectives of the Glen Gray Act of 1894 was to secure Africans to work in the diamond and gold mines of South Africa; any native who could prove that he had been employed for at least three months of each year outside his district was exempt from the 10-shilling tax. In Nigeria the progressive imposition of direct taxes payable only in the colonial currency resulted in every household's having to turn either to wage labor or to the production of cash crops. The French introduced the *prestation*, a tax payable in the form of labor, but this was replaced by a "road" tax when the natives reacted unfavorably.[33]

These taxes, along with the utility of money for the purchase of manufactured goods, succeeded in getting people to work. There was a period of transition, however, during which the laws did not fully achieve their purpose. In many cases the men worked just long

---

[31] Hailey, *op. cit.*, pp. 676, 1362–63, 1369; and Bronislaw Malinowski, *The Dynamics of Culture Change*, ed. Phyllis M. Kaberry (New Haven: Yale University Press, 1945), pp. 23–24.

[32] Oliver, *op. cit.*, pp. 94–95.

[33] Coleman, *op. cit.*, p. 57; Hailey, *op. cit.*, pp. 387, 643, 651, 759, 1362–63, 1400; and Lugard, *op. cit.*, pp. 234, 414.

enough to pay the taxes and to buy what they wanted—and then disappeared. When a land tax was introduced in the Dutch East Indies, many of the natives arranged to have the fee paid for them by others—Chinese traders, tribal chiefs, or Europeans—in exchange for some of their surpluses.[34] The practice of wage labor, then, became widely accepted in the colonies only after a money economy was established.

If the natives prove to be unsuitable, other ethnic groups may be imported to provide the necessary labor. In South Africa the Boers encountered difficulties from the beginning. White labor was rebellious and expensive. Slaves were imported from Angola, but they proved to be poor field laborers. Workers were then brought in from Madagascar and from the Malay Archipelago. When Africans did not work well in the cane sugar and cotton plantations, Indian coolies were imported, the first indentured workers reaching Natal in 1860. The demand for plantation, mine, and railroad construction labor was so acute between 1869 and 1911 that the Natal administration offered to allocate crown lands to indentured Indians who decided to remain after the termination of their contracts. After the Boer War some Chinese were also imported.[35] In Polynesia the natives were often found unsatisfactory as laborers. When neither fear of economic want nor prospects of gain made plantation labor attractive to the natives of Hawaii, labor agreements were signed with the governments of China, Japan, and Portugal. From 1880 to 1905 the planters spent an estimated $9 million to entice workers from these and other countries.[36] The tin mines in Malaya, the rubber plantations in Java, and the rice fields in Burma and Indochina also required a large supply of inexpensive labor, and the European colonists actively promoted Chinese and Indian immigration.[37] Thus, the practice of importing labor is widespread. Some observers insist that imported labor is easier to manage than local "free" labor; they are not bound by village ties, and there is less turnover. Many of the color lines in

---

[34] Boeke, op. cit., pp. 94, 106; and Wertheim, op. cit., pp. 230–49.

[35] Hailey, op. cit., pp. 393, 400, 1357, 1358; Johnston, op. cit., pp. 128, 270–71, 290; and Kuper, Watts, and Davies, op. cit., pp. 25–30.

[36] Lind, An Island Community, op. cit., pp. 14, 188–201; and Oliver, op. cit., pp. 91–93, 190–91.

[37] Ta Chen, Emigrant Communities in South China (New York: Institute of Pacific Relations, 1939), p. 53; E. H. G. Dobby, Southeast Asia (London: University of London Press, 1954), 113–24; Furnivall, Colonial Policy and Practice, op. cit., p. 89.

the world today are what they are because so many contract laborers elected not to return to their homes.

The economy of the United States has been constructed on the basis of voluntary immigration. Indeed, the presence of so many immigrants in the labor force has given American industry and labor organizations a distinctive pattern.[38] Immigrant labor was welcomed by many employers because of the physical strength, steady work habits, willingness to accept low wages, dependability, and sobriety of many peasant groups. All parties were reasonably satisfied, and our population today bears the marks of its diverse origins.

California, in comparison to other states, has a disproportionate number of large farms, which depend for their operation upon a large supply of labor. In 1930 the largest 10 per cent occupied 80 per cent of all the agricultural land in the state. The preservation of this farm structure through the importation of successive waves of immigrants provides an especially illuminating example of the manner in which a system of ethnic stratification develops as an outgrowth of the pursuit of economic interests.

From 1769 to 1833 agricultural life was largely confined to the Spanish missions. Although the land grants were large, the priests were not concerned with profit, nor were the Indians who worked for them interested in the accumulation of worldly goods. In 1834, when the transition to civil life occurred, the land was transferred to laymen for private profit; the Indian labor was kept on the plantation-like ranches, in many instances in peonage. Americans who began coming into the state adopted the same system, and some even imported Negro slaves to work their land. With the discovery of gold in 1848, however, floods of anti-slavery people entered from the North, and California joined the union as a free state. At the end of the gold-rush period, there were enough disappointed gold-seekers and Chinese coolies to maintain the large-scale farming.

At first it was assumed that more farmers would come from the East as soon as the railroads were completed and that family-type farms would replace the large holdings, which were regarded as a transitional pattern. During the prosperity of the 1870's, however, the availability of an abundance of Chinese labor made possible the conversion to intensive cultivation of lands that had been extensively

[38] Herman Feldman, *Racial Factors in American Industry* (New York: Harper, 1931), pp. 132–79.

cultivated. When opposition to the Chinese developed in urban centers, the landowners did not resist, because they still thought the arrangement was temporary. When the land was evaluated in anticipation of returns utilizing cheap labor, however, it became so expensive that few could afford to buy it. After the passage of the Chinese Exclusion Act in 1882, the landowners organized to prevent the Chinese already in the state from being driven away. The labor problem was temporarily solved after 1889, when a depression threw many white people out of work. For the next decade much of the agricultural labor was provided by those driven out of urban centers by unemployment.

With the coming of prosperity at the turn of the century the white workers returned to jobs in the cities, and another threat of a labor shortage developed. The Chinese had been reduced in number through death and emigration, and because of the new law no more could be imported. At this point large-scale importations of Japanese labor began. Although the employers were dependent upon the Japanese from 1902 to 1907, they were not pleased with them. The Japanese were too aggressive in establishing themselves as independent operators and entering into competition with their former employers. Although agitation against the Japanese was carried on primarily by the workers in urban areas, the landowners did little to oppose it. The supply of Japanese labor was cut off by the Gentlemen's Agreement of 1907.

During the hard times from 1908 to 1916 there was again an abundance of white labor from the cities. Then the prosperity of World War I resulted in another critical shortage. This time the need was met through the use of patriotic women and children and the importation of some Mexicans. From 1920 to 1930 the farm labor supply was filled by an increasing number of Mexicans. When protests arose and a demand was made for a quota system for Mexicans, the employers were conspicuous in their opposition. During this decade Filipino workers were also imported, although many employers were less enthusiastic about them. In 1934, when the Philippine Republic won its provisional independence, the immigration quota was set at 50 per year, and this cut the supply of workers. During the depression years of the early 1930's the supply of agricultural labor was ample, but as the New Deal got under way there was once again a shortage. This time it was filled by recruiting people from the "dust bowl" in Arkansas and Oklahoma. Although the farm owners denied it, there is evidence that they engaged in promotional activities to entice "Arkies" and "Okies" into the state.[39] With the outbreak of World War II all persons of Japanese ancestry, their loyalty under suspicion, were evacuated from the Pacific coast. The "Arkies," "Okies," and Filipinos abandoned their farm jobs for more lucrative positions in war plants, and there was another critical labor shortage. This vacuum was filled by the large-scale immigration of Mexican labor, in which the federal government took an active part. In recent years the farm system has been maintained by armies of seasonal workers. Thus, the heterogeneous population of California is the by-product of attempts to perpetuate a particular type of agricultural production.

The voluntary migration of seasonal workers has helped relieve labor shortages and has provided occasions for inter-ethnic contacts. The practice is not new, especially in Europe. From the fifteenth century Polish *Sachsengänger* migrated regularly to Germany; from the sixteenth century large "agricultural gangs" from Ireland have helped in the English harvest; prior to the Bolshevik revolution as many as 4 million people moved about in Russia to supplement their income as "factory nomads"; before World War II seasonal workers from Spain and Italy went annually to Latin America.[40] During the past century an increasing number of Africans have been drawn into seasonal work. The development of diamond mines at Kimberley gave rise to the first extensive emigration of native labor from the reserves in South Africa, and the discovery of gold on the Witwatersrand in 1886 created a new and increasing demand for labor. During World War I men from Bechuanaland were employed by the government in the African Labour Corps; they were sent to France to work on the docks, railways, and quarries. During World War II some 9,500 men were sent to North Africa and the Middle East in the African Pioneer Corps. During the summer of 1943 about 35 per cent of all men in the area were away from home—as factory

[39] Varden Fuller, "The Supply of Agricultural Labor as a Factor in the Evolution of Farm Organization in California," in U.S. Senate, *Hearings Before a Subcommittee of the Committee of Education and Labor,* 76th Congress, Part 54 (Washington, D.C.: Government Printing Office, 1940), pp. 19, 777–898; and Carey McWilliams, *Factories in the Field* (Boston: Little, Brown, 1939).

[40] Carter Goodrich, "Migratory Labor," *Encyclopedia of the Social Sciences,* Vol. X, pp. 441–45.

workers, domestic servants, municipal employees, farmhands, clerks, and railway workers.[41]

In tropical Africa, especially in Uganda, it has now become a common practice for men to enter employment temporarily and then to return to their farms on the countryside. The towns are much like army barracks accommodating successive waves of recruits. Over 100,000 men enter the Union of South Africa each year, but the majority of them return to their homes after six months or a year, thereby maintaining close contacts with the kraal. In Bechuanaland seasonal fluctuations in the number of men making trips home correlate with the agricultural calendar, and the history of Uganda reveals that the periods during which the natives enjoyed a high farm income, particularly after the introduction or extension of some cash crop, are characterized by a marked decline in the migration of seasonal workers. In Northern Rhodesia a smaller number of men were found to leave farms from areas in which the production of cash crops is feasible. Thus, African farmers are offering their services as migrant laborers during periods when they are not needed at home, thereby supplementing their income.[42]

The flow of labor into areas in which it is needed is facilitated by recruiting campaigns. Agents are sent into regions with surplus manpower to publicize opportunities. One common procedure is the "contract labor" system, where a man is legally bound to work for a prearranged period in return for having his transportation and initial expenses paid. Since the men being recruited are often illiterate and ignorant, many have been exploited by recruiters, labor gang bosses, steamship lines, and employers. Some hapless workers have been forced into debt and have had their period of required service extended indefinitely. Countless cases of such exploitation have been reported among immigrants to the United States, among Chinese coolies in Southeast Asia, and among migrant workers in Africa.[43] In recent years the interests of the workers have been protected through government regulations. In South Africa, for example, the

[41] Schapera, op. cit., pp. 25–64.
[42] Cf. William J. Barber, "Economic Rationality and Behavior Patterns in an Underdeveloped Area," Economic Development and Cultural Change, VIII (1960), 237–51; Elkan, op. cit., pp. 3–4, 34–36; and Hailey, op. cit., pp. 1278, 1379, 1394–95, 1441.
[43] Purcell, op. cit., p. 345; and Watt Stewart, Chinese Bondage in Peru (Durham, N. C.: Duke University Press, 1951).

Native Labour Proclamation of 1941 sets limits on the number of men who can be recruited from each area for outside work. It prohibits the recruiting of boys under 18 except with the permission of the Resident Commissioner and the consent of their parents. All recruited natives must be brought before a District Commissioner or his representative to sign the contract, and the attesting officer must satisfy himself that the recruit fully understands the terms of the contract and that he has not been subjected to coercion, undue influence, or misrepresentation. A medical certificate must be presented certifying that the recruit is physically capable of performing the duties specified in the contract. The law also requires that the labor agent or employer must provide each worker with a travelling pass, transport him to his destination, and see that safeguards are maintained for his health and comfort during the journey. Under some circumstances the employer is also liable for the worker's repatriation. Thus, a migrant worker has all his travelling arrangements made for him; he is admitted without question into the Union; and he can start working immediately upon arrival. All the terms under which he is employed are subject to government approval and supervision.[44]

Immigrants who travel great distances to find work are usually unmarried young men, many of them away from home for the first time. A study of those who were away from Bechuanaland during World War II reveals, for example, that 49.4 per cent of the unmarried male adults were away, in comparison to only 23.4 per cent of the married men. Furthermore, most of the married men were working with the army rather than in private firms. The age distribution of the migrants reveals that nearly half the men between 15 and 44 were away. In many cases the migrants have no intention of remaining at their destination; they intend only to accumulate enough of their savings to establish themselves at home. For many, going to see the white man's world is an adventure, a conspicuous landmark in their life. They are attracted not only by the tales of more experienced elders but also by the fact that girls show a marked preference for those who have been away. The migrant workers return home well dressed, with money for gifts, airs, and glamorous stories; in contrast, those who remain at home to farm and to tend cattle have nothing to wear but loinskins. Some find their new life in the

44 Schapera, *op. cit.*, pp. 76, 94–102, 112–14.

city sufficiently attractive to stay. In Bechuanaland an estimated 6 out of every 100 who leave never return.[45]

The youthful migrants often find themselves in settings in which traditional norms have been weakened and where they are introduced to new values. Although the extent of social disorganization among them is often exaggerated, many become demoralized, and their discontent is frequently revealed in absenteeism, high job turnover, destruction of property, and strikes. Orgiastic religious cults and radical political movements often gain support in colonies where restless workers are living. As the newcomers become acculturated, their discontent tends to grow. Furthermore, as the men learn the language and develop new skills, they acquire competitive advantages and attempt to raise their status. This makes them less attractive to many employers. In the United States the second-generation children of immigrants were not so welcomed by their employers as their fathers, although they were sometimes preferred to other Americans. Because they could speak English, they would complain about working conditions. Being ignorant of the poverty their parents had known, they were dissatisfied, demanded opportunities for advancement, and did not hesitate to quit for better jobs.

Even in communities in which labor unions exist, immigrants often experience difficulty in obtaining help to improve working conditions. Much of the opposition to ethnic minorities comes from the workers with whom they are in direct competition, and labor unions of the dominant group rarely welcome outsiders. This was long the pattern in the United States. When the A.F.L. was first formed, its leaders announced a policy of nondiscrimination. Before long, however, they realized that their ideals were standing in the way of expansion, and in 1895 the policy was ended. In 1934, in the midst of unprecedented growth of American unions, A. Philip Randolph of the Brotherhood of Sleeping Car Porters demanded the termination of the color line but was defeated. The C.I.O., which was organized during this period, has adhered to a policy of nondiscrimination from the beginning; since it was not a craft union, it depended upon a large base.[46] When the two organizations merged after World War II, the new federation adopted a policy of equality, but there has

---

[45] *Ibid.*, pp. 36–39, 61, 115–17. Cf. Raymond Firth, *Social Change in Tikopia* (New York: Macmillan, 1959).

[46] Herbert R. Northrup, *Organized Labor and the Negro* (New York: Harper, 1944), pp. 8–16.

been considerable variation in the extent to which it has been followed. In a recent study of the treatment of minority groups in 21 union locals in Los Angeles, for example, Greer found that the fate of minority peoples was a by-product of activities that had no ethnic reference. Whether or not Mexican or Negro workers were included depended upon the hiring practices of the industry, and this in turn depended upon the supply and demand for labor. As much as 70 per cent of the total membership of some unions was drawn from minority groups, but in other unions members from minorities made up about 5 per cent. The higher percentages were found in unions of industrial workers; occupations that require customer service and craft unions had the lower percentages. Although intellectuals often pointed to the importance of class solidarity, irrespective of ethnic identity, they had little power within the organizations.[47] In Africa and Asia members of minority groups who were rebuffed formed unions of their own. These militant organizations have not protested industrial conditions as such; in many cases the unions have become the industrial wing of nationalistic movements. They are appendages to political parties and derive their strength from this connection.[48]

As the productive system of a community takes shape, the more arduous tasks are generally relegated to members of minority groups. If these people prove unsuitable, manpower needs are met by bringing in members of other ethnic groups. Patterns of ranking emerge in the competition among these people for land and for jobs. Through these ecological processes, then, the foundations are laid for a complex system of stratification.

The Formation of Service Occupations

As members of minority groups are increasingly drawn into a a new and complex economic system, certain kinds of services become essential. Where differences between the ethnic categories are marked, however, members of the dominant group may refuse to provide them. In the various immigrant colonies in the United States,

[47] Scott Greer, *Last Man In: Racial Access to Union Power* (Glencoe, Ill.: The Free Press, 1959).

[48] Cf. Elkan, *op. cit.*, p. 65; Arnold L. Epstein, *Politics in an Urban African Community* (Manchester, England: Manchester University Press, 1958); and Charles D. Stewart, "The Work Force," in Williamson and Buttrick, *op. cit.*, pp. 104–34.

for example, people became ill, longed for special food that had to be imported from the old country, and wanted news in their native tongue; doctors, retail merchants, and journalists were needed. Retail trade requires showing some measure of deference toward one's clientele, and those of high status are not always willing to make such concessions. Some kinds of services—barbers, clergymen, teachers, undertakers—require close or extended personal contacts with clients, and the members of some dominant groups are unwilling to enter into such relationships. Some kinds of transactions—insurance and credit, for example—require taking risks, and businessmen in positions of privilege may be unwilling to take chances with ethnic minorities. Owners of mines and plantations depend upon a healthy and reasonably satisfied labor force; even when they are willing to provide medical care, the workers may prefer to be treated by someone with whom they can identify more closely.

There are also a number of intermediary positions that must be filled. In ethnic colonies people occasionally need legal advice or find it necessary to communicate with those who speak a different tongue. Lawyers and interpreters are needed. Peasants with surpluses for sale generally know little of the world market. Although middlemen are often condemned for excessive profits, they constitute an essential link between the outside market and the multitude of local craftsmen and farmers who would otherwise have difficulty in disposing of their wares. These men also bring in raw materials and sometimes even provide the necessary capital. Managers of plantations and factories need labor recruiters and foremen who can interact directly with the workers. People in positions of privilege often want menial tasks done for them, and those who work as domestic servants must acquire some knowledge of the culture of their employers. Bureaucracies, governmental or industrial, are staffed by a variety of white-collar workers—typists, bookkeepers, shipping clerks; these people must have some degree of literacy. Where contacts with clients in the minority group are required, individuals are needed who are not bound by its traditional culture but who know something about it.[49] Policemen and social workers who are bilingual are much in demand. In any complex economy a variety of specialized services are required, and in time a group of specialists develops to provide them.

[49] Cf. Yale Brogan, "Entrepreneurship and Technological Change," in Williamson and Buttrick, *op. cit.*, pp. 196–241.

Such services are often performed by persons of mixed parentage. Women of minority status are either exploited or voluntarily consort with men of the dominant group, and their offspring frequently receive favorable treatment. Even when they are not accepted in the dominant group, the father often provides them with an education and other advantages, and this gives them opportunities for moving up the economic ladder. During the colonial era the Mestizos in Mexico were exempted from the tribute exacted of Indians. Their residence was not fixed; the Indian costume was not prescribed for them; and they had to pay taxes like the Spaniards. They were also subject to the Inquisition; whereas the Indians, believed to be children, were not. They became the artisans, the foremen, the noncommissioned officers in the army, and the poorer curates.[50] Eurasians in the Dutch East Indies rarely received training that went beyond the elementary schools, and most of them became petty officials and clerks. But a few of them were educated in Europe and became wealthy entrepreneurs and estate owners.[51] If the service occupations are largely monopolized by such persons, the upward mobility of ambitious individuals in the minority group is complicated by a genetic barrier. Where a mixed group is identified with certain occupations, there develops a distinct ethnic group, marked off by physical and cultural characteristics, which stands in the way of the talented people below. Much of the hostility toward these people becomes more understandable when seen in this light.

In some communities these services are provided by a third ethnic group, and the Jews have often been identified with this intermediate position. The Jews in Europe had certain competitive advantages because of their cultural attributes—literacy, technical knowledge, and the fact that they were not bound by the papal decree forbidding Christians from engaging in usury. In medieval Spain, under the Moors and during the early period of Christian reconquest, the Jews worked in various skilled occupations, as traders, and as moneylenders. They maintained schools at their own expense and did scholarly work. The rulers often left tasks requiring financial and administrative competence in Jewish hands, and some Jews became fiscal agents—the collectors of royal and municipal taxes, of tributes owed to lords and to military orders, and even of tithes for Christian

[50] Gruening, *op. cit.*, p. 24.
[51] Justus M. van der Kroef, "The Eurasian Minority in Indonesia," *American Sociological Review*, **XVIII** (1953), 484–93.

church officials.[52] During the early days of capitalism, when many merchants and princes found it necessary to borrow large sums of money, the Jews in many cases were the only people to whom they could turn. During the seventeenth and eighteenth centuries individual Jews rose to positions of influence in various European courts by financing state affairs. The national states that emerged after the French revolution required such huge sums of capital and credit, however, that only the combined wealth of the most affluent Jews could meet the needs. By this time other businessmen had been released from the papal restriction, and the Jews lost their exclusive position.[53] Although only a small proportion of European Jews were fiscal experts, the group has been characterized throughout the world as the handlers of money. During the nineteenth century, when the Ijebu controlled the main trade routes into the interior of Nigeria and supplied most of the middlemen in the slave traffic, they were called the "Jews of Yorubaland." [54]

Such services have also been provided by other ethnic groups, especially the Arabs, the Chinese, and the Indians. Throughout the world Chinese immigrants have started as coolies, deserted these arduous tasks to go into retail trade, and through thrift and industry have become wealthy merchants and plantation owners. In Southeast Asia many of the merchants serving the natives, the doctors and lawyers, and the money-lenders are Chinese. In the early 1580's the Chinese in Manila were assigned a separate quarter, the Parian, which soon became the center of the city's commercial life. The Chinese had a virtual monopoly over retail business and dominated the craft trades.[55] In many parts of Africa people from the Middle East—Greeks, Syrians, and Lebanese—filled the gap between large European firms and petty African traders.[56] In Indonesia Arab middlemen travelled from village to village to buy up surplus cash crops, to lend money, and to pay taxes for peasants; these traders often served as guides to the strange world beyond the village.[57] Traders from India

---

[52] Americo Castro, *The Structure of Spanish History*, trans. Edmund L. King (Princeton, N. J.: Princeton University Press, 1954), pp. 471–87, 498.

[53] Hannah Arendt, *The Origins of Totalitarianism* (New York: Harcourt, Brace, 1951), pp. 11–28. Cf. Toynbee, *op. cit.*, Vol. VIII, pp. 272–313.

[54] Coleman, *op. cit.*, p. 228.

[55] Phelan, *op. cit.*, p. 11; and Schurz, *op. cit.*, pp. 63–98. Cf. Coughlin, *op. cit.*; Purcell, *op. cit.*; and Willmott, *op. cit.*, pp. 36–80.

[56] Coleman, *op. cit.*, p. 47. Cf. Hourani, *op. cit.*, pp. 24–25.

[57] Van der Kroef, "The Arabs in Indonesia," *op. cit.*

established themselves in East Africa even before the coming of the Portuguese in the fifteenth century, and toward the end of the nineteenth century Indian soldiers formed the backbone of the police and military forces. Nearly all of the Indians in the area today live in towns or trading centers, 77 per cent of them in the 17 largest urban centers. They do a large volume of retail trade, market agricultural products, and own most of the small factories. Most of the doctors, lawyers, and accountants in private practice are also Indian.[58]

Trade is for profit, and successful business requires a certain degree of detachment. Where sentiment enters the picture, it may constitute a disadvantage. An outsider who maintains social distance may more easily develop the rationality needed to trade with people unaccustomed to a money economy. In the Fiji Islands, for example, when the natives brought their farm produce to sell in the open market, the Chinese and Indian vegetable merchants sometimes waited until late in the afternoon before they began to buy. The natives needed money and did not want to go home again with the load; by that time they were willing to dispose of their products at a considerably lower price. A Fijian bound by sentimental ties would have had difficulty in exploiting the situation in this way. Attempts by Fijians to form merchandising companies had failed, for the native storekeeper could not refuse credit to his relatives and friends, who borrowed all his goods and forced him out of business.[59] Foreigners have succeeded as middlemen in Africa and Southeast Asia, because as outsiders they are least affected by personal obligations in their transactions with the local inhabitants.

In some communities the services are provided by the more able and ambitious members of the minority group. Although some Negro freedmen ventured into business before the Civil War, the Negro middle class developed largely during the period following emancipation. Barbers, restaurant keepers, and mechanics were able to use the experience they had acquired during slavery to go into business for themselves. Small retail stores were opened. The Freedmen's Bank was established to serve the financial interests of the emancipated

[58] Elkan, *op. cit.*, p. 9; Lawrence W. Hollingsworth, *The Asians of East Africa* (London: Macmillan, 1960); and McCulloch, *op. cit.*, p. 3.
[59] John W. Coulter, *Fiji: Little India of the Pacific* (Chicago: University of Chicago Press, 1942), pp. 59, 62–63.

Negroes, and insurance firms were founded to meet their distinctive needs. Many of the Negroes in business depended upon the segregated community for their market, and those in the professions and in white-collar jobs often served in organizations set up exclusively for the use of Negroes.[60] In the various immigrant colonies in the United States arrangements had to be made to take care of orphans, the indigent, and the needy; the newcomers did not know enough about welfare services and did not wish to appeal to outsiders for help. They formed their own mutual aid societies and even recruited educated men from the old country to minister to their needs.[61] In this manner a new bourgeoisie may emerge within the minority group.

The development of a new middle class disrupts the status system within the minority group. With the transformation of the economy many previously esteemed career lines become obsolete. The introduction of modern medicine, for example, leaves the shaman with little to do, although some of the older people may continue to consult him. Conquest renders the former aristocracy unnecessary; even under indirect rule the traditional leaders lose power and prestige. In many cases those who had once been respected are forced to do menial work to eke out their livelihood.[62] In most societies prestige is associated with the control of resources, and the emergence of white-collar workers and entrepreneurs constitutes the beginning of a new class structure. The money economy is a great equalizer, for even a commoner can earn money to purchase goods. In Kampala, Uganda, people who own farms on the outskirts of the town are developing into a new elite. They work as clerks, artisans, foremen, and supervisors and enjoy a dual income from the job and from their farm. Compared to the migratory workers who must travel great distances, there is less job turnover among them, and their stability leads to their being selected for the better jobs.[63] The new leadership in Africa consists largely of professional men trained in Europe, former servants of Europeans who learned their culture, low-ranking bureaucrats, policemen, shopkeepers, and intellectuals. These men have a world

---

[60] E. Franklin Frazier, *Black Bourgeoisie* (Glencoe, Ill.: The Free Press, 1957), pp. 29–59; *The Negro in the United States* (New York: Macmillan, 1949), pp. 387–413; and Myrdal, *op. cit.*, pp. 304–32.

[61] Robert E. Park and Herbert A. Miller, *Old World Traits Transplanted* (New York: Harper, 1921).

[62] Cf. Daniel Lerner and Lucille W. Pevsner, *The Passing of Traditional Society* (Glencoe, Ill.: The Free Press, 1958), pp. 19–42.

[63] Elkan, *op. cit.*, p. 6.

view and a set of values quite different from those of the people among whom they were born. They have demanded economic growth and have played an important part in nationalistic movements.

Those who occupy similar positions in an economic system often develop similar interests. Occupation assigns men and families to a position in society. One's place of residence, form of labor, political affiliation, aspirations for the future—all are somehow related to work. People with similar economic interests often interact and cooperate, and through frequent communication they develop a common culture. Furthermore, they tend to form characteristic self-conceptions and an occupational ideology. Stereotypes develop; certain modes of conduct are believed to be typical of those in a given station in life; special symbols are cultivated and displayed, and legends grow up around them. Standards of consumption, financial folkways, family mores, and modes of dress and decorum are set by occupational groups. The new bourgeoisie generally emulates the status symbols of the dominant group. The upper classes in Uganda, for example, copy the culture of the English aristocracy, as far as it is known in Uganda. English dress is copied, and the elaborate complex of fashionable social events is also imitated.[64] Thus, even when services are provided by members of the minority group, class differences emerge to make these people culturally different from the clients whom they serve.

Once class lines form, they tend to solidify. Various organizations—professional associations, guilds, unions—are formed, and they frequently establish a code for recruitment and training. In many cases, especially where property rights and technical skills are involved, occupations are passed on from father to son. In Timbuctoo before the French conquest, for example, there was a guild system of hereditary crafts. The slipper-makers were Arma; the tailors were Alfa; the masons, butchers, and barbers were Gabibi; the smiths were Arab or Songhoi. These distinctions were supported by supernatural sanctions and by force. Even when the French prohibited the use of violence to keep men out of certain occupations, many of the crafts were still protected against poachers by popular will.[65] Soon after the Spanish conquest of the Americas, craft guilds were established

[64] Berthold F. Hoselitz, *Sociological Aspects of Economic Growth* (Glencoe, Ill.: The Free Press, 1960), pp. 139–58; and Hoyt, *op. cit.*
[65] Miner, *op. cit.*, pp. 52–55.

very similar to those in Europe since the late Middle Ages. There was a graduated system of instruction from apprentice to journeyman to master. Although Indians, Negroes, and Mestizos made up the bulk of the journeyman workers, they were barred from the rank of master and thereby excluded from lucrative participation in the technical trades.[66]

When class lines coincide with ethnic lines, the groups become separated into occupations that are believed to be natural for them. In medieval Spain, for example, the accomplishments of Jews as artisans, businessmen, interpreters, pharmacists, physicians, tax collectors, and scholars confirmed the popular belief that Jews had special aptitudes for such work. Many Spaniards disdained such activity; most of them were poor farmers who longed through military enterprise to become *hidalgos*, who paid no taxes and did no work.[67] The association of an ethnic group with a particular occupation is of considerable importance, especially in an industrial society, where the job one holds is usually the most important single index of status. A sense of unity arises from common experiences at work, and common class interests reinforce a sense of being of a kind. Class marks, such as working clothes, roughness of the hands, and argot, are added to inherited symbols of differentiation. Under these circumstances the system of stratification tends to become more rigid.

When a third ethnic group becomes the middle class, it becomes a buffer between the conquerors and their subjects. The interposition of a readily distinguishable group between management and labor creates a formidable barrier to upward mobility. Class conflict reinforced by ethnocentrism accounts for much of the hostility that eventually develops against such buffer groups. The rulers of medieval Spain did what they could to protect the Jews, but the resentment of debtors and taxpayers led to popular demands that Jews be expelled along with the Moors, even though it was recognized that no one would be able to take care of the many essential tasks performed for centuries by these groups.[68] During the seventeenth century the Filipinos, smarting under hardships and dislocations resulting from the Spanish conquest, enthusiastically cooperated with their suspicious rulers in a succession of bloody massacres of the successful Chinese.[69]

[66] Haring, *op. cit.*, pp. 269–71.
[67] Castro, *op. cit.*, pp. 609–31.
[68] *Ibid.*, p. 508.
[69] Phelan, *op. cit.*, pp. 11, 145–46.

In many American cities the merchants who set up trade in Negro slum areas were often Jews; many of the housewives who hired Negro domestic help were Jews; the property owners who rented and sold to Negroes were also Jews. It is not surprising, then, that there has been considerable anti-Semitism among Negroes in urban centers.[70] Throughout Africa south of the Sahara Indian traders have been subject to bitter criticism. They have been accused of charging exorbitant rents for poor accommodations, of excessive profiteering in retail trade, and of remitting their money out of the country. What a businessman may regard as necessary to protect his investment may appear to his victim a "heartless" act, and moneylenders have often been accused of cruelty. Furthermore, some African politicians have regarded successful Asians as threats to their own ascendancy and have opposed cooperation with them.[71] Thus, the Africans who rioted in Durban turned their wrath on the people who loomed before them as major obstacles.

Summary and Conclusion

The invasion of a community by an alien group upsets the pre-existing economy. In some cases the disruption is minor, but in others the economic system is completely displaced. The situation of contact constitutes a transformed context for all of the parties involved, and a new economy develops as all inhabitants make collective adjustments to modified life conditions. The type of economy that develops is one favoring the interests of the ethnic group that wins dominance, although it is not necessarily an imposition of the productive system the rulers had in the past; the others must adjust to the circumstances. A new division of labor emerges through competition, and the outcome depends upon the cultural traits that give each group advantages or disadvantages in the particular situation. However, the relative competitive strength of groups changes with acculturation. The pattern that eventually crystallizes is of crucial importance, for systems of ethnic stratification are closely related to the structure of sustenance activities.

[70] Arnold M. Rose, *The Negro's Morale* (Minneapolis: University of Minnesota Press, 1949), pp. 128–40; and Harold L. Sheppard, "The Negro Merchant: A Study of Negro Anti-Semitism," *American Journal of Sociology,* LIII (1947), 96–99.

[71] Hailey, *op. cit.,* pp. 294, 298–99, 398, 581; and Lugard, *op. cit.,* pp. 480–83.

There has been much controversy over Karl Marx's contention that the productive system gives rise to the social structure of a community. Scholars who have attempted to test this hypothesis through the examination of class stratification have encountered many difficulties. In many cases the lines of demarcation between various classes are obscure, and the theory may be easier to evaluate through the study of ethnic stratification. The formation of color lines reveals that there is a close relationship between the allocation of duties and rewards in the economic system and social status. This does not necessarily mean that economic organization determines all other aspects of society; all phases of social life are closely interrelated, and because of this they tend to modify each other. This becomes more apparent in the dissolution of color lines, when class interests often supersede ethnic identity.

CHAPTER 8

The Development
of Group Consciousness

Not long after the turn of the century Charles H. Cooley wrote that an individual's conception of himself is essentially a "looking glass self," a reflection of what is mirrored in the responses of other people. Each imagines how he must appear from the standpoint of those around him, imputes judgments to them, and then forms an estimate of his worth.[1] Since that time a number of child psychologists have confirmed Cooley's hypothesis. Each individual develops a sense of personal identity—a stable conception of the kind of human being he is—in response to the manner in which he is consistently treated by his associates. If a child is treated with affection and consideration, he grows up believing that he is a valuable object and develops a sense of pride. If he is ignored and treated contemptuously, he grows up convinced that he is a worthless object and develops a sense of inferiority. The children of servants are frequently denied many of

---

[1] Charles H. Cooley, *Human Nature and the Social Order* (New York: Scribner's, 1922), pp. 183–84.

the privileges of others their age and grow up convinced that they are different in kind. The same principle appears to hold in the formation of ethnic identity.

Systems of social stratification rest upon classifications of human beings, for patterns of differential treatment depend upon being able to make distinctions between categories. In every community there is some scheme in terms of which people categorize themselves and one another. Because most of us live in communities in which ethnic categories seem to be clearly defined, we assume that the distinctions we make represent the natural divisions of mankind, that they have always existed, and that the ancestors of these people made the same distinctions among themselves. Although a study of history reveals that each ethnic group is but a temporary alignment of human beings, an alignment in which a common genetic background plays but an incidental part, we seldom realize how often and how much the lines of demarcation can change. The central problem of this chapter is to ascertain how new categories of human beings come into existence. Interest centers here upon the subjective aspect of ethnic stratification, upon the manner in which beliefs about common ancestry arise and crystallize. What men do depends upon what they mean to each other, and our task is to see how these meanings arise.

The Delineation of Ethnic Categories

When the ethnic groups coming into contact differ considerably, in culture and in physical appearance, the existing categories are usually retained for at least a few generations. Where cultural differences are great, the people encounter serious difficulties in comprehending one another's activities. Curiosity or reciprocal utility may bring them together, but each side carefully maintains social distance. This is especially true in cases of military conquest, where the victors set themselves up as the dominant group.

Even when the differences between the groups are clear in the beginning, however, the line becomes blurred after a few generations of contact, as marginal individuals develop. Even where intimate contacts are forbidden, illicit sex relations occur across the color line. Traders and other intermediaries acquire some of the cultural characteristics of the minority group in order to carry on their work, and some may intermarry. Members of the subordinate group do menial work in the homes of their rulers and thereby acquire some of the standards and values of the dominant group. A case of inter-ethnic contact in which the peoples involved differed as much as the natives of Australia and the European colonists would be difficult to find. The naked, dark-skinned people were unable to offer organized resistance. They had no tribal chiefs, no land ownership, and no government. Since there was no single language understood by all of them, they could not even communicate with each other. The differences were so great that the Aborigines were designated as the "lowest race in the world," as "survivals" of the Stone Age. Since their material culture and technical development were so simple, they were viewed as savages by the colonists, who contended that the creatures knew nothing of human sentiments and were interested only in gratifying animal appetites. Even anthropologists set them apart in a separate category as "Australoid." Yet, after fewer than 200 years of contact the Aborigines are disappearing into the Australian population. Their old culture is rapidly becoming extinct, and many of the "half-caste" are so much like Europeans that they are able to "pass" by moving to new communities.[2]

Sometimes the categories already existing at the time of initial contact are adopted. More often new categories develop gradually over a long period of time. Initial uncertainties are eventually replaced by more clearcut classifications, and people who were once heterogeneous come to be characterized in specific ways. As the division of labor in the newly developing economy crystallizes, it becomes convenient to distinguish between those who perform different tasks and who thereby develop somewhat different orientations toward life. People who can be usefully placed together are set off in a separate category, even though they may initially not regard themselves as being alike. Sometimes new distinctions are made between men who had once been united. In the Spanish colonies in the Americas, for example, a distinction developed between the Peninsulares, Spaniards born in Spain, and the Criollos, persons of Spanish descent born in the Western Hemisphere. The Criollos were excluded from many government positions and were relegated to lower status, no matter how proud their lineage. They were the less important officials, the landholders, the business and professional men, and the artisans. In spite of the similarity in culture a sharp distinc-

[2] Berndt and Berndt, *op. cit.*, pp. 46-51; Oliver, *op. cit.*, pp. 115-19.

tion arose within the privileged elite.[3] In most communities, then, *new classifications of human beings develop to coincide with the evolving pattern of differential treatment.*

Men who find themselves in lowly positions sometimes become aligned politically and may eventually develop consciousness of kind. In the European colonies all natives were treated alike, regardless of the numerous distinctions they made among themselves. Even the colonists who recognized differences in language and custom treated all natives as inferior human beings. Immigrants into a powerful country like the United States often have little choice but to accept their low status. Those who had migrated from northern Italy found that their claim of being superior to the Sicilians was not acknowledged by Americans. They were all called "Wop" or "Dago," forced to live in small enclaves in a poorer part of town, and accused of harboring bootleggers and gangsters. A more conspicuous case is the American Negro. Although most of the slaves were seized on the west coast of Africa, they were from a number of different ethnic groups. In the beginning those who worked together on the same plantation spoke so many different languages that they had to learn English in order to communicate with each other. Regardless of ethnic identity they were assigned the same status, and after four centuries as a minority group American Negroes now conceive of themselves as being of a kind.[4] Thus, minority groups arise from differential treatment based upon classification. People who find themselves set apart eventually come to recognize their common interests.

Persons enjoying a position of privilege, especially if they are outnumbered by their subjects, also tend to become united into a single category. This was the case in the enclaves of Europeans and Americans living in the cities of Asia and Africa. On the frontier settlements of the American West the pioneers were drawn from diverse sources, spoke different languages, and had different customs; but they united against the Indians. People in such colonies regard themselves as manning the outposts of civilized society, facing an area beyond that is unknown and perhaps uninhabitable by their kind. Since they believe they face danger, they become dependent upon

---

[3] Haring, *op. cit.*, pp. 30–31, 211–12; and Herring, *op. cit.*, pp. 187–88.
[4] Cf. Louis Wirth and Herbert Goldhamer, "The Hybrid and the Problem of Miscegenation," in Klineberg, *Characteristics of the American Negro, op. cit.*, pp. 256–62; and Rose, *op. cit.*, pp. 11–56, 76.

each other for mutual defense as well as for the accomplishment of other objectives. Minor differences among them tend to be over-looked, and a strong sense of solidarity often develops. Contacts are readily established, since people in frontier communities are generally more individualistic and less conventional. Status distinctions of the past tend to be minimized, and within the group men are judged on the basis of their personal attributes rather than in terms of previous indices of status.[5] Even where differences among them are acknowl-edged, they are superseded by their many common interests. Through-out the world the white man has been able to establish a united front against native peoples.

Whether or not a conquering group attempts to retain its "racial purity" usually depends upon its sex ratio. In many cases the invaders consist primarily of young men, and the unbalanced sex ratio results in extensive intermingling with native women. With the arrival of women from the motherland, however, ethnic distinctions assume new importance. In Peru, for example, as in much of Latin America, the early *conquistadores* were accompanied by only a few women, and the Catholic church allowed marriages between Spaniards and converted natives. Concubinage was also widespread, and many chil-dren of mixed ancestry were accepted in the dominant group. In 1544, some upper-class Spanish women accompanied the new vice-roy, and the distinctions between the Peninsulares, the Criollos, the Mestizos, and the Indians solidified.[6] Similarly, the Chinese immi-grants in Thailand mingled more freely with the Siamese women until about 1910, when the rise of Chinese nationalism and the immigration of more Chinese women slackened the pace of intermarriage and assimilation.[7]

Where there are disagreements over where the color line is to be drawn, the definitions of the dominant group are enforced. Even when those in subordinate positions protest and insist upon making distinctions among themselves, they can win recognition of their claims only with the consent of the rulers. In the southeastern region

[5] Cf. James G. Leyburn, *Frontier Folkways* (New Haven: Yale University Press, 1935); and Frederick J. Turner, *The Frontier in American History* (New York: Henry Holt, 1920), pp. 1–38.

[6] Philip A. Means, *Fall of the Inca Empire* (New York: Scribner's, 1932), pp. 69–86, 208–11. Cf. Ralph L. Beals, "Indian-Mestizo-White Relations in Spanish America," in Lind, *Race Relations in World Perspective, op. cit.,* pp. 418–20; and Haring, *op. cit.,* pp. 212–13.

[7] Coughlin, *op. cit.,* pp. 22–24, 74–80; and Purcell, *op. cit.,* pp. 118, 212–13.

of the United States, for example, there are several groups called "Indian" that are in fact mixtures in varying degree of Indians, Negroes, and white people. In Robeson County, North Carolina, there are approximately 15,000 people called "Croatan Indians" who are Indians only by courtesy. Faced with the possibility that all non-white people would be placed into a single category and treated as Negroes, the group tried to escape that stigma by stressing its Indian ancestry. In 1885 they were legally declared a separate "race" and named Croatan. To strengthen their position the legislature specified that the Croatans themselves were to be the final judge of genealogy. In their struggle for status and respectability they persuaded the legislature of the dominant group to give them the right to exclude people whose Negro ancestry was too visible.[8]

This principle is manifested most clearly in the definition of persons of mixed ancestry. Almost invariably children of mixed parentage attempt to identify with the dominant group, but there are a variety of practices for their classification. In the United States anyone with a single known Negro ancestor was classified as a Negro, regardless of physical appearance or culture. In Brazil, however, the term *branco* does not mean an individual of undiluted European descent but a predominantly white person; the category may even include a person of high status whose complexion is quite dark.[9] Mixed marriages were not forbidden in the Dutch East Indies, since there were so few European women available. Theoretically a Eurasian had status equal to Europeans; actually, they were called "Lippers," ridiculed by the Dutch settlers, and set apart socially. They developed as a separate group and also maintained their distance from the Indonesian natives.[10] In the Caribbeans a person with only a single Negro ancestor was considered white after the second generation. The stigma of the slave past still persists, however, and among the epithets used in moments of anger are: "Go home and look at your grandmother!"[11] The manner in which persons of mixed parentage are classified has much to do with the way in which a color

[8] Guy B. Johnson, "Personality in a White-Indian-Negro Community," *American Sociological Review*, IV (1939), 516-23.

[9] Donald Pierson, "Race Relations in Portuguese America," in Lind, *Race Relations in World Perspective, op. cit.*, pp. 433-62.

[10] Van der Kroef, "The Eurasian Minority in Indonesia," *op. cit.*

[11] Williams, *op. cit.*, p. 64.

line develops, and in each community the practice is established by the dominant group.

By the time the categories become established, social types develop. People on either side of the line of demarcation being drawn become sensitive to the particular features in terms of which the distinctions are made. Those who are inferior in status are usually characterized as having many childlike attributes, and those who come into contact with them do so with a patronizing attitude. The people who are so treated soon become aware of what is expected of them, and they conduct themselves in ways likely to elicit maximum returns. Enough people in each category conform publicly to these characterizations to make them meaningful. These popular concepts come to designate useful distinctions in that they enable people to anticipate to some extent what those with whom they must deal are likely to do. The features emphasized in others are those which are relevant to one's interests, and newly-formed ethnic categories are then reinforced through selective perception. Thus, popular beliefs arise which serve to maintain social distance and justify differential treatment.

An illustration of the manner in which ethnic categories are formed is provided by what happened when Negro troops were first stationed in Oahu, Hawaii, during World War II. Until 1943 the residents of Hawaii had rarely come into direct contact with American Negroes, although they had read about them in newspapers, heard Negro comedians on the radio, and had seen them in stereotyped roles in motion pictures. The initial contacts were marked by ambivalence; there was some fear and suspicion but also considerable curiosity. They were American soldiers, but they seemed different from the rest. Skin color was not the basis of differentation, for many of the Negro soldiers were lighter in complexion than the local residents. The initial definitions of the newcomers were shaped in informal communication. One widespread rumor was that a Filipino girl who had merely returned a greeting was relentlessly pursued until she finally had to flee to the home of her father; the soldier even followed her there, and the father had to call the police. People were warned against being too friendly with the Negroes, for they might have difficulty in getting them to leave. The initial impressions were not entirely unfavorable, however. Many of the Hawaiian boys preferred Negro troops to others. The "Bennies" had taken away their girl friends by offering them rides on jeeps, but the Negroes permitted the boys to ride their vehicles and played games with them. Some Hawaiians thought that Negroes were polite, for they were quick to pick up objects dropped by girls and were always waiting at bus stops for all of the other people to enter ahead of them.

The presence of a large number of white soldiers from the mainland had much to do with the importation of stereotyped conceptions. At first, many Hawaiian girls treated the Negroes like all other soldiers, but they soon found themselves under pressure to make distinctions. Girls who danced with Negroes at the U.S.O. were ostracized; in time most hostesses refused to dance with Negroes, even though they had initially assumed that they were to entertain all servicemen. The commanding officer of the Negro unit issued special orders for all his men to stay away from the local populace, although no such orders were issued to other troops. In addition, people could not help but observe that the Negroes were serving in segregated units. Once the conception began to take shape, definite expectations emerged. Certain modes of conduct were deemed acceptable; others, unacceptable or unwise. As lines of demarcation crystallized, then, group sanctions arose to support them.

As the conception of the Negro soldier began to take definite shape, it was reinforced by other practices. Whenever a crime was committed by a Negro soldier, newspaper and radio reports noted his ethnic identity; other soldiers who committed similar offences were referred to as "servicemen." All service dances were operated on a clearly differentiated basis. They were open to all soldiers, but everyone understood that requests for dances from Negroes would not be honored. Realizing that there was little possibility of being accepted, Negro soldiers did not bother to approach the hostesses. Thus, the expectations of people on both sides of the color line became clearly established. As differential treatment became institutionalized, the classification became fixed and was continually reinforced. In Oahu parents began to discipline their children by threatening to call a Negro to take them away.[12] Thus, in the course

---

[12] Judy Kubo, "The Negro Soldiers in Kahuku," *Social Process in Hawaii*, **IX** (1945), 28–32. Cf. Lloyd L. Lee, "A Brief Analysis of the Role and Status of the Negro in the Hawaiian Community," *American Sociological Review*, **XIII** (1948), 419–37.

of the interaction of people with different cultural backgrounds, common understandings arise as to what are the significant categories of human beings, the attributes of people in each category, and the symbols in terms of which they can be identified. As these conceptions crystallize, they become the basis for ethnic stratification.

In most communities, then, the development of a new scheme of classification coincides with the evolving pattern of differential treatment. Whenever cultural differences between people affect the transactions that take place, a distinction is likely to be made. Useful distinctions tend to be retained, and they persist as long as they remain serviceable. During the first century of the Christian era, for example, few Romans made distinctions between Jews, Christians, and other peoples of the near East. Religious and other cultural differences were recognized, but the Romans did not attach much importance to them. When they themselves were converted to Christianity, however, they began to note religious differences, for they then assumed new significance.[13] Ethnic categories, like all other categories used by human beings, emerge in a selective process in which *utility* is the key selective factor.

That ethnic categories are determined by convention rather than the genetic make-up of people is revealed by the very fact that they are so readily transformed. The expedient character of the distinctions is further betrayed when inconvenient cases are redefined by fiat. In Nazi Germany the category of "Jew" was carefully defined under the Nuremberg Laws. A number of scientists and highly skilled professional men who could be removed only at considerable loss to the German war machine were classified, however, as "honorary Aryans" and given privileges denied to other Jews.[14] In the Union of South Africa a person is considered a "European" if he is one either in appearance or by general acceptance and repute. This definition is politically expedient, for the dominant group would be weakened numerically if it were actually to draw the line on the basis of unmixed European ancestry.[15] In the summer of 1954, when the Union government invited the delegates to the Commonwealth Parliamentary Association conference in Nairobi to be guests on a special

---

[13] Gilbert Highet, *Juvenal the Satirist* (Oxford: Clarendon Press, 1954), p. 150.
[14] Ruth Benedict, *Race: Science and Politics* (New York: Modern Age, 1940), p. 214.
[15] Kuper, Watts, and Davies, *op. cit.*, p. 50.

tour of the country, embarrassment arose because the Pakistani visitors would be classified as "Asians." To meet the awkward situation the government designated the Pakistani delegation "temporary Europeans." They were free to go where they pleased, and the regulations barring "non-Europeans" from purchasing alcohol were suspended for them, even though this was not likely to affect the conduct of Moslems.

Differential Treatment and Identification

The degree to which consciousness of kind develops among people varies with consistency of differential treatment. In many cases those in subordinate positions do not initially regard themselves as being alike, but a sense of identity gradually emerges from a recognition of their common fate. At first the lines of demarcation drawn by the dominant group are not accepted, but those who do not acknowledge these distinctions lack the power to enforce their objections. In some instances people who are treated alike continue to maintain distinctions among themselves for centuries; in most cases, however, those who occupy the same status eventually develop a sense of unity.

Members of a dominant group often feel obligated to act before their subjects in an assertive manner, even when it is inconvenient or painful for them to do so. In the European colonies there was much concern over the preservation of "white prestige"; especially where only a small number were responsible for the control and guidance of millions, Europeans felt a special obligation to conduct themselves in ways that left their reputations untarnished. Lord Lugard, an eminent British official, noted that the white man's courage must not be doubted, his word and pledge must be inviolate, and his sincerity must be transparent. The arrogant display of power or the selfish pursuit of profit could be fatal. Lugard argued further that those dealing with "uncivilized races" must maintain high standards of conduct not only to maintain their influence and authority but also for their own moral and spiritual balance.[16] Many colonists were less idealistic, but they recognized the need to erect a façade. Some believed that in dealing with natives the best policy was to maintain their dignity by indifference and their authority by dis-

---

[16] Lugard, *op. cit.*, p. 59.

courtesy. In New Guinea, for example, the Rabaul *Times* openly cautioned newcomers to refrain even from talking to any natives other than houseboys or boss boys.[17] This consistent manner in which the rulers act, even when no personal malice is involved, is what puts subject peoples in their "places."

Minority peoples are often segregated from their rulers; because of the resulting differential communication, this practice facilitates the formation of new ethnic categories. Residence in a common area restricts the possibilities of establishing friendly contacts with outsiders. Just as workers living together in mining towns more readily develop a fierce sense of class consciousness, so those living in segregated ethnic quarters develop a sense of being alike. The Jews have been able to maintain their identity for many centuries in their millets and ghettoes, and the natives in Africa have developed a sense of unity in the compounds and locations into which they have been herded. In the United States many Negroes attend segregated schools. Although the curriculum is much like that in other schools, all their contacts are with other Negroes. Their teachers are usually Negroes, and instruction is often given from a "race angle." American history is often interpreted differently, and the students tend to form a distinctive outlook and a sense of being different from outsiders.[18] Thus, the ease with which people within segregated areas can communicate with each other reinforces the barriers between them and outsiders. Differences within the segregated community tend to be minimized.

In many cases barriers are erected against the upward mobility of talented persons of subordinate status. They are often restricted to menial occupations and are not given ready access to technical knowledge. This practice also facilitates the formation of a common outlook, for people who are limited to given occupations tend to develop a distinctive world view around their peculiar interests. Furthermore, when ambitious individuals realize that they will not be advanced no matter what they may achieve, they are forced to identify with those with whom they share a common fate. By articulating the discontent of the people and focusing their attention upon the rulers as sources of evil, these individuals often become agitators who facilitate the growth of group consciousness. Although the

[17] H. I. Hogbin, *Transformation Scene: The Changing Culture of a New Guinea Village* (London: Routledge & Kegan Paul, 1951), p. 227.
[18] Rose, *op. cit.*, pp. 97–98.

Criollos enjoyed a position of privilege in the Spanish colonies in America, they became increasingly hostile toward the Peninsulares, who outranked them. In Mexico the immigrants from Spain were referred to derisively as Gachupines, "the men with the spurs"; in South America they were resented as Chapetones, "tenderfeet." [19] When the various colonies demanded their independence, the nationalistic movements were led by men of Spanish descent who had been humiliated by this distinction.

People who are treated alike are more likely to realize that they have common interests, and this is the first step toward the development of a sense of unity. Even when members of the ruling elite are of diverse origins, they are able to conceive of themselves as valuable objects if they are all treated with deference. Even when people of minority standing had once fought one another, succeeding generations born into the same position find the distinctions made among themselves trivial in comparison to the difference between themselves and their rulers. Consciousness of kind on the part of people who share a subordinate position usually does not arise through reasoning or deliberate design. Mutual identification emerges from repeated experiences of denial and humiliation. Recognition of the fact that individual differences do not matter results in their joining forces. Differential treatment does not automatically produce new groups, however. Only when people become *aware* of being treated alike on the basis of some arbitrary criterion do they begin to establish identity on that basis. Those who are treated alike gradually come to conceive of themselves in the same manner.[20] The formation of a minority group in this manner constitutes the evolution of a new ethnic group; the Nigerians, for example, were not a single ethnic category prior to their conquest by the British.

The typical defensive stance so often found in minority groups is a response to their treatment by members of the dominant group. Some observers of the American scene have contended that Negroes are forced to act as they do by the activities of white men.[21] The fate of the white people who migrated from the South to Chicago reveals that the same kind of orientation may develop wherever men are

---

[19] Herring, *op. cit.*, p. 187.
[20] Giddings, *loc. cit.*
[21] Cf. James Baldwin, *Notes of a Native Son* (Boston: Beacon Press, 1955); and Stanley M. Elkins, *Slavery: A Problem in American Institutional and Intellectual Life* (Chicago: University of Chicago Press, 1959).

singled out for differential treatment, even when ethnic identity is not involved. Many of the migrants had not been "poor trash" in the South; they had been part of the privileged group. In Chicago, however, they found themselves despised as "hillbillies" and treated as one of the many ethnic minorities—Greeks, Irish, Jews, Italians, Mexicans, and Negroes. They were regarded as ignorant and addicted to vicious brawling; they had a reputation of keeping their homes in filthy condition and of letting their children run wild. To many Chicagoans these people seemed uncivilized. Many had trouble finding housing, for landlords would not rent to strangers speaking with a Southern accent. When they applied for jobs, they discovered that "foreigners" were often preferred to them as workers. They recognized the difference in customs in the treatment of Negroes; although they did not like what they saw, they realized that they could not change it. But they did resent the preference shown by many employers for Negroes, although some realized that many Negroes were better trained and more accustomed to the work requirements of an industrial society. The scorn with which they were treated for their low standard of living resulted in a defensive group consciousness. They lived together in segregated areas where they were able to retain some semblance of their old way of life.[22]

The history of the Mennonites illustrates the manner in which new ethnic categories come into existence. Ethnically heterogeneous people united by their religious beliefs, they were transformed into an ethnic group through their isolation from a hostile world. In the early sixteenth century various Anabaptist groups that had been persecuted elsewhere gathered in the Netherlands and consolidated. Refugees who streamed in from other parts of the Holy Roman Empire were absorbed. When the Counter Reformation began in Holland, many of these people moved to Poland, forming colonies on the Vistula. They continued to speak Dutch, imported literature from Holland, and maintained their culture. After 200 years, however, German became the official language of the church. When laws were passed against them by their Prussian rulers, they moved to the Ukraine, where special laws favored them. Here they settled in homogeneous colonies defined by church affiliation and country of origin. They were permitted self-government, and this resulted in changes in social structure. Members of the church had to hold secu-

22 Killian, *op. cit.*

lar offices, and the use of force became necessary to maintain control. Members of the new generation had to be accepted into the church without evidence of their individual conversion. Thus, cardinal principles of their religion had to be compromised to meet the exigencies of communal life, and within three generations the Mennonites in Russia became an ethnic group. Intermarriage with outsiders became taboo. After 1870, when government policy was changed to encourage assimilation, about a third of the people in the colonies emigrated, many of them coming to the United States. There are no Mennonites left in Russia today, and they are scattered over three continents. A sense of unity still remains, however, and consciousness of kind is kept alive by correspondence, common periodicals, and personal visits.[23]

Consciousness of kind did not develop among the Eurasians in India until they realized that they would be treated alike regardless of the differences among them. Persons of mixed parentage lived in the various cities of India from about 1500, and their numbers grew over the next three centuries. They were rejected by the British and the Indians alike because of their "mixed blood," but they did not develop a sense of identity. The Eurasians were usually Christians, spoke a European language, and were European in culture; but they were a heterogeneous group genetically, linguistically, and in economic position and political views. For a long time their religion and the national origin of their European parent were regarded as more important than their being of mixed parentage, and most Eurasians acted as independent individuals. There was no Eurasian community at the end of the eighteenth century. The crucial years during which the new group emerged were from 1784 to 1833, when the British were struggling to consolidate their empire in India. Since Eurasians outnumbered the Europeans, they became the object of fear and suspicion. The British began to regard them as a threat and through a series of legal acts placed them in a disadvantageous position. They were not permitted in the army because they were neither European nor native, and they were barred from many civil service posts. They were treated as a group apart and were forced to set up separate schools and clubs. The first activity of the Eurasians as a group came in 1823, when a meeting was called in Calcutta to

[23] E. K. Francis, "The Russian Mennonites: From Religious to Ethnic Group," *American Journal of Sociology,* LIV (1948), 101–07.

form the Parental Academic Institution for the education of their children. Two years later an East Indian Club was formed there. After the uprising of 1857 the British began to despise them more openly. Recognizing that they had been set apart as a specific class, the Eurasians became more aware of their common fate, stopped trying to "pass" into the dominant group, and became more concerned with one another. They then formed their own community. Thus, the initial definition of the category was by the British officials in England; this was taken up by the Europeans in India and finally was accepted by the Eurasians themselves. The 1950 census included only 200,000 acknowledged Eurasians, but they were recognized as an ethnic category in the new constitution and were given political representation as a unit.[24]

The importance of differential treatment in the growth of consciousness of kind is also revealed by the failure of unity to develop in many of the European colonies governed through indirect rule, where each conquered group was ruled through its own chief and treated somewhat differently. In such cases the natives retained their culture and ethnic identity. Despite their numerical superiority the peoples of the Far East were dominated by European powers for centuries, for they were unable to achieve political unity. Many continued to live under the rule of local chieftains whose world did not extend much farther than their immediate territory. The various Arab groups have also had difficulty in forming a united front; they were ruled separately and developed along different lines. This was also true of hundreds of African tribes that were subjugated. When some of their members became educated in European ways, they were expelled or left of their own accord to work in the cities. Those who remained behind retained their old loyalties. Thus, the nationalistic movements that developed in the cities have been hampered by factionalism in the rural areas. The people may unite temporarily to oppose the white man, but they still regard one another as outsiders.

Once an ethnic category has been established, social distance is reduced among the people who are placed together, and they become alike in fact. Communication channels are formed among those who once regarded one another as alien. The establishment of newspapers and radio stations greatly facilitates the development of

[24] Dorris W. Goodrich, *The Making of an Ethnic Group: The Eurasian Community in India* (Ph.D. dissertation, University of California, Berkeley, 1952).

consciousness of kind. Despite the variety of circumstances under which American Indian tribes were subdued, they all experienced similar difficulties once they were in reservations. Intertribal councils were formed, and warfare among themselves was abolished. Since the young people attended government schools, they were able to substitute English for their limiting sign language. Using the railroads and the mail service of the white man also facilitated contact. There have been a number of pan-Indian movements since 1890, and there are now several organizations that represent all Indians.[25] The rise of the Negro press, devoted largely to reports of injustices against Negroes or of achievements of Negroes, has facilitated the growth of group consciousness. Every city with a sizable concentration of Negroes has at least one newspaper, and their total circulation runs into the millions. Hardly a week goes by without some incident in which a Negro is mistreated; although other Americans hear only of the incidents in their local community, Negroes all over the country learn of most of them in their own press. Magazines such as *Ebony* and the *Negro Digest* also picture life and achievement within this social world. It is easy to understand, then, similarities in the perspectives of Negroes distributed throughout the nation. The foreign language press similarly unites colonies of immigrants.[26] Since communication within the group is facilitated at the same time that relative isolation from outsiders develops, a distinctive outlook is formed. As they develop a common culture, people in the emerging category develop distinctive characteristics that set them off from others.

Those who identify are able to relax in one another's company, and a "we feeling" emerges. This sense of communality develops in informal gatherings—dances, picnics, and parties. Voluntary associations in minority groups, no matter what the formally stated purposes may be, tend to become recreational associations.[27] Here people meet one another on equal terms. Personal reserve breaks down, and they act more spontaneously, each revealing his individuality. There is a feeling of intimacy and closeness, of knowing others well enough to guess their feelings at a glance. Each person feels more "at home." In the spontaneous discussions that occur in such contexts, many

25 James S. Slotkin, *The Peyote Religion: A Study in Indian-White Relations* (Glencoe, Ill.: The Free Press, 1956), pp. 18–19.

26 Rose, *op. cit.*, pp. 102–12. Cf. Robert E. Park, *The Immigrant Press and Its Control* (New York: Century, 1922).

27 Cf. Drake and Cayton, *op. cit.*, p. 440.

items of information that are kept secret from the dominant group are brought out in stories, in jokes, and in allusions. There are many items of common knowledge to those within every minority group that are not revealed to outsiders. This reinforces the isolation from outsiders, for they do not seem to "understand." As each group develops its own vocabulary of motives, the activities of outsiders become more difficult to anticipate; in some cases their deeds become incomprehensible. This reinforces the conclusion that they are fundamentally different kinds of human beings.

As the separation of people along the new lines of demarcation becomes widely accepted, there is a tendency for a new physical type to develop. Since most intimate contacts are with people who conceive of themselves as being alike, romantic affairs and marriages are likely to be restricted to members of the new group. Those who had previously regarded one another as outsiders now identify and accept the union of their children. This is sometimes difficult for some of the elders, but they become reconciled to the inevitable. If the group maintains its isolation for any length of time, a distinctive physical type may develop through inbreeding. Although American Negroes customarily trace their ancestry to the more than 300,000 slaves brought in from Africa, the new category that has developed in the Western Hemisphere is markedly different in appearance from most Africans. American Negroes have many Caucasoid characteristics, and on the whole they are much lighter in complexion.[28] Where there are genetic differences between ethnic groups, then, they develop *after* identification has been partially established.

Once mutual identification has been established, the mistreatment of another person in one's own category is experienced as a personal injury; an insult aimed at another member of the group is taken as a personal affront. Similarly, a brilliant achievement by someone with whom one identifies arouses personal pride. Thus, many American Negroes were elated when Joe Louis distinguished himself as a prizefighter and were embarrased by his subsequent woes. There is a feeling of kinship, and people emphasize what they hold in common. Demands are made for "race loyalty," and there are strong reactions against "stoolpigeons" who betray the secrets of the group. Once an individual identifies himself as a member of a group, he feels obligated to live up to its expectations. People of his kind

[28] Cf. Myrdal, *op. cit.,* pp. 113-53.

become his reference group; the outlook he shares with them becomes the standpoint from which he sees his world. Thus, *his conduct becomes subject to the social control of a limited segment of the community* in which he lives. When this happens, the new category becomes a social group. Until a sense of mutual identification develops, the category is merely a convenient classification. Once the people *think* they are alike, however, they are transformed into a social group capable of concerted action.

The lines along which human beings identify depend not so much upon genetic continuity as upon avenues of communication—conditions that isolate from without and facilitate intense interaction within. This process is clearly revealed in the formation of the ethnic groups that invaded Rome. Toward the close of the second century A.D., the Goths were one people, but the various tribes migrated toward the lower Danube and the Dniester at different paces, settling down in different areas. After years of separation a sense of difference developed, until the Visigoths and the Ostrogoths became distinct groups. At about the same time other ethnic groups were being formed in the area that is now Germany. The small tribal units lived in islands of cleared land surrounded by almost impenetrable forests and were isolated from one another. As the pastoral peoples of the East began to expand, the tribes in the West could not move away, for they faced the Roman Empire to the west and the south. The only alternative to emigration was the converting of woodlands into farms and pasture land. As the forests were cut down, the previously isolated groups were brought into contact. During the century that followed, these unions led to the formation of such groups as the Alemanni, the Franks, the Saxons, and the Thuringians.[29]

Thus, ethnic groups are not the natural biological divisions of mankind, but temporary alignments of people created by communication channels. As Oswald Spengler put it, peoples are created by events.[30] When people of diverse origins find themselves in circumstances that facilitate communication among them, they develop a common culture and eventually consciousness of kind. In some cases

---

[29] John B. Bury, *The Invasion of Europe by the Barbarians* (London: Macmillan, 1928), pp. 6–11, 15–17.

[30] Oswald Spengler, *The Decline of the West*, trans. Charles F. Atkinson (New York: Alfred A. Knopf, 1939), Vol. II, p. 165.

isolation from outsiders results from ecological processes; usually it is the product of differential treatment. Any condition that facilitates communication among people who are set apart leads to the formation of a new group.

The Development of Group Solidarity

Ethnic groups differ considerably in group solidarity. Some minorities merely recognize the fact that they have been set apart and long for the day when they can become assimilated into the dominant group. For a long time the American Negroes could point to no common heritage; few slaves were proud to be Negro, and freedmen tried to dissociate themselves from the category. There are other groups, however, that develop a fierce sense of unity, cherish their symbols, and insist upon protecting their values at all cost. Group pride is more easily established among rulers, but it is also found in minority groups, as in the case of the Jews. The Méti on the Canadian frontier never considered themselves the humble hangers-on to white civilization; they were proud of their Indian ancestry. Most of them were Catholic, spoke French, and dressed in blue capote, red belt, and corduroy trousers. Louis Riel, their leader, acknowledged the humble origin of his "race," but he emphasized that they honored their mothers as much as their fathers. They had a keen sense of independence, and for almost a century their intense consciousness of kind resulted in conflicts with the waves of settlers who invaded their hunting lands. The ethnocentrism of such groups bolsters personal pride and inures them against the pain of low status.[31]

The formation of a new group and its ability to stand united in the face of adversity depend in part upon identification symbols, especially upon the wide acceptance of its name. The cohesiveness of a group depends largely upon the extent to which the members are aware of it as a unit, and the existence of an acceptable label for self-designation facilitates the establishment of consciousness of kind. For a long time the peoples in the Balkans could not join forces to throw off the yoke of the Turks and other conquerors because they had no name to designate the oppressed collectivity. The importance of having a suitable name has been recognized by political leaders. The

[31] Stanley, op. cit., pp. 6–12. Cf. W. O. Brown, "The Nature of Race Conciousness," Social Forces, X (1931), 60–97.

conquerors of China in 1644 were originally the Ju-chen, a relatively small Tungus people on the periphery of the empire. In 1635, when their leader T'ai-tsung became an open contender for the imperial throne, he renamed his people "Manchu" to destroy all traces of their former submission to China. To strengthen its ranks raids were made into the Tungus hinterland. The captives were absorbed through intermarriage, and as parts of the new unit they joined forces to overthrow the Ming dynasty.[32]

When the commonly used name is unacceptable to members of the minority group, it can become the source of considerable controversy. In India the term "Eurasian" dates back to the eighteenth century, and since that time it has been in frequent use. But the newly formed group called itself "East Indian" for a time, and then a preference arose for "Anglo-Indian," even though many of them were not of English descent. In 1911, this designation became official.[33] In 1885, the North Carolina legislature gave the Indians in Robeson County the name of "Croatan" and by implication recognized their proud legends, but the name soon went sour. For the first time outsiders had a term they could apply to these hitherto nameless people; they shortened it to "Cro" and pronounced it with a sneer, and before long the term became an epithet. The group then decided that "Croatan" was not its true name, and in 1911 the legislature was persuaded to call them "Indians of Robeson County." When someone suggested that these people were really Cherokee, the group again asked for legislative help. In 1913, over the protests of the Eastern Cherokee of the Great Smoky Mountains, they were legally renamed the "Cherokee Indians of Robeson County." Since no one called them Cherokee, however, some of their intellectuals later contended that they really originated from the Sioux.[34] The extent to which such newly-formed groups struggle over their name gives some indication of the importance of such labels.

The criteria of differentiation vary from one community to another, and a variety of status symbols arises to provide means of identification. These symbols are important, for the ease with which members of a category can identify one another facilitates the establishment of personal contacts. Skin color, mode of dress, style of

[32] Michael, op. cit., pp. 39–47, 75.
[33] H. W. B. Moreno, "Some Anglo–Indian Terms and Origins," Proceedings of the Indian Historical Records Commission, V (1923), 76–82.
[34] G. B. Johnson, "Personality in a White-Indian-Negro Community," op. cit.

speech, or any other perceptible feature may become generally accepted as the distinguishing mark. These symbols generally become objects of value—positive or negative. Some become marks of shame, and others become objects of great pride. The Méti in Canada, for example, wore their belt under their capote; most white men wore their belt above it. This was a badge of distinction and the symbol of the group. Those who are proud of their group display their symbols openly and criticize others who fail to do so. Those who are ashamed of their symbols conceal them as best they can and may even criticize their associates for having these characteristics.

Ethnic groups that regard themselves as the charter members of a community have an additional basis for unity, even if their ancestors had slaughtered one another for centuries. The term "charter member" was used by Anderson to designate that group that regards itself as the original inhabitants of an area into which others had migrated. In ethnic stratification the question of who occupied the land first may be of considerable importance, for charter member groups often develop a typical orientation—whether they are in dominant or subordinate status. They conceive of themselves as the people who "really" belong in the area; others are either guests or unwanted intruders. Because of their identification with the territory they feel a special responsibility for looking after it. They are the ones who become most concerned about the exploitation of resources. Whether in historical fact they were the first to occupy the territory does not matter; what is important is that they *believe* the land is theirs. In the New England community studied by Anderson, the old Yankee Protestants regarded themselves as the original settlers and were so viewed by the other ethnic groups, even though it was known that the Indians had been there first.[35] When an ethnic group identifies with the land in this way, it is easy to understand the apprehensions that arise when the people are confronted with the possibility of being outnumbered by immigrants, as in the Chinese invasion of Malaya. Much of the bitterness of the nationalists in modern Asia and Africa arose from the fact that the minority peoples regarded themselves as charter members and the Europeans as intruders. Much of the tension between Arabs and Jews in the Middle East exists because both groups regard the territory that is now Israel as their own.

[35] Anderson, *op. cit.*, pp. 21–24.

Group solidarity is also enhanced by conflict, for opposition isolates the adversaries from each other. There was not much consciousness of kind among the ancient Greeks until the age of Pericles, when a law against intermarriage was passed. This coincided with the development of the antithesis between Greeks and "barbarians." Although this was the period of the rise of democracy, when there was concern over the kind of people who participated in government, it was also a time of external conflict. There was the constant threat of war with Persia.[36] Persecution by the dominant group often solidifies an otherwise heterogeneous minority. Prior to European colonization the Maori of New Zealand owed no loyalty to aggregations larger than a tribe. As the settlers encroached upon their rights, however, they confederated into a kingdom for the first time. When the colonial government attempted to enforce an unpopular land sale in 1860, there was organized resistance, and the bloody war that followed lasted for 10 years.[37] The dangers of conflict force men to work together for survival, and suffering together for a common cause often intensifies consciousness of kind. The combatants identify with the collectivity, and the public good is placed above self-interest. Barriers against neighbors come down, and past disagreements are conveniently forgotten. The symbols of ethnic identity become marks of honor, the banners of the good who struggle against evil.[38]

The existence of a common enemy plays an important part in uniting a group. People are more likely to maintain intact their values, their historical memories, and their conception of themselves when they have constant reminders from their enemies. Among American Negroes the white man is viewed as one who segregates and lynches, is cruel, animal-like, brutal, and most of all, is hypocritical. Spectacular events as lynchings and riots attract attention and reinforce these beliefs. Reflection on "what *they* have done to us" supports further the sense of being alike. Richard Wright indicates that as he grew up, the price he had to pay for admittance into the company of older boys was subscribing to the appropriate "race" sentiments. The

[36] Aubrey Diller, *Race Mixture Among the Greeks Before Alexander* (Urbana: University of Illinois Press, 1937), pp. 159–60.

[37] Oliver, *op. cit.*, pp. 121–24.

[38] Cf. Lewis A. Coser, *The Functions of Social Conflict* (Glencoe, Ill.: The Free Press, 1956); and George H. Mead, "National Mindedness and International Mindedness," *International Journal of Ethics*, XXXIX (1929), 385–407.

touchstone of fraternity was the hatred of white people.[39] The role of the enemy in developing group solidarity has been recognized by many politicians. Confronted with a dangerous adversary, the members feel that they share a common responsibility to defend and preserve their values. Those who believe that they are being unjustly opposed will rally together. If there is no common foe, an astute leader may even invent one.

Where it not for their long history of persecution, the Jews would probably have disappeared as a group. As Theodore Herzl, the founder of modern Zionism, wrote long ago: "We are a people—the enemy makes up a people." [40] There is considerable evidence that the excesses of the Nazi regime rekindled consciousness of kind among Jews throughout the world who were well on their way to becoming assimilated into other groups. The horrors made them more conscious of their ancestral ties, aroused a sense of responsibility for assisting other Jews in trouble, and stimulated a sense of identity that was disappearing. The same is true of the Chinese in Southeast Asia, who were united by persecution. They became increasingly aware of their identity as a consequence of the revolution against Manchu rule and the resistance to the Japanese invasion of their homeland. The rise of nationalism throughout Southeast Asia and the attacks against their economic position by the natives further intensified their consciousness of being Chinese.[41]

As lines of demarcation become clearly established, organizations are founded to promote the interests of the new group. Among American Negroes the National Association for the Advancement of Colored People has long been a prominent protest organization, and other bodies have organized boycotts and demonstrations in various communities against firms refusing to hire or serve Negroes. When the Eurasians in the Dutch East Indies were rejected by the Europeans with whom they tried to identify, many formed

[39] Richard Wright, *Black Boy: A Record of Childhood and Youth* (New York: New American Library, 1951), p. 67. Cf. Rose, *op. cit.*, pp. 112-17; and Edgar T. Thompson, "Race Relations in the Modern World," *Journal of Negro Education*, **XIII** (1944), 270-79.

[40] Louis Wirth, "Education for Survival: The Jews," *American Journal of Sociology*, **XLVIII** (1943), 686. Cf. Max Lerner, *America as a Civilization* (New York: Simon & Schuster, 1957), p. 510.

[41] Cf. W. Macmahon Ball, *Nationalism and Communism in East Asia* (Carlton, Australia: Melbourne University Press, 1956), pp. 5, 111; Purcell, *op. cit.*, pp. 154-55, 522, 614.

their own community. In 1919 the Indo Europeesch Verbond was organized to promote economic assistance to Eurasians as well as their social emancipation. This organization was conservative and pro-Dutch, but in 1949, after the Indonesian revolution, the Partai Indo Nasional was formed to represent the Eurasian minority in the new nation.[42] In Africa there have been a large number of organizations to mobilize popular sentiment for elevating the natives' status.[43]

Intellectuals of the new ethnic group usually create a literature that binds them together—poetry, fiction, history, and stirring polemics. Among American Negroes the Association for the Study of Negro Life and History was founded in 1915, and it has not been content just to dig out forgotten facts for publication in its *Journal of Negro History*. Considerable effort has been expended to publicizing them so that Negroes will know about them and be proud of their "race." Findings have been made available to Negro newspapers and organizations, and a special effort has been made to reach the children. In addition, books intended for popular consumption have been published and sold at low cost.[44] Especially since World War II the Negro press has made frequent reference to events in Africa, and some Negro intellectuals have tried to discover their "true" identity through a study of African culture. In Africa, attempts have also been made to glorify ways that are typically African, especially in a movement called "Negritude." [45]

Since nationalism is the prevailing political framework of our time, many new ethnic groups have attempted to establish a national state of their own. In some cases they have succeeded in winning political sovereignty before they had become fully united, and serious difficulties have arisen. In Israel a homeland was established for an ethnic category with an old history, containing members who had become assimilated to so many different cultures that people who claimed to be alike were in fact quite different—culturally and physically. Were it not for memories of the Nazi program of extermina-

[42] Van der Kroef, "The Eurasian Minority in Indonesia," *op. cit.*

[43] W. O. Brown, "Race Consciousness Among South African Natives," *American Journal of Sociology*, XL (1935), 569–81. Cf. James S. Coleman, "Politics of Sub-Saharan Africa," in G. Almond and J. S. Coleman (eds.), *The Politics of the Developing Areas* (Princeton, N. J.: Princeton University Press, 1960), pp. 247–368.

[44] Rose, *op. cit.*, pp. 40–41.

[45] Georges Balandier, "Race Relations in West and Central Africa," in Lind, *Race Relations in World Perspective, op. cit.*, pp. 149–52.

tion and the constant danger of attack from the neighboring Arabs, it is doubtful that group solidarity could have been achieved. In Indonesia there was so much diversity that the central government had difficulty in establishing its rule. In emerging Afro-Asian nations enmities checked under European rule threaten to explode again.

Summary and Conclusion

Lines of demarcation between ethnic categories develop to coincide with the evolving patterns of differential treatment, and the people so classified then begin to conceive of themselves as a kind. The distinctions that have the greatest utility in social interaction become widely accepted and tend to persist as long as they remain useful; unless there is some point to making distinctions, they are not likely to survive. Sometimes the classifications that exist at the time of initial contact are retained, but in many cases they are replaced by new ones that are more useful. Consciousness of kind arises among those who find themselves in the new category from a recognition of common interests; among the underprivileged it develops from being subjected to differential treatment. Consciousness of kind reduces social distance, facilitates communication, and eventually results in the formation of a common culture. Thus, the people become more alike in fact. Should they develop special pride or become involved in conflict, group solidarity is enhanced. Once the lines are drawn, organizations are founded to promote the interests of the new groups. The product is the classification of the people of a community into definite categories, which after a time come to be regarded as the natural "races" of mankind.

The processes whereby ethnic minorities come into existence are the same as those through which any ethnic group emerges. Patterns of differentiation develop initially through competition and then crystallize into conventional norms concerning who can live where, do what kind of work, and marry whom. Lines of demarcation are reinforced as consciousness of kind seals the boundaries of the groups. One implication of this is that if classifications of human beings arise from utility, they are likely to change when they are no longer useful. We often fail to recognize the fluidity of color lines even though new ethnic groups are constantly coming into existence and old ones are disappearing.

CHAPTER 9

The Establishment

of Legitimate Authority

After slavery became an established practice in the Greek city-states, intellectuals of the day devoted considerable time to debating its justification. The Sophists insisted that the differences between slaves and free men were fixed by custom, that slavery had been established by force, and that it was therefore unjust. Aristotle defended the institution. He argued that the contrast between the superior and the inferior was universal in nature—man was superior to other animals, male to female, soul to body, and reason to passion. It was expedient and just for the superior to rule over the inferior, for the arrangement was advantageous to both. Some men were slaves by nature; they were capable of nothing better. He conceded that slaves, unlike other animals, had the ability to understand the rational acts and orders of their masters, but he denied that they could behave rationally on their own initiative. Aristotle admitted that some, particularly those who had been subjugated by conquest, were slaves only by convention, and he was especially disturbed by the enslavement of his fellow Greeks. In general, however, he was convinced that conflict could be avoided only if inferior people accepted the status imposed upon them by eternal law.

Since that time the same arguments have been repeated in numerous historical contexts in attempts to justify or to attack various systems of ethnic stratification. This suggests that there may be something about the situation that elicits similar sensitivities. Those who have defended color lines have sometimes been condemned as "racists" and have been held responsible for the "consequences" of their ideas; their arguments have been regarded as the "cause" of exploitation, and much effort has been put into their refutation. Debates of this kind usually occur among intellectuals *after* political control has been established. They also occur when a stratified system is breaking down. To place these ideological controversies in their proper context, then, we must first ascertain how distinctions between ethnic groups and status differences become crystallized into custom and law.

The Establishment of Political Control

Where disagreements arise over rival ways of life, the pattern sponsored by the people with power becomes dominant. This leads to the question: What is power? Because the word *power* is a noun, it is often viewed in a static sense, somewhat like a brick that can be carried about or passed around from one person to another. Actually, the term refers to a social relationship, for there must be two or more parties involved. It is a relationship in which one party is able to enforce its demands on the other. A father has power over his child; a master has power over his slave; an employer has power over his employee; a blackmailer has power over his victim. Furthermore, power is a reciprocal relationship; it persists only as long as the second party continues to submit. Should the commands be challenged, power relations persist only if the ruler has the capacity to take punitive measures. Of course, those with power need not mete out punishment personally; institutional arrangements usually are available. Expectations of such punishment are included in the perspectives of all participants. Any human relationship can be converted into a power relationship when one party can demand a particular line of conduct from another and can enforce compliance. Authority is institutionalized power; the right to use force is vested in certain positions. An official has power, not because of his individual strength, but because of his status.[1]

The most obvious instrument of coercion is the use of violence. Fighting ability, control over the family hairbrush, or the loyalty and high morale of the armed forces can provide one party with instruments for punishing those who refuse to submit. As the techniques of violence become increasingly specialized, untrained men are no match for experts. A band of outraged peasants would be foolhardy to challenge a mechanized infantry unit. The mastery of firearms and of the tactics based upon their use was decisive in the conquest of much of the world by Europeans after the sixteenth century. Where the effectiveness of these tactics was limited by local circumstances, domination could not be established. For two centuries after their conquest of the Philippines, for example, Spaniards were able to control only the coastal regions of Mindanao. Horses and firearms were neutralized by mountain barriers, jungles, and the hot and humid climate. Not until the second half of the nineteenth century did the steamboat make accessible the interior river system of the island and make possible the establishment of Spanish authority.[2] Where disparity of power is great, use of actual physical coercion is rarely necessary; assurance that force will be used is generally sufficient to win submission. In fact, excessive use of violence is generally an indication that a power relationship is disintegrating and that the rulers are being challenged.

Once the ascendancy of an ethnic group has been established, further conflicts are minimized through the use of the police power of government. Government constitutes an effort to remove conflicting interests from the arena of brute struggle and to submit them to some rational agency for adjustment. Astuteness in government can be a source of great power, as the Manchus demonstrated in their conquest of China in 1644. The small Tungus tribe from the border area first developed the political organization necessary to control an agricultural economy and its rural labor. When the Ming dynasty collapsed, both Chinese revolutionaries and other external groups

---

[1] Cf. Robert Bierstedt, "An Analysis of Social Power," *American Sociological Review*, XV (1950), 730–38; and Harold D. Lasswell, *Power and Personality* (New York: W. W. Norton, 1948), pp. 7–19.
[2] Phelan, *op. cit.*, pp. 142–44.

competed for the throne. The Manchus proved to be the strongest, not only because of the mounted archery that gave them military strength but also because they had developed institutions suited to the situation. Power rested upon the taxation of agriculture, and the Chinese bureaucratic system and its ideology were adopted for this purpose. Deserters from Chinese ranks as well as others were incorporated into the Manchu group and rewarded with places in the government. The Manchus were thus able to rule the empire for 300 years.[3]

Power may also rest upon control of economic resources. Those who can manipulate the production and distribution of goods are in a position to withhold the necessities of life from those who refuse to comply with their demands. Strikes and boycotts can be effective instruments of coercion if the parties are interdependent; then, the withholding of essential work or purchases can be a powerful weapon for enforcing demands. The power of middlemen and merchants in many areas arises from their ability to control credit and to drive people into bankruptcy. In the area that is now Burundi the Watusi made up about 10 per cent of the population of 1.7 million, but they were supported in comfort for more than 50 years by the Bahutu. Their power and prestige rested upon the disposition of cattle. This was done through the *ubuhake*, a feudal system in which persons of lower status offered their services to those of higher rank in return for the right to use one or more cows. Since the Watusi owned all the cattle, they could take back these sources of livelihood whenever they were displeased with their clients. When a Watusi became impoverished, he became a client to another Watusi lord and was in turn able to have his own clients.[4]

In the last analysis, however, the right of certain parties to monopolize the instruments of coercion rests upon consensus. Government officials can count on the support of their military and police units only as long as the people and the soldiers themselves acknowledge their authority. A monopolist can control supplies only as long as thousands of others support the existing economic system, respect his property rights, and obey his orders. This suggests that control

[3] Michael, *op. cit.*
[4] Jacques J. Maquet, *The Premise of Inequality in Ruanda* (New York: Oxford University Press, 1961); and "The Problem of Tutsi Domination," in Simon and Phoebe Ottenberg (eds.), *Cultures and Societies of Africa* (New York: Random House, 1960), pp. 312–17.

over the educational system and the various channels of communication is a source of power. Through communication the perspectives of men are shaped, and if people can be taught to support the existing order, there is little likelihood of a serious challenge. Dominant groups often defend their ascendancy through differential education. Education in the numerous schools and colleges scattered throughout the Spanish colonies in the Americas, most of them conducted by religious orders, was essentially aristocratic. They were for Peninsulares, Criollos, and well-to-do Mestizos. Although the crown decreed that a school be established in every Indian pueblo, this order was not obeyed. Indians were given religious instruction, but they were rarely taught to read and write.[5] Similarly, the Watusi trained their young exclusively in the military arts, and they perpetuated the dogma of their innate superiority by pointing to their height and distinctive appearance.[6]

This suggests that the theory of Ludwig Gumplowicz that political institutions are formed through conquest and subjugation is not entirely without foundation. Gumplowicz, a nineteenth-century Austrian sociologist who lived in the multi-ethnic Habsburg Empire, contended that in organizing a new community, conquerors set themselves up as the ruling class and relegated their defeated foes to the servant class. Ethnic differences exist between the rulers and their subjects, and class struggle is a survival of the original hostility between conqueror and subject. Thus, the conflict by which a state originates and expands is paralleled by a struggle within the community for control, although this contest is political rather than military. As each group constantly strives to increase its power, the general effect is the establishment and maintenance of some kind of organization. In most cases the rulers are not satisfied with ascendancy; they try to transform might into right. Since they have many advantages, they soon come to think of themselves as inherently superior and attempt to justify their exploitation of others in terms of claims of "racial" superiority. Gradually, however, the ruling class undergoes a softening and is displaced by the bourgeois class.[7]

There are many cases in which the rule of one ethnic group over

---

[5] Haring, *op. cit.*, pp. 224–32.

[6] Maquet, "The Problem of Tutsi Domination," *op. cit.*

[7] Ludwig Gumplowicz, *The Outlines of Sociology*, trans. F. W. Moore (Philadelphia: American Academy of Political and Social Science, 1899). Cf. Hans Kohn, "Race Conflict," *Encyclopedia of the Social Sciences*, Vol. XIII, pp. 36–41.

another is established roughly in the manner outlined by Gumplowicz, but stratified societies also develop in other ways. Immigrants who go voluntarily into powerful states simply submit to the authority structure they find there. Certainly the various immigrant groups entering the United States were under no illusions about setting themselves up as rulers.

There have also been cases in which ethnic groups or their leaders have requested foreign rule in order to avoid what they feared would be a worse fate. During the second century B.C., Attalus III of Pergamum, a kingdom in what is now western Turkey, feared that disorders might follow his death, since he was without an heir. He foresaw the danger of local rulers seizing power and of the various Hellenic states becoming involved in factional quarrels. Therefore, he bequeathed his domain to Rome, which he regarded as the only sovereign power capable of controlling the situation.[8] During the nineteenth century some Bantu groups in South Africa accepted the protection of the British in order to escape the Boers, and the Acoli and other tribes of the Sudan and Central Africa welcomed European colonial power to escape the slave raiders.[9] During the 1860's the influx of European adventurers into the Fiji Islands resulted in lawlessness and chaos that the local authorities could not control. The natives suffered from war, epidemics, drunkenness, and the depredations of labor recruiters. To stop this both Fijian and European leaders tried to arrange the cession of the islands to one of the great powers. Great Britain resisted until 1874, when it assumed responsibility for governing the islands.[10]

Even in cases of conquest, colonial governments differ considerably in their policies. In Oceania, for example, the Americans and the Japanese aimed toward assimilating the natives to the dominant group; the British, Dutch, and Australians worked toward preserving the indigenous culture and ethnic identity of the natives; the French worked toward assimilating the "advanced" natives while keeping the remainder of the population in a state of "association" with France. In Africa areas in which the climate was moderate became European settlements; places like Morocco, Algeria, Southern Tu-

[8] David Magie, *Roman Rule in Asia Minor* (Princeton: N. J.: Princeton University Press, 1950), Vol. I, pp. 26–33.

[9] Southall, *op. cit.*, p. 233.

[10] Oliver, *op. cit.*, p. 85; and Peter Worsley, *The Trumpet Shall Sound* (London: MacGibbon & Kee, 1957), p. 19.

nisia, Tripoli, Egypt, Ethiopia, and parts of Somaliland, where climatic conditions and soil were satisfactory but where the numerical strength or warlike spirit of the natives made colonization difficult, became "tributary states"; and tropical regions, where climatic conditions made settlement impossible for Europeans, became plantation colonies, vast territories to be governed autocratically through native chiefs.[11]

In some cases the conquering group sets up its own legal and police system, and subject peoples must adjust to a new type of government. Most European colonies were administered by a colonial service in which the high officials were appointed and where the bureaucracy consisted of career civil servants. The spread of European authority into the interior of Africa, however, was gradual and encountered many difficulties. The maintenance of law and order from the British standpoint, for example, meant destroying practices of "barbarism, slavery, and superstition," and this required severe punishment of blood offenses. Tribal police had to be recruited and trained. Taxation was at first in small amounts, much like a tribute to the chief, but as time went on, taxes were increased and regularized. For the French the centralization and codification of law was important, but this proved a difficult problem for the colonial administration. Trial by a jury of one's peers, for example, proved impractical in African groups with different traditions. Thus, African customary law had to be recognized, and it was administered by separate courts for Africans only. In 1946, the native penal code was abolished, and all inhabitants in French tropical Africa were placed under the same penal code as metropolitan France.[12] After a generation or two, the people become accustomed to the new regime and accept it; then the rule imposed by the conqueror becomes legitimate authority.

Many conquered areas are ruled indirectly through the traditional leaders of the vanquished. Successful imposition of this type of political control depends upon the degree of formal regulation already there; where a central government already exists, a puppet regime is much easier to set up. The Inca theory of sovereignty as

[11] Felix M. Keesing, "Changing Life of Native Peoples in the Pacific Area," *American Journal of Sociology*, XXXIX (1934), 443–58. Cf. Adam, *op. cit.*, pp. 6–20; Johnston, *op. cit.*, pp. 443–45; and Kennedy, *op. cit.*

[12] Adam, *op. cit.*, pp. 22–23, 29–54; Lugard, *op. cit.*, pp. 578–79; and Southall, *op. cit.*, p. 284.

residing in the person of the king, for example, facilitated Spanish rule. In the Inca government authority was arranged vertically in an orderly sequence of ranks from the top officials to those in charge of units of 10 families. Each official was directly responsible to the one above him and eventually to the sovereign. Hence, to capture the person of the ruler was to capture all authority in the Inca Empire—what is now Ecuador, Peru, and Bolivia.[13] British colonial policy in Africa, as announced by Lord Milner, was to rule subject peoples through their own chiefs, but the manner in which this principle was translated into practice varied from one colony to another. In some cases a representative government was established in which a small group of educated natives served as spokesmen for the many. In a few cases complete independence was set up as a goal with a period of tutelege for preparation. In most cases, however, rule was through native chiefs, who appointed and dismissed subordinate officials, allocated land in their control, and adjudicated disputes. But the range of their authority was carefully defined by ordinance. Furthermore, the native rulers were not permitted to raise or control armed forces, nor were they given the sole right to impose taxes.[14] All they did was to enforce tribal customs that did not conflict with colonial practice.

When the aims of conquerors are too transparent, indirect rule is not accepted. After their conquest of Manchuria in 1931, the Japanese set up three Manchurian provinces with puppet regimes in each. They won over, by cajolery or coercion, a local military or political figure, and the support of his adherents followed. These politicians were then required to install Japanese "advisers," who controlled the action of the nominal Chinese rulers. The Japanese also tried to pose as champions of minority aspirations; although Manchuria by this time was predominantly Chinese, the Japanese tried to foster Manchu national sentiment by selecting an heir of the Ch'ing dynasty as the ostensible ruler. Promised the favored position they had enjoyed under the Ch'ing empire, the Mongols were initially responsive. When the Japanese Army overran Inner Mongolia in 1937, however, it did not unite this region with the Hsingan area to form a separate Mongol state; the Mongols then realized that the Japanese had no intention

[13] Means, *op. cit.*, pp. 10–11, 47. Cf. Charles Gibson, *The Inca Concept of Sovereignty and the Spanish Administration in Peru* (Austin: University of Texas Press, 1948).

[14] Lugard, *op. cit.*, pp. 194–207.

of strengthening them. On paper Manchukuo had a modern judicial, legal, and police system, but actually it was an imposition of Japanese concepts and methods. The nominal leaders were kept under constant surveillance. The courts, police, and prisons were staffed by more Japanese nationals than other branches of the administration. Large numbers of Koreans, once an oppressed minority in the area, were employed in the police force, and some proved to be brutal. The secret police, the equivalent to the dreaded *Kempeitai* in Japan, suppressed all disaffection toward the regime. There was little doubt among the people that the area was ruled by the Japanese Kwantung Army, and very little popular loyalty developed toward the state of Manchukuo.[15]

When successfully established, indirect rule has proved a very stable form of government. Under this system the native rulers maintain some of their power and a semblance of authority, and this tends to make them less resentful of foreign domination. The practice also preserves native institutions not incompatible with colonial policy and minimizes the disruption of native society. Even when a chief is required to follow the "advice" of the colonial governor, his credentials go back to antiquity. He represents legitimate authority, and he is a symbol of the moral order.[16] In such cases the legal authority of the colonial government is reinforced by the traditional authority of the native chief. The system has been condemned by many nationalist leaders as an outmoded feudal arrangement; it is difficult to overthrow, for the traditional leaders develop a vested interest in the colonial government. In the Dutch East Indies, for example, the Dutch preserved the traditional social gradations, and their contacts with the Indonesian people were through the native aristocracy. The communal *adat* (customary law) and the village society were left intact. When European-educated nationalists proposed a program to modernize the villages, they received little support from the people. In many respects the young intellectuals found themselves to be foreigners in their own land. The nationalist movement thus became a struggle between town and country, between the Europeanized and the tradition-bound generations.[17]

15 F. C. Jones, *op. cit.*, pp. 19–68.

16 Cf. Frazier, *Race and Culture Contact in the Modern World*, *op. cit.*, pp. 191–202; and Coleman, *Nigeria*, *op. cit.*, p. 172.

17 Justus M. van der Kroef, "Social Conflict and Minority Aspirations in Indonesia," *American Journal of Sociology*, LV (1950), 450–63.

A well-established color line is supported by legitimate authority. There are many kinds of rule with power in the hands of a variety of officials, but whatever the arrangement, someone controls the means of violence and is able to coerce the recalcitrant to comply. There are recognized rules of conduct, often explicitly stated as laws, and there are formal procedures for their enforcement. But laws are difficult to enforce unless they are supported by consensus. A conqueror can rule for a time through brute force, but his position becomes difficult unless he can win some kind of acceptance. This is facilitated through indirect rule, when the bases of traditional authority can be exploited.

The Formalization of Status Gradations

All institutional patterns have a history, and the conventional norms that make up a color line take shape in a succession of collective adjustments. Beginning with trial-and-error attempts to solve practical problems arising in situations of contact, procedures gradually develop. As the expectations the participants have of one another become fixed in habit, the patterns become customary. All social institutions are products of collective adjustments to extant life conditions, and this is true of the common understandings that constitute the color line.[18]

An example of the manner in which these arrangements develop is the odd and discontinuous history of the various "Jim Crow" practices of the American South. Segregation was impractical under slavery; it developed during the Reconstruction period after the Civil War. Social equality never existed in the region, but Negroes were at first accepted in public transportation vehicles, at polls, in the police and militia, in theaters, and at exhibitions. To be sure, this was not a peaceful era; it was one of brutality and violence, and there were a large number of lynchings. Negroes were exploited, but they were not ostracized. Even those who believed Negroes to be inferior did not feel that they should be publicly humiliated. The withdrawal of federal troops from the South in 1877 forced Negroes to turn to upper-class white people for protection, and for more than a decade their *noblesse oblige* provided a bulwark against agitators, who

[18] Cf. Robert T. Park, *Society*, ed. E. C. Hughes *et al.* (Glencoe, Ill.: The Free Press, 1955), pp. 13–21; and Sumner, *op. cit.*, pp. 2–4.

were predominantly of the lower class. Only after relaxation of the opposition were various "Jim Crow" laws passed. Northern politicians were seeking a reconciliation with the South, and upper-class Southerners wanted to make peace with the working people; both did so at the expense of Negro rights. With increasing demands for the disfranchisement of Negroes to eliminate "corruption," tension mounted, and this led to stronger demands for separation. Before 1900 Negroes were legally segregated only on trains, but soon after that the code was expanded to many other areas. These regulations tightened the color line and froze the relationships between the groups. Policies that are sometimes described as the immutable folkways of the South are of quite recent origin, and they evolved as various categories of people adjusted successively to changing circumstances.[19]

The pass laws of South Africa also began as an attempt to meet a practical problem—of keeping track of native migrations. Under the Proclamation of 1809, nomadic Hottentots without passes were treated as vagrants, liable to be contracted out as laborers. In Transvaal and the Orange Free State passes were used not only to control "vagrants" but also to stabilize the supply of farm labor by making movements more difficult. Through the Native Registration Act and the Natives Accommodation and Registration Act, the Federation of Rhodesia and Nyasaland then decreed that unemployed Africans had to carry passes authorizing them to seek employment or to visit town. As the policy of *apartheid* hardened in the Union of South Africa after World War II, the passes were used for identification purposes—of placing individuals permanently into legally defined categories. Thus, what had once been permits became instruments for hardening the lines between ethnic groups. For Africans they became a hated symbol of oppression.[20]

In most cases the spatial segregation of ethnic groups develops initially through natural selection, but after a period of sustained contact conventional understandings develop as to who should occupy what areas for what purpose. Some of these norms may subsequently be enforced by law. The Jewish ghetto in Frankfurt, for example, was not the product of ill will on the part of local administrative of-

---

[19] Doyle, *op. cit.*, pp. 109–57; and C. Vann Woodward, *The Strange Career of Jim Crow* (New York: Oxford University Press, 1955).
[20] Hailey, *op. cit.*, pp. 1418–23. Cf. Franck, *op. cit.*, pp. 87–98.

ficials. It developed originally from the voluntary self-segregation of Jews who wished to pursue their way of life undisturbed; the preparation of food according to their rituals and the enforcement of dietary laws was easier when they lived together. Such communities formed near synagogues and existed for a long time before laws were passed, especially after the sixteenth century, forbidding Jews from living elsewhere. These communities enjoyed a form of extraterritoriality. At the same time all residents of a ghetto were held responsible for the deeds of any member, and the entire community was taxed as a unit. From the standpoint of the city officials the ghetto became a convenient administrative unit for the control and supervision of aliens.[21] Similarly, the "Black Belt" in Chicago during the interwar years developed as Negro migrants from the South settled in the places where they could afford to live and where they encountered the least opposition. As wave after wave of immigrants entered the city, the area of initial settlement became much too small, but for many years the boundaries were maintained through tacit agreements, restrictive covenants, and terror. Thus, a spatial pattern that had developed through natural selection was maintained through a number of "unwritten laws." During World War II there was an explosive increase in the Negro population in Chicago; the ecological pressure became too great, and the boundaries collapsed.[22]

In the allocation of work to different ethnic groups the initial division of labor develops through competition and natural selection; it then becomes institutionalized, and there is a progressive restriction of the area of free competition.[23] As clearly-defined ethnic roles develop, they become funded with values, and many of the roles become institutional offices. Once they are recognized in the community, the practitioners begin to take pride in their performance. They become jealous of their badges and take steps to prevent their unauthorized use. If they enjoy high rank within the minority group, they often set up standards of achievement and training, and they insist upon judging the newcomers and upon having something to say about their accreditation. When people identify closely with an

[21] Wirth, The Ghetto, op. cit., pp. 41–62.
[22] Cf. Drake and Cayton, op. cit.; and Otis D. and Beverly Duncan, The Negro Population of Chicago (Chicago: University of Chicago Press, 1957).
[23] Edward B. Reuter, "Competition and the Racial Division of Labor," in Edgar T. Thompson (ed.), Race Relations and the Race Problem (Durham, N. C.: Duke University Press, 1939), pp. 46–60.

office, they become afraid that other occupants might misbehave and hurt its reputation; they therefore set up an informal code of ethics. Career lines become well defined, and a practitioner is able to compare his own performance with that of his predecessors in office. Thus, self-evaluation does not include people in other ethnic categories. Once tasks are allocated to ethnic categories, these offices are protected against poachers by the entire community. If someone in the dominant group tries to take up an occupation usually followed by members of a minority group, people on both sides of the color line object that it is improper. The work is not necessarily regarded as degrading, but certain kinds of people are thought to be naturally suited for certain tasks—as if they had been born to do it.[24]

The manner in which various types of work continue to be assigned to particular ethnic groups is revealed by figures from the U. S. Census for the past 100 years. Hutchinson concludes that the following continuities in occupational patterns of the foreign-born were still noticeable in the 1950 report. Irish immigrants continued to be associated with personal or domestic service and with unskilled labor. Scandinavians had a high relative concentration in agriculture for half a century or more. They were predominantly farmers and farm managers, in contrast to Mexican male migrants, who were predominantly farm laborers. Hungarians continued to be associated with heavy industry; French-Canadians were conspicuous as operatives in textile mills and other factories; Greeks were heavily represented in the restaurant and food businesses; and Italians were markedly numerous among bakers and masons. Hutchinson also notes that, for several decades, the foreign-born were poorly represented in clerical, managerial, official, and other high-status positions.[25]

Patterns of differential action, however they were initially formed, eventually become fixed in custom. After a dominant group has controlled the community for several generations, virtually all persons accept the arrangements as proper. The lines of demarcation between groups seem perfectly natural; indeed people have difficulty conceiving of any other way in which human beings might be classified. Most Americans, for example, have trouble in understanding

---

[24] Cf. Everett C. Hughes, *Men and Their Work* (Glencoe, Ill.: The Free Press, 1958), pp. 56–77.
[25] Hutchinson, *op. cit.*, pp. 63–278.

the classification of people in Latin America, when an obviously dark-skinned person is not regarded as a "Negro" and where the word may even be used as a term of endearment. The alleged attributes of various ethnic categories are similarly accepted as a matter of course, and the patterns of differential treatment go unquestioned. Many of the salutations and other rituals that symbolize the different status positions become so habitual that they are enacted automatically, without thought. They are performed in much the same manner as most American men open doors for women and permit them to pass ahead of them. They become matters of proper usage. When particular ways of interacting are repeated over and over, the participants come to share common expectations of one another.

The formation of social institutions in multi-ethnic communities is sometimes explained in terms of the transplantation of practices from the old country—in terms of the theory of diffusion. To be sure, some borrowing does take place, but this is an inadequate explanation of the formation of the color line. The labor practices that developed in the various European colonies, for example, were not derived from the culture of any of the ethnic groups involved. The stockade in South Africa in which workers were detained against their will was certainly not an imposition of a Dutch, British, or native practice. Indeed, most of the people in the Netherlands or in Great Britain probably would have been horrified, had they been aware of what was done. The borrowing of culture traits is not the principle in terms of which the emergence of systems of ethnic stratification is to be explained.

Whenever alien peoples come into contact, life conditions in the community are altered, and all parties must adjust to the new circumstances. New patterns of coordinated activity emerge in the attempts that are made to cope with the peculiar needs of that situation. In South Africa, for example, conditions in the mining communities were such that special measures had to be taken to ensure a stable supply of labor. Illiterate workers could not understand why they had to continue working under disagreeable conditions simply because they had put marks on a piece of paper. Work contracts were meaningless to them, and they had to be restrained by force. Of course, people in all ethnic groups fall back upon the resources of their culture; when confronted by a problem, each starts with the traditional solutions. A number of the practices of the group with superior technology are likely to be adopted, giving a new community the outward appearance of transplantation. Even where one group is clearly more powerful than the others, however, suitable procedures previously used by minority groups may also be adopted. Furthermore, in most cases new practices are also improvised. The needs must be met in some way, and where no adequate patterns exist in the culture of any of the groups, new ones must be invented. In the formation of the new patterns the interests of the dominant group are more conspicuously represented, but the new system cannot be regarded as the imposition of a ready-made scheme.[26]

That the pattern of differentiation in each community is a unique adjustment to the peculiar circumstances encountered there is demonstrated by the fact that a color line varies somewhat in different communities, even when the same ethnic groups are involved. Many people think of the "Jim Crow" practices in the United States as if they were a homogeneous set of norms; actually the status of Negroes differs from one community to another—even within the South. A Negro who is travelling finds it necessary to ascertain in each instance what is permitted and what is not. In a study conducted in the 1930's Johnson documented a bewildering variety of practices. There were no hotel facilities for Negroes in the South, except in large cities where Negroes operated their own; visitors were obliged to stay with their friends. In the Northern cities prominent Negroes were accepted in the large hotels, for refusal could have resulted in damage suits. Most Negroes, however, did not seek such accommodations, since by tacit agreement the employees made things so uncomfortable that a Negro hotel was preferable. Negroes were not permitted to eat in restaurants in the South, although in some communities Negro patrons could eat in the kitchen. In the North, chain restaurants, department-store counters, and small, inexpensive places were open to Negroes; but patrons had to know how to "pick their spots," for some owners were very disagreeable. Since they were required by law to serve everyone, restaurants did not refuse Negro patrons; but they gave poor service, overcharged, or put emetic or heavy seasoning in the food. These were understood ways of letting Negroes know that their patronage was not wanted—without saying anything to invite a lawsuit.

The greatest variation was found in the extent to which Negro

[26] Cf. Malinowski, *op. cit.*; and Sahlins and Service, *op. cit.*, pp. 45–68.

patronage was invited in stores. In rural communities of the South Negroes and white people met on friendly terms in country stores. Patronage of the same store was understood not to imply social equality; all the people knew each other, and they supported one another in observing local customs. In the larger communities in the South, few distinctions were made in chain stores; the transactions were impersonal and hurried, and there was little time for observing rituals. Two exceptions were the meat counter, where the service was somewhat more personalized, and apparel stores, where Negroes were not permitted to try on clothing before making purchases. Considerable variation was found in the border states. In Baltimore, for example, the downtown stores made no secret of their view that Negro trade was not wanted, and Negroes generally did their shopping in neighborhood stores in outlying areas. In other cities few distinctions, if any, were made among customers. In the North, especially in large urban communities, customers were generally treated alike. Some of the exclusive stores discouraged Negro patronage, but they also discouraged other kinds of clientele as well. None of the larger stores in New York or Chicago had a policy of differentiating between customers on an ethnic basis, and whatever unpleasantness a Negro might encounter was a personal reaction on the part of the particular clerk.[27] There have been a great many changes since Johnson's study was made, but there is still no uniformity in the treatment of Negroes; the customs vary from one community to another.

The adjustment of different Indian tribes to the westward expansion of American settlers also varied from one region to another. The Indian policy of the U. S. Government grew bit by bit, developing under the press of circumstances and the pressures of diverse groups.[28] Everywhere Indians were reduced to subordinate positions, but the pattern of accommodation differed, depending upon the circumstances under which the contacts occurred. The Puyallup in Washington were initially accepted on terms approaching equality; there were many joint enterprises and intermarriages. The individualistic pattern of the Indian culture made it easier for those who wanted to assimilate to do so. In time, however, new settlers arrived

[27] Charles S. Johnson, *Patterns of Negro Segregation* (New York: Harper, 1943).
[28] Cf. Francis P. Prucha, *American Indian Policy in the Formative Years* (Cambridge: Harvard University Press, 1962).

who made distinctions. Then, the sale of land brought great wealth to the Indians, and this led to idleness, alcoholism, dependency, and depopulation. The Shoshoni of Nevada borrowed freely from white men during their early sporadic contacts. With the influx of more settlers, however, their food supply was exhausted, and they were reduced to depending upon charity, odd jobs, and prostitution. The Utes of Colorado had horses, economic surpluses, and war plans. They organized into efficient bands, and they had to be subjugated by force. The survivors of the war split into two groups; one tried to adopt the American way of life, while the other continued the old ways in a poor area not wanted by white men. The Arapaho of Wyoming were placed on a reservation within their own land. The area was not suited to agriculture, and with the destruction of buffaloes, they became dependent upon white men. The culture of the white man was inconsistent with their own, and they accepted the technology and religion but retained many of their other ways. Their tribal solidarity remained strong and prevented defection. The Fox in Iowa had a long period of not too close contact with the settlers before they were finally surrounded, and they had more opportunities to adjust. They accepted the white man's technique of land purchase as well as his methods of production, and there was only a gradual diminution of their resources. They became an accepted enclave, and their culture and sense of group solidarity remained intact. Some groups, like the San Ildefonso of New Mexico, were largely unaffected by contact with the newcomers.[29]

When the norms that make up a color line enjoy a high degree of consensus, they become presuppositions underlying conduct and are rarely discussed. They are not discussed because they appear obvious to everyone. The institutional order is then well established. The classification of people, the kind of work assigned to each category, the limitations placed upon informal association—all are taken for granted. All parties feel uncomfortable and out of place in situations in which these norms are relaxed. Such arrangements become a part of a *moral order* when they come to be regarded by everyone as just, fair, and proper. Violations of such norms generally arouse emotional reactions in people, both in the minorities and in the dominant group. Thus, patterns of differential action and lines of demarcation that

---

[29] Ralph Linton (ed.), *Acculturation in Seven American Indian Tribes* (New York: D. Appleton-Century, 1940).

emerged through natural selection become institutionalized as they are supported by popular beliefs.

The Development of Race Ideologies

All stable authority rests upon popular beliefs over which there is a high degree of consensus. As Rousseau put it, "The strongest is never strong enough to be always master, unless he transforms his strength into right, and obedience into duty." Rulers usually justify their exercise of power by finding a legal and moral basis for it. Without such justification those who govern feel insecure, sometimes even doubting their own right to rule. Unless power is justified by linking it to accepted values, the governed are less willing to obey and question the right of others to hold power. When consent to the exercise of power is gained, government is no longer based upon naked force. Where power is made legitimate, it becomes authority.[30]

Institutional arrangements that prove painful or inconvenient to a substantial part of the population are generally called into question, and they are sooner or later justified in a set of popular beliefs. Whenever conspicuous differences of rank lead to embarrassing questions, ideologies emerge to explain the gradation. One of the most effective ways of justifying the status quo is by religion. In India, for example, the doctrines of *karma* and reincarnation—that a person of a lower caste will be reborn into a higher caste if he fulfills all his duties in his present life—helped to allay the discontent of the underprivileged and made their station in life more bearable.[31] When such beliefs are widely accepted, the institutional arrangements appear inevitable and natural even to those who suffer.

If an ideology is challenged, basic beliefs may be proclaimed openly in books, resolutions, speeches, party platforms, and other public statements. The Nazi Party, for example, incorporated all kinds of anti-Semitic statements into its public pronouncements. The *Bhagavad Gita*, a popular and influential book of Hindu literature, justifies the caste system by maintaining that the Creator apportioned the duties of the four castes in accordance with inherent qualities

---

[30] Cf. Robert M. MacIver, *The Web of Government* (New York: Macmillan, 1947).

[31] Ghurye, *op. cit.*, p. 64. Cf. J. H. Hutton, *Caste in India* (Cambridge: Cambridge University Press, 1946), p. 110.

of the members. Another Indian epic, the *Mahabharata*, maintains that the Sudra cannot own property in an absolute sense because their masters can appropriate their wealth at will. In fact, the Sudra are described as "the servants of another" to be expelled or slain at will.[32] Ideologies are also transmitted more informally. The *Rigsthula* is an epic poem that describes the ethnic make-up and the relationships among the various categories of people in Viking society. The tall, blond, narrow-skulled Norsemen rank high, and the short, brunette, roundheaded people are placed below them.[33] In the United States the myth of the "nigger baby" is popularly believed by Negroes and white people alike, and for many the superstition serves as a deterrent to "passing." As long as people who have a lone Negro ancestor are convinced that their lineage may be betrayed at any time by the birth of a very dark offspring, they will continue to identify themselves as Negro even when their physical features are Caucasoid. Although geneticists have indicated that this is extremely unlikely, it remains a widely entertained belief.[34]

Many of the beliefs that make up a well-established ideology are implicit in action that is strongly praised in the group. Differential treatment implies a category of people who are fundamentally different and worthy of being treated in a distinct way. As long as such acts continue to win approval, the premises upon which they rest are reinforced. In the long run rituals are important. Unless they are supported by rituals, doctrines tend to be subverted by the facts of experience, and they are not likely to be stabilized in a changing world unless they are supported by habitual practices that take place without conscious reflection. Widely-accepted dogmas call for a sort of loyalty. A man who fails to support the doctrine of his group is regarded as a heretic or a traitor.[35]

In recent times the most common justification for ethnic stratification has been racism, an ideology that has an interesting history. The idea of inherited differences is old, but it became part of a politi-

---

[32] Ghurye, *op. cit.*, pp. 50, 59–61, 65.

[33] Christen T. Johassen, "Some Historical and Theoretical Bases of Racism in Northwestern Europe," *Social Forces*, XXX (1951), 156–60.

[34] Cf. Julian Lewis, *The Biology of the Negro* (Chicago: University of Chicago Press, 1942).

[35] Cf. Romanzo Adams, "The Unorthodox Race Doctrine of Hawaii," in E. B. Reuter (ed.), *Race and Culture Contacts* (New York: McGraw-Hill, 1934), pp. 143–60; C. S. Johnson, *op. cit.*, pp. 194–227; and Park, *Race and Culture, op. cit.*, pp. 301–15.

cal ideology during the rise of national states in Europe and the scramble for colonies. Apologists for the French revolution spoke of a "race" of aristocrats in contrast to a "nation" of citizens. The emphasis upon "race" among Germans was prominently connected with their struggle for unification. This line of thought was a welcome expedient to those who sought noble ancestry to justify their national aspirations. Each group sought to emphasize its peculiar national traits as evidence of superiority, and in the struggle for national supremacy each country interpreted the cultural traits that presumably gave it temporary victory as earmarks of inborn superiority. Racism would probably have disappeared along with other irresponsible and refutable opinions had it not been for its usefulness in justifying imperialism.[36]

In spite of differences in detail, race ideologies have certain features in common. One of the basic beliefs is that human beings are divided into different species, some inherently superior to others. During the formation of colonial policy in the sixteenth century a controversy arose among Spanish intellectuals as to whether Indians were rational beings or an intermediate species between man and beast. Bartholomé de las Casas argued that all peoples of the world were alike and urged humanitarian treatment; he argued that the Indians compared favorably with peoples of ancient times, were rational, and fulfilled every one of Aristotle's requisites for a good life. Others, such as Juan de Sepulveda, argued that Indians were of a different breed and should be enslaved. There was so much disagreement that the government devised a series of experiments to test these contentions.[37] The same belief forms the cornerstone of the orthodox position of the American South: the Negro is biologically inferior; the lowest white man is better than the highest Negro; peasantry is all that the Negro can attain. It follows, therefore, that Negroes should be educated only in ways that prepare them to serve white men.[38]

[36] Cf. Arendt, *op. cit.*, pp. 158–84; Jacques Barzun, *Race: A Study in Modern Superstition* (New York: Harcourt, Brace, 1937); Yves R. Simon, "Secret Sources of the Success of the Racist Ideology," *Review of Politics*, VII (1945), 74–105; and Louis L. Snyder, *Race: A History of Modern Ethnic Theories* (New York: Longmans, Green, 1939).

[37] Cf. Lewis Hanke, *The First Social Experiments in America* (Cambridge: Harvard University Press, 1935); and *The Spanish Struggle for Justice in the Conquest of America* (Philadelphia: University of Pennsylvania Press, 1949).

[38] Thomas P. Bailey, *Race Orthodoxy in the South* (New York: Neale, 1914), pp. 92–115.

The government of the Union of South Africa also maintains that there are ineradicable biotic differences between natives and Europeans. Its policy, therefore, is not regarded as a matter of expediency but in accordance with natural law.[39]

The implication is that a person's thought and behavior depend upon his organic make-up. Behavior patterns, like physical appearance, are said to be inherited. Psychological characteristics, such as being quick-tempered, are also inherited. The key idea is that "blood will tell." The degradation of an inferior "race" is permanent, ineffaceable, and transmissible to the next generation. Since these traits are inborn, they cannot be removed through education. There are many, including educated people, who believe that Negroes are incapable of serious intellectual activity. The accomplishments of American Negroes are explained in terms of the high percentage of "white blood" in their veins. Sir Harry Johnston, an eminent British colonial administrator and an influential authority on Africa, characterized Africans as the natural servants of others—a people possessed of great strength, docility, cheerfulness, short memory for sorrows and cruelties, gratitude for kindness and just treatment, and ability to toil in heat and unhealthy climates. He insisted that the Zimbabwe civilization in Rhodesia, now in ruins, must have been built by some foreign invader, for he was convinced that Africans could not have possibly built the stone forts, aqueducts, round towers, and other buildings.[40] The belief in the inheritance of behavior patterns accounts for the interest in the "stock" from which a stranger is descended. If this knowledge can be used to anticipate what the other person is likely to do, one can be prepared to deal with him. Seen in this light, concern over the alleged dangers of "mongrelization" also become more understandable. If one sincerely believes that there are inherited differences in mental and behavioral traits, intermarriage and amalgamation could appear catastrophic.

During the sixteenth and seventeenth centuries, when the maritime discoveries first brought strange peoples to the attention of Europeans, many scholars attempted to account for the differences in terms of the theory of polygenesis—the plural origin of races. This was an attempt to explain the observed differences among peoples in a reasonable way, but the theory was condemned and rejected because it was contrary to the accepted religious account of the

[39] Hailey, op. cit., p. 434.
[40] Johnston, op. cit., pp. 23–29, 150–52.

origin of man. As Darwin's theory of evolution gradually replaced the Biblical account, however, evolutionary theory was misused to explain the same observations: different races were at different stages of evolution.[41] Thus, evolutionary theory provided a convenient rationale for colonialism. The colored peoples were less developed; therefore, they had to be treated like children until they "evolved." The natives were regarded as sub-human, some closer to apes than to civilized man. Nor are Europeans the only people with such views. To the Japanese, who tend to be hairless on the body, body hair is regarded as an indication of proximity to wild animals. Both the Ainu and Europeans are thought to be less civilized, and the epithet for the white man is *keto*—or "hairy barbarian."

Another key idea of racism is the dogma that the hope of human civilization depends upon the preservation and growth of a particular "race." During the nineteenth century Arthur de Gobineau wrote in *Essai sur l'inegalité des races humaines* that nations fall because of degeneration—the adulteration of blood through intermarriage. All civilization derives from the Aryan "race," and none can exist without its help. European peoples degenerate only through the mixture of their blood with foreign elements. In *Foundations of the Nineteenth Century*, Houston S. Chamberlain contended that the turning point of European history came when Teutonic peoples became conscious of their all-important mission as founders of a new civilization. Everything of value in modern times can be attributed to the Teuton, and degenerative processes of history are the work of Jews.[42] To those who take such views seriously, progress would depend upon eliminating some "races" and keeping others pure. If the biologically superior are subjected to the rule of the incompetent, a just state cannot survive. The welfare of everyone would depend upon the purity of the rulers. Although this position has been refuted repeatedly by many scholars, it continues to be seriously entertained by people of several proud ethnic groups. Adolf Hitler was much influenced by the writings of Chamberlain, and part of the Nazi program was an attempt to implement these ideas.[43]

European colonization has sometimes been justified candidly in

[41] Bock, *op. cit.* Cf. Carleton S. Coon, *The Origin of Races* (New York: Alfred A. Knopf, 1962).

[42] Snyder, *op. cit.*, pp. 103–61.

[43] Cf. Franz Boas, *The Mind of Primitive Man* (New York: Macmillan, 1911); Snyder, *op. cit.*, pp. 162–79; and David Spitz, *Patterns of Anti-Democratic Thought* (New York: Macmillan, 1949), pp. 137–62.

terms of the interests of the motherland. The colonies were regarded as sources of raw materials, as markets, as outlets for surplus capital, and as places to send surplus population—penal settlements and convenient depositories for the poor, the loafer, and other "useless" people. As one British official put it, the hungry people of Europe have the right to benefit from the wasted bounties of nature that are not used by Africans who do not know their value. It is in the interest of the natives as well as of the rulers to attract capital to open up and exploit the natural riches of Africa.[44] In addition, there were strategic military and naval considerations—to gain a foothold from which to attack other powers in time of war.[45]

From the very beginning colonialism faced many critics at home, and when the economic justifications were rejected, the proponents argued that they were bringing the benefits of civilization to the natives. From the start of the Spanish adventure in the New World the conversion of Indians to Christianity was a major objective, and the exploitation of natives was tempered somewhat by the desire to increase the number of Christian subjects. The people of Peru were described as barbarous, bestial, idolatrous, and inherently vicious; the Inca regime was depicted as an oppressive tyranny, and Spanish colonial rule was said in contrast to be benign and enlightened, bringing to the ignorant and distressed natives the benefits of freedom and civilization. In the Philippines the Spaniards claimed they were liberating the Filipinos from the oppressive sway of the devil.[46] Apologists for British colonialism spoke of the "white man's burden." One eminent British colonial administrator set the aims of colonialism as putting an end to slavery, establishing law and order, inculcating in the native a sense of responsibility, liberty, and justice, and above all seeing that they were educated. It was contended that the natives were unable to rule themselves properly; some even claimed that the subject peoples did not want to govern themselves and liked to be dominated. The theory of the "white man's burden" also imposed upon the rulers the responsibility of maintaining a high standard of

[44] Johnston, op. cit., p. 232; and Lugard, op. cit., p. 615.
[45] Klaus E. Knorr, British Colonial Theories, 1570–1850 (Toronto: University of Toronto Press, 1944), pp. 64–65.
[46] Harold Osborne, Indians of the Andes: Aymaras and Quechuas (London: Routledge & Kegan Paul, 1952), pp. 16–19; and Phelan, op. cit., pp. 4–7, 25–26. Cf. Haring, op. cit., pp. 179–208.

conduct; the prestige of the white man had to stand high.[47] Clearly, many of these justifications were addressed toward the colonists themselves as well as toward the subjugated peoples.

Nor is racism the exclusive property of dominant groups; there are many minority groups that proclaim their innate superiority in spite of their subordinate standing. For centuries many Jews have believed that they were the "chosen people," the elect of God. Although this claim has recently been attacked by a number of Jewish intellectuals, there are still many Jews who are convinced of their privileged role on earth.

Social scientists and men of affairs have devoted considerable effort to refuting race ideologies, especially after the excesses of the Nazi regime. Some have written of Chamberlain and Gobineau as if they were villains who were responsible for the inter-ethnic tensions of the modern world. Since the basic ideas in racism have been disproved so thoroughly and so often, some scholars have expressed astonishment that they have not disappeared. But the persistence of ideologies is better understood in terms of their utility in political contexts than in terms of their truth or falsity. As Marxists and Freudians have frequently pointed out, there is a curious coincidence between the spread of an ideology and the interests for which it serves as a useful cover. Race ideologies are political tools, and their expedient nature is revealed by the compromises made when their usefulness is in doubt. The Nazis constantly stressed the supremacy of the Nordic "race," and they were embarrassed when the Japanese joined the Axis Powers. Japanese residents in Germany were simply exempted from the racial laws of the Third Reich; they were able to marry Germans without polluting Aryan "blood." Hans Gunther, a professor at the University of Jena, declared that some Nordic people were among the ancestors of the Japanese; Alfred Rosenberg, inspector general of Nazi mental training, laid down as official doctrine to be taught in German schools that the biological guarantee of Germany's leadership was shared by the Japanese.[48] Race ideologies are not only justifications of existing practices but also serve as the rallying ground for aspiring peoples; they play an

[47] Cf. Lugard, op. cit., p. 5; Kennedy, op. cit., pp. 311–16; and Maunier, op. cit., Vol. I, pp. 29–36.
[48] Benedict, op. cit., p. 214.

important part in sustaining political movements. Many American Negro and African leaders today are finding black racism a convenient device for solidifying their control over a heterogeneous population.

Although ideologies often serve as useful justifications of political programs, they are not necessarily constructed for that purpose. There are some cases, however, in which deliberate design appears to have been involved. The Incas of Peru conceived of themselves as the people who had been chosen by the Sun God to raise the other Indians from their subhuman ways. As the first thrust of conquest gave way to colonial organization, they attempted to remove from the minds of their new subjects cherished memories of their past greatness. Remembered history was organized by the victors; memories of the past were systematically edited. Local traditions were supplanted. The official rememberers, who were the Inca historians, suppressed all traditions anterior to their own, and with their quipu knot-string records recounted only the official version. When the monarch Pachacuti centralized historical records and created an official Inca history, he apparently eliminated all accounts not directly concerned with the Inca dynasty. The result, if not the purpose, of this selective manipulation of remembered history was to represent the Incas as the sole bearers of civilization. They were *the* civilizers; before their arrival all of South America was presumably a cultural void. They were so successful that there is today no record of the pre-Inca period in South America, other than what can be inferred from archaeological findings.[49]

Most ideologies are not deliberately produced artifacts, even though harassed victims may contend that they are. They develop through a selective process, being shaped over a long period through the contributions of thousands of individuals. Students of the sociology of knowledge have pointed out that ideas that tend to support or facilitate the pursuit of predominant interests tend to be accepted, while other, equally valid ideas pass unnoticed or are rejected. Ideas are not always accepted or rejected on the basis of evidence; in many cases the choice is in terms of their utility. In any situation

---

[49] Victor W. von Hagan, *Realm of the Incas* (New York: New American Library of World Literature, 1957), pp. 24–40; and Osborne, *op. cit.*, pp. 15, 30–31, 131.

of inter-ethnic contact thousands of remarks are made; most of them are uttered a few times and are forgotten. But ideas consistent with prevailing interests or justifying deeds that have already been committed seem strangely more appealing and "true." These views tend to be taken more seriously and are repeated. This is not to suggest that men are dishonest nor that they set out deliberately to salve their consciences. Some men are liars, but most do their best to find meaningful interpretations of the events in which they are involved. All perception is selective, and men who find themselves under pressure are especially responsive to whatever enables them to retain their self-respect. A race ideology, far from being the diabolical invention of evil men, is another way of looking at the world. Race ideologies are like other political ideologies; they emerge through a selective process and justify social institutions.[50]

Once they have crystallized, however, ideologies may enjoy some measure of independence and may subsequently be applied in contexts quite different from those in which they originated. They may survive long after the conditions under which they developed have disappeared. If the beliefs become embodied in sacred books, they become rigid, for they must be accepted or rejected in totality.[51]

Ideas, especially those organized systematically into a scheme, are important, but they must be seen in their proper perspective. In most cases they are not so much the "cause" of political action as rationalizations after the fact. This is not to suggest that questions of truth and falsity should not be raised. One of the tasks of scholars is to expose mistaken beliefs and fraudulent claims, for this is the only way in which men will be able to develop a better understanding of their environment. But one should not be dismayed if disproving an idea does not kill it, for ideas that happen to support strong collective interests are often retained even when they are not supported by evidence nor even logically consistent with each other. Should such an ideology be disproved, it would only be replaced by a substitute.

[50] Cf. Karl Mannheim, *Ideology and Utopia*, trans. Edward A. Shils and Louis Wirth (New York: Harcourt, Brace, 1936); and Weber, *Essays in Sociology, op. cit.*, pp. 267–359.

[51] Cf. Stanislaw Andrezejewski, "Are Ideas Social Forces?" *American Sociological Review*, XIV (1949), 758–64.

Summary and Conclusion

The type of stratified society that develops in a situation of contact depends largely upon the relative power of the contending groups. Power rests partly upon numbers but mostly upon the cultural attributes of a group. Various social patterns—the classification of people, status symbols, differential treatment of categories—however they may initially be formed, became customary through repetition. To minimize further conflicts within the community the dominant group, once it is established, utilizes the power of government to guarantee its ascendancy. After these institutions are established, ideologies emerge that provide justifications. When the norms that constitute a color line come to be taken for granted, they become part of a moral order. Each person is then able to locate himself within an ethnic category, see his life in terms of one of the accepted career lines of his station, and evaluate himself in terms of generally accepted standards.

Many social patterns represent the institutionalization of arrangements that developed through ecological processes. The division of labor arises through competition; it is fixed in custom through communication; if challenged, it is enforced by political power. If it becomes painful or inconvenient, it is justified by ideologies. Once formalized, the customary resists change until life conditions change again. Thus, a color line is a phase of an on-going process. The term refers to a temporary period of stability, when a stratified system is regarded as natural and right by the participants.

PART III

Sustaining

Processes

CHAPTER 10

The Stratified Community
as a Moral Order

According to the Nagas, who live on the slopes of the Himalayas, God created a model of man out of something like dough and put it into an oven to bake. Being inexperienced at first, He took it out too quickly, and the creature was still white and unfinished; this was the first white man. Being dissatisfied, God tried again. But this time He left the model in too long, and the second man was burned to a dark color; this was the first Negro. Still dissatisfied, God tried a third time and finally succeeded in producing the perfect, golden brown Indian.[1] Nor are these folk people of northern India the only ones persuaded of their own excellence; creation myths of this type are to be found throughout the world. Not all of the ethnic groups convinced of their superiority enjoy high social status, but beliefs of this kind support systems of ethnic stratification everywhere.

Any social system is subject to stresses and strains. Thwarted ambitions and frustrations are inevitable in any kind of society, but

[1] Santha Rama Rau, *This Is India* (New York: Harper, 1954), p. 16.

they are even more likely in one in which the unequal distribution of rewards is based upon ancestry, since some of the more intelligent and ambitious members of minority groups are bound to become dissatisfied. But systems of ethnic stratification, once they are established, tend to be stable. The "untouchables" of India, the Jews in medieval Europe, the Eta in Japan—all have lived under conditions of subservience for centuries. Since Americans live in a rapidly changing society in which upward mobility is encouraged, they find the quiet acceptance of subordination difficult to comprehend, but on more than one occasion slaves who had been freed have returned voluntarily to their former masters. In the study of sustaining processes interest centers upon the procedures whereby various patterns of interaction are perpetuated and reaffirmed, the ways in which deviation from conventional norms is kept to a minimum. What are the processes through which systems of ethnic stratification are maintained even in the face of pressures to change?

Any system of stratification is unlikely to be perpetuated for long without the wholehearted support of the dominant group. If people in positions of privilege are not convinced of the rectitude of their way of life, they are likely to feel guilty and to support programs of reform. Therefore, we may begin the study of sustaining processes by examining the perspectives of people in dominant groups. What are the characteristic beliefs found among those in positions of privilege, and how are such perspectives maintained?

The Subjective Aspect of Domination

Where a system of ethnic stratification is well established, a high degree of consensus exists regarding the classification of people. Although emphasis upon biological lineage varies from community to community, people are divided into readily recognizable categories, each category being defined in stereotyped terms. There are well-known symbols of identification by which each individual is placed into a scheme. The assumption is that human beings have always been divided into these categories and that they will always be so divided.

The members of each ethnic category have a "place" in the community. "Place" refers to status, one's position in the social hierarchy. Each individual has certain rights and duties, depending upon his classification and quite independent of his personal characteristics. Differences in status are not always recognized explicitly by those who observe them, but people seem to be able to make the proper distinctions intuitively. The social system in the South prior to the Civil War, for example, was clearly stratified. At the top was the aristocracy, consisting of plantation owners, wealthy merchants, and members of the learned professions. Just below them came the upper middle class, consisting of small planters, commercial farmers, and the lesser merchants and professional men; most of these people were slaveholders or were closely associated with them. The lower middle class consisted of independent farmers and of artisans, most of whom had no slaves. Although "poor whites" were at the bottom of the hierarchy of the white population, they were still ranked above all Negroes. In a very real sense, the "white man's floor was the Negro's ceiling." The gap between Negro and white extended far beyond slavery. Even free Negroes were subject to many of the regulations applying to slaves; persons of dark complexion were presumed to be slaves, even though it was known that many of them were not. Slave traders and overseers occupied an anomalous position; they were generally seen in stereotyped terms and were despised by the slaves and their masters alike, but both were essential to the economy, and their authority was recognized.[2] The relationships among these various categories were clearly understood by all parties; there was little question of who enjoyed precedence over whom or of how each was to behave in the presence of the others. Each person knew where he belonged and adopted the mannerisms and pretentions common to those in his category.

A person stays in his "place" by fulfilling the obligations traditionally assigned to the category in which he is located. He is conscious of the rights and responsibilities of his station in life and tries his best to meet them. A man who knows his "place" observes the appropriate rituals. If he is in an inferior position, he addresses those of higher rank with deference and waits to be addressed before speaking up. If he is not expected to dress well, he does not, even though he may be able to afford fine attire. If his dwelling is expected to be humble, he complies. Although severe limitations are placed upon the life chances of a person of low status, there are still oppor-

---

[2] Wilbert E. Moore and Robin M. Williams, "Stratification in the Ante-Bellum South," *American Sociological Review*, **VII** (1942), 343-51.

tunities for him to win recognition and self-respect. One may do his work in a slovenly manner, or he may do it efficiently. A person can develop pride in being a good servant, an efficient truck driver, or a skilled craftsman. He can be proud of the special responsibilities he is given in recognition of his skill. If he is reliable, he is trusted as an individual and is given special privileges. Those who know their "place" take pride in being able to discharge their duties well in comparison to their peers. They accept their humble station and try to make the best of it. People in positions of privilege also have a "place." They are expected to live elegantly; they must dress well, even when they cannot afford it; they are expected to honor disagreeable responsibilities. Thus, persons of high rank are often expected to officiate in various community ceremonies, even if they are bored and would prefer to be doing something else.

A man who knows his "place" has no aspirations beyond those regarded as appropriate for his category. If he is especially competent, he may work for honorary positions with more responsibility and authority, such as gang boss or special assistant to an official. As such he would receive higher pay and special privileges. But there is no hope of moving into positions that are reserved for people in the dominant group. Many accept this fate with resignation. For example, a low-caste drumbeater in Ceylon observed, "From the Puranic ages we have been classified as tom-tom beaters; that is the way it was and that is the way we like it. We would like to be of higher position, but what is the use of wishing for what is impossible? If we were, who would then beat the drums? And if the Henaya were not a Henaya, then who would wash? Everything would be upset and it would not be good for people." [3] In his study of a small community in Guatemala, Tumin found that when a political office was offered to an Indian, he declined on the ground of inadequate preparation. This excuse provided a cover for the conviction that it would be unwise and perhaps dangerous for an Indian to get out of "place." [4] Nor are the requirements of "place" the exclusive concern of people of humble standing. Children who are born into privileged groups are expected to acquire the manners and the special skills regarded as essential for people of their rank. Even when a boy prefers to col-

---

[3] Bryce Ryan, *Caste in Modern Ceylon* (New Brunswick, N. J.: Rutgers University Press, 1953), pp. 259–60.
[4] Tumin, *op. cit.*, pp. 177–78.

lect butterflies or to build racing cars, he is required to pursue an accepted career—cattle-raising, military life, plantation management, scholarship—combined with cultivated leisure.

Each minority group is defined in stereotyped terms. The peoples are usually regarded as inferior objects, often as childlike creatures. In European colonies kindly missionaries frequently referred to their heathen converts as "children"—simple souls whom patience would win to the ways of "civilized" men. They were pleased when the natives were obedient, but many of them would have been horrified at the thought of treating the "savages" as their equal. South of the Mason-Dixon line American Negroes are viewed in many circles in a somewhat similar manner. Their inexpert use of the English language, like that of a young child, is seen as an indication of incomplete development. Negroes are said to be irresponsible; it is argued, therefore, that there is little point in improving their lot, for the advantages would only be wasted.[5] People in positions of privilege frequently contend that paying higher wages to members of minority groups would be foolish; the money would be squandered anyway. A Chinese woman who studied medicine in Tokyo later reported that the Japanese were kind to her in many ways, but she found it very difficult to cope with their overbearing superiority.[6] Especially since China's defeat in the Sino-Japanese War of 1895 the Japanese had looked down upon the Chinese as inferior people, and this contempt was no doubt manifested in their treatment of Chinese immigrants.

People in most dominant groups conceive of themselves as valuable objects; their ascendancy is believed to be due to their inherent superiority. In ethnic stratification these qualities are assumed to be inherited genetically; people of good "stock" are the bearers of highly valued characteristics—dependability, honesty, intelligence, and courage. Those who have ruled for many generations are so convinced of their superiority that they do not even discuss it. During the heyday of the British Empire, for example, many Englishmen would have regarded boasting of their paramount attributes as being in poor taste. This did not mean, however, that they had any doubts about the virtues of Englishmen. Where there is a high degree of consensus

---

[5] Cf. Allison Davis, Burleigh B. Gardner, and Mary R. Gardner, *Deep South* (Chicago: University of Chicago Press, 1941), pp. 15–20; and Dollard, *op. cit.*, pp. 364–89.

[6] Chao, *op. cit.*, pp. 132–49.

on the relative worth of ethnic categories, such estimates may persist even among people in intimate association. Banton discovered, for example, that some of the Englishwomen who had married colored immigrants in London looked upon their spouses as good husbands but did not accept them as their equal.[7] In most communities intellectuals provide scholarly "proof" to support these popular beliefs. During the period preceding the Civil War many American scientists tried to demonstrate that Negroes were of a different species.[8] Beliefs of this kind enable men to maintain a color line with confidence and a sense of righteousness. The unequal distribution of values is seen as inevitable and morally justified.

People of good will sometimes believe that ethnic minorities live in a constant state of terror, hated by their oppressors. Sometimes this is the case, but such instances are rare. Occasionally individuals in privileged positions abuse their authority, but in most societies there are safeguards against this. In stable stratified communities the usual orientation of people in dominant groups toward those in minorities does not involve malice or hostility; the most common attitude is one of *condescension.* In the South the attitude of many slaveholders was one of paternalistic benevolence; the prevailing image was that of the contented "darky" and his kindly master. There was no objection to Negroes' having a good time, nor to their attempting to improve their lot within the confines of their "place." Capable men were often helped, and whenever a local Negro won regional or national recognition, everyone in the community was proud of him and rejoiced. Even today many white people in the South can say in complete honesty that they feel no antipathy toward Negroes. People in minority groups are not hated; they are viewed with affection as long as they are childlike and lovable and remain in their "place."

In well-entrenched dominant groups there often arises a tradition of *noblesse oblige,* the responsibility of the fortunate to protect and to look after the welfare of the less fortunate. In some cases it becomes part of a code of honor. Just as children in minorities are expected to learn their "place," those in privileged families are trained

[7] Banton, *The Coloured Quarter, op. cit.,* p. 80. Cf. Maunier, *op. cit.,* Vol. I, pp. 139-48.

[8] Cf. William Stanton, *The Leopard's Spots: Scientific Attitudes Toward Race in America, 1815-59* (Chicago: University of Chicago Press, 1960).

from childhood to uphold the responsibilities of their position—to be considerate and to treat their subordinates well. Although there are many local variations in custom, those who rule are often held accountable for the misdeeds of their charges; they are expected to pay damages or to make other amends. In some societies women of high rank are trained to look after the needs of their subordinates, just as wealthy women in the United States distribute baskets to the poor. In the antebellum South sons of plantation owners were trained to look after their slaves. Especially where it had become a family tradition, slaveholders took a sincere interest in the welfare of certain individuals. They extended to Negroes they knew regard and affection that they did not have for many white men, and they sometimes assumed responsibility for them at crucial moments of financial or legal trouble. Many white people have made substantial contributions to the welfare of Negroes—giving generous gifts to schools, hospitals, and other institutions. In many European colonies the "white man's burden" was more than a slogan; the colonists built roads, introduced more effective medical care, abolished slavery, and established universities. The standard of living has generally been improved, even where there has been extensive exploitation.

Especially in situations in which there are great differences of power, common understandings arise prohibiting certain types of depredation. In the antebellum South a master had the legal right to use his slaves as he chose, but customary controls were imposed by other slaveholders, limiting the extent of exploitation. Cruel men who mistreated the helpless were ostracized and sometimes even punished. Slave traders and overseers had to resort to repressive measures to maintain control; because of this they were often rejected.[9] People in minority groups are not unaware of such codes, and they judge individuals in the dominant group largely in terms of the standards that the latter set for themselves. Those who pay honor expect the bearer to conduct his life in accordance to certain rules; he is expected to act with dignity and integrity.[10] Those who treat their subordinates with consideration and meet their own obligations often win staunch loyalty. They are served with devotion by people who never complain of their lowly status.

[9] Cf. Wilbur J. Cash, *The Mind of the South* (New York: Doubleday, 1954), pp. 85–89.
[10] Speier, *op. cit.*, pp. 83–85.

When individuals of different ethnic categories are in sustained contact—master and his personal servant, hunter and his bearer, overseer and his assistant—the interpersonal relationship that develops is often one of dependency. One person by convention and law has all the authority, and whatever rewards the subordinate receives rest upon the initiative of his master. Gaining the good will and affection of the master gives a person of low rank a sense of security. For one thing, he is protected by his master's position against exploitation by others in the dominant group. For some individuals, depending upon another may also be satisfying because it relieves them of responsibility and initiative. While it saps their self-respect and undermines their capacity for independent action, it enables them to get along. Many people in minority groups have advanced themselves by getting favors rather than by insisting upon their rights.[11]

Some observers have noted that the establishment of such ties may also be gratifying to the master, in spite of the added responsibilities and inconveniences. Mannoni has suggested that colonies tend to attract men who have an inferiority complex and need such reassurances. These are men who cannot exert power among their peers, weak men who cannot bear to compete on equal terms. They cannot accept people as they are and find it difficult to live in a world in which others have to be respected. They therefore fill their world with imaginary associates who are always subservient. In a colony such a person may become a magnificent leader of people who give him unquestioned homage.[12] But the kindly treatment of those who are subordinate is viewed as a gift rather than a moral obligation. The kind of orientation that American Negroes call the "patronizing attitude" is based on the assumption that the donor is a superior being who is doing something for his subordinate out of kindness. What is done is not a response to a legitimate claim of the person of lower rank but a privilege that has been extended as a bounty. This is psychologically gratifying to the donor, for he can conceive of himself as having done something virtuous that was really unnecessary. By his benevolence he reinforces his self-respect. When the recipient of such "kindness" is not quick in showing his gratitude, the reaction

[11] Cf. Hortense Powdermaker, "The Channeling of Negro Aggression by the Cultural Process," *American Journal of Sociology*, **XLVIII** (1943), 751-52.
[12] Dominique O. Mannoni, *Prospero and Caliban: The Psychology of Colonization*, trans. Pamela Powesland (New York: Frederick A. Praeger, 1956), pp. 97-110.

is one of hurt feelings, of resentment over not being appreciated after going to all the trouble, and the gift may even be withdrawn. Favors are extended only as long as the subordinates are appreciative and remain in their "place." When a system of stratification is breaking down, this attitude is resented by people in minority groups more than open hostility, for it rests upon the silent assumption of their inferiority; an object of hostility is at least acknowledged as an opponent worthy of taking seriously.

In a stable system of ethnic stratification *there is no direct competition among people in the different ethnic categories.* They do not compete for jobs, for homes, for recognition, nor for mates. Friction is kept to a minimum, as people of the different strata maintain their distance and perform their respective tasks. Thus, systems of stratification that emerge from competition generally crystallize into forms in which continued competition becomes impossible. Members of the dominant group are fully protected; there is no possibility of their being defeated.

To the extent that there is consensus concerning the "places" of the various ethnic groups the system remains stable and cooperation occurs smoothly. Differences in rank are taken for granted: in many cases the dominant group shows neither snobbery nor exclusiveness, nor does the minority group show sullenness. Differences in status are accepted quietly and do not prevent cooperation and friendliness among those who must work together. In most cases there are no egalitarian ideologies. People just assume that there are different kinds of human beings and that it is natural for some to rule and for others to obey. Ambitious members of minority groups may occasionally long for a better fate, but they view it more as a dream than as something that could actually occur. The prevailing orientation is conservative: the traditional ways are believed to be just and decent. As long as all the participants conform to the accepted norms—doing the things that each person regards as proper—the system of unequal rewards is perpetuated. A well-established system of stratification, then, is a moral order.

Once we understand that a color line consists of a set of conventional norms defining the relationships among various categories of people, many puzzling occurrences become comprehensible. Many of the distinctions that appear invidious to an outside observer are not made from malice; in many cases these practices are symbolic of status. "Jim Crow" practices in the South, for example, cannot be explained in terms of repugnance to skin color. When buses were still segregated in the South, many outsiders were amazed to learn that a Negro nurse carrying a white child was required to sit in the white section. But segregation did not arise from distaste for physical proximity. The status of the child determined where he was to sit, and the nurse was expected to accompany him. There was never any objection to close and intimate contacts between Negro and white. Servants, nurses, fellow workers, and those in various service occupations were in constant association. In some homes white children were much closer to the Negro servants than they were to their own parents. Negroes were required to ride in the rear of buses, not because they were thought to be dirty, but to symbolize the difference in rank. Similarly, when the British excluded Hindus from their clubs in India, there was no fear of physical contact. There was no charge that the Indians were dirty; if anything, the Indians found the Europeans offensively unclean. Membership in certain voluntary associations was symbolic of high status, and there were a great many Englishmen who did not qualify for admission either. What made this exclusion policy so obnoxious to so many Indians was precisely this quiet assumption of English superiority.

This also helps to account for a frequently observed phenomenon that was the source of considerable misunderstanding in a number of European colonies, one that has been reported in widely different contexts as "lack of gratitude" on the part of natives and interpreted as further evidence of their primitive character. A European who had done a favor for a native, such as providing him with drugs that enabled him to recover from a severe illness, was then astonished when the native, instead of expressing thanks, demanded further gifts. The native acted as if he had a special claim upon the colonist who did him a kindness. Mannoni suggests that the native did not see the favor as a gift, but as an indication of the establishment of an interpersonal relationship in which he was the dependent party. His attitude might be summarized as follows: "You did something for me that you were under no obligation to do. I am yours to command, but you must look after me." Such a reaction is predicated upon inequality of status. When a person in a competitive society receives a favor from someone of equal rank, he repays it; otherwise he is conscious of his debt and dislikes or avoids his benefactor. Gratitude is something that can be demanded only where people are equal; it implies a rejection of dependence.[13]

The emotional reaction that is aroused whenever a color line is violated often appears to an outside observer to be excessive. Attempts by Negroes to improve their economic position, for example, are viewed by some white people in the South as an insult.[14] When a white woman marries a Negro, some people become ill and vomit. In South Africa natives are considered savages and are often assumed to be like wild animals. Sexual intercourse between natives and Europeans therefore appears to be a form of perversion, and a sense of revulsion is elicited because such acts are defined as "unnatural" as well as immoral.[15] The neuromuscular sets that constitute disgust are formed during childhood in most cases through prohibitions of the handling of excreta, and it is not surprising that characteristic facial expressions and muscular movements arise later in life whenever one inadvertently does something that is thought to be dirty.[16] Any violation of the moral order offends one's sense of congruence, and human beings cannot afford to let their view of the world go to pieces. They must continue to have a sound basis for their own conduct.

Ethnic Categories and Social Distance

Since ethnic stereotypes are abstract concepts, one would think that contacts across a color line would disclose their inaccuracies. Yet different ethnic groups have lived side by side for many generations without altering their conceptions of one another. How is this possible? Somehow people maintain their isolation in spite of physical proximity. In most communities relatively few individuals in each ethnic group come into direct contact with outsiders. Much of the information about others is indirect; most people know about other ethnic groups largely by hearsay. In his study in a city in northern Japan of the Eta—an endogamous pariah group based upon the occupation of slaughtering meat—Donoghue found that all of the Japanese interviewed had heard of *Shin-machi*, the segregated area in which the Eta lived. Most of them had never been there, however,

[13] *Ibid.*, pp. 9–10, 43–47, 70–80. Cf. Lévy-Bruhl, *op. cit.*, pp. 410–30.
[14] Dollard, *op. cit.*, pp. 298–99.
[15] MacCrone, *op. cit.*, pp. 298–302.
[16] Cf. Andrus Angyal, "Disgust and Related Aversions," *Journal of Abnormal and Social Psychology*, **XXXVI** (1941), 393–412.

and many did not even know where it was. None had knowingly associated with an Eta, and several were curious to know what these "barbarians" looked like; yet they were all convinced that the Eta were dirty, dangerous, and afflicted with frightful diseases.[17] Even those who do come into direct contact usually do so in institutional settings—as master and servant, buyer and seller, policeman and suspect. In such transactions the patterns of appropriate conduct for all of the parties are prescribed by custom. Even where there is repeated contact, *the modification of ethnic stereotypes is not likely to occur unless there is a reduction of social distance.*

Where any particular relationship would fall on the continuum of social distance depends upon the type of knowledge the participants have of one another. Since men interact in terms of the conceptions they form of each other, the same person may mean different things to different observers, and all kinds of imaginary traits may be imputed. Conceptions of other people are constructed from a variety of sensory cues—their speech, their facial expressions, their deeds—from which inferences are made about their inner experiences. In intimate contacts the other person sometimes confirms these hypotheses by confessing some of his secrets, but each person retains some area of privacy. Furthermore, in many relationships, especially with strangers, men deliberately hide their actual dispositions through diversionary gestures. There is a wide range of variation in what men learn about one another, and social distance can be measured along these lines.[18]

In those relationships in which social distance is great, knowledge of the other party is highly specialized and categorical. In these impersonal contacts people approach one another as representatives of categories. Other people are known only in specific roles—waiter in a restaurant, gun bearer on a safari, clerk in a grocery store. The unique personality of the other party is either irrelevant or of secondary importance. When a destitute person is seen as a beggar, his plea for alms falls upon deaf ears or elicits a perfunctory response; his hunger and humiliation are not vicariously felt. Because men live in a symbolic environment in which objects have been classified and

[17] John D. Donoghue, "An Eta Community in Japan: The Social Persistence of Outcaste Groups," *American Anthropologist*, **LIX** (1957), 1000–17.

[18] Simmel, *op. cit.*, pp. 307–44. Cf. Erving Goffman, "The Nature of Deference and Demeanor," *American Anthropologist*, **LVIII** (1956), 473–502.

labelled, they are able to interact effectively even with total strangers —simply by placing them into the proper category.

When knowledge that the participants have of one another is so impersonal, concerted action can occur only in situations in which social structure is well established, where conventional roles are clearly defined. Since they know little or nothing about the other person's idiosyncracies, they have no other way of anticipating his reactions. The fact that most people act in customary ways makes their mutual adjustment possible. Most economic transactions are of this nature. Each individual is able to orient himself to the other's plan of action, but successful role-taking can occur only within this specialized context. Cooperation involving people about whom little is known would be precarious were it not for the institutional setting.

Social distance is at a maximum in situations in which each person maintains his personal reserve. As long as one is self-conscious and confines himself to playing conventional roles, he does what others expect of him rather than what he actually wants to do. Politeness is a way of concealing one's individuality: a polite man does not disclose his unique personal reactions; all he displays is a façade. When men maintain their discretion, they conceal their joys, sorrows, and hopes behind a mask. The communication that takes place in such contexts is largely formal. What appear to be expressive movements, those involuntary manifestations of emotional reactions, are often not spontaneous; they are more like the practiced smile of a salesman. When men are intent upon doing the proper thing, each person tries to hide his personal feelings; like people riding in street cars behind impassive faces their worries and aspirations remain hidden.

In relationships in which social distance is at a minimum, knowledge of the other person is highly individualized. In intimate circles each individual is recognized as having a distinct personality, and his various idiosyncrasies are taken into account in dealing with him. The better one gets to know someone, the more he stands out as a distinct individual with numerous features that distinguish him from everyone else. Such knowledge can be acquired only when there is a relaxation of personal reserve, and most people act more spontaneously in the company of intimate associates, often admitting some of their inner thoughts and forbidden reactions. In addition, through facial expressions, many inclinations that are ordinarily hidden from strangers are inadvertently disclosed to friends. Although this is sometimes embarrassing, it facilitates the establishment of sympathetic identification. The spontaneity that accompanies the relaxation of personal reserve shows a person for what he is; his mask comes off. People who are well acquainted make allowances for one another's quirks and weaknesses; hence, the outcome of the transactions in which they participate may depend more upon the personalities of those involved than upon conventional norms.

Furthermore, because those who are in sustained association do so many different things together, their knowledge of one another becomes unspecialized. In impersonal contacts one's knowledge of others is limited to what is essential for carrying out a particular type of transaction—such as medical treatment in a clinic, classroom instruction, or the purchase of goods. In intimate associations, however, others are observed performing a variety of tasks, and the participants become familiar with one another's views and reactions in many different contexts. Not only are more things known about close friends and relatives, but the knowledge is diversified. Friends are generally familiar with one another's background of experience, and in many cases they even share each other's dreams for the future. Precisely because they have more rounded conceptions of one another, each can better anticipate what the other is likely to do—even in new situations.

Increasing knowledge about the personal characteristics of others facilitates the establishment of sympathetic identification. Differences in behavior patterns often arise from diverse definitions of a situation, but misinterpretations are difficult to correct unless people trust one another. In Madagascar, for example, the inability of Europeans to appreciate the faith that the natives placed in divination resulted in frequent misunderstandings. When a Malagasy changed his plans without apparent reason or gave up a profitable enterprise for one that was less lucrative, he did not admit to a European that he was following the advice of a fortune teller. Retaining his façade, he invented excuses that were sometimes absurd, and these irritated Europeans even further.[19] If these people had known one another more intimately, they would have been able to speak more candidly, even about things that were a bit embarrassing, and could thereby have developed a better comprehension of one another's perspectives.

[19] Mannoni, *op. cit.*, pp. 72–73.

What this suggests is that human beings are basically alike. Similar impulses are aroused in similarly defined situations; a pious European might also give up his profits on the advice of ecclesiastical authorities. But the resemblance is not immediately apparent because men so frequently conceal their inner dispositions. A man who has erotic interests in the voluptuous wife of a friend may regard himself as depraved until another friend, seemingly immune to her charms, confesses similar inclinations. With the relaxation of personal reserve and the disclosure of such inhibited reactions, those who are close to one another come to appreciate that behind their customary masks they are fundamentally alike. Each person is unique and reacts somewhat differently from anyone else; yet his distinctive responses become more understandable when *his* definition of the situation becomes clear. Paradoxically, then, the more one appreciates another person as a unique individual, the easier it becomes to identify with him as a human being. The ability to enter imaginatively into the minds of others and to sympathize with them is ordinarily blocked by self-consciousness and personal reserve. Relaxation facilitates this type of role-taking.[20]

Where social distance is great, people stand in a relationship of mutual utility. Although strangers interact politely, for all practical purposes the other party is only a "thing" to be manipulated in the pursuit of one's own interests. If for any reason there is a temporary reduction in social distance, however, a remarkable transformation takes place. A man who happens to glance directly into the eyes of a beggar suddenly experiences pangs of guilt and reluctantly makes a generous handout; a stranger who catches the ecstatic joy of an innocent child spontaneously breaks into a grin and offers him candy; a driver who notices the face of a disappointed hitchhiker remonstrates to himself for passing him by. Momentarily, the "it" becomes a "you"—a human being with whom there is sympathetic identification. Momentarily one projects himself to the standpoint of the other and responds as a human being, appreciating the plight or the joy of the other person.[21] As social distance is reduced, then, the other person is seen as a creature like oneself rather than as a representative

---

[20] Cf. Cooley, *op. cit.,* pp. 136–67; and Park, *Race and Culture, op. cit.,* pp. 244–55.

[21] Cf. Martin Buber, *I and Thou,* trans. Ronald G. Smith (New York: Scribner's, 1958).

of a class of objects. Ethnic categories, therefore, become increasingly difficult to retain as personal reserve is relaxed.

Precisely because of such identification, sentimental considerations take on overriding importance when social distance is reduced. Among one's intimate associates, conventional obligations are often overlooked, and laws that get in the way are ignored. When one knows someone else well, he becomes acutely aware of his unique interests, his concern over his self-esteem, and his sensitivity about matters in which he is involved. With intimacy comes mutual concern. Hence, an impartial enforcement of customs and laws becomes difficult. Thus, the first generation of English rulers in India managed to establish close personal ties with Indians but were often corrupt. Because of scandals they were replaced by civil servants who regarded their power as a public trust rather than a personal opportunity. But the moral redemption of British administration was accompanied by increasing social distance between the English settlers and their Indian neighbors. Aloofness was the price of integrity.[22]

The importance of sympathetic identification is revealed in the manumission of household slaves. In most continuing relationships there is some reduction of social distance. As people become better acquainted, they relax bit by bit, revealing more and more of their unique preferences. Once a minimum identification is established, special obligations of a personal nature develop, which in turn facilitate even closer contacts. Since intimacy rests upon a mutual appreciation of one another's inner experiences, its development depends upon the relaxation of reserve on the part of both parties. With the reduction of social distance there is more spontaneity, less consciousness, and increasing ease of interchange. Men cannot share their sorrows, hopes, and joys for a long time and still not appreciate one another as human beings. Sudden bereavement brings master and slave close together—in great sorrow in which feelings are difficult to conceal and where the presence of any understanding human being can mean so much. When the sorrow is genuine, inhibitions are relaxed. Countless situations of this kind must have modified the relationships between masters and their personal slaves, and the rapid growth of the free Negro population in the United States from 1790

[22] Toynbee, *op. cit.*, Vol. VIII, pp. 207-13.

to 1860—from 59,557 to 488,070—gives some indication of the frequency with which slaves were set free.[23]

Since the social contexts in which people experience their greatest sense of security are characterized by a reduction of social distance, some sociologists have praised such relationships as desirable. Furthermore, in most groups there are conventional norms that persons who are in intimate contact *should* like one another; the assumption, therefore, is that all intimate relations are friendly and desirable. Even a superficial glance at clinical materials reported by psychiatrists indicates that this is not true. Close contacts are not necessarily cordial. People who know one another quite well may develop intense antipathies; indeed, the most bitter hatreds of which men are capable seem to be directed against those with whom they have been in intimate association. This value judgment is misleading, and it also overlooks the fact that most categorical contacts are not unfriendly. What does one know about the friendly waiter in a restaurant he regularly patronizes? He knows that the man is an efficient waiter, that he is familiar with the preferences of his customers, and that he gives generous portions of butter. But what does one know about the man's personal ambitions, his hopes for his children, or his relations with his wife? And without such knowledge what does anyone know about the waiter as a human being? Yet, even without such knowledge, transactions occur smoothly, pleasantly, and without hostility. Men in frequent contact cannot remain indifferent to one another, but the sentiments that develop may be either friendly or unfriendly.

Some sociologists have contended that people who interact frequently tend to like one another.[24] In general, this is true, but it is not necessarily so. Neither physical proximity nor frequency of contact necessarily results in the reduction of social distance nor in the formation of favorable sentiments. There are many situations in which traditional barriers make the relaxation of personal reserve awkward. Master and servant in the same household learn a great deal about one another, much more than either is willing to admit; as long as each pretends not to know, however, the servant remains in his "place." In slum areas members of different ethnic minorities

23 Cf. Frazier, *The Negro in the United States, op. cit.,* pp. 60–62.
24 Cf. George C. Homans, *The Human Group* (New York: Harcourt, Brace, 1950), pp. 111–13; and Suchman *et al., op. cit.,* pp. 47–56.

live side by side and engage in countless transactions together; in spite of the apparent cheerfulness of their contacts, however, they often view one another with contempt. Further indications that people who live together do not necessarily understand one another come from the testimony of Africans visiting or studying in Europe that they find it easier to associate with Europeans who had never lived in colonies; Malagasies living in France get along quite well with most Frenchmen, but they carefully avoid those who had spent any time in Madagascar.[25] Englishmen who had served in positions of authority in colonies appear to be well informed, but they tend to be less tolerant toward colored immigrants in the Britsh Isles.[26] In 1957 Franck questioned 1,142 Europeans living in the Rhodesias on what Africans should or should not be permitted to do and found "liberal" attitudes more frequently among those who had been there for less than five years. The longer their residence, the more stereotyped their conception of the natives and the more opposed they were to making any concessions.[27] It appears, then, that the Europeans who remained at home do not have the stereotyped conceptions and in many cases treat foreign visitors as individuals; former colonists, however, act in terms of their deeply ingrained beliefs.

In communities in which the differentiation of ethnic groups has become traditional, most people are not likely to get close enough to each other to test their beliefs. In their colonies Europeans were often baffled by the mixture of success and failure in their efforts to understand the behavior of the natives. In many cases they gave up and concluded that communication was impossible, that there was an impassable barrier between the "civilized" and the "uncivilized." Many insisted that the mentality of natives was incomprehensible and that there was no point in wasting time trying to understand it.[28] Similarly, in many rural communities in Europe the contacts of the native population with infiltrating nomadic groups or with expanding neighboring peoples have not always led to the establishment of primary relations. Although Gypsies have lived for centuries in various countries in Europe, most of their contacts have remained categorical, and they have retained their strange customs and exclusiveness. They

---

25 Mannoni, *op. cit.,* pp. 33, 126.
26 Banton, *The Coloured Quarter, op. cit.,* p. 43.
27 Franck, *op. cit.,* pp. 243–47.
28 Mannoni, *op. cit.,* pp. 19–20.

have been persecuted almost everywhere they have appeared, being accused of stealing, witchcraft, well-poisoning, kidnapping, and even cannibalism. In Hungary they were enslaved until 1781; in Rumania, until 1866. In spite of their numerous contacts with many peoples the Gypsies have until very recently retained a common language and a common culture.[29] There were many cases in medieval Europe in which invaders maintained their distance. The Germans in eastern and central Europe during the twelfth and thirteenth centuries established urban colonies in the midst of peasant societies, and they remained isolated.

There are cultural differences in the extent to which the relaxation of personal reserve among strangers is permitted. In addition, a personal equation is also involved. There are marked personality differences in the capacity of individuals to enter into intimate associations with other people. Some establish rapport with others and make friends easily. Others are guarded and defensive and unable to relax even in the presence of people they have known most of their lives. Some establish intimate ties with only a handful of persons in their lifetime.[30] Furthermore, the perspectives of some people are rigid. Contradictory evidence passes unnoticed or is explained away, and anyone who presents views different from theirs is suspected of having vicious motives. Thus, some individuals retain their stereotyped conceptions in spite of numerous opportunities for revision.

The Reaffirmation of Ethnic Categories

When several ethnic groups occupy a common territory, people in other categories are bound to be observed. Since their actual conduct frequently does not resemble the stereotyped models, the question arises as to how such meanings can retain their stability in spite of inadequate or contradictory evidence. The belief that dogs and cats are natural enemies is perpetuated because most dogs and cats do not in fact get along, but how can the belief that one's neighbor is of an indolent "race" be sustained when one sees him working every day? How can people in minority groups continue to believe

[29] Cf. Max Handman, "Gypsies," *Encyclopedia of the Social Sciences*, Vol. VII, pp. 231–32.
[30] Cf. Rosalind F. Dymond, "Personality and Empathy," *Journal of Consulting Psychology*, XIV (1950), 343–50.

that their rulers are malicious and selfish, when each year they are the recipients of generous gifts and bonuses? The hypothesis may be advanced that *most stereotypes are reinforced unintentionally in contexts that have little or nothing to do with ethnic identity.* Evidence is not examined critically precisely because ethnic identity is irrelevant in these transactions, and attention is focused upon other matters.

Since aversions toward ethnic categories often appear at an early age and seem to be spontaneous, some people believe that "racial" antipathies are inborn. There is no evidence to support this contention.[31] Virtually all meanings are learned; and as with most other meanings, ethnic stereotypes are learned while participating in organized group activities. It has been noted that the meaning of any object consists of the manner in which one is disposed to act toward it. These behavior patterns are shaped through the consistent responses of *other people.* The reactions of other people initially lead a child to do some things and to refrain from doing others; the approved procedures are repeated and in time become fixed so that he is able to act properly even when he is by himself. One learns to address his mother with respect because of the consequences of not doing so; his parents and other elders all express shock and disapproval. The meanings of other categories of people are learned in the same manner. How does a Catholic child learn to address a nun? In the beginning the child does not make a distinction between nuns and other human beings, but before long he observes the differences in the conduct of his elders whenever a sister is present. Should he use profanity in her presence, he is punished far more severely than he had ever been for similar offenses in other company. He is also given explicit instructions about showing respect. Thus, in time even a dull child learns that there is an important difference between women in clerical garb and other women. When he approaches a nun with deference, he is praised for observing the appropriate custom. Thus, the responses of other people play a decisive part in socialization; meanings are crystallized through the *consistency* in the responses of a number of persons in a succession of transactions. Other people give instructions on the proper modes of conduct; they provide models of action to be imitated; and they enforce the customary

---

[31] Cf. Eugene L. Horowitz, "Race Attitudes," in Klineberg, *Characteristics of the American Negro, op. cit.,* pp. 158–84; and Bruno Lasker, *Race Attitudes in Children* (New York: Henry Holt, 1929).

standards through punishment and reward.[32] Ethnic stereotypes are similarly shaped in social contexts.

Although some antipathies may result from unfortunate experiences with a representative of an ethnic category, a great many meanings take shape independently of direct contact. Each person has a working conception of categories of people he has never encountered. Stereotyped meanings are shaped in social interaction; each child learns to classify human beings in the manner that is accepted by the adults in his group. At first, children cannot distinguish between ethnic groups at all, but this ability develops quite early and increases quickly while children are still in elementary school.[33] In a study conducted in Charlottesville, Virginia, white students from the fourth to eleventh grades were asked to compare Negroes and white people on 60 traits. The younger children disagreed considerably, but the degree of consensus in the characterizations increased with age. The younger children had a less favorable conception of Negroes; they were unwilling to attribute any positive traits to them. With increasing age, however, the portrayals began to approximate the adult stereotype, which is not entirely negative. Older children would attribute to Negroes traits such as cheerfulness, having a good sense of humor, and being religious.[34] The importance of adult influence is shown in a number of other studies that reveal that the attitudes of children resemble those of their parents.[35]

The proper way to approach people in each ethnic category in the community is sometimes taught, although it is rarely a subject covered by formal instruction in schools. The teaching is informal and differs somewhat from family to family. In a study of the acquisition of the concept of "Negro" in the South, Quinn found that explicit instructions were sporadic; they were usually given only when a child had inadvertently violated the color line. If a child invited a Negro playmate to her birthday party, she was told that she

[32] Cf. Shibutani, op. cit., pp. 471–534.

[33] Mary E. Goodman, Race Awareness in Young Children (Cambridge, Mass.: Addison-Wesley, 1952); and J. Kenneth Moreland, "Racial Recognition by Nursery School Children in Lynchburg, Virginia," Social Forces, XXXVII (1958), 132–37.

[34] Robert Blake and Wayne Dennis, "The Development of Stereotypes Concerning the Negro," Journal of Abnormal and Social Psychology, XXXVIII (1943), 525–31.

[35] Cf. Allport and Kramer, op. cit.; and Eugene L. and Ruth E. Horowitz, "Development of Social Attitudes in Children," Sociometry, I (1938), 301–38.

could not do this. In response to her queries the parents would then explain that such things were not done, providing any of a variety of justifications. Or a child might refer to a Negro woman as a "lady," and corrective instructions would follow. By making a succession of social errors, which were then corrected by elders, a child learned to distinguish between himself and Negroes. Some indirect learning was also permitted. Children would be allowed to overhear conversations about the immoral conduct of Negroes, when similar behavior on the part of white people was hidden from them until they were older. There was little deliberate effort at indoctrination unless a child persisted in confounding the categories.

In the course of forming their own self-conceptions and learning the responsibilities of their station in life, children of the dominant group are given additional details for the construction of stereotypes. In the South, for example, white children were instructed never to make disparaging remarks in public about Negroes, especially in the presence of Negroes. They were also taught to treat Negroes with consideration. The implication was that a white person *could* mistreat a Negro but that he should not; in contrast, he could not mistreat another white person with impunity. Thus, a distinction was made between human beings with the power to retaliate and those who depended upon the good will of others. The children were cautioned against taking unfair advantage of the powerless, but they were also taught not to reveal their own weaknesses in public. They learned of the glorious history of the South, of the manner in which Negroes and Indians had been subjugated, and of the considerate manner in which these inferior people had been looked after—for their own good.[36] Thus, the different ethnic categories are distinguished, and the child of the dominant group is placed clearly into one of them. In learning the meaning of the category of "Negro" the child also learns the category of "white." Little by little he learns to assume the responsibilities of the latter.

Stereotyped meanings are also shaped in a variety of other contexts. Epithets are used when making disparaging or derogatory remarks, often by children who are unfamiliar with the ethnic group. American children frequently decide priority in games by counting: "Eeny, meeny, miny, mo; Catch a nigger by the toe; . . ." This de-

[36] Olive W. Quinn, "The Transmission of Racial Attitudes among White Southerners," *Social Forces*, XXXIII (1954), 41–47.

vice is used daily by countless children who have never seen a Negro and do not even understand what they are saying; it is merely a way of deciding who is to enjoy the temporary advantage of being first. When discussing financial transactions, children sometimes use the expression overheard in adult talk: "Jew the man down." Many of the youngsters who use this expression do not realize that the verb refers to an ethnic group. In both these cases attention is focused upon something other than ethnic identity; children are trying to find an orderly way to settle disputes over priority, or a financial transaction is described in commonplace terms. Although ethnic identity is irrelevant, the meaning is in each case consistent. Negroes are represented as inferior objects, and Jews are seen as adroit in handling money. These illustrations also suggest why so many ethnic categories are vague; there is no explicit instruction. Some stereotypes are formed, then, as incidental by-products of transactions that have nothing to do with stratification.

Stereotyped meanings are also constructed as adults attempt to discipline their children. In many American communities children who do not keep themselves reasonably clean are warned that if too much dirt accumulates on their skin, they will become permanently dark, like Negroes. They are then teased and ridiculed, the implication being that a Negro is a contemptible object. When Negro soldiers were first stationed in Oahu, Hawaii, in 1943, parents admonished their daughters: "Be careful. You know what a Negro will do to you!" [37] Among the Teton–Dakota Indians parents disciplined their children by telling them that the white man would take away those who did not behave.[38] In this context parents are preoccupied with getting obedience, not with inculcating an ethnic stereotype. The reference to ethnic groups is incidental, but the implication is that the fate of a person in the clutches of an outsider would be so horrible that any sacrifice—even being well behaved—is preferable. The tone of the voice and the look of terror suggest that the alternative would be dreadful.

This provides a clue on the formation of those strange, unaccountable emotional reactions toward ethnic groups that are so difficult to control. When a person who has several Chinese friends

[37] Kubo, op. cit.
[38] Scudder Mekeel, "Education, Child-Training, and Culture," American Journal of Sociology, XLVIII (1943), 680.

experiences a sudden, uncanny fear upon seeing a photograph of a man dressed in mandarin garb, he knows there are no rational grounds for the reaction; nonetheless, it fills him with terror. The psychiatrist Sullivan suggests that such meanings develop when an experience that is differentiated into a unit becomes associated with sensory cues with which it has no necessary, logical connection. His hypothesis is that meanings of this type are shaped in anxiety-provoking situations, the details of which have been forgotten. It is quite possible that these meanings develop in contexts in which other people express their own fears and hostilities, in many cases unintentionally through expressive movements. Some individuals manifest obvious fear when talking about a minority group they regard as dangerous, just as they reveal their disgust when expressing contempt for another group they regard as hopelessly primitive. In family circles, even where the alleged characteristics of ethnic groups are not discussed openly, parents often betray meanings through facial expressions and nervousness that they are trying to hide in their conscious speech. Thus, emotional dispositions of all kinds are communicated without deliberate intent.[39]

Meanings are premises of action, and they are reaffirmed by the responses of other people. The meanings of various objects around us may be regarded as assumptions about the characteristics of these objects. These presuppositions are reinforced whenever action based upon them is carried out successfully, and they are also reinforced as other people observing the action respond as expected. Stereotyped conceptions of ethnic groups are reaffirmed, then, whenever acts based upon these assumptions gain approval. A boy may insult or hurl a stone at someone in a minority group on the assumption that the category is defined as fair game. If the victim runs away and his friends approve his act or join him, their response reaffirms his belief. Even if someone objects that the victim is helpless to fight back, this reinforces his belief that the object is inferior. Assumptions such as these need never be stated; they can be sustained by the approval of overt acts based upon them. Confirmation may occur through expressive movements; when an ethnic group is being discussed, one may reveal his emotional dispositions toward it—fear, anger, disgust, or affection. If such manifestations are received sympathetically, the orientation is strengthened. Such interchanges fre-

[39] Sullivan, *op. cit.*, pp. 28–29, 38–39, 83–84, 304–305.

quently occur without malice; the people who contribute to the perpetuation of pejorative meanings often do so without any conscious awareness of their deeds.

Ethnic stereotypes are also reinforced through selective perception. It has often been contended that one aggressive Jew injures hundreds of others who do not fit the stereotype, since the many outsiders who come into contact with him go away convinced that *all* Jews have the same attributes. Actually such reaffirmation may occur without the presence of a single Jew—aggressive or otherwise. When a person who is anti-Semitic meets a charming individual who happens to be Jewish, he does not inquire into his ethnic identity, and the category of "Jew" is not credited for the favorable impression. On the other hand, an obnoxious act by anyone whose appearance even approximates the stereotype—dark hair, prominent nose, sallow skin—elicits the response: "Look at that dirty Jew!" The manner in which this rude individual crowded in at the head of a line or had cheated an elderly lady in a transaction is cited as further proof that Jews are "pushy." But there is actually no evidence that the individual is in fact a Jew; he might have been an Armenian, a Greek, an Italian, a Turk, or even an Arab! Acts that reaffirm a stereotyped conception attract attention, and those that run contrary to expectations usually pass unnoticed. Selective perception occurs everywhere, but it probably plays a more important part in the continued differentiation of groups that are not highly visible, as in the case of minority groups in Europe.

Ethnic stereotypes are also reinforced in a variety of communicative acts, both in the formal media of communication and in informal interchanges. In American literature before 1930 Negroes were generally characterized as contented slaves, wretched freedmen, brutes, tragic mulattoes, exotic primitives, or comics. In almost all portrayals Negroes were set apart from white people. The comic Negro—with his love of watermelons, crap games, and chicken, his use of big words he does not understand, his hysterical cowardice, and his love of grandiloquent titles—was a particularly familar character. In many ways this stereotype resembled that of the comic Irishman built up by English authors during the period of Irish persecution.[40] Berelson and Salter examined eight of the most widely-read Ameri-

---

[40] Sterling A. Brown, "Negro Character as Seen by White Authors," *Journal of Negro Education*, II (1933), 180–201.

can magazines for the two years of 1937 and 1943 and found that virtually all of the heroes and heroines in the stories were of the dominant group—generally assumed to be "American." Most of the characters clearly placed in a minority group not only had subordinate roles but were characterized in stereotyped terms. There was an abundance of lazy but good-natured Negroes, Japanese houseboys and gardeners, Chinese cooks, and Jewish pawnbrokers. Although the color line in the United States during the period covered in the study was actually undergoing change, readers of popular magazines were being exposed continually to stereotyped conceptions. There was little in the way of a serious consideration of the problems confronting ethnic minorities, and representatives of the various categories were not presented in situations in which some of their shortcomings could be explained.[41] This is not to suggest that American writers were involved in a conspiracy to perpetuate stereotypes; on the contrary, much of this was undoubtedly unintentional. Many of the authors did not know any better, and those who did probably realized that accurate portrayals would strike their editors and readers as being implausible. Without malice, writers who wished merely to entertain and to earn a living inadvertently reinforced stereotypes. Since World War II there has been a concerted effort within the communications industry to present various minority peoples in less standardized forms.

Ethnic stereotypes are also reinforced in the spontaneous interchanges that take place among friends from day to day. Many of the jokes commonly told about people in ethnic minorities are pointless unless one takes the stereotyped conception for granted. Jokes about Negroes named Rastus, Sambo, or Mandy, of Jews named Abe or Cohen, or of Irishmen named Pat or Mike often provide surreptitious approbation for acts that are prohibited. Jokes about Negroes and chicken-stealing often conceal malice; they provide subtle barbs that strike telling blows.[42] Jokes are told to entertain, and those who relate them usually do not realize that they are reinforcing prevailing stereotypes with each punchline.

Members of ethnic minorities are usually aware of the stereo-

[41] Bernard Berelson and Patricia J. Salter, "Majority and Minority Americans: An Analysis of Magazine Fiction," *Public Opinion Quarterly*, X (1946), 168–90.
[42] Cf. Milton L. Barron, "A Content Analysis of Intergroup Humor," *American Sociological Review*, XV (1950), 88–94; and John H. Burma, "Humor as a Technique in Race Conflict," *ibid.*, XI (1946), 710–15.

typed conceptions that other people have of them, and some deliberately play the part in order to get what they desire. Much of what came to be regarded as the "racial" characteristics of Negroes was nothing more than the artful and adroit accommodation of their manners to what they knew to be the predilections of their white neighbors. Knowing what was expected of them, some Negroes craftily exploited this knowledge to eliminate friction and to achieve their aims.[43] In some cases members of minority groups may deliberately act out the stereotype for financial gain. After World War II some Japanese–American wrestlers discovered that they could earn a better living by playing the part of the "heavy" who committed treacherous acts. Negro actors and actresses have achieved fame by playing stereotyped roles, and stars like Stepin Fetchitt and Hattie McDaniel have been criticized for this in the Negro press. This is a difficult issue that confronts many actors in minority groups, for they would probably remain unrecognized unless they played roles that were plausible to outsiders. By achieving stardom, they demonstrate the potentialities of the people with whom they are identified; at the same time their very success reinforces the traditional meanings.[44]

Even in the most rigidly stratified society, friendships are established across the color line. Those who get to know one another intimately realize that their friends do not fit the stereotype, but the friend is usually regarded as an exception. When this happens, the stereotyped conception remains unchanged, for there can be no exception unless there is a standard form from which the deviation is to be noted. In East London (in South Africa) Mayer found that many pleasant relationships had been established between individual Africans and Europeans; it was not uncommon, however, for a Xhosa to praise the understanding and kindness of a particular foreman or employer and still fulminate against the "white man's cruelty." Similarly, many Europeans who complained of the "natives" in abstract terms spoke warmly of particular individuals they knew.[45] The same process is found even where personal ties are not involved. In a community in which Negroes are excluded from technical positions

---

[43] Cf. Robert R. Moton, *What the Negro Thinks* (New York: Doubleday, 1929), pp. 27–28.

[44] Cf. Buell G. Gallagher, *American Caste and the Negro College* (New York: Columbia University Press, 1938), pp. 368–71.

[45] Philip Mayer, *Townsmen or Tribesmen* (London: Oxford University Press, 1961), p. 51.

on the ground that they are incapable of intellectual work of a high order, a competent Negro who had proved himself elsewhere may be hired. In such cases, however, the new man acquires a reputation of being a genius, a person so extraordinary that he is regarded as a freak. Although he may be accepted, the door remains closed to other Negroes. Thus, even the presence of unusual individuals does not challenge deeply ingrained stereotypes.[46]

Summary and Conclusion

Once a system of ethnic stratification has become established, it tends to be self-sustaining. The norms of conduct enjoy a high degree of consensus, and most people do not even consider the possibility of deviating from them. Mankind is assumed to be naturally divided into the prevailing categories, and members of the dominant group believe that they enjoy their ascendancy by virtue of their superiority. They look upon people in the subordinate strata, not in hatred, but with condescension. Stereotyped conceptions are perpetuated in spite of their inaccuracies because most people do not get close enough to outsiders to test them; social distance is maintained. The critical examination of stereotypes is especially difficult because the beliefs are shaped and continually reaffirmed in a variety of activities having nothing to do with ethnic identity; reinforcement occurs in contexts in which attention is focused upon other matters. In a stratified society a great many acts are predicated upon a recognition of differences, and the mere performance of these acts in customary ways supports the beliefs upon which the distinctions rest.

Reformers often view the color line as something that is deliberately created by vicious men who hate the people they rule. Although there are some occasions when cruel devices are intentionally instituted in order to protect unfair advantages, this is the exception rather than the rule. By and large, the conventional norms that constitute the color line persist, not because of the machinations of evil men, but because most men are moral. People, in dominant and minority groups alike, try to live in the ways they regard as decent and just; they do the accepted things. To an outside observer some of the beliefs on which these traditional procedures rest may appear absurd,

[46] Cf. Hughes and Hughes, *op. cit.*, p. 172.

nothing more than convenient justifications for the advantages enjoyed by the ruling elite. But most of the participants in a stable social system do not see things in this light. Questions about the unfairness of unequal rewards arise in situations in which a color line is breaking down, as in the United States today, but they are rare in stable societies. As incredible as it may seem to most Americans, systems of ethnic stratification are upheld for long periods by the willing support and cooperation of the people who are being subjugated.

CHAPTER 11

The Accommodation

of Stable Minorities

Until quite recently every major city in the United States had a number of esoteric settlements bearing colorful names—among them, Bronzeville, Dago Hill, Finntown, Little Bohemia, Little Tokyo, Polonia, and Wop Roost. The people who lived in them not only looked different but often behaved differently. They ate strange foods, dressed in odd costumes, maintained different standards of sanitation, and spoke a different language. Peculiar smells and sounds emanated from these areas; some of the streets appeared dark and foreboding. Storefronts often bore unintelligible signs, and even from the benign standpoint of a curious tourist they sometimes appeared sinister. Segregated ethnic communities apparently are as old as city life itself, and such cultural islands are found throughout the world. There are the Christian millets in the Moslem world and the Jewish ghettos in European cities. Even in colonial areas where the natives far outnumber their rulers, there are special native quarters, like the Casbah in Algiers, which are understood to be reserved for people of a certain kind.

For a great many people in ethnic minorities these segregated communities provide a haven of refuge in what may otherwise seem an unfriendly world. Millions of men and women live their entire lives within the confines of such settlements, learning of the outside world only from hearsay. Most of these colonies are transitory and disappear after a few generations. But some ethnic groups—such as the Armenians, the Jews, and the Parsees—have managed to retain their culture and identity for centuries by succoring one another in such concentrations. Interest in this chapter centers upon the typical behavior patterns that characterize minority groups in stable, well-established systems of stratification.

The Social World of Minority Groups

In conquered areas the subjugated groups usually outnumber their rulers. Under these circumstances the conquerors are the ones who establish their exclusive settlements, such as the International Settlement in old Shanghai. In these surroundings, served by native labor, the rulers enjoy a different way of life. They establish various institutions like those of their motherland to bring a "bit of home" into their lives. They use their own language and require those who serve them to learn it. Only a very small proportion of the people in minority groups come into direct contact with their rulers. The contacts that do take place are formal—employer and laborer, master and servant, missionary and convert, teacher and student, doctor and patient—and the participants interact only as representatives of ethnic categories. When the required services have been rendered, those of minority status usually return home.

The cultural differences between the rulers and their subordinates are often quite noticeable, and this distinction is perpetuated through segregation. Most conquerors interfere as little as possible with the culture of their subject peoples, as long as their practices are not threatening or offensive. Generally subject groups are forced to participate in a new economic system and to accept new political institutions. Certain mores of the dominant group must also be accepted, at least in public. Europeans in tropical colonies, for example, forced the natives to abandon nudity, polygamy, and certain crisis rites that they found bizarre, and the British in India abolished the suttee—the practice of burning widows on the funeral pyre of their husbands. Beyond this minimum, however, meddling with the indigenous culture has been found to arouse widespread resentment and add unnecessarily to the problem of maintaining order. Thus, while acknowledging foreign rule, some minorities have been able to retain their heritage and way of life for many centuries. Some changes, of course, are inevitable; culture represents a collective adjustment to life conditions, and subordinate peoples must revise some of their customary procedures to cope with the modifications resulting from the conquest.

Immigrants who settle in well-established communities are usually outnumbered by the host population; then, the immigrants establish separate quarters. Although segregation is sometimes forced by external hostility, in most cases the formation of ethnic islands is voluntary. People who conceive of themselves as living in the midst of an alien world usually prefer to form a closed society. They maintain their exclusiveness and often reject the attempts of outsiders to participate in their affairs. Immigrants do their work wherever they are required to go, but at night they return to their refuge. Even those whose employment requires their living elsewhere maintain their ties and return on holidays and on special occasions. In such a segregated area, members of a minority group can speak their own language; it is often the only place where they can feel "at home." Most persons in minority groups prefer one another's company, feel uncomfortable in the presence of outsiders, and engage in leisure activities largely among themselves. Even among American Negroes, after several centuries of contact, life goes on almost exclusively within a separate social world.

The culture that develops in immigrant communities is usually a hybrid culture. It contains some of the institutions of the "old country," some of the practices copied from the dominant group, and some procedures that are distinctive adjustments to the new environment. The customs that are transplanted from the motherland are rarely brought over intact. Most noticeable of these are language, food habits, and ritualistic salutations. These patterns are generally so deeply ingrained that they can be transformed only with great difficulty. But some acculturation is inevitable. Sometimes the people must do things in the manner prescribed by the dominant group, and sometimes they simply recognize the superiority of a new practice and adopt it. Typical institutions also arise in response to the special problems of immigrants. There are usually several first-aid institutions, established by the better-educated immigrants to meet the practical needs of their fellows—boarding houses, banks, steamship agencies, labor organizations, and real estate agencies. Mutual aid and benefit societies are also founded to provide sickness benefits and to pay for burials. Nationalistic organizations also arise to serve the motherland, reaffirm nationalistic sentiments, and improve the status of the minority group in the new land. Special institutions—press, theater, school, and church—also develop. A new culture arises out of the meaningful exchange of experiences among those who share a common fate in a strange land.[1]

Culture is the product of communication, and *a minority group develops a distinctive outlook to the extent that it has its own communication channels*. There is a wide range of variation in this; some minorities are so different from their rulers that the people live in separate social worlds, while others are only slightly different. Most well-established minorities have their own communication channels, which supplement those of the community as a whole. Of particular importance is the use of a different language. In immigrant settlements the language of the motherland is used, although with a number of neologisms. In conquered areas the natives generally continue to use their own vernacular for some time; the survival of languages such as Gaelic, Polish, and Hebrew reveals the reluctance of subject peoples to part with their mother tongue. Even when almost everyone in the minority has learned the language of the dominant group, special words and phrases are used with nuances of meaning generally unknown to outsiders. Within each ethnic community, then, there tends to develop a special universe of discourse. This is a matter of great importance, for human experiences are classified in terms of words. Just as direct translations of literature from one language to another are not always possible, certain experiences are incomprehensible to people who speak another tongue. Thus, the use of different lan-

[1] Cf. Coughlin, *op. cit.*, pp. 32–66; Elena Padilla, *Up from Puerto Rico* (New York: Columbia University Press, 1958); Park and Miller, *op. cit.*, pp. 119–44; Moses Rischin, *The Promised City: New York's Jews, 1870–1914* (Cambridge: Harvard University Press, 1962); and Caroline Ware, "Ethnic Communities," *Encyclopedia of the Social Sciences*, Vol. V, pp. 607–13.

guages results in the formation of diverse outlooks. The crucial importance of differential communication is revealed by the survival of the Tewa Indians, who have been living with the Hopi in Arizona since the end of the seventeenth century. According to legend, the Tewa moved into the area to help the Hopi ward off attacking Utes. After their victory the Hopi refused to give them what they had promised, and a curse was invoked that sealed the Tewa language and way of life from the Hopi forever. Ceremonial practices are still carefully guarded. The Hopi who live among them may actually know the Tewa idiom, but their attempts to use a few words are met with such mocking laughter that they do not continue. Most Tewa are still convinced that it is impossible for a Hopi to learn their tongue. Unlike other tribes that have joined the Hopi, they have retained their culture, their sense of identity, and their sense of superiority.[2]

The separation of educational facilities reinforces differences in outlook. In many stratified societies children in minority groups are educated in very different ways. In some European colonies educational facilities were not provided for the natives. The children of the colonists attended special schools in which they received an education roughly equivalent to that of respectable people in the motherland; some of the wealthier children were even sent there for advanced training. But the natives continued to be socialized in traditional ways, and the gap between the groups was perpetuated. In the United States education is compulsory for everyone, but in the South most Negroes are still required to attend separate schools. Segregation persists even though it has been ruled illegal. In the North there is no legal separation; however, since pupils are assigned to schools by place of residence and most Negroes live in segregated areas, in fact most of the schools are segregated.[3] The outlook that is formed in segregated schools is different, for in their informal contacts students learn from one another many distinctive values. Even when children of different ethnic categories attend the same schools, what they get out of their experience may be quite different. In Guatemala, for example, Ladino children expect to go on to secondary schools and from there on to lucrative work. But Indian children realize that they will quit in a few years; they can only hope

---

[2] Edward P. Dozier, "Resistance to Acculturation and Assimilation in an Indian Pueblo," *American Anthropologist*, LIII (1951), 56–66.

[3] Cf. C. S. Johnson, *op. cit.*, pp. 173–85.

to learn to say a few simple words, to write their names, and to count in Spanish so that they will not be cheated.[4] Many minority groups set up their own schools in which children can be taught their parents' language and heritage. To the extent that the youngsters can be persuaded to accept these offerings, they form conceptions of themselves that differ from those of outsiders. The Jews, though widely dispersed, have retained their sense of identity and their culture through the inculcation of a religious heritage. The traditional method of teaching—repetition and rote learning—provided a reliable medium for the continuation of Jewish traditions. The hostility of the outside world has also contributed to group solidarity, for wherever Jews have been given opportunities outside the ghetto, this special education has been forsaken for richer opportunities elsewhere.[5]

Since the development of the media of mass communication, many minority groups have been served by their own newspapers. In the United States almost every concentration of immigrants is serviced by at least one newspaper. Most immigrants probably read more here than they did at home. Peasant communities are fairly stable, and gossip is sufficient for making adjustments. But in a turbulent metropolis it is necessary to keep informed. A laborer may suddenly find himself unemployed unless he is up with the news, and this information has to be supplied in a language he can understand. In addition, there are many events of no interest to the larger public that are of special concern to those within the community.[6] In the same way the Negro press provides a mirror in which American Negroes can see themselves. It gives a picture of the world of white people quite different from that provided by the metropolitan dailies.[7] All minority presses tend to be provincial, seeing events exclusively from the narrow standpoint of a single group.

If sufficient news is not forthcoming from legitimate channels, it circulates by way of clandestine contacts. During the Civil War, for example, the slaves were able to keep track of the movements of the armies. Meetings were held at various plantations to which they could slip away in the night. As the good news came over the "grapevine" that all slaves would soon be free, there was more singing than

---

[4] Tumin, *op. cit.*, p. 182.
[5] Wirth, "Education for Survival: The Jews," *op. cit.*
[6] Cf. Park, *The Immigrant Press and Its Control*, *op. cit.*
[7] Cf. Myrdal, *op. cit.*, pp. 908–24; and Frazier, *Black Bourgeoisie*, *op. cit.*, pp. 174–94.

usual.[8] Informal communication channels play an important part in the formation of minority group perspectives.

Diversity of outlook is also assured by differential association. Members of ethnic minorities associate primarily with others of their kind; contacts with outsiders are categorical and impersonal. Even when opportunities for contact are available, there is lack of interest. The economic and educational limitations ordinarily associated with low status often result in a lack of confidence. Thus, there is a suspicion of anything that is strange and a tendency of minority peoples to withdraw even when such action is not demanded of them.[9] From childhood they had been told of the crimes and indignities perpetrated by members of the dominant group. Such incidents are actually quite rare, but the frequency with which the tales are repeated, often with embellishments, creates a general impression of constant danger. All people, including those in minority groups, feel comfortable only among those with whom they identify. What is sometimes called "clannishness" becomes more understandable once we realize that ethnic groups consist of people who think differently. Members of different ethnic groups find it difficult to relax in one another's presence because they cannot anticipate intuitively what the other person is likely to do. Hence, they must always be on guard—partly in self-defense and partly not to give offense. Ethnocentrism is an effective barrier to communication across the color line.

The distinctive perspective developed in each minority group is perpetuated through selective perception. The media of mass communication are generally available to those in minorities who are bilingual, but there is a selective sensitivity to news. One of the characteristics of minority peoples is their extreme preoccupation with the affairs within their own world; they have a detailed knowledge of the transactions within their own group but only a vague notion of what goes on outside. Among the Molokans in Los Angeles, for example, there was generally little interest in the items reported in the metropolitan dailies. A Molokan could not raise his status among his fellows by getting his name or picture in the newspapers; if anything, he lost status for getting into trouble. Hence, news of the

---

[8] Doyle, *op. cit.*, pp. 105–06.
[9] Cf. Genevieve Knupfer, "Portrait of the Underdog," *Public Opinion Quarterly*, XI (1947), 103–14; and C. S. Johnson, *op. cit.*, pp. 267–93.

outside was largely ignored, and the people learned of what was important to them through gossip.[10] Furthermore, there is a tendency to interpret reports solely or largely in terms of their implications for their own group; outside events arouse interest only insofar as they have direct and obvious bearing upon the minority group. Even when the same events are being considered, they are seen in a different light. During World War II, for example, Negro and white soldiers in the U.S. Army tended to have similar attitudes toward all matters unrelated to ethnic identity. However, Negroes often defined situations in "racial" terms even where ethnic considerations were irrelevant; many complaints common to all soldiers were seen by Negroes as instances of "discrimination." Although Negro soldiers generally supported the war effort and questions of national loyalty rarely arose, there was considerably more cynicism among them about the noble objectives of the Allied Powers. There were doubts over whether their participation in the war would actually improve their lot. For many Negroes there were two struggles—the fight against the Axis powers and the struggle to elevate their own status in line with the avowed goals of the war. It is not surprising that some segments of the Negro community were not wholeheartedly behind the war effort.[11] As a consequence of selective sensitivity to news and an interpretation of it from a special standpoint, members of each ethnic minority continue to use a perspective different from that of others in the same community.

Since minority groups are drawn into the economic system of the larger community, inevitably some of their numbers will have to work for outsiders. Their job often assumes a significance for them, however, that it does not have for their co-workers. In a study of Bantu-speaking clerks in South Africa, Sherwood found that the European supervisors tended to see their charges in terms of a stereotyped conception. They evaluated them in terms of their obedience to European authorities—whether they were submissive, self-effacing, and methodical in their work. But the clerks themselves were concerned more with the services they could render to the Bantu-

---

[10] Pauline V. Young, *The Pilgrims of Russian Town* (Chicago: University of Chicago Press, 1932), pp. 88–90. Cf. Herbert J. Gans, *The Urban Villagers* (New York: The Free Press of Glencoe, 1962), pp. 181–96; and Thomas and Znaniecki, *op. cit.*, Vol. II, pp. 1367–96.

[11] Samuel A. Stouffer, *et al.*, *The American Soldier* (Princeton: Princeton University Press, 1949), Vol. I, pp. 486–599.

speaking public, and they evaluated their work in terms of being helpful, sympathetic, tactful, and patient. They were aware of the expectations of their supervisors, but they were more responsive to the expectations of their own people.[12] Certain occupations are highly coveted by members of minority groups, even though they may not command much respect among others. To a poor Negro who is exceptionally skilled in fisticuffs, for example, boxing is not just a sport; it becomes a means of escaping the slums and moving into an elite class. Among American Negroes professional athletes have an honored position that they do not enjoy in the larger society. Within each minority group, then, there develops a somewhat different status hierarchy, and many persons not highly regarded by outsiders may be accorded considerable deference. Bootleggers, money-lenders, smugglers, gambling-house operators, dope peddlers—all despised in the larger community—may enjoy high status in a minority world.

Although members of minority groups may perform menial tasks when employed by the dominant group, their standing in their own social world is usually not so humble. Since the overall status of the group is clearly subordinate, a man who works as a servant or a doorman expects to defer to outsiders. In his own social world, however, he may be a high-ranking official in an important fraternal association or the leader of a nationalistic movement. Within the segregated community a man lives a life in which he is his own master in a world in which men are equal. When he returns from work, he assumes in the privacy of his own home the dignified role of *pater familias;* he expects to be obeyed and respected as a patriarch. A person's prestige within the minority group is more or less independent of his rank in the outside world. Southerners have sometimes referred to Negroes as "Dr. Jekyll and Mr. Hyde" in contrasting their dual roles—the one which they are forced to play before white people and the one they assume among their own people.[13] Seen in this light the preference of many persons in subordinate groups for company of their own kind becomes more understandable.

Members of segregated ethnic minorities live by a distinctive set of values, and they generally enforce their own social codes.

[12] Rae Sherwood, "The Bantu Clerk: A Study of Role Expectations," *Journal of Social Psychology,* **XLVII** (1958), 285–316.

[13] Dollard, *op. cit.,* pp. 257–58. Cf. Marian W. Beth, "The Elite and the Elites," *American Journal of Sociology,* **XLVII** (1942), 746–55; and Tumin, *op. cit.,* p. 171.

The more a community is isolated, the more easily can leader exercise control over the conduct of its members. Many behavio patterns that seem incomprehensible to outsiders make sense when seen in terms of the customs of the settlement. A strong sense of consciousness of kind usually develops; those in well-established minorities claim the unconditional loyalty of everyone in the group, and in turn, when a member is in need, they stand united behind him. Each individual knows this, and it gives him a sense of security.[14] One important consequence of this strong sense of identification is that other members of the group come to constitute one's reference group. The minority group becomes the primary audience for whom one performs. The aspirations of young people in minorities must be seen in terms of the expectations imputed to their kind. When a young man who graduates from a professional school with highest honors declines an opportunity to launch a career as a specialist and returns to his home to enter a humble practice, outsiders are usually puzzled. But he is not concerned with the opinions of people outside his social world; he is acting for those with whom he identifies. The values of "barbarians" may be recognized, especially by those who are better educated, but they are only of slight interest. In immigrant communities many are only sojourners who regard their stay in the country as a temporary interlude during which to earn money; these people are usually insensitive to the views of the dominant group.[15] Individuals who are so responsive to the prevailing values of an enclave are effectively controlled by it; they may even engage in behavior that is illegal in the outside world. Concern over ostracism, gossip, or ridicule forces them to comply with the demands of their kind.

Most minority groups have their own regulatory institutions to coerce those who deviate from their customs, although informal social sanctions are generally sufficient. Since many of the conventional norms of minority groups differ from the dominant group's customs and some may even be illegal, offenders are usually not reported to the police. In general, people in minority groups do not appeal to outside agencies, even when a serious offense has been committed.

[14] P. Young, op. cit., pp. 74–75.
[15] Cf. Paul C. P. Siu, "The Sojourner," American Journal of Sociology, LVIII (1952), 34–44; and Kian M. Kwan, "Minority Members and Their Assimilation," Ohio University Review, III (1961), 63–67.

Among the overseas Chinese, for example, there are family associations that exercise considerable control over their members. Quarrels are often settled by a council of elders whose decisions are enforced by men entrusted with such duties.[16] To some extent all minority groups practice self-rule and punish offenses by traditional procedures.

In some cases the ruling body of a minority group is officially recognized by the government, and responsibilities are delegated to it. In the ancient Hellenistic cities of Asia Minor and North Africa the *gerousia*, the council of elders of the Jewish communities, operated along side the Greek city councils. The Seleucid and Ptolemaic kings of Egypt used these self-governing agencies for the collection of taxes. In the Arab world each millet was given responsibility for policing itself; in a sense, there was extraterritoriality. Jewish officials were given recognition under the caliphates as intermediaries in fiscal matters and as interpreters of the law.[17] In Aragon and Castile rabbis had great power; they tried criminal and civil suits and sometimes even imposed the death sentence. Many kings and central governments in Europe found this practice useful. Since local officials sometimes regarded such autonomy as an infringement of their authority, there were times when the central government had to protect the Jews against them. Not until the rise of the modern state and their emancipation from the ghettos did most Jews renounce their autonomy and begin to regard themselves more as a separate religious group.[18] Similarly, in many of the European colonies in Africa the government recognized existing chiefdoms and allowed the native leaders to continue their rule, limited by certain laws imposed from above.

Reconciliation to Subordinate Status

The various ethnic groups in a community, whether they like it or not, become jointly involved in a common economic system. Although they live in separate social worlds, to some extent they must

[16] Cf. William Hoy, *The Chinese Six Companies* (San Francisco: Chinese Consolidated Benevolent Association, 1942); and Purcell, *op. cit.*

[17] Hourani, *op. cit.*, pp. 113–14; Toynbee, *op. cit.*, Vol. VIII, pp. 184–86; and Tritton, *op. cit.*

[18] Simon Dubnow, "Jewish Autonomy," *Encyclopedia of the Social Sciences*, Vol. VIII, pp. 391–94. Cf. S. Davis, *op. cit.*, pp. 102–09.

cooperate. Members of minority groups often become dependent upon existing arrangements for their livelihood; furthermore, there may be other compensations for their low status. For example, in spite of the harsh repressive measures used by the Japanese after their conquest of Manchuria in 1931, most Chinese acquiesced to the puppet regime. Many benefited from the industrial development; the propertied classes saw their new rulers as a safeguard against Communism, and those who were conservative welcomed the revival of the traditional teaching of Confucius that accompanied Japanese rule.[19] After the Zulu had been put down in 1880, they found that there were certain advantages to British rule—abolition of tribal warfare, aid in fighting epidemics, famine relief, and greater employment opportunities for earning money to purchase coveted goods.[20] Many people in minority groups, then, are able to pursue satisfactory careers, and some may even develop a vested interest in the status quo.

Although rebellious individuals are to be found in all groups, most people in stable minorities become reconciled to their subordinate status, at least for a time. Some are convinced that "this is the way things are"; for others it is a strategy for survival.[21] Some people are fatalistic: they not only regard their own status as inevitable but even acknowledge the superiority of the dominant group. The system of stratification seems to be part of the natural order; like the weather, one may complain about it but has to put up with it. They are so accustomed to their subordinate roles that they would not know how to act if suddenly given their freedom. When emancipated after the Civil War, the slaves were overjoyed, but many of them remained with their old masters. There was little else to do. They were highly skilled in performing specific tasks on a plantation and not trained to compete on the open market for jobs; in many cases their only contacts were with the people on the plantation. If they had been treated well, they felt that they were better off staying where they were.[22] Similarly, when the Belgians conquered the Congo, they launched an energetic suppression of African serfdom. They freed the Lendu, who had been enslaved by the Alur and the

19 F. C. Jones, *op. cit.*, pp. 52–54.
20 Max Gluckman, *Custom and Conflict in Africa* (Glencoe, Ill.: Free Press, 1955), pp. 140–51.
21 Cf. Dollard, *op. cit.*, pp. 250–66.
22 Cf. Frazier, *The Negro in the United States, op. cit.*, pp. 109–22.

Hema. But many of the Lendu refused to leave and had to be forced out of bondage. After a few generations of freedom the Lendu now insist that they had always been free and cherish their independence.[23] The extent to which members of minority groups are fatalistic in accepting their subordinate status apparently depends upon the flexibility of the system of stratification. In rigidly stratified societies people in minorities often know of no other way of life. But where there are possibilities of upward social mobility, acceptance of low status is not quite so complete. At least outwardly, however, there is a tacit acceptance of subordination.

But the fact that minority peoples accept their subordinate status does not necessarily mean that they conceive of themselves as inferior human beings. Overt obeisance is not necessarily matched by inward assent. This is especially true where the culture of the minority group remains undisturbed. They form conceptions of themselves from the standpoint of their own culture, and because of their ethnocentrism they find themselves adequate and others wanting. They look upon their lowly status as a temporary inconvenience that is the result of past mistakes, a situation that will someday be corrected. In colonial areas many assume that the intruder will eventually leave, and immigrants often dream of returning to their motherland with great wealth. Members of the dominant group are viewed as an unfortunate nuisance. Their power is acknowledged; that they may be able to do some things more effectively is grudgingly conceded, and some of their practices may even be imitated. But in private these outsiders are often referred to with derogatory epithets. In Madagascar, for example, many natives were dependent upon French colonists, but they did not feel inferior. For the Malagasy his world was with his peers, not with the European interlopers. His meaningful world was made up of people of his kind, and he left it only occasionally to deal with Frenchmen.[24]

There are some ethnic minorities that acknowledge their own inferiority. People who have occupied a lowly station for many generations and are unfamiliar with egalitarian ideologies cannot conceive of themselves as being as deserving as those of high rank. In the antebellum South many slaves saw themselves through their master's eyes. Many conceived of themselves as natural servants and took

[23] Southall, *op. cit.*, pp. 152–53.
[24] Mannoni, *op. cit.*, p. 62.

pride in the family standing of their master, looking down upon slaves of lesser households. This orientation arose from the unusual history of the group. Ancestral traditions were broken soon after the slaves were brought to the United States, where they were forced to work among strangers, to learn a new language, and to mate with people from other parts of Africa. Ties with the ancestral past were severed; collective memories were disrupted, and there was no perspective to use other than that of the dominant group.[25] Many outcastes in India were not troubled by their degradation; they had no serious desire to rise, nor did they believe in the possibility of rising. For centuries they had lived by the Hindu faith and were resigned to their fate.[26] In Guatemala the Ladino lives off the Indians' labor, uses military power for his own ends, exercises rights over Indian women that he does not permit of his own, forces their deference, excludes them from his company, and does not allow them to eat at his table. Yet, the Indians express only incidental and inconsequential resentment. They conceive of themselves as poor and hardworking. They contend that things are as they are because God intended them to be so.[27] As strange as this may seem to Americans, who assume that everyone desires upward mobility, there are many minority groups that accept their inferior status and become eager recipients of paternalism in return for their subservence.

On the other hand, there are ethnic minorities that conceive of themselves as intrinsically superior to their barbarian rulers. The Egyptians of the days of Herodotus manifested the same feeling toward Greeks as many Asians showed toward European colonists —a feeling of inherent superiority. This is bound to be the attitude of those whose civilization is deeply rooted in the past toward peoples whose ascendancy is recent and insecure, those who are still striving for a settled mode of cultural expression. When the Egyptians were conquered by the Greeks, they had to submit to Greek rule. They conformed externally and even learned the Greek language. They recognized many of the superior features of Greek culture and technology, but they looked upon the newcomers as upstarts who

[25] Doyle, op. cit., pp. 68–80. Cf. Frazier, The Negro in the United States, op. cit., pp. 3–21. For a contrary view, see Melville Herskovits, The Myth of the Negro Past (New York: Harper, 1941).

[26] J. C. Heinrich, The Psychology of a Suppressed People (London: Allen & Unwin, 1937), p. 3.

[27] Tumin, op. cit., pp. 169–70.

did not have a long history.[28] The Indonesians in Surinam (Dutch Guiana) have low status. They are poor and uneducated, and they accept dirty tasks such as sewer-cleaning that others refuse to do. In spite of this, however, they take pride in the refinement of the traditions of their motherland. They look down upon the Creoles because of their mixed ancestry, calling them *blanda item*— "black white men"—an Indonesian epithet for Eurasians. They are equally contemptuous of the Hindu population, dismissing them as "coolies." [29] In spite of their lowly station such people cling stubbornly to their belief in their own superiority, and they buttress their forlorn hopes with tales of the glorious past.

The socialization of a child in a subordinate group differs from that of others in that he must learn that he is different and that he cannot expect the same privileges as many other people. Sooner or later each child in a minority group learns how human beings are classified and where he is located within this scheme. Many learn about ethnic differences in the same manner as they learn about sex, informally from their peers; they therefore absorb the popular beliefs of the community. In one study 100 Negro children in the South were asked how they first discovered that they were Negroes. They learned by being treated differently in a variety of contexts—a store, a restaurant, the home of a neighbor, while playing with white children, a train, a circus. Some learned when they were taunted by other children; others learned when they had to attend separate schools. Several children learned when they were admonished by their parents not to hurt white children.[30] Parents in minority groups often dread the day when they must tell their children and wonder how to go about it. They want their offspring to develop respect for themselves and to have a healthy outlook on life. The youngsters cannot help but notice the inequities. Like all children they first assume that their parents are omnipotent; they demand fair play, and they are disillusioned when results cannot be produced. Some children learn of their lowly status by observing the submissive behavior of their parents. For a few children learning their ethnic identity can be a traumatic experience. Many parents provide some kind of his-

[28] S. Davis, *op. cit.*, p. 27.

[29] Justus M. van der Kroef, "The Indonesian Minority in Surinam," *American Sociological Review*, XVI (1951), 672–79.

[30] Edward K. Weaver, "How Do Children Discover They Are Negroes?" *Understanding the Child*, XXIV (1955), 108–12.

torical account, real or fictitious, in terms of which their subordination is explained. In colonial areas youngsters are told of a war fought unfairly by the invaders, and immigrants often boast of the glory of the "old country." Negro children are told in family circles of their slave ancestors and of their mistreatment by white people. In these ways the children are inculcated with the ideology of the minority group.

Identification symbols become the focus of attention, and young people in minority groups often become very sensitive about them. When inherited marks are the key symbols of differentiation, they assume special significance. Once a Negro child realizes that he is deprived of what others can have because of the color of his skin, he wonders whether blackness in itself is bad. Being told that "God loves us all" is often not enough. Studies reveal that Negro children with darker complexions become aware of ethnic differences much younger than the others. Working with drawings of different colors, Clark and Clark found that darker-skinned children used the colored pictures to identify themselves more frequently than those who were lighter.[31] They also found that the concepts of ethnic differences as indicated by skin color and of the low evaluation of darkness develop gradually from year to year and is fixed by the age of seven.[32] In another study Negro and white children in Philadelphia were given dolls—one black and one white—and were asked to dress them in appropriate clothing and to place them in toy houses. The children in both categories placed the dark dolls in inferior housing, regardless of where they themselves lived in the city.[33] Studies of American Negro children show, therefore, that at a relatively early age they learn to identify themselves in terms of skin color and to place themselves at a lower station in the community.

As they become older, members of ethnic minorities begin to realize that people in the dominant group have a number of beliefs about them that are incorrect. At first they may protest, but in time most of them conclude that outsiders are prejudiced, and a few may

[31] Kenneth B. and Mamie P. Clark, "Skin Color as a Factor in Racial Identification of Negro Pre-School Children," *Journal of Social Psychology*, XI (1940), 159–69.

[32] Kenneth B. and Mamie P. Clark, "Emotional Factors in Racial Identification and Preference in Negro Children," *Journal of Negro Education*, XIX (1950), 341–50.

[33] Marian J. Radke and Helen G. Trager, "Children's Perceptions of the Social Roles of Negroes and Whites," *Journal of Psychology*, XXIX (1950), 3–33.

even acknowledge that some of the traits that make up the stereotype are actually found in their group. At the same time they acquire a stereotyped conception of the dominant group. A study made in New Orleans of the Negro's conception of the white man reveals a fairly consistent set of beliefs. White men were regarded as people who feel superior, who hate Negroes and want to keep them down, who are brutal and deceitful. White people think they "know" the Negro but underestimate his ability; they judge all Negroes by the "worst type of Negro." White people who call themselves "liberal" do nothing but talk, giving lip service to democratic principles. But the conception was not entirely negative. White people were credited with superior mechanical ability, ambition, intellectual capacity, shrewdness, businesslike mentality, and group solidarity.[34] Long before adulthood, then, most American Negroes have some comprehension—not always accurate—of their standing in the community. Especially in the South they learn that a "good nigger" is expected to be obsequious and humble. This role is learned by observation and imitation, and it is a mask that comes off as soon as Negroes are among themselves.[35] This understanding serves as the basis for bitter jokes as well as for strategies to exploit the privileged.

In general, members of ethnic minorities try to avoid direct contact with the dominant group. They are so unaccustomed to such meetings that they experience much discomfort in the presence of an outsider—even a very friendly one who has proved himself a benefactor. Although they may trust a particular individual in the dominant group, they approach the group as a whole with suspicion. In Guatemala, Indians avoid Ladinos whenever possible. They want to avoid being ordered about at their whim and fancy, being "drafted" for disagreeable labor, being subjected to unpleasantness over attempts to exploit women.[36] Similarly, most American Negroes try to stay away from white people. There is a feeling that they are not welcome. They are uncertain over the reception they will receive, and they want to avoid trouble. They confine their contacts to those that are unavoidable, do what they must as quickly as pos-

[34] Tilman C. Cothran, "White Stereotypes in Fiction by Negroes," *Phylon*, **XI** (1950), 252–56; and "Negro Conceptions of White People," *op. cit.* Cf. G. Jahoda, *op. cit.*, pp. 54–57.

[35] Cf. Powdermaker, "The Channeling of Negro Aggression by the Cultural Process," *op. cit.*, p. 757.

[36] Tumin, *op. cit.*, p. 171.

sible, and then return to their own kind. Such defensive insulation usually follows a succession of rebuffs and unpleasant experiences. Thus, people in minority groups move freely and act naturally within their own group, and they manage to put up with rebuffs from outsiders and to discount them. They are thereby able to protect their pride.

Tacit acceptance of subordination is reflected in the manner in which children are taught the responsibilities of their station—in some cases to serve others faithfully. In many families children learn that a good person is one who knows his limitations and does not develop unrealistic aspirations. They are trained to exercise restraint and are warned of the dire consequences of failing to do so. If a child announces his aspirations for a position that is beyond his reach, his parents and friends discourage him, sometimes even resorting to ridicule. Should he persist, he will quickly discover that he will not be taken seriously when he applies for a job for which he is not regarded as suited. His friends accuse him of overreaching, and even the very ambitious soon realize that their path is blocked by immovable barriers. Children are taught to take pride in doing their work well, whatever it may be. If they are to be house servants, they are taught the intricate details of doing such work. Over and over, they are reminded that one can develop self-respect through personal integrity. Thus, many patterns of differentiation are maintained by social control within the minority group. In many American cities Negroes assume that they will not be accepted and do not bother to apply for positions not customarily held by Negroes. They gain a sense of security from knowing what is expected, and they avoid trouble by staying in their "place." By following the line of least resistance, they win security for themselves and inadvertently support the color line.[37]

Even when upward mobility into the larger community is possible, it is usually discouraged. The unusually gifted are encouraged to remain among their kind, even when the outside world may offer greater rewards. Where differences between the categories are great, members of minorities who are too successful risk getting "out of place." They are embarrassed even when they are accepted. Whenever such unusual individuals get into trouble, there are fears

[37] Cf. Frank F. Lee, "Social Controls in the Race Relations Pattern of a Small New England Town," *Social Forces*, **XXXIII** (1954), 36–40.

that the few might endanger the entire group, and they are condemned as "troublemakers." This accounts for some of the carping criticism directed at persons who stand out. Autobiographical accounts of men who have somehow managed to climb out of the lowest rungs of a stratified society frequently reveal the extent to which they were taunted for their ambitions and discouraged by people who loved them. Many of their neighbors dismissed them as insane, and their parents spent many hours worrying about their fate. Where the physical differences are not great, it is sometimes possible to change one's ethnic identity and status by leaving the area in which he is known. Since the Eta are indistinguishable in appearance from other Japanese, why do they not go to large cities and drop their stigma? For one thing, the economic sacrifice would be considerable. Many are skilled craftsmen in the leather industry; outside their settlement they would have to compete for unskilled jobs without benefit of family connections. Furthermore, there are many tales among the Eta of the disastrous fate of those who had been discovered. After sacrificing so much to establish themselves, they had lost their job, and sometimes their family. Some who had attempted escape return to tell of their mistreatment. Courage is required to face the hostility of outsiders, and most people prefer to stay home with their own kind.[38]

Minority groups in stable settings usually struggle against both assimilation and intermarriage. Intermarriage with the dominant group is opposed by almost all minorities, although the intensity of opposition varies considerably. In Guatemala Tumin found that many Indians did not object to their children marrying a Ladino, but they felt that it was unwise. They argued that Indians were poor and needed partners who could work along with them, but a Ladino would not know how to work.[39] Other groups are very strict, and the prohibitions apply in particular to attractive young women. Women in minorities who marry into the dominant group or who become concubines or mistresses may enjoy many material advantages, and their children may have even greater opportunities. But they are generally shunned as prostitutes by the people among whom they grew up; they may even be disowned by their own families. Especially strict are the Indonesians, who are proud of their cultural

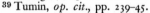

38 Donoghue, *op. cit.* Cf. Wirth, *The Ghetto, op. cit.,* pp. 263–81.
39 Tumin, *op. cit.,* pp. 239–45.

tradition. In Surinam, where their status is very low, marriages between Javanese women and Creole or Hindu men do occur. But the women place themselves beyond the pale in the eyes of their people, and even their offspring are condemned as *blanda item*.[40] Members of minority groups, like others, believe that each ethnic category is a different species of mankind; they therefore believe that mixture is contrary to nature.

Although it is commonly believed that the color line is maintained by pressure from above, in many cases there is far greater pressure within minority groups to preserve their integrity. Members of many ethnic minorities oppose segregation as a matter of principle, but they have no desire to mingle with outsiders. Even when there is no external hostility, many voluntarily congregate in their own settlement. They fear the contamination of their group and its culture. Many minority groups have no desire to emulate the practices of the dominant group, and parallel cultures may persist for many generations.[41] Sometimes special tactics are used. The Hutterites, a religious cult that migrated to the northwestern part of the United States and Western Canada, have not been able to maintain the degree of isolation that was possible in Russia. But they have been able to preserve their unity by controlling innovations. The colonies are visited by salesmen, officials, doctors, teachers, and others, and the younger people are attracted by outside values. As pressures mount to accept some cultural innovation, it is formally approved. By bending with the wind, they have managed to prevent breaking. They now use up-to-date farm machinery and trucks, but they still retain their communal ties.[42] Among people who feel themselves unfairly persecuted, external pressure tends to reinforce group solidarity, and the task is much easier.

When a system of ethnic stratification is well established, most of the people in the subordinate strata have no choice but to accept their fate and to make the most of it. While many accept it fatalistically, there are some who develop intense hostility against the dominant group, its symbols, and its values. This is especially true of those

[40] Van der Kroef, "The Indonesian Minority in Surinam," *op. cit.*
[41] Cf. John Gillin, "Parallel Cultures and the Inhibitions to Acculturation in the Guatemalan Community," *Social Forces*, XXIV (1945), 1–14.
[42] Joseph W. Eaton, "Controlled Acculturation: A Survival Technique of the Hutterites," *American Sociological Review*, XVII (1952), 331–40. Cf. Freed, *op. cit.*

who are in frequent contact with their rulers, where they can see their weaknesses and foibles. As they look at the ceilings placed over them, they feel frustrated. They feel that the established order is unfair but that there is nothing to be done about it. Resentment that one is powerless to express is often transformed into abiding hatred. Those who seldom have direct contact with members of the dominant group learn of them through hearsay, and the accounts are often unfavorable. Rulers are seen as cruel, unreasonable, arrogant, and selfish. The stereotype of the white man in Negro literature reflects such resentment. Cothran studied 12 Negro novels, dealing primarily with Negro life and introducing white characters only in minor roles, and found them depicted as immoral, inferior, and having unfair views of Negroes.[43] In some communities, then, contentedness is superficial, and beneath the surface there are latent hostilities waiting only for an opportunity to explode. Some individuals must be perpetually on guard, lest they betray their festering hatred and invite retaliation. There is an intuitive recognition of this condition in the obsessive fear of revolt on the part of European settlers in Africa and of white people in the American South. In stable systems of ethnic stratification, what hatred there is is more often found among people in the minorities rather than among their rulers.

Cathartic Outlets for Frustration

Frustrations are inevitable in any society, and in one in which there is unequal access to values, they are often blamed upon the dominant group. But it may be dangerous to voice protests openly. Subordinate groups are conscious of the power of their rulers. They realize that their welfare rests to a large extent upon maintaining some semblance of good will, and they are careful not to do anything that is likely to bring on retaliation. Resentments, if they are expressed at all, are channeled through furtive means. In some communities there are approved channels for draining tensions. In the antebellum South there were special holidays for slaves. These were celebrated in accepted style, and any slave who did not make the most of these occasions was suspected.[44] In Timbuctoo opportunities

---

[43] Cothran, "White Stereotypes in Fiction by Negroes," *op. cit.* Cf. Heinrich, *op. cit.*, pp. 15–17.

[44] Cf. Herbert Aptheker, *American Negro Slave Revolts* (New York: Columbia University Press, 1943), p. 64; and Dollard, *op. cit.*, pp. 287–314.

for expressing hostilities were afforded by *alkura*, a game resembling
hockey, which was played by teams representing different quarters
of the city. During the rough and tumble of a contest, a slave could
hit a nobleman with impunity, and it was understood that blows received in the game were to be taken without ill will. Although only
the players had the satisfaction of beating one another with sticks,
others were able to enter into the spirit of the contest. In inter-
ethnic rivalries the women often goaded the men on and taunted the
losers.[45]

Anything thought to be offensive to the dominant group is concealed, and considerable effort is expended to create the impression
that everyone is satisfied and happy. There are some things that members of minority groups hardly ever reveal to outsiders; common understandings exist that "dirty linen" should not be washed in public,
and the few who may do so are severely condemned. Whenever a
crime is committed within a minority settlement, an attempt is
made to prevent the authorities from finding out about it. Of course,
major offenses that cannot be hidden are reluctantly reported, but
other matters are settled within the group. Any behavior that reflects
adversely on the group is discouraged by ostracism, ridicule, and
sometimes, violence. Those who rebel are labelled as "troublemakers"
or "radicals." Sometimes an attempt is made to dissociate the community from the deeds of these individuals; they are disowned by
the group. Matters to which the dominant group is believed to be
especially sensitive are hidden with special care. When sex relations
with women of the dominant group are discovered, the men involved
are discouraged. In fact, the mere revelation of a desire to engage in
such relations may elicit immediate disapproval. If someone in a
subordinate group commits a particularly heinous crime against a
member of the dominant group, people in the minority may even
cooperate with the authorities in hunting down the offender and
prosecuting him. Members of ethnic minorities usually assume that
the fate of all persons of their category is bound together. The mis-
deed of a single individual could result in severe retaliation that may
injure many innocent people. Nor is this an idle fear; there have been
instances in which a single dramatic crime has resulted in a massacre.
The sense of mutual responsibility is a protective device of considerable importance. Everything is done to present the appearance of
humility and acceptance of the status quo.

[45] Miner, *op. cit.*, pp. 240–42.

One safe way of reducing the tensions of frustration and resentment is aggression against a substitute object—other members of the minority group. Several observers have suggested that the high incidence of quarreling, crime, and homicide among American Negroes is to be explained in terms of their inability to vent hostility against white people. Furthermore, the courts, especially in the South, take a more lenient view toward offenses against fellow Negroes. It has been suggested that the fighting among the various Zulu tribes has been similarly cathartic.[46]

Considerable tension is drained in all minority groups by the telling of jokes. Tales of skillful exploitation of the foibles of the dominant group spread rapidly. There are countless anecdotes about the manner in which someone had cleverly exploited an outsider's stereotyped conception. For American Negroes the best jokes are those in which "Jim Crow" practices backfire on a Southerner, when a Negro who had been treated as a "darky" subsequently is discovered to be incomparably superior to the white man. A gnawing sense of inadequacy is transformed temporarily into a vision of triumph. Members of minority groups also laugh at themselves; in fact, most of the jokes about an ethnic minority are told by the people in that category. Negroes tell many jokes about Negroes in which the point rests upon the stereotype.[47] In doing so, they are unintentionally reinforcing existing definitions, but the catharsis of mutual laughter provides a much-needed safety valve.

In most minority groups there are a number of standard strategies for deceiving and exploiting their rulers. In Guatemala the Indians arrange to be conveniently absent whenever they know they will be called for "voluntary service." [48] Most American Negroes believe that white people are easily fooled by flattery and by the antics of an "Uncle Tom." Indeed, it has been suggested that contrived humility is a form of concealed aggression. In Christian ideology suffering is a prelude to eventual triumph over one's adversary; the greater the suffering, the greater is the reward. A Negro may even temporarily enjoy his deferential role, for through it he feels superior. He is un-

---

[46] Cf. Dollard, *op. cit.*, pp. 267–86; Powdermaker, "The Channeling of Negro Aggression by the Cultural Process," *op. cit.*, p. 753; and Gluckman, *op. cit.*
[47] Cf. Burma, *op. cit.*; and Russell Middleton and John Moland, "Humor in Negro and White Subcultures," *American Sociological Review*, XXIV (1959), 61–69.
[48] Tumin, *op. cit.*, p. 179.

doubtedly the better Christian, and he will win the final victory; white people enjoy only a temporary advantage. Furthermore, he feels superior because he knows he is fooling the white man; he can even enjoy part of his success now. Outsiders never know his real thoughts. He gets things from white people that they would never give him if they knew his real feelings.[49] Some people in subordinate groups deliberately play the role of a fool. Like Falstaff, they act the part of an idiot to survive and to say truthful things that are not otherwise permitted. The "untouchables" in India, like American Negroes, cover up their bitter resentment by playing the buffoon and receiving favors that are denied to others.[50] This mask comes off when these people are among themselves.

Feelings of resentment and reactions against oppression are often reflected in the art and literature of minority peoples. Creative work provides a medium for expression, and among the various minority groups in Europe there has developed a rich protest literature, which pokes fun at the dominant group and presents a more sympathetic view of their own plight. The Czechs, who have been ruled by one conqueror after another, have long laughed at the antics depicted in *The Good Soldier Schweik*, a novel by Jaroslav Hasek that provides a satirical account of European armies. The hero carries out farcical sabotage, and this book has been credited with inspiring some of the resistance work during World War II. Works of this kind are also abundant in Jewish literature. Most writings of this kind are accepted by intellectuals of the dominant group as art, and they are usually not suppressed.

American Negroes have also developed an abundant literature. The delightful stories of Simple by Langston Hughes provide hilarious accounts of the failings of both Negroes and white people; at the same time they point to the injustices suffered by Negroes. Many read these stories for entertainment, but the philosophical observations of the seemingly harmless hero challenge a number of silent assumptions concerning the color line. On the whole, however, humorous pieces are comparatively rare in the work of Negro authors; much of their literature is grim and contains a more direct protest.

---

[49] Cothran, "Negro Conceptions of White People," *op. cit.*, p. 462; and Powdermaker, "The Channeling of Negro Aggression by the Cultural Process," *op. cit.*
[50] Cf. Gerald D. Berreman, "Caste in India and the United States," *American Journal of Sociology*, LXVI (1960), 125-26.

There is evidence that these writings have influenced intellectuals in Africa, who are now producing similar writings of their own.[51]

The folk art, folklore, and folk music of less literate minority groups throughout the world also reflect the preoccupations, the trials, and the aspirations of the underprivileged. Perhaps even more than published writings, they express sentiments typical of down-trodden people. The plastic and decorative arts of the various ethnic groups subjugated by European colonists disclose their conception of the white man. The figures often appear ridiculous—with their cigars, hats, and firearms. In many cases it is apparent that the conquerors were reproduced in mockery.[52] Rumanian folk songs reveal the hatred of the peasants for the various alien groups that ruled them. In the folklore of Bessarabia there are many expressions of popular resolution to resist the czars' efforts to assimilate them to the Russian way of life. The bitterness of Moldavian and Wallachian peasants toward the Phanariote Greeks of Constantinople, who for more than a century acted as administrative agents and tax collectors for the Ottoman Empire, is reflected in their numerous *doine*, a type of pop-ular song.[53] The *kalela* dance is a popular pastime in the Copperbelt of Northern Rhodesia. At the head stands the "king," elected by the others to organize the dancing team. A key role is the "doctor," dressed in a white operating gown with a red cross in front, who gives encouragement to the dancers. There is also a "nursing sister," also dressed in white, who goes about with a mirror and handkerchief to allow each dancer to inspect himself and to wipe sweat from his face. It is believed that the *kalela* dance had its origin in the *mbeni*, which apparently developed shortly after World War I. In it the central figure was the "governor." He stood in the center of the courtyard resplendently attired and decorated with medals. The rest of the dancers circled slowly around him, led by a drummer. They moved in military formation, officers and enlisted men, each with ap-

[51] Charles I. Glicksberg, "For Negro Literature: The Catharsis of Laughter," *Forum*, CVII (1947), 450–56. Cf. Langston Hughes (ed.), *An African Treasury* (New York: Pyramid Books, 1961); and Peggy Rutherfoord (ed.), *African Voices: An Anthology of Native African Writing* (New York: Grosset & Dun-lap, 1961).

[52] Cf. Julius E. Lips, *The Savage Hits Back* (New Haven: Yale University Press, 1937).

[53] Leon Feraru, *The Development of Rumanian Poetry* (New York: Institute of Rumanian Culture, 1929), pp. 30–33; and Tereza Stratilesco, *From Carpathian to Pindus* (Boston: J. W. Luce, 1907).

propriate badges of his rank fashioned out of lead. It is clear that these early dances were a pantomime of the local European community, providing opportunities for vicarious participation in roles from which Africans were excluded. They also provided an excellent medium for the expression of hostility through satire. The dancers no longer wear military uniforms, but correct clothing is still emphasized; they now wear the smart clothing of European business and professional men.[54]

Folk art apparently develops through a selective process. All kinds of songs and tales are composed, but only the items that appeal to a large number of people are preserved. In a study of Negro spirituals Park notes that the content of these songs gives clear expression to the attitudes that Negro slaves would not have dared to express openly. But no one could be accused of fomenting trouble while singing a song. The songs that were remembered and handed down to succeeding generations were those that best expressed the sentiments of downtrodden slaves. The songs that were repeated until they had crystallized into spirituals were those that most adequately voiced the wishes of the people who sang them. The songs that have survived to this day are the ones that reflected the more permanent moods.[55] It has been suggested that the tales of Uncle Remus about Brer Rabbit were so popular among the slaves because the rabbit, a weak creature, always gets the best of his more powerful foes through humbug and resourcefulness. In the same way, the tales of Robin Hood provided the conquered Saxons with a safe way of laughing at Normans.[56] It seems that people take advantage of any opportunity for giving vent to their inner feelings, and folk traditions arise in situations in which they will not be held accountable for their deeds. The folk art of oppressed peoples, then, is likely to manifest the hopes that they cannot proclaim openly.

Religious movements are frequently found among dissatisfied people, and many of them attract large followings in minority groups. Unlike political movements they make no attempt to alter the existing social order. Religious movements are introverted; instead of trying to change what is found undesirable, converts modify their

---

[54] J. Clyde Mitchell, *The Kalela Dance* (Manchester, England: Manchester University Press, 1956).

[55] Park, *Race and Culture, op. cit.*, pp. 284–300.

[56] Cf. Peter Haworth (ed.), *Rumours and Hoaxes: Classic Tales of Fraud and Deception* (Oxford: Basil Blackwell, 1928).

own outlook so that the same world no longer appears so futile. Religious movements provide a new set of values, a different set of criteria for evaluating oneself. It becomes possible for a person to alter his self-conception without changing his overt conduct. At least in the beginning, there is no threat to the status quo.[57]

Esoteric cults often find followers in the lowest rungs of society. In his classic study of the origin of religious groups Niebuhr spoke of the people attracted to cults as the "disinherited." Whenever the already-established church no longer serves the interests of outcasts, they break off to set up their own. If the new group prospers and becomes too respectable, there is another schism and those unable to keep up establish another cult.[58] The Independent Church movement in South Africa, for example, began in 1892 with the founding of the Ethiopian Church in Witwatersrand. This came at a time when tribal traditions were losing their appeal; with the penetration of European culture villages had ceased to be the center of the native world. Those who had migrated to cities were disappointed. They had to submit quietly to white men who treated them harshly; they worked long hours for meager wages; and they were plagued by disease and loneliness. Magena M. Mokone, a native minister, broke away from the Wesleyan Church and together with other discontented Africans formed a new organization. Christian missionaries had interpreted the psalm, "Ethiopia shall soon stretch out her hands unto God," as a prediction of the evangelization of Africa, and Mokone adopted this interpretation. Other African ministers followed Mokone's footsteps and established separate churches of their own. Tribal differences, diversity of economic and educational attainment, questions of sex, arguments over polygamy, disputes over money and property, and internal struggles for power and prestige resulted in further schisms within the Independent Church.[59] In the United States there have been a succession of "holy roller" groups with their emotional, energetic services. The outward manifestations of the ecstatic feeling of sanctification when God forgives their sins include glossolalia, visions, involuntary twitching, running, shouting, writhing, or rolling on the floor. Because of the primitive

---

[57] Cf. Herbert Blumer, "Collective Behavior," in Alfred M. Lee (ed.), *Principles of Sociology* (New York: Barnes & Noble, 1955), pp. 214–16.

[58] H. Richard Niebuhr, *The Social Sources of Denominationalism* (New York: Henry Holt, 1929).

[59] Bengt G. M. Sundkler, *Bantu Prophets in South Africa* (London: Lutterworth Press, 1948), pp. 38–39, 81, 178, 236, 295.

expression found in many of these cults, middle-class Negroes have dissociated themselves from them. But such religious cults inspire hope in minority peoples, give them a feeling that someone cares, and restores in them a sense of dignity. The fellowship offers warmth and consolation. The presence of the color line in the organized church is one of the main reasons for the initial secession.[60]

Also found among minority groups is a variety of revivalistic movements of a reactionary nature. They are reactionary in that they focus attention upon the distant past—when life was presumably better—before the coming of the conqueror. Sometimes an effort is made to reinstate a long-forgotten language and various status symbols that had been important in the past. A number of such movements developed among the American Indians during the latter part of the nineteenth century—the Grass Dance, the Hand Game, the Great Message, Shakerism, Peyotism, and the Ghost Dance. Most of these movements were pan-Indian and not restricted to any single tribe. They came at a time when the Indians had given up hope of ousting the settlers. Since warfare had been prohibited and there was not much hunting to be done, the young men were without the traditional ways of achieving status and had to endure ridicule and humiliation.[61] In the Ghost Dance of the Sioux it was contended that through the intervention of the Great Spirit, the earth would shortly be transformed into a paradise, enjoyed both by the living and the resurrected dead. In preparation for this return to the golden age believers must immediately return to their aboriginal mode of life, all foreign influences being cast aside. There were visions of buffalo hunting and living in a land without smallpox. New rites included ceremonial bathing and an elaborate dance. Eventually the movement exhausted itself when all the dancing and the adherence to new rules failed to bring on the millennium. Those who were not disillusioned were suppressed a few years later. At first the movement had been dismissed as harmless, but when the Sioux uprising was mistakenly connected with it, it was suppressed through military action.[62]

---

[60] Cf. Anton T. Boisen, *Religion in Crisis and Custom* (New York: Harper, 1955), pp. 176–91; Arthur H. Fauset, *Black Gods of the Metropolis* (Philadelphia: University of Pennsylvania Press, 1944); and Frazier, *The Negro in the United States, op. cit.*, pp. 52–53, 334–66.

[61] B. Barber, *op. cit.*; and Fred Voget, "The American Indian in Transition," *American Journal of Sociology*, LXII (1957), 369–78.

[62] Alexander Lesser, "Cultural Significance of the Ghost Dance," *American Anthropologist*, XXXV (1933), 108–15; and James Mooney, "The Ghost Dance Religion and the Sioux Outbreak of 1890," *Fourteenth Annual Report of the Bureau*

A number of similar nativistic movements developed in the South Seas. The "cargo cults" were also attempts to point backward to the glorious days before the coming of the white man. Although the movements differed somewhat from island to island, they appear to have had certain characteristics in common. A prophet announced the imminent destruction of the world in a cataclysm; then, dead ancestors would appear, bringing with them all the goods the people desired. There would follow a period of eternal bliss. To prepare for the wonderful day it was necessary to build storehouses to receive the goods—called "cargo" in pidgin English. In some of the cults, as in New Guinea, the people stopped working, killed their pigs, and waited for the millennium. Many of the colonists looked upon the cults in amusement, and they pointed to their bizarre character as further evidence of the childlike nature of their charges. Some of the movements were clearly anti-European; in the Tuka movement on the Fiji Islands, for example, it was contended that all officials, missionaries, and traders would be driven into the sea. In 1944, when American troops drove out the Japanese and ships began unloading tons of war materials on the beaches, some of the natives thought the great day had finally arrived.[63]

The Sioux outbreak in the Teton in 1890 was crushed by the U.S. Army with such ferocity that no Plains Indian tribe ever dared to rebel again. Demoralized and resigned to their fate, an increasing number turned to Peyotism, a movement that was nativistic but completely non-violent. When the fruit of the peyote—a small, turnip-shaped cactus that grows wild near the Rio Grande River—is eaten or brewed as a tea, one experiences intense color vision and hallucinations. The religion, which is intertribal and nationalistic, is a compromise that blends old Indian ways of worship with Christian theology. Eating the peyote is regarded as a solemn sacrament; the Indians claim that it enables them to talk directly to God, just as their ancestors had talked to the Great Spirit. Worshippers, except when singing, praying, or drumming, are lost in quiet contemplation of their dreams. The values emphasized are brotherly love, honesty, care of the family, and self-reliance.[64] The charge that Japanese offi-

---

of *American Ethnology, 1892–93* (Washington, D.C.: Government Printing Office, 1896), pp. 653–1136.

[63] Worsley, *op. cit.* Cf. Coleman, *Nigeria, op. cit.*, pp. 174–77.

[64] Cf. B. Barber, *op. cit.*, p. 668; and Slotkin, *The Peyote Religion, op. cit.*

cials deliberately distributed drugs to render the people of Manchuria more docile has not been proved, but the sales figures suggest that their efforts to control the use of narcotics were not diligent. In 1937 almost half of the total profits from state monopolies came from the sale of opium.[65]

Although religious cults are sometimes transformed into explosive revolutionary movements, on the whole these activities do not threaten the established social order. They often attract the sympathetic attention of intellectuals of the dominant group, who find them quaint and interesting. Activities such as these give people in hopelessly subordinate positions an opportunity to pad their forlorn hopes and to reinforce their pride. They are like safety valves; they pacify frustrated individuals by permitting them to drain their tensions and thereby make their lives more bearable.

Summary and Conclusion

In well-established systems of ethnic stratification people in minority groups live in their own social world and pursue the values of their own culture. Those in the subordinate strata are just as much a part of the moral order as their rulers; most of them conduct themselves in ways that they regard as correct. They accept the classification of human beings used in the larger community, and they conceive of themselves as different, although they do not necessarily concur with the derogatory evaluation placed upon them. Customary procedures within the minority group generally discourage contacts with outsiders, hinder upward social mobility, stifle protest, and prohibit intermarriage. *Attempts of ethnic minorities to maintain the integrity of their group thus tend to reinforce the already-existing system of stratification.* Subordination is accepted. Feelings of resentment are released harmlessly in ways that are not likely to offend the dominant group; tensions are drained surreptitiously in jokes, popular songs, or folk tales. Rarely is a direct assault made upon the existing order.

Since Americans take it for granted that everyone desires to better his lot, they find it difficult to believe that many people in minority groups are not only content to remain in their "place" but feel uncomfortable out of it. Yet groups have occupied subordinate

[65] F. C. Jones, *op. cit.,* pp. 134–35.

positions for centuries without directing a single challenge at the existing order. Suggested changes are often branded as immoral, and they are opposed by the very people who would benefit from them. This is not to suggest that oppressed people are as contented as they often appear, nor does it mean that some of them are not envious of the advantages of the ruling elite. But most of them do not entertain seriously the possibility of rebelling against the status quo. Thus, systems of ethnic stratification, which are formed initially through natural selection, are reinforced by custom, as all of the people view the existing arrangements as proper and just.

CHAPTER 12

Sanctions and

Regulatory Institutions

The names of Gabriel Prosser, Denmark Vesey, and Nat Turner have been burned indelibly into the history of the antebellum South as leaders of the three major slave insurrections. Their exploits have been recorded in song and popular lore, and their names inspire dread or hope, depending on which side of the color line one stands. But these men stand out as exceptions, and their efforts failed to win the backing of their fellows. A great many slaves were dissatisfied with their lot; the number who escaped, even before the "underground railroad" became established, gives some indication of the extent of their discontent. Although uprisings occurred more frequently than is generally supposed, the vast majority of slaves served their masters faithfully. Even during the Civil War, when their own freedom was at stake, they made no serious effort to throw off the yoke.[1] The people in the South had long lived in dread of a major slave revolt;

[1] Cf. Aptheker, *op. cit.*; and Joseph C. Carroll, *Slave Insurrections in the United States, 1800–1865* (Boston: Chapman & Grimes, 1938).

yet, no concerted movement toward freedom ever developed. How is this to be explained?

Apologists for slavery have cited this relative absence of rebellion as evidence for the absurd contention that Negroes are naturally suited for servitude. But what else could the slaves have done? Once a moral order is established, it is rarely challenged. When it is, deviant behavior can generally be put down with comparative ease. Conspirators usually have difficulty in winning the support of the very people for whom they are fighting. This suggests that there are formidable barriers to change. What are some of the common procedures through which challenges to the color line are minimized or crushed?

Many of these practices seem admirably suited for perpetuating a system of exploitation. In spite of appearances, however, most of them were not deliberately created for the purpose of maintaining the color line. Occasionally an astute leader advocates unscrupulous control to protect the ascendancy of the dominant group. Usually, however, these measures develop through a process of trial and error in which fortuitous events play an important part. Only after they have become established do they acquire the appearance of purpose.

The Perpetuation of Social Distance

When people live side by side in the same community, some kind of contact is inevitable. The same persons see one another frequently, grow old together, and watch each other's children develop to manhood. Under such circumstances the color line can be maintained only through the regulation of social distance. Inequities are difficult to enforce unless members of the dominant group continue to see their subjects in stereotyped terms. Once people identify one another as being basically alike, the unequal distribution of values becomes more difficult to defend. Most systems of ethnic stratification are fortified by conventional or legal barriers to the establishment of familiarity.

Some kind of residential segregation is found in most stratified societies, and this facilitates the perpetuation of social distance. Even when men of diverse categories work together during the day, they go home to different areas at night. They understand that their working together does not mean that they must also share their recreational activities. Segregation need not consist of isolation in ethnic islands; in many cases, quarters for servants and field hands are located near the places where they work. When a group is segregated, most of each person's informal contacts are with those with whom he identifies. People become so unaccustomed to outsiders that they are unable to relax in their presence; they remain stiff and formal and do not reveal their individuality.

Once they have been established, the boundaries of segregated areas are defined in custom or in law. The practice of enclosing natives in their traditional territory and denying them the right to leave their district without permission is an old one. In the Roman Empire Trajan tried to shut off conquered peoples in their native lands to prevent their entering too freely into contact with Romans.[2] The lines of demarcation of many of the Jewish ghettos in Europe were also set by law. In response to petitions against Asian immigration the government of Transvaal enacted in 1885 a law setting aside "as a sanitary measure" streets and locations for the settlement of these immigrants.[3] In American cities, to the extent that areas inhabited by different ethnic groups have stability, the boundaries have been fixed by custom rather than by law. Exclusive residential areas have until recently been protected by tacit agreements among home owners not to sell to members of minority groups. Since the U.S. Supreme Court ruled that such private covenants could not be enforced through the courts, they have been less effective as barriers.[4] Where there is a high degree of consensus over the desirability of segregation, laws are not necessary, for most people would not even consider the possibility of invading territory reserved for some other group.

One of the most extreme programs of segregation ever attempted is now being instituted in the Union of South Africa. *Apartheid*, the policy of the Nationalist Party, has not yet been carried out. Its announced objective is complete and permanent separation of the three major categories: European, Native, and Coloured—the last including Indians, Chinese, Malays, and the Cape Coloured. Many laws implement the policy, but the cornerstone is the Group Areas

[2] Maunier, *op. cit.*, Vol. II, pp. 479–81.
[3] Hailey, *op. cit.*, p. 389.
[4] Cf. Jack Greenberg, *Race Relations and American Law* (New York: Columbia University Press, 1959), pp. 275–312.

Act of 1950. Not only are the ethnic groups to be separated, but each is encouraged to develop its own culture. Thus, revitalized tribalism is an important part of the program, and there are plans for setting aside additional land as reserves in which each tribe could develop its own "national character." Since so many of the natives already live in cities and perform essential labor, the separation is to be gradual. Some of the reserves are to be industrialized so that in time only a small number of necessary natives would be left in the urban centers. It is stated quite candidly that the purpose of this ambitious project is to protect the interests of outnumbered Europeans in the face of the rapidly expanding population of the minority groups. The white people in South Africa are obsessed with the fear of being overwhelmed by a native population many times their size, as it begins to approach them in outlook and technical skill. The policy is, therefore, a desperation measure.[5]

Since all of the inhabitants of any community are jointly involved in a common web of life, contact cannot be avoided even when there is segregation. There develops in each community a set of common understandings concerning what people of different categories may do together and what they must do separately. In Guatemala, for example, Ladinos and Indians cooperate where it is necessary; otherwise they remain apart. There are some activities, such as agriculture, in which members of the two categories are mutually interdependent. There are other activities, such as prostitution and service as God-parents, in which Indians and Ladinos need each other for profit. In religion, politics, and education the two groups are compelled to cooperate by custom and law. Still other transactions, such as meeting in the plaza or the streets, are simply unavoidable. In all of these contexts the Ladino plays the dominant role and the Indian takes orders, and customary procedures are observed.[6] In general, there is less objection to joint participation in economic transactions than in anything else. Here the roles assumed by the participants—employer or employee, buyer or seller, landowner or tenant—are all impersonal.

In most communities the greatest objection arises to informal social contacts across the color line. Special efforts are made to avoid situations in which young people can get together on a friendly basis,

[5] Cf. Dvorin, *op. cit.*, pp. 56–131, 157–71.
[6] Tumin, *op. cit.*, pp. 172–74.

where erotic attraction might overcome prohibitions not yet firmly established. Even where other forms of segregation are not practiced, members of minority groups are excluded from situations in which personal reserve is likely to be relaxed. Each ethnic group has its own clubs; outsiders may enter only as servants or as honored guests. In Jamaica, for example, one cannot gain admission to clubs or dances without tickets, which are sold only to those who are socially acceptable.[7] In many American communities men who greet one another in a jovial manner during the day only exchange nods or weak smiles when they happen to meet in a theater lobby in the evening in the company of their wives and children.[8] In congenial situations people tend to interact on an equal basis and to respond to each other as unique human beings. Social situations such as eating, mating, and friendship are filled with uneasiness and anxiety unless the participants can address each other with mutual respect. It is in the camaraderie of congenial settings that binding sentiments are formed, and when such personal ties involve members of different ethnic categories, they may interfere with the observance of customary practices.[9]

In most stratified communities transactions that are performed jointly are governed by ritualistic observances to maintain an air of formality. Etiquette is often based upon differences in rank; the status of an individual determines the forms considered proper in addressing him. It usually involves acting differently when approaching a person of another rank; people who commonly use chairs often stand in the presence of someone of higher rank, but there are people who show respect by sitting down. Such rituals become symbolic of respect; they are ways of reassuring one another that differences of status are recognized. Thus, European colonists insisted upon being addressed as "Boss" or "Bwana" by the natives, not because they enjoyed hearing the sound, but because it was a symbol of status. Since etiquette implies respect for the person to whom it is addressed, a breach of etiquette is resented as a personal slight. This is true even of a person of lower rank, who feels insulted even though he may not be able to do anything about it.[10]

[7] Henriques, *Jamaica, op. cit.*, pp. 133-34.
[8] Cf. Anderson, *op. cit.*, pp. 124-25.
[9] Cf. Simmel, *op. cit.*, pp. 40-57.
[10] Cf. Goffman, *op. cit.*; and A. M. Hocart, "Etiquette," *Encyclopedia of the Social Sciences*, Vol. V, pp. 615-17.

Etiquette enables men to act freely within the limits set by convention. It is a way of maintaining social distance; it makes possible proximity and frequent contact of different categories of people over a long period of time without either side relaxing personal reserve. To be polite a person must remain self-conscious, and self-consciousness is a way of checking impetuous behavior through which one might reveal some of his personal characteristics. A person who is polite is less likely to reveal his individuality; all he shows is a "front" that reveals only that he knows his manners. One can sit next to a polite guest for an entire evening and not learn anything about him as a human being. People can work together in an amicable atmosphere year after year and never get to know anything about one another's personal life. In their colonies, for example, the British demonstrated by their conduct that they did not want the natives to feel that they belonged to British society. While they were not unkind, the rituals upon which they insisted symbolized the separateness of the ruler and the ruled. The natives grudgingly expressed admiration for the moral rectitude, financial incorruptibility, and legalistic fairness of British officials, but bonds of friendship and affection were completely lacking.[11]

A very elaborate system of etiquette developed in the antebellum South governing the relationships between masters and slaves. Much of it was revived after the Reconstruction period to symbolize the superiority of white people, and these practices are still very much resented by American Negroes. Master and slave were in constant contact, but in most cases their association remained highly formal. In public encounters Negroes did not initiate conversations; they had to wait until they had been addressed, and were always required to be courteous. In conversations a slave had to keep his eyes on the ground. He was required to remove his hat or to touch it as if he were going to remove it at each sentence; if he were not wearing a hat, he pulled at his forelock while the conversation lasted.

The name with which an individual is addressed is indicative of the social relationship between him and the speaker, the degree of intimacy between them, and the esteem in which he is held. On the plantation slaves addressed their owners as "Mars" or "Miss" with their Christian name. "Missey" was more intimate and was used by a female slave in addressing a woman to whom she was quite close.

11 Kennedy, *op. cit.*, p. 320. Cf. Banton, *White and Coloured, op. cit.*, pp. 73–91.

All white people were addressed respectfully as "Suh," "Boss," "Mistah," "Kuhnel," or "Ma'am." Negroes who were known were always called by their given name; others were addressed as "nigger," "you," "boy," or "girl." Older slaves were addressed somewhat more respectfully as "Mammy" or "Uncle" with the Christian name. Titles such as "Mr.," "Mrs.," or "Miss" with the surname were never used in addressing Negroes, nor were they ever referred to as "man" or "woman." If a Negro became so prominent that he could no longer be called "boy," he was addressed as "doctor" or "professor." Many were relieved when Booker T. Washington was awarded an honorary LL.D., for it had become embarrassing to address a person of his stature by his first name. Many white people regarded him as a great man and admired him, but they were unable to call him "mister."

There were a number of conventions covering other exigencies. Master and slave never ate together. On large plantations the slaves ate in a "cookhouse" or in their own cabins; on small farms the slaves ate in the kitchen. When someone in the owner's family was married, the slaves lined up after the ceremony to wish the couple well; when a slave became a bride, a woman in the master's family prepared her trousseau. When a master died, the presence of his slaves at his deathbed was expected, and the slaves usually attended the funeral. If a slave died, the master sometimes gave the other slaves a day off and arranged for the burial rites. Slaves never visited the "big house" on a plantation; when they had to go there on an errand, they never entered through the front door. On certain occasions slave quarters were visited by the owner or his guests; the slaves were then expected to greet the visitors with a handshake and perhaps to give them a small gift, such as eggs or vegetables. Master and slave did not ordinarily shake hands in public, but there were occasions on which it was expected, as in leave-taking or returning from an extended trip. On such occasions the Mammy often kissed the women and children.

Conduct away from the plantation was also regulated. When shopping, a maid dropped behind her mistress and came up to her when needed. Negro and white man conversed in public if the relationship between them was well known, but even then indiscriminate interchange was kept to a minimum. If a Negro met some white people on a street where there was not enough room, he was expected to step out of the way and to allow them to pass. Where slaves sat on trains and stagecoaches depended upon whether or not they were travelling alone. When accompanying their master, the servants stayed with him. When they travelled alone, slaves were given second-class accommodations. Segregation practices in churches varied. In general, the greater the proportion of Negroes in the congregation, the more distinctions were maintained in worship. When there were only a few Negroes, they sat in separate sections; when the number increased, they held separate services. Sometimes they were given a separate church with a Negro preacher. In some homes the slaves were invited to join in family prayer services.[12]

Similar ways of symbolizing status differences are found in many other societies. In Guatemala, for example, Indians are always courteous in addressing a Ladino, especially a Ladino woman. They remove their hats and address them by title—"Don" or "Senora." But a Ladino merely shouts "hey" or "boy" to call an Indian. When an Indian meets Ladinos on a narrow sidewalk, he steps aside to let them pass. Indians rarely visit Ladino households on a friendly basis, but business calls must sometimes be made. On such occasions the Indian asks for permission to enter the house, although a Ladino enters an Indian home without asking. Indians and Ladinos do not eat together; when they participate jointly in baptisms and similar gatherings, special arrangements are made to serve food separately.[13] In Australian towns and ranches white people rarely used or even knew the real name of an Aborigine. This would have been considered being "too friendly with the niggers." Commonly used appellations included "Piggie," "Monkey," "Spider," "Cranky," "Misery," "Tommy," "Jacky," "Maggie," and "Polly."[14] In New Guinea the colonists called the natives by names such as "boy," "coon," "boong," and "bloody black bastard."[15] Refusal to eat together is a widespread practice in stratified societies. In India, Hindu and Moslem not only did not share their meals, but even the water served on passenger trains was labelled "Hindu water" and "Moslem water."[16]

Although these symbols of rank may appear to have been im-

[12] Doyle, *op. cit.* Cf. Davis and Gardner, *op. cit.*, pp. 15–58; and C. S. Johnson, *op. cit.*, pp. 117–55.

[13] Tumin, *op. cit.*, pp. 184–207.

[14] Berndt and Berndt, *op. cit.*, pp. 194–95.

[15] Hogbin, *op. cit.*, p. 227.

[16] K. T. Behanan, "Cultural Diversity and World Peace," in Wayne Dennis (ed.), *Current Trends in Social Psychology* (Pittsburgh: University of Pittsburgh Press, 1948), pp. 61–62.

posed by the dominant group, etiquette usually enjoys a high degree of consensus. The slaves in the antebellum South probably did not enjoy performing these rituals, especially when addressing someone they did not respect. To many people, however, etiquette was only a matter of good form. When an outsider appeared who did not know the rules, the slaves were embarrassed. A Yankee who failed to observe protocol and called a Negro "mister" was not regarded as a fine person who refused to "discriminate"; rather the slaves often looked upon him as an ignorant, uncouth foreigner who did not know his manners.[17] Violations of etiquette by members of the dominant group are generally punished by informal social sanctions rather than by law; the most potent weapons are ridicule and gossip. In extreme cases those whose deviation is too flagrant may even be ostracized.

Even when friendships are established across the color line, the individuals usually relax only when they are alone together and observe etiquette when they are in public. In this way they do not threaten the general standards of the community. In stable systems of ethnic stratification, then, the preservation of the color line is largely a matter of conformity with local customs.

The Perpetuation of Power Differentials

The laws and customs that constitute the color line can be enforced only as long as minority groups do not become so powerful as to challenge authority. Therefore, any innovation likely to enhance the competitive advantages of minority peoples is usually opposed by at least some segment of the dominant group. In some communities constant vigilance is maintained. In the antebellum South, for example, there were laws regulating almost every conceivable activity of the slaves. They were forbidden to assemble without the permission of a responsible white person, to own or carry arms of any kind, to engage in any economic transaction without the permission of their master, to be off plantation grounds or on city streets after 10 o'clock in the evening without written permission, or to testify in court in cases involving a white person. Even after defeat in the Civil War and acceptance of the Emancipation Proclamation the newly organized legislatures of the Southern states passed a number of laws—known as the "black codes"—which

[17] Doyle, op. cit., pp. 68–80.

re-enacted the old slave laws and virtually reduced free Negroes to their previous condition of servitude. The minimum rights of Negroes had to be established through military rule, and many of these were lost again after the withdrawal of the Union Army.[18] Changes in the attributes of ethnic groups alter the balance of power, and there are a variety of procedures that tend to discourage such transformations.

In modern national states the central government theoretically enjoys a monopoly over the techniques of coercion. It controls the police force and the army, and various individuals and groups can utilize violence only under conditions that are specified by law. The government is usually in the hands of the dominant ethnic group. Thus, recalcitrant members of minority groups are faced with overwhelming odds. Behind the Southern slaveholder and his agents stood an elaborate system of military control—the police, the state militia, and numerous voluntary associations that were well armed. These bodies, which were mobilized at the slightest hint of rebellion, periodically searched for and disbanded secret assemblies of slaves.[19] Various ethnic groups, like all other groups in the community, can pursue their interests only by attempting to influence governmental policy. Except in unsettled times they must work within the legal framework.

As long as participation of minority groups in government is limited, they are not able to use the machinery in support of their own interests. The reluctance of rulers to grant the franchise to subordinate peoples becomes more understandable when seen in this light. In any government in which officials are elected, a large electorate of minority peoples could force the representatives to grant concessions. In the American South, for example, Negroes have long had the constitutional right to vote, but through a variety of subterfuges they have been effectively denied the opportunity to exercise these rights. One study revealed that the extent to which politics in a state rested upon opposition to Negroes varied directly with the proportion of Negroes in the population.[20] This suggests that once Negroes do win the franchise, the complexion of Southern politics

18 Aptheker, *op. cit.,* pp. 70–71; and Frazier, *The Negro in the United States, op. cit.,* pp. 126–32.
19 Aptheker, *op. cit.,* pp. 67–68.
20 V. O. Key, *Southern Politics* (New York: Alfred A. Knopf, 1950). Cf. Samuel Lubell, *The Future of American Politics* (New York: Doubleday, 1956), pp. 106–36.

Scandinavian migration in relatively large numbers to Australia and New Zealand began in the latter half of the nineteenth century. The British colonial government, anxious to populate the areas with white people, not only welcomed them but also actively promoted their immigration.[27] Ever since the Treaty of Portsmouth in 1905 gave Japan a firm foothold in Manchuria, its statesmen planned to colonize the area with Japanese farmers. Several schemes were launched to persuade them to emigrate, and by 1941 there were more than 100,000 colonists in rural settlements. From 1932 steps were also taken to discourage Chinese immigration. Not only was there a drop in the total number of Chinese immigrants, but an ever larger proportion of the Chinese who did migrate went into industrial rather than agricultural work.[28] The importance of increasing the size of one ethnic group *vis à vis* another can be seen by reviewing the history of the annexation of California and Texas by the United States.

Attempts by European rulers to develop homogeneous populations have resulted in the persecution and the mass expulsion of minority groups. Jews have been expelled from various parts of Europe, generally as a result of popular pressure. One of the most dramatic cases of mass expulsion was the banishment of the Moors from Spain in 1610. Attempts to enforce religious conformity had resulted in a century of civil strife and led to the belief that the presence of such a large alien group was dangerous; the Moors could align themselves with any enemy that might invade Spain. Since the Moors were the best artisans and agricultural workers, some Spanish leaders argued for retaining a selected number, at least until enough Spaniards had been trained to take their places. But their pleas were overruled, and an estimated 500,000 Moors were expelled. The sudden departure of such a large segment of the population disrupted the economy to such an extent that Spain never recovered from the blow.[29] The drive for hegemony was intensified during the nineteenth century when Europe was swept by a number of nationalistic movements. The rise of Turkish nationalism led to a succession of population exchanges, starting before World War I and continuing afterward under the supervision of the League of Nations. Under the Lausanne Treaty

[27] J. Lyng, *The Scandinavians in Australia, New Zealand, and the Western Pacific* (Melbourne: Melbourne University Press, 1939).

[28] F. C. Jones, *op. cit.*, pp. 82–97, 167–68.

[29] Cf. Henry C. Lea, *The Moriscos of Spain* (Philadelphia: Lea Bros., 1901).

all of the Greeks in Turkey, except those living in Constantinople, were deported in exchange for all Moslems in Greece, other than those in western Thrace. In all about 200,000 Greeks and 350,000 Turks were uprooted.[30]

Another source of political power is control over goods and services, and wealthy minority groups are sometimes able to institute reforms. No minority group is likely to develop economic power, however, as long as there are job ceilings, as long as their members are excluded from high-paying jobs and skilled occupations that enjoy prestige. A man's occupation is usually his major source of income, and the restriction of occupational roles generally results in disparate incomes. Even when men work together in common enterprises, they perform different tasks, tasks that are ranked differently and paid for on a different scale. In South Africa, for example, the ceiling for Africans is semi-skilled labor; unions have pushed through legislation that reserves all skilled jobs for Europeans, thus depriving natives of an opportunity to compete. The bulk of the native labor force remains in the unskilled category. Africans in various professions can practice only among their own people and must scrupulously avoid competition with white persons.[31] In the United States the ceilings placed over Negroes are not quite as severe nor rigid, but a great many Negroes are still excluded from occupations for which they are well qualified.[32] Although job ceilings are not always established deliberately, such customary procedures make it difficult for subordinate groups to develop enough power to challenge the color line. In fact, competition on even terms is impossible.

In agricultural communities land laws and differential rates of taxation prevent minority groups from competing and minimize the possibilties of their acquiring economic power. For example, the Alien Land Law of California, first passed in 1913, prohibited the ownership of land by "aliens ineligible for citizenship." Since immigrants from Asia could not become citizens at that time, they were hindered in their efforts to establish independent farms. Those who cannot own land must either engage in share-cropping, lease land, or

---

[30] Cf. Stephen P. Ladas, *The Exchange of Minorities: Bulgaria, Greece, and Turkey* (New York: Macmillan, 1932); and Joseph J. Senturia, "Mass Expulsion," *Encyclopedia of the Social Sciences*, Vol. X, pp. 185–89.

[31] Hailey, *op. cit.*, p. 419.

[32] Cf. Drake and Cayton, *op. cit.*, pp. 214–62; Feldman, *op. cit.*, pp. 20–77; and Richard Sterner, *The Negro's Share* (New York: Harper, 1943).

work for someone else. Experienced farmers are reluctant to improve the land on which they are working as long as there is a possibility of its being taken away from them as soon as its value has been enhanced.[33] Merchants and entrepreneurs in minority groups have also been handicapped by special licensing regulations. In response to petitions against Asian immigration the government of Transvaal enacted a law in 1885 that not only denied Asians citizenship and the right of property ownership but required the registration of all Asians who wanted to trade in the territory. The Gold Law of 1908 reserved to Europeans the right to mine minerals, and no person of color could acquire rights in the proclaimed mining areas.[34] In various parts of Southeast Asia similar controls have been imposed upon the activities of Chinese farmers and businessmen.

Although qualified professional men from ethnic minorities are generally granted licenses to practice, their activities are often curtailed by informal understandings that develop within the profession. Studies of the medical profession in American cities reveal, for example, that hospitals vary considerably in prestige and that the doctors in the better organizations are not necessarily the most competent. Graduates of medical schools vie for internships in hospitals with the greatest prestige, but interns are not selected on the basis of competence alone. A certain minimum proficiency is expected, of course, but other criteria are decisive; men are selected who fit the pattern of the hospital in terms of ethnic identity, class background, and type of specialization. Although county hospitals and public clinics often draw staff members from all ethnic groups, elite Protestant hospitals are generally closed to all doctors but those on their staff. These doctors are drawn from the "right" medical schools, trained in the "right type" of hospital, and must be sponsored by a senior colleague already on the staff.[35]

Most members of subordinate groups become part of the labor force, but they have difficulty in organizing to protect their interests. They are often excluded from membership in labor unions, and in

---

[33] Cf. Eliot G. Mears, *Resident Orientals on the American Pacific Coast* (Chicago: University of Chicago Press, 1928).

[34] Hailey, *op. cit.*, p. 389; and Kuper, Watts, and Davies, *op. cit.*, p. 26.

[35] Oswald Hall, "The Stages in a Medical Career," *American Journal of Sociology*, LIII (1948), 327–36; and David N. Solomon, "Ethnic and Class Differences Among Hospitals as Contingencies in Medical Careers," *ibid.*, LXVI (1961), 463–71.

many communities they are not even allowed to organize among themselves. In South Africa the natives may organize if they wish, but they are forbidden by law to strike; hence, they are deprived of their major weapon. In many cases minority groups are kept in their "place" through unequal wages, even for the performance of the same tasks. In the Union of South Africa the disparity is especially marked. According to the Census of Industrial Establishments, the average annual income for 1944–45 for Europeans drawing salaries was £540. Wages varied as follows: Europeans, £341; Coloured, £149; Asians, £145; and Africans, £91. In the mines European workers earned on the average approximately 14 times as much as non-Europeans.[36]

Legitimate authority rests upon consensus. Since the beliefs that support a social order are learned, control over the educational system is important. After their conquest of Manchuria in 1931 the Japanese lost no time in renovating the school curriculum to develop views more favorable to the new regime, to instill a spirit of "Manchukuo" nationalism, and to counteract the spread of "liberal" and Marxist views.[37] Although a number of European colonial administrators have advocated raising the educational level of their subjects, others have long opposed such a policy, arguing that it would raise the competitive advantages of minorities. As long as the natives remain illiterate, they cannot compete for the more skilled and technical positions; furthermore, they are less likely to aspire for equality.[38] On the other hand, employers in industrial enterprises want better-trained labor; hence, they advocate the establishment of trade and vocational schools to teach skills that would make minority peoples more useful workers. In the United States Booker T. Washington won the cooperation of many white people by advocating such limited training for Negroes, and he became embroiled in a controversy with other Negro leaders on this very issue.[39] Although some members of the dominant group have a cold, calculated policy to facilitate subjugation, others sincerely believe that inferior people are incapable of absorbing knowledge, that they would be happier if left uneducated. Just as defenders of the status quo so often oppose edu-

[36] Hailey, op. cit., pp. 165, 1276, 1280, 1388; Richmond, op. cit., p. 105; and Sundkler, op. cit., p. 34.
[37] F. C. Jones, op. cit., pp. 44–48.
[38] Cf. Lugard, op. cit., pp. 426–28, 442, 456.
[39] Cf. Myrdal, op. cit., pp. 879–907.

cational benefits for minorities, those who advocate change stress its importance. Communist and nationalist agitators trying to mobilize discontented minorities often stress the importance of literacy and education. Learning to read is a definite part of many nationalistic programs; among other things, propaganda then becomes easier.

Where the media of mass communication are controlled by the dominant group, news items and views contrary to its interests tend to be suppressed. In the antebellum South, for example, all news of slave revolts was concealed, since the white people feared that such information might incite other slaves. Even though there were a number of minor incidents, no concerted movement toward freedom ever developed.[40] In most countries today the mass media are regulated by licensing laws, and those charged with circulating "inflammatory" materials encounter difficulties in continuing their operations. In totalitarian states control is easier. In the Soviet Union Jews have been deprived of rights accorded to all other ethnic minorities. In 1948 the government presses stopped publishing material in Yiddish. Although this prohibition was relaxed in 1959, only six books were published between 1959 and 1962. Jewish history may not be taught, even in the Russian language. Prayerbooks in Hebrew have not been printed, and no Hebrew Bible has been published in Russia since 1917.[41]

Social unrest may develop in spite of such regulations. Popular uprisings are discouraged, however, by the incarceration or exemplary punishment of "agitators." In Natal, under a proclamation of 1928, the freedom of Africans to assemble for anything other than religious or other specified purposes was curtailed. Gatherings of more than ten persons in any native area had to be approved by the district magistrate. Under a proclamation of 1932 any native held to be a danger to public peace became liable to summary arrest and detention.[42] Several observers of the American South have described lynching as a form of terrorism to maintain the color line. Many apologists for the practice have admitted that it was a means of keeping Negroes in their "place," and most of the victims have been men accused of being "uppity." They were subjected to violence as an

[40] Carroll, *op. cit.*

[41] Moshe Decter, "The Status of the Jews in the Soviet Union," *Foreign Affairs,* **XLI** (1963), 420–30.

[42] Hailey, *op. cit.,* pp. 432–33.

example of what could happen to others who acted as they did. The murder, then, was a symbolic act. Until quite recently, local officials have been reluctant to prosecute those who had participated in lynching parties.[43] An illustration of the extent to which some officials will go to suppress what they regard to be a dangerous practice is provided by the harassment of the peyote cult by the U.S. Indian Bureau. An order prohibiting the religion was issued even before it was investigated. When a subsequent anthropological inquiry revealed that the practice was not dangerous, the study was rejected. In 1907, when legislation to suppress traffic of alcohol among Indians was under consideration, representatives of the Bureau recommended that peyote be included. Congress refused to pass the law, but the Indian Bureau went ahead with its program anyway. It persisted even when a court held that religious persecution was unconstitutional. Not until 1935 were the restrictions finally lifted.[44] It is not surprising that so many protest movements among minority peoples become clandestine and subversive.

In well-established systems of ethnic stratification, people of minority standing are generally sufficiently adjusted to their way of life that there are no widespread demands for change. Should injustices arouse resentment, there is actually very little that can be done; the disparity of power is too great. In many cases minority groups are so weak that there is no serious thought of revolt. In some cases the major problem is that of survival in the midst of poverty and disease, and concern for status is lost in the struggle to meet more immediate needs.

The Regulation of Social Mobility

Even in the most backward of minority groups there are bound to be individuals of exceptional ability who learn quickly the ways of the dominant group. Unless avenues are provided for these people to gain some kind of satisfactory status and self-respect, they can be dangerous. Should they have some of the qualities of "natural leaders," they may become bitter rebels who assume leadership of revolutionary movements. Even where there is little likelihood of their

---

[43] Cf. Oliver C. Cox, *Caste, Class, and Race* (New York: Doubleday, 1948), pp. 548–64.
[44] Slotkin, *The Peyote Religion, op. cit.*, pp. 50–56.

overthrowing the established order, they can be a nuisance. In most stratified societies, therefore, there are special arrangements for accommodating individuals of unusual competence. They are often granted special privileges denied to others.

Many conquerors have found that it is easier to rule their subjects indirectly by controlling the traditional sources of power in the subordinate group. Parts of India and Malaya, for example, were ruled by the British through native princes, and after World War II there were still over 300 sultans and regents in the Dutch East Indies.[45] In such colonies the social organization of subordinate groups is left largely undisturbed. Since the people are permitted to pursue the values of their own culture, they can achieve satisfactory careers. They are therefore less likely to rebel.

Being a puppet ruler is by no means an easy task. An ideal African chief, for example, had to be an efficient tax collector, cooperate enthusiastically with official policies, show no favoritism among his subjects, and be immune to corruption. He was expected to remain ahead of his people and to set examples for them—by educating his children and by maintaining high standards in housing and latrine construction. But he should not be so far ahead as to lose his influence or to become dangerous. At the same time, he was expected to maintain his dignity and to be a "natural leader" of his people.[46] But such officials enjoy many benefits denied others of their ethnic group. In some communities they are accepted in the elite circles of the dominant group. Furthermore, they retain high status among their own people. Since they can enjoy some measure of self-respect, they are less likely to become leaders of a revolt. In Europe it was comparatively easy for aristocrats of different ethnic groups to join forces to maintain order. They shared a common culture, spoke one another's languages fluently, and lived by a similar code of ethics. The aristocrats had much more in common with each other than they had with the ordinary people with whom they were identified.

When leaders of minority groups become dependent upon the support of their rulers, they often become defenders of the status quo. During the Manchu rule over China, from 1644 to 1911, the frequent Mongol invasions over the Great Wall were stopped by granting special privileges to the Mongol leaders. The Manchu rulers

[45] Kennedy, *op. cit.*, p. 327.
[46] Cf. Southall, *op. cit.*, p. 306; and Gluckman, *op. cit.*, pp. 51–52.

increased the number of Mongol chiefs, and those who owed their position to the new regime were readily drawn into allegiance with it. Then, each chief was required to visit Peking periodically—accompanied by his retinue—and the cost of travel and the need of maintaining appearances while at the capital impoverished the chiefs and increased their dependence. Before long they began to encourage Chinese colonization of the plateau of Mongolia at the expense of their own people. They had to sell land to immigrants to reimburse their coffers. While they enjoyed high status and the pleasures of Peking, the Manchu dynasty was able to rule undisturbed by border raids from the north.[47] In South Africa the Zulu people expected their chiefs to represent them and to stand up for them against the colonial government, but the power of the chiefs had been curtailed. They had lost their wealth, and they could no longer levy tributes or requisition labor. They became so dependent upon their rulers that they were in no position to revolt.[48] In some cases puppet rulers even cooperate in the crushing of uprisings by the more militant youth in their group.

Immigrant communities, for the most part, are also left alone as long as the people do not break laws, and they are usually governed, formally or informally, by their own leaders. Within the social world of minority groups the more ambitious are able to rise above the ordinary ranks and to pursue satisfactory careers. Professional men, for example, can generally find enough clients within the group to earn a comfortable living, and they often command deference markedly greater than that enjoyed by their colleagues in the dominant group. Although successful professional men in minority groups oppose segregation as a matter of principle, many of them realize that separation protects them against open competition.

Systems of ethnic stratification vary considerably in the extent to which upward social mobility is permitted. In some cases, as individuals in minority groups acquire the culture of the dominant group, they are granted some recognition and limited privileges. In the small New England community studied by Anderson, mobility was possible because of ties of friendship that developed across the various color lines. To hold back the son of a man with whom one had done business for 20 years would have been difficult, and most

---

[47] Lattimore, "Chinese Colonization in Inner Mongolia," *op. cit.*, pp. 293–94.
[48] Cf. Gluckman, *op. cit.*, pp. 154–60.

men did not even think of it—"He is an Italian, but he is all right."
On the other hand, because the people knew one another and their
respective family histories, there were definite limitations on how far
one could advance. No matter how great a fortune a man might
amass, he encountered people in the community who remembered his
grandfather and the part of town in which the old man had lived.
This kept him from being fully accepted in the social elite.[49]

To the extent that biological lineage is emphasized, however, social mobility becomes more difficult. One cannot become a member
of the dominant group, regardless of his ability, except by being born
into it. In the Union of South Africa a registration system has been
established to place each individual into one of the legally defined
ethnic categories. Preparatory to enforcement of the stringent regulations of the *apartheid* program, a registration of the people was
begun in 1955. Some persons of "doubtful racial origin" suddenly
found their lives drastically reshaped. In one short review ses-
sion, a number of people who had always regarded themselves as
"Coloured" were reclassified as "Native" and thrust to the bottom of
the social ladder. This registration, in which each individual received
an identity card containing his classification and photograph, would
eventually make it impossible for borderline cases to "pass" into a
higher category. When a system is rigid, it tends to persist for a
longer period. However, when a dominant group is so sharply set
off from all others, its members encounter more difficulty in establishing friendships with outsiders with whom they share common interests or in forming alliances with leaders of minority groups
who favor the status quo. When life conditions change, such rigid
systems tend to be challenged in an open revolt, often in a violent
uprising.

Intermarriage is discouraged almost everywhere, and it is prohibited in those areas in which genetic lineage is a paramount consideration. Where the differences between ethnic groups are believed
to be inherited, each group can maintain its integrity only through
endogamy. Where marriages must be registered with the government, this prohibition constitutes a serious barrier to changing the
boundaries of the color line. During the English occupation of Ireland the Statute of Kilkenny was passed to forbid English administrative officials from marrying the Irish in the belief that this would

[49] Anderson, *op. cit.*, pp. 56–72.

prevent their developing too strong an interest in the Irish cause.[50] In the Union of South Africa the Prohibition of Mixed Marriages Act of 1949 made it illegal for a European to marry a non-European. Irregular sex relations became punishable under the Immorality Act of 1950.[51] Although color lines in the United States are undergoing change, intermarriage is still infrequent. Among those who wish to retain their distance from Negroes, the greatest opposition is to sex relations and marriage. There are several states that prohibit intermarriage; these laws vary somewhat in their definition of ethnic categories, and in most cases marriages contracted in other states are recognized as legal. Even where the practice is not illegal, officials at the license bureau, clergymen, and friends try to discourage the couple. There are also family pressures, often resting on the belief that such marriages are bound to fail.[52]

The prohibition of intermarriage undeniably reaffirms the color line. The intimate ties of married life usually break down stereotyped conceptions on the part of the participants and their friends, and the offspring often have physical and cultural characteristics that make them more difficult to classify. Where intermarriage occurs on a large scale, the conventional symbols of ethnic differentiation eventually become useless. But opposition to intermarriage is usually more than an attempt to defend the status quo; it is also an emotional reaction to failure. People who conceive of themselves as representatives of a "pure race" and take pride in their ancestral heritage feel obligated to do their part in preserving it. Many think of their progeny as the part of themselves that they leave to the future; there is ego-involvement, and the thought of having progeny bearing some of the stereotyped characteristics of an alien group is revolting.

A system of ethnic stratification may also be perpetuated through cooptation, a procedure whereby the more competent members of minorities are incorporated into the ruling class.[53] As these people are accepted and given the responsibilities of high rank, they often develop strong allegiances to their new associates. Minority groups

---

[50] Ware, *op. cit.*, p. 608.

[51] Hailey, *op. cit.*, p. 165; and Richmond, *op. cit.*, p. 105.

[52] Cf. Joseph Golden, "Social Control of Negro–White Intermarriage," *Social Forces*, **XXXVI** (1958), 267–69; Greenberg, *op. cit.*, pp. 343–54; Myrdal, *op. cit.*, pp. 60–67; and Wirth and Goldhamer, *op. cit.*

[53] Cf. Philip Selznick, *TVA and the Grass Roots* (Berkeley: University of California Press, 1953).

are deprived of the leadership that might have been provided by their most able men, and the dominant group is buttressed by additional talent. In a study of a community in Colorado in which 58 per cent of the people were Spanish-speaking, Watson and Samora detected no concerted effort by the minority group to improve conditions, even though considerable resentment existed against the conventional patterns of differentiation. No one in the subordinate category was willing to act as a spokesman for the group. Further inquiry revealed that the few individuals who stood out among the Spanish-Americans were successful in terms of American values, assimilated people who were viewed with suspicion as *Agringados*—"gringo-ized." These few were accepted by the Anglo–Americans as individuals, and they enjoyed respected positions in the community.[54] A number of social theorists have pointed to the effectiveness of this device, and French colonial policy was based upon this principle. In contrast to other European colonial powers France advocated a policy of gradual assimilation. As individual subjects acquired French culture, their status was to be modified, and the final step was full French citizenship. The educated native elite was to be the spearhead in a move toward incorporating all properly qualified people into "Greater France." These ideals, however, were not always implemented; in fact, they were largely negated by the political chaos at home.[55]

A system of domination can be perpetuated, then, by the orderly incorporation of assimilated peoples into the dominant group. Prior to their subjugation by Belgians the Alur of Uganda believed in their destiny to rule, and they extended their domination to the chiefless societies on the periphery of their territory by imposing their own aristocracies. Peripheral tribes such as the Lendu requested to be ruled by an Alur chief, who was desired as a rainmaker, an arbiter of quarrels, a protector from violence, and an enforcer of law and order. Then, the assimilation process would begin. Each Lendu family would be attached to an Alur household, not as slaves but in a definitely subordinate position. The male serfs were given wives by the master, who had the right to dispose of any resultant daughters, but the descendants were free men. Although incorporation into Alur society was theoretically possible only by becoming a part of its

---

[54] James B. Watson and Julian Samora, "Subordinate Leadership in a Bicultural Community," *American Sociological Review*, XIX (1954), 413–21.

[55] Kennedy, *op. cit.*, pp. 328–30.

kinship system, in practice it was possible to fabricate the necessary ancestry. The chiefs accepted as a subject and gave protection to anyone who pledged his allegiance. Thus, the Alur grew through the continuous assimilation of foreigners who had first accepted a chief. The alien groups were attached first as junior members and subject classes and gradually acquired equal status and full membership.[56]

Persons of low status who have exceptional talent constitute a problem in all stratified societies. The acceptance of all who assimilate may blur the "purity" of the dominant group, but it is thereby able to retain its ascendancy. Providing channels for the orderly advancement of such individuals facilitates the preservation of a system of stratification in which most of the people in subordinate groups continue to be denied full privileges.

Summary and Conclusion

Systems of ethnic stratification are more likely to survive if some measures are found for preserving social distance between people in the different categories, for maintaining the relative competitive advantages of the various ethnic groups, and for rewarding people who have exceptional talent. Social distance is usually maintained by convention. People in different ethnic groups generally avoid one another, and when it is necessary to interact, their conduct is governed by etiquette. By limiting the ownership of land, promotions to higher-paying jobs, and the establishment of businesses by minority peoples, the economic power of minority groups is kept to a minimum. Through control of education and of communication channels, support for the dominant group is reinforced while competing ideas are censored and agitators eliminated. As long as the means of violence remain the monopoly of the dominant group, it is extremely difficult for any subjugated people to revolt. Brilliant men in minority groups who are denied an opportunity for advancement may become leaders of troublesome insurrections, but in many cases channels develop that enable them to win self-respect. Once a system of social stratification becomes well established, it becomes extremely difficult to alter.

A stable system of ethnic stratification is a moral order. When it

[56] Southall, *op. cit.*

has persisted over many generations, there is a high degree of consensus over procedures, and the existing order is accepted as a part of nature. The persistence of patterns is a matter of conformity; each person does what he is convinced is correct. From childhood people of high rank and low are taught the rights and responsibilities of their station in life. Members of minority groups lead a separate existence, and their attempts to preserve the integrity of their group further support the existing order by reinforcing their isolation from the dominant group. Neither the laws against violating the color line nor the power to enforce them are too frequently needed in a well-established society, for even the underprivileged accept their fate without question. Should any kind of challenge develop, however, the means are at hand to defend the status quo. Thus, many social institutions persist long after the conditions that brought them into existence have disappeared.

PART IV

Disjunctive

Processes

CHAPTER 13

Social Change

and Collective Protest

Much of the current interest in "race relations" arises from concern over tension and conflict. The extended periods during which people of different ethnic categories live together in peace and mutual respect tend to be overlooked, and discussions of the subject frequently bring to mind organizations such as the Ku Klux Klan, the Mau Mau, the Nazi Storm Troopers, and the Sinn Fein. Because of their spectacular character, bombings, assassinations, riots, guerrilla warfare, lynchings, and pogroms attract a disproportionate share of attention, and even historians tend to focus upon these outbreaks of violence, which are episodic and ephemeral and constitute but a small part of what happens in the contact of peoples.

In the study of disjunctive processes we are concerned with the characteristic patterns of individual and collective behavior that develop when different ethnic groups are opposed to one another. Since minority peoples often charge that they are being persecuted, inter-ethnic conflict is often thought to be one-sided. To be sure, in some incidents the victims are helpless to fight back. In most cases, however, conflict is a joint transaction; as the popular expression goes, "It takes two to make a fight." Conflict arises when people in different categories pursue incompatible values. Both sides cannot succeed; one must give up its claims, and the struggle is to see which party will make the sacrifice. Rivalry and conflict can be found in a wide variety of contexts, ranging from two brothers' fighting over a toy to a desperate war of extermination, and all such transactions have certain features in common. Insofar as conflict is a joint transaction, the course of events can be understood only as a succession of reciprocating adjustments that the combatants make to one another. What each side does is a response to the actual or anticipated moves of its opponents; thus, the course of events is built up in social interaction.

The more spectacular clashes between ethnic groups generally occur in periods of transition, when the degree of institutionalization of stratified systems is low. Disorders of all kinds arise in situations characterized by uncertainty, either before a color line has been established or when it is breaking down. Ironically, where the color line is well established, tension is usually at a minimum. To be sure, the calm of a stable society is occasionally disturbed by a mutiny led by a resourceful rebel who becomes a thorn in the side of the authorities. But such incidents are rare and seldom a serious threat to the ascendancy of the dominant group. In stable societies minority peoples are either reasonably satisfied with their lot or do not dare challenge the existing order. What, then, are the conditions under which an already-established color line breaks down?

Before studying disjunctive processes a word of warning must be interjected. Explanations of conflict are often complicated by the tendency of participants to account for what happens in terms of the vicious traits and motives of their adversaries. Unfortunately some social scientists have followed suit in explaining violence in terms of the depravity of assassins. Although violence is not a necessary part of conflict, vicious deeds are often committed, and these generally elicit wild accusations. Such accusations are a part of the process of conflict, and they are not to be confused with a sociological explanation of it.

The Weakening of Stratified Systems

Since conflicts are not likely to occur unless members of minority groups challenge the prerogatives of their rulers, we may begin our study by examining the conditions under which minority groups become dissatisfied with their lot. The social institutions of any community represent collective adjustments to life conditions. If these circumstances change, some of the accepted procedures become inadequate, and new and better-suited arrangements eventually develop. This suggests that the various forms of opposition between ethnic groups constitute a phase in a larger process through which social structures are transformed.

Among the most important changes in life conditions are technological innovations. A social system is geared to a given material environment, and the introduction of new techniques generally disrupts the old patterns. The new ways often create new tastes, and they force changes in social relationships so that they can be utilized more effectively.[1] Sometimes a new elite group is formed, while those who had previously enjoyed high standing suddenly find themselves obsolete. For example, the invention of an automatic cotton picker has diminished the demand for cheap farm labor in the South, and it has driven many marginal farmers into bankruptcy. Both Negro and white people have been leaving the South in large numbers, and the pattern of ethnic stratification throughout the United States is being altered. Transformations may occur with the sudden loss of people with specialized skills, as in the departure of the Moors from Spain. There can be little question that the widespread adoption of automation will also lead to changes in the structure of our society. As the demand for highly skilled specialists increases and the need for unskilled labor decreases, many social dislocations can be anticipated.

When there are drastic changes in the prevailing mode of production, new interests develop that clash with customary procedures. Marked changes follow the introduction into a community of mass production—with its specialization of tasks, separation of ownership from management, and huge, impersonal labor force. In the South, for example, absentee employers were not concerned with the pedi-

[1] Cf. William F. Ogburn, *Social Change* (New York: Viking Press, 1937).

gree of their workers; there was no opposition to hiring Negroes, especially if they were willing to work for somewhat lower wages.[2] Wherever there is a shortage of labor, employers tend to encourage a spirit of tolerance and good will so that they can recruit the necessary manpower from alien sources. The voluntary segregation of minority groups also collapses from economic necessity. When the Molokans lived in agricultural settlements in Russia, they were largely self-sufficient. When they settled in Los Angeles, however, they could not possibly produce everything that they needed, and they were forced to seek employment outside their colony.[3] Gypsies were traditionally coppersmiths, musicians, bear tamers, peddlers, horse dealers, and fortune tellers; and there is little demand for their specialties in industrial societies. In the United States their campsites have virtually disappeared. Many have gone to cities, where they now express an interest in vocational training, permanent housing, and an education for their children. Perhaps one reason for the recent granting of independence to their colonial subjects by so many European powers is that the practical advantages of colonialism have been declining. As the natives insist upon higher wages and better economic opportunities, they no longer serve as a source of cheap labor. Furthermore, the growing unrest among subject peoples makes the cost of maintaining order too great.[4]

One of the consequences of such changes in the economic system is that people in minority groups may acquire new competitive advantages. The industrialization of Europe, for example, gave many of the Christians and Jews living in the millets of the Middle East advantages over their Moslem neighbors. Because of their aptitude for European languages and ways of thought, governments and commercial organizations drew a disproportionately large number of their minor employees from these minority groups, thus helping to create a *bourgeoisie*.[5] When members of minority groups acquire skills that make them an integral part of the labor force, they become indispensable to their employers. Those in the dominant group whose livelihood depends upon the cooperation of these people are among the first to make concessions. The practice of hiring Negroes in the

---

[2] Davis and Gardner, *op. cit.*, p. 478. Cf. Rudolf Heberle, "Social Consequences of the Industrialization of Southern Cities," *Social Forces*, XXVII (1948), 29–37.
[3] P. Young, *op. cit.*, pp. 122–23.
[4] Cf. Kennedy, *op. cit.*, p. 345; and Strachey, *op. cit.*
[5] Hourani, *op. cit.*, pp. 25–26.

urban North, for example, was not altered by the subsequent influx of large numbers of white people from the South. Negro workers had already proved their worth, and employers were not willing to risk alienating them just to accommodate newcomers of uncertain value. In many cases the Southerners found themselves treated contemptuously as "hillbillies"; most of them had to accept the prevailing conditions of work or do without jobs.[6] Higher wages and better jobs mean not only a better standard of living but greater purchasing power. Although some scholars question whether the economic position of Negroes has actually improved relative to other Americans, the purchasing power of Negroes is now so great that few entrepreneurs can afford to antagonize them.[7] Furthermore, better economic circumstances also give minority groups organized bargaining power. During World War II, when imports to Nigeria fell, Nigerians were forced to produce many of their own goods. War production not only increased the productive capacity of the area but stimulated the growth of labor unions from 12 with 4,337 members in 1940 to 177 unions with 165,130 members in 1955.[8]

The repudiation of customary practices while pursuing economic interests is relatively easy in a capitalistic society, where a high value is placed upon profit and upon private property. It is further facilitated by the impersonal character of money, for as the popular saying goes, "One man's money is as good as another's." Many merchants are not particular with whom they trade, and where there is respect for the operation of a free market, others are reluctant to interfere. Should people in minority groups produce goods more cheaply or be willing to sell their labor for a lower price, there are bound to be businessmen who will find them attractive. In addition, economic gains of minority groups are protected by reluctance to interfere with property rights, one of the cornerstones of a laissez-faire economy. Even under the "black codes" of the Reconstruction period, for example, when Negroes were stripped of most of their rights, their right to own property was not taken away.[9] One of the

---

[6] Lewis M. Killian, "The Effects of Southern White Workers on Race Relations in Northern Plants," *American Sociological Review*, XVII (1952), 327–31.

[7] E. Franklin Frazier, "The Negro in the United States," in Lind, *Race Relations in World Perspective, op. cit.*, pp. 348–57. Cf. Gary S. Becker, *The Economics of Discrimination* (Chicago: University of Chicago Press, 1957).

[8] Coleman, *Nigeria, op. cit.*, pp. 255–59.

[9] Allison Davis, "Caste, Economy, and Violence," *American Journal of Sociology*, LI (1945), 13–14.

major barriers faced by proponents of *apartheid* in South Africa is that the program conflicts with economic interests. If the proposed separation of ethnic groups is actually carried out, many industries would not be able to operate. Thus far, this phase of the program has not been implemented.[10]

Another type of change in life conditions is the transformation of demographic structure. A social system is geared to a particular demographic balance. The educational institutions of a community depend upon a particular age distribution, just as prostitution is more likely to be profitable where the sex ratio favors males. The preservation of a rigid color line also depends upon retaining roughly the same proportion of people in each category; any change in relative numbers may disrupt the old patterns. The demographic structure of a community may be upset by migration. People in a minority group may leave, or a large number of one ethnic minority may enter. For example, only half of the 6 million people in Malaya in 1960 were Malay; about 37 per cent were Chinese and 11 per cent were Indian or Pakistani. The Chinese were so numerous and their economic power so great that their political demands could not be ignored. The demographic structure of a community may also be altered by differential rates of growth. We live in the kind of society we do partly because the American pioneers who pushed westward enjoyed a much higher reproduction rate than the Indians. The demographic structure may also be altered by a changing sex ratio. When the sex ratio is balanced on both sides of the color line, segregation is easier to maintain. Should the sex ratio in one ethnic group become unbalanced, however, there is likely to be pressure for permitting intermarriage.

Of particular importance in inter-ethnic contacts is an increase in the density of population. The growth of cities alters many customary practices; cities have tended to be melting pots, and industrial cities in particular have been graveyards for traditions. Sentimental ties to one's own group are often weakened, and new patterns of conduct are attempted. The Molokans found it extremely difficult to maintain their isolation in Los Angeles. Their adversary was protean, informal, insidious, and therefore difficult to handle. There were no direct attacks upon them by Americans. But the desire to dis-

---

[10] Leo Kuper, "The Control of Social Change: A South African Experiment," *Social Forces*, XXXIII (1954), 26–28.

tinguish themselves as a select group diminished among the younger people, and the comforts of the new way of life to which they were exposed became more appealing.[11] Nigerian cities were aggregations of tribal units, and tribal homogeneity was to a large extent preserved in the heart of each of the quarters. But in the peripheral sectors there was a weakening of ancestral ties; new tastes were created, new values adopted, and new patterns emulated. In these areas people felt insecure and frustrated, and it was here that nationalist activities centered.[12] Even in the well-established caste system of India the exigencies of city life have forced many Hindus to alter their notions of ritual purity. In restaurants one had to eat food prepared by people of other castes, generally without even knowing who they were, and in hotels one had to eat in the company of whoever happened to be present.[13]

Drastic changes in systems of ethnic stratification sometimes follow a major catastrophe. Disasters that affect the entire community—such as floods, epidemics, famine, or invasion by a common foe—strike everyone in the same manner and require cooperation for survival. In periods of grave crisis customary barriers are usually relaxed somewhat in the face of more pressing considerations. The exigencies of life force men to respect one another for their intrinsic qualities rather than for the conventional status symbols they bear.

The relative position of various ethnic groups may also be altered by war and conquest. This has been a frequent occurrence in Europe and in the Middle East, where national boundaries have changed back and forth. The annexation of Bosnia and Herzogovina by Austria–Hungary in the early twentieth century stimulated the development of Slav nationalism. The earlier loss of German-speaking Silesia to Prussia and the strengthening of the Slavic peoples by the acquisition of Polish and Ruthenian areas also changed the relative numerical strength of the various ethnic groups in the Empire.[14] When Timbuctoo was conquered by the French soon after the turn of the century, the guild system of hereditary crafts broke down, for the new rulers forbade the use of force to keep former slaves out of the occupations they desired. Furthermore, the Arma were no longer able to

---

[11] P. Young, *op. cit.*, p. 158.
[12] Coleman, *Nigeria, op. cit.*, pp. 72–79.
[13] Ghurye, *op. cit.*, pp. 186–87.
[14] Robert A. Kann, *The Habsburg Empire* (New York: Frederick A. Praeger, 1957), p. 31.

pillage the wealthy Gabibi, who in turn found it unnecessary to plunder their subordinates to recoup their losses. Since armed robbery was prohibited, the upper classes in the various ethnic groups had to learn to live by commerce.[15] During the Japanese occupation of Southeast Asia in World War II the European colonists were placed at the bottom of the social scale. Although the Japanese were disliked, the puppet regimes they sponsored helped develop native leadership and stimulated nationalistic sentiment.[16]

Perhaps the most important change in life conditions is the transformation of values. When new ideas are introduced, especially those that challenge values previously taken for granted, an ethnic group is on its way to developing new cultural attributes. The doctrine of "white supremacy," which many subjects in European colonies had accepted, was first challenged by the success of the Japanese in the Russo–Japanese War. The defeat of the Russians in 1905 was the first concrete proof that white men were not invincible. The numerous dislocations of World War II resulted in additional doubts. Throughout Southeast Asia achievements of the Japanese in employing the industrial inventions and military methods of the white man gave the idea of the inferiority of colored people a stunning blow.[17] In New Guinea the presence of Negro troops in the U.S. Army was convincing proof to the natives that colored people, if given an opportunity, could attain the same level of accomplishment as white people.[18] In Nigeria, which was a station for troops and supplies going to the battlefields of North Africa, failure of a large number of European troops unconnected with colonial governments to observe customary aloofness provided opportunities to learn that the white man had all the vices of the colored.[19]

Despite the efforts of rulers to insulate their subjects from outside influence, knowledge of conditions in the rest of the world often reach minority peoples. Travellers bring word of life in other lands. Those who had once regarded their conditions as inevitable learn that there are people much like themselves who enjoy a very different

[15] Miner, op. cit., pp. 55–57, 181, 252–53.

[16] Cf. Wertheim, op. cit., pp. 152–66.

[17] Rupert Emerson et al., Government and Nationalism in Southeast Asia (New York: Institute of Pacific Relations, 1942), p. 16. Cf. Chaudhuri, op. cit., pp. 104–05; and Kennedy, op. cit., p. 312.

[18] Hogbin, op. cit., p. 288.

[19] Coleman, Nigeria, op. cit., pp. 253–54.

way of life. When members of minority groups learn of democratic ideals, they become critical and restive. During the nineteenth century the ideas of the Enlightenment could not be kept out of Latin America. The people rejected the doctrine of the divine right of kings, and independence came to the entire area within 50 years of the French Revolution.[20] The ideological conflict in World War II focused attention upon such basic issues as political liberty, economic opportunity, intellectual freedom, and social justice. The publication of the Atlantic Charter and the subsequent discussion of the third clause, ". . . the right of all peoples to choose the form of government under which they will live . . . ," aroused nationalistic aspirations throughout the colonial world. The pursuit of a virulent racist policy by the Nazis made such views even more important. Allied propaganda urging freedom and equality for all played an important part in sowing discontent among subjugated peoples, and in areas dominated by the Axis powers many of the natives joined resistance movements and fought courageously. The British Labor Party pledged itself to an anti-colonial policy, and public opinion in the ruling nations also underwent transformation. The entire institution of colonialism was weakened, and Prime Minister Churchill's postwar declaration that he would not preside over the liquidation of the British Empire was interpreted as a betrayal of a promise. When some colonial powers attempted to re-establish their hold after the war, they discovered that their presence was no longer welcomed. Once the ideals of freedom and equality had been released, they could not be conveniently recalled.[21]

In industrial societies the most important channel of upward social mobility is education. In Africa, the Europeans taught that education was an indispensable prerequisite to economic progress and political privilege, and the Africans accepted this belief. The educational gains of minority groups usually result in the transformation of perspectives. The people not only learn new skills but new ideas as well. Merely learning to read opens new vistas, and educated Africans have played an important part in transmitting new ideas of freedom to their illiterate fellows. News of the achievements of American Negroes provided inspiration throughout Africa. In India,

[20] George A. Blanksten, "Politics of Latin Amerca," in Almond and Coleman, *op. cit.*, p. 490; and Haring, *op. cit.*, pp. 237–43.
[21] Cf. Coleman, *Nigeria, op. cit.*, pp. 79–80, 231–49; and Kennedy, *op. cit.*, pp. 338–40, 345–46.

the educated Hindu learned that European history was a struggle for freedom, and the revolutionary leaders of Europe became the heroes of Indian intellectuals. Missionary education gave an increasing number of Africans powerful weapons, for the Christian ideals of equality and brotherhood challenge the ethical basis of colonial rule.[22] Thus, education not only raises the competitive advantages of minority peoples but also gives them access to ideas that challenge the existing order. The schools now being established throughout the world through foreign aid funds and by UNESCO will not only help people to raise their standard of living but will undoubtedly alter their thinking about social status.

As ethnic minorities acquire new cultural characteristics, they are better able to compete for jobs and for space. Through their new competitive advantages they acquire more political power. Systems of ethnic stratification begin to break down when minority peoples develop new self-conceptions and refuse to accept subordinate roles. As they become more aware of their worth in comparison to members of the dominant group, what they had once accepted as natural becomes unbearable. What had once appeared to be special privileges for superior persons is redefined as the rights of all human beings. If American Negroes had not made the progress in education and occupation that they did during the past decades, they would probably be less articulate and less effective in their protests. This widening gap between their improved economic position and their traditional social status has led to militancy in their demands.[23] The failure of people in the dominant group to recognize the fact that conditions have changed results in misunderstandings, and this *discrepancy between social status and power* is what leads to difficulties.

Once something has occurred to disturb the existing social order, there is a period of transition before a new social system is established. This period varies considerably in length, but it is almost always marked by misunderstanding and tension. Social structure rests upon consensus; concerted action is possible because men share common understandings. Social change of any kind involves a change of perspectives, and this is not likely to occur simultaneously for every-

---

[22] Cf. Coleman, *Nigeria, op. cit.,* p. 101; Franck, *op. cit.,* pp. 116–37; and Leakey, *op. cit.,* p. 71.

[23] Frazier, "The Negro in the United States," *op. cit.,* pp. 339–70. Cf. McKenzie, *op. cit.,* p. 137.

one in a community. A transitional period is one in which consensus has broken down. It is a period of uncertainty, for people are not quite sure of what to expect of one another. Frequently there is external conformity to outdated norms. Status symbols of the old order may still be honored ostensibly, even when they are no longer accepted. Some members of the dominant group realize that their claims to superiority are unjustified, and people in minorities may feign subservience to avoid possible trouble. There may be a flat contradiction between overt behavior and inner dispositions. As long as each person believes that the others still support the old order, external compliance with traditional patterns continues. What makes the re-establishment of consensus so difficult is that many refuse to reveal their inner feelings. Thus, human beings often support one another for some time on views that only a few of them actually hold. Under these circumstances the resentment of those in minority groups becomes intensified.

The transformation of the color line does not result in the abolition of inequality. In most cases one system of social stratification is replaced by another, and distinctions are made on some other basis. A system of ethnic stratification may become transformed into a class system. This is frequently the case in a capitalistic economy. As members of a subordinate group in increasing numbers acquire the culture of the dominant group, ethnic identity becomes secondary, and people begin to identify on the basis of occupation and income level. In some cases, ethnic groups change their relative ranks, while the system itself remains the same. This is what has happened in the United States. A century ago the Irish were at the bottom of the social scale, doing the least desired jobs and being despised for it. Then, as they improved their lot, they were replaced by a succession of new immigrants. The system itself has not changed fundamentally, but the strata have been occupied by different ethnic groups. Thus, when a system of ethnic stratification breaks down, it is not likely to be replaced by an unstratified society.

Upward Mobility and Marginal Status

Systems of ethnic stratification vary in the extent to which social mobility is tolerated, but some individuals in the minority group usually manage to improve their lot. Even in quite rigid societies there are ways in which higher status can be acquired by a few through ability or personal effort. Thus, in the antebellum South it was possible for a slave to purchase his freedom. Monetary rewards seem to have been fairly prevalent, particularly in the border states. From these gratuities, from money received for "overtime" work, and from pennies accumulated from the occasional sale of vegetables and chickens, Negroes were able to purchase their freedom. There was some hope, even if it was limited. Exceptional individuals are sometimes able to move into advantageous positions through the sponsorship of an influential member of the dominant group. Upward mobility of individuals of unusual talent is somewhat easier in periods of crisis, when customary barriers are not so rigidly enforced. In a changing society, then, some individuals are likely to attain a rank that exceeds customary expectations.

At first there are only a small number who escape their traditional lot, and individuals in this vanguard occupy *marginal status*, a position dangling between two social worlds. They encounter all kinds of difficulties. They develop new interests and tastes and no longer feel at ease in the company of those among whom they grew up. At the same time they are not able to participate in the society of people who think and behave as they do. They qualify formally for positions in the dominant group, but they have difficulty in getting informal acceptance.[24] In the antebellum South, when a Negro was emancipated, he was legally free, but his social status was ambiguous. A free Negro, especially if he remained in a slave area, was a misfit, and white people did not know exactly how to act toward him. Occasional privileges were granted, but most successful freedmen avoided trouble by reverting to the etiquette for slaves.[25] In many European colonies natives educated along Western lines were not admitted in equal standing in the clubs and homes of colonists. A Nigerian trained at Oxford or a Vietnamese educated at the Sorbonne was out of place. His dress, his manners, and his bearing were different, and all his real interests were reserved for "Europeans only." Other natives stared at him, and even among his own relatives he felt uncomfortable. One African writer reports that his sister dressed in her best clothing just to walk with him.[26] Those who are

[24] Cf. Hughes, *Men and Their Work, op. cit.,* pp. 102–15.
[25] Aptheker, *op. cit.,* pp. 76–78; and Doyle, *op. cit.,* pp. 86–99.
[26] Peter Abrahams, *Tell Freedom* (New York: Alfred A. Knopf, 1954), pp. 268–75.

among the first to acquire the culture of the dominant group are on the margin between two ethnic groups, partly in and partly out, and not a full participant in either.

In transitional societies those who have advanced too quickly find themselves in a succession of situations in which they have no clearly defined role, and their fate is not an enviable one. Marginal status is ambiguous, and those who occupy it are often attacked by people on both sides. They are resented by members of the dominant group who find it difficult to justify their special privileges in the face of the ability of some of their new competitors. During the colonial era in Mexico, for example, the Mestizos were hated by the Indians as allies of the Spaniards and mistrusted by their rulers as potential leaders of Indians.[27] Before the Civil War free Negroes were walking refutations of the entire ideology of the South. There were fears that they would corrupt the morals of slaves and would enter into competition with white people. Laws were passed making it a capital offense for them to assist slaves in conspiracies or uprisings. Other laws regulated their presence in the streets after dark and restricted their educational opportunities, their freedom to move from one state to another, and their entrance into certain trades. Just before the outbreak of the Civil War some states passed laws that virtually re-enslaved Negroes who were free. The apprehensions were unjustified, for many freedmen claimed that the appropriate division should be between free and slave and not between Negroes and white men. They accepted the prevailing attitudes toward slavery and tried hard to maintain a sharp distinction between themselves and the slaves. Many of them stayed away from "common" Negroes and avoided marriage with persons with dark complexions.[28] It is not surprising, then, that marginal persons are also attacked by members of minority groups. They are often accused of "thinking they are too good for us." Sometimes the accusation is justified, for some successful men try to escape their past and look with contempt upon those they left behind. But even those who are not snobbish are subjected to carping criticism. Such individuals therefore tend to become isolated from both groups; this is a fate they share with innovators in all areas of social life.

In European colonies individual natives who were separated from their tribal origins before this practice became widespread found

---

[27] Gruening, *op. cit.*, p. 24.
[28] Aptheker, *op. cit.*; Doyle, *op. cit.*; and Rose, *op. cit.*, p. 12.

themselves in similarly anomalous positions. Those who were among the first to leave their villages to work for the colonists, especially if they had an opportunity to learn the language and to study, found themselves without ties to any particular group. They saw enough of European culture never to be able to return to what they regarded as the "superstitions" of their tribal past; many of them came to despise their parental ways. But they were excluded from the society for which they had been trained, and there were no accepted career lines open to them. That many such individuals suffered personal demoralization is a matter of record. Their lives became aimless, and they sometimes abandoned themselves to seeking hedonistic pleasures. But they remained dissatisfied, for it was difficult for them to develop self-respect.[29]

The more articulate and ambitious children of immigrants also find themselves in a similar situation. In countries like the United States, where education in the schools of the dominant group is compulsory, the younger generation acquires many of the values of the larger society. As they examine the low standard of living of their parents from this new perspective, they feel apologetic. They strive to change conditions at home so that they will not be ashamed to bring their schoolmates there. They complain bitterly of the "old-fashioned" ways of the immigrant generation. Their attitudes of superiority are resented by their elders, who regard the new ideas as foreign and evil. At the same time, they are not really a part of the dominant group either. Their manners suffer because they can imitate only the gross phases of American life, merely copying what is readily visible with little understanding of what they are doing. They lack the contacts that would give them a better appreciation of the values upon which their behavior patterns rest. The older children, the first to struggle against the customs of their parents, must bear the brunt of the conflict. Their younger siblings generally have an easier time because the path has already been cleared for them.

Children of mixed marriages or of illicit relations across the color line, especially in communities in which such contacts are severely condemned, may also find themselves in marginal positions. If persons

---

[29] Bronislaw Malinowski, "The Pan–African Problem of Culture Contact," *American Journal of Sociology*, XLVIII (1943), 649–65. Cf. Lloyd Fallers, "The Predicament of the Modern African Chief," *American Anthropologist*, LVII (1955), 290–305.

of mixed ancestry are accepted as members of the dominant group, they often disappear into the general population. But if they are not accepted, as is so often the case, their position is marginal. They are often labelled "half-breed" or "half-caste," usually a term of opprobrium. Mixed ancestry often carries with it a stigma of illegitimacy. Initially children of mixed parentage attempt to identify with the dominant group. They are very careful to differentiate themselves from the minority group, and in this they are often helped by the parent of higher rank. Even if they are rebuffed, they continue their identification with the rulers. Many try to protect their precarious status by drawing a sharper line between themselves and those who are clearly subordinate. They may even mistreat members of minority groups to demonstrate their separateness. Such airs of superiority are deeply resented. In the uprising in Madagascar in 1947 the Malagasy were as hostile toward the "half-caste" as they were toward Europeans.[30] The Eurasians in Indonesia were unpopular for the same reason. They had shown open sympathy for Dutch colonists and contempt for the natives; with the departure of the Dutch their position became very difficult.[31] After a long succession of rebuffs, some persons of mixed parentage may turn against the dominant group, but this is not a common occurrence.

The concept of the marginal man was originally formulated by Park in his study of the consequences of migration. He regarded such persons as by-products of the emergence of new societies, and he contended that the study of such individuals is instructive in that they reveal in their inner experiences the processes of social change.[32] On the basis of a number of autobiographies of marginal men, Stonequist outlined what he regarded to be a typical life cycle. Although this sequence is not always found, it occurs with sufficient regularity to merit consideration. In most cases consciousness of ethnic differences develops suddenly in a dramatic experience. The single incident, perhaps being denied something that is coveted, results in the reorientation of his life. He alters his conception of himself and his aspirations for the future. In reflecting over the incident, he becomes increasingly self-conscious. The initial reaction is to identify with

[30] Mannoni, op. cit., p. 118. Cf. Everett V. Stonequist, The Marginal Man (New York: Scribner's, 1937), pp. 29, 50.

[31] Van der Kroef, "Social Conflict and Minority Aspirations in Indonesia," op. cit.; and "The Eurasian Minority in Indonesia," op. cit.

[32] Park, Race and Culture, op. cit., pp. 345-92.

the dominant group; he regards the minority group as inferior and feels that its differential treatment is deserved. He points to himself as an exception and insists that he be exempted from the customary restrictions, for he is capable of living by the standards of the dominant group. Since he believes that his own misfortunes arise from the characteristics of the minority group, he becomes a severe critic of it. He exhorts the people to give up their undesirable practices and to conform to the values of their rulers. If he is rebuffed in these efforts, he becomes isolated, dangling between the two social worlds.[33] Marginal men often develop a keen interest in the problem of interethnic contacts.

Park believed marginal men to be neurotic. He spoke of them as a personality type arising in the conflict of cultures. The marginal man is condemned by fate to live in two social worlds at the same time, and the opposition between groups is incorporated in him as inner conflict. He is often confused. He sees himself from the standpoint of the dominant group and develops an inferiority complex. As he compensates for his sense of inadequacy, he may become aggressive or develop other compulsions. Traits commonly found in the marginal man include ambivalence, excessive self-consciousness, restlessness, hypersensitivity, moodiness, and lack of self-confidence. He has doubts about his role in many situations; he is unsure of his relationships to his friends and fears their rejection. He is often lonely and spends much time daydreaming. He sees life as a bad experience and has difficulty in enjoying himself. He is highly critical of other people and feels that they treat him unjustly.[34] As in the case of many innovators, Park overstated his case and failed to make some necessary distinctions. He failed to differentiate between being in a marginal position and the development of personality disorders, which are not necessarily connected. All persons who occupy marginal status do not become neurotic.[35]

Many persons in marginal positions somehow manage to come to terms with their ambiguous world without serious personality dis-

[33] Stonequist, op. cit., pp. 121–26.

[34] Park, Race and Culture, op. cit. Cf. Stonequist, op. cit.; and Wirth and Goldhamer, op. cit., pp. 335–57.

[35] Cf. Milton M. Goldberg, "A Qualification of the Marginal Man Theory," American Sociological Review, VI (1941), 52–58; and Arnold W. Green, "A Re-examination of the Marginal Man Concept," Social Forces, XXVI (1947), 167–71.

orders. Kerckhoff and McCormick proposed the hypothesis that the individuals most likely to develop neurotic traits are those who identify too completely with the dominant group and at the same time are rejected by it. Furthermore, difficulties increase in severity with the extent of rejection. To test these propositions they studied 84 Chippewa Indian children. Degree of identification with the dominant group was measured through questions on self-identification, preferences for associates, aspirations, and acceptance of Indian ideas and practices. Degree of rejection was measured indirectly by questioning white classmates about their "Indian" appearance. Identification with modern American standards was greatest among the children who were least "Indian" in appearance, but these children were accepted and suffered no marked personality disorders. Indian children who identified with their ancestral culture were also reasonably well adjusted. Difficulties were experienced most by those who identified themselves with the dominant group but were likely to be rejected because of their appearance.[36] Thus, some persons in marginal positions become resigned to inferior rank and accept it. Those who have incorporated the outlook and values of the dominant group, reject their inferior status, and demand what they are not likely to receive are the ones most likely to encounter difficulties.

Many of the problems confronting such individuals arise from their having to perform for two different and incongruous reference groups. Since contradictory demands are made upon them by the two audiences, they experience inner conflicts. When a man participates in two social worlds, each of which is a moral order, he cannot live up to all his obligations. Where standards are inconsistent, he will be wrong in the eyes of one of the groups no matter what he does. He may be plagued by a sense of guilt, even when he has done his very best. Such persons sometimes have difficulty in developing a consistent self-conception. As Cooley pointed out, a man comes to conceive of himself as a particular kind of human being in response to the manner in which others treat him. But what happens to a man who looks simultaneously into two mirrors and sees sharply different images of himself? For example, a native clergyman in a colonial area

[36] Alan C. Kerckhoff and Thomas C. McCormick, "Marginal Status and Marginal Personality," *Social Forces*, **XXXIV** (1955), 48–55. Cf. Elton F. Jackson, "Status Consistency and Symptoms of Stress," *American Sociological Review*, **XXVII** (1962), 469–80.

may view himself as a respectable servant of God; then, he hears his ethnic identity ridiculed and suddenly sees himself as an inferior object. Some marginal men despise themselves; human beings develop a low level of self-esteem when they feel themselves unable to live up to their moral code.[37]

People who occupy marginal status may resolve their difficulties in several ways. If there are enough marginal men in a given community, they may form a society of their own. This does not always happen, however, for such persons often despise one another and shun each other's company. Once such groups have been established, the members become preoccupied with maintaining its position above the minority group. Societies of detribalized natives often develop where they happen to congregate. In the slums of Johannesburg, for example, Africans of diverse tribal backgrounds are developing a new culture that differs both from their ancestral ways and those of Europeans. Persons of mixed parentage, if rejected by both sides, sometimes find solace in one another's company. The Cape Coloured in South Africa and the Creoles in Louisiana are among those who acknowledge mixed ancestry and have formed their own groups.

Some individuals are able to exploit their marginal position by finding or creating jobs in which their familiarity with both cultures can be used to advantage—such as interpreter, negotiator, or foreman of special work groups. Sometimes special positions are created for them. Thus, an ecclesiastical junta in Mexico in 1539 decided to admit a few carefully chosen Indians and Mestizos to minor orders to aid priests in parish work. Although this decision was subsequently reversed, exceptions were always made, and friars of minority groups were not uncommon. They were generally assigned to the rural parishes, however, and there was little hope of advancement.[38] Such persons often find it necessary to ingratiate themselves to enhance their usefulness; self-interest frequently becomes their policy. Although they are sometimes regarded by outsiders as leaders of the minority group, in many cases they are quite unpopular.

Most marginal men meet their difficulties by leading segmented

[37] Stonequist, *op. cit.*, pp. 145–46. Cf. Robert J. Lifton, *Thought Reform and the Psychology of Totalism* (New York: W. W. Norton, 1961), pp. 117–32; and Wulf Sachs, *Black Anger* (Boston: Little, Brown, 1947).

[38] Haring, *op. cit.*, p. 216.

lives. They divide their activities into compartments and become somewhat different persons while participating in each social world. This type of partial dissociation is common among those living in complex societies; daily they move from one set of roles to another, shifting their perspectives to meet the requirements of each situation. Embarrassment occasionally arises when they must deal simultaneously with people from two social worlds, but in general they can keep the contexts separate and lead divided lives. If some marginal individuals appear to lack spontaneity, it may be that they cannot afford to relax. They must always be on guard lest they say or do the wrong thing at the wrong time. It is easier to keep incongruous perspectives separated if most relationships with other people are formal.[39]

After being confronted by a succession of disagreeable incidents, some persons withdraw. Such retreat may take several forms. Some reject most of their associates and submerge themselves completely within a small group. They then have a single, reasonably consistent set of expectations to meet. One may retreat into a life of scholarship or into a religious cult. Or he may join a group of outcasts, like lepers. One place where they frequently find a home, however, is among the *avant garde*. Informal circles of aspiring artists, writers, and musicians and those who seek their company are often insensitive to ethnic identity and sympathetic to the cause of downtrodden people. Since they are themselves outcasts from polite society, they lose no status in associating with those who have been rejected elsewhere. For some individuals the isolation may be more complete. One may become a hermit or a lone worker in a field that does not require too much collaboration. Withdrawal may on occasion even take the form of chronic alcoholism, drug addiction, or psychosis. People may free themselves from their inner conflicts and guilt feelings by abandoning their goals. They withdraw from human society and absolve themselves of all responsibilities. Some may even commit suicide.

Some marginal men become innovators—artists, writers, or scientists. What characterizes the work of such persons is the setting of lofty goals and perfectionist standards, which they pursue with

---

[39] Cf. Hughes, *Men and Their Work, op. cit.*, pp. 102–15; and William J. Goode, "A Theory of Role Strain," *American Sociological Review*, XXV (1960), 483–96.

compulsive dedication. Whether the aim is the development of a new art form, a scientific theory, or a new religion, they put forth prodigious effort. Hoffer proposes the hypothesis that fanatics in any field are persons who are unable to form a satisfactory self-conception. They are people who have rejected the values of the group in which they grew up and have a long history of disturbances in interpersonal relations. They identify with some larger program of unquestioned worth and then sacrifice everything—including their life and their family—for the "cause." This becomes their way of struggling for self-esteem. Neurotic striving, then, is a way of compensating for sharp feelings of inadequacy. The neurotic character of their striving is revealed by their inability to cease struggling when they have succeeded, even after they have won world-wide acclaim. Even after winning acceptance in the dominant group, they keep going, looking for more fields to conquer. Such individuals often lead miserable lives, but through their dedication they sometimes make outstanding contributions in their fields, thereby enriching the lives of countless others.[40]

The manner in which a difficult situation is resolved depends, of course, upon the personality of the individual and the circumstances in which he finds himself. Sometimes marginal men who have been rebuffed by the dominant group identify themselves with the minority group. Since they often have advantages of education and contacts with the rulers, they are able to provide badly-needed services and technical skills. Some marginal men become champions of the oppressed, leaders of revolutionary or reform movements. This may account in part for so many political leaders of minority peoples being compulsive, rigid, and intransigent. Much of the egocentrism and the expediency that so often characterizes their conduct may arise from an explicit recognition of the relativity of morals, an insight a marginal person is more likely to have than one who has only lived in one society. The jealousy with which some minority group leaders look at one another and the vindictiveness with which they glare at their defeated foes may be products of long-festering hatred. In a society in which upward mobility is encouraged, many exceptional leaders may be individuals who lead pathetically disorganized lives. Great heroes, admired throughout the

---

[40] Cf. Eric Hoffer, *The True Believer* (New York: Harper, 1951); and Karen Horney, *Neurosis and Human Growth* (New York: W. W. Norton, 1950).

world for their achievements, are often thoroughly disliked by their intimate associates.[41]

The fate of those who occupy marginal status is important, for these individuals play key roles in the transformation of a stratified society, especially as critics and as models. Because of their in-between position, marginal men may become acute and able critics of the dominant group and its culture; as political leaders they often call attention with embarrassing accuracy to the foibles and weaknesses of their rulers. They combine the knowledge of the insider with the critical attitudes of the outsider. They are also in an excellent position to develop some measure of objectivity and to escape ethnocentrism. They often have more insight and are likely to question things that others take for granted.[42] Furthermore, through their sometimes neurotic endeavors they set the pace for others. They show what can be done, and their achievements are sometimes outstanding. Successful individuals in minority groups help eliminate the belief in the inherent inferiority of the category. The development of a small, rising class of educated natives among colonial subjects demonstrated the falseness of the doctrine of the inferiority of colored peoples. Such living examples provide models for those who come after them. Through their compulsive endeavors many marginal men hasten the breakdown of the color line, even when they are not making direct assaults upon it.

The Development of Collective Protest

Although many suppose that popular uprisings occur when oppressed people become so poverty-stricken that they are no longer able to withstand the misery, this is apparently not the case. Oddly enough, the period preceding revolutions is characterized by a gradual increase in the wealth, cultural attainment, and power of the subordinate group.[43] As Marx pointed out, people in abject poverty—

[41] Cf. Harold D. Lasswell, *Power and Personality* (New York: W. W. Norton, 1948); Gerhard E. Lenski, "Status Crystallization," *American Sociological Review*, XIX (1954); 405–13; and Elton Mayo, "Routine Interaction and the Problem of Collaboration," *ibid.*, IV (1939), 335–40.

[42] Cf. Stonequist, *op. cit.*, p. 155; and Simmel, *op. cit.*, pp. 402–08.

[43] Cf. Crane Brinton, *The Anatomy of Revolution* (New York: Prentice–Hall, 1952), pp. 30–41; James C. Davies, "Toward a Theory of Revolution," *American Sociological Review*, XXVII (1962), 5–19; and Robert A. LeVine, "Anti-European Violence in Africa," *Journal of Conflict Resolution*, III (1959), 420–29.

the *lumpen proletariat*, as he called them—are so preoccupied with the problem of survival that they have little time to worry about politics. Although wars, famines, and similar calamities sometimes precede rebellions, such events serve only to intensify resentments that have been developing for a long time and make it easier for agitators to crystallize support for a movement. What is important is not drudgery, but changes in perspective. When people in under-privileged positions see their world in a different light, they detect new possibilities and become dissatisfied even when they are materially better off. Thus, in Madagascar, the Malagasy uprising came during the period of prosperity following World War II; the people had just been granted more liberties and given guarantees against forced labor and arbitrary punishment.[44]

In the last analysis, then, the most important change is psychological—the manner in which people define their situation and their roles in it. Systems of ethnic stratification rest upon popular acceptance of classifications of people and of the assignment of rights and duties to each category. When a system is changing, *the most significant transformation occurs in the self-conceptions of an increasing proportion of individuals in the minority group.* Those who had previously accepted their inferior rank as inevitable develop new aspirations and new ideals of a good life. Hence, even if objective conditions do not change or even when they improve, they feel that the circumstances are unbearable. Indeed, the improvement of their lot may have much to do with their developing the notion that they are just as deserving as members of the dominant group. That they had been able to improve their lot is taken as evidence that they are not inherently inferior. When people begin to believe in their own worth, they can no longer accept invidious distinctions without resentment. They begin to regard themselves as being deprived of something that is rightfully theirs. Decent and respectful treatment is no longer seen as a privilege that is extended to them out of kindness, but something that they deserve. Having to remove one's hat and to answer "Yes, Bwana" or "No, Bwana" appears normal as long as subordination is accepted as natural, but it rankles a man who conceives of himself as a person entitled to live in dignity. Whereas paying deference to someone in the dominant group had previously been

[44] Mannoni, *op. cit.*, pp. 135–36.

regarded merely as good manners, it is now seen as a symbol of sub-servience and cowardice.

Difficulties arise when the dominant group fails to acknowledge changes that have occurred and continues to treat its subjects in the same manner. Even when self-conceptions change, the system of stratification remains the same as long as the dominant group still has the power to enforce its ascendancy. A direct challenge may not be made, but people who feel oppressed begin telling their children that they are being robbed of something that belongs to them, and a younger generation arises with a festering sense of injustice. The recent militant protests of American Negroes become more under-standable in this light. Negroes have made substantial educational gains, but they still have difficulty in converting their training into jobs for which they are qualified. This discrepancy places a man in a status dilemma; the contradiction lies in his being assigned a humble and limited status while bearing characteristics that ordinarily assure higher rank. An educated Negro cannot accept the status to which Negroes are customarily assigned; he usually develops a feeling of intense resentment.[45] The customary attitude of the dominant group, even when it is kindly, becomes a source of resentment. Members of the dominant group often remain condescending; many see themselves as protectors of the interests of minorities. But the protected are always at the mercy of their protectors; they get only what they are given. Resentment is especially strong in colonial areas in which people of subordinate rank are "charter members" of the community. The natives may have accepted subordination in the be-ginning when confronted by the superior technology of the con-querors, but once they feel that they can manage their own affairs, they see their rulers as intruders. A longer period of tutelage is felt to be unnecessary, nothing more than an excuse for further exploi-tation.

At first discontent has no particular direction. People are rest-less and dissatisfied, but they are not able to pinpoint the blame. They thrash about and complain; they move around in an erratic and aim-less way, as if trying to find something but not knowing just what it is. Tension and uneasiness arise when aggressive impulses are ex-perienced, which, in the absence of definite goals, lead to random

---

[45] Cf. Hughes and Hughes, *op. cit.*, pp. 188–99; and Ralph H. Turner, "Negro Job Status and Education," *Social Forces*, **XXXII** (1953), 45–52.

behavior. There are vague apprehensions, alarms, fears, rumors, and exaggerated charges. At first, the complaints are about the inconveniences and hardships of daily life. Africans living in the urban slums of South Africa, for example, complain about poor housing accommodations and the inadequacy of their wages to meet the high cost of city life. They also complain of taxes. The flat-rate tax—either in the form of a hut tax or a poll tax—is much resented, not only because people generally dislike the idea of paying taxes, but because of the great difficulties that they encounter in finding the means of payment.[46] As an increasing number in minority groups become dissatisfied, social unrest becomes more widespread. What is important is that the restless become increasingly responsive to one another. As they begin to realize that they share common grievances, social distance breaks down among people of subordinate standing, even if they are still of several different ethnic categories. More effective communication then becomes possible among the aggrieved.

Widespread discontent often leads to sporadic outbreaks of violence, but for a time a program of action does not develop. These initial mutinies are usually suppressed, and the "troublemakers" are imprisoned or killed. There have been many such scattered and unconnected uprisings in Africa. In 1903, the Bondelzwarts—Hottentots north of the Orange River, who had mixed with the Boers—rose against German authority. Although they numbered only about 5,000 fighting men at most, they occupied the German forces for four years. While the Germans were preoccupied with the Bondelzwarts, the Bantu Damara also broke out in rebellion. They destroyed all the German homesteads they could find. In 1905, there was a more serious uprising in German East Africa, when several tribes joined in an effort to oust their rulers. Officials, missionaries, planters, and traders were murdered, and it took nearly a year and a half to subdue the rebellion. An estimated 120,000 natives died in this struggle from fighting, the famine resulting from the destruction of crops, and disease.[47] In 1929, dissatisfaction over abuses in native courts and a rumor that women were to be taxed touched off a women's movement that spread quickly through the most densely populated provinces of Eastern Nigeria. Riots broke out. Europeans and native chiefs cooperating with them were attacked indiscriminately, and there was

[46] Hailey, *op. cit.*, pp. 643, 680, 1284.
[47] Johnston, *op. cit.*, pp. 413, 417–18.

widespread destruction of property.[48] As violent as these rebellions were, none of them seriously challenged the hold of the colonial powers in Africa.

Serious demands for reform usually develop over a period of several generations. As in the case of other mass movements, the evolution of collective protest is irregular and episodic. An energetic leader in one locale may push a number of reforms, but with his passing the movement may lapse. Members of different factions within the minority group often clash over the best strategy, and the more conservative elders caution young firebrands of the dangers of challenging their rulers. Protests develop in many areas of interest; demands are made for new arrangements in education, in labor relations, in taxation, in the use of public facilities. Periodically, trivial incidents attract attention, and they may result in mass demonstrations. The efforts of dissatisfied minorities are often groping and uncoordinated. They lack organization, and for a time there is no established leadership. What leadership there is consists of pace-setters rather than directors. Initially they are nothing more than "voices in the wilderness"; then, some of the spokesmen gain a following. In general, progress is uneven.[49]

It is through agitation that such amorphous discontent gains specific direction. The onslaught on the existing order is initially led by sympathetic intellectuals of the dominant group, by marginal men, and by successful business and professional men of the minority group. Whenever things are not going well, discontented intellectuals are among the first to call attention to the difficulties. At first most of them believe that a change of leadership or the passing of new laws will solve the problems. When this fails, some of them desert the camp of the privileged. They insist that existing conditions are unjust and point repeatedly to the corruption and ineptitude of the regime. They cooperate with the more affluent members of the minority group, who are upset either because they are not being accepted socially or because they cannot make the profits to which they feel entitled. After World War II Nigerian entrepreneurs, who desired to break into the lucrative export-import trade, found themselves frozen out of this field by the superior competitive position of European and Levantine firms. Ambitious traders who had made

---

[48] Coleman, *Nigeria, op. cit.,* p. 174.
[49] Cf. Blumer, "Collective Behavior," *op. cit.,* pp. 199–202.

profits in the wartime expansion of the cocoa industry had hoped to use their capital to establish direct relations with foreign manufacturers. The great economic power exercised by a small group of European firms gave rise to a popular image of alien collusion and exploitation. It was at this time that various entrepreneurial groups began to back nationalist movements.[50] Such agitation provides "explanations" of the discomforts and crystallizes sentiments. What men do depends upon their definition of the situation, and the aim of an agitator is to get people to see things in a particular way.

When those who are dissatisfied are not organized, communication among them is limited. One important channel of communication is the printed page—books, newspapers, and leaflets. The protest literature that develops in such contexts calls attention to many injustices and demands reform. The writings of such American Negroes as James Baldwin, Claude McKay, and Richard Wright are of this character, as is the novel on South Africa by Alan Paton, *Cry, the Beloved Country*. *Uncle Tom's Cabin*, a novel by Harriet Beecher Stowe first published in 1851, played a significant part in the growth of the abolitionist movement, for it provided a powerful weapon for the opponents of slavery. One of the most influential books of this kind was *Noli Me Tangere*, first published in 1887, by the national hero of the Philippines, José Rizal. Its theme was the evil of Spanish colonialism. The people found that Rizal wrote of things they knew from experience; the characters were familiar and the injustices described were those they had endured. Such literature intensifies dissatisfactions, awakens hopes, and implants suggestions. It leads to the asking of questions that had never been raised before. The more intelligent and literate members of the dominant group begin to wonder about the moral order. Such literature also makes possible communication among people who are widely dispersed. Of course, agitation is facilitated when linguistic barriers are somehow overcome. The use of Swahili, a language not burdened with the stigma of being a white man's tongue, as the *lingua franca* in Kenya, Tanganyika, and Zanzibar by all ethnic groups has helped nationalist leaders communicate over great distances.[51] The usual reaction of officials to the appearance of propaganda is suppression, but this is rarely effective. If anything, it focuses attention upon the material and arouses the

[50] Coleman, *Nigeria, op. cit.*, pp. 80–87, 251–52; Hailey, *op. cit.*, p. 1458.
[51] Coleman, "Politics of Sub-Sahara Africa," *op. cit.*, p. 348.

curiosity of those who might otherwise not have read it. *Noli Me Tangere* was banned by Spanish authorities, and the author was sentenced to death in absentia, but the book swept through the islands like a forest fire. It was copied by hand and passed about surreptitiously from house to house.[52]

The contributions of angry intellectuals on both sides of the color line are important, for they expose the weaknesses of the existing order and encourage demands for justice. They publicize scandals that occur in the dominant group, revealing that people of high rank are not too different from others. Those who engage in debaucheries or cultivate sophisticated tastes that provide a stark contrast to the deprivations of the poor are exposed. Waste, extravagance, and unnecessary splendor are often financed through corruption, and this is also attacked. The exposure of illegal and immoral activities by those in high position leads to heated discussions. Questions are raised that undermine faith in the moral order. Intellectuals also try to give apt expression to the inchoate desires of less articulate people, provide slogans, and thereby facilitate the spread of discontent. Some of them also provide justifying ideologies for social movements, and by describing utopian schemes they shape and crystallize the hopes and aspirations of the downtrodden.

Such writings also provide members of minority groups with a sense of dignity and self-respect. Some intellectuals publicize the worth of minority peoples. Through selection and exaggeration they sometimes build up a glorious historical past to which the underprivileged can look with pride. The people develop a new perspective, a new way of looking at the world and their place within it. Once such an outlook is formed, those who are convinced that they deserve better things will naturally demand changes. If various attempts at reform fail, many conclude that the overthrow of the existing regime by force is justified.[53]

In ethnic minorities that are beginning to object to their station in life consciousness of kind is intensified. Men become selectively responsive to matters involving identity; awareness of differences between groups becomes acute. There is hypersensitivity to slights and

---

[52] Cf. José Rizal, *The Lost Eden*, trans. Leon M. Guerrero (Bloomington: University of Indiana Press, 1961).

[53] Cf. Lyford P. Edwards, *The Natural History of Revolution* (Chicago: University of Chicago Press, 1927), pp. 50–66.

innuendoes, and innocent acts are often misinterpreted to conform to suspicions. Since the struggle to desegregate schools developed in the United States, there has been much more concern over skin color and other symbols associated with the position of Negroes. A white man trying to be friendly may find himself accused of being prejudiced for calling a Negro acquaintance by his first name. In 1956, the Board of Education in Toronto ordered the removal of *Little Black Sambo* from the bookshelves of the city's schools after hearing complaints from a delegation of Negroes. This led to a storm of protest from librarians, some of whom pointed out that the children's story was set in India, not in the American South.

An awakened sense of injustice is eventually focused upon a few selected objects, and issues become defined with increasing clarity. Customary procedures that are regarded as roadblocks are singled out for condemnation. Throughout Asia people have been especially sensitive about extraterritoriality, the practice of granting to foreigners special immunities from local law enforcement agencies. That intruders could not be punished for violating laws of the land seemed unjust.[54] In South Africa, the passbook has been singled out as the symbol of oppression. In 1960, a demonstration over passbooks at Sharpsville resulted in violence in which 72 were killed and over 250 wounded. In Kenya, discontent centered on the question of land. European settlers, unfamiliar with Kikuyu laws, had made payments to anyone who happened to be occupying the land they desired. According to Kikuyu custom, however, land could not be acquired by conquest, nor could a sale be made without the approval of the extended family to which it belonged. The British settlers had come just at a time when the area had been temporarily depopulated by a succession of calamities, and they had thought it to be unused. To the Kikuyu land represented not only livelihood but also his connection to the traditional society of his tribe. Thus, even though only a small portion of Kikuyu land had actually been taken, most of the coveted highlands having belonged to the Masai, agitation centered on the question of regaining lost land.[55] American Negroes have had many grievances. For a long time they focused their wrath upon

---

54 Cf. Philip M. Brown and Arthur N. Holcombe, "Exterritoriality," *Encyclopedia of the Social Sciences*, Vol. VI, pp. 36–39.

55 Leakey, *op. cit.*, pp. 1–13, 28–30, 64–77. Cf. St. Clair Drake, "Some Observations on Inter-ethnic Conflict as One Type of Inter-group Conflict," *Journal of Conflict Resolution*, I (1957), 166–76.

"Jim Crow" practices in public accommodations: segregation in schools, refusal of service in public establishments, and segregation in public transportation. In the 1960's attention centered increasingly on charges of police brutality. Since any social system is too complex for most people to understand, an oversimplification of the difficulties is inevitable. Changes in a handful of practices would hardly alter the structure of a community, but the concentration of attention upon a limited number of objects facilitates the mobilization of sentiments.[56]

In some areas commercial enterprises that play a prominent part in the economy are singled out as symbols of exploitation. Many Latin Americans are convinced that the nationalization of the United Fruit Company would solve many of their problems. In Nigeria the AWAM, the Association of Western African Merchants, became the symbol of oppression. Six European firms had joined to make import agreements and to allocate export quotas. The economic power exercised by this small group of European firms appeared to have the support of the colonial government, since nothing was done to curb the association's activities. Agitators pointed out that the annual profits of these firms exceeded the annual expenditures on education, that the salaries of 3,000 European employees exceeded the wages paid to 100,000 natives, that the bulk of European salaries and firm profits were not reinvested in Nigeria, that the mining royalties paid to one firm over a 10-year period equalled nearly one-sixth the total Nigerian budget. Protests against the monopoly became especially vocal during and after World War II. When wartime shortages forced the growth of local industries, the local products were noticeably cheaper than imports. This provided the "proof" for which the agitators had been waiting. They charged that the industrialization of Nigeria was being prevented by the British, who wanted to protect their home manufacturers.[57]

The struggle is often visualized in minority groups as a contest between leaders of the two sides. Various individuals who are prominently involved are singled out and labelled. Outspoken leaders of the minority group as well as the "white angels" who come to their aid become the heroes and are personified with sterling attributes.

[56] Cf. Walter Lippmann, *The Phantom Public* (New York: Harcourt, Brace, 1925).
[57] Coleman, *Nigeria, op. cit.*, pp. 80–90, 253.

At the same time outspoken defenders of the status quo are also picked out and personified as selfish, wicked men. Thus, the complex political struggle is defined in the minds of the people in relatively simple terms: heroes and villains are engaged in a succession of skirmishes. Obnoxious practices and personifications become the symbols around which participants of minority movements can be rallied and urged to donate time, money, and services.

The new definitions and self-conceptions are reinforced through sanctioned communication. The things that people say, like almost everything else men do, are subject to social control. Certain kinds of remarks find a receptive audience, while others are greeted coldly, if not with open hostility. As discontent intensifies, remarks that tend to support the color line are condemned, and only those views pointing to injustices are tolerated. Reports that tend to give members of the dominant group credit for sympathy and understanding are dismissed as "propaganda," and those who repeat them find themselves under fire as traitors. In time, those who are not in sympathy with the protest movement learn to remain quiet. It is through such selective communication that a new perspective is molded and crystallized in the minority group.

Summary and Conclusion

When life conditions change, systems of ethnic stratification break down. Members of ethnic minorities alter their cultural characteristics and thereby acquire new competitive advantages. As their capacity to make their way in the existing social order is enhanced, there is a discrepancy between power and status. The retention of old privileges by the dominant group is resented by people who feel deprived of what is legitimately theirs. Some members of ethnic minorities acquire the culture of the dominant group more rapidly than others, and as they advance in the social scale, they find themselves in ambiguous situations. They are out of "place" and are often attacked from both sides. Although marginal men may adjust in a variety of ways, some of them identify with the subordinate group, after first attempting to win acceptance in the dominant group and being rejected. They may become leaders of minority movements, and their personal problems sometimes complicate the political scene. As increasing numbers in minority groups develop new self-conceptions, they reinforce one another's discontent. Agitation gives direction to their unrest, and in time dissatisfaction centers upon a few selected objects that are held responsible for their discomforts. It is at this point that demands are made for social reform.

Since demands for social reform arise only after minority groups have improved their lot to the point where they can challenge their rulers, defenders of the status quo might conclude that the most effective way of protecting their interests would be to keep their subjects so close to the margin of existence that there is no time for politics. Such a policy has been pursued by some groups in the past, in some cases with success. But sooner or later subjugated people acquire new skills that enable them to compete more effectively, and rigid systems of ethnic stratification are eventually overthrown in violent uprisings. Especially in our age, when humanitarian ideals are a central part of most political ideologies, such outright exploitation is not likely to work. A dominant group that is uncertain of the rectitude of its stand, a group that is split into bickering factions, is not likely to retain its ascendancy.

CHAPTER 14

Inter-Ethnic Tension

and Conflict

Aesop's fable of the snake and the wasp is one that men in the twentieth century might well ponder. A wasp settled on the snake's head and stung it repeatedly. No matter what it did, the snake could not get back at its tormentor; finally, in great anger, it put its head under the wheel of a wagon, and the two died together. Like many other fables this tale is meaningful because it points to a not uncommon human trait. There have been many wars in which the participants hated one another so intensely that they preferred death to negotiation. To an outside observer such determination appears stupid, but to the combatants this often appears to be the only honorable thing to do. Nor is such rigidity limited to warfare. There are industrial conflicts in which the owner of a plant chooses bankruptcy over meeting union demands. In the Union of South Africa today many Europeans openly acknowledge courting disaster with *apartheid*. In spite of such premonitions, however, they refuse to alter their course. They prefer risking death for themselves and their children and the destruction of everything they have built to granting reforms that might placate some of the Africans.

Since human beings are presumably rational creatures, how is such conduct to be explained? Nothing can be gained through collective suicide; yet this type of mentality appears to be recurrent in conflict situations. We can gain some understanding of it through a comparative study of such transactions. What are the conditions under which conflicts occur? What are some of the typical patterns of activity that arise in conflict situations, and how do these patterns develop?

Conflict and Social Change

Members of ethnic minorities who suffer heavy losses in conflict often claim that they are the victims of unjust persecution. From their standpoint this is frequently the case. But losers are not alone in believing that they have acted honorably; the victorious are also convinced that they have done the right thing, that they had been goaded into violence. Discussions of conflict are often accompanied by moral judgments, but the fixing of blame does not provide an understanding of disjunctive processes. A more fruitful way of approaching the problem is to identify the conditions under which ethnic groups become so intensely opposed to one another that they attempt to damage or destroy each other.

Conflicts frequently occur in situations that are inadequately defined, as in the period before a color line has been established. Following the initial contact of ethnic groups ensues a period of trial and error; neither side has yet made firm commitments, and each is waiting to see what the other will do. The settlement of the American frontier north of the Rio Grande provides a good example of this type of context. Although the Indians had established friendly relations with trappers and explorers, their interests clashed with those of settlers. As pioneers encroached upon free land, they threatened the way of life of the hunters. Neither side understood the motives of the other, and there followed a succession of wars resulting in the near extermination of the Indians.[1] As the large-scale migration of Negroes into the cities of the North got under way after World War I, there developed a shifting color line. In some respects life

[1] Cf. Stanley, *op. cit.*; and Maunier, *op. cit.*, Vol. II, pp. 471–86.

was more difficult there for Negroes than it was in the South because the response of each white person was unpredictable; he might be hostile, friendly, or indifferent. Negroes had to guess in each transaction, and many misunderstandings arose.[2] After World War II colored immigrants in the British Isles found themselves in a similarly uncertain environment. Unlike the colonies, there were no established patterns of interaction, and each individual had to adjust to each situation.[3] When systems of ethnic stratification are being built up, people are not quite sure of what to expect of one another. Each person has to act on his own, for there is as yet no customary procedure to follow. As misunderstandings arise, people become hesitant, and there is widespread frustration.

Many conflicts, however, occur between groups that have been living together for some time. Violence sometimes erupts during or soon after catastrophes, when tensions that have been generated in a prolonged war, depression, revolution, or epidemic are dissipated in attacks upon unpopular minorities. Soon after the Russian Revolution, for example, some of the restless mobs unleashed their anger against the Jews in their midst.[4] Many of the "race riots" in the United States have occurred either during or immediately after a war. In such situations people are under severe strain. There are a variety of ways in which such tensions may be released, and violence against vulnerable people is one of them. Crisis situations provide opportunities for those with grudges to express themselves, and they are able to commit aggressive deeds that would otherwise not be tolerated. Unsuccessful businessmen find it convenient to have their competitors eliminated, and those who owe money have a simple way of cancelling their debts. When people are upset, agitators can more easily put the blame for their woes upon some unpopular group.

The type of situation in which inter-ethnic conflicts probably occur most frequently is one in which a well-established color line is breaking down. When the customary procedures no longer enjoy consensus, outward conformity is not matched by inner dispositions. People in minority groups who are no longer willing to accept their subordinate rank become resentful. Members of dominant groups

[2] Cf. Drake and Cayton, *op. cit.*, pp. 263–86.

[3] Cf. Banton, *The Coloured Quarters, op. cit.*, p. 13; and Clarence Senior, "Race Relations and Labor Supply in Great Britain," *Social Problems*, IV (1957), 302–12.

[4] Cf. Elias Heifetz, *The Slaughter of the Jews in the Ukraine in 1919* (New York: Thomas Seltzer, 1921).

make concessions from necessity but resent having to do what they regard as improper. The history of the American South is dotted with violent incidents, and they are related to the rising status of Negroes. The practice of lynching began two or three decades before the Civil War, when white men suspected of tampering with the slave system were flogged, tarred and feathered, and occasionally hanged. After 1831 the South was forced to take a defensive position on slavery. The agitation of Abolitionists was especially resented because so many in the South had inner doubts about the practice. Furthermore, some of the pamphlets circulated were inflammatory, and fears arose of insurrection should they get into the hands of the slaves. The violence reached its peak in the last decade before the Civil War and was resumed in the Reconstruction period, when both white people and former slaves had to learn new ways of associating with each other. Negroes were legally free, but their social status was otherwise undefined. Many continued to accept the ascendancy of the white man, but others rebelled and became disrespectful. The wearing of hats become a symbol of their new status, and some Negroes insisted upon keeping their hats on even when they were indoors. There were rumors of thievery, vagabondage, and starvation. During this period the Ku Klux Klan was first formed, and Negroes and carpetbaggers were terrorized through the same tactics that had been used against the Abolitionists, until the color line was once again re-established. An estimated 4,000 people were lynched from 1880 to 1930; three-fourths of them were Negro.[5] It appears, then, that violence is most likely to occur where minority groups are no longer willing to accept the evaluation placed upon them by the dominant group.

What is particularly upsetting to many people when a color line is breaking down is that they see one another in incongruous roles. Each person has a relatively fixed conception of himself, of various categories of people, and of other objects that make up his symbolic environment. Most Americans feel no emotional reaction upon walking into a Chinese laundry, seeing Filipino farm hands, eating in an Italian restaurant, hiring a Japanese gardener, or having baggage carried by a Negro porter. Such experiences are consistent

[5] Cf. Francis W. Coker, "Lynching," *Encyclopedia of the Social Sciences*, Vol. IX, pp. 639–43; Doyle, *op. cit.*, pp. 109–35; and Clement Eaton, "Mob Violence in the Old South," *Mississippi Valley Historical Review*, XXIX (1942), 351–70.

with their beliefs. But seeing someone from any of these ethnic categories as a guest at an exclusive cocktail party would occasion some surprise. What is the reaction of most Americans upon seeing an attractive white women being escorted by a handsome Negro? During World War II many Americans shuddered at the thought of white women in concentration camps operated by the Japanese, just as they were horrified at the thought of Belgian women in the hands of Congolese soldiers during the outbreak in 1961. Why? What makes these situations more horrible than any other case of potential exploitation? Somehow they seem to be unnatural; what is perceived clashes with set expectations, and one's conception of his world is momentarily challenged. When things do not happen within the range of anticipated possibilities, a person feels uncomfortable. People in ethnic minorities who are out of "place" violate well-established notions of propriety.

Similarly, members of ethnic minorities who have altered their self-conceptions feel that others are not treating them with sufficient respect and not acknowledging their proper claims. A person in the dominant group may approach an acquaintance of minority standing with condescension, taking the stereotyped characterization of this category for granted. He has the best of intentions and does his best to be pleasant, considerate, and helpful. If the party of lower rank regards himself as inferior, the two will get along quite well. But if he believes himself to be as good as anyone else, he becomes offended at the implication of inferiority. He objects to being treated like a child, and he may express his resentment openly, much to the dismay of the man who had approached him in good will. For people who are upwardly mobile a patronizing attitude is really more damning than open antagonism. To many American Negroes, for example, the calm assumption of inferiority is a far keener hurt than the aggression of an adversary who admits that they are worthy of fighting.[6] Since Dr. Albert Schweitzer has devoted much of his life to the welfare of Africans, most Americans and Europeans assume that he is revered by those who know of his work. Actually, he is a controversial figure among African nationalists. Some regard him as domineering and patronizing—a figure out of the nineteenth century. They charge, "He is doing things for us, not with us," and resent

[6] Cf. Edwin R. Embree, *Brown America: The Story of a New Race* (New York: Viking Press, 1931), pp. 204–05.

him. Thus, much of the tension found in such situations arises from the breakdown of consensus concerning the classification of people, their characteristics, or their proper roles.

If other people do the unexpected, the situation becomes uncertain, and one cannot act out a conventional role. There is delay, misunderstanding, and necessity of adjusting. This can be irritating. Acting at cross purposes often results in frustration for people on both sides of the color line. Much of what happens in such contexts is irrational, for the reactions are more emotional and spontaneous than deliberate and planned. Psychologists have attempted to account for the hostility that develops under such circumstances in terms of what has been called the "frustration–aggression hypothesis." According to this theory, a frustrated organism will attack the agent held responsible for the interference. For example, a man who is in a hurry to answer a telephone and stumbles over a chair may turn back in fury and kick the chair. If the object believed to be responsible cannot be attacked, one may direct his aggression against a more vulnerable substitute. A person who has lost an argument against a formidable foe may kick a stray dog in the street, or a man who has been tormented during the day by his employer may turn upon his wife when he gets home. Another possibility is that a frustrated person may turn upon himself. People do punish themselves for their failures and, in extreme cases of guilt, may even kill themselves.[7] As everyone knows from his personal experiences, there is much truth to this theory. Unfortunately, however, it has been applied uncritically and indiscriminately in the field of inter-ethnic contacts.

The frustration–aggression hypothesis is valuable as an explanatory scheme, as long as two major limitations are recognized. First, as psychoanalysts have frequently pointed out, frustration does not *always* lead to aggression. Tensions may be dissipated in a variety of ways—by daydreaming, through slips of the tongue, through accidents, or by sublimation. Aggression is but one of many possible reactions to frustration, and the problem remains of ascertaining the conditions under which frustration results in aggression rather than some other compensatory response. In all probability the manner in which frustration is handled is a personality trait. Some individuals have hair-trigger tempers and attack at the slightest provocation;

---

[7] Dollard *et al., op. cit.* Cf. Theodore M. Newcomb and Eugene L. Hartley (eds.), *Readings in Social Psychology* (New York: Henry Holt, 1947), pp. 257–96.

others are quite placid and manage to sublimate most of their hostile impulses. Still others are upset by certain types of frustration but not by others. Second, the hypothesis applies only to *individual* behavior and not to *collective* phenomena.[8] Under ordinary circumstances an angry individual is not likely to attack a member of an ethnic minority or, for that matter, anyone else. Such assaults become possible only when large numbers of people are sufficiently aroused to engage in violence or at least to condone it. Thus, in explaining inter-ethnic tension and conflict one must ask how individual frustrations become *shared* so that they provide a basis for concerted action. In unsettled times large numbers of individuals experience frustration, but they must be able to *communicate* with one another before sufficient consensus develops to mount a concerted attack upon unpopular people.

Where a system of ethnic stratification is not firmly established, persons of different ethnic categories are brought into *direct competition* with each other. There is no such competition in a stratified society because the conventional roles of people in different classifications are clearly separated; each has different responsibilities. But where these conventional norms are no longer observed, men begin to compete with one another as human beings—without benefit of or hindrance from customary barriers or advantages. They compete with one another for favorable ways of earning a livelihood, for space regarded as desirable, for mates, and for whatever other values prized in the community. Since victory so often depends upon cultural characteristics, persons of minority standing who have acquired competitive advantages that they are not supposed to have make headway beyond what is expected of them. Under these circumstances competition, which is unconscious and impersonal, is transformed into rivalry. When competitors are able to single out the opposition and identify it clearly, the struggle becomes more deliberate and personal. Instead of merely doing one's best in striving for values, a conscious effort is made to outdo an opponent. Rivalry and conflict develop most frequently in those situations in which men compete on relatively even terms, especially where opposition is so intense that conventional norms governing competition are overlooked.

Men generally become more upset in rivalry over women than

[8] Cf. Jessie Bernard, "A Sociological Study of Conflict," in *The Nature of Conflict* (Liège, Belgium: UNESCO, 1957), pp. 46–55.

they do over anything else. The fact that there is far greater opposition to women of the dominant group becoming involved with men of lower rank than there is to the seduction of women of minority groups suggests that self-esteem is involved. Women are seen as prizes for which men compete. In erotic attraction human beings respond to one another largely as unique individuals, *not* as enactors of conventional roles. Social status is often only a secondary consideration; sometimes it is irrelevant. Each potential partner is evaluated for what he is as a human being, and he succeeds or fails on the basis of the estimate placed upon his personal qualities. Both in Great Britain and in the United States the greatest hostility against Negroes arises when there are contacts between colored men and white women. Control of this phase of the color line may be even tighter in the United States than it is in the caste system of India.[9] In recent years one of the major complaints against "beatniks" has been that they condone sex relations between white women and Negro men.[10] This type of association is seen as repugnant and unnatural, and the objection is strengthened by the widely-held belief that Negroes are sexually more virile and satisfying than white men. Those who have serious doubts about their attractiveness to women cannot afford to lose in this type of rivalry. The intensity of emotional reactions suggests that it is especially difficult for men who have the advantages of high status to admit defeat.

Violence frequently erupts in communities in which different ethnic groups are struggling for the use of land. The riot in Shanghai in 1874 resulted from such rivalry. The International Settlement had been established by treaty, but the areas adjacent to it were being sold to the highest bidder. As European and American purchases increased, tension developed, and violence finally broke out when the French tried to build a road through a Chinese cemetery.[11] The four areas of Africa in which there has been the most trouble are those with the largest settlement of Europeans: Algeria, the Central African

[9] Cf. W. Lloyd Warner and Allison Davis, "A Comparative Study of American Caste," in E. T. Thompson, *Race Relations and the Race Problem, op. cit.*, pp. 219–45; Banton, *The Coloured Quarter, op. cit.*, p. 71; and J. A. G. Griffith *et al.*, *Coloured Immigrants in Britain* (London: Oxford University Press, 1960), pp. 68–72.

[10] Cf. Francis J. Rigney and L. Douglas Smith, *The Real Bohemia* (New York: Basic Books, 1961), pp. 50–52, 163–65, 182.

[11] F. L. Hawks Pott, *A Short History of Shanghai* (Shanghai: Kelly & Walsh, 1928), pp. 93–98.

Federation, Kenya, and the Union of South Africa. By contrast, there has been comparatively little tension or violence in Nigeria, where European and other foreign peoples made up only a small proportion of the total population; furthermore, only a few of the Europeans in Nigeria considered themselves permanent residents, most of them being missionaries, employees of European firms, or civil servants.[12] The "race riots" in Chicago in 1919 and in Detroit in 1943 both arose from the struggle for space resulting from mass migrations of Negroes from the South. There were approximately 210,-000 Negroes living in Detroit in 1943, segregated into a ghetto called Paradise Valley. There was simply not enough room, and Negroes were forced to bid for better housing accommodations. In addition, competition for goods and services, already scarce in the wartime economy, intensified antagonisms.[13] In a comparative study of violence in the United States Grimshaw found that, except during the peak of rioting, the incidence of violence was highest in "contested areas" in which Negroes and white people were vying directly for housing.[14]

Rivalry for jobs and for economic security also results in tension and sometimes in violence. We have already noted (in Chapter 4) that considerably more hostility toward minority groups is found among the unsuccessful, and agitation against outsiders is most sympathetically received among those who are struggling with them. In American history there is a direct correlation between peaks of agitation against ethnic minorities and valleys of economic difficulty. All of the major "anti-foreign" political movements—the Native American Party of the 1830's, the Know Nothing Order of the 1850's, the American Protective Association of the late nineteenth century—won their largest following in hard times. Various regional movements—against Orientals on the Pacific Coast, against Italians in Louisiana, against French-Canadians in New England—have also coincided with depressions in these areas.[15] In the South all transactions between Negroes and white people other than trade have been

---

[12] Coleman, *op. cit.*, pp. 33–34.

[13] Alfred M. Lee and Norman D. Humphrey, *Race Riot* (New York: Dryden Press, 1943). Cf. Chicago Commission on Race Relations, *The Negro in Chicago* (Chicago: University of Chicago Press, 1922).

[14] Allen D. Grimshaw, "Urban Racial Violence in the United States," *American Journal of Sociology*, LXVI (1960), 114–15.

[15] Donald Young, *Research Memorandum on Minority Peoples in the Depression* (New York: Social Science Research Council, 1937), pp. 133–41.

subject to conventional control. But storekeepers, contractors, farmers, and others providing services for Negroes had to treat their clientele with some deference. Violence has occurred most frequently in those areas where a large number of Negroes were better off economically and could insist upon some relaxation of the color line. The largest number of lynchings have occurred not in the regions with the highest percentage of Negroes, but in areas where Negroes constituted less than 25 per cent of the population. Where the colored population was sparse, Negroes were less involved in the plantation system and competed more directly with poor white people.[16] In the Union of South Africa the entry of immigrants from Asia into new industrial occupations during World War I aroused considerable resentment. Sentiment against them also ran high in the European communities in East Africa, when it was widely believed that Asian traders had made excessive profits during the German East African campaign.[17]

The persecution of minority groups in Europe is also related to economic rivalry. The massacre of Armenians in the Ottoman Empire in 1894 and 1895 came after the Christian minority had improved its economic position. The affluence of the artisans and the merchants aroused envy and fear among the Turks and the Kurds. Armenians had traditionally purchased protection against nomadic intruders from the Kurds, but the introduction of a new system of tax assessment left little money for these payments. Many Turks regarded the Armenians as potential allies of powerful Christian nations, especially Russia, and the Kurds saw them as a threat to Islam. The mobs were frequently made up of people who disliked the traders to whom they owed money.[18] The 690 anti-Semitic pogroms that took place in Russia from 1903 to 1906 occurred under similar circumstances. In 1882 all Jews had been segregated to the Pale, a series of provinces along the western frontier from Riga to the Black Sea. The same laws excluded from agriculture all Jews who were not already in it; thus three out of five inhabitants in the urban cen-

---

16 Coker, *op. cit.*, pp. 640–41; A. Davis, *op. cit.*; and Eaton, *op. cit.*, p. 369.

17 Hailey, *op. cit.*, pp. 391, 395.

18 Joachim Barckhausen, *Männer und Mächte am Bosporus* (Berlin: Schützen Verlag, 1938), pp. 226–27; Edwin M. Bliss, *Turkey and the Armenian Atrocities* (Philadelphia: J. H. Moore, 1896), pp. 277–79, 503; and Frederick D. Greene, *Armenian Massacres or the Sword of Mohammed* (New York: G. P. Putnam's Sons, 1896), pp. 41, 59.

ters of the Pale were Jews, for 1.3 million had been forced off the land. Confined to the towns, the Jews had to compete for limited industrial, service, and trade opportunities. Since the conditions were harsh, they sometimes resorted to illegal tactics to eke out a living, and this led to further antagonism. Popular passions were turned against the Jews in a succession of massacres beginning with the Kishinew riot of 1903.[19]

When members of ethnic minorities engage in aggressive action, their hostility is often directed against other minority groups rather than against the rulers. In Hawaii a succession of immigrant groups entered as plantation workers and then rose in the economy. In stages, as they became conscious rivals for positions of dignity and responsibility, attitudes of indifference or tolerance were replaced by suspicion or open hostility.[20] Just as the primary targets of African rioters in Durban in 1949 were the Indians, in the European colonies in Southeast Asia hostility was directed against the Chinese and the Indians. In the Philippines a widespread belief developed that the livelihood of Filipinos was endangered by Chinese remittances to relatives in China.[21] The usurious practices of the *chettyar* money-lenders no doubt accounted for some of the hostility against the Indians in Burma, but by and large alien minorities in Southeast Asia became targets of nationalist animosity because they appeared to be a barrier to the economic advancement of the native population.[22] Thus, aggression is directed against the group that is singled out and identified as the opponent, and this group may or may not be responsible for the aggravating conditions.

The frequency with which hostility is directed against economically successful minority groups has led some theorists to contend that economic competition is the "cause" of inter-ethnic conflict. This is not true, for many people who are locked in competition do not fight, and people have been attacked who were not regarded as economically threatening. In any changing society some discontent and unrest is inevitable; those who have been uprooted from traditional positions are frustrated and find themselves under consider-

---

[19] H. Otto Dahlke, "Race and Minority Riots," *Social Forces*, XXX (1952), 419–25.

[20] Lind, *An Island Community, op. cit.*, pp. 268–74.

[21] Purcell, *op. cit.*, pp. 614, 630.

[22] Furnivall, *Colonial Policy and Practice, op. cit.*, pp. 86, 294, 336; and Jacoby, *op. cit.*, p. 79.

able tension. Relative success makes minority groups more vulnerable, for attacking an "unfair" rival is easier than acknowledging personal failure. Those who are encountering difficulties are less likely to resist agitation against their opponents. But inter-ethnic conflict is a complex transaction that can develop in many ways. *The course of events in each situation takes shape in the social interaction of the participants with each other*, and the content of communication provides a better clue of what is likely to happen. The existence of competition and rivalry, with marked success by minority peoples, makes the task of agitators easier; however, it cannot be singled out as the "cause" of hostility.

The Formation of Contrast Conceptions

From time immemorial men involved in conflict have committed the most vicious deeds against one another. They have fought with great courage and determination, only to wonder afterward whether victory was worth the sacrifice. This has happened over and over, and one wonders why men do things in the heat of conflict that subsequently fill them with amazement or remorse. Attempts have been made to explain atrocities in terms of sadistic instincts, but this is not sufficient. Such tendencies may very well exist in some individuals, but they are ordinarily suppressed. We must account for their being released under some circumstances and not under others. Since the things men do depend upon their definition of the situation, behavior in combat must be explained in terms of typical definitions formed in such contexts. Human beings interact in terms of the conceptions they form of themselves and each other, and participants in conflict apparently construct typical personifications through selective perception. What is perceived often depends more upon the sensitivities of the perceiver than upon the attributes of the object. To what kinds of sensory cues are people in conflict situations sensitized? What kinds of conceptions are they likely to construct, even independent of the activities of their foe?

In conflict situations there tends to be a sharper definition of group boundaries and greater consciousness of kind. When the actual differences between opponents are slight, they tend to be exaggerated by accentuating status symbols. Ethnocentrism is intensified, and the disposition to evaluate the strange in terms of the known tends to convert the realization of differences into moral judgments.[23] Thus, in conflict situations there is a bipolarization of the participants into the good and the evil. A particularly fruitful concept is the *Gegenidee*, coined by Voegelin in an attempt to account for anti-Semitism in Germany. In building up the idea of the "Jew" attributes were selected that Germans unconsciously disliked in themselves. Only by attributing such qualities to someone else could a positive characterization of the ideal German be constructed. The Jew became the *Gegenidee*, the contrast conception, built up through the projection of all the traits rejected by Germans in forming their self-conceptions. Copeland subsequently used this concept to describe inter-ethnic contacts in the American South. He believed that Negroes and white people were defined in moral antithesis, white people attributing to Negroes all those traits that were the opposite of the qualities they valued in themselves.[24] But white people have not always conceived of Negroes in this manner—only when they were involved in conflict. When people are gripped with anxiety, they tend to see things in clearly delineated terms, and thinking generally becomes more stereotyped. The enemy is transformed into unrelieved evil, and one's own side is seen as possessing all the virtues.

People on both sides form similar conceptions of their opponents. In situations in which the color line is breaking down, those who are upwardly mobile insist that they are as worthy as members of the dominant group, although some of them may have inner doubts. Since they view themselves as equal, perhaps even as superior, they resent being relegated to inferior status. They are especially sensitive to slights. Some become so hypersensitive that they appear to be walking about with a "chip on their shoulder," looking for trouble. Any suggestion of inferiority, though unintended and without hostility, elicits sharp reactions. When a friendly white custodian refers to a Negro physician as a "boy" and to his colleague as a "gentleman," there is an angry explosion. Members of the dominant group are defined as roadblocks, as barriers—in short, as frustrating objects.

[23] Cf. Murdock, *op. cit.*; and E. T. Thompson, "Race Relations in the Modern World," *op. cit.*

[24] Lewis C. Copeland, "The Negro as a Contrast Conception," in E. T. Thompson, *Race Relations and the Race Problem, op. cit.*, pp. 152–79; and Eric Voegelin, "The Growth of the Race Idea," *Review of Politics*, II (1940), 283–317. Cf. Arthur Gladstone, "The Conception of the Enemy," *Journal of Conflict Resolution*, III (1959), 132–37.

They are hated as tormentors—unfair, unjust, and indecent people who are deliberately attempting to hold down the deserving to perpetuate their own advantages. Even those who had not felt this way in the past develop such views as the opposition between groups is intensified.

Members of the dominant group who accept the status quo are disturbed upon coming into contact with those of lower status who insist upon equal rights. Such individuals are viewed as a threat to their well-being. Much of what is commonly called "race prejudice" consists of the defensive hostility that might be expected of people who feel that their positions of privilege are in peril. They are convinced that minority groups are clearly inferior and that everyone could be happy if they would only be content to remain in their "place." The discontented few who threaten to upset the entire social order are viewed as dangerous objects—not only for what they might do for themselves but as agitators who might arouse others. Persons assuming a defensive stance become acutely sensitized to those qualities that make their opponents so formidable. They frequently charge that members of minority groups are clannish, that they work too hard, that they lie and cheat for each other, that they are unfair. Militant protest is condemned as "aggression," and insistence upon rights is dismissed as "insolence." In the American South a Negro with aspirations beyond his customary rank was accused of being "uppity," just as a Bantu in the Union of South Africa who was not subservient was called "cheeky." As long as American Negroes accepted their subordinate position, the prevailing attitude toward them was one of condescension and good will; when Negroes became upwardly mobile, however, this was transformed into hostility.

Participants in conflict situations characteristically impute vile motives to their opponents. Motive imputation is always inferential, and much depends upon the person who is making the inference. Since any overt act can be interpreted in several ways, the identical deed may be seen as courageous or dastardly, depending upon the intention that is imputed. Each person is sensitized to those features in the behavior of others that will justify his feelings; of the hundreds of things an opponent does, one notices only those attributes that support his hatred, overlooking or explaining away everything else. Whatever the enemy does is interpreted in the least favorable light. If he fights courageously, he is called a fanatic; if he withdraws in the face of formidable opposition, he is called a coward. If he makes an honorable suggestion for a truce, it is viewed with suspicion and a search is made for ulterior motives. The result is that the other party is personified as the combination of the most horrible traits imaginable. Everything that is condemned within one's own group is imputed to the enemy. He is cruel, treacherous, sordid, perfidious, destructive; he is a fiend who commits atrocities against women and children, against the old and the blind.[25]

In contrast, one's own group and its allies are personified as noble and self-sacrificing people who fight only in self-defense. The contrast between friend and foe is enhanced as each combatant forms an idealized self-conception. Men rarely acknowledge fighting out of greed; they fight for lofty ideals—freedom, democracy, God. Divine justice is always on one's own side, the right side. That the opponent could make the same claim is inconceivable, for good is fighting against evil. Every form of common exertion has the blessing of all the holy sentiments, and steps sometimes have to be taken among Christians to calm the doubts of those who give the Biblical injunctions against hatred and violence an inconvenient interpretation. As one Bantu in South Africa is quoted as saying, "You say the devil is black, but I picture a white man with blue eyes and yellow hair." According to one native preacher, "I know that the Lord Jesus Christ was a white man; yet I could not pray to Him and love Him as I do if I did not picture Him as black and with wool like myself."[26] In some parts of Asia and Africa, where hostility against white men has become intense, dark complexion has become a symbol of purity, a certificate of nobility, a passport to belonging. Some nationalist leaders have called for the unity of all men of color, as if they had something in common besides their grievances.

Once contrast conceptions are formed, they are continually reinforced through selective perception. Sensory cues inconsistent with expectations are overlooked. The manner in which convictions can be reaffirmed even in the absence of definite evidence is illustrated by Cameron's discussion of paranoid perspectives. A woman who has purchased a daringly new hat that may be too far ahead of the fashion

---

[25] Cf. Harold D. Lasswell, *Propaganda Technique in the World War* (New York: Alfred A. Knopf, 1927), pp. 77–101; and Leo Lowenthal and Norbert Guterman, *Prophets of Deceit* (New York: Harper, 1949), pp. 38–89.

[26] Olive Schreiner, *Thoughts on South Africa* (New York: Stokes, 1923), p. 127.

trend is afraid that people will laugh at her. The first time she ventures into the street with it she encounters a strange man who is smiling. The man is smiling to himself about a practical joke that he had played on a friend the night before, but the woman concludes that he was amused at her hat and runs inside to change it. The difference between this woman and a person with paranoid delusions that F.B.I. agents are following him is that she can communicate with her friends. When they reassure her that the hat is not comical, she can marshal her courage and venture forth again. But the person who is paranoid is isolated, and there is no one with whom he can check his impression. He suspects those who try to reassure him of being a part of the F.B.I. conspiracy, and their testimony is discounted.[27] This is not to suggest that all people in conflict are paranoid, but they are cut off from their enemies in much the same manner. Those in minority groups who are convinced that members of the dominant group are out to "get" them frequently "test" the sincerity of others. If service in a restaurant happens to be slow—perhaps because it is a very busy day—this is interpreted as "discrimination." Attempts of the management to reassure them are rejected as "excuses." Rigidity of beliefs about others is often related to danger; the more frightened a person is, the more his ideas tend to become fixed.[28]

As conflict increases in intensity, the concept is further reinforced by sanctioned communication. What a person might say under ordinary circumstances is circumscribed only by considerations of good taste and tact, but in conflict situations there is additional pressure to say only good things about one's cause and bad things about the opposition. Thus, information that might correct contrast conceptions tends to be cut off. Since the enemy is diabolically clever and his propaganda is deadly, anyone who might say anything in his behalf is suspected of having been duped or even of complicity. Anyone who points out that his own side is not faultless is seen as a traitor and is sometimes ostracized. Not surprisingly, then, leadership on both sides tends to fall into the hands of extremists. Recognized leaders of minority groups find themselves under pressure to take a militant stand. When the facts of the Nazi attempt to exterminate

[27] Norman Cameron, "The Development of Paranoic Thinking," *Psychological Review*, L (1943), 219–33.
[28] Cf. Forrest LaViolette and K. H. Silvert, "A Theory of Stereotypes," *Social Forces*, XXIX (1951), 257–62.

Jews became known after World War II, for example, American Jewish leaders found that they had to take a militant stand against anti-Semitism. Men who had changed their name and in private life put up with mildly anti-Semitic acquaintances found themselves making fiery demands in public. Had they not done this, they would have lost their following.[29] During the Mau Mau emergency in Kenya from 1952 to 1955, Jomo Kenyatta, the acknowledged leader of the Kikuyu, was reported no longer able to control the extremists. Had he arranged some kind of compromise with British authorities, he himself might have been slain by the Mau Mau.[30] As the desegregation issue became more intense in the American South, white people who took a moderate position were attacked as "nigger lovers." Similarly, a Negro who took a moderate view was attacked by other Negroes as an "Uncle Tom" or a "white man's nigger." Even the more conservative leaders of the N.A.A.C.P. were forced to take an outspoken stand.

Sumner long ago pointed to the utility of contrast conceptions. In conflict situations the differences between groups are so intensified that an ethical dualism becomes possible. The accentuation of differences is especially easy when people are already convinced that the opposition is genetically different. Since the enemy is viewed as something less than human—perhaps even as a threat to humanity—norms and obligations that hold in one's relationships with other human beings do not apply to him. A double standard of morality develops. Treachery, trickery, bribery, anything to gain an unfair advantage—the very forms of conduct that would be severely condemned within the group—are highly praised when the victim is an opponent. In war men receive high decorations for doing the very things for which they would be incarcerated at home.[31] The most vicious carnage becomes possible because of the complete lack of identification. A machine gunner would have difficulty in strafing hundreds of women and children on the streets if he were able to identify with them. Thus, as conflict develops, contrast conceptions tend to make themselves come true. Each side is forced to act in ways that make the other angry, and hostility begets a hostile response.

---

29 David Riesman, "The Militant Fight Against Anti-Semitism," *Commentary*, XI (1951), 11–19.

30 Drake, *loc. cit.*

31 Sumner, *op. cit.*, pp. 12–15.

After a while, when the opponents attribute evil intent to each other, they are largely justified.

The construction of contrast conceptions also facilitates the mobilization of group solidarity. In large-scale conflicts sacrifices must be borne by a large number of people. Once contrast conceptions are widely held, men voluntarily join the struggle, and loyalty to one's ethnic group becomes an overriding consideration. They willingly do without items they need in order to enforce a boycott called against another ethnic group. Merchants whose livelihood depends in part upon trading with the enemy suffer heavy losses. Workers do not unite on a class basis. Where there is inter-ethnic tension, the different groups maintain their distance, and employers have sometimes exploited such popular hatreds to maintain control. Labor unions in the South have faced special difficulties since the school desegregation issue attracted national attention. Since national officers of the AFL–CIO publicly supported desegregation, local leaders have had difficulty in recruiting and in getting contributions for the union fund.

Contrast conceptions bolster determination to fight to the bitter end. There can be no thought of surrender to monsters; the fate of those who surrender would be worse than death. Hence, men prefer to die with honor than to give in to the forces of evil. There have been many wars in which hopelessly outmatched soldiers have fought on courageously to the last man. Even when there appears to be some possibility of compromise, combatants cannot be induced to consider it until they have been worn down to the point of exhaustion. Even then, negotiation is extremely difficult. When men distrust each other, anything that is suggested tends to be misinterpreted. Each party is so defensive that effective communication is almost impossible. When negotiations fail, this further reinforces the conviction that the enemy is vicious. In extremely bitter conflicts reconciliation is not possible until most of the active participants have died; then, members of a new generation who have only heard of the atrocities are able to re-establish communication.

A remarkable feature of conflict is that the conception of the enemy formed on one side is almost a mirror image of the conception formed on the other. Arabs and Jews have made somewhat different accusations against each other, but the presuppositions upon which each took action against the other are almost identical. The same can be said for the British and the Cypriots, the Indonesians and the Dutch, the Japanese and the Koreans. Similar personifications are also found in other kinds of conflict. Assumptions made about the opponent in strikes, in revolutions, in wars, and even in intense football rivalries are alike. In spite of the diversity of contexts the opposition is claimed to be immoral, unfair, vicious, and incapable of appreciating human sentiments. Many conservative Americans regard Communists as devils. Communists have similar conceptions of their foes—"imperialists," "deviationists," and "counter-revolutionaries." Guerrilla fighters are often called "bandits" and are similarly characterized by the organized unit that hunts them down, whether it be the Japanese Army in Manchuria, the French Army in Indo–China, or the U.S. Marines in Venezuela. One need only compare the assumptions made by many Jews about the "anti-Semitic Gentile" and the conception of the "Jew" held by Gentiles who are anti-Semitic; they frequently accuse one another of the same things! It is only natural that they dislike each other; no one could like human beings with the attributes that make up contrast conceptions.

But hatred is directed against an abstract object, and in many cases this does not interfere with actual contacts with friends and acquaintances on the other side of the color line. Except at the height of conflict, people in opposing ethnic groups continue to carry on their trade and other relationships as if nothing had happened. Contrast conceptions are artificial constructs; they are made up through selective perception, imagination, and the projection of rejected impulses to someone else. Concrete individuals who are well known are usually not associated with them; they are exceptions.

When peace is re-established, the combatants are invariably astonished to discover that their erstwhile foes are human beings after all. Upon meeting warriors from the other side, men discover that they are not fanatic cannibals. In prisoner-of-war camps guards and prisoners often discover that they have much in common—their dislike of military routine and longing for home, their dislike of petty and meaningless tasks, the enlisted men's dislike of officers. The fact that they are so surprised is an indication of the inaccuracy of their working conceptions during combat.

Combatants often do have opposing interests, and much of their tenacity rests upon their correctly defining the enemy as an obstacle to their success. Nonetheless, much of the ferocity of conflict arises from the spontaneous reactions of men to images they construct in their minds. They invent frightful objects, become horrified, and then respond gallantly to the challenge to overcome them. They impute foul motives to people they do not even know and then react emotionally. Throughout history human beings have spent considerable time fighting against villains and ogres conjured in their imagination.

Outbreaks of Physical Violence

There is considerable variation in the ease with which individuals are aroused to take aggressive action. Some are quick-tempered and vicious; they not only take advantage of every opportunity to attack but enjoy tormenting people. Others are willing to fight when they consider it necessary or prudent to do so. Still others are very reluctant to fight and insist upon searching for alternative solutions until the very end, when violence becomes necessary. Still others will not engage in aggressive action under any circumstances, neither pushing their own interests nor resisting the encroachments of others. Frustrations of some sort are inevitable, but individuals have different frustration thresholds. Some are easily angered, while others are more understanding and tolerant.

In all societies aggression is subject to social control; it is usually prohibited or closely supervised. From early childhood people are taught to inhibit their aggressive tendencies, and the conventional roles they play generally require their dissipating hostile impulses through harmless channels. Even in moments of anger most men "count to ten" before they attack. When the strain becomes too great, however, considerations of decorum are brushed aside, and in common parlance, they "lose their temper" or "blow their top." Such outbursts represent a temporary lapse of social control, and in most cases the person is subsequently ashamed of what he has done. Thus, although there are individuals in all communities who are hostile toward ethnic minorities, they are not free to give vent to their aggressive dispositions. *Aggression receives group sanction only when a substantial portion of the people agree that such action is justified.* Even in a riot only a small proportion of the people in the community actually participates actively; rioters are usually drawn from the restless youth who have not yet acquired respectable status.[32] In the riots in London and Nottingham in the summer of 1958 colored immigrants were attacked by "Teddy boys," who took advantage of the unpopularity of Negroes to indulge in violence. Similar attacks in the past had been stopped by adults, but in this case the young men received encouragement and support.[33] The problem, then, is to account for the manner in which frustrations and resentments become collective so that respectable people support or condone activities they would otherwise condemn.

Outbursts of violence are episodic and ephemeral, and they occur after a long period of tension during which appropriate definitions develop. The lynching of Abolitionists in the South became common after the latter had deluged the region with inflammatory pamphlets. People were enraged by accusations of immoral conduct, and they were fearful of economic loss. Rumors of slave uprisings led by renegade white men periodically swept Southern communities. After the Compromise of 1850 there was even greater intolerance of anti-slavery views, and men suspected of distributing literature were set upon and attacked. The violence reached its climax after John Brown's raid in 1859. Most of the victims were white men; slaves were valuable property, and they were protected by their owners.[34] The massacre of Armenians in Turkey also developed out of a background of tension. The success of European minority groups in organizing nationalistic movements led many Armenians to aspire to a similar revival, and agitation and acts of terrorism by some nationalists served to provoke Turkish officials and to alarm the Moslem population. Whereas the Armenians had previously accepted their subordinate position, nationalist propaganda inspired many of them to demand greater political and economic rights, and many Turks viewed this growing dissatisfaction as a serious threat to their dominance. The possibility that one of the great powers might use the "Armenian question" as an excuse for an attack on the Ottoman Empire was another source of concern, and some Armenian nationalists tried to provoke such foreign intervention by inciting disorders.

[32] Cf. Kenneth B. Clark, "Group Violence: A Preliminary Study of the Attitudinal Pattern of Its Acceptance and Rejection," *Journal of Social Psychology*, XIX (1944), 319–37.

[33] Griffith *et al.*, *op. cit.*, pp. 89–90.

[34] Eaton, *op. cit.*

It was in this context that massacres broke out from the Black Sea to the Mediterranean.[35]

Hostility mounts through selective communication, through the constant repetition of hostile sentiments and the suppression of favorable comment. While interviewing Englishmen about the colored immigrants in Stepney, a borough of London, Banton found that many opened with disapproving statements. After the conversation had proceeded for a while, however, a more sympathetic attitude was frequently revealed. In an area in which many had strong feelings against the immigrants it was safer to start with mild disapproval and then to make personal reservations later on, after the others had indicated their views.[36] The initial attacks usually consist largely of communicative acts, and agitators on both sides find increasingly receptive audiences. Ill feeling between ethnic groups is manifested in open name-calling, ridicule, and taunting. In Turkey in the period immediately preceding the massacres, there was an increase in the use of terms of personal abuse in addressing Armenians in public, a practice that had previously been on the decline.[37] "Discrimination" becomes more obvious as some members of the dominant group become anxious to let their associates know where they stand. Negative jokes about the other group provide more avenues for expressing hostility. Jokes that imply unfavorable attributes and the laughter of listeners reinforce contrast conceptions.[38] Rumors also add to the tension. Events are reported in inflammatory ways. Frightened men often give vent to startling remarks; if they wish to secure a hearing, they may exaggerate or speak with greater force than the circumstances warrant. If an atmosphere of social unrest already exists, such exaggerations pass quickly from person to person, for there is no disposition for calm inquiry. In Turkey there were widespread rumors that arms were being gathered by Armenians for use against the government.[39] During World War II, when Negroes in increasing numbers began to resist "Jim Crow" practices, there were frequent

---

[35] Sarkis Atamian, *The Armenian Community* (New York: Philosophical Library, 1955), pp. 88, 150–52; and Bliss, *op. cit.*, pp. 278–79, 345–50, 478.

[36] Banton, *The Coloured Quarter, op. cit.*, p. 124.

[37] Barckhausen, *op. cit.*, pp. 350, 414, 434.

[38] Cf. Burma, "Humor as a Technique in Race Conflict," *op. cit.*

[39] Halide Edib Adivar, *Memoirs of Halide Edib* (New York: Century, 1927), p. 284.

rumors in the South of Negro women forming "Eleanor Clubs," named after Mrs. Roosevelt, through which they would seek complete equality; reportedly Negro women would refuse to work as cooks unless the white mistress agreed to spend one day a week in the Negro home.[40] Tales that would otherwise be rejected as fantastic are seriously entertained in crisis situations. Within each group the expression of hostility against outsiders provides an acceptable outlet for tensions and reinforces a sense of belonging together; it gives each person his credentials for membership. As feelings of this kind mount on both sides of the color line, social distance between opponents is increased, and there is less chance for checking the accuracy of the charges. Once people become suspicious of one another, they are less likely to notice contradictory evidence.

Through such one-sided communication the contrast conception becomes widely held, and it becomes increasingly difficult to restrain hostility. Attention is increasingly focussed upon a single object, which becomes defined in a particular way. In the Los Angeles riots of 1943, when sailors indiscriminately beat Mexicans, the "zoot suit" —the long coat and trousers pegged at the cuffs worn by boys with long, well-greased hair—became the symbol around which the rioters rallied. Turner and Surace found that during the decade preceding the riots the treatment of Mexicans in the media of mass communication had gradually become less favorable and that the concept of "zoot-suiter" had been built up as a negative symbol—being associated with sex crimes, delinquency, gang attacks, and draft-dodging.[41] When antagonistic dispositions have formed, actual contacts with the opposition intensify hostility. In a study conducted in Philadelphia in 1952 most white policemen were found to believe that the percentage of Negroes arrested in their district was higher than it actually was. In fact, the higher the actual rate of Negro arrest in a district, the greater was the overestimation of the rate. The more Negro offenders the officers actually handled, the more exaggerated was their belief in Negro criminality and the more strenuously they

---

[40] Howard W. Odum, *Race and Rumors of Race* (Chapel Hill: University of North Carolina Press, 1943). Cf. Emory S. Bogardus, *Immigration and Race Attitudes* (New York: D. C. Heath, 1928), pp. 233–36; and Chicago Commission on Race Relations, *op. cit.*, pp. 25–33.

[41] Ralph H. Turner and Samuel J. Surace, "Zoot–Suiters and Mexicans: Symbols in Crowd Behavior," *American Journal of Sociology*, XLII (1956), 14–20.

opposed the introduction of Negro policemen as co-workers.[42] Tension mounts as the participants reinforce each other's excitement through circular interaction, in which the expressive movements of one angry individual elicit a sympathetic response from those who see him, these reactions in turn reinforcing the hostility of the first person.[43] As collective excitement mounts, there is a successive transformation of perspectives, and the enemy becomes so heinous that aggressive action becomes imperative.

Periods of rising tension are often marked by individual acts of terrorism—bombings, arson, assassination, and beatings. Such intimidation usually occurs in communities in which the legal ways of maintaining the color line have been exhausted. The bombing of the homes of people in unpopular minorities who have moved into previously homogeneous residential areas occurs after all other efforts to exclude them have failed. In 1958, 27 bombings and attempted bombings were reported in the South. The victims were Negro schools, community centers, and churches, and Jewish synagogues. Exasperated law enforcement officials then formed the Southern Conference on Bombings to coordinate their efforts to control extremist groups. In 1962, as it became apparent that the Algerians would soon win their independence, the O.A.S.—an extremist organization of the French *colons*—adopted a "scorched earth" policy, which included the wanton murdering of Algerians. Nor are terrorists confined to the dominant group; members of minority groups who find their upward mobility blocked sometimes become desperate and engage in illegal violence. These are the acts of individual terrorists; they do not represent the concerted effort of an entire group, even when they may be approved by a large percentage of the people. They are the acts of a few disgruntled and impetuous individuals or of small cults, acts that are usually carried out in secret, even in situations in which the police are not likely to search too diligently for the offenders.

The hostility of some individuals may be manifested in subtle ways, so subtle that it may be very difficult to detect. When people in different ethnic groups are working together on dangerous jobs

[42] William M. Kephart, "Negro Visibility," *American Sociological Review*, XIX (1954), 462–67.
[43] Cf. Blumer, "Collective Behavior," *op. cit.*, pp. 170–71; and Park and Burgess, *op. cit.*, pp. 788–92.

that require precise coordination, injuries can be inflicted by care-lessness or by "accident." Examples of such transactions include in-fantry combat, operating a crane, loading heavy materials, or football games. Although charges of intentional malfeasance may be made, such accusations cannot easily be proved. Yet studies show that in such crews men who are most liked by their fellows tend to be ac-cident-free, while the highest accident rates are recorded by those who are unpopular.[44] This suggests that the ability of men of different ethnic categories to participate together without mishap in dangerous transactions may constitute a barometer of their sentiments toward one another. There is an intuitive recognition of the possibility of such "accidents," and in periods of tension there are many unsub-stantiated charges of foul play. This is especially true of athletic con-tests in which the participants are drawn from opposing ethnic groups.

Tension finally mounts to the point where a sense of urgency develops. Mob action involves the cooperation of a large number of people, and in this respect it differs from individual acts of terror-ism. Mob action takes place in the open and implies a temporary breakdown of conventional norms. As conflict becomes more intense, there is usually a closing of ranks by those in each ethnic category. With increased group solidarity the conventional barriers of social distance are lowered among those who are fighting on each side. A person can unhesitatingly approach comrades and allies, taking it for granted that their interests are alike. This makes interaction more spontaneous and more effective. Once extreme tension has developed mob action is touched off by some dramatic event. The "zoot suit" riot in Los Angeles started when a group of 11 sailors on leave re-ported that they had been set upon by a number of Mexican boys while walking through a slum area. On the following night about 200 sailors cruised through the Mexican section in taxis in search for victims. When the local newspapers gave prominent publicity to these incidents, large numbers of servicemen from all branches went looking for Mexicans, stripping and beating anyone they could find in a "zoot suit" and even attacking Mexicans who were dressed con-

---

[44] Cf. Boris Speroff and Willard Kerr, "Steel Mill 'Hot Strip' Accidents and Interpersonal Desirability Values," *Journal of Clinical Psychology*, VIII (1952), 89–91.

servatively.[45] Violence broke out in Alabama in May 1961, when a mixed group sponsored by the Congress of Racial Equality rode into the state to test compliance with federal court orders forbidding segregation on buses and at bus terminals. The "freedom riders" were met by hostile mobs in Anniston and Birmingham; the riders were beaten, tires were slashed, and one of the buses was burned. Often the incident that touches off the violence is in itself trivial. Such incidents become important, however, in that they arouse talk, provide a focus of attention, and present restless people with a pretext to do something.

The course of mob action is shaped as the participants mill about, and agitators play an important part. Through agitation attention becomes focused upon certain objects. Agitators provide oversimplified explanations; if they are not challenged by influential and responsible men in the community, the mob may get out of hand. As angry men mill about, the dominant mood becomes ugly: it hangs heavy over the collectivity like the atmosphere, and those who are present feel something "in the air." As tension mounts further, deliberate and rational discussion becomes more difficult. Men in mobs are intolerant; those who raise questions about the propriety of violent action are silenced or driven away, and those who persist may even be set upon and attacked. There tends to be a self-selection of participants; those who are not in sympathy with the prevailing mood leave or are chased away. The development of inter-ethnic tension is a cumulative process. Once it gets under way, it is difficult to alter or stop. Participants become more and more suggestible, responding uncritically to proposals that coincide with already-formed beliefs and rejecting those that do not.

Agitators are sometimes individuals who stand to profit from aggression against the victims, but this is not always the case. Extremists of all kinds play on the passions of people who are aroused. Sometimes they are individuals who have some real grievance against the minority group. A man whose wife had been raped by a member of a minority group harbors a festering hatred for the entire category, but under ordinary circumstances his remarks do not find such an appreciative audience. Sometimes the agitators are professional

[45] John F. Burma, *Spanish-Speaking Groups in the United States* (Durham, N. C.: Duke University Press, 1954), pp. 110–12.

agents. Some are self-appointed spokesmen who win a popular following, and some are agents of political parties. They may be members of special cults whose interests are served by trouble between ethnic groups. In most cases, however, agitators are thrill seekers who seize upon the opportunity to give vent to their feelings. They are men who ordinarily live routine lives and are not too highly respected by their fellows. They enjoy the attention they receive. They are able to win transitory followings to the extent that they are able to give apt expression to the prevailing sentiments.

As tension mounts, mob violence can be prevented only if the authorities take a firm stand. There have been cases in which the officials, sharing the same hostile feelings as the people, have actually encouraged violence. In the Armenian massacres Turkish police and military units either participated or gave no indication of disapproval. The attacks were sometimes initiated by frontier regiments of Kurds or by Turkish soldiers; popular participation followed. Peasant villages were surrounded and destroyed. In urban areas Armenian residential or business districts were sealed off and systematically attacked; in such cases the assaults began and ended with the sound of a bugle. Many of the men were killed; women and children were sometimes offered the choice of accepting Islam as the price of being spared. Many women were held captive and raped. Some Armenians were able to escape into hideouts in the surrounding countryside, and a number were protected by Turkish friends and neighbors. There was much looting: the dead and the wounded were generally stripped of their clothing; even doors and windows were taken, and what could not be detached and carried away was destroyed.[46] There have also been cases in which the officials permitted trouble to start and then had difficulty in restoring order. Sometimes they lacked the courage to take an unpopular stand. In some cases— as in the rioting during the partition of India and Pakistan in 1947 —the authority structure simply broke down. Estimates of the number killed in these riots range up to a million. The position taken by the authorities is decisive. Most cases of popular violence can be brought under control through the concerted efforts of the police and the army.

If law enforcement officers, who are usually of the dominant

[46] Barckhausen, *op. cit.*, p. 226; Bliss, *op. cit.*, pp. 421–22, 479; and Greene, *op. cit.*, pp. 34–37.

group, stand by or themselves take an active part, members of minority groups may be slaughtered. This is apparently what happened
at the pogrom in Kishinew on April 6, 1903. Prior to the carnage
there had been rumors of "ritual murder," the alleged annual killing
of Christian children as a part of Jewish rites, and considerable excitement had developed. Some officials carried on a campaign, ex-
torting money from wealthy Jews. Newspapers repeated the charge
of "ritual murder" and accused Jews of being swindlers, liars, parasites, and exploiters of Christians. The editors organized a Christian
Welfare Society to purchase weapons and to print handbills describing an imperial ukase that granted permission to inflict "bloody punishment" on Jews during the three days of the Christian Passover;
the police made no effort to block distribution of these leaflets. The
rioters included soldiers, policemen, civic servants, priests, peasants,
and laborers. The manner in which the pogrom was carried out indicates organization. About 200 men in red shirts split into 24 sections of 10 or 15 each and attacked simultaneously in 24 different
places in the ghetto. Communication was maintained among these
units by students riding on bicycles. In the beginning the rioters only
looted and destroyed property. About 3:00 A.M., however, a larger
mob formed, and this time they not only plundered but also administered beatings, raped, and killed. When Jewish leaders tried to
get official intervention, local authorities refused to cooperate, although wealthy families were able to secure protection by brib-
ing the police. For two days there was no interference from the
police. By the time troops arrived, the rioters were almost exhausted
and were dispersed without the firing of a single shot. The result
was 44 killed, 583 wounded, 700 homes wrecked, 600 shops looted,
and 10,000 people needing relief.[47]

In the American South the lynching of Negroes was for a long
time a customary practice, and it was difficult to control because of
the connivance of local officials. When a Negro accused of a crime
was dragged out of jail by outraged lynchers, local officers were conveniently absent and unable to protect their prisoner. There was
little point in bringing the lynchers to trial, for they would be freed
by the jury. However, indications are that the climate of opin-

---

[47] Dahlke, op. cit.; and Simon M. Dubnow, History of the Jews in Russia and
Poland (Philadelphia: Jewish Publication Society of America, 1920), Vol. III, pp.
66–86.

ion in the South is changing. In 1947, in Greenville, South Carolina, 26 men who admitted being part of a lynching mob were not only arrested but were charged with murder. At the instigation of the governor, the incident was investigated, a special prosecutor appointed, and the case was brought to trial. Although the 26 men were acquitted without even a word of defense testimony, the trial attracted national attention, for it was one of the few times that lynchers had actually been forced to stand trial. Officials were serving notice that they would no longer tolerate such violence. In 1955, the two men who were charged with the murder of Emmett Till, who had boasted of sex relations with a white girl in Chicago, were freed by a Mississippi jury. This did not mean, however, that the two could continue to live in the community as they had in the past. Both were from a family that had operated a chain of small stores catering to Negro trade, and all of these had to close because of a Negro boycott. When his store closed, one of the killers was unable to find a job and had to go to school under the G.I. Bill of Rights. The other decided to go into farming but found that the landowners who had contributed funds for his defense refused to rent to him. He also had difficulty in getting a loan from banks in the area, even though he had more collateral than most renters. Friends who said they had contributed money for his defense made excuses and kept their distance. Furthermore, the sheriff would not allow him to carry a gun, even though he had received several threatening letters and had reason to fear for his life.[48]

Vicious deeds are tolerated only in situations in which people are collectively excited. Once tension has been dissipated, conventional perspectives are restored, and many of the participants reevaluate their acts. Even those holding extreme views sometimes find it difficult to justify what they have done, and there have been cases of lynching mobs in which some of the participants have subsequently committed suicide. Guilt feelings are not aroused, however, when the violence can be explained in acceptable terms. Apparently no widespread sense of shame developed among the Turks who had participated in the slaughter of the Armenians. For some time survivors who ventured on the streets were greeted with derision, especially if they wore Armenian costumes. The official Turkish ex-

[48] Cf. William B. Huie, *Wolf Whistle* (New York: New American Library, 1959).

planation stressed the provocation of Armenian agitation and terrorism, and the Turkish people were satisfied that a rebellion had been suppressed.[49]

Summary and Conclusion

Inter-ethnic tension and conflict are found in changing societies. In situations in which the color line has not yet been established or where it is breaking down, there is disagreement over the relative positions of ethnic groups. Under these circumstances many occasions arise for rivalry between members of different ethnic categories. Those who do not perform effectively become frustrated and vent their anger against the interfering objects. As conflicts develop, the perspectives of the participants are transformed. People are divided into the good and the evil, and through selective perception and imagination the opposition is personified as wicked. Collective tension develops as frustrated men communicate with each other, reinforcing one another's apprehensions and anger. Agitators provide suggestions and models of action. When the prevailing mood becomes one of hostility, violence sometimes erupts after some trivial incident. In conflict situations the aggressive few, who are usually held back, are given group sanction to release their inhibitions. They attack the enemy, who has become especially vulnerable through redefinition. Violence is seen as justified, since it consists only of overcoming evil.

Reformers have long advocated the elimination of both conflict and the color line. Ironically, one arises when the other is being eliminated. As long as a system of ethnic stratification remains stable, there is relatively little tension or violence. People in minority groups do not enjoy equal rights and are sometimes exploited, but there is little they can do about it; most of them learn to accept their fate. Only when subordinate groups begin to improve their lot and to aspire for more do they come into competition with more powerful foes; then, violence frequently breaks out. But tension and conflict are transitory. They occur in changing situations and serve as the crucibles out of which new social relationships emerge. The resolution of conflict often results in the establishment of new patterns of behavior. Conflict, then, is an incidental part of the process of social change.

49 Adivar, op. cit., p. 386; and Bliss, op. cit., p. 523.

CHAPTER 15

Interest Groups

and Political Tactics

Early in the nineteenth century, in his memorable account of the fledgling republic, Alexis de Tocqueville expressed amazement at the ease and frequency with which Americans formed voluntary associations. Whenever they were displeased with something, they formed a special committee to propose changes; if some form of public entertainment was desired, they banded together and pooled their resources to assure its establishment. This spirit still pervades all aspects of American life. From childhood Americans are taught to rely on their own resources to overcome the difficulties of life. Groups are organized to meet problems of all kinds and to promote public safety, commerce and industry, and even morality and religion. Many Americans believe that anything can be improved through joint effort, and there has recently been a proliferation of groups working in the field of "race relations." Millions of dollars are spent every year for propaganda, lobbying, and litigation by voluntary associations fighting for or against changes in the existing system of ethnic stratification.

Since this type of activity is so commonplace in the United States, most Americans fail to realize that there are many societies in which voluntary associations cannot be formed so easily. The type of protest that can be lodged depends upon the political structure of the community. In a totalitarian dictatorship the formation of reform movements is prohibited. In an absolute monarchy there is little recourse for the aggrieved but to petition the crown for justice and hope for the best. Failing in this, insurrection or acceptance of one's fate are the only alternatives. Brutality can be curbed only by those who have access to sources of political power. In sixteenth-century Spain, for example, power was concentrated in the crown and in the Catholic Church. Bartolomé de las Casas, the famous "Protector of the Indians" who became a central figure in the Spanish conquest of the Americas, was a Dominican friar. He denounced the cruelty of his countrymen, demanded reforms, and for a time even persuaded Emperor Charles V to abolish the *encomienda* in Mexico.[1] The Chinese counselor who accompanied the Mongol conqueror Genghis Khan was sometimes able to save defeated peoples from being massacred by pointing out that they could be forced to pay taxes and that their labor would be needed to provide food and other supplies for the armies.[2] In this chapter we shall confine our attention to societies in which some public agitation for change is permitted. How do people organize to reform or defend the status quo? What are the characteristic maneuvers used, and what are the conditions under which each of these tactics is effective?

The Emergence of Reform Movements

In societies in which public policy is shaped at least in part through popular will, the first organized attempts to alter a system of ethnic stratification are usually reform movements. Social movements are collective enterprises through which people who are dissatisfied with some phase of the social order try to bring about desired changes. Since social structures consist of conventional understandings, they cannot be altered without the cooperation of other

[1] Cf. Lewis Hanke, *Bartolomé de las Casas: An Interpretation of His Life and Writings* (The Hague: Martinus Nijhoff, 1951); and Simpson, *op. cit.*, pp. 36–60.
[2] René Grousset, *The Rise and Splendour of the Chinese Empire*, trans. A. Watson-Gandy and T. Gordon (Berkeley: University of California Press, 1953), pp. 225–27.

people. Before a political movement can be successful, therefore, the perspectives of many other people must be transformed. Thus, considerable effort must be devoted to persuading, cajoling, or even coercing others to see things in the desired manner. There are a variety of ways in which a fight can be made to improve the lot of ethnic minorities. In complex mass societies successful political action generally requires a sizable organization and skillful maneuvering. Without them it is difficult to mobilize public support for a cause.

In situations in which a minority group is depressed and not in a position to fight for itself, the first organizations are usually established in their behalf by sympathetic members of the dominant group. This is true of many reform movements—against child labor, for women's rights, for benefits for the aged. Reformers are often persons of high status, sometimes even wealthy and influential. A good example of a reform movement is the drive to abolish slavery. There was considerable agitation against slavery in Europe, and as early as 1792 Denmark outlawed the practice. In the United States the movement got under way in the early nineteenth century, and much of the activity centered around the publication of the *Liberator* by William Lloyd Garrison. The New England Anti-Slavery Society was organized in 1832, and a national organization was formed in the following year. Many prominent men lent their support, and the members went to churches, courtrooms, schools, and public meetings to plead their cause; they also distributed pamphlets. The killing of Elijah Lovejoy in 1837 for his anti-slavery utterances further reinforced the movement, and slavery became a national issue. When the Republican Party was organized, it adopted as a prominent part of its platform opposition to the further extension of slavery. The publication of *Uncle Tom's Cabin*, the news of "bleeding Kansas," and the Dred Scott decision kept the issue before the public. Many people outside the South became determined not to compromise. Only a small percentage of the Abolitionists were Negroes.[3]

The objectives of reform movements are limited in scope. Reformers demand the modification of a few objectionable practices—forced labor, refusal to sell alcohol to Indians, inadequate hospital facilities for the poor, ethnic segregation in public schools. From the

[3] Louis Filler, *The Crusade Against Slavery, 1830–1860* (New York: Harper, 1960); and Frank J. Klingberg, "Abolition," *Encyclopedia of the Social Sciences*, Vol. I, pp. 369–72.

standpoint of a reformer the status quo is basically healthy and desirable. His aim is to bring into line some feature of society he believes to be inconsistent with the rest of it. In his discussion of the "rank order of discrimination" Myrdal indicates that during the period just before World War II, the reforms American Negroes wanted most were changes that white people would have been least reluctant to approve. Negroes wanted most to eliminate differential treatment in securing land, credit, jobs, and other means of livelihood, and all but the most rigid segregationists would have agreed that a Negro had the right to earn a living. Next, Negroes wanted equal treatment by the police and in courts of law, and many white people agreed that this would only be fair. After that, Negroes objected to political disfranchisement, segregation in the use of public facilities, and barriers against dancing, bathing, eating, or drinking together. Complete equality in intermarriage and sex relations was last among Negro aspirations, and here the opposition of the dominant group would have been formidable. These findings have been confirmed by other studies.[4] Thus, the granting of the reforms most wanted by Negroes at that time would not have overturned the American social system.

Although reformers are often accused of radical activity, they are basically conservative. The objective in social reform is not the overthrowing of an existing social order, but the reaffirmation of prevailing values. Reformers cite values that are generally accepted—such as equality, justice, and freedom—and call attention to discrepancies between these avowed ideals and existing conditions. They are asking that the treatment of minority groups be brought into conformity with accepted standards of the society. In contrast, a revolutionary movement attacks basic values; Communists, for example, do not advocate freedom of speech. This suggests, then, that whether a social movement is to be classified as reform or revolutionary depends not so much upon what it advocates as upon the accepted values of the society. What some Americans would regard as a mild program of reform might elsewhere be viewed as a dangerous subversive movement. Reform movements do not challenge the high status of the dominant group. It is for this reason that they so often

[4] Myrdal, *op. cit.*, pp. 60–67. Cf. W. S. M. Banks, "The Rank Order of Sensitivity to Discriminations of Negroes in Columbus, Ohio," *American Sociological Review*, XV (1950), 529–34.

enjoy the support of some of the most powerful individuals in the community.[5]

Voluntary associations with similarly moderate objectives also develop among the more successful members of minority groups. Most of them draw powerful support from outsiders and would have difficulty in getting a hearing without their patrons. In Nigeria, the early protests were objections to particular measures rather than fundamental challenges to imperial rule. In 1895, there was protest over a proposed house and land tax in Lagos; in 1908, there was objection to the water rate. Membership in these early political associations in Lagos was limited to a few leaders who tried to defend what they considered the natural rights of Africans and their acquired rights as British subjects.[6] In Kenya, the educated Kikuyu wanted to build good, clean houses for their families but found that this was impractical without land ownership. Some were able to buy land, but there was not enough to go around. The Kikuyu Central Association was founded in 1922, and one of its objectives was the recovery of the "lost lands" of the tribe.[7] In the Central African Federation, the better educated of the various ethnic groups at first supported a program of "gradualism." The United Federal Party in Southern Rhodesia and the Central African Party in Northern Rhodesia were moderate. Branches of the Capricorn movement included Europeans of liberal persuasion and moderate Africans. The Congress movement in Northern Rhodesia, after the Zambia African Congress had split off from it, was led by the more prosperous Africans and was so reasonable that it was the only Congress movement in the territories not banned by 1959.[8] Opposition to extremists on both sides comes from business and professional men in the minority group and from religious leaders and intellectuals of the dominant group. They are all substantial citizens who are well established, and they have no desire to overthrow the existing social order. These people are culturally alike, and their views are often so congenial that they even find it easy to meet socially.

In spite of the wild charges that have been directed against the

[5] Cf. Blumer, *op. cit.*, pp. 211–14; and Francis Delaisi, *Political Myths and Economic Realities* (New York: Viking Press, 1927), pp. 4–71.

[6] Coleman, *Nigeria, op. cit.*, pp. 178–82.

[7] Hailey, *op. cit.*, pp. 451–52; and Leakey, *op. cit.*, pp. 67–77.

[8] Coleman, "Politics of Sub–Saharan Africa," *op. cit.*, p. 299–300; and Franck, *op. cit.*, pp. 254–61.

National Association for the Advancement of Colored Peoples by white extremists in the South, it is basically a conservative group. It appears radical to some Southerners only because they regard any change in the color line as revolutionary. Early Negro leadership was even more conciliatory. Booker T. Washington taught patience, hard work, and good will toward white people. He believed that Negroes had a long way to go and cautioned against political agitation. The N.A.A.C.P. was founded in 1910 by leaders who were more militant than Washington, but its approach has also been cautious. Most successful Negroes have accepted the values of American society, and they live much like other successful Americans. In the course of acquiring their education they have developed a partial identification with the dominant group. They may support movements that extol the merits of Negroes, but they do not struggle for political independence. They stress assimilation into American life and advocate reforms that will make this easier—to get the vote, to get a better education for their children, to get equal treatment before the law. They see their future in the United States and want a more equitable share of it. The N.A.A.C.P. does not challenge the social order.[9]

Such organizations usually do not enjoy the support of rank and file members of the minority group, nor do they always fight for the interests of the entire group. In many conflict situations the more affluent members of minority groups side with their rulers, for they are culturally closer to them. Leaders of reform movements often speak in behalf of oppressed people, but they themselves are seldom among the dispossessed. They are men who have done well in the existing system in spite of their disadvantages, and they are not anxious for drastic changes. In Nigeria, where African-owned newspapers played an important part in politics, the press was by no means anti-British. The *Nigerian Pioneer*, launched by Sir Kitoyi Ajasa in 1914, always took a conservative line. Ajasa defended the colonial government on most issues and opposed leaders and movements that aroused government displeasure.[10] The Indian National

[9] Cf. Guy B. Johnson, "Negro Racial Movements and Leadership in the United States," *American Journal of Sociology*, XLIII (1937), 57–71; Myrdal, *op. cit.*, pp. 810–57; Mary W. Ovington, *The Walls Came Tumbling Down* (New York: Harcourt, Brace, 1947), pp. 100–282; and Wilson Record, *The Negro and the Communist Party* (Chapel Hill: University of North Carolina Press, 1951).

[10] Coleman, *Nigeria, op. cit.*, pp. 184–85.

Congress began as a narrowly-based association primarily concerned with the interests of the small middle class. It got its start by agitating for more civil service positions for graduates of the British-introduced university system, and it became a mass movement only after World War I. Under Gandhi's leadership local units were established in villages and towns throughout India, and the basis was laid for civil disobedience campaigns on a large scale. It gained support from other parts of the population through its crusade against "untouchability." [11]

More radical associations also develop among minority peoples, usually drawing their support from the less successful. Students, labor leaders, and intellectuals who are not well established tend to be more militant in their demands for change. The Sinn Fein movement opposed Irish representation in the British Parliament, arguing that lobbying in London for "home rule" was folly. When members of Parliament were granted a salary of £400 a year, agitators asked how anyone in the pay of the British government could oppose it.[12] In colonial Africa leaders who actually had the backing of the rank and file were radical; they demanded immediate independence. They exercised more influence from their jail cells than moderate leaders, some of whom had even been stoned by other Africans. These extremists disliked and distrusted Europeans, even those who were liberal; the only white men who could reach them were small groups of Marxists and some Quakers. Moderate groups such as the Capricorn movement were attacked as "cooling off" bodies, and Africans who joined them were accused of being "stooges." Marxist slogans were frequently used; the mixed groups were labeled "tools of Western imperialism" and "opiates of the intelligentsia." [13]

In some communities other powerful organizations make common cause with a minority group, especially when their interests happen to coincide. When employers can divide their labor force along ethnic lines, they have a strong weapon against a union in that the minority group is always available for breaking strikes. There-

---

[11] Akshayakumar R. Desai, *Social Background of Indian Nationalism* (Bombay: Popular Book Depot, 1959), pp. 224–51; and Myron Weiner, "Politics of South Asia," in Almond and Coleman, *op. cit.*, pp. 185–86.

[12] John F. Boyle, *The Irish Rebellion of 1916* (London: Constable, 1916), pp. 13–17.

[13] Cf. Franck, *op. cit.*, pp. 254–61; and Coleman, "Politics of Sub-Saharan Africa," *op. cit.*, pp. 299–300.

fore, some industrial unions have tried to incorporate workers from all ethnic groups into their membership. Although it is still segregated, African labor has become increasingly aware of the value of collective action.[14] In the United States some predominantly white unions have even elected Negroes to high office. A study revealed, however, that this happened only when there was a sizable Negro membership and when the union was facing opposition—in winning loyalty away from employers or in competing for members against other unions. A Negro candidate was usually sponsored by white leaders who recognized the expediency of the move in meeting the crisis.[15] Political machines in many American cities have drawn considerable strength from mutually satisfactory relationships with various minority groups. In "melting pot" politics a precinct captain in a segregated area would render personal services for newcomers not too familiar with American institutions. He would look after welfare cases, secure protection against fire, get hospitalization for the poor, or check with the police when one of his constituents was arrested. In return, the minority group promised to deliver its votes to the party. As large numbers of Negroes migrated to the North during the early part of this century, some became active participants in "machine politics" in Chicago. By promising votes in the "Black Belt," Negro politicians were able to get patronage and other political favors, including the placing of qualified Negroes in various appointive positions.[16] In the United States much political power resides in the hands of politicians who do not hold office, and many of these men draw their strength from the minority groups they serve.

Minority groups are often aided in their struggle for a better life by humanitarian organizations set up to assist anyone in need. The American Civil Liberties Union supports anyone being deprived of his constitutional rights, and this organization has fought for many individuals in minority groups. Various religious groups, especially among the Protestant denominations, have played an important part in social reform. Among the most widely respected is the American Friends Service Committee, which is accepted even in parts of the world where no other Americans are wanted. Although missionaries

[14] Hailey, *op. cit.*, p. 1431.
[15] William A. Kornhauser, "The Negro Union Official," *American Journal of Sociology*, LVII (1952), 443–52.
[16] Harold F. Gosnell, *Negro Politicians: The Rise of Negro Politics in Chicago* (Chicago: University of Chicago Press, 1935).

in Nigeria apparently did not succeed in convincing Africans of their sincerity, they actually prodded the colonial government in behalf of the natives. Nigerians resented their assumption of native inferiority and their silence on subjects like inequality and denial of opportunities. The missionaries depended upon the colonial government for leases of land and for financial subsidies for their schools, but within this framework they were actually vigorous critics on behalf of the Africans—both behind the scenes and on government advisory committees.[17]

Sometimes an ethnic minority may receive aid from organizations outside the country. A minority group may appeal to its ethnic "brothers" in another country for help or in some cases plead for international control. The Treaty of Berlin of 1878 encouraged the hopes of some Armenians in Turkey for international intervention in their behalf. The Hunchaks, an Armenian nationalistic organization, tried to invite such intervention by creating political turmoil.[18] Immigrant communities are sometimes backed by the government of the country from which the immigrants came. During the reign of the Kuomintang, the overseas Chinese were bound to their motherland in many ways. They remitted money to their families in China, and many sent their children there to be educated. In addition, the overseas Chinese had official representation in the Chinese government, for six of 274 senators were selected from among them.[19] Furthermore, the Chinese government would protest through consular channels whenever its citizens were mistreated. Natives in various European colonies have been aided by political parties in the motherland, who have demanded all kinds of reforms. The British Labor Party was always against imperialism; it charged that the "white man's burden" was too heavy, that British taxpayers had to support the ambitions of chauvinists, and that the natives were misgoverned. They advocated "constructive trusteeship"—a policy geared to preparing the natives to determine their own destiny.[20] In recent years there has been much concern over the aid given minority movements in colonial areas by Communists in their "people's liberation" parties. Under Marxist doctrine the composition and the mission of Com-

[17] Coleman, *Nigeria, op. cit.,* pp. 105–11.
[18] Adivar, *op. cit.,* p. 386; Atamian, *op. cit.,* pp. 150–52; and Bliss, *op. cit.,* p. 478.
[19] Chen, *op. cit.,* pp. 56–57.
[20] Coleman, *Nigeria, op. cit.,* pp. 235–36. Cf. Lugard, *op. cit.,* p. 608; and Strachey, *op. cit.,* pp. 215–16.

munist units in colonies differ from those in industrial communities; they participate in a united front that appeals to all segments of the minority group. In Southeast Asia results of this strategy have been mixed; it has been very successful in Indo–China but has encountered obstacles elsewhere.[21]

In areas in which inter-ethnic tension is chronic, voluntary associations may be formed to promote better understanding and to meet special problems. In the period following World War II "action groups" of all kinds were organized in almost every major American city. These groups have been financed by contributions from wealthy patrons, by grants from foundations, and by subscription. Most of them have hired a professional staff—to carry out fact-finding surveys, to testify before local officials for or against pending ordinances, to engage in lobbying, to make public appeals in support of their program, to give lectures to interested bodies, to counsel individuals with problems, to assist in litigation, to promote contacts through recreational programs, to plan the introduction of unpopular minorities into better jobs or housing, to intervene in behalf of minorities with the police. The staff members have worked in cooperation with other organizations with similar interests, with minority groups, and with governmental agencies. Such work has become so complicated and requires so many technical skills that the field is becoming professionalized.[22]

Although outsiders often get the impression that minority groups are united in their demands, there are usually so many shades of opinion that concerted action is very difficult. Differences with respect to goals and tactics reflect the diversity of class interests, religious affiliations, and tribal or sectional loyalties. Some of the factions form contrast conceptions of each other; they see their rivals within the minority group as dangerous troublemakers or as sycophants of the dominant group. The N.A.A.C.P., for example, has always opposed radical activities among Negroes. When Marcus Garvey launched his movement to establish a homeland for American Ne-

[21] Lucian W. Pye, *Guerrilla Communism in Malaya* (Princeton: Princeton University Press, 1956), pp. 17–46; and Frank N. Trager, *Marxism in Southeast Asia* (Stanford, Calif.: Stanford University Press, 1959).

[22] Cf. Charles S. Johnson, "National Organizations in the Field of Race Relations," *Annals of the American Academy of Political and Social Science*, **CCXLIV** (March 1946), 117–27; and Robin M. Williams, *The Reduction of Intergroup Tensions* (New York: Social Science Research Council, 1947).

groes in Africa, he attacked the more successful Negroes, even casting aspersions against their lighter complexion. The N.A.A.C.P. not only opposed this movement, but many of its officials, along with other Negro intellectuals, signed a petition to the Justice Department asking that Garvey be prosecuted and deported.[23] The Congress movement in Nigeria fell apart when its supporters began fighting among themselves. The tendency to think in terms of tribal affiliations rather than the artificial territorial unit under British control led to many difficulties, and the internal struggle was aggravated by personal quarrels among the various leaders.[24] A study of politics in Luanshya, Northern Rhodesia, shows how demands for reform were weakened by antagonisms between union leaders and the spokesmen of the African National Congress.[25] Many of the leaders of minority movements are marginal men, and this tends to create additional problems. Men who are ambitious, egoistical, and suspicious are easily alienated from each other and have difficulty in working together, even for a common cause.

Cooperation among the various organizations in a community that profess to be working for the welfare of minority groups is often only nominal. Groups that side with minorities as a matter of expediency continue to work with them only as long as it is useful. People of good will have lofty ideals, but when their support of unpopular causes becomes too costly, they tend to withdraw; many are "fair weather liberals." Union leaders, clergymen, professional reformers, and marginal men get together with the best of intentions; the more they communicate with each other, however, the more they realize that they are from different social worlds, pursue different values, and actually agree only on quite limited objectives. Especially where more than one ethnic minority is involved, cooperation becomes extremely difficult. Minority groups in the Austro–Hungarian Empire, for example, could agree on the existence of inequities, but they had little else in common. The interests of industrialized Czechs were quite different from those of Ruthenian peasants in eastern Austria, and Polish nationalists in Austrian Galicia regarded the Ruthenians among whom they lived as pariahs of the Slavic peoples. Hence, they were reluctant to cooperate in action against the

[23] Wilson Record, "The Negro Intellectual and Negro Nationalism," *Social Forces* XXXIII (1954), 10–18.

[24] Coleman, *Nigeria, op. cit.*, pp. 192–210.

[25] Epstein, *op. cit.*, pp. 86–197.

established order; the risk was too great, and they did not have sufficient confidence in one another.[26] In 1951, a Coloured Peoples Society was organized in London to handle common problems of housing, child welfare, and entertainment confronting ethnic minorities in England. But the West Indians, Africans, and East Indians could not get along. Yoruba and Ibo would side against someone from Ghana, and then they would argue with each other over domestic issues in Nigeria. Popular support was only lukewarm.[27] Reformers can generally agree on a broad, superficial level. When they actually begin working together, however, they are often shocked at the conduct of their new comrades. Some may even conclude that the status quo is preferable to the changes being proposed.

The Mobilization of Conservative Forces

As demands for social reform become more insistent, those who want to preserve the status quo also mobilize their resources. Although most of the support for conservative programs comes from people who are well established in the social order, this is not necessarily the case. Those who would be regarded by outside observers as dispossessed and perhaps even as victims of exploitation often have staunch loyalties to the existing order. Demands for changes, especially when they come from people of low status like themselves, strike them as being sacrilegious.

In each community there are many organizations that represent vested interests. Landowners and businessmen often oppose reforms that will cut into their profits or disturb their way of life. Organizations such as the California Joint Immigration Committee, which played a prominent part in the anti-Oriental agitation in the West, represent people who are well established.[28] The Church in many areas has been a pillar of conservatism. Although the Roman Catholic Church has taken a leading role in the fight against segregation in the United States, elsewhere it has generally sided with the old order. In the period preceding the expulsion of the Moors from Spain, for example, it was the Church that insisted upon enforcing orthodoxy.

[26] Robert A. Kann, *The Habsburg Empire* (New York: Frederick A. Praeger, 1957), pp. 46–47, 140.
[27] Banton, *The Coloured Quarters, op. cit.*, pp. 228–33.
[28] Cf. Morton Grodzins, *Americans Betrayed* (Chicago: University of Chicago Press, 1949), pp. 19–61.

Priests and lay leaders inflamed the people into action.[29] In Latin America, many revolutionary movements have shown hostility toward the Catholic Church; justly or unjustly, it has been identified with wealthy landowners and high-ranking military officers. Officials of the Russian Orthodox Church were involved in the massacre of Jews at Kishinew, and many young men studying for the priesthood took an active part in the pogrom.[30] The status quo is also defended by partiotic organizations. In the United States the American Legion, the Daughters of the American Revolution, the Native Sons of the Gold West, and similar organizations have consistently opposed "subversive" and "foreign" elements in the country. Such groups have been especially active in lobbying for restrictive immigration laws.[31] That people who are well established would regard any social movement advocating drastic changes as dangerous is understandable.

Since Marxist intellectuals and leaders of industrial unions have strongly condemned racism in various parts of the world, it is widely believed in "liberal" circles that workers are against making ethnic distinctions. In many communities, however, the strongest support for the color line comes from members of the working class.[32] This is to be expected, since these people are most likely to become involved in direct competition with members of minority groups for jobs, housing, and status. Furthermore, ethnic stratification rests upon erroneous popular beliefs that are least likely to be corrected among those with less education.

Secretly allied with such conservative groups are some of the privileged individuals of minority groups. In European colonies that were governed through indirect rule, the chieftains and their aides had a stake in the status quo. In South Africa the Bantu National Congress is a native group that supports *apartheid*. It was organized at a meeting of African herbalists, whose position would be undermined by the widespread acceptance of European medicine.[33] In many European colonies children of mixed parentage were among

---

[29] Cf. Lea, *op. cit.*

[30] Dahlke, *op. cit.*

[31] Cf. William Gellermann, *The American Legion as Educator* (New York: Columbia University Press, 1938).

[32] Cf. Seymour M. Lipset, "Democracy and Working Class Authoritarianism," *American Sociological Review*, XXIV (1959), 482–501.

[33] Leo Kuper, *Passive Resistance in South Africa* (New Haven: Yale University Press, 1957), pp. 35–36.

the most ardent supporters of the color line. In Indonesia, for example, Eurasians became the backbone of the Dutch colonial administration and were thoroughly disliked.[34] The stand taken by such persons often sounds reasonable. They are not unaware of some of the grievances and concede that some changes may be desirable. They may even support, at least in principle, a program of "gradualism." For this reason the agitation of revolutionary leaders is often directed against these traditional leaders as well as against the dominant group.

The ideologies of conservative groups have certain characteristics in common in spite of the diversity of contexts in which they develop. Many conservative people believe that the existing social order is inevitable because it rests upon human nature. A system of ethnic stratification is thought to be natural because some men are inferior to others. Giving too much power to persons of insufficient mental capacity can be disastrous. The proponents of *apartheid* justify their program in terms of the "natural theory of segregation"— that members of the same "race" instinctively want to live together. Segregation is therefore normal; it would enable each group to give full expression to its distinctive culture, and the inferior "race" would be spared the humiliations that are inevitable when it came into contact with others.[35] Thus, without denying that some ethnic groups are better off than others, these people would accept it as fate.

Conservative parties often justify existing arrangements in terms of the theory of the "survival of the fittest." They point to their cultural attainments in contrast to those of minority groups and contend that they deserve special privileges because of their inherent superiority. The inferior and the weak do not have the right to claim equality. Humanitarian values are neither rejected nor opposed, though in some cases they are ridiculed. They are described as ideals. It would be wonderful if all men were idealists, but since they are not, unfortunately such utopian visions cannot be made the basis of public policy. Only dreamers take such ideals seriously, and government cannot be placed in the hands of such impractical people.

Conservative people often doubt that the world can be changed through rational effort. There are limitations to what can be accom-

---

[34] Van der Kroef, "The Eurasian Minority in Indonesia," *op. cit.*
[35] Kuper, Watts, and Davies, *op. cit.*, pp. 21, 35, 144, 212; and Richmond, *op. cit.*, p. 23.

plished by human beings. In conservative ideologies the notion of organic growth is emphasized; changes will occur if they are a part of nature. There is no point in rushing things, for that would only result in more disorder and unhappiness. The world is best when left alone. In contrast to reformers, conservative thinkers tend to view history as an accidental conglomeration of events. There are no trends; things merely happen as they do. But reformers tend to view history as an ordered sequence of events, moving inexorably toward utopian existence. They emphasize the possibility of speeding up the process through rational effort. Thus, in many cases those advocating changes and those defending the status quo not only disagree upon specific issues but also approach their respective environments with incompatible assumptions.[36]

Groups are seldom formed merely to suppress the aspirations of a minority group. Most conservative associations have a broad range of objectives, and keeping a minority group in its "place" is but one of them. Occasionally, however, groups are founded in which the preservation of the color line is a primary objective, and these organizations tend to assume more extreme positions. The Ku Klux Klan was first organized in Tennessee in 1866 by a group of former Confederate officers and spread quickly throughout the South. From 1867 to 1870 it counteracted the excesses of carpetbaggers and Negro politicians through intimidation. In 1872, when a number of reforms were instituted by Congress, such illegal activities became unnecessary, and the organization disbanded.[37] In 1915, a second Ku Klux Klan was founded. This organization was more like a political party and was more active in the Midwest than in the South. The membership claimed Anglo-Saxon descent, and its announced purpose was defense of the country against Jews, Catholics, and other "foreigners." Negroes were also included among the "un-American" influences. In 1955, as Negroes won one victory after another in their struggle for civil rights, there was another revival of the Ku Klux Klan. As in the White Citizens Councils that sprang up in various communities in the South, opposition to integration was the sole

---

[36] Cf. Samuel P. Huntington, "Conservatism as an Ideology," *American Political Science Review*, LI (1957), 454–73; and Karl Mannheim, *Essays on Sociology and Social Psychology*, ed. Paul Kecskemeti (New York: Oxford University Press, 1953), pp. 74–164.

[37] Walter L. Fleming, *Documentary History of the Reconstruction* (Cleveland: A. H. Clark, 1907), Vol. II, pp. 327–77.

common denominator in the membership.[38] Such extremists often take positions with which there can be no compromise. Extremists among the Afrikaners in South Africa, for example, claim that they are a "chosen people." They call their political foes *Kaffirboeties*— "black man lovers"—and attack their "British–Jewish ideas of liberal-democracy."

When hostility against an ethnic minority becomes an integral part of a social movement, it thereby acquires the vehicles of organization and systematic dissemination as well as group sanction. The antipathy then becomes significant in the formation of public policy. The fate of the Jews in Nazi Germany is an example of what can happen when a powerful organization adopts a racist ideology. Chamberlain had written that all civilization was the product of the conquering German tribes and that it decayed whenever there was intermarriage with inferior "races." When Hitler rose to power in 1933, this theory became the official doctrine of the German government. According to Hitler, Aryans were the creators of all that is admired on earth, and other "races" were either maintainers or destroyers of culture. The Jews never had a culture of their own, always being guided solely by expediency. Only Germans were capable of understanding the true meaning of German culture; therefore, the aim of National Socialism was the union of all Germans in the Third Reich. None but persons of German "blood" could be citizens; others were only guests and were covered by special laws. Public offices could be filled only by Germans. Many who were not eligible for citizenship were deported, and the further immigration of aliens was prohibited. Finally, a battle to the death was pledged against the enemy of the state: the Jews.[39] Since this philosophy was so easily contradicted by the accepted scholarship of the world, many did not take Hitler seriously; they regarded his utterances merely as domestic propaganda, an expedient way of winning a following in Germany. It was not until after World War II that details of the genocide program were revealed. In fact, many of the details were not generally known until 1961, when the trial of Adolf Eichmann was held in Israel.

---

[38] Frank Bohn, "The Ku Klux Klan Interpreted," *American Journal of Sociology*, XXX (1925), 385–407; and James W. Vander Zander, "The Klan Revival," *ibid.*, LXV (1960), 456–62.

[39] Snyder, *op. cit.*, pp. 180–98.

The political scene is frequently complicated when unscrupulous men who have no strong convictions about ethnic identity attack unpopular minorities when they find it expedient. They use popular beliefs as a fulcrum for promoting their own interests. In the decade before World War I Russians attempted to cut the traditional ties between Lithuanians, especially the intellectuals, and the more numerous Poles. During the war German occupation officials also encouraged a Lithuanian revival, not because of enthusiasm for Lithuanian culture but because the Germans were also rivals of the Poles. These moves led some Polish politicians to complain that Lithuanian nationalism had been invented in Berlin or Moscow rather than among the Lithuanians.[40] During World War II a prominent labor leader running for mayor of Detroit was defeated through a campaign of anti-Semitism, even though he was not a Jew. The opposition had little to show on record, and it campaigned on the charge that the Jews would "take over" the city and force everyone to accept Negroes.[41] In September 1957, the civilized world gasped at the spectacle of the governor of Arkansas calling out troops to prevent a handful of Negro children from entering a high school in Little Rock. What was even more astonishing was the disclosure that the governor had a reputation as a "moderate" on matters concerning the color line. At the time, he asserted that he had "nothing against" Negroes, and his record sustained his claim. Since the incident the governor has had little trouble in winning elections.

Social reform may become extremely difficult if a powerful organization depends for its existence upon the perpetuation of a color line. A government may attempt to preserve a system of ethnic stratification in another country to protect its own interests. In the late nineteenth century German officials feared that any change in the relationships of various ethnic groups in the Austro–Hungarian Empire might lead to revisions of a foreign policy favorable to Germany. Therefore, the Germans refused to revise the Compromise of 1867, which defined the status of each group in the Dual Monarchy.[42] In the American South the Democratic Party no longer represents the

---

[40] Alfred E. Senn, *The Emergence of Modern Lithuania* (New York: Columbia University Press, 1959), pp. 2–11.

[41] Carl O. Smith and Stephen B. Sarasohn, "Hate Propaganda in Detroit," *Public Opinion Quarterly*, X (1946), 24–52.

[42] Kann, *The Habsburg Empire, op. cit.*, p. 19.

interests of many of the people, and one way of retaining power is by raising the "race" issue. Although there are many conscientious public servants, some politicians go from one part of their state to another, crying for "white supremacy," reviving the passions of the Reconstruction days, and boasting of their efforts to stop integration. The attention of their constituents is thereby deflected from other issues, and embarrassing questions are less likely to be raised.[43]

In the heat of conflict reformers often accuse their opponents of selfishness and of evil motives. But many conservative persons are sincerely defending their cherished values. They neither enjoy the miseries of the poor, nor are they insensitive to their plight. But they are fearful of the prospect of their descendants living in a society in which relationships "against nature" are sanctioned—where inferior people rise to positions of power and where intermarriage and miscegenation are commonplace. The educated often dismiss racists as "crackpots" and assume that they really know better, but many agitators are sincere in their beliefs. Although the weight of scientific evidence is against their views, they actually conceive of themselves as superior human beings by virtue of what they have inherited from their ancestors.

Political Tactics and Public Policy

In a democratic society, especially in a large one like ours, those who wish to promote a program of action find that they must organize to get a hearing. No matter how meritorious a proposal, it is not likely to catch the attention of the public or of officials without some kind of group support. In a society in which public officials are elected, representatives of organizations are usually listened to with a deference proportional to the number of people they represent. Voluntary associations, whether reform or conservative, devote much time trying to influence government policy. Some engage in more direct action—such as organizing boycotts or mass demonstrations—but this is not likely to be as effective as having one's program carried out by the government. Reformers try to utilize the police power of the state to alter the prevailing system of ethnic stratification, and conservative parties try to keep things as they are. Public policy is

43 Cf. Key, *op. cit.*

shaped in the give-and-take of the various interest groups representing different segments of the population.[44]

Where laws are enacted by elected officials, one very important type of political activity is seeking the passage of favorable laws. Reformers are continually trying to outlaw practices through which social distance and power differentials are preserved and social mobility is controlled. The fight to secure the civil rights of American Negroes through legislation goes back to 1865, when slavery was abolished by the ratification of the Thirteenth Amendment to the Constitution. In the following year the guarantee of "equal protection of the laws" was also written into the Constitution, and in 1870 the Fifteenth Amendment was ratified—that the right to vote could not be denied on the basis of "race, color, or previous condition of servitude." Since then, there has been a concerted effort to outlaw various "Jim Crow" practices as well as to secure better enforcement of these laws. Throughout the United States reformers and representatives of minority groups have operated as pressure groups in lobbying for legislation guaranteeing fair employment practices. New York and New Jersey passed F.E.P.C. laws in 1945, and within the next decade a number of other states and large cities also passed them. These laws forbid employers to take ethnic identity into account in hiring help and prohibit labor unions from denying membership to qualified workers on an ethnic basis. The commissions check on complaints of "discrimination" and try to iron out difficulties through persuasion. In some states public hearings may be held, and offenders may be prosecuted.

In countries in which laws are interpreted by the courts, disputes over the respective rights of various ethnic groups are frequently taken before the judiciary. But litigation is expensive. When members of minority groups cannot afford it, they are often assisted by reformers and philanthropists. Although the U.S. Supreme Court has not always ruled in favor of Negroes—as in the Dred Scott case— their rights as American citizens have gradually become more clearly defined in a succession of favorable decisions. In 1915, it declared unconstitutional the "grandfather clause" used by Southern states to restrict Negro suffrage by exempting from educational tests and

---

[44] Cf. Arthur F. Bentley, *The Process of Government* (Evanston, Ill.: Principia Press, 1949); and David B. Truman, *The Governmental Process* (New York: Alfred A. Knopf, 1955).

property qualifications voters whose progenitors had voted prior to 1867. In 1927, it overruled a Texas law barring Negroes from Democratic Party primaries. In 1940, it overturned the conviction of a Negro in a trial from which Negroes had been excluded from jury service. In 1946, it outlawed "Jim Crow" practices on inter-state buses, and it ruled in 1948 that restrictive covenants could not be enforced by the courts. In a memorable decision on May 17, 1954, it outlawed segregation in the public schools.[45] In the United States the rulings of the Supreme Court cannot be challenged; in South Africa, however, Prime Minister Malan was able to alter the court and in effect to overrule its decisions.

Reformers often have an advantage over their opposition in that they are reiterating already-accepted values of the society. Because they are respectable, reform movements are able to challenge their opponents openly. Furthermore, since influential and wealthy patrons can support such movements without any loss of status, considerable pressure can be brought to bear upon government officials. In many cases reformers assume a self-righteous stance and accuse their opponents of being "undemocratic." In a changing society, however, genuine disagreements may arise over values. Among the Europeans in South Africa, for example, there is no consensus on the ideal status for natives. The philosophy of Cecil Rhodes of "equal rights for all civilized men" has many followers; they contend that Africans ought to have the same rights as other citizens as soon as they acquire the culture of the dominant group. Others, mostly Afrikaners, are convinced that there is a fundamental difference in kind between black and white, with no possibility whatsoever of equality in church or state.[46]

In communities in which ethnic minorities have already demonstrated their capacities, conservative politicians do not publicly challenge the contention that the underprivileged deserve a better lot. They insist, however, that popular beliefs are deeply rooted; the "average man," who is not familiar with scientific findings, cannot help feeling as he does. They may even agree that it is immoral to deprive a person of opportunities he deserves, but they point out that,

[45] Greenberg, *op. cit.*, pp. 79–114, 133–53, 208–312. Cf. Clement E. Vose, "Litigation as a Form of Pressure Group Activity," *Annals of the American Academy of Political and Social Science*, CCCXIX (1958), 20–31.

[46] Cf. Dvorin, *op. cit.*, pp. 30–60.

human nature being what it is, a perfect society cannot be expected. Such popular "prejudices," they contend, cannot be eliminated by passing laws against them, nor can morality be legislated. This matter has become controversial among students of the law as well as among sociologists.[47] Cardozo and Holmes, the protagonists of common law, regarded legal norms as products of society, principles that developed out of conventional norms. If ethnic stratification is customary, therefore, laws that are contrary to tradition cannot be enforced. The difficulty of controlling lynching in the South and the dismal failure of prohibition are often cited as examples. What is needed is education, not laws. Many reformers have countered that the process of passing legislation and attempting to enforce the statutes are ways of educating people; the very publicity that accompanies such campaigns is informative. Furthermore, most people obey laws without even thinking of their merits; for example, they pay taxes even when they disagree with the uses for which the money is spent. But reformers need not take such a defensive position. Reform movements are themselves a part of society; they are collective protests that arise when previously accepted procedures are no longer suited to new life conditions. Laws that are pushed through by reformers are crystallizations of conventions, just as much as the laws sustaining the old order. Such contradictions arise because of the diversity of standards during the transition from one kind of social order to another.[48]

A color line may be maintained or altered to some extent through administrative decree, and pressure groups often try to accomplish their aims through this channel. Many of the major advances made by American Negroes have been through executive orders. In 1863, President Lincoln put into effect the Emancipation Proclamation; in 1941, President Roosevelt established a federal F.E.P.C. to eliminate "discrimination" in war industries; and in 1948, President Truman issued an executive order abolishing ethnic segregation in the armed forces. In Hungary during the early part of the twentieth century

---

[47] Cf. Greenberg, *op. cit.*, pp. 1–30; and Harry V. Ball, George E. Simpson, and Kiyoshi Ikeda, "Law and Social Change: Sumner Reconsidered," *American Journal of Sociology*, LXVII (1962), 532–40.

[48] Cf. M. G. Aronson, "Cardozo's Doctrine of Sociological Jurisprudence," *Journal of Social Philosophy*, IV (1930), 5–44; Sumner, *op. cit.*, pp. 82–118; and Rupert B. Vance and Walter Wynne, "Folk Rationalizations in the 'Unwritten Law'," *American Journal of Sociology*, XXXIX (1934), 483–92.

Magyar rulers consistently favored the Serbs against the Croats; this policy was followed as a matter of expediency and reflected no special interest in the Serbs. They believed that by granting desirable concessions to less dangerous groups the growth of common purpose among different minorities could be inhibited, rivalry and distrust stimulated, and the relative position of stronger groups weakened.[49] In the excitement following the Japanese attack on Pearl Harbor, various pressure groups on the Pacific Coast agitated so effectively that they persuaded federal officials that resident Japanese and their children constituted a threat to American security. As a result, 110,-000 persons of Japanese ancestry were evacuated from their homes in 1942 and sent to camps in the interior. Less than a year after the costly move, which disrupted agricultural production in a time of great need, federal officials realized that they had made a mistake and began to release the internees. Soon afterward, thousands of young men who had been thus imprisoned were drafted for service in the U.S. Army.[50] In Durban, when segments of the European population realized that the *apartheid* program would require their moving out of desirable residential areas, they clamored against the change. The city council yielded to pressure and conceded nearly all the demands. Thus, the Europeans gained additional holdings of desirable areas and at the same time were able to keep their own settlements.[51]

Since governmental authority is supported by consensus, however, the most important task of all interest groups is to influence public opinion. Laws are not likely to be effective without public support. Alexander the Great encouraged intermarriage and tried to adopt some of the customs of conquered peoples, but the policy was not popular with the Macedonians. During his lifetime his authority was not questioned, but soon after his death his colonization schemes were abandoned.[52] Although people in the South have resisted the desegregation program of the federal government, Southerners are by no means agreed on this issue. There are many who favor obeying the laws even if they do not regard them as just. A study of Guilford County, North Carolina, shows that readiness to accept

---

[49] Robert A. Kann, *The Multi-National Empire* (New York: Columbia University Press, 1950), Vol. I, p. 255.

[50] Grodzins, *op. cit.*

[51] Kuper, Watts, and Davies, *op. cit.*, pp. 38, 66, 110, 136, 142, 158, 164, 184, 190-98, 220.

[52] S. Davis, *op. cit.*, pp. 8-14.

desegregation varies directly with exposure to the media of mass communication, most of which originate in the North.[53] This suggests that Southerners whose perspectives extend beyond their local communities realize that American public opinion is overwhelmingly against them and are willing to make more concessions. Similarly, many literate Europeans in the Union of South Africa realize that public sentiment throughout the world is against *apartheid*, and they assume an apologetic or defensive stance. Even extremists are sensitive to public opinion; when they realize that it is against them, they devote considerable time to justifying their position.

The importance of public opinion is revealed by the failure of Protestant clergymen in Little Rock, Arkansas, to take action. When the crisis over the desegregation of schools arose in 1957, most clergymen outside the South took a strong stand against segregation, and the ministers in Little Rock were placed in an extremely difficult position. If they spoke up as Christians, they knew they would lose at least a part of their congregation. Campbell and Pettigrew found that most of the clergymen were personally in favor of integration. However, they realized that within their respective church hierarchies each minister is judged in terms of how his church prospers. This meant that they could not succeed within their profession without the support of their congregation. Public opinion in Southern communities was so inflamed that anyone who spoke against the traditional practices was immediately ostracized as unsympathetic to the cause. Hence, even ministers whose national organization had taken a firm and uncompromising stand were reluctant to attack segregation.[54] When a high degree of consensus exists within a community about a subject such as the color line, those who hold alien views are dismissed as "foreigners" who do not "understand." Even if they are highly respected as individuals, their views on the specific issue will be discounted as incompetent.

Reformers usually enjoy an advantage in propaganda, for one cannot argue against the accepted values of a community without making himself vulnerable. The strategy of many reform movements is to make a public issue of their program, for simply by provoking

[53] Melvin M. Tumin, "Exposure to Mass Media and Readiness for Desegregation," *Public Opinion Quarterly*, **XXI** (1957), 237–51.
[54] Ernest Q. Campbell and Thomas F. Pettigrew, "Racial and Moral Crisis: The Role of Little Rock Ministers," *American Journal of Sociology*, **LXIV** (1959), 509–16.

discussion some sympathetic support can be elicited. Promotional campaigns are carried out openly, for there is no need for underground operations. The media of mass communication are used, and various public meetings are held, often protected against cranks by the police. In the United States reform groups point to the fundamental tenets of Christian and democratic ethics—such as fair play and equality of opportunity. Defenders of the status quo have difficulty in meeting such attacks, for they would be arguing against justice and decency. Since the position taken by many reform movements is unassailable on ethical grounds, rebuttal must take a different form. One of the most common tactics used is ridiculing the movement and its leaders. The leaders are caricatured as visionary and impractical, though undoubtedly men of good will. Thus, the desirability of equal opportunity is not challenged, but it is contended that inferior people are incapable of appreciating the advantages; therefore, the change would be wasteful.

Another common procedure is identification of the reform program with some dangerous object that everyone fears, thereby ascribing to it all kinds of hidden and sinister purposes. Those who defend the color line often contend that any change will result in widespread miscegenation. Once people can be convinced that giving Negroes a better education is the initial wedge to widespread sex relations across the color line, the program can be attacked by appealing to emotional reactions through such time-tested slogans as "blood and water do not mix." Those supporting reform can be asked, "Do you want your daughter to marry a Negro?" In recent years one of the most effective ways of attacking any reform movement in the United States has been to identify its leaders as Communists or as dupes of Communism. As reformers are forced to spend more and more time proving that they are not Communists, attention is turned away from the basic issues. Sometimes "smear" tactics are used against an individual reformer. His sincerity may be questioned. Since some reformers assume a "holier than thou" attitude, their opponents take delight in exposing some past deed that is inconsistent with their stated ideals, thus labelling them as hypocrites.

Those who become involved in public controversies rarely grapple with basic problems. Most of the discussion centers around rationalizations, the arguments used to justify the practices at issue. The argument used by Hungarian rulers in the late nineteenth century against equal rights for Rumanian peasants was that earlier settlement in the area gave the Magyars a superior claim. The Rumanians then proved that they were at least in part descendants of ancient Roman legionnaires, thereby establishing the fact that some of their ancestors had occupied Transylvania since the time of the Emperor Trajan. In spite of their scholarly triumph the status of the Rumanians remained unchanged.[55] Reformers fighting for better housing for minority groups in the United States have been much concerned with the contention of real estate interests that the introduction of an unpopular minority into an area lowers property values. Men of good will have spent considerable time arguing against this, and studies by economists have been cited to prove that under certain conditions this is not true.[56] But this is an argument over a rationalization, and widespread acceptance of the rebuttal would merely elicit another excuse. The question of whether in a democratic society property values are more important than the equitable treatment of all human beings is rarely discussed.[57] Controversies often center on peripheral matters, such as status symbols. When *Rabbit's Wedding*, a children's book by artist Garth Williams, was published in 1959, some segregationists were upset because the male bunny was black and the female bunny was white. A newspaper in Montgomery, Alabama, attacked it as "integration propaganda" aimed at children in their most formative years!

Of particular importance in mass societies is control of the media of mass communication, for what is presented over these channels can play an important part in the formation of public opinion. Propaganda, if carried out cleverly, can have a serious impact upon values. On many occasions inflammatory attacks against ethnic minorities have been made through the press. Preceding the pogrom in Kishinew, for example, newspapers repeatedly accused Jews of "ritual murder" and even exhorted readers to kill them.[58] In the United States, especially since World War II, the mass media have tended to support reform. During the war, when national unity was a prime objective, there were frequent criticism in the press and radio of the mistreatment of minority groups; it was emphasized that the United

---

[55] R. W. Seton-Watson, *Transylvania: A Key Problem* (Oxford: Classics Press, 1943), p. 1.

[56] Cf. Luigi Laurenti, *Property Values and Race* (Berkeley: University of California Press, 1960).

[57] Hughes and Hughes, *op. cit.*, pp. 145–55.

[58] Dahlke, *op. cit.*

States was a nation of immigrants. This trend has been continued since the war. The motion picture industry has played a major part in the attack on "discrimination" with productions like *Crossfire*, *Gentlemen's Agreement*, and *Pinky*. In recent war pictures, in which audiences are likely to identify with American soldiers, men from various minority groups have been included in integrated units and shown in heroic roles, even when the picture is about a period in American military history preceding President Truman's executive order. The "pig-tailed" Chinese coolie and the stereotyped Negro clown no longer appear; Indians are no longer portrayed as savage killers of brave settlers, but as honorable people who had been cheated by dishonest white men. In addition, the overwhelming majority of American press coverage outside the South has been against "Jim Crow" practices. Cartoons show segregationist leaders as ignorant, outdated, and hypocritical.

While those who are not in sympathy with what is presented over the media of mass communication often fear that such propaganda determines public opinion, the effectiveness of such appeals depends upon the perspective of the audience. The views of those who already agree are reaffirmed, and some of the undecided may be influenced. But those who are not in sympathy with the appeals usually remain unmoved; many propaganda campaigns have failed miserably. Studies of audience reactions to motion pictures with a "message" reveal that in many cases people are not even conscious of having been the targets of special appeals. The message was neither accepted nor rejected; those who were against minority groups failed to understand it or twisted it around until it was misrepresented. Thus, the appeal of a motion picture such as *Gentlemen's Agreement* tends to be blunted by the failure of anti-Semitic people to perceive the theme.[59] Indeed, some studies of reactions to this movie reveal that many anti-Semitic viewers labelled it as "propaganda"; this reinforced their hostility against Jews. This response pattern has been called the "boomerang effect." [60] These results are

---

[59] Cooper and Jahoda, *op. cit.;* and Russell Middleton, "Ethnic Prejudice and Susceptibility to Persuasion," *American Sociological Review,* XXV (1960), 679–86.

[60] S. H. Flowerman, "The Use of Propaganda to Reduce Prejudice: A Refutation," *International Journal of Opinion and Attitude Research,* III (1949), 99–108; Paul F. Lazarsfeld, "Some Remarks on the Role of the Mass Media in So-Called Tolerance Propaganda," *Journal of Social Issues,* III (1947), 17–25; and Irwin C. Rosen, "The Effect of the Motion Picture *Gentlemen's Agreement* on Attitudes Toward Jews," *Journal of Psychology,* XXVI (1948), 525–36.

consistent with other findings on the effectiveness of mass appeals.[61] Those with firm convictions are left untouched by propaganda campaigns.

Interest groups may also back their demands with economic pressures. If minority groups succeed in winning too many concessions, some extremists in the dominant group may retaliate through economic sanctions. For example, Negroes in the South who have played an active part in the N.A.A.C.P. have been dismissed from their jobs, denied credit, or cut off by wholesalers. In some cases stores have refused to sell them essential supplies. Some Negro colleges have been forced to discipline their more outspoken students, since much of the operating expenses is met by funds donated by white people. Of course, minority groups have also used the boycott as a means of retaliating against tenacious foes. Soon after World War II, when the British government attempted to bring to trial for treason members of the Indian National Army who had cooperated with the Japanese, they found themselves unable to act because of strikes that broke out throughout the continent. The British had unquestioned superiority in weapons, but they were powerless without Indian labor.[62] In Nigeria, discontent developed during the war over the rising cost of living without a corresponding rise of wages, and in 1945 a general strike was called. The refusal to work of people performing indispensable services—railway workers, postal and telegraph workers, technical workers in government—virtually paralyzed the land. The strike shocked both Africans and Europeans into a realization of the great power Nigerians possessed when organized.[63]

Strikes and boycotts are effective only where people in the opposing groups are actually interdependent. Where there is a division of labor along ethnic lines, the economy would come to a standstill

---

[61] Cf. Bernard Berelson, Paul F. Lazarsfeld, and William N. McPhee, *Voting: A Study of Opinion Formation in a Presidential Campaign* (Chicago: University of Chicago Press, 1954), pp. 215-33; Herbert H. Hyman and Paul B. Sheatsley, "Some Reasons Why Information Campaigns Fail," *Public Opinion Quarterly*, XI (1947), 413-23; and Shirley A. Star and Helen M. Hughes, "Report on an Educational Campaign: The Cincinnati Plan for the United Nations," *American Journal of Sociology*, LV (1950), 389-400.

[62] Daniel and Alice Thorner, "India and Pakistan," in Ralph Linton (ed.), *Most of the World* (New York: Columbia University Press, 1949), pp. 640-46.

[63] Coleman, *Nigeria, op. cit.*, pp. 255-59.

with the refusal of one ethnic group to work. Furthermore, the refusal of a large ethnic group to purchase goods would send many merchants into bankruptcy.[64] American manufacturers in highly competitive industries have recently been especially careful not to offend minority groups. One soap or cigarette is much like another, and the boycott of a brand by a substantial portion of one's potential market is something most manufacturers would not care to risk. Several hundred Negro radio stations as well as a large number of magazines and newspapers regularly carry the advertisements of major manufacturers. The 1955 boycott of segregated buses in Montgomery, Alabama, was won by the Negroes because the loss of their patronage cost the company about 65 per cent of its income. Strikes and boycotts involve painful sacrifices for the minority group, too, and they are not effective without widespread cooperation. If leaders of a minority group can get sufficient group solidarity, this can be an effective weapon, but many strikes fail because of lack of unity.[65]

Passive resistance is another weapon used by interest groups. It involves a renunciation of the use of force. Although its advocates contend that non-violence is not merely an expedient way for the weak but a demonstration of the strength of one's moral conviction that violence is evil, it is especially useful in communities in which the dominant group is so powerful that it would be folly to challenge it. The doctrine apparently originated in the Orient, where it has been used from time immemorial as a weapon against oppression. In India, for example, a man who had suffered a wrong would sit before his tormentor's house and starve himself to death. This can be an effective form of retaliation, for his death would expose the culprit to shame and public censure. Gandhi made use of these tactics from 1930 to 1933 in an attempt to wrest concessions from the British. Passive resistance was probably not as effective as its proponents contend, for many Congress members were intimidated by police brutality, and public opinion in Great Britain was not visibly moved; however, the boycott on British goods and the refusal to pay taxes that accompanied the campaign were probably felt. The important

---

[64] Cf. E. T. Hiller, *The Strike: A Study in Collective Action* (Chicago: University of Chicago Press, 1928), pp. 12–24.

[65] Cf. Epstein, *op. cit.*, pp. 157–97.

result, however, was that *Hartal*—the day of mourning and non-cooperation—succeeded in awakening Indians to an awareness of their own power.[66] This type of attack was revived in South Africa in 1946 by Indians protesting the "ghetto act." In 1952, in the campaign against pass laws, the African National Congress and the groups allied with it—Indians, Africans, and Coloured—all joined in a united front to conduct a passive resistance campaign. Civil disobedience included the refusal to pay taxes and the deliberate violation of pass laws and submission to arrest. Protests did not remain entirely passive, however, and there were sporadic outbreaks of violence.[67] This doctrine has been espoused in the United States by the Congress of Racial Equality in its struggle against segregation. It should be pointed out that passive resistance can be effective only in communities in which a humanitarian ideology prevails. It is not likely to work against a ruler like Genghis Khan; his opponents were often killed whether they resisted or not.

In democratic societies there are thousands of voluntary associations, ranging from small cults to huge political parties. Since only a few of these groups enjoy a monopoly in their sphere of operation, each struggles constantly—through persuasion, bargaining, and perhaps coercion—for more favorable conditions in which to pursue its interests. What is ordinarily called "politics" consists in large measure of the tactical maneuvers of interest groups. The extent to which a reform movement is successful depends largely upon the ability of its tacticians. Even when it is successful, however, an organization cannot relax, for the political scene is ever changing. When one group pushes through its program, life conditions for all others change, and they are all forced to adjust to the new circumstances. Conflicts are often terminated by setting up a working arrangement, such as a labor contract. The accommodation lasts until life conditions change again, when one group or the other decides to take advantage of the new situation to make additional demands. On the political scene, then, the course of events develops in the interaction among interest groups.

---

[66] Krishnalal J. Shridharani, *War Without Violence* (New York: Harcourt, Brace, 1939), pp. 130–42. Cf. H. N. Brailsford, "Passive Resistance and Non-Cooperation," *Encyclopedia of the Social Sciences*, Vol. XII, pp. 9–13.
[67] Cf. Kuper, *Passive Resistance in South Africa, op. cit.*

Summary and Conclusion

When there is widespread discontent in minority groups, reform movements arise and vie for public support. When the political structure permits orderly change, the initial attempts at improving the lot of minority peoples occur within the accepted legal framework. The first organizations are usually established in behalf of the underprivileged by sympathetic members of the dominant group and by the more successful in the minority. Such groups have a vested interest in the status quo. Radical movements may also arise among the dispossessed, but they often encounter opposition even within the minority group. The mobilization of minority groups for action is not easy, for there are usually a number of factions reflecting almost every shade of opinion. The leaders often compete with one another, and in many cases they dislike one another more than they do the dominant group. In highly critical situations they may develop a façade of unity, but this often collapses with pressure. When there is a real possibility of some drastic changes being made, conservative forces are also mobilized. Reformers generally make mass appeals to public opinion; other tactics include litigation and operating as pressure groups. When these measures do not produce satisfactory results, attempts may be made to apply economic pressure— through strikes and boycotts. Since reformers support the avowed ideals of the moral order, they have certain advantages over their adversaries.

Societies that permit changes to be made move slowly toward their avowed ideals, as one reform movement after another succeeds in putting through part of its program. The changes occur slowly in small, barely discernible increments. Those who are active in reform often become discouraged, for they cannot see tangible results of their hard work. Members of minority groups often wonder if an egalitarian ideology will ever be implemented. Yet, little by little the dominant group surrenders its special privileges. One need only look at the shifting climate of opinion in the United States during the past half century to see the changes that have been made toward a more equitable distribution of rewards. Whereas the public use of ethnic epithets was once widespread, it is now generally frowned upon. Although many people once felt that "discrimination" was justified, such individuals have now been forced on the defensive; they feel compelled to explain their stand. Open violence against minority groups is widely condemned and has been renounced even by many extremists in the South. These changes are apparently the cumulative product of thousands of separate efforts in thousands of communities, each altering a bit the outlook of the people involved. Thus, even when reformers fail in a particular situation, sometimes their efforts are not in vain, for there is a cumulative effect that is not discernible for many decades. Members of ethnic minorities now take for granted many rights they would not have dreamed of 50 years ago. When societies change in this manner, there is far less likelihood of a bloody uprising.

CHAPTER 16

Nationalism and

Secessionist Movements

The topic of revolution arouses the deepest fears and the highest hopes of men, depending upon their social status. To those who are well established, revolutions constitute a threat to civilization; they are frightful affairs in which the rabble, led by deranged agitators, runs through streets plundering and killing. On the other hand, to the oppressed the possibility of revolting may offer the only gleam of hope in an otherwise dark and forlorn world. Revolutions are seen as glorious uprisings in which their tormentors, fat from overindulgence and debauchery, are given their just due. They are led by adventurous young heroes who, like Robin Hood, are adept at escaping the corrupt police. The intensity of these emotional reactions makes the objective study of revolutions difficult, for one's working conception of the phenomenon so often depends upon his political sympathies. Thus, scholars rooted in the status quo tend to devote themselves to the study of agitators, of crowd behavior, and of subversive groups. On the other hand, scholars sympathetic with revolutionary movements tend to focus their attention upon conditions that lead to the collapse of the old regime.

The word "revolution" is used to refer to a variety of phenomena, but our interest centers upon sudden, drastic changes in government brought about through the concerted effort of the oppressed; as Bodin noted, the mark of a revolution is a change in sovereignty. Most scholarly interest has centered upon uprisings in which one class displaces another and forms a new government. Examples of such upheavals include the French Revolution of 1789, the Russian Revolution of 1917, and the Chinese Revolution of 1948. We shall focus upon attempts of ethnic minorities to overthrow their rulers. Examples include the establishment of "home rule" in Ireland in 1916, the Israeli war of independence of 1948, and the numerous nationalistic movements in Asia and Africa since World War II. Revolutionary movements apparently follow a consistent course, and the aim of this chapter is to examine this process. What are the characteristic patterns of activity found in the uprisings of ethnic minorities against the legitimate order, and what are some of the conditions under which they occur? This study will enable us to understand better what is happening in the so-called "underdeveloped areas" of the world today.

The Emergence of Subversive Groups

Revolutionary uprisings are preceded by a long period of social unrest during which a number of subversive groups emerge to compete with one another for popular support. Such underground organizations are generally formed only after leaders of minority groups become convinced that their aspirations cannot be attained under the existing regime. Engaging in subversive activities is a desperation measure, taken only as a last resort. Revolutionary parties such as the Vietminh won a following in Indo-China only after many generations of moderate reformers experienced frustration.[1] In South Africa, as the Nationalist Party consolidated its position and started to carry out its policy of *apartheid*, native leaders in increasing numbers turned from futile public protests to underground movements. Some of them have been organized into cells, and the educated youth are beginning to use Communist slogans, even blaming some of their

[1] Ellen J. Hammer, *The Struggle for Indo-China* (Stanford, Calif.: Stanford University Press, 1954), pp. 78-79.

misfortunes upon "American warmongers." In the United States the Black Muslim movement made headway among Negroes only after World War II, when increasing numbers became convinced that there was no chance of living with dignity in a white man's world.[2] The belief that reform is impossible develops gradually and is sometimes not acknowledged by the leaders themselves until after their conversion to a revolutionary orientation. After the struggle has been won, they are reluctant to acknowledge any kind of loyalty to the old regime, but most responsible leaders remain loyal almost to the end, when they conclude reluctantly that peaceful reorganization is impossible.

Because of their illegal tactics subversive groups are often regarded as organizations of terrorists, but many of them have quite innocuous beginnings—as clubs, discussion groups, or religious cults. The organizations so dreaded by defenders of the status quo generally have humble beginnings and become conspiratory and violent in response to persecution. Among the early nationalist movements in India were the Indian Association, a literary and social club of educated Hindus, and a variety of pistol cults and physical culture clubs.[3] The Sinn Fein movement, credited with much of the terrorism in the Irish opposition to English rule, did not advocate violence, although some of the extremists in the group took action on their own.[4] In Africa, nationalistic tendencies have frequently developed in religious groups. The agitation of African preachers apparently contributed to the Zulu rebellion in 1906. John Chilewbwe's uprising in Nyasaland in 1915 was connected with the Watch Tower movement, and a few years later prophets of this organization were preaching in Northern Rhodesia the message that in time the Europeans would become the slaves of the Africans.[5] In spite of their secular objectives, nationalist movements in Burma and Indonesia began as religious associations—the Young Men's Buddhist Association in Burma and the Serekat Islam in Indonesia.[6] When a reform movement goes underground, its objectives change to include overthrowing the government. In addition, the leadership is often replaced; dedicated,

[2] Lincoln, *op. cit.*, pp. 3–49.

[3] Bruce T. McCully, *English Education and the Origins of Indian Nationalism* (New York: Columbia University Press, 1940), pp. 299–320. Cf. Chaudhuri, *op. cit.*, pp. 219–44; and Desai, *op. cit.*

[4] Cf. Francis P. Jones, *History of the Sinn Fein Movement and the Irish Rebellion of 1916* (New York: P. J. Kenedy & Sons, 1917).

[5] Sundkler, *op. cit.*, pp. 60, 66, 72, 102.

[6] Pye, "Politics of Southeast Asia," in Almond and Coleman, *op. cit.*, p. 109.

sometimes rigid, men who are able to withstand deprivations and can fight with determination usually take the places of more moderate reformers. Marginal men often play an important part in revolutions.

Although subversive groups often receive money, arms, technical advice, and sympathetic support from outsiders, it is not accurate to say that revolt is fomented from abroad. Most revolutionary movements have strong local support, and many participants are drawn from the rank and file of the minority group. In the years immediately after World War I nationalism became a mass movement in India under the leadership of Gandhi. A person such as Gandhi can become the symbol of a movement, giving it focus and concrete representation. As Communists have learned through their failures, outsiders cannot win local support for a revolutionary cause unless appeals are addressed to the people in terms they can understand. The discontented welcome assistance from any source, but they will not respond to meaningless propaganda.[7] The ideology of a revolutionary movement is likely to reflect the resentments, interests, and aspirations of the people.

The leaders usually consist of a hard core of revolutionaries—often marginal men, disillusioned aristocrats, professional agitators, and sympathetic intellectuals. Since participants in subversive groups are severely punished when caught, a movement cannot survive without a core of dedicated men. Such leadership is usually forged in the course of the struggle; out of common misery and danger there arises a small circle of men who know they can count on each other. Revolutionary movements are often led by intellectuals who had been denied positions for which they had been trained. The standardbearer of the Mexican revolution, for example, was Father Miguel Hidalgo y Costilla, who had been denounced before the Inquisition for heresies, moral lapses, and speaking approvingly of the French Revolution. Although he escaped conviction, he was banished to a small village, where he rallied the Indians to revolt.[8] Among the early Indian nationalists was Surendra Banerjea, who had been dismissed from the civil service in 1873, had appealed the case in England, and had lost. When he was also denied admission to the bar, he studied the life and writings of Mazzini and entered native politics.[9] In Ni-

---

[7] Harold D. Lasswell and Dorothy Blumenstock, *World Revolutionary Propaganda* (New York: Alfred A. Knopf, 1939). Cf. P. Abrahams, *op. cit.*, pp. 297–98.

[8] Herring, *op. cit.*, pp. 254–55.

[9] McCully. *op. cit.*, pp. 296–97.

geria where the characteristic attitude of Europeans toward educated Africans was one of contempt, amusement, condescension, or veiled hostility, many nationalist agitators were drawn from the ranks of frustrated native bureaucrats.[10] Sympathetic outsiders are also attracted to the cause of the oppressed. The Greek struggle for independence against the Ottoman Empire aroused widespread sympathy throughout Europe, and such eminent men as Lord Byron joined the ranks of the partisans. This not only inspired the Greeks but gave their movement considerable publicity.[11] More recently, Communists have tried to participate in revolutions against colonial powers. They had only limited success in Burma and Thailand, but in Vietnam Ho Chi Minh, a professional revolutionary, played a central role. In Indonesia, nationalist ideology has been strongly influenced by Marx, but the Communist Party has not been dominant.[12]

Although misery in itself does not provoke revolution, misery that can be attributed plausibly to the dominant group greatly facilitates the work of revolutionaries. People are usually prodded by agitators, and their work is made easier when they can cite concrete cases to back their charges. Invidious comparisons are especially effective. Underprivileged people become discontented when they learn of others in humble positions like themselves who enjoy a better life. The accomplishments of American Negroes have provided for many Africans living proof that people with dark complexions are not necessarily limited to base occupations. Furthermore, many of the restless tend to travel about; they feel an urge to move about, though usually without any specific destination. This is important, for wanderers bring back amazing tales. Outsiders bearing similar accounts are not trusted, but when a local boy comes home with details of a utopian existence elsewhere, those who know him begin to question some of their firmest beliefs.[13] Once nationalistic aspirations develop, all inconveniences are attributed to alien rule, and the people begin to dream of independence.

The decadence of some of the rulers—their abuse of privileges

[10] Coleman, *Nigeria, op. cit.,* pp. 116–25, 145–48, 152–55.
[11] William Miller, *The Ottoman Empire and Its Successors* (Cambridge: Cambridge University Press, 1927), p. 84.
[12] Trager, *op. cit.* Cf. Hammer, *op. cit.,* pp. 74–93; and George W. Shepherd, *The Politics of African Nationalism* (New York: Frederick A. Praeger, 1962), pp. 143–55.
[13] Edwards, *op. cit.,* pp. 23–25.

and their hedonistic outlook—leads many to question the moral order. People are usually provoked into an epidemic desire for action by the blunders and the ineptitude of the privileged group, and the record of each major revolution contains a long list of provocations. Some scholars have suggested that revolutions do not succeed so much from the efforts of revolutionaries as from the unintentional abdication of those in positions of privilege.[14] When an elite group can no longer live up to its own code of honor, it is disintegrating. *Noblesse oblige* requires personal sacrifice; when men of high rank are so preoccupied with personal pleasures that they are unwilling to meet their obligations, they cannot command respect. Unpopular laws also help build opposition against the existing order. Downtrodden people may be able to tolerate an autocrat who is a capable ruler, but not one who is irresponsible. Indeed, in many cases members of the dominant group have little respect for themselves or their associates, making it almost impossible for them to join ranks in a concerted stand to defend their interests. Men do not question a moral order without good reason, even when they are of subordinate status. The weakening of sentimental attachments to traditional values is gradual. Continued provocation leads to complaints, to disillusionment, and finally to alienation.

The period of revolutionary unrest is marked by sporadic outbursts of violence. There are raids upon storehouses, occasional street demonstrations, and insults hurled at officials. These objections are initially scattered and relatively ineffective, but the authorities often take harsh action. They jail agitators for their "inflammatory" speeches and shut down presses for printing "rumors." In many cases a previously-divided minority group is welded together through ruthless suppression. Harsh measures often breed fanatics; they also provide martyrs, who become symbols of the movement. Many of the leaders of the new African nations have been imprisoned for their political activities—Dr. Hastings Banda of Nyasaland, Jomo Kenyatta of Kenya, Patrice Lumumba of the Congo, Albert John Luthuli of the Union of South Africa, Kwame Nkrumah of Ghana. Mahatma Gandhi and Jawaharlal Nehru spent considerable time in British jails, and the Dutch made a hero of Sukarno by incarcerating him. The Irish uprising of 1916 did not initially enjoy popular support, for many were opposed to taking action while England was at war

14 Brinton, *op. cit.*, pp. 28–71.

with Germany. But the crushing of the insurrection and the execution of its leaders rallied the people to demand "home rule." Although many of them did not know what it was, Irishmen rallied around the Sinn Fein, an organization which at that time was almost dead.[15] During the civil disobedience campaign called by Gandhi soon after World War I the people were to observe *Hartal*—a day of mourning. Everyone was to stop normal activities for 24 hours and to observe a fast. The campaign was to be one of non-violence, but the government struck back. Processions were stopped by military units, and large crowds were fired upon in Delhi, Calcutta, and Amritsar. This intensified resentment and led to national unity.[16] In Indo–China, a series of strikes and riots were countered savagely by military force; there were mass arrests, and native leaders were exiled to the penal colony of Pulo Condore. This united the people and reinforced their determination to resist.[17] The most effective argument against any form of oppression is not that it is wicked but that it is foolish and self-defeating.

When confronted by political opposition, members of the dominant group often react like angry schoolmasters rebuking naughty pupils. They are outraged at the "insolence" of disobedient children. While a few ask for calm and understanding, many lash out in anger. They appear to gain psychological satisfaction from resorting to violence of a theatrical sort; they make a scene, strike a pose, create a spectacle for themselves and their friends, and apparently derive some solace from it.[18] Often the dominant group shows an astonishing inability to comprehend the resentment of its subjects, seeing them only as children incapable of adult interests. The reaction of French *colons* in Algeria to the tragedy at Dienbienphu was one of outrage, and subsequent events in North Africa suggest that nothing was learned from the lesson of Indo–China.

Since most subversive groups do not have sufficient power for a direct assault on the government, they are forced to resort to guerrilla tactics and to terrorism. Guerrilla warfare is generally used by the weaker side and is facilitated by difficult terrain, a sympathetic populace, and a general condition of lawlessness. Guerrillas cut lines

[15] F. P. Jones, *op. cit.;* and P. S. O'Hegarty, *The Victory of Sinn Fein* (Dublin: Talbot Press, 1924), pp. 1–11.
[16] Shridharani, *op. cit.*, pp. 117–30.
[17] Kennedy, *op. cit.*, p. 330.
[18] Cf. Mannoni, *op. cit.*, p. 88.

of communication, intercept supplies, annihilate foraging parties, and hold small detachments close to their barracks. In 1831, 1846, 1861, and 1863 Polish patriots harassed Russian and Austrian troops, and prior to the breakup of the Ottoman and Austro–Hungarian Empires the Balkan area was full of guerrilla bands. Long before the revolution in North Africa French legionnaires had to fight Moslem irregulars in the deserts.[19] Much of the fighting in Algeria by the National Liberation Army was of this nature. Tiny units moved at night in the back country; the usual fighting unit consisted of 30 men. But this kind of tactic tied down a huge, modern French army for several years. The Malayan Communist Party provided the principal opposition to the Japanese during World War II. When the war ended, it became active in "front" groups and in unions, but after 1948 it returned to its program of open violence. Although the party claimed to represent all Malayans, it was actually dominated by Chinese. From June 1948, to April 1949, for example, 581 out of its 601 casualties were Chinese.[20]

Conspiratory associations also engage in terroristic practices. Assassinations and bombings are carried out, sometimes to eliminate key political figures, but often for political effect—to show people that the police are not all-powerful and to frighten members of the dominant group. In spite of Gandhi's insistence upon non-violence, the history of India is dotted with the terroristic acts of small groups of nationalists. In the summer of 1952 the Mau Mau outbreaks in Kenya attracted world-wide attention. Small bands of Kikuyu tribesmen surprised isolated farms and murdered all the Europeans. They also killed natives who had cooperated with the police. The Europeans were terrified, and for the duration of the emergency they all wore sidearms. No African was trusted, for there were rumors of betrayal by servants who had served faithfully for more than 20 years.[21] Other groups that have attracted attention as terrorists include the Sinn Fein in Ireland, the Huks on the Philippines, and the E.O.K.A. (National Organization of Cypriot Fighters) in Cyprus. It should be pointed out that members of the minority group

[19] Cf. Carleton Beals, "Guerrilla Warfare," *Encyclopedia of the Social Sciences,* Vol. VII, pp. 197–99.

[20] Ian Morrison, "Aspects of the Racial Problem in Malaya," *Pacific Affairs,* XXII (1949), 239–53; and Pye, *Guerrilla Communism in Malaya, op. cit.,* pp. 47–111.

[21] Leakey, *op. cit.*

often suffer most from such tactics, both as victims of attacks and from the retaliation of the police and the army.

Much of the work of subversive organizations consists of agitation and propaganda within the minority group. Even when there are many grievances, the more successful members are often reluctant to take action; even those who are sympathetic with the rebel cause fear retaliation. But revolutionary parties must win popular support. One objective is increased popular discontent. Agitators call attention to injustices, point to flagrant violations of the moral code, make invidious comparisons with minorities in other lands, and urge people to demand their rights as human beings.[22] The popularization of slogans—such as *"merderka!"* in Indonesia and *"uhuru!"* in Africa—helps to unite otherwise divided people in a common cause. The promotional devices used differ with the requirements of the situation. Pamphlets are often distributed. Between 1945 and 1952 nationalistic propaganda in Kenya was distributed through newsletters, most of them mimeographed. Since few Europeans could read Kikuyu and a system of monitoring had not yet been set up, this agitation went on largely unchecked.[23] Where the press is suppressed or where the people are largely illiterate, a variety of other tactics are used—plays, public meetings, games, and comic books.

In most revolutions several subversive groups compete for popular support. A number of protest groups form spontaneously, each with its own program and leadership. Although outsiders may regard the distinctions among them as trivial or imaginary, minor differences in doctrine are of utmost importance to revolutionaries. It should also be remembered that many of the active participants in revolutions are men who have suffered severe deprivations; many are marginal men plagued by doubts about themselves. The excessive egotism so commonly found among long-frustrated men often plays an important part in pre-revolutionary conspiracies. Power-oriented men are often petty, and they watch one another jealously to see that no individual gets too far ahead. After the Indian Association had been established in 1879 to agitate against Civil Service regulations, it was hampered by many internal conflicts. Bitter personal quarrels among the editors of Indian newspapers ruined the possibility of concerted

[22] Cf. Lincoln, *op. cit.*, pp. 98–134; and Louise Nalbandian, *The Armenian Revolutionary Movement* (Berkeley: University of California Press, 1963), pp. 67–178.
[23] Coleman, "Politics of Sub-Saharan Africa," *op. cit.*, p. 348.

action, and in 1877, the National Mohammedan Association was formed, allowing Moslems to band together under their own leaders.[24] When the Mongolian princes led their uprising against the Chinese, some wanted an autonomous Mongolia in which princes and lamas would be restored to power; but others wanted to form a government that would remove Mongol princes as well as the Chinese, and they appealed to an old Mongol law that princes held power only with the consent of the tribe.[25] When different ethnic groups try to make common cause against a ruler, there are even more conflicts. They may agree upon an ultimate goal, but the various leaders fight bitterly among themselves. Differences among native leaders became quite obvious in the strife in the Congo after 1961.

Subversive groups are secret societies, and many of their activities are attempts to forge group solidarity under unfavorable conditions and to protect themselves. One of the major objectives of subversive groups, one that is often overlooked, is the weakening of their rivals. Since they cannot attack one another openly without risking loss of popular support, conflicts between them are ruthless and underhanded. The intrigues often result in animosities that persist even after the revolution has been won. It is not unusual for revolutionaries to eliminate dangerous rivals by betraying them to the secret police. Some of them hate each other so much that they would even prefer to deal with the police. Since subversive groups operate outside the legal order, they must enforce their own rules. Both the Hunchak and Dashnak organizations used terror to exact money from wealthy Armenians who counselled patience.[26] To protect themselves they must kill those suspected of betraying them. The Mau Mau put considerable pressure on the Kikuyu people, even murdering those who opposed it. Once a Kikuyu had been informed about the organization, he had to take a sacred oath of secrecy in order to protect it. Those who had taken the oath were urged to have nothing to do with Kikuyu who were still outside. Anyone suspected of being in sympathy with Europeans, especially if there was reason to believe he had cooperated with the police, was killed.

[24] McCully, *op. cit.*, pp. 299–316.
[25] Owen Lattimore, "The Historical Setting of Inner Mongolian Nationalism," *Pacific Affairs*, IX (1936), 339. Cf. "The Eclipse of Inner Mongolian Nationalism," *op. cit.*
[26] Atamian, *op. cit.*, pp. 141–42.

Witnesses mysteriously disappeared.[27] During World War II more "traitors" were killed by the guerrillas in Malaya than the total Japanese casualties in Malaya and Singapore. After 1948, ten times as many Chinese were killed as all others. The guerrillas were mostly Chinese, and people in the Chinese communities knew the location of camps, trails, and headquarters. Rather than cooperate with the police; however, they stood mute.[28]

Sometimes conflict between the factions becomes so bitter that the revolutionary movement as a whole collapses. In many cases the rival groups work out a *modus vivendi* until their common objective is realized. In some revolutions these differences become more apparent after success, when the victors begin to fight among themselves. Sometimes one of the groups becomes dominant, either eliminating or absorbing all the others. It may have a program that appeals to the majority of the people, or it may have been blessed with astute leadership. No group is likely to succeed, however, unless it can persuade a substantial portion of the discontented populace that its program is the most promising. The successful group emerges, therefore, in a selective process. The struggle for power among different subversive groups is important, for the leadership and the ideology of the successful faction place their stamp on the entire revolution. The peculiar history of a small group affects the type of social structure that eventually develops. The myths, saints, and ideology of a revolution are shaped in these smaller groups.

Some revolutionary leaders are refined and command respect in the dominant group. Since "grass roots" leaders who have risen from the ranks are often unimpressive in appearance, however, the rulers sometimes fail to take them seriously. This is often a fatal error. When partisans who have been captured are brought before them, officials frequently laugh contemptuously at their bedraggled clothing and poor equipment. But Americans who are unimpressed with the guerrilla fighters in the "underdeveloped areas" today need only recall the contemptuous attitude of the British Army toward the "minutemen" in 1776. Even those who acknowledge the skills of rebel leaders in guerrilla warfare are often convinced that such

---

[27] Leakey, *op. cit.*, pp. 53–54, 98–108.
[28] Morrison, *op. cit.*, p. 248; and Pye, *Guerrilla Communism in Malaya, op. cit.*, p. 69.

"barbarians" could never conduct the affairs of a complex government. Those who are inclined to scoff at the leadership in the newly-created nations of the twentieth century should be reminded of the circumstances that produced such men as Benito Juarez, Genghis Khan, or Abraham Lincoln. To be sure, such men are rare, but there can be no guarantee that some partisan leaders are not geniuses. In a revolutionary era, when people have long been oppressed, some of the finest minds turn to fighting.

The Development of Nationalism

One of the most important bases of identification today is nationality. The ideal of nationalism is national unification, in which each ethnic group occupies contiguous territory and governs itself. Thousands of people who share a common culture and conceive of themselves as being of a kind have survived for a long period of time without their own government, but the ideal is that they should constitute an independent polity and determine their own destiny. Nationalism is a state of mind; it is based largely upon common traditions. People with a common culture have a similar outlook toward life. They share common memories and feel united because they can understand each other and can cooperate more easily than they can with outsiders. Once an independent government has been established, nationality becomes a legal concept. It is a form of identity defined by laws concerning birth and ancestry. A citizen owes his supreme loyalty to his nation, and children are taught to place love of country above all else.

Nationalism has played an important part in Europe from the eighteenth century, and similar movements are now sweeping the rest of the world. In eighteenth-century Europe the idea of popular sovereignty gradually displaced the notion of loyalty to a ruling house, and the conviction that each ethnic group should have something to say about its destiny followed. The idea that the natural goal of every ethnic group is the creation, maintenance, and enhancement of the power of its own state was propagated by Mazzini and was reinforced by President Wilson's pronouncements toward the end of World War I. One of the major problems of the age was that of reconciling the sovereignty of states with the autonomy of ethnic groups.[29] After World War I the principle of self-determination was used in the unrestrained partition of the losers. More recently nationalistic movements have developed in Asia, the Middle East, and Africa, where there has been an epidemic demand for independence from foreign rule.

As nationalistic movements develop, consciousness of kind is intensified. When Hitler insisted that all Germans should be united under the Nazi regime, persons of German descent throughout the world became more conscious of their ethnic identity. Although many overseas Germans rejected Nazism, they became more conscious of ancestral ties. The growth of a sense of unity is sometimes facilitated by the acceptance of a myth of common descent. The people of Israel are defined in the Torah as the "chosen people" with a divine mission. Zionism was born when a group of Jewish thinkers recast the history of their group within the framework of the European concepts of "race" and "nation" and demanded as a homeland territory their forebears had once occupied. From 1795 to 1919 the area inhabited by Poles was divided into three territories, each ruled by a different country—Russia, Austria, and Prussia. There was no Polish government, but the Poles maintained their own culture and sense of solidarity across political boundaries. In secret they taught their children their language and traditions, and they finally won their independence after World War I. The national land is often regarded as a group possession on which foreigners are interlopers.[30]

Intellectuals play an important part in the growth of nationalism. A great many people in minority groups are either content with their lot or feel that nothing can be done about it. Discontent generally develops first among intellectuals, often after they have suffered some personal humiliation because of their ethnic identity. In Poland, for example, aristocrats were reconciled to their position, and peasants were concerned primarily with acquiring wealth. Only the intelligentsia kept the torch of national aspiration burning.[31] Intellectuals

---

[29] Cf. Dominian, *op. cit.*; Carleton J. H. Hayes, *The Historical Evolution of Modern Nationalism* (New York: Richard R. Smith, 1931); and Hans Kohn, *The Idea of Nationalism* (New York: Macmillan, 1944).

[30] Cf. Florian Znaniecki, *Modern Nationalities* (Urbana: University of Illinois Press, 1952), pp. 81-111.

[31] Louis L. Gerson, *Woodrow Wilson and the Rebirth of Poland* (New Haven: Yale University Press, 1953), pp. 7-14.

find out about different ways of life, provide explanations for inequities, downgrade the dominant group, give voice to the inchoate discontents, resentments, and hopes of the people, and formulate utopias toward which they can aspire. They articulate grievances and formulate explicitly a series of demands. They give content and form to popular lament and eventually formulate some kind of ideology.

The incipient stages of nationalistic movements are often revivalistic. An effort is made to develop pride within the minority group. There is often a cultural renaissance in which intellectuals try to recover and popularize the group's history. The Mexican revolution, for example, was accompanied by a self-conscious exaltation of the virtues of the Indian, contrasted with the vices of the Spaniard.[32] Prominent artists, among them Diego Rivera, played an important part in the continued growth of Mexican nationalism, just as Chopin, Dvorak, Grieg, and Sibelius did in giving the folk music of their countries greater stature and more permanent form. In many cases associations are formed to promote national culture. Soon after World War I the first Pan-African Congress was convened in Paris, and the emergence of the Garvey movement among American Negroes at that time helped to create consciousness of kind. There followed a "Negro renaissance" in which African intellectuals turned increasingly to the study and glorification of African history and culture. They learned to appreciate the worth of their indigenous arts and crafts and especially their unwritten literature. African intellectuals began to develop a sense of being alike, of having a common destiny, of being rooted in a common past.[33] This feeling has played an important part in subsequent political action. The Black Muslim movement among American Negroes has followed in this tradition; this, along with emphasis upon high moral standards, has enabled its participants to develop self-respect.[34] The nationalism that has recently developed in Ghana has a pan-African outlook and emphasizes economic and cultural independence of European civilization.[35]

The mother tongue is an important characteristic of a people.

---

[32] Robin N. Humphreys, *The Evolution of Modern Latin America* (New York: Oxford University Press, 1946), p. 22. Cf. Anthony F. C. Wallace, "Revitalization Movements," *American Anthropologist*, LVIII (1956), 264–81.

[33] Coleman, *Nigeria, op. cit.*, pp. 188–91. Cf. Elkin, *op. cit.*

[34] Cf. Lincoln, *op. cit.*, pp. 80–83, 204–09; and E. U. Essien–Udom, *Black Nationalism: A Search for an Identity* (Chicago: University of Chicago Press, 1962).

[35] Cf. Shepherd, *op. cit.*, pp. 84–105.

Memories are stored in that language, and the emotional life of the group gets its most faithful expression in it. Most ethnic groups feel that their language is the cornerstone of continued existence and defend their right to use it. It is not strange, then, that many nationalistic movements are accompanied by linguistic revivals. Sometimes local dialects or infrequently used and almost forgotten languages are resuscitated. In India, there was a revival of Sanskrit language and literature, and the superiority of Aryan culture—lost in ruthless conquests—was proclaimed.[36] In Norway, especially since its separation from Sweden in 1905, nationalists have promoted the use of Landsmaal, an attempt to unify various local dialects into a standard tongue. They contended that the official language, Riksmaal, had been imposed by the Danes during their rule, which ended in 1814. They claimed further that country people, who spoke Landsmaal, were the true bearers of pure and unadulterated Norwegian culture.[37] The Irish gave expression to their emancipation from English rule by the revival of ancient Gaelic script, and nationalism in Turkey led to the abolition of Arabic script. The new linguistic norms are often standardized through their use in epics, legends, and popular fiction. Some of the previously unwritten European languages were given standard form through translations of the Bible and other classics.[38] In recent years such revivals have posed serious problems, for some of the old languages are not adequate for handling technical problems of the industrial age.

Unity often rests upon the sharing of a common past. Those who believe they have the same traits because of common origin often point with pride to great men of their kind. They can thereby make their claims of superiority more plausible to themselves, even if they fail to persuade others. Intellectuals often develop for the people a special version of history, sometimes involving a fictitious lineage and an idealization of the past. Certain individuals, long forgotten by other historians, are revived, given new significance, and proclaimed as national heroes. During the unification of Italy, for example, historians began to write of the entire peninsula rather than the separate city-states, and they went back to ancient times, tracing

36 McCully, *op. cit.*, pp. 242–54.
37 Ottar Tinglum, "Landsmaal–Riksmaal: The Feud Between the Dialects and the Official Language of Norway," *American Journal of Sociology*, **XXXIV** (1929), 686–92.
38 Cf. Znaniecki, *op. cit.*, pp. 23–56.

their continuity from the glories of the Roman Empire. In Finland a national epic, the *Kalevala*, was manufactured. Certain events in India—as the Sepoy Mutiny of 1857—have been reinterpreted to become landmarks in the evolution of a great people. The treatment of this uprising by British historians had attributed the whole affair to rumors about the introduction of new rifles requiring native soldiers to bite into greased cartridges—an act repulsive to Moslem and Hindu alike. These accounts gave the impression that the whole incident was a mistake, based upon the superstitions of ignorant people. In the histories written by Indians, however, the uprising is depicted as a glorious rebellion in which heroic attempts were made against overwhelming odds to right a number of wrongs; nothing is said of greased cartridges.[39] Mestizo politicians in Mexico now proclaim their Indian "blood" and point to the Aztec and Maya civilizations as their true past. They speak of the Spaniards as interlopers. Although Cortez actually won only because he had the help of 50,000 Indians, most Indians are illiterate and know little of recorded history.[40] It is difficult to develop group pride without some historical support.

As people who had once been considered inferior human beings re-evaluate themselves, pride develops over the very identification symbols that had once been marks of shame. The traits for which a group feels it had been persecuted are emphasized. When Garvey started his movement to found a separate state in Africa for American Negroes, he inverted the evaluation of skin color and insisted upon black superiority. He attacked members of the Negro upper class, many of whom were lighter in complexion. He did not exclude them entirely, however, offering to make light-skinned individuals "honorary Negroes" in his new state.[41] In Irish nationalism the emphasis was placed upon Catholic religion, Gaelic language, and Irish folklore. *Sinn Fein* means literally "ourselves alone." Their doctrine was that Irishmen should depend only upon themselves and not seek outside help. They should think, speak, and write in Irish, dress in Irish clothing, develop Irish resources, support Irish industries, and

[39] Cf. Sashi B. Chaudhuri, *Civil Disturbances During the British Rule in India* (Calcutta: World Press, 1955); and Asoka Mehta, *1857: The Great Rebellion* (Bombay: Hind Kitabs, 1946).

[40] Gruening, *op. cit.*, pp. 69–88. Cf. Sydney G. Fisher, "The Legendary and Myth–Making Process in Histories of the American Revolution," *Proceedings of the American Philosophical Society*, **LI** (1912), 53–76.

[41] Record, "The Negro Intellectual and Negro Nationalism," *op. cit.*

progress on purely Irish lines.[42] As consciousness of kind developed in Africa, natives who imitated slavishly the dress and customs of Europeans were deprecated in their own press as "black white men."[43]

This suggests that many nationalities are new classifications of human beings, formed in the struggle against a common foe. There are economic, political, and military advantages to the consolidation of smaller units; after they have been formed, intellectuals make up mystical references to "race." Prior to the British conquest, India was a loosely-knit country of a half million small, self-contained villages. Differences in language and custom divided the population; there were sentimental attachments to ancestral religion and manners, but no love of country. Use of the English language promoted unity among educated Indians; as English became the *lingua franca*, it enabled Indians far apart in space and outlook to exchange views. In addition, under British rule all subjects, regardless of their status in their own society, enjoyed similar rights and developed similar grievances.[44] When Nigeria was unified under British rule in 1914, the area was divided geographically and culturally. No common language existed, and the people identified themselves as Ibo, Hausa, Fulani, or Yoruba. The British did not consciously plan to create a Nigerian nation; when the boundaries were drawn, the area was seen only as an administration unit. But British policies actually unified the country, establishing a common transportation and communication system and introducing a common currency, language, and educational system. Christianity also provided a trans-tribal bond, uniting individuals in formerly hostile communities. Use of the English language gave Nigerians access to a new world of ideas, awakened new aspirations, provided a medium for the expression of their grievances, and enabled them to communicate with educated men in different tribes. In addition, because of fear of corruption the colonial administration assigned educated Nigerians to areas other than those from which they came. The result was that these men developed a Nigeria-wide outlook.[45] The area that is now Indonesia was inhabited by many ethnic groups: Achinese, Bataks,

---

[42] Boyle, *op. cit.*, p. 11; and F. P. Jones, *op. cit.*, pp. 1-45.

[43] Lugard, *op. cit.*, p. 589.

[44] Desai, *op. cit.*, pp. 152-58; and McCully, *op. cit.*, pp. 211-13, 227-28, 238-40, 282-91.

[45] Coleman, *Nigeria, op. cit.*, pp. 104, 113-14, 141-58, 320.

Dayaks, Javanese, Sundanese, Madurese, Balinese, Timorese, and many others. But all ethnic groups were against the Dutch; they were united by the administrative boundaries of the Dutch colonial government. Nationalism began with demands to control the government, and the government in question covered the entire territory.[46]

Ironically, leaders of revolutionary movements against colonial powers are often intellectuals who had been trained by the very people being evicted. European colonial governments frequently encouraged natives to get an education to create a supply of public servants. The middle-class natives went to school because they wanted better jobs, but there were more graduates than the government could hire. These educated but unemployed intellectuals became the focus of discontent.[47] The colonists often regarded these men as ungrateful, and the educated natives themselves were ambivalent, seeing much of value in the culture of the dominant group that their fellows could not appreciate. Many of the leaders were highly accomplished persons who could easily have taken their place with the best of the dominant group, had the latter not chosen to exclude them. In South Africa it was the educated Bantu who bore the brunt of differential treatment, because many of them came into close contact with Europeans without being their servants. There was an accepted place for natives as servants, but an independent African was ostracized by the Europeans. Many were marginal men, who were actually not at home in the company of those whom they led. For example, Dr. Hastings Banda, leader of the African Congress Movement in Nyasaland and hero of the Rhodesias, was educated in England, worked as a physician in London for 20 years, and did not speak any native language.[48] Leaders of Mongolian nationalism were members of the princely class who were not in line for hereditary posts. Many had received a Chinese education and were self-conscious of being culturally Chinese but being identified as Mongol.[49] The im-

---

[46] Van der Kroef, "Social Conflict and Minority Aspirations in Indonesia," *op. cit.;* and Wertheim, *op. cit.,* pp. 21–29.

[47] Cf. Furnivall, *Colonial Policy and Practice, op. cit.,* pp. 124, 376–78; and Hunter, *op. cit.,* pp. 560–74.

[48] Franck, *op. cit.,* pp. 248–66. Cf. Thomas P. Melady, *Profiles of African Leaders* (New York: Macmillan, 1961); and Immanuel Wallerstein, *Africa: The Politics of Independence* (New York: Random House, 1961), pp. 45–61.

[49] Lattimore, "The Historical Setting of Inner Mongolian Nationalism," *op. cit.,* p. 400.

portance of missionary education in Africa is shown by the number of nationalist leaders who are Christians. Nor are the sources of nationalist ideologies so difficult to trace. Early Indian nationalist theories drew their chief inspiration from European nationalism, and British self-criticism—exemplified in the writings of Burke, Mill, Macaulay, and Laski—has bulked large in African nationalist literature.[50] Inspiration has also come from other European sources. The first Marxist cadres among the Vietnamese were formed in France, and Ho Chi Minh began his career as a revolutionary there.[51]

Emigré intellectuals also play an important part in winning support abroad for national aspirations. Those who are studying away from home often become acutely aware of the low esteem in which their ethnic group is held, and differential treatment abroad leads to a sharp desire to increase national prestige. In the late nineteenth century, when Armenian intellectuals abroad realized that they were regarded as backward and cowardly, their sense of shame stirred them into active efforts to organize reform movements.[52] Polish intellectuals in the United States felt similarly humiliated and became spokesmen for Polish nationalism. Many Indian students discovered India as a nation while studying abroad. Most of them had been ignorant of their nation's history and culture and had been more conscious of differences of caste and language.[53] Sometimes intellectuals in exile are more free to take action than those at home, for they have a chance to organize without being hounded by the police. Thus, Armenian nationalists were able to publish books abroad in their native tongue; the first Armenian Bible was published in Venice.[54] A leading role in the Greek revolution against the Ottoman Empire was played by the Philiki Hetairia, an organization of Greeks in Odessa. Emigré intellectuals of several ethnic groups sometimes join forces; Armenian Hunchaks, for example, joined Macedonian, Albanian, Cretan, and Greek revolutionaries to form the Oriental Federation of Nationalist Groups to synchronize their struggle

---

[50] Coleman, *Nigeria, op. cit.,* p. 414; "Politics of Sub-Saharan Africa," *op. cit.,* pp. 278–83; and McCully, *op. cit.*

[51] Cf. Pye, "Politics of Southeast Asia," *op. cit.,* pp. 105–06; and Robert Shaplen, "The Enigma of Ho Chi Minh," *The Reporter,* XII (January 27, 1955), 11–19.

[52] A. O. Sarkissian, *A History of the Armenian Question to 1885* (Urbana: University of Illinois Press, 1938), pp. 115–16.

[53] John and Ruth H. Useem, *The Western-Educated Man in India* (New York: Dryden Press, 1955), pp. 57–67.

[54] Nalbandian, *op. cit.,* pp. 34–36.

against the Ottoman regime.[55] Without sympathy and tangible support from foreign governments many revolutionary movements would probably fail.

All nationalistic movements do not develop the same objectives. Most people want independence; they aim for the development of a nation that can take its place on the basis of equality in the family of nations. Many Malagasy, for example, realized that independence would mean trouble; they expected more corruption, more forced labor, heavier taxes, and more severe penalties for infractions; but they preferred to control their own destiny rather than trusting their fate to outsiders whom they neither understood nor trusted.[56] Where the leadership includes successful businessmen, desire for a larger share of the dominant group's profits plays an important part; they see possibilities of greater profits once they are able to control the government. Sometimes the demand for self-rule comes only after a succession of bad experiences. In Papua the natives disliked the Dutch so much that they did not oppose the coming of the Japanese during World War II. When the new conquerors freed prisoners, coolies, and mission trainees and allowed them to return home, the Papuans became even more receptive to their propaganda. Before long, however, they were disillusioned; Dutch rule had been replaced by something much worse. By the time the war ended, they wanted independence from *all* foreigners—including Indonesians.[57] Many nationalists have a utopian mentality; they regard independence as the key to all good things in life.

But there are some movements in which no attempt is made to win national sovereignty. In 1848, the Czech leader Havlicek opposed the creation of an independent Bohemia, for a small state would have had difficulty surviving in the midst of great powers. He advocated instead a close union with other Slavic peoples.[58] Political control may remain in the hands of others or be placed in the hands of a coalition of ethnic groups—as long as there are constitutional guarantees of the rights of each nationality and opportunities for each to develop its culture without undue interference. Marxism de-

---

[55] Miller, *The Ottoman Empire, op. cit.*, p. 65; and William Miller, *A History of the Greek People, 1821–1921* (London: Methuen, 1922), p. 13.

[56] Mannoni, *op. cit.*, p. 134.

[57] Worsley, *op. cit.*, pp. 123–45.

[58] Cf. Kann, *The Multi-National Empire, op. cit.*, Vol. I, p. 166; and *The Habsburg Empire, op. cit.*, pp. 20, 30.

veloped in Europe at a time when minority groups were struggling for autonomy, and such guarantees have become a part of official Communist ideology. The policy of the Soviet Union is that its minority groups are autonomous; although it is not likely to happen, they are theoretically free to secede from the U.S.S.R. Constitutional provisions to permit the retention of native languages and cultures have been carried out for all groups but the Jews.[59] A similar policy has been adopted by Communist China. The Ningsia Hui Autonomous Region was established in 1958, giving the Chinese-speaking Moslems some measure of control over their own development. Other autonomous regions include Inner Mongolia, the Sinkiang Autonomous Region of the Uigur people, and the Kwangsi Autonomous Region of the Chuang people. Tibetans may eventually receive similar treatment. This does not mean, of course, that these people can actually secede; any such suggestion would quickly be put down as "counter-revolutionary."

Some nationalistic movements develop racist ideologies. The Nazi movement was pan-German and sought to incorporate within the frontiers of the Third Reich all areas inhabited by persons of German descent. Various pan-Slavic and pan-Arabic movements have also had racist overtones. Racism involves not only self-exaltation but also the pursuit of interests at the expense of other ethnic groups. Even in the French Revolution such considerations were not absent. The conservative philosopher de Boulainvilliers had contended that the French aristocracy was made up of Franks (from Germany) who had subdued the Gauls (Celts) and that the inequality of classes was irreparable because of "racial" differences. In 1789, in *Qu'est-ce que le Tiers-État?* Sieyès replied that the revolution represented the overthrow of these oppressors by the Celts—the righting of a historical wrong.[60] In most African nationalistic movements the leaders indicated their intention of protecting the rights of European minorities that would be created by independence. There were many agitators, however, who preached an anti-white philosophy. Extremists opposed "multi-racial" organizations as "cooling chambers," designed to pacify but not to rectify. They thrived in an atmosphere of "race"

[59] Bernhard J. Stern, "Soviet Policy on National Minorities," *American Sociological Review*, IX (1944), 229–35. Cf. Decter, *op. cit.*

[60] Cf. Jacques Barzun, *The French Race* (New York: Columbia University Press, 1932).

struggle. European settlers made things easier for them by their intransigence; they demonstrated that white people who were sympathetic to African aspirations were politically ineffective and often repudiated by their own kind. This led to the widespread conviction that it would be necessary to wrest control from white people. Africans who rejected this strategy were not able to speak out, for they would have faced ostracism, boycott, and perhaps violence. Most Africans became convinced that sooner or later the day of reckoning would come, and they did not want to be caught on the wrong side. In the United States, the Black Muslims are the only nationalistic group to win a substantial following among Negroes. In February 1961, in the midst of a Security Council debate on the Congo, a group of American Negroes suddenly burst past the U.N. guards and stormed into the gallery. The wild melee that followed focused public attention upon the extent to which an old cult had grown into an aggressive national movement. It affirms the American Negro's bonds with Africans and proclaims the superiority of the black "race." It claims allegiance only to the "flag of Islam" and, scorning integration, demands separate areas for the settlement of the two "races." Although the estimated membership is small, it has won many sympathizers as an increasing number of Negroes are abandoning their past restraints.[61]

The Seizure and Consolidation of Power

Although we generally think of revolutions in terms of violence and disorder, drastic political changes can occur without them. The granting of independence to the various British colonies after World War II has been accomplished with little bloodshed. By the time a revolutionary uprising becomes imminent, formerly privileged groups have become considerably weaker; in some cases they are inept, inefficient, and actually incapable of enforcing their ascendancy through force. The formerly underprivileged, by contrast, have risen in power and actually control many activities, even though they may continue to observe customary deference toward those of higher rank. If both strata realize that changes have occurred, abdication can be arranged through negotiation. In Nigeria, for example, the gov-

[61] Cf. Lincoln, *op. cit.*; and James Baldwin, *Nobody Knows My Name* (New York: Dell, 1962).

ernment announced plans for revising the constitution in 1945, and this initial proposal was subsequently revised in response to Nigerian protests. An increasing number of Nigerians were placed in civil service positions; indirect rule was replaced by elected councils on which educated Nigerians could eventually replace traditional leaders; and education was expanded along the lines proposed by the nationalists. Nigeria became an independent nation in 1960.[62] Violence occurs when those of high rank fail to realize that they are no longer strong enough to defend their privileges. On August 17, 1945, Indonesia proclaimed its independence. Demoralization of the Japanese Army and six weeks' delay in the arrival of Allied forces enabled the Indonesian Republic to become entrenched. The Dutch claimed that the new regime was a Japanese creation, but the Dutch colonial government was weak and at first had to depend upon the reluctant assistance of British and Australian troops. As preparations got under way for the return of Dutch soldiers, fighting broke out throughout the archipelago. The struggle was intensified in 1946, when the Dutch sent in 100,000 soldiers for "police action." But the rebels could not be subdued, and in 1950, under considerable pressure from the United Nations, independence was granted.[63]

Where there is violence, mass participation in a revolution is usually touched off by some trivial event—an assassination, the bombing of a public building, a demonstration that gets out of hand, or the arrest of a popular hero. This is not the beginning of the revolution, but it is the crucial point at which the challenge is made openly. The event is important because it leads to a clearly recognized split between defenders of the status quo and those who are against it. After the schism is acknowledged, all previously uncommitted parties are forced to take a stand on one side or the other. The event may also be important in disclosing dramatically the incompetence of people in the privileged category. The defenders no longer have enough power, and the event reveals this so decisively that those who had hesitated from fear of retaliation now join the movement. In some revolutions the initial step is not easy to identify, for the transition from agitation to other forms of action is neither drastic nor sudden. After the revolution is over, historians may point to some particular event—as the storming of the Bastille—as the starting point.

[62] Coleman, *Nigeria, op. cit.*, pp. 309–17.
[63] Wertheim, *op. cit.*, pp. 76–88.

But the participants in such events certainly do not visualize themselves as living through a decisive moment.

Estimates of the inability of the dominant group to retaliate are frequently premature, and many rebellions have been crushed. The Sepoy Mutiny of 1857 was an abortive attempt to overthrow British rule in India. The activities of the Armenian nationalists came just at a time of Islamic revival; hence the repressive measures of the Ottoman government went beyond the stamping out of revolutionaries. Many officials wanted to get rid of the Christians in their midst and organized a series of massacres from 1894 to 1896; estimates of the number of Armenians killed range from 50,000 to 300,-000, and the revolutionary movement was crushed.[64] The Taiping rebellion was an uprising of the Chinese against Manchu rule; the government was saved largely through Western intervention. In the Boxer Rebellion young Chinese intellectuals banded together in an abortive attempt to eliminate foreign rule and to raise China's standing in the eyes of the world. Failure of a revolt generally results in ruthless oppression; leaders are hunted down and executed. Such failures usually intensify the opposition among various subversive groups and may lead to enduring divisions, even among those who have fled into exile. Partisans accuse each other of faltering at decisive points. Among the Armenians in America, for example, divisions have persisted even beyond the generation that actually participated in the movement.[65]

Where a revolution is successful, the transfer of power consists of formal recognition by the dominant group of changes that have already occurred. Violence, if there is any, generally lasts only for a short period. The dominant group is disarmed, and a provisional government is established. Oppressive laws are repealed, and practices that are obnoxious to the minority group are outlawed. Members of the privileged group who had been unable to see the facts are now forced to re-evaluate their situation. The new government is usually a motley affair, containing revolutionaries of all stripes, necessary bureaucrats from the old order, ambitious politicians without convictions, disillusioned reformers, and "grass roots" leaders. Commanders of military units who have a strong personal following may

[64] Cf. Nalbandian, *op. cit.*, p. 102.

[65] Atamian, *op. cit.*; and K. S. Papazian, *Patriotism Perverted* (Boston: Baikar Press, 1934).

also play decisive roles. In the beginning different subversive groups join forces to drive out the old rulers and to set up a new government. After many of the needed reforms have been instituted, there follows a brief period of optimism. But a new regime is bound to encounter difficulties, and before long a number of innocent people are injured or inconvenienced. Those who had utopian hopes are soon disillusioned.

After victory, subversive groups that had united temporarily to oust the dominant group renew their struggle, and the outcome has an important bearing on the revolution. In virtually all revolutions there are more than two adversaries; defenders of the status quo are usually divided into several factions, and revolutionaries include men of moderate bent who merely want a few reforms as well as those who demand drastic changes—sometimes even extermination of the dominant group. Furthermore, the composition and the strength of each faction is altered as the leaders align and realign their forces with each issue that arises. Sometimes the struggle yields a single widely-accepted leader. After World War I Masaryk and Benes provided the new republic of Czechoslovakia with statesmen of international reputation, just as Gandhi and Nehru provided leadership for India after World War II. But independence may find the victors so splintered that the selection of high officials becomes very difficult. Despite the claims of nationalist agitators of their readiness for self-rule, no widely accepted leadership may develop. When the Greeks secured their independence from the Ottoman Empire, for example, they cast around for a foreign prince to serve as head of state, for no Greek was willing to acknowledge another Greek as his sovereign.[66] When different ethnic minorities combine forces to oust their rulers, the rivalries sometimes become disastrous. Competition between closely related ethnic groups plagues the internal stability of the new government, as in Yugoslavia and to some extent in Czechoslovakia.

A struggle for power frequently develops between the moderate faction, which is satisfied with the reforms that have been instituted, and the radical faction, which wants further changes. The rivalry between moderate reformers and radical revolutionaries develops in almost all revolutions, although in many cases one of the factions is not strong enough to make itself felt. The moderate leaders often win in the beginning because they hold the balance of power between

[66] Miller, *The Ottoman Empire and Its Successors, op. cit.,* pp. 83–84.

extremists on the right and the left. But the strength of the radical elements increases with disillusionment. Men who participated in the uprising expecting the fulfillment of utopian dreams are still dissatisfied and demand more changes. The conservative parties also pick up strength from the disillusioned. Sometimes the radical factions resort to violence to back their demands, and this leads to even greater alienation on the part of the reformers.

If radical leaders rise to power, the moderate factions sometimes align themselves with the conservative people who are still left, and they may make a joint effort to recover control. Disillusioned revolutionaries who had been squeezed out by their rivals sometimes join the plot to overthrow the provisional government. From the standpoint of the radical faction such an attempt would constitute a counter-revolution, an attempt to go back to the old order, although actually very few people want to go back that far. Members of the dominant group are hardly in a position to appeal for popular support, since it was their action that had brought about the uprising. Sometimes defenders of the old regime resort to terrorism. When the French government signed a peace pact with the Algerian nationalists in 1962, for example, the O.A.S. stepped up its campaign of violence in an apparent attempt to goad the Algerians into reprisals. This would have brought the French Army back into action and might have postponed for some time a settlement favoring the Algerians. More often, however, members of the dominant group appeal to foreign powers for aid, and by doing so they almost invariably strengthen the hand of the radical leaders. In Indo–China, for example, the French tried to enlist American aid, and there were many officials in the U.S. government who wanted to send troops. The intervention of foreign armies generally unifies the various revolutionary factions; in addition, the people, regardless of their political views, usually respond to an appeal to defend their country against invasion. Although many rebellions are successfully put down through the intervention of alien troops, invasion often seals the doom of the conservative parties. Moderate leaders also lose strength as they become identified with old order; sometimes they are even redefined as traitors.[67]

[67] Cf. Brinton, *op. cit.*, pp. 134–93; Edwards, *op. cit.*, pp. 98–131; and Alfred Meusel, "Revolution and Counter-Revolution," *Encyclopedia of the Social Sciences*, Vol. XIII, pp. 367–76.

Even if a counter-revolution is successful, the old order is seldom re-established as it was. Radical leaders are imprisoned or driven into exile, and some extremist organizations are outlawed. But the basic reforms instituted by the provisional government are frequently retained. If the dominant group tries to reimpose the old order, further rebellions arise. On the northern coast of South America the Criollo population, led by Bolivar, revolted against Spanish rule and set up a provisional government in 1810. But with promises of freedom the Spaniards enlisted the aid of various ethnic minorities that disliked the Criollos—the Indians, the Negro slaves, and the Pardos, persons of mixed ancestry. In a successful counter-revolution the first Venezuelan Republic was overthrown in 1812, and the Criollos were subjected to considerable mob violence. When the Spaniards did not keep their promises and tried to re-enslave their allies, however, the sympathies of the minorities turned toward the Criollo cause. In 1821 the different groups banded together to drive out the Spaniards. Then the struggle between the Criollos and the other ethnic groups was resumed, and Venezuela and the Colombian Republic were finally separated.[68] Although Indians and Mestizos started the Mexican revolution in 1810, the Criollos completed it; Spaniards were driven out or immobilized, but except for that there was little change, for the conservative faction won the struggle among the revolutionaries. A succession of uprisings followed and continued until the twentieth century.[69]

The character of the new government and its policies depends upon who wins the internal struggle for power among the revolutionaries. If one of the radical factions wins, members of the dominant group may be deprived of their privileges at once. For example, when the Mongolian People's Republic was formed, a small group of Bolshevik Mongols captured control of the government. The privileged classes were eliminated, and the other innovations were so drastic that the people distinguished between being "new-minded" or "old-minded" to describe themselves and their attitudes toward the changes.[70] If the moderate leaders maintain control, however, the

[68] Cf. George D. Flinter, *A History of the Revolution of Caracas* (London: T. & J. Allman, 1819); and William D. Marsland, *Venezuela Through Its History* (New York: Thomas Y. Crowell, 1954).

[69] Humphreys, *op. cit.*, pp. 117–22.

[70] Lattimore, "The Historical Setting of Inner Mongolian Nationalism," *op. cit.*, 401–04.

transition is likely to be more gradual. One program that all revolutionary governments put through is official recognition of the minority culture, but the traditional culture glorified by nationalists often proves difficult to adopt. Some old customs are revived, as are some of the practices proscribed by the former rulers; in many cases, however, the people are surprised and embarrassed to learn how much they have become acculturated to the ways of their erstwhile rulers. In former European colonies that have recently won their independence, for example, the aim of the nationalists is modernization. Most of the leaders are men educated in European ways; regardless of what they may say of the glorious history of their group, they have no real attachment to the traditional past. There is certainly no desire to revert to pre-European times. What they want is recognition and respect for their people in the industrial era.

The native tongue of the victorious minority group is given official recognition. Not only are all official communications in the new language, but considerable pressure is placed upon other ethnic groups to learn the standard tongue. Remnants of what had been the dominant group are required to learn the new idiom, as zealous patriots sometimes refuse to speak to them in the old language, even if they can speak it fluently themselves. After World War I several ethnic minorities freed from the empires of the Central Powers established their own states in which their respective tongues became the official language—among others, Polish, Czech, and Rumanian. When Finland became an independent nation, it elevated its local dialect into the national language. Israel adopted Hebrew as its official language, even though many Israelis spoke other languages more fluently and there was already an extensive modern literature in Yiddish. Although some of the older people encountered difficulties, the younger Israelis have all been learning Hebrew in school; hence, the inability of Jews from different parts of the world to communicate with each other will be overcome in a single generation.[71]

When a nationalistic movement is successful is establishing a new state, the assimilation of remaining minorities is often attempted, although at times a pluralistic arrangement may be established, as in the case of Czechoslovakia. Disagreements over language sometimes lead to further civil strife. Language is one of the major problems that has plagued India since its independence. Sanskrit and English

[71] Cf. Patai, *op. cit.*

are the two common tongues on the continent. Since so much of the scientific and technical literature of the world is available in it, English is obviously more convenient, but it is a symbol of the colonial past. Since 45 per cent of the populace speak it, Hindi was declared the national language, but others became fearful that Hindi-speaking people would exercise undue influence upon the central government. Therefore, on November 1, 1956, states were established on a linguistic basis. Each was granted the right to establish its own university in which instruction would be given in English and in its own language.[72] When Malaya achieved independence from British rule in 1957, the prime minister announced that he wanted every citizen to be a Malayan in national loyalty and to be able to speak Malay as the national tongue. But the Chinese, who dominated economic life in the area, objected vigorously to the policy of "Malayanization" in language and culture.

Some nationalistic movements become militant after their victory, demanding not only the assimilation of newly-created minorities but also the annexation of adjacent territories. After winning its independence, Poland disavowed the principle of "self-determination." It pursued a policy of forceful incorporation of other minorities, and Russians, Lithuanians, and Jews within its borders were not treated generously. It even opposed plebiscites in areas in which others were likely to win.[73] A new state sometimes directs more attention to unredeemed territories than to the establishment of internal order. After the Greek war of independence the great powers excluded from her narrow boundaries the richest lands, leaving only the thin soil of Chios and Thessaly.[74] Since then, the Greeks have successfully extended their frontiers through annexation. Indonesia demanded the annexation of West Irian; in 1958, when the Dutch government refused to negotiate this issue, the Indonesians retaliated by nationalizing the major Dutch industries.[75]

Any new government faces many serious problems. Even when the regime enjoys popular acceptance, many difficulties still remain. There are many economic problems, for the mere winning of a war does not insure the elimination of poverty nor the establishment of

[72] Hingorani, *op. cit.*
[73] Gerson, *op. cit.*, pp. 121-37.
[74] Miller, *A History of the Greek People, op. cit.*, pp. 18-19.
[75] Wertheim, *op. cit.*, pp. 84-85.

an adequate economic system. Many mistakes are due to inexperience in government. Men who made superb guerrilla leaders are not always suited for bureaucratic work. Leaders who are marginal men may have difficulty in controlling their vindictiveness, and their excesses must be curbed. Many of the revolutionary leaders are rivals who have no great affection for one another, and a scramble for power begins soon after the common foe has been overthrown. In 1957, the Indonesian government was endangered with bankruptcy as local officials in the Celebes, Sumatra, and Borneo refused to allow a share of the foreign currency earned on their islands to go to the central government. Regional military commanders maintained autonomy. The new leaders sometimes find themselves in dangerous situations; revolutionary heroes are periodically exposed as traitors and shot. In addition to all this the danger of counter-revolution is always present.

Remnants of the dominant group, however corrupt or hedonistic, constitute a constant source of danger as potential counter-revolutionaries. Many old-timers find it difficult to adjust to the new regime. Colonists are often bitter: they had worked hard to build up the country, and they feel that the natives are ungrateful. Many are still contemptuous of their former subjects and leave in disgust. But the colonists who return to their motherland face serious problems. The Dutch had been in Indonesia for over 300 years; many had never been in the Netherlands, nor had their parents; furthermore, much of their wealth was invested in Indonesia. By 1956, however, life became so unpleasant for them that they left for "home" at the rate of 14,000 a year. After years of bloody conflict in Algeria, the French *colon* was faced with the same difficult choice; he could remain in minority status under Arab rule or "return" to France and take his chances in a strange country. The privileged classes in Indo-China, given a reprieve when the seven-year civil war ended in partition in 1953, continued their life unchanged. While the Communists organized the north and rebuilt their underground in the south, Vietnamese officials squabbled for spoils and for power. The French community had been hurt economically, but life in Saigon remained the same. The *Cercle Sportif*, a fashionable club, continued to bar Vietnamese from membership; brothels operated under police protection; opium dens were easy to find. Corruption, graft, and bribery continued unabated, and many were preoccupied with the problem of getting around the currency regulations.[76] To be sure, the former rulers are no longer able to order others about, but many of them still have considerable economic power as well as powerful connections.

Revolutions have often been condemned because of the terrorism that sometimes occurs, although the extent of violence is often exaggerated, especially by refugees and opponents of the new regime. Without condoning the practice, it is important that we make some effort to understand this feature of revolutions. The systematic planning and execution of terror is done with definite purposes in mind. One is the dissipation of tensions: when there has been too much excitement, leaders may stage a massacre of scapegoats so that the people will become exhausted—and too tired to complain about the inefficiency of the new regime. Another objective is not death and destruction, but the creation of an atmosphere of fear: the aim is to maintain order by frightening potential opponents. Key individuals in opposing factions are arrested without warning. This often creates the impression that the new regime is all-powerful, with eyes and ears everywhere, and prepared to deal directly with any opposition. Executions are often staged publicly—to be seen by large numbers. Those who might object to new policies can be immobilized through fear. Revolutionaries who have used such tactics have attempted to justify their deeds by insisting that in the long run bloodshed was minimized. They admit killing some innocent persons, but they insist that many more would have died had the populace not been cowed into obedience. Terrorism is not always an expression of blind hatred for those who had once oppressed the people, nor is it necessarily sadism on the part of long-frustrated leaders. In many cases it involves cold, deliberate calculation.[77]

Those who refuse to become assimilated may be imprisoned, slaughtered, or deported. The words of Louis Kossuth, the Hungarian nationalist, calling for the liberties of oppressed peoples, moved men everywhere. When the Magyars later achieved most of their national claims, however, the rights of ethnic minorities on Hungarian territory were not honored; instead a program of "Magyarization" was launched in an attempt to absorb Rumanians, Serbs, Croats,

[76] Peggy Durdin, "Saigon in the Shadow of Doom," *New York Times Magazine* (November 21, 1954), 7, 40–46.
[77] Cf. Edwards, *op. cit.*, pp. 156–84.

Slovaks, and Germans.[78] Although conquered peoples have often learned the language of their rulers, there have been few systematic attempts to impose a tongue upon minority groups until recent times. Czarist Russia forbade the teaching of Polish, and the Italians tried to wipe out the use of German in the territory ceded from Austria after World War I.[79] In Indonesia the Dutch, the Eurasians, and the Chinese had to learn the Indonesian language and assimilate or risk unemployment. In 1957, when the controversy over West Irian intensified anti-Dutch sentiment, six Dutch consulates were ordered closed, and the progressive evacuation of all non-essential Dutch nationals was ordered. Many Dutch industries were nationalized, and the government announced that compensation would be discussed after the West Irian question had been settled. By December 1957, there were only about 46,000 Dutch left on the islands. Indonesians had once distinguished between the *trekkers*, those who expected to return to Holland, and the *blijvers*, those who expected to remain, but the distrust of white men became so great that everyone was expected to leave.[80] Tunisian independence deprived the Jews of French protection, leaving them at the mercy of the Arabs. Although the government deplored anti-Semitism and assured the Jews repeatedly that they would be treated like other Tunisians, it did nothing to moderate the clamor of the press. Only a few incidents actually occurred, but many Jews became frightened and prepared to leave for Israel. Although Arab nationalists insist it was the French who set Jews and Arabs against each other, the claim of colonial powers of the necessity of protecting minorities that would be formed under a new regime has not been entirely without foundation.

A revolutionary movement might be regarded as successfully terminated with general acceptance of the new government. Recognition by foreign powers and resumption of trade and diplomatic relations are indications of such acceptance. When it becomes obvious that the struggle is over, some remarkable changes in political sympathies take place. People overlook their past records and insist that they had been influenced by the propaganda of the old regime; now, however, they realize that they had been sympathetic to the

---

[78] Kann, *The Habsburg Empire, op. cit.,* pp. 19, 44–45.
[79] Sapir, *op. cit.,* p. 30.
[80] Cf. Van der Kroef, "Social Conflict and Minority Aspirations in Indonesia," *op. cit.,* 462–63; and Wertheim, *op. cit.,* pp. 162–64.

revolutionary cause all along. With the resumption of foreign contacts amnesty is often granted to political prisoners; there is a return to some of the old practices to which there are no serious objections and a general search for more pleasure and relaxation. The term "thermidor" is used to refer to this period of convalescence.

Summary and Conclusion

Attempts to overthrow the existing social order occur only when the leaders of minority groups become convinced that all other hope is gone. They then organize subversive movements. Subversive groups are illegal, and they usually resort to special tactics—terrorism and guerrilla warfare. The program and the ideology of revolutions develop as these groups struggle for survival. The direction in which an uprising develops arises in a selective process through which one of the subversive groups emerges as the spokesman for the oppressed. One of the most important bases for identification in modern times is nationalism, which enables once-separate peoples to unite against a common foe. Once a movement is under way and people begin to identify with one another, intellectuals usually invent a history for the newly-formed category, and a sense of pride evolves. The overthrow of the dominant group is but one phase of revolution. After victory the inner struggle among different factions continues. All revolutionary regimes face characteristic difficulties, partly from lack of experience and partly from rivalries among the new rulers. The course of events in these uncertain times depends upon the beliefs of the leaders and upon their tactical skills.

Since World War II Americans have been alarmed and puzzled at the continued success of Communists in the "underdeveloped areas" of the world. In spite of unprecedented generosity in foreign aid Americans are apparently becoming more unpopular. How is this state of affairs to be explained? Nationalists will grasp at any straw that will bring relief from an unbearable condition, and they have welcomed Communist assistance. But the longing for freedom by peoples who for many generations have felt stifled by colonial policies should not be confused with the organized tactics of a single political movement. The unpopularity of Americans does not arise from Communist propaganda alone but from the assistance given inadvertently to counter-revolutionary movements, to colonial powers, and to members of minority groups who enjoy special privileges and had always aligned themselves with their rulers. Although American sympathy has traditionally been for the underdog, American officials have placed valuable resources in the hands of those who have stood against the rising tide of nationalism. Thus, in many parts of the world the United States has become identified with the forces of oppression.

PART V

Integrative

Processes

CHAPTER 17

The Transformation
of Minority Groups

In *Pygmalion*, an imaginative play by George Bernard Shaw, Professor Higgins, in order to win a wager, transforms a street urchin into a lady acceptable on the highest rung of London society. He purchases new clothing for her, replaces her Cockney accent with correct English, and teaches her the manners and affectations of the privileged elite. During the height of their triumph, however, difficulties arise. Eliza, the newly-created lady, becomes upset because she is not fully accepted by her creator; although she has won the admiration of many others, Professor Higgins has continued to treat her merely as the subject of an interesting experiment. In many ways Eliza's plight is not unlike that of some people in ethnic minorities, who are transformed through the kindly intervention of missionaries and teachers but are not accepted after they have mastered their lessons.

The upward mobility of minority peoples need not result in revolution and secession. Most cases of inter-ethnic contacts result in the eventual integration of diverse groups into a new ethnic category. The process begins with the breakdown of the culture of one of the groups and terminates with the development of a common culture and a common sense of identity. There is considerable variation in the time this requires. In some cases, as in the European immigration to the United States, integration occurs in a few generations; in many cases, however, the process takes several centuries, during which there may be intermittent conflicts in which one of the groups is reduced in number. Furthermore, a few ethnic minorities, such as the Armenians, the Gypsies, and the Jews, have managed to retain their consciousness of kind for many centuries; these cases, however, are exceptions rather than the rule.

When integration does occur, how does it take place? We may begin by considering the characteristic changes that occur in minority groups after a period of sustained contact. The integration of once-separate groups means that one or both undergo some kind of transformation. In most cases the culture of the minority group is the first to change—to approximate that of the dominant group. The process is a long and tortuous one, usually including a transitional period characterized by social disorganization and bitter conflicts between generations. The period of transition is one filled with bewilderment, alienation, and despair, and many of the difficulties that engage the attention of social workers and reformers are apparently manifestations of this process of change. In addition, there are ecological changes. As some members of the minority group acquire competitive advantages, a new class structure develops, resulting in further cleavages within an already-divided group. These gradations generally hasten integration.

Acculturation of Minority Groups

In almost all instances of inter-ethnic contact people of subordinate rank have sooner or later learned the ways of the dominant group. The concept of *acculturation* refers to the process of acquiring the culture of another ethnic group. This is the initial step in the breakdown of ethnocentrism, and when it occurs, there are many changes in behavior patterns. At first alien norms are adopted in a superficial manner, but gradually the new values become an integral part of emerging perspectives. The problem of acculturation has long been of interest to anthropologists, who have described and attempted to explain differential culture change—the manner in which some aspects of culture are modified more readily than others and some ethnic groups change more quickly than others.[1]

The direction of acculturation apparently depends more upon prestige than upon power. In most cases the dominant group is not only more powerful but enjoys greater prestige as well. In those few instances in which the minority group enjoyed greater prestige, however, it was the rulers who adopted the culture of their subjects. We have already noted that China has been subject from the earliest times to a succession of invasions—from Mongolia, from Manchuria, from Turkestan, and from Tibet. But after each conquest the prestige of Chinese culture remained high, and the Chinese looked upon their rulers as "barbarians." One by one the invaders were absorbed into the general population of China.[2] Similarly, when the Roman Empire was overrun by various invaders from the north, the conquerors adopted Roman ways and eventually became integrated into the life of their subordinates. Of course, there are many cases in which some particular aspect of the culture of a minority group may acquire prestige and become accepted by the dominant group, as in the case of the jazz music of American Negroes.[3] In general, however, the prestigious way of life is emulated.

Soon after the establishment of inter-ethnic contacts a universe of discourse begins to develop. A common language is needed for trade and to deal with authorities. Where a small ruling class does not learn the language of its subjects, a third language may develop as servants speak their masters' tongue brokenly and in simplified idiom. Pidgin English, trade jargons, and various creole dialects were apparently formed in this manner and were perpetuated because of their utility.[4] In most cases, however, the language of the dominant group is established as the official tongue, and learning it becomes the first step toward acculturation. For a time, many people in the mi-

---

[1] Cf. Melville J. Herskovits, *Acculturation: The Study of Culture Contact* (New York: J. J. Augustin, 1938); and Leonard Broom *et al.*, "Acculturation: An Exploratory Formulation," *American Anthropologist*, LVI (1954), 937–1002.

[2] Lattimore, *Inner Asian Frontiers of China, op. cit.*

[3] Cf. James S. Slotkin, "Jazz and Its Forerunners as an Example of Acculturation," *American Sociological Review*, VIII (1943), 570–75.

[4] Cf. John E. Reinecke, "Trade Jargons and Creole Dialects as Marginal Languages," *Social Forces*, XVII (1938), 107–18.

nority group are bilingual, but eventually their old tongue falls into disuse. With the establishment of the Ptolemaic dynasty in Egypt, for example, Greek became the official language and remained so until the Arab invasion. The strong Hellenistic influence on Egyptian culture is still apparent.[5] In medieval Spain many Christians were converted to Islam and identified with their Moorish rulers. The Muwalladun, as they were called, were strongly influenced by Arab learning and literature. Other Spaniards, called Mozarabs, retained their Christian faith but became assimilated to the Moorish way of life. For centuries after the Christian reconquest of such cities as Toledo, the Mozarabs continued to use Arabic as the language of law and commerce and were permitted a certain amount of autonomy by their Spanish rulers.[6] Almost all children of immigrants to the United States have learned the English language. The learning of a new language is of fundamental importance, for language is a basic social institution. Linguistic symbols not only provide the avenues through which other transactions take place but are the vehicles of thought. Those who learn a new language learn to categorize their experiences differently and are introduced to a new world of objects.[7]

The question of the order in which new practices are adopted has been a difficult one to study, for anthropologists have usually worked with data that are not dated.[8] It is generally agreed, however, that the alien practices likely to be adopted most readily are those that can pass a pragmatic test—such as useful tools or effective medical care. The various peoples who have come into contact with Europeans in the last three centuries have been most interested in weapons and in manufactured tools; the utility of these devices is obvious. European techniques of medical care are also winning out in competition with the ministrations of folk specialists; the recovery of patients provides a decisive test. But the traditional curer has not been

---

[5] S. Davis, op. cit., p. 38.

[6] Castro, op. cit., pp. 317–21; and E. Lévi-Provençal, Histoire de l'espagne musulmane (Paris: Maisonneuve, 1950), Vol. I, p. 76.

[7] Cf. L. Carmichael, H. P. Hogan, and A. A. Walter, "An Experimental Study of the Effect of Language on the Reproduction of Visually Perceived Form," Journal of Experimental Psychology, XV (1932), 73–86; and Leonard W. Doob, Communcation in Africa: A Search for Boundaries (New Haven: Yale University Press, 1961), pp. 194–202.

[8] Cf. Margaret T. Hodgen, "Glass and Paper: An Historical Study of Acculturation," Southwestern Journal of Anthropology, I (1945), 466–97.

eliminated; among the Pondo in South Africa modern medicine is accepted in many cases, but witchcraft and magic are retained for the management of disorders believed to be beyond anyone's ability to cure—often spheres in which the efficacy of European devices is untestable.[9] In Ecuador illnesses with supernatural etiologies are treated by witch doctors, but even these folk specialists send their patients to hospitals for tuberculosis, appendicitis, or diphtheria. But attempts to institute programs of preventive medicine have failed, for their results are not readily visible.[10]

Initially many new practices are learned of necessity. Peasants who migrated to the United States, for example, had to participate in large corporations to earn a living, and there they learned the meaning of time and of punctuality. When the more successful opened their own businesses, they had to learn about tax laws, licensing, and standards of sanitation.[11] Such new meanings, however, are initially viewed from the traditional standpoint. When the Eskimos in Gambell, a village on the Bering Sea, first adopted manufactured goods, they used them for the pursuit of conventional Eskimo goals. Outboard motors were placed on their native craft; rifles were used for hunting; and kerosene-burning pressure lamps supplemented their seal-oil lamps.[12] In time, however, the more obvious customs of the dominant group became status symbols for a new way of life. In many parts of the world today wristwatches, fountain pens, and automobiles are sought eagerly by people who actually have little use for them. In central China before the Communist revolution the Mongols who remained behind in areas colonized by the Chinese learned to speak Chinese, became farmers, and adopted so many practices of the sedentary life that in a few generations they could be recognized as Mongols only by a few remaining customs.[13] In Mexico, Indians who are acquiring the national culture first learn to speak Spanish; then, they get rid of their *huaraches* and *calzones;* then, they put floors, windows, and chimneys on their houses; and then they

---

[9] Hunter, *op. cit.*, pp. 272–348.

[10] Charles J. Erasmus, "Changing Folk Beliefs and the Relativity of Empirical Knowledge," *Southwestern Journal of Anthropology*, VIII (1952), 411–28.

[11] Mary B. Treudley, "Formal Organization and the Americanization Process," *American Sociological Review*, XIV (1949), 44–53.

[12] Charles C. Hughes, *An Eskimo Village in the Modern World* (Ithaca, N. Y.: Cornell University Press, 1960), p. 17.

[13] Lattimore, "Chinese Colonization in Inner Mongolia," *op. cit.*, pp. 295–96.

begin to boil their drinking water and to take other sanitary precautions against diseases.[14]

Since knowledge of the alien culture is quite limited during the early phases of contact, the imitation may in the beginning appear ridiculous. Members of the dominant group often view with amusement and contempt the efforts of those who are becoming acculturated. The hybrid culture of the children of immigrants often appears to observers to be superficial when compared to that of the immigrants themselves. The inability of some members of minority groups to comprehend fully what they are doing often reinforces beliefs concerning their inherent inferiority. A common observation is that these people are "not ready" and that changes "take time." Such attitudes are found frequently among members of elite groups looking at those who are upwardly mobile.

An appreciation of values is the final step in acculturation. Values are basic presuppositions about what is good and bad, beautiful and ugly, desirable and undesirable. Unlike tools and technical devices there are no obvious external criteria for judging values. In most cases they are so much taken for granted that they are not discussed; values are rarely called into question or tested. It is for this reason that immigrants so often misinterpret much of what they see, even if they have made a careful study of the new culture. For example, a European refugee intellectual would probably know more about American history than most Americans but still not be able to comprehend many aspects of American life that any native child could grasp readily. Using the distinction that William James made between a "knowledge of" something and an "acquaintance with" it, Schuetz suggests that the knowledge of the refugee is explicit rather than intuitive. The natives are so saturated with their own culture that they do not raise questions about the premises of their conduct.[15] The mastery of values usually occurs only after more than one generation of contact; children seem to take over intuitively and without resistance those elements of a culture that an adult alien finds most difficult to understand. They develop the kind of orientation toward life and toward themselves that is characteristic of the dominant group; studies in the United States reveal, for example, that the more ac-

---

[14] Whetten, *op. cit.*, pp. 355–71.

[15] Alfred Schuetz, "The Stranger: An Essay in Social Psychology," *American Journal of Sociology,* **XLIX** (1944), 499–507.

culturated a person of minority standing, the more his score on projective tests resembles that of the average American.[16]

Not all members of the minority group acquire new meanings at the same time. The differential rate of acculturation depends to some extent upon opportunities for contact. The extent to which different groups of the Pondo in South Africa have departed from their indigenous culture is related to their accessibility; where roads were not easily made, they have not gone out to meet Europeans, and more conservative views prevail in these tribes.[17] Traders, servants, prostitutes, and others who become directly involved in transactions with outsiders are among the first to learn of alien behavior patterns; among the Chinese in modern Thailand, for example, the pace-setters in acculturation are the businessmen who must travel a great deal, the wealthy merchants who must deal with Thai officials, and the intellectuals.[18] The Mundurucu Indians in Para, Brazil, live in three different settlements, each marked by a different degree of acculturation to Brazilian life, and those who are most directly involved in trading and in the rubber industry have changed most from their traditional way of life.[19] Mere physical proximity, if association is not cut off through the barriers of segregation, provides more opportunities for learning. In New Zealand, traditional Maori life can still be found in the rural areas, where segregation is largely self-imposed; the communities are highly cohesive, and many of the younger people speak Maori fluently. But most of the Maori who have settled in urban areas no longer follow their old customs, and the old culture is dying out. Only a few of the younger generation know the Maori language, and much of their social life is indistinguishable from that of their European neighbors.[20]

In many cases organized resistance develops within the minority group against the acceptance of alien ways. Those who adopt the customs of the dominant group are condemned as wicked "radicals," horrible examples of what can come of friendly association with

[16] Cf. Alan C. Kerckhoff, "Anomie and Achievement Motivation," *Social Forces*, **XXXVII** (1959), 196–202; and Gardner Lindzey, *Projective Techniques and Cross-Cultural Research* (New York: Appleton–Century–Crofts, 1961), pp. 226–57.

[17] Hunter, *op. cit.*, pp. 548–54.

[18] Coughlin, *op. cit.*, pp. 67, 86–91.

[19] Robert F. Murphy, *Headhunter's Heritage: Social and Economic Change Among the Mundurucu Indians* (Berkeley: University of California Press, 1960), pp. 1–26.

[20] Ausubel, *op. cit.*

foreigners. In the American Southwest the Zuni Indians have built wooden houses with electric lights and running water, but they have not abandoned their kinship obligations, their religion, nor many other features of their traditional way of life.[21] Especially when subjugation has been preceded by bitter conflict, social distance is maintained; the Pondo tribes in South Africa that actually fought against the British have absorbed European culture much more slowly than those who had not once been enemies.[22] In some cases resistance may continue for centuries. After a long succession of wars the Saxons of lower Germany were conquered by Charlemagne toward the end of the eighth century. Christianity was imposed on the group; the area was incorporated into the Frank Empire; and many Saxon nobles were accepted in the Frankish court. But the Saxons frowned upon intermarriage, and strangers continued to be distrusted. Paganism persisted, and there were several rebellions. When the empire was finally dissolved, Saxon institutions once more superseded the exotic Carolingian practices.[23] It is apparent, then, that acculturation is not an irreversible process.

This suggests that any condition that makes possible the establishment of communication channels across the color line facilitates acculturation. Special educational facilities, efficient transportation, or the absence of conflict or segregation encourage association and learning. The Christian churches have played an important part in opening channels in the recent past. In the various European colonies missionaries have opened a new world to many natives, just as the churches have played a decisive role in the Americanization of many immigrants to the United States.[24] The Eskimos in Gambell were introduced to the modern world by the establishment of an Army Air Force Base nearby in 1942. Planes were used to fly sick people to hospitals on the mainland and to bring in food during periods of famine. In 1954, air mail service and a biweekly commercial passenger air service were established, and now young people go regularly to

[21] Evon Z. Vogt, "The Acculturation of American Indians," *Annals of the American Academy of Political and Social Science*, CCCXI (May 1957), 137–46.

[22] Hunter, *op. cit.*, pp. 548–54.

[23] James W. Thompson, "The Early History of the Saxons as a Field for the Study of German Social Origins," *American Journal of Sociology*, XXXI (1926), 601–16.

[24] Cf. Broom *et al.*, *op. cit.*, pp. 980–84; Park, *Race and Culture*, *op. cit.*, pp. 331–41; and Treudley, *op. cit.*

the mainland in search of employment. With more effective communication the traditional way of life is disappearing.[25] In many of the native locations in African cities there was such a serious shortage of housing that residential segregation by tribes could not be maintained; any house that fell vacant went to the next man in line. This absence of segregation resulted in the loosening of tribal loyalty and the learning of new ways and provided a basis for the development of a national consciousness that transcended tribal loyalty.[26]

Development of the media of mass communication has greatly facilitated all contacts in the modern world, and acculturation is now easier, faster, and more widespread. Once-isolated peoples are now able to learn of different ways of life—even without direct contacts with outsiders. The radio and motion pictures have played an especially important part, for literacy is not needed for an appreciation of either. Motion pictures have been especially effective, probably because they facilitate sympathetic identification with the characters and are sufficiently entertaining to attract wide audiences. They have introduced new models of conduct and new status symbols to many otherwise-isolated communities. There has been an extensive development of all communication channels in the areas now undergoing industrialization, and all of them are characterized by rapid cultural change.[27]

When the dominant group provides schools, especially if education is part of a program of nationalization, acculturation is usually facilitated. The widespread belief among Europeans that popular education was one of the duties of government probably had much to do with the rapid acculturation of subject peoples in their colonies. In 1813, the House of Commons voted to provide an English education for Indians, partly to train natives for government service and partly to win over those who were most likely to be influential.[28] Similar programs were established in other colonies. There can be little doubt that compulsory education had much to do with the comparatively rapid acculturation of various immigrant groups in the United States. The Americanization movement began early in the

---

[25] C. C. Hughes, op. cit., pp. 222–338.
[26] Mitchell, op. cit., pp. 21–22.
[27] Cf. Leighton and Smith, op. cit.; Powdermaker, Copper Town, op. cit., pp. 223–90; and Lyle W. Shannon (ed.), Underdeveloped Areas (New York: Harper & Row, 1957), pp. 96–119.
[28] McCully, op. cit., p. 20.

twentieth century, when the population was largely of foreign origin. At that time over 100 different languages and dialects were being spoken, there were more than 1,300 foreign language newspapers, and an estimated 5 million people could not speak English. Although the many private and governmental agencies involved often worked at cross purposes, the movement was highly successful.[29] In central Asia the Soviet government is eliminating illiteracy among the Tadzhiks, Uzbeks, Kirghiz, Turkmen, and Kazakhs by teaching them the Russian language, and the best students are sent to Moscow for advanced training. Since only the Cyrillic alphabet is used, even local literature is printed in it, and the new generation is becoming thoroughly Russian in outlook.

Acculturation occurs more rapidly in situations in which children are educated apart from their parents. In Timbuctoo prior to the French conquest the Tuaregs separated the children of their slaves from their parents; the result was the almost complete acculturation of the Bela to Tuareg ways.[30] In Australia zealous missionaries placed the Aborigine children in their care in dormitories and did not permit them to visit their families, and in time the children lost interest in the semi-nomadic life of their elders. They were not only converted to Christianity but also lost their aptitude for survival in the deserts.[31] The Eskimo children in Gambell who wanted to go beyond elementary school had to go to the mainland to the Indian Bureau high schools. Since the $200 plane fare made it difficult for them to return home each summer to renew their ties, many were cut off from their families until graduation. By the time they returned, they had changed; they were independent and self-assertive. They had adapted to a new way of life and had learned to see their future in terms of careers in an industrial society.[32] On the *kibbutz*, the collective settlements of modern Israel, children live in communal nurseries and are brought up with their peer group through high school. Although they are not entirely separated from their parents, they spend considerably more time with their own age group.[33] Such sep-

---

[29] Howard C. Hill, "The Americanization Movement," *American Journal of Sociology*, XXIV (1919), 609–42.

[30] Miner, *op. cit.*, pp. 39–40.

[31] Berndt and Berndt, *op. cit.*, pp. 112–13.

[32] C. C. Hughes, *op. cit.*, pp. 312–22.

[33] Melford E. Spiro, *Children of the Kibbutz* (Cambridge: Harvard University Press, 1958).

aration from parental influence probably has much to do with the very rapid development of a distinct culture in Israel.

Acculturation may take place without assimilation; minority groups may alter their culture but still retain consciousness of kind. *Assimilation* refers to both the acquisition of the perspective of the dominant group and the attempt to identify with it. A person who is assimilating develops a new reference group; he performs for an audience that transcends the minority group.[34] In many cases people who acquire new behavior patterns use them primarily among themselves and do not venture forth into the larger society.[35] Many members of American minorities speak English and are otherwise acculturated, but they continue to conceive of themselves as a people apart and act only for others like themselves. The Zuni Indians, for example, have been in contact with white men since the sixteenth century but have retained their way of life. Most of them can read and write English, but those observed speaking too much English may be ridiculed. They have adopted many technical devices, but these are used to implement Zuni goals.[36] The Jews in the city of Chicago have been pushed out of their ghetto by waves of immigrants from the South—Negro and white—and have moved to various areas of secondary settlement. New synagogues have been established, and religious schools are well attended. The people have become so acculturated that they regard members of a recently-arrived Hasidic sect as "foreign." Yet, parents fear intermarriage and go to considerable lengths to make their children conscious of their ethnic heritage.[37]

Acculturation is only the first step toward the *integration* of ethnic groups, which takes place when assimilated people are accepted by their rulers. In many European colonies native intellectuals educated in Europe were more like the colonists than they were like other natives. Some of them did not even know a native language. As long as they were not accepted, however, they could not be

---

[34] Cf. Borrie *et al., op. cit.,* pp. 89–98; and Park and Burgess, *op. cit.,* pp. 734–84.

[35] Leonard Broom and John Kitsuse, "The Validation of Acculturation: A Condition of Ethnic Assimilation," *American Anthropologist,* LVII (1955), 44–48.

[36] John Adair and Evon Z. Vogt, "Navaho and Zuni Veterans: A Study of Contrasting Modes of Culture Change," *ibid.,* LI (1949), 547–71; and George Devereux and E. M. Loeb, "Antagonistic Acculturation," *American Sociological Review,* VIII (1943), 133–48.

[37] Erich Rosenthal, "Acculturation Without Assimilation: The Jewish Community of Chicago, Illinois," *American Journal of Sociology,* LXVI (1960), 275–88.

integrated into the larger society. Similarly, many middle-class American Negroes are culturally indistinguishable from other Americans, but as long as they are excluded from important sectors of American life, they remain a minority group. Acculturated and assimilated individuals who are not accepted are much like those who are converted to a new religion but not confirmed by the church. Like Eliza in *Pygmalion* they have all the necessary qualifications but are not granted status.

Community and Family Disorganization

Although some exceptions have been reported, most minority groups that are acquiring the culture of another group become temporarily disorganized. As ethnocentrism breaks down, there is a transitional period during which people are uncertain about the appropriate modes of thought and conduct. The group loses its solidarity, being split into several factions. The disorganization of immigrant communities in the United States has been described in many sociological studies. European colonization dealt heavy blows to the traditional life of many subject peoples. Many of the Africans who left their farms to work in mines and plantations became detribalized, not only from their contacts with Europeans but also from their association with co-workers from other tribes. The same phenomena have been observed in many communities that are now undergoing industrialization without extensive contacts with outsiders; this underscores the crucial importance of communication. Because of its spectacular character social disorganization attracts attention. The difficulties are often cited as evidence that minority peoples are of "inferior blood" and therefore incapable of living like civilized men, and popular beliefs that such people are unreliable, indigent, or over-sexed, or have criminal tendencies tend thereby to be reinforced. Sympathetic intellectuals often write novels and political tracts depicting the plight of individuals torn loose from the moorings of their traditional culture, and these accounts focus more attention upon the difficulties.

The most widely-entertained theory of social disorganization was developed by Thomas and Znaniecki in their classic study of the migration of Polish peasants to the United States. Their contention was that social "problems" of all kinds constitute a manifestation of the decreasing influence of traditional values. Cultural patterns persist only insofar as each individual inhibits and redirects his personal desires to act in accordance with group expectations. When individuals are no longer willing to conform, conventional norms collapse; immorality and crime represent an unwillingness of men to comply. Some violation of conventional norms is going on all the time, but under some conditions the transgressions become so widespread that they can no longer be checked by the usual group sanctions. Thomas and Znaniecki regarded this as a transitional state, one that persists only until a new set of shared understandings emerges.[38] Thus, in the native locations in South Africa tribal discipline is no longer effective, but no substitute for it has yet developed.[39] Similarly, a study of illegitimacy in Latin America reveals that rates are lower in urban areas, where people have moved further toward the development of a new national culture, than they are in rural communities, where new cultural patterns have not yet been formed. Furthermore, the incidence of illegitimacy is lower in countries that have moved farther toward the establishment of new national cultures.[40] Social disorganization, therefore, is a phase of social change, and it is likely to occur in any society during periods when one moral order is being replaced by another.

As ethnocentrism breaks down, people begin to question some of their values. Coming into contact with outsiders not only exposes them to new models of conduct but also demonstrates that violation of the sacred taboos of one's group is not necessarily fatal. Matters that had previously been taken for granted are called into question, and embarrassing questions are raised about practices long regarded as right and natural. In Nigeria, for example, missionaries insisted upon the abolition of initiation ceremonies, a crucial part of the education of young people; polygamy, dancing, secret societies, ancestor worship, witch doctors, and semi-nudity were also attacked. The result was the inculcation of disrespect for all the old ways.[41] In Burma under British rule many time-honored customs as well as the influence

---

[38] Thomas and Znaniecki, op. cit., Vol. II. Cf. J. Thorsten Sellin, Culture Conflict and Crime (New York: Social Science Research Council, 1938), pp. 57–116.
[39] Ellen Hellmann, Rooiyard: A Sociological Survey of an Urban Native Slum Yard (Cape Town: Oxford University Press, 1948), p. 116.
[40] William J. Goode, "Illegitimacy, Anomie, and Cultural Penetration," American Sociological Review, XXVI (1961), 910–25.
[41] Coleman, op. cit., pp. 97–100. Cf. Maunier, op. cit., Vol. II, pp. 500–705.

of Buddhist monasteries were destroyed; with secularization the bonds that had held the people together were weakened. During the 1940's one out of every 215 persons was in jail, and the high incidence of crime there was notorious.[42] It appears that raising questions about sacred beliefs is the first step toward challenging anything that proves to be inconvenient.

Common forms of activity during transitional periods include unconventional sex practices, alcoholism, and theft. In the urban centers in South Africa sexual promiscuity was widespread among migrant workers. No longer bound by tribal regulations, young people pursued opportunities more freely. Bantu marriage customs were difficult to enforce on the locations, for very few men could raise enough money for the *lobolo* (bride price). Attractive women were not expected to remain chaste, and few married before having children; illegitimacy was accepted as "normal." Since the women needed protection, they entered into a variety of temporary alliances. Prostitution and venereal diseases became commonplace.[43] The Australian Aborigines first accepted alcohol in barter for women, and the effect was devastating. After the area had been settled by Europeans, Aborigines were not permitted to purchase alcohol without special permits, but drunkenness remained one of the most frequent offenses.[44] In Rooiyard, one of the slum areas in Johannesburg, women hard-pressed for money found the illegal brewing of beer one way of making ends meet. The illicit liquor trade became necessary for the survival of many families, and those who failed to do this were condemned as "bad wives." The beer-drinking party became a popular form of recreation, and widespread intoxication led to so much disorder that parents concerned with the welfare of their children often sent them away to live with relatives in the country.[45] In the United States, because of the lack of uniformity in police statistics, there is no conclusive evidence that the crime rate is higher in one ethnic group than another. Considerable agreement exists among law enforcement officers, however, that in most cities the greatest difficulties arise in areas settled by recently-arrived immigrants.[46]

---

[42] Emerson *et al.*, *op. cit.*, p. 165; and Furnivall, *Colonial Policy and Practice*, *op. cit.*, p. 108.

[43] Hailey, *op. cit.*, p. 1386; Laura Longmore, *The Dispossessed* (London: Jonathan Cape, 1959); Mayer, *op. cit.*, pp. 243–69; Schapera, *op. cit.*, pp. 173–75.

[44] Berndt and Berndt, *op. cit.*, pp. 67, 216–45.

[45] Hellmann, *op. cit.*, pp. 14–15, 20–46, 50, 79, 92.

[46] Cf. Frazier, *The Negro in the United States, op. cit.*, pp. 638–53; Oscar Han-

Especially noticeable in disorganized minority groups are juvenile gangs that become involved in crimes of violence. In recent years many have patterned their activities after the way of life depicted in American gangster films. Some, like the "zoot-suiters," are marked by colorful attire. Since World War II policemen in every major American city have been harassed by incidents involving Negro and Puerto Rican gangs.[47] In New Zealand there are similar gangs of young Maori—identifiable by their sideburns, leather jackets, and motorcycles. Their favorite activities include seeing American gangster movies, rock-and-roll dancing, affected talk, brash drinking, sexual promiscuity, and sporadic violence.[48] In the locations of South African cities the natives rarely venture forth at night because of their fear of *tsotsi* gangs. Since violence is usually directed against members of the minority group, the youth are hated, feared, and strongly condemned. An incident during the East London, Cape Province, riot of 1952 is revealing. Initially there was widespread native support for public demonstrations against the pass laws. After the disorders had begun, a white woman, a doctor of the Dominican Order, was brutally slain, mutilated, and burned. Because of the defenselessness of the victim, the lack of provocation, and the unnecessary brutality, people in the location saw it as a "typical *tsotsi* crime" rather than an ordinary murder. Sentiment against the gangs was so strong that united opposition to white people broke down, and many Africans left town in disgust.[49]

Segregated ethnic colonies are frequently located in slum areas where young people are exposed to activities of the underworld and of other outcast groups. They sometimes become involved in the intricate networks of understandings that tie together racketeers, prostitutes, corrupt politicians, and the police. It is not strange that so many children of immigrants to American cities have become professional criminals. Criminal behavior must be learned; one cannot become a hold-up artist or a professional killer merely by purchasing a pistol, and crimes like safe-cracking require a high degree of skill.

---

dlin, *The Newcomers: Negroes and Puerto Ricans in a Changing Metropolis* (Cambridge: Harvard University Press, 1959), pp. 96–104; and Sellin, *op. cit.*

[47] Cf. Kenneth B. Clark and James Barker, "The Zoot Effect in Personality," *Journal of Abnormal and Social Psychology*, XL (1945), 143–48; Albert K. Cohen, *Delinquent Boys: The Culture of the Gang* (Glencoe, Ill.: The Free Press, 1955); and Harrison E. Salisbury, *The Shook-up Generation* (New York: Harper, 1958).

[48] Ausubel, *op. cit.*, p. 67.

[49] P. Mayer, *op. cit.*, pp. 82–83. Cf. Longmore, *op. cit.*, pp. 189–92.

This training must be acquired either in reform schools or by serving apprenticeships with experienced specialists. One cannot be led into a life of crime without opportunities for contact and education, and this is much easier for those who live among criminals.[50]

Difficulties are often aggravated when avenues for the advancement of those who become acculturated are not sufficient. Those who acquire new skills and values find it difficult to return to their old life; their perspectives have changed too much, and they have developed too many new interests to be content. When young migrant laborers returned to Bechuanaland, for example, many of them found tribal life dull after the glamour and bustle of the city. The old forms of amusement were no longer appealing. Tribal warfare had been outlawed; hunting was less frequently practiced; and traditional public dances had been forbidden or abandoned. Sheer boredom drove many back to the cities, where they were restricted to menial work.[51] The situation in British India was notorious. University-educated Indians acquired a liberal arts education that stressed European values. While a few were able to find positions in the civil service, there was little for the rest to do. They were not equipped for most vocations, and because of their education they considered many of the available jobs beneath their dignity.[52] Resentment arises when avenues of upward mobility are closed. Radical and esoteric social movements are frequently found in periods of transition.

When acculturation is confined largely to the younger generation, family disorganization frequently results, for the two generations do not share the same perspective. Immigrants who had grown up in a homogeneous society as members of the dominant group have proud memories of their ancestral past. Their children, who have never known anything but subordinate status, cannot understand such pride and conclude that their parents must be stupid. The older generation defends the traditional ways; the younger generation finds these norms impractical. Especially where members of the two generations speak different languages, they not only have dif-

---

[50] Cf. Richard A. Cloward and Lloyd E. Ohlin, *Delinquency and Opportunity: A Theory of Delinquent Gangs* (Glencoe, Ill.: The Free Press, 1960); and William F. Whyte, *Street Corner Society* (Chicago: University of Chicago Press, 1943).

[51] Schapera, *op. cit.*, p. 117.

[52] B. B. Misra, *The Indian Middle Classes* (London: Oxford University Press, 1961), pp. 147–210.

ferent views of the world but cannot communicate effectively enough to correct misunderstandings. Inter-generational conflicts have been commonplace in families of immigrants to the United States. Most of them came from peasant societies and settled in industrial centers, where their children attended American schools and acquired American middle-class values. The children quickly became aware of the low standing of their ethnic category, and many became contemptuous of the things that their schoolmates ridiculed.[53] Nor are such differences confined to the United States. The young Javanese born in Surinam, unlike their parents, have no desire to return to Indonesia. They want to shed hampering mores and to organize protest groups to demand better working and living conditions.[54] In Guatemala, Tumin found that the older Indians expressed no desire to become Ladinos nor to live like them, but the younger Indians held that transition to Ladino status was both desirable and possible.[55] As students of the sociology of knowledge have pointed out, each generation faces somewhat different problems, sees its world in a somewhat different light, and arrives at its own way of coping with its environment. A recent study of three generations of American Jews shows that each generation has had a somewhat different standing in American society and has revolted against the previous generation's way of being Jews.[56]

In spite of the diversity of historical contexts in which such differences develop, many features of the ensuing conflict occur with remarkable consistency. Each generation is convinced of the rectitude of its position, and bitter quarrels take place between parent and child. In many cases the younger generation learns new sources of hedonistic satisfaction, individualistic types of economic motives, and different vanity values. The elders remain ethnocentric; they defend their moral order—ways that to them are right and natural. What their children propose appears wicked. The elders are often left confused and bewildered. They see their own culture—the sacred ways

[53] Cf. Thomas and Znaniecki, op. cit., Vol. II; Warner and Srole, op. cit., pp. 124–55; and P. Young, op. cit., pp. 98–216.

[54] Van der Kroef, "The Indonesian Minority in Surinam," op. cit.

[55] Tumin, Caste in a Peasant Society, op. cit., p. 69.

[56] Judith R. Kramer and Seymour Leventman, Children of the Gilded Ghetto (New Haven: Yale University Press, 1961), pp. 3–27. Cf. Karl Mannheim, Essays on the Sociology of Knowledge, ed. P. Kecskemeti (London: Oxford University Press, 1952), pp. 276–320; and S. N. Eisenstadt, From Generation to Generation (Glencoe, Ill.: The Free Press, 1956).

of their ancestors—mocked by their own children. They hear their native tongue ridiculed as a "foreign language." They become convinced that they have failed somewhere in educating their offspring and muse uncomprehendingly at the changes that disrupt their lives and threaten the destinies of their descendants. Many eventually accept the changes as inevitable, but some resist bitterly to the end. Among the Australian Aborigines, for example, the old and well-informed refuse to pass on their traditional knowledge to uninitiated youngsters, whom they see as irresponsible. As the number of old people dwindles, their culture will probably die with them.[57]

Members of the younger generation are equally convinced they are right and find the beliefs of their elders dull and "old-fashioned." Many of them, even those regarded as more "advanced" or "evolved," try to understand their parents and frequently make tedious efforts to explain their position. In most cases, however, they give up in disgust. They frequently become infuriated because the older people are unable to understand what they regard as obvious. Some even suspect that their elders are deliberately trying to obfuscate the issues in order to get their own way. The children often conclude that their parents are unreasonable and obstinate, that they have closed their minds to realities of the modern world. Where cultural differences between generations are great, the young people sometimes lose all respect for their elders. Among the younger Aborigines in Australia the traditional ceremonies are regarded as primitive and disgusting, and some of the young Eskimos in Gambell see their elders as "dumb people." [58] On the other hand, many children make minor concessions to their parents. For example, many assimilated American Jews have their sons circumcised so that the wife's parents will not feel hurt. Many observe *Yortzeit*, the anniversary of the death of their parents, even while ignoring all other religious occasions.[59] The few parents known to be sympathetic to the plight of the younger generation are singled out as "modern" and "understanding," and their children are regarded with envy. Such rare individuals are often consulted by the young and asked to intercede in family quarrels.

Some of the most serious disagreements arise over appropriate

[57] Berndt and Berndt, *op. cit.*, pp. 40, 88–93, 226. Cf. James H. S. Bossard, "The Bilingual as a Person," *American Sociological Review*, X (1945), 699–709.

[58] Berndt and Berndt, *op. cit.*; and C. C. Hughes, *op. cit.*, pp. 312–22.

[59] Kramer and Leventman, *op. cit.*; and Herbert J. Gans, "Park Forest: Birth of a Jewish Community," *Commentary*, XI (1951), 330–39.

patterns of boy-girl relationships and the selection of mates. In most peasant cultures perpetuation of the family is the basic consideration, and marriage is a family affair in which the desires of individual participants are secondary. Although the principals are usually consulted, they are seldom allowed to make the final decision, since young people are believed to be too blinded by sentimental considerations to take into account the best interests of the family. But the practice of courtship by individuals and the selection of mates on the basis of romantic love is regarded as an inalienable right by most people reared in industrial societies. Elders are usually horrified by this practice; such courtships are fraught with dangers of premarital pregnancy, which in many societies would preclude a desirable match. In many immigrant families in the United States misunderstandings arising from this issue resulted in mutual rejection. When the daughter of an immigrant began to wear lipstick, her disapproving parents would accuse her of wanting to become a prostitute. The angry girl, sensitized to her parents' negative traits, would criticize them mercilessly, asking why such superior people as they claimed to be had to live in slum areas like beggars. Each side would attribute foul motives to the other, and opposition would build in intensity in a cumulative manner. Contrast conceptions were constructed, and with the breakdown of communication there were even fewer possibilities of correcting false impressions. Many children rebelled against what seemed to them to constitute unreasonable restriction, since all their schoolmates were free to go out on dates. Many were hurt that their parents did not trust them as other parents trusted their children. In desperation some youngsters left home as soon as they were old enough to fend for themselves. Periodically an ethnic colony would be shocked by a spectacular suicide pact carried out by lovers who found it impossible to pursue their wishes.[60] Similar struggles are found among the various peoples now undergoing industrialization. In Rooiyard young African women felt silly with facial tattoos and expressed their preference for lipstick and powder. They wanted European-style clothing to attract more desirable men. They showed little or no interest in the opinions of their parents concerning their suitors and had decided views on their right to choose their future husbands.[61] In Gambell, the Eskimo children educated in Indian Bureau schools insisted upon their right to choose their

[60] Cf. P. Young, op. cit., p. 108.
[61] Hellmann, op. cit., pp. 10, 78, 83. Cf. Longmore, op. cit., pp. 64–74.

own mates. Young girls disliked the hard life at home, and many envisioned an easier and happier life with a white husband on the mainland.[62]

Many arguments arise over the proper roles of youth in relation to their elders. In many peasant societies there is a strong emphasis upon filial piety. Children are expected to work without compensation, to obey orders without question, and to care for their parents in old age. The parents, thinking of the extended family as the all-important unit, assume that everything they are doing is to create a legacy for their children. Where there has been contact with alien cultures, however, many children do not want what their parents plan to leave them. In most industrial societies a man, his wife, and their children constitute the basic unit. The younger people tend to stress individualistic values and demand independence. Many of the acculturated youth in American minority groups contribute financially to the support of their parents, but they resent patriarchal rule. When they make a concession to their elders, it is a compromise, more from personal consideration for their parents than from conviction.[63] Wherever the youth are becoming acculturated, complaints about the new generation are commonplace. In Bechuanaland, young migrants returned from the city were accused of neglecting their tribal duties and of being insolent toward the chief. They were described as "cheeky" and ill-mannered, showing little respect for their parents and still less for other elderly people.[64] As once-isolated Moslem communities came into contact with outsiders, one of the first demands from the young women was for removing their veils. Although displaying the face was regarded as wicked by their elders, to them it became a symbol of freedom. In modern Uzbekistan, for example, most people are Moslem and many still bow toward Mecca. But the young women rarely wear veils, and many are leaving for the cities. Similar transformations in conceptions of feminine roles have been reported from other areas undergoing industrialization.[65]

Misunderstandings also arise over the meaning of work, for members of the two generations often operate with different vocabularies

[62] C. C. Hughes, op. cit., pp. 279–303. Cf. Willmott, op. cit., pp. 277–82, 290–95.
[63] P. Young, op. cit., pp. 100–13.
[64] Schapera, op. cit., pp. 169, 185.
[65] Cf. Maria Leblanc, "Acculturation of Attitude and Personality Among Katangese Women," Journal of Social Psychology, XLVII (1958), 257–64.

of motives. This is especially true when one generation is involved in farming while the other is finding its way into an industrial economy. Those who are recruited and trained as industrial workers develop new tastes, new criteria for evaluation, and new habits—such as punctuality and literacy.[66] Among elders who have mastered a craft there is considerable pride in their skills as shoemaker, barber, cabinet-maker, or cook. The younger generation in an industrial society, however, tends to be impatient with the years of hard work that mastery of such crafts requires and feels that the financial returns are insufficient. They seek instead jobs that pay well and promise reasonable security. While they are not indifferent to the acquisition of skills, they do not place as much emphasis upon doing their work well, and to their elders this attitude appears slovenly. In most instances an industrial worker plays such a small part in the division of labor that there is no final product that he can point to with pride as an example of his own work. Numerous misunderstandings of this kind have arisen between Negroes who have emigrated from the American South and their children. The parents were usually from a rural background; they were religious and accustomed to hard work. They had made their way out of the South at considerable sacrifice in search of opportunities to live with dignity. Many of their children, however, acquired the youth culture of the slum areas. They believed that hard work was for "suckers." They learned to steal, to fight, and to laugh at religion. Many of them saw their parents as relics of the past.[67] In a recent study in New Zealand Ausubel found that the aspirations of Maori youth were much like those of European boys. He found, however, that there was little environmental support to implement these aspirations.[68]

A high degree of individualism is usually found in disorganized societies.[69] Those who are caught in the transitional state are not so much immoral as amoral. Since they know of more than one culture, they realize that no moral code is absolute. Their outlook becomes rational and utilitarian, and they become concerned with personal gain. Many pursue hedonistic interests and do not consider long-

[66] Slotkin, *From Field to Factory, op. cit.,* pp. 33–122.

[67] Hortense Powdermaker, *After Freedom: A Cultural Study in the Deep South* (New York: Viking Press, 1939), pp. 325–33.

[68] Ausubel, *op. cit.,* pp. 70–71.

[69] Thomas and Znaniecki, *op. cit.,* Vol. II, pp. 1134–70. Cf. Harold Finestone, "Cats, Kicks, and Color," *Social Problems,* V (1957), 3–13.

range plans; they indulge their impulses rather than suppress them for greater gains in the future. The growth of individualism may be further facilitated by participation in a money economy. Those who are incorporated into a money economy tend to emphasize success through individual effort rather than security through family ties. Furthermore, economic values more and more supersede sentimental but profitless ties. Group solidarity is weakened. Especially where there have been bitter conflicts, people become increasingly unconcerned with what happens to a group that contains so many disagreeable individuals. As the ethnic group loses its attractiveness and importance, there is less obligation to comply with its norms, and many find it relatively easy to realign their loyalties with others. Former clan- and tribe-oriented people gain a new awareness of themselves and their potentialities as they begin to think of themselves as individuals.

Although the incompatibility of roles they encounter is not nearly as great as that faced by marginal men, young people who become involved in conflicts with their parents find themselves in similarly difficult situations. No matter what they do, someone will be dissatisfied. Such persons are often guilt-stricken, and studies reveal that there is a higher incidence of various mental disorders among those who are undergoing acculturation.[70] This is readily understandable. Those who quarrel with their parents are confronted with the necessity of hurting those whom they love and to whom they are so indebted or doing something they are convinced is wrong or stupid. When the quarrels become too intense, some abandon their family and former friends. It is difficult for a person who is doing something of which he is ashamed to maintain his self-respect, but it is equally difficult for him to regard himself as a worthwhile individual without getting some measure of support from those he loves and respects. Life histories of those growing up in disorganized societies frequently contain accounts of excessive drinking, debauchery, ostentatious display, and other compensatory acts. Such conflicts are found in virtually all minority groups undergoing change, but the individuals involved rarely air their personal problems in public. Hence, year

---

[70] Paul K. Benedict and Irving Jacks, "Mental Illness in Primitive Societies," *Psychiatry*, **XVII** (1954), 384; Arnold W. Green, "The Middle Class Male Child and Neurosis," *American Sociological Review*, **XI** (1946), 31–41; and Lindzey, *Projective Techniques and Cross-Cultural Research, op. cit.*, pp. 226–57.

after year thousands of young people go about haunted by guilt feelings, regarding themselves as evil for having hostile impulses toward their parents. They do not realize how commonplace such misunderstandings are.

Minority groups undergoing change differ considerably in the extent to which they become disorganized. Sometimes the disruption is spectacular and extensive; sometimes it is barely noticeable.[71] Whether or not the split occurs along generational lines apparently depends upon the extent to which the two cultures differ and the speed with which the changes occur. Those who migrated to the United States from northwestern Europe made their adjustments with relative ease. Their Protestant background, their industrial and urban experience, their higher literacy rate, and their individualistic orientation toward marriage all facilitated integration. Furthermore, where acculturation takes place slowly, acute conflicts between parent and child are not so likely. What made conflicts so violent in the families of so many immigrants from southern and eastern Europe and among those in areas now undergoing industrialization is the fact that drastic changes occurred within a single generation. In some cases changes took place so quickly that parent and child could barely communicate, neither understanding the language of the other. The degree to which the way of life of minority groups is accepted by the dominant group may also be of importance. If it is possible for those in subordinate positions to maintain their self-respect, social disorganization may be kept to a minimum.

The Development of Class Differences

Distinctions of rank exist within all minority groups, but class differences often become more pronounced when they are undergoing transformation. In some cases the elite group within the minority is the remnant of its old aristocracy. In Peru, for example, the Spanish conquerors mixed with the Inca nobility, setting the former rulers even farther apart from the other Indians. In all European colonies governed by indirect rule native aristocrats enjoyed many advantages; those of noble birth were often educated in European uni-

---

[71] Cf. Coughlin, *op. cit.;* Lerner, *op. cit.;* and Margaret Mead, *New Lives for Old* (New York: William Morrow, 1956).

versities, thereby making them culturally even more different from their subjects.

Education is especially important in those situations in which cultural differences between the ethnic groups are great. The new elite often consists of those who are educated in schools of the dominant group. In most European colonies missionaries played an important part in enticing able young people away from traditional norms. Many of these individuals became marginal men, but in time there were enough of them to form a special class of their own. When missionaries recruited clergymen and encouraged the formation of an indigenous church, they gave educated Africans at least one avenue of advancement—a career approximating "senior service" or the rank of a white man.[72] Many of the schools established in the American South after the emancipation of slaves were built by religious groups, and the influence of missionaries over the past two centuries can be seen in the ideals of piety, thrift, and respectability so emphasized in the Negro middle class today.[73] With the completion of the Suez Canal in 1869 sea travel from India to England became easier, and there was an increasing flow of Indians to British schools. Most of these students received a literary education, and the new Indian middle class contained many in the learned professions.[74] In the Dutch East Indies, too, the government's "ethical policy" of helping the natives help themselves resulted in the training of many in Europe.[75] Thus, in most European colonies the traditional and hereditary elite was eventually displaced by a more heterogeneous, educated elite. In Africa today education is the most important factor in social differentiation; knowledge is the key to prosperity and prestige.

In most cases, however, the new privileged class is a *bourgeoisie*—the people in service occupations. This type of class structure arises initially from the differentiation of tasks required to meet peculiar needs of the minority group in the new economy that develops as the result of contact. We have noted (in Chapter 7) that the American Negro middle class arose after emancipation among those who performed necessary services for the segregated communities—

[72] Colemen, *Nigeria, op. cit.*, p. 102.

[73] Frazier, *Black Bourgeoisie, op. cit.*, pp. 60–85. Cf. P. Mayer, *op. cit.*, pp. 35–36.

[74] McCully, *op. cit.*, pp. 215–17; Misra, *op. cit.*, pp. 147–210; and Useem and Useem, *op. cit.*

[75] Robert van Niel, *The Emergence of the Modern Indonesian Elite* (Chicago: Quadrangle Books, 1960).

banking, insurance, newspapers, retail stores, and mortuaries. Segregated Negro communities today contain entrepreneurs, professional men, and white-collar workers; they are almost replicas of the American class system outside, although the proportion of people in each class is somewhat different. There are also class differences within Jewish communities in America. The first generation of Jewish immigrants worked in sweat shops, lived in ghettos, and sacrificed to educate their children. In the second generation more were in the professions and in business. Among them distinctions were based upon money, material accumulation, and intellectual attainment. They shared the Yiddish-speaking culture of the ghetto, but there were vast differences among them. The Jews in the United States today constitute a heterogeneous category.[76] In Africa, World War II contributed greatly to economic growth, and this gave rise to a new native middle class. Those directly or indirectly connected with export production profited. Industrialization was also stimulated, and native workers were able to improve their lot, some advancing to the ranks of semi-skilled workers. With the decline of traditional influence and the improvement of economic position the new African *bourgeoisie* became increasingly concerned with education and with political issues, and these developments paved the way for nationalism.[77] Thus, as members of minority groups are drawn increasingly into the money economy of industrial societies, the relative importance of occupations changes. A man who had been a grocer becomes a merchant of affluence. Sons of chieftains, instead of planning to be farmers, aspire to become shopkeepers or to enter a profession. Those who play the more important roles in the emerging economy thus acquire prestige and power.

People in the same income level often develop a common outlook, and the culture of the well-to-do in subordinate groups is usually a reproduction of the way of life of the dominant group. Once established in the new nation of Liberia, for example, former American slaves struggled to perpetuate the traditions of the old Southern aristocracy. They lived in mansions, disdained manual labor, wore high hats and long-tailed coats, and walked with canes.[78] In

---

[76] Kramer and Leventman, *op. cit.*, pp. 62–74.
[77] Hailey, *op. cit.*, pp. 253–54.
[78] Raymond L. Buell, *Liberia: A Century of Survival* (Philadelphia: University of Pennsylvania Press, 1947).

Egypt, during the period before World War II, foreigners who controlled the economy were not subject to Egyptian law and enjoyed many advantages. Egyptian entrepreneurs who could not purchase foreign citizenship tried to identify with the outsiders in other ways; many took pride in their frail Arabic, which they used only in speaking to their servants.[79] Where there are several minority groups in the same community, those in the same income level often develop patterns of conduct that cut across ethnic boundaries. In Mauritius, an island in the Indian Ocean, Muslim importers, Hindu planters, Chinese merchants, and the professional men in each of these categories not only share economic interests but are also evolving a similar way of life.[80] As the more privileged members of minority groups acquire some of the symbols of the larger society, they educate their children in the culture of the dominant group. The son of a Negro professional man in the United States today, for example, has a far better chance of attending a university than the son of a white tenant farmer in the South. Indeed, Edwards found that 60 per cent of the Negro professional men in Washington, D.C., were children of white-collar parents.[81] Like other professional men in the country most of them had inherited their advantages.

Because of the walls of segregation American Negroes with the same income and education as middle-class white people have had a position of special privilege in their own communities. Rejecting the folk culture that developed among the slaves, they have accepted unconditionally the values of white people—their canons of respectability, their standards of beauty, and their consumption patterns. Nowhere is conspicuous consumption more apparent than among successful members of ethnic minorities, and American Negroes are no exception. They purchase expensive automobiles, build homes in the best residential areas available to them, furnish them lavishly, wear expensive clothing, consume imported wines, and form exclusive fraternal organizations. Anyone attending a cotillion for debutantes of Negro society—or that of any other American minority group— would be amazed at the extravagance of the affair. An attempt has

---

[79] Edward R. F. Sheehan, "The Birth Pangs of Arab Socialism," *Harper's Magazine*, CCIV (February 1962), 85–91.

[80] Burton Benedict, "Stratification in Plural Societies," *American Anthropologist*, LXIV (1962), 1239–40.

[81] G. Franklin Edwards, *The Negro Professional Class* (Glencoe, Ill.: The Free Press, 1959), pp. 49–75.

been made to maintain the style of living of propertied white people, even though income is not comparable. The outlook of this social world has been reaffirmed by the Negro press with its disproportionate coverage of social affairs. Even the fertility rates of Negroes resemble those of white people. As income, rent paid, and other indices of class position rise, the fertility rate goes down.[82]

Since the well-to-do in minority groups have many competitive advantages, they can afford far better housing than many members of the dominant group. Where residential segregation is not rigidly enforced, they usually move into better neighborhoods. Where segregation is still in effect, they establish secondary areas of settlement— areas that are partially segregated but in more desirable parts of the community. As they achieve higher economic position, they move into mixed areas, where they live with the successful members of other ethnic minorities.[83] Since World War II many of the affluent members of American minorities have congregated in suburban tracts, sometimes even establishing separate tracts of their own. In Park Forest, Illinois, a garden apartment housing project 30 miles south of Chicago, approximately 100 out of the 2,000 families are Jewish, most of them young business or professional men. Their way of life is much like that of their Gentile neighbors, except that they also participate in special activities with other Jews. They are brought together by their food preferences, their distinctive use of gestures, and their similar interests. Although most families refuse to live by Jewish traditions at home, the parents want their children to learn enough about them in Sunday School so that they would have some basis for deciding later on whether or not they wished to be Jews. They have all but rejected Jewish traditions, and while maintaining some ethnic ties, they are pursuing the suburban style of life.[84]

As the more privileged members of minority groups become culturally more like people in the dominant group, it is easier for them

[82] Frazier, Black Bourgeoisie, op. cit.; and Everett S. and Anne S. Lee, "The Differential Fertility of the American Negro," American Sociological Review, XVII (1952), 437–47.

[83] Wirth, The Ghetto, op. cit., pp. 246–61. Cf. op. cit.; and Warner and Srole, op. cit., pp. 33–52.

[84] Gans, "Park Forest," op. cit. Cf. Stanley son, "Suburbs and Ethnic Residential Patterns, American Journal of Soc y, LXVII (1962), 673–81; Kramer and Leventman, op. cit.; Rosenthal, op. cit.; and John R. Seeley, R. Alexander Sim, and Elizabeth W. Loosley, Crestwood Heights (New York: Basic Books, 1956).

to establish contacts across the color line. Although this does not mean that the barriers are retracted, there is more likelihood that such people will reach some kind of mutual understanding. Those who perform similar tasks in an economic system—entrepreneurs, small businessmen, landowners, artisans—often develop similar interests. Businessmen on both sides of the color line may meet periodically to deal with common problems, and professional men in a community find it convenient to cooperate in dispensing their services. Those who pursue artistic or intellectual interests are also brought together, as are those who share the same hobbies. Even when considerable reserve is maintained, it is relatively easy for those sharing the same cultural background to interact. They all speak the language of the dominant group fluently, dress alike, eat and drink the same food, and share the same values. That friendships develop is not surprising. A study made among the Negroes in Indianapolis showed that those of higher status showed far less opposition to white people than did the less fortunate. Furthermore, higher-status Negroes were less likely to perceive white people in stereotyped terms than Negroes of lower status.[85] In Central and South Africa the various Capricorn movements are made up of educated people on both sides of the color line who share "liberal" views on "race relations." They are able to get along quite well with each other but are unable to persuade others in their respective ethnic groups that a peaceful solution to their difficulties is possible.

Although the more successful continue to conceive of themselves as members of an ethnic minority, they tend to despise those of the lower classes and to maintain social distance from them. They usually limit their associations to persons of their own class, and their children generally marry others of the same station. Since they are acculturated, they look upon other members of the minority group from the standpoint of the dominant group. In India, for example, those who had lived and studied in England became so thoroughly Anglicized that they looked upon native life through English eyes; many shared the disgust of their rulers.[86] Among American Negroes the *bourgeoisie* has refused to identify with the Negro masses, referring contemptuously to them as "niggers." The economically successful do not feel the brunt of being Negro; they can afford good houses

85 Westie and Howard, *op. cit.* Cf. Hill, *op. cit.*
86 McCully, *op. cit.,* p. 222.

and avoid the slums, and they can afford their own cars and thereby avoid "Jim Crow" transportation.[87] In modern Nigeria the chasm between the new elite and the masses is even greater. Except where they are bound by family ties there is little close contact. Members of the elite are heirs of the British colonial officials and do not identify with the masses except on certain political issues. Although they maintain tribal ties and pay respect to tribal authority, their way of life is completely different.[88]

Such individuals are generally acknowledged by rank-and-file members as the most successful in the minority group, but they are seldom leaders of the people. In British India most natives looked upon the European-educated Indian as an alien and had no confidence in him. Since so many of the educated were marginal men, they were charged with being rootless—neither wholly English nor wholly Indian.[89] In the United States such successful persons are often approached by officials and by reformers of the dominant group whenever the cooperation of a minority group is desired. The fact that those who are recognized outside a minority group may not have a following within it is generally not appreciated. Lewin once referred to this phenomenon as "leadership from the periphery." [90]

Even if they are resented, however, their way of life provides models toward which other members of the minority group can strive. From those who have been exposed, knowledge of the world of the dominant group gradually trickles down to the others. Since people in minority groups have easier access to their own elite than they do to the dominant group, it is by observing the successful that they acquire conceptions of proper behavior, patterns of consumption, and job aspirations. This process may be observed in many historical contexts. When the Romans conquered Gaul, they left the natives largely to themselves, and the move toward acculturation originated among the subject people themselves. It started with the richest and noblest families and worked downward. In time more and more people progressed to citizenship, became attached to Rome

[87] Frazier, Black Bourgeoisie, op. cit.; "Race Contacts and the Social Structure," American Sociological Review, XIV (1949), 7; and Rose, op. cit., pp. 67–73.
[88] Hugh H. and Mabel M. Smythe, The New Nigerian Elite (Stanford, Calif.: Stanford University Press, 1960), pp. 99–102.
[89] McCully, op. cit., pp. 222–24.
[90] Kurt Lewin, Resolving Social Conflicts (New York: Harper & Row, 1948), p. 196.

as their native land, and adopted Roman language, religion, and customs.[91] Thus, as the more affluent acquire some of the symbols of the dominant group, those of lesser rank within the minority also adopt them. Little by little, all of them begin to resemble the dominant group, and in time the social structure of the minority group duplicates that of the larger society of which it is a part.

When the color line begins to change, some of the privileged members of minority groups discover that their class interests are diametrically opposed to the interests of their ethnic group. Many business and professional men of minority standing find that they have a vested interest in the existing system of ethnic stratification. Among American Negroes, for example, many businesses can survive only as long as segregation persists; once the more efficient and less expensive goods and services of the dominant group become available to everyone, many of their customers would turn to the new sources. Many professional men enjoy great prestige behind the wall of segregation, where they do not have to compete with white professional men. When schools in the South are finally integrated, many Negro teachers who hold highly-paid jobs may find themselves unable to compete on an equal basis with white teachers; this means that many would either lose their positions or suffer humiliating demotions. When segregation is ended, minority group publications lose their importance; actors who play stereotyped roles as well as those who serve as intermediaries would be left without means of livelihood. In some cases older, wealthier, and better-established business and professional men have tacitly cooperated with members of the dominant group to preserve the status quo.[92] Those who stand to gain by the perpetuation of the color line cannot argue openly for segregation, but they frequently use other justifications—among them the claim that people prefer to be with their own kind. Nor is this true only of American Negroes. In Mongolia, Chinese, Japanese, and Manchu invaders were able to make special arrangements with princes and priests, who were the privileged classes, to facilitate the subjugation of other Mongols.[93]

The competitive advantages and power held by privileged members of minority groups are often used to advance themselves in the

[91] Keller, *op. cit.*, pp. 56–58.
[92] E. Franklin Frazier, "The Negro Middle Class and Desegregation," *Social Problems*, IV (1957), 291–301.
[93] Owen Lattimore, "Prince, Priest, and Herdsman in Mongolia," *Pacific Affairs*, VIII (1935), 35–47.

existing system of stratification rather than to alter the system itself. When a small group has a monopoly on power, wealth, and education, officials from that group often do not serve the community as a whole but the elite itself. For example, in many of the areas now undergoing industrialization, appointments to white-collar jobs that do not require advanced skills depend more upon friendship than upon ability. There are cases of units in governmental agencies made up entirely of relatives, co-villagers, and friends of the department head.[94] Such practices usually create a class of discontented intellectuals. Younger men who find their aspirations blocked by the color line are on the forefront of the fight against "discrimination." Such individuals are often regarded as dangerous "radicals" by the well-established in the minority group. In the United States agitators have frequently been accused of having Communist sympathies. Even where demands are acknowledged to be just, conservative elders argue that such persons are irresponsible and may invite retaliation through their boldness. Those who are well established advocate a cautious policy of winning additional favors through good will and hard work. In European colonies native chieftains fought against "troublemakers" and argued that their own people were "not ready" for reforms. They argued that it was necessary to "go slow." In following the careers of young "radicals" it is interesting to note how many of them alter their views once they themselves become well established.

The persistence of class differences within minority groups varies with the extent to which social mobility is possible. Even when remnants of the color line still persist, many persons on each class level feel more comfortable in one another's company than they do among other members of their ethnic group. As people of the same classes live in similar neighborhoods and are educated in the same schools, they associate with one another more and more in spite of their ethnic differences. Personal reserve is often retained more in contacts across class lines than across ethnic lines. To the extent that upward social mobility is possible across ethnic lines, then, persons who are fully assimilated disappear into the dominant group. In the centuries of Hungarian rule over Rumanians and various Slavic-speaking peoples in Transylvania, some acculturation occurred constantly. Although all classes were affected, it was especially the

[94] Berthold F. Hoselitz, "The Recruitment of White Collar Workers in Underdeveloped Countries," *International Social Science Bulletin*, VI (1954), 3–11.

members of the middle class and nobility who were eventually absorbed into the Magyar population.[95] When this happens, the underprivileged stratum becomes a lower class, containing the less successful of all ethnic groups. Class loyalties gradually replace ethnic loyalties, as is the case in much of Latin America today.

This suggests that the "caste-class" theory of "race relations"—widely entertained by American sociologists—describes a transitional period during which the more successful members of ethnic minorities have developed a different way of life. During the days before the Civil War all white people, regardless of class, were placed above all Negroes in the social hierarchy. But after emancipation the dividing line between the ethnic groups changed from a horizontal line to a slanted one, for upper-class Negroes were rated above lower-class white people. A Negro professional man was held in higher esteem by many white people than a white sharecropper. According to the theory, sometime in the future the color line will become vertical, so that two separate class societies will coexist side by side.[96] The line between the two ethnic groups is called a "caste line," presumably because mobility across it is almost impossible; this is an unfortunate misuse of the term "caste." [97] It seems unlikely, however, that ethnic barriers can be perpetuated under such circumstances. In the long run the formation of privileged classes facilitates integration. People associate first on a class basis, and ethnic differences are gradually minimized; members of the privileged classes become so similar that they identify with one another. Furthermore, the successful participate in social reform and self-improvement programs and thus aid in raising the general standard of living within the minority group. Privileged persons also set examples in terms of which the entire minority group may be remodeled.

Summary and Conclusion

When ethnic groups are in sustained contact, some members of the minority group begin to acquire the culture of their rulers. At first the imitation is superficial, and only a few individuals are in-

[95] R. W. Seton-Watson, *Racial Problems in Hungary* (London: Archibald Constable, 1908).
[96] Park, *Race and Culture, op. cit.*, pp. 230–43; and Warner and Davis, *op. cit.*
[97] Cf. Cox, *op. cit.*, pp. 3–118, 489–508.

volved; in time, however, this develops into widespread participation in a new way of life. Technological practices are accepted first; then, changes in customs follow, and in the end even the values of the dominant group are accepted. The breaking of ethnocentrism in the minority group usually results in social disorganization. In a transitional period there are no clear-cut norms of conduct, and intergenerational conflicts are frequent—clashes between those who still cling to traditional values and those who are acquiring a new outlook. Those who become acculturated more quickly, usually people in more advantageous positions in the minority group, often become separated from the others. As a new elite group develops, it forms into a special class. The more privileged members of minorities imitate the status symbols of the dominant group, and they reproduce a small version of the larger society. They sometimes develop a vested interest in the perpetuation of the color line, for they cannot enjoy many of their advantages without it. This sometimes leads to painful conflicts between ethnic loyalties and class loyalties.

When the more capable members of minority groups become absorbed into the dominant group, they are often condemned as traitors who failed to utilize their talents to fight for their kind. Such criticism rests on the assumption that loyalty to ethnic group *should* supersede all other loyalties—perhaps because "blood is thicker than water." This is a moral question, not a sociological problem. In point of fact, most of the independence movements in areas once colonized by Europeans have been led by marginal men and by members of the educated elite. These men are culturally European and have very little in common with their countrymen. They are almost unanimous in advocating programs of "modernization," for they are concerned with the position of their country on the international scene. This suggests that many of the minority peoples of the world today are being led to some measure of self-determination by men whose perspectives transcend those of any particular ethnic group.

CHAPTER 18

Factionalism in
Changing Minorities

Although ethnic minorities usually appear tightly knit and homogeneous to outsiders, many are split between those who struggle to preserve the group as a distinct unit and those who favor assimilation into the larger society. For more than 100 years the Xhosa from surrounding tribal reserves have been migrating into East London in South Africa. Among themselves the more than 65,000 who live in the locations make a sharp distinction between "School People" and "Red People." The former are products of missions and other schools; they are literate, Christian, dressed in European style, and adapted to the European way of life. The latter smear their clothing and bodies with red ochre and stand by their traditional way of life. Although they live side by side and are often intertwined by bonds of kinship, they remain aloof from one another, engage in very few common activities, and regard each other with mutual distrust.[1] After

[1] Mayer, *op. cit.*

their subjugation by Federal troops the Southern Ute Indians were so disagreed on this matter that they finally separated into two parts. The Ute of Ignacio adopted farming and sought formal education. Acculturation was rapid, and the younger generation won a strong voice in community councils. But the Ute of Towaoc retreated to a region where poverty afforded a shield against white penetration. Although receiving government rations, they resisted acculturation and continued their nomadic existence. Social control remained in the hands of elders, and only a few of the younger people learned to speak English.[2] Virtually all American minorities have been divided on this issue; opposition has been especially bitter among American Jews. Similar conflicts have been conspicuous among the Maori in New Zealand, the Karen in Burma, and the Chinese in Indonesia.

Although well-established minority groups are often characterized by social solidarity, cohesion is difficult to maintain in societies in which some measure of upward mobility is possible. Where members of minority groups can alter their status, the fundamental issue becomes one of identification. Is the ethnic group worth preserving, or should people try to become assimilated into the larger society? Sometimes opposition on this point coincides with the conflict between generations, but in many cases there are differences among those in each generation. The conflict sometimes coincides with class differences, but this is not always the case.[3] In some communities different minority groups move in different directions. In the American Southwest, for example, the Navaho Indians are rapidly becoming acculturated, but the Zuni have retained their own way of life; in Kenya, the Masai have resisted change and have tried to live according to their ancient ways, but the Kikuyu have embraced European standards—accepting Christianity, trade unions, and formal education. The problem with which we shall be concerned in this chapter is the manner in which changing minority groups are split into factions, the characteristics of each faction, and the manner in which individuals align themselves to one faction or the other.

[2] Linton, *Acculturation in Seven American Indian Tribes, op. cit.*, pp. 119–203.
[3] Cf. Toynbee, *op. cit.*, Vol. VIII, pp. 580–629.

Are the Metis "Edging into Mainstream?"

Assimilation into the Larger Society

Where acculturation is widespread, especially in communities in which some avenues for social mobility are open, a number of people in minority groups advocate assimilation. Those who desire to assimilate acquire the values of the dominant group, see the minority group from its standpoint, and seek to better their lot by escaping subordinate rank. They are optimistic that the barriers of segregation will eventually come down, and they strive for the kind of situation in which there would be the fullest opportunity for participation in community life without any kind of ethnic differentiation. Although it is not always thought of in these terms, successful assimilation means the disappearance of the minority group as an identifiable entity. Advocates of assimilation are not necessarily against the minority group; in many cases what other members of the group do does not concern them. But as individuals they do not care to be part of it, and they do not care especially whether the ethnic group as such is perpetuated or not. This type of orientation toward the larger society is found in most minority groups in the United States and among the more educated natives in colonial areas.

The decisive change that occurs in assimilation is the *displacement of reference groups.* The transformation of perspectives is usually a gradual process; a newcomer in a community comes to assume the outlook shared by his new associates and to redefine himself from this standpoint. Such transformations take place in many contexts—the son of a sharecropper who works his way through college by playing football and eventually becomes a cardiac specialist, or the first offender who becomes acclimated to the values of the underworld. The initial step consists of recognizing differences between oneself and the others and experiencing a sense of uneasiness. From his ethnocentric standpoint a person initially sees strangers in terms of their utility, and there is no attempt made to identify with them. While the relationships may be friendly, all parties maintain their reserve. At first a newcomer is not much concerned with the opinions of outsiders, but he soon realizes that they place an estimate upon him and that the respect with which he is treated depends upon this evaluation. Thus, in spite of himself he becomes sensitive to their opinions and begins to struggle for some sort of acceptable standing among them. Seeking status in the outside world, however, necessarily involves role-taking; one must develop some appreciation of the values of the outside world in order to understand how he is appraised in it. Little by little the novice begins to grasp an alternative point of view.

With sustained association communication becomes more effective, and the person begins to appreciate more clearly the manner in which his group is seen from the standpoint of the larger society. As he adopts the standards of the dominant group, he judges himself in these terms. Children of immigrants to America, for example, became very self-conscious after mingling with outsiders. They felt humiliated over their bad table manners, their foreign accent, their lack of general information, and their inability to invite their new friends to their dirty homes.[4] If the ethnic group is one that is despised or ridiculed, he becomes especially sensitive to those particular features that are singled out as objectionable. He works hard to eliminate these characteristics in himself or to make them less conspicuous. A person who is being converted is able to see the social world of the minority group with greater detachment; to him its outlook appears to be small and confined. Once a social world is felt by its participants to be "narrow," it is no longer coterminous with the universe but is seen as only a part of it. Many sons of Chinese shopkeepers in the United States, for example, refuse to follow their father's trade, for it provides insufficient prestige in the larger world; a career in Chinatown is not attractive. Such people have no intention of returning to the home of their ancestors, and they are more concerned with winning rights in the larger community.[5] If there are no barriers against upward mobility, the assimilating person is absorbed into the dominant group. If upward mobility is not possible beyond a certain ceiling, he trains his children to improve their station in life.

Assimilation involves the transformation of one's self-conception; hence, it is a difficult and painful experience. There is initially a period of alienation during which old meanings and habits are rejected. Many who become assimilated are pushed away from the minority group by severe deprivations. Sensitivity to new possibilities

<hr />

[4] P. Young, *op. cit.*, p. 177.
[5] Kwan, *op. cit.*, pp. 72–76. Cf. Beulah O. Kwoh, "The Occupational Status of American-Born Chinese Male College Graduates," *American Journal of Sociology*, **LIII** (1947), 192–200.

always precedes change, and those who are satisfied with their life do not become seriously interested in strange and meaningless modes of conduct. In some cases there is a traumatic experience in which one suffers deep humiliation because of his ethnic identity. A transitional period usually follows during which the individual plays two sets of roles, one in the minority group and one in the larger society. This is generally the most difficult part of assimilation. A person who is forced to play two sets of roles often becomes stilted; his conduct becomes studied, for he cannot act spontaneously. He is torn by inner conflicts and guilt feelings. He may chastise himself for being snobbish or unfair to those who remain attached to the minority group, but he is convinced that they are old-fashioned, misinformed, and narrow-minded. He knows that he hurts those around him, and yet he cannot accept their way of life. He has difficulty in forming a consistent and acceptable self-conception, for he plays incongruent roles for two different reference groups. During this period an individual is especially defensive and hypersensitive about the question of ethnic identity; he is not sure of what he is. Success in assimilation depends largely upon the willingness of the dominant group to accept the person who has adopted its values. With the support of new associates one can lose himself in their society and reject the old. Without it he is left without roots, and he may occupy marginal status throughout his life.[6]

Most people who are assimilating are bilingual, but they prefer to speak the language of the dominant group. They are reluctant to use their ancestral tongue, especially in public, even if they are able to speak it fluently. They believe that faulty use of the official language of the community is disgraceful, take great pains to master the intricacies of the tongue, and are critical of their fellows whose performance is substandard. Children of immigrants are often ashamed of the "accent" of their parents and beg them not to express themselves so loudly in public. In Hawaii there is much sensitivity about the use of pidgin English. Those advocating assimilation insist on the use of "good English," even at the cost of being accused of becoming

---

[6] Cf. David I. Golovensky, "The Marginal Man Concept," *Social Forces*, XXX (1952), 333–39; Park, *Race and Culture, op. cit.*, pp. 357–71; Georgene Seward (ed.), *Clinical Studies in Culture Conflict* (New York: Ronald, 1958); and Laura Thompson and Alice Joseph, "White Pressures on Indian Personality and Culture," *American Journal of Sociology*, LIII (1947), 17–22.

"high hat." [7] Since those who master a new language categorize their experiences somewhat differently, they actually approach life with a different set of presuppositions. Other members of the minority group are frequently puzzled. The person undergoing assimilation may still appear much as he had in the past, but he begins to act quite differently.

Since their reference group is the larger community, those who are assimilating tend to conceive of themselves as *inferior* objects and look with envy upon members of the dominant group. Realizing that they are still identified with an ethnic minority, many learn to despise it; they are ashamed of themselves and develop an apologetic stance. Some writers have referred to this phenomenon as minority-group "self-hatred." [8] For example, a native pastor in New Guinea is reported as declaring that his people were descendants of Ham and ascribing their low economic position to the curse on their ancestors. [9] Once the young Eskimos in Gambell broke their ethnocentrism, they identified with the white man on the mainland. They visualized themselves in terms of the model of an American citizen—a man who has a steady job, owns furniture and electrical gadgets, drives an automobile, belongs to a Christian church, and votes in elections. In contrast, they saw the way of life of their ancestors as "primitive." [10] Similarly, in East London the "Red People" are sneered at for their "uncivilized pagan ways." Their habits are condemned as dirty and unhygienic, and they are referred to as the "smeared ones" and the "wooly ones." [11] Some individuals develop a sense of personal inferiority that many of their associates feel is unjustified. For example, if an attractive woman of the dominant group should profess her love for such a man, he may balk at reciprocating even though he may adore her. In areas dominated by Europeans the "white woman" has come to mean something very special; the ideals of the reference group make her the best of all women, viewed longingly as a creature

---

[7] John E. Reinecke, "Pidgin English in Hawaii: A Local Study in the Sociology of Language," *American Journal of Sociology*, XLIII (1938), 778–89. Cf. George C. Barker, "Social Functions of Language in a Mexican-American Community," *Acta Americana*, V (1947), 185–202; and Bossard, *op. cit.*

[8] Lewin, *op. cit.*, pp. 186–200. Cf. Jean-Paul Sartre, *Anti-Semite and Jew* (New York: Grove Press, 1960), pp. 92–100.

[9] Hogbin, *op. cit.*, p. 242.

[10] C. C. Hughes, *op. cit.*, pp. 343–46.

[11] P. Mayer, *op. cit.*, pp. 35–36. Cf. G. Jahoda, *op. cit.*, pp. 29–31.

beyond all hope. Thus, he finds it difficult to conceive of himself as being worthy of genuine affection from such a desirable woman. He may see himself as an object of a passing infatuation or may even suspect that she has some ulterior motive. In many cases classification of oneself as a base object is reinforced by a sense of guilt from being alienated from one's parents and former friends. Some men who are trying desperately to assimilate become involved in a succession of affairs with women of the dominant group, as if they found it necessary to prove over and over that they are worthy of being loved.

Since they adopt the values of the larger society, proponents of assimilation strive to make themselves worthy of those by whom they wish to be accepted. This leads to emulation of the status symbols of the dominant group. Until very recently there was little "race pride" among American Negroes. Light pigmentation of the skin had long been an index of superiority. Color differences sometimes became the basis for invidious distinctions among children in the same family, and close friendships were often limited to persons of approximately the same shade of darkness. Negroes who were light sometimes expressed fear of other Negroes because they were "so black." [12] Skin color, of course, cannot be changed, but through preferential mating one may lighten the shade of his offspring. Thus, the more successful tended to marry lighter mates, preferably those with Caucasoid features. When some 400 Negro adolescents in Oklahoma were asked to characterize the kind of person they wanted to marry, most of them chose people with pigmentation lighter than their own and with more Caucasoid traits.[13] Entrepreneurs have made fortunes in Negro communities selling hair-straighteners and a variety of fraudulent schemes for lightening skin color. Some Negroes have also thought of intermarriage as another way of altering the characteristics of their descendants. In fact, those who favor assimilation tend to scoff at ideals of "racial purity"; even when they themselves choose mates of the same ethnic category, they favor intermarriage in theory and encourage others who are contemplating the possibility.

Those who are assimilating try to eliminate in themselves the

[12] E. Franklin Frazier, *Negro Youth at the Crossways* (Washington, D.C.: American Council on Education, 1940), pp. 51–53; C. S. Johnson, *Patterns of Negro Segregation, op. cit.,* pp. 242–73; and Rose, *op. cit.,* p. 88.
[13] Mozell C. Hill, "Social Status and Physical Appearance Among Negro Adolescents," *Social Forces,* **XXII** (1944), 443–48.

traits that are disapproved; they do their best to alter those symbols of ethnic identity that they see as marks of shame. Language is an important status symbol, and "foreign" languages are avoided. As the Arabs spread their control over most of the Iberian peninsula in the eighth century, many Spaniards were attracted by the grandeur of Moorish technology, science, economic organization, literature, and government. Although many who were assimilated to the Moorish way of life were bilingual, they were conscious of their intellectual inferiority. Since so many disdained the use of the Spanish language, a bishop of Seville is reported to have translated the Bible into Arabic for the use of Spaniards as well as Moors. Efforts are also made to change tell-tale names. In some cases the changing of names is a matter of expediency, but many names are changed to obscure ethnic identity. In medieval Spain the assimilated had both a Spanish and an Arabic name.[14] In Kansu, the Chinese who moved into Tibetan villages not only adopted Tibetan garb and language but also disregarded their surnames, for Tibetans have only personal names.[15] Many American Jews have changed their names and moved into a community in which they were not known and have become merged into the general population. Inherited marks are not so easily changed, but there have been many cases in which hair dyes and plastic surgery have been utilized.

Advocates of assimilation often believe that the minority group actually deserves the differential treatment it receives, and they engage in vitriolic criticism of the group. Australian Aborigines who are more "advanced" declare that the others do not get ahead because they have no "guts" and "ask" for bad treatment.[16] While the Jews who had migrated to Australia from Eastern Europe blamed Gentiles for anti-Semitism, the more assimilated Australian-born Jews tended to blame it on Jews themselves as well as Gentiles. When asked how anti-Semitism was to be overcome, the latter suggested changing the conduct of the Jews.[17] Those who are assimilating sometimes initiate reform movements within the minority group to alter practices condemned by outsiders. When an ambitious person is

[14] Philip K. Hitti, *The History of the Arabs* (London: Macmillan, 1960), pp. 515–16; and Lévi-Provençal, *op. cit.*, pp. 75, 233.

[15] Ekvall, *op. cit.*

[16] Berndt and Berndt, *op. cit.*, p. 265.

[17] F. E. Emery and F. M. Katz, "Social Theory and Minority Group Behaviour," *Australian Journal of Psychology*, III (1951), 22–35.

placed into a category and cannot escape the rank no matter what he achieves, one solution to his difficulty is improving the entire category. During the nineteenth century, when Hungary was pressing its national claims against Habsburg Austria, the most active advocates of assimilating Hungarian minorities were the already-Magyarized Jews, Slovaks, and Serbs. The revolutionary leader Louis Kossuth, an assimilated Slovak, denied to Hungarian minorities the very rights he sought for all Hungarians from Austria.[18] There is special sensitivity to traits included in the stereotype of the group, and attempts are made to compensate for them. If a group is accused of being uncouth, members go out of their way to be well-mannered; those accused of being dirty become immaculately clean; those suspected of disloyalty make ostentatious displays of fealty. Leaders often exhort others to make themselves presentable so that the entire group can benefit from it. Among the outcast Eta in Japan the more successful express embarrassment and disgust at the way of life of the others, conduct periodic inspections of health and sanitation facilities, call for the wearing of clean clothing, insist upon moderation in drinking, urge getting an education, and promote honest business dealings.[19] The proponents of assimilation fight against all efforts to preserve the traditional culture of the group. They regard advocates of cultural pluralism as dangerous and may even form contrast conceptions of them, since they are seen as the party responsible for keeping the minority group in its "backward" condition and for blocking acceptance in the larger community.

As an increasing number become assimilated, there tends to be residential dispersion, infiltration into more occupations, and increased social contacts with outsiders.[20] Some do their best to avoid other members of the minority group. They are fearful of drawing undue attention to themselves and live inconspicuously in mixed neighborhoods or among members of the dominant group. They generally refuse to join minority group organizations; in fact, many question the desirability of having them at all. They argue that such gatherings only call attention to the group and its undesirable traits. Furthermore, by facilitating exclusiveness they tend to perpetuate the dis-

[18] Seton–Watson, *Racial Problems in Hungary*, *op. cit.*, pp. 65, 104.
[19] Donoghue, *op. cit.*
[20] Cf. Clarence E. Glick, "The Relation Between Position and Status in the Assimilation of Chinese in Hawaii," *American Journal of Sociology*, XLVII (1942), 667–79.

tinctive culture that sets them apart. People who are upwardly mobile are often ashamed to see themselves as they had once been; they resent being reminded of their origins and turn against those they left behind. In minority groups of low visibility many successfully merge into the larger population. Among American Jews, for example, there are many who are Jews only by vague family reminiscences and otherwise know nothing of the culture of the group. They conceive of themselves as "Americans" and answer "Jew" only if someone persists in asking about the religion of their parents.[21] After World War II a small number of Jews returned to Germany; when others expressed their astonishment, they replied simply that they did not feel at home anywhere else in the world. They had been assimilated to German life and had long forgotten their Jewish ancestors. These people were in fact Germans.[22]

Some are so intent upon removing all ties with the minority group that they deny all connections, including their ancestry. They believe that their future is endangered by being identified with the category; they are ashamed of being in it, and they do not wish to risk losing their "good connections." The younger generation of Aborigines in Australia, educated in English schools, try to conceal their background and ignore their darker relatives on the street. They refuse to acknowledge their darker grandparents, insisting that they are entirely different from those "wild blackfellows." [23] One of the renowned scholars of Moorish Spain was Ali Ibn-Hazm (994–1064), whose grandfather had been converted from Christianity. He preferred not to claim Spanish descent and insisted that he was a Persian.[24] In the United States today many persons born and reared in ethnic colonies insist in fluent Oxford English that they know nothing about the minority group. An extreme case of rejection of ethnic affiliation is the conduct of some assimilated Jews during the Spanish Inquisition. Recent converts were acutely aware that the old Christians were suspicious of their sincerity, and some of them turned with enthusiasm upon Jews who had not been converted. Since judgments in the Inquisition were often based on the word of informers, there were many opportunities for personal attacks. Many severe blows

21 Bram, *op. cit.*
22 William Attwood, "Germany's Lonely Jews," *Look*, XVI (September 23, 1952), 29–31.
23 Berndt and Berndt, *op. cit.*, pp. 93–97, 244–64.
24 Hitti, *History of the Arabs, op. cit.*, p. 558.

against Jews were struck by erstwhile rabbis. Rabbi Salomon Halevi, who had been the chief rabbi of Burgos, embraced Christianity in 1390. After a few years of study he became chief chaplain to the king, then papal nuncio, and finally Bishop of Burgos. His attitude toward the Jews was especially harsh.[25]

People who are assimilating are often accused of being excessively ambitious, and many selfish motives are imputed to them. In most cases, however, the orientation does not develop as a deliberate scheme for self-advancement. Many children of immigrants in the United States simply absorbed the American outlook in public schools. They did not set out to escape their ancestral past; they simply grew up seeing their world differently from their parents. When a person is assimilating, he sees his career and that of his children as those of active participants in the larger society. It is for this reason that such individuals are often the most militant battlers for civil liberties. They protest "discrimination" even when other members of the minority group believe the struggle is hopeless. They are convinced that members of ethnic minorities who live up to the standards of the dominant group will be given an opportunity to succeed. They assume that those who form the vanguard will have to work harder in order to prove themselves worthy of acceptance.

Since some persons in minority groups assimilate and others do not, the question arises: what are the conditions under which such drastic transformations of perspective occur? First of all, people who assimilate are drawn from those who have had *opportunities for contacts* with the dominant group, and this often depends upon one's position in the minority group. Some children of low rank, for example, are reared outside of ethnic colonies. Their parents may be employed on estates, or they may prefer not to be associated with the group. The youngsters grow up among the privileged, knowing little or nothing about the "foreigners" with whom they are identified. Sometimes contact is indirect—through the media of mass communication. Usually, however, contacts are direct and sustained—schoolmates, teachers, playground directors, clergymen, or fellow workers. Such associations provide the communication channels through which ethnocentrism is broken, through which a sympathetic understanding of another way of life is acquired. Studies of Japanese-Americans reveal, for example, that Christians tend to be more assimilated than Buddhists, confirming a view widely held among the

[25] Castro, *op. cit.*, pp. 526–38.

Nisei themselves.[26] Before World War II Christians on the Pacific Coast worshiped in segregated churches, but members of different ethnic groups maintained friendly contacts with other churches of the same denomination and periodically held joint affairs. The Buddhists, on the other hand, lived in groups that were exclusively Japanese, and opportunities for contacts with outsiders were more limited. People cannot learn new patterns of behavior without opportunities to observe them.[27]

Among those in minority groups who have established sufficient contact to learn something about the outside world, some assimilate and others remain comfortably lodged in their ethnocentric outlook. Why are some receptive to new possibilities while others resist change? The decision is not an easy one; it is a choice between alternative ways of looking at the world. Whether a man remains within a social world or leaves it depends in part upon the *extent to which he believes his personal values can be realized* in the conventional roles open to him. A person who is well established and can see himself fulfilling a satisfactory career within a segregated area is not so likely to be interested in altering the status quo or in departing for an uncertain life elsewhere. To be sure, business and professional men in minority groups are often the more acculturated, but the more successful among them rarely advocate changes. But to a person of low standing in the minority group, to one in a marginal position, or to a young man whose career is still uncertain, the possibilities of a more exciting life elsewhere may be appealing. Common sources of alienation from a group include failure, a sense of unjust deprivation, or the existence of barriers to advancement; inferior rank, rejection, and personal frustration set a man against his group. Dissidents are especially responsive to new possibilities; the disgruntled, the maladjusted, and the frustrated are pre-eminently the acceptors of innovations.[28] A study of Galilean and Mormon mis-

[26] Melvin L. DeFleur and Chang-Soo Cho, "Assimilation of Japanese-Born Women in an American City," *Social Problems*, **IV** (1957), 244–57; and Eugene S. Uyeki, "Correlates of Ethnic Identification," *American Journal of Sociology*, **LXV** (1960), 468–74.

[27] Cf. Cloward and Ohlin, *op. cit.*, pp. 144–52; and Borrie *et al.*, *op. cit.*, pp. 206–22.

[28] Homer G. Barnett, "Personal Conflicts and Cultural Change," *Social Forces*, **XX** (1941), 160–71; and *Innovation: The Basis of Cultural Change* (New York: McGraw-Hill, 1953), pp. 378–410. Cf. Cloward and Ohlin, *op. cit.*, pp. 108–43; and Leonard W. Doob, *Becoming More Civilized* (New Haven: Yale University Press, 1960), pp. 71–101.

sions among the Rimrock Navaho reveals, for example, that the Indians who wished to identify with white men were those who felt that they could not achieve satisfaction through conventional Navaho patterns. Some were ignorant of Navaho ways, and others who were familiar with them felt unfulfilled. The churches were filled with misfits.[29] Among immigrants to Israel, Eisenstadt found that the choice of reference groups was made largely in terms of an individual's estimate of the possibilities of achieving satisfactory status through each alternative.[30]

The orientation of those who are assimilating is also reinforced by *cordial interpersonal relations* with individuals of the dominant group or with others who feel as they do. People who are involved in such situations are usually caught in a web of conflicting personal obligations. A perspective is learned with the cooperation of particular individuals, and one develops a sense of obligation to those who teach him. In difficult situations in which a person cannot make up his mind, he often reverts to the learning context and asks what these people would say if he were to violate the norms they had taught him. In such dilemmas a person often chooses in terms of his sentiments toward these individuals. It is very difficult to go against the known wishes of those one loves. Just as there are many young women who have given up lovers to please their parents, there are many people of ability in ethnic minorities who have declined opportunities for advancement in the larger society from not wanting to go against the wishes of their parents or from fear of being labelled as snobbish by their close friends. Studies in areas undergoing industrialization show that individuals are more likely to accept innovations if they are favorably disposed toward the instructor and especially if they identify with him and impute to him a desire to see them change.[31] In his study of Jewish–Gentile intermarriage Mayer found that those who intermarried against the wishes of their parents were not only attracted by their mates but were also supported by mutual friends who approved of the relationship.[32] The

[29] Robert N. Rapoport, "Changing Navaho Religious Values," *Papers of the Peabody Museum of American Archaeology and Ethnology,* XLI (1954), No. 2.
[30] S. N. Eisenstadt, "Reference-Group Behavior and Social Integration," *American Sociological Review,* XIX (1954), 175–85.
[31] Doob, *Becoming More Civilized, op. cit.,* pp. 102–34.
[32] John E. Mayer, *Jewish–Gentile Courtships* (New York: Free Press of Glencoe, 1961), pp. 179–98.

extent to which a person lives up to the expectations imputed to a reference group depends, then, upon his sentiments toward the particular individuals who were responsible for teaching him that point of view and toward others who agree and approve.

There are also cases in which assimilation is reinforced by disjunctive interpersonal relations with other members of the minority group. Often individuals who are most anxious to assimilate are those who have been involved in a long succession of conflicts, especially with their parents. They want desperately to escape because they can no longer tolerate the people they encountered in their unhappy childhood. In his study of the acculturation of Navaho Indians, Vogt found that men who preferred to go the way of the white man were those who lacked satisfying affective ties with other Navahos.[33] Many innovators are persons who are antagonistic toward traditional authority. When one's sentiments toward certain individuals are hostile, there is little incentive to comply with their wishes; in fact, one may even go out of his way just to spite them. In Great Britain Banton found that English women who consorted with Negroes were in many instances those who had been rejected by the English—in many cases women who felt abandoned by their parents. Many had been born illegitimate, and they indicated that they appreciated the consideration they received from the immigrants.[34] Studies also show that people who intermarry before the practice becomes widespread reveal a sense of alienation from individuals in their own ethnic group. They often show a record of conflict with their parents and an idealization of some alien culture; in many cases both partners reject their respective groups.[35] Choice of reference group may also be facilitated by complementary sentiments. A person who dislikes his parents may be taught a new outlook by outsiders whom he views with affection and respect.

---

[33] Evon Z. Vogt, "Navaho Veterans: A Study of Changing Values," *Papers of the Peabody Museum of American Archaeology and Ethnology*, **XLI** (1951), No. 1, pp. 105–06. Cf. Barnett, *Innovation, op. cit.*, pp. 291–377; and Doob, *Becoming More Civilized, op. cit.*, pp. 116–19.

[34] Banton, *The Coloured Quarters, op. cit.*, pp. 150–81.

[35] Linton Freeman, "Homogamy in Interethnic Mate Selection," *Sociology and Social Research*, **XXXIX** (1935), 369–77; Joseph Golden, "Patterns of Negro–White Intermarriage," *American Sociological Review*, **XIX** (1954), 144–47; and James S. Slotkin, "Jewish–Gentile Intermarriage in Chicago," *ibid.*, **VII** (1942), 34–39.

The Struggle for Cultural Pluralism

The major opposition to assimilation comes from advocates of cultural pluralism, those who favor the separate development of each ethnic group. In most minorities there are persons who remain loyal to traditional values and who shun opportunities for moving out into the larger world. In charter-member minorities many feel they have been overpowered by barbarians who are superior only in their military technology. Among immigrants a number are unable to see anything of merit in the new country; they see it as an expedient place in which to make a living, a place inhabited by strange people who have no appreciation of the more important things in life. They accept their subordinate positions only because they conceive of themselves as visitors, and they look forward to the day when they will return "home." Such persons desire to remain separated from the dominant group and to live in enclaves in which their way of life can be preserved. In fact, the development of such an outlook is greatly facilitated by segregation, as in the case of the reservations for American Indians. Their view toward outsiders is not necessarily hostile; unlike those who advocate *apartheid*, they do not wish to hold down other groups by force. What they desire is to be left alone; the ideal of cultural pluralism is separate but equal existence.[36] Although this type of orientation is found in many different historical contexts, both the programs advocated and their justifications are similar.

The philosophy of cultural pluralism, the coexistence of different ethnic groups under a common government that guarantees autonomous cultural development of each, has long been advocated by minority peoples in Europe. Switzerland, where four national languages are officially recognized and where other cultural differences are respected and protected, has been held up as an example of what can be done.[37] The French-Canadians have also enjoyed a certain measure of autonomy.[38] In Tewa Village, a pueblo on the Hopi Res-

[36] Wirth, *Community Life and Social Policy, op. cit.*, pp. 237–60, 354–67.
[37] Kurt Mayer, "Cultural Pluralism and Linguistic Equilibrium in Switzerland," *American Sociological Review*, XVI (1951), 157–63.
[38] E. C. Hughes, *French Canada in Transition, op. cit.*; and Horace Miner, *St. Denis: A French-Canadian Parish* (Chicago: University of Chicago Press, 1939).

ervation in northern Arizona, descendants of the Tano have retained their identity and culture. They resisted the attempts of Spaniards to convert them, and for the past 250 years they have lived on friendly terms among the Hopi without being absorbed.[39] This type of orientation is found especially among those who are pessimistic of their chances of gaining adequate status in the larger society; hence, they ask for reasonable control over their own affairs. Although it has long been one of the dominant philosophies in Jewish ghettos, it gained considerably more support among Jews throughout the world after the excesses of the Nazi regime. Those who fear the resurgence of anti-Semitism and are pessimistic of living safely among Gentiles are the ones who strongly advocate separation and independent development.[40] Until very recently most American Negroes favored assimilation, but with increasing pessimism over the possibilities of ever being accepted, many are becoming more responsive to the appeals of the Black Muslims, who advocate establishment of a separate state.[41]

The reference group of such persons is their own ethnic group in historical perspective, all those with whom they believe they share common ancestry—living, dead, and yet unborn. A substantial portion of the audience of many immigrants remains in the country whence they came. Before the Communist revolution a Chinese emigrant who planned to return home, for example, viewed his activities as an episode in a career in China—purchasing some land, building a home for his family, providing a dowry for his daughters, and arranging a suitable marriage for his sons. He worked hard and saved for these occasions. The bones of those who died abroad were sent back to China for burial; other places were for economic opportunity but not for eternal life. A sojourner was not concerned with civil rights; he took it for granted that he was an alien and did not even consider the possibility of gaining equal status.[42] Those who had been subjugated by invaders dream of native life as it presumably was before the conquest. Among the Xhosa the "Red People" see white men as foreigners who defeated them in battle. They look back to a happy past before the Kaffir Wars, and they envision a future with-

---

[39] Dozier, *op. cit.*
[40] Wirth, "Education for Survival: The Jews," *op. cit.*, p. 689.
[41] Lincoln, *op. cit.*
[42] Siu, *op. cit.* Cf. Kwan, *op. cit.*, pp. 63–67.

out white men, when they will again be independent.[43] An American Jew who is orthodox lives largely within the Jewish community. His audience consists of other orthodox Jews; he cares little about outsiders, although he may be concerned that they show sufficient respect for the group. In many ways these people are like sectarians; they see themselves and their world as the only values of real significance. Accomplishments elsewhere are unimportant, perhaps even undesirable. Some are even reactionary in that they continually emphasize a glorious past; they stress the achievements of their ancestors and dream of the restoration of past greatness. There is a tendency to exaggerate the importance of the group in history, as trivial events are blown up into magnificent affairs. Sometimes the leaders speak of destiny—a sacred mission of the people.

Most proponents of separate development conceive of themselves as valuable objects, and they do not apologize for themselves nor their customs. Men who are engrossed with their own way of life form self-conceptions through the eyes of their peers, not those of their rulers; they are satisfied with what they see. Of course, an individual may have personal reasons for feeling inadequate, but this has no relation to his ethnic identity. Unlike those who are assimilating, they do not compare themselves with people of higher status and greater power. When their rank in the community is low, they assume that the barbarians around them are not intelligent enough to appreciate them. They are sometimes highly resentful of differential treatment in the hands of people they regard as inferior to themselves. They conceive of themselves as a group apart, a separate entity, not as part of a larger population. This type of self-conception results in different behavior patterns. Among the colored minorities in Great Britain, for example, West Africans and West Indians tend to see England as their "mother country" and try to assimilate, but most Pakistanis and Sikhs merely earn their money or get their education and return home; the latter are unconcerned with assimilation.[44]

Those who favor separation are proud of their group symbols. They may realize that some of these marks happen to symbolize low status in the larger community. If so, the very characteristics that are

[43] P. Mayer, op. cit., pp. 30–31.
[44] Banton, The Coloured Quarter, op. cit., pp. 73–74. Cf. Mannoni, op. cit., pp. 39–40, 62.

seen as marks of shame by those who want to assimilate become sacred symbols to be defended at all cost. Rather than humiliation, there is resentment. If the group is criticized for wearing different clothing, traditional garb will be worn proudly, even defiantly. The major argument that is used against altering status symbols is that one should not pretend to be someone he is not. Thus, the "Red People" in East London declare, "I am not one of the Xhosa who try to ape the white man; I only want to appear what I am, a real Xhosa." [45] All attempts to eliminate the disapproved traits are opposed. The changing of names is condemned; it is argued that members of an ethnic group should be able to recognize their own kind with ease. One frequent charge is that "only criminals change their names." [46]

Although they may have a fluent command of the language of the dominant group, champions of cultural pluralism tend to discourage using languages other than their own. In countries with compulsory education laws, their children undergo special hardships, for they must attend separate language schools after regular school hours. In countries in which the use of languages other than the official tongue is outlawed, secret schools are established, or the children are taught at home. Attempts are sometimes made to win official recognition of their language so that it can be used in school and in government notices. Even when there are no official attempts to suppress the idiom, difficulties arise, for younger people find the vernacular of the dominant group far more useful in getting employment and for everyday use. The development of a literature in the minority tongue is recognized as important; a language cannot survive in competition with others that are more widely used unless there is something of value that can be expressed in it, and intellectuals often set about to create a body of literature. In recent years, with the rise of nationalism throughout the world, groups that have never had a distinctive language are trying to develop them. One eminent Eurasian intellectual in India bemoaned the fact that Eurasians had no mother tongue. He insisted that English was not their native tongue, even if it was the only language they knew! [47]

Those who desire separation are often characterized by a high

[45] P. Mayer, *op. cit.*, p. 30.
[46] Adamic, *op. cit.*, pp. 39–42.
[47] Charles I. Glicksberg, "Eurasian Racialism," *Phylon*, XII (1951), 13–19.

degree of ethnocentrism. In-group feelings are periodically reinforced through ritualistic acts, the celebration of traditional holidays, and religious observances. Their outlook is limited, and they inculcate their offspring with this parochial standpoint. When children demand reasons for the insistence upon separation, they are told that the only people who can really be trusted are those of their own kind and that even friendly people on the other side of the color line will desert them in time of need. This position is reinforced by many legendary accounts of mistreatment by outsiders and by tales of injustice and snobbery; persons who have assimilated are reported to be lonely and unhappy and are singled out as pathetic examples of what happens to those who disobey their parents. In East London elders among the "Red People" point to widespread illegitimacy, lack of respect for parents, learning to value only money, and criminal activities that even white men cannot control as examples of what happens to Xhosa who get "mixed up" with alien ways.[48] Some immigrants go so far as to send their children to the old country for an education. This was for a long time a widespread practice among both Chinese and Japanese in the United States. When such children returned after graduation, they found themselves to be strangers in their own family, unable to communicate with their brothers and sisters. Furthermore, many found that they could not communicate with their parents, whose views seemed outdated, since they had not been "home" for many decades. Many had to study English at night school in order to qualify for menial jobs; even then, many parents were still convinced that they had done the right thing.[49]

Many advocates of separate development disdain the dominant group's culture and attack those who are assimilating as deserters. Since such a high value is placed upon the ethnic group, its symbols, and its culture, there is great concern over the possibility of its dissolution. Those convinced of the group's sacred mission feel that anyone who fails to meet his responsibilities is a traitor. Thus, in British India many orthodox Hindus complained of natives who copied the manners, gestures, and customs of the English. They talked of moral decay and loose living among those who had come to despise the habits of their countrymen and shuddered over stories

[48] P. Mayer, op. cit., pp. 36–40, 72, 90–165.
[49] William C. Smith, Americans in Process (Ann Arbor: Edwards Bros., 1937), pp. 181–85.

of beef-eating and brandy-drinking.[50] As Jews in the United States become acculturated, there is nothing to set them apart from other Americans other than consciousness of kind. Because it is relatively easy for Jews to "pass" Jewish leaders recognize explicitly that the group must struggle for its preservation by opposing assimilation. Among the more orthodox Jews anyone who favors assimilation is seen as a villain, for assimilation, like genocide, is defined as a crime. They point out that Jews have maintained their identity for centuries against great odds and at great cost; therefore, it is the sacred duty of each Jew to protect the entity for which so many have fought and died. Changing names, not observing food taboos, and altering religious rituals have all come under fire. Nor is this reaction new in the history of the Jews; in the past, whenever the group was treated with tolerance, special care was taken to protect its solidarity.[51] In some circles of American Negroes a person who willingly accepts his subordinate position and fits into the larger society is condemned as a "white man's nigger." The mistress of a white man is reviled as a "white man's strumpet," and a man with a strong predilection for white women is condemned as a "sheet lover." Anyone who curries favor in a servile manner is disdained as an "Uncle Tom," in contrast to one who fights for the welfare of Negroes, who is praised as a "race leader." [52] Among the Xhosa in East London a person who is highly assimilated is sometimes called an *Itshipha*, a derogatory term derived from the English word "cheap." [53] When Katanga seceded from the Congo Republic in 1962, difficulties were compounded because its leader, Mr. Moise Tshombe, was disdained by fellow African leaders as a "white man lover." He was a man of affluence who spoke French fluently and had little difficulty in mixing with Europeans; few questioned his ability, but most nationalists distrusted him.

If the dominant group launches a program to assimilate all its minority peoples, advocates of cultural pluralism organize active resistance to it. European minorities have long resisted nationalization campaigns of the various groups that have ruled them, and similar opposition has developed in minority groups throughout the

[50] McCully, *op. cit.*, p. 204.
[51] Cf. Manasse, *op. cit.*, p. 204; and Rosenthal, *op. cit.*
[52] Samuel M. Strong, "Negro–White Relationships as Reflected in Social Types," *American Journal of Sociology*, LII (1946), 23–30.
[53] P. Mayer, *op. cit.*, p. 6.

world. During World War II young men were drafted for the U.S. armed forces from all Indian reservations, but the manner in which the Zuni treated its veterans, in contrast to the fate of war veterans among the Navaho, illustrates the determination with which a policy of separation can be pursued. The Zuni made every effort to get their men deferred from military service by insisting that their eligible young men were priests; those who were inducted carried Zuni symbols with them to the battlefields; and wherever they were sent, they were kept informed of affairs at home. When they returned, they were required to undergo a cleansing rite. If they deviated from traditional practices, sanctions were imposed to bring them back into line. There was little interest in the experiences they had away from the reservation, and the more "progressive" of the veterans eventually left the village. In contrast, the Navaho made no attempt to escape the draft, and they welcomed returning veterans as victorious warriors. There was much curiosity about the outside world, and many of the veterans were seen as future leaders who had first-hand knowledge of the white man's ways. The Zuni have retained their own way of life through centuries of contact and felt that a fight among white men was none of their concern; the Navaho felt themselves a part of the war and contributed as Americans.[54]

Those who favor separation tend to live with their own kind and participate almost exclusively in their own organizations. Many of them admit that they feel uncomfortable in the presence of outsiders and do not care to have anything to do with them. Many of the immigrants to the United States could hardly wait to move out of the tenements in which they first settled, but many others have remained in segregated colonies long after they were able to afford better housing. They preferred living where they could speak their own language, be close to places of worship, and be able to shop for their favorite foods.[55] Among the Xhosa "Red People" kept up an unbroken contact with their rural homes, visiting as frequently as possible and participating in family affairs on weekends; their roles at home remained unchanged. In East London those from the same village lived together, drank beer together, and exchanged nostalgic tales of home. This constant association facilitated the collective dis-

[54] Adair and Vogt, op. cit.
[55] Firey, op. cit.

cipline of those who might be tempted to alter their ways.[56] When
such individuals become involved in political action in the larger community, it is to demand formal recognition of their group as a separate
entity with some measure of self-rule. Some individuals gain political
power by emphasizing differences and then becoming leaders of one
of the separate segments of the community.[57]

Those who emphasize separation usually stress the importance
of biological lineage. Persons of low visibility who manage to "pass"
into the general population are singled out for condemnation. They
are accused of being dishonest, of pretending to be something they
are not. Since those who "pass" successfully are both acculturated
and assimilated, the implication is that what they *really* are is determined by their genes. Some advocates of cultural pluralism are ardent
racists; others who profess to be "liberal" disavow racism but assume
that one's inherited make-up should determine his life and fate—his
"true identity." Since there is so much emphasis upon the importance
of ancestry, it is not surprising that intermarriage is condemned.

Individuals in minority groups vary considerably in the extent to
which they favor autonomous development. Sometimes one member
of a family assimilates readily while another holds himself aloof from
the dominant group. Many proponents of separation are characterized
by a *lack of opportunity for favorable contacts with outsiders*. Those
who grow up knowing of only one way of life actually are not presented with a choice, for they see all others through an ethnocentric
perspective. Many immigrants who defend the traditional values of
their culture are people who spend a large part of their lives in the
new country without ever learning the language of the dominant
group; their lives are confined to the segregated colony. Children
who are sent to the old country for an education also become defenders of old traditions; linguistic problems make it difficult for them
to learn anything about the outside world. Knowing little about what
goes on outside their enclave, they are unable to evaluate critically
the various negative reports they hear about the dominant group.
Upon making contact, therefore, they assume a defensive stance and
are careful to maintain social distance. Minor misunderstandings confirm suspicions and reinforce beliefs about the diabolical character-

[56] P. Mayer, *op. cit.*, pp. 90–165.
[57] Cf. B. Benedict, *op. cit.*, p. 1243.

istics of outsiders. Thus, even when opportunities arise for friendly contacts, they are declined. When such individuals become well established in the minority community, they have too much to lose by any drastic change. Elders and successful persons in the minority group are usually the defenders of a policy of self-rule.

As in assimilation, the perspective of those who favor separate development is frequently supported by interpersonal relations—sentiments toward particular individuals known to support or reject the same point of view. The orientation is reinforced by cordial sentiments toward members of the minority group and hostile sentiments toward outsiders. In immigrant circles young people who are close to their parents generally remain responsive to traditional values even when they know about the outside world. It is very difficult for a "favorite child" to disappoint his parents.[58] In communities in which upward mobility is difficult, the most ardent proponents of cultural pluralism are men who have tried to assimilate and have failed. Those who have been rebuffed by the dominant group strike back with vengeance and determination. Before World War II the Maori professional men in New Zealand tried to assimilate as quickly as possible; they adopted the standards of Europeans, intermarried, and even denied their ancestry and past affiliations. But many were driven back by ill treatment and hostility. Now they are eager to affirm their Maori heritage and are developing national sentiment. Intermarriage has also become less common.[59] The perspective may be supported by complementary sentiments—hatred of people outside and love of those within who provide a sense of warmth and safety.

Contrary to expectations, the extent to which ethnic groups actually differ from one another is not necessarily related to the development of widespread demands for autonomous development. The philosophy of cultural pluralism is quite strong in ethnic minorities that are barely distinguishable from their rulers. It is most commonly found in Europe, where ethnic groups are physically indistinguishable and are often difficult to identify even in terms of cultural traits. Such minorities are often feared by the dominant group as a threat to national security, and for this reason an effort is made to assimilate them. In turn, minority peoples fear extinction of their cultural heritage and fight back. In the United States

[58] Cf. P. Young, *op. cit.*, pp. 119-20.
[59] Ausubel, *op. cit.*, pp. 115-16.

cultural pluralism is most conspicuous among Jews, who are least unlike the general population. On the other hand, demands for separation are also found in ethnic groups that are easily distinguished from others—among the Chinese in various parts of the world and among emigrants from India.

Dual Allegiance in Changing Minorities

In his study of Italians in New Haven, Connecticut, Child found three types of orientations: some rejected Italian culture and identified strongly with America; others rejected American culture and identified strongly with Italy; still others were apathetic and avoided the problem of choosing between the two.[60] A similar division can be found in most minority groups in transition. Most of the people assume an ambivalent orientation, seeing something worthwhile both in assimilation and separate development; extremists on both sides are regarded as unreasonable and unrealistic. A common feeling is that advocates of assimilation want to change too quickly, that most of the people are not yet ready to compete on equal terms with members of the dominant group. It is pointed out that the most ardent champions of assimilation are individuals who have had special advantages of education, of wealth, or of having one parent in the dominant group. On the other hand, those who call for the reaffirmation of traditional values are also rejected as "old-fashioned." Children of immigrants in the United States, for example, have for the most part little interest in the old country. While they can understand the feelings of their parents, they believe that their elders are being unrealistic in wishing that life in America could be ordered in terms of Old World standards. Children who are born in conquered areas appreciate the superior culture of their rulers, and they are generally unimpressed by talk of the old days when there were native kings; leaders of nativistic movements are often dismissed as visionary. When activities of extremists on either side arouse the ire of powerful figures in the dominant group, most members of the minority group tend to become irritated with the agitators. Unimpressed with

[60] Irvin L. Child, *Italian or American* (New Haven: Yale University Press, 1943). Cf. Doob, *Becoming More Civilized, op. cit.*, pp. 149–70; and Mary B. Treudley, "An Ethnic Group's View of the American Middle Class," *American Sociological Review*, XI (1946), 715–24.

the objectives, they see little point in inviting retaliation. Many American Jews would be quite happy to see both the pro-assimilation American Council for Judaism and the pro-separation Zionist Organization of America go elsewhere with their quarrels.

The reference group of most people living in ethnic colonies consists of other inhabitants in the colony. After a generation or two of segregated living, a distinctive culture develops, and those who share this way of life become concerned primarily with the views of others like themselves. They are not interested in their ancestors; children of immigrants are not concerned with what people in the old country would think of them, and most natives in conquered areas have long since stopped worrying about their forebears. Their aspirations are limited; from childhood they see their career as unfolding entirely within the colony. A young man who aspires to become a doctor, for example, leaves the enclave for his special training, but his intention is to return after his internship to serve patients of his kind. He looks forward to winning recognition within the colony, marrying a beautiful girl in the group, and bringing up his children in the same area. Such individuals visualize their career within the ghetto, a community within a community.[61] At the same time, these people are not unfamiliar with the culture of the dominant group. In the United States most children of immigrants speak English as their native tongue, and they learn much about American life through the media of mass communication. Although confined to their own colonies, they use the symbols of the larger society to gain status within the minority group. They accept many of the standards of the dominant group but perform for an audience of their own kind.[62]

The culture of minority groups undergoing transformation is a hybrid culture, containing norms that are traditional as well as some values of the dominant group. Many educate their children in the new ways while preserving some features of the old. As the elders decline in numbers, sales of foreign language newspapers fall, and religious practices rigidly rooted in tradition are abandoned.[63] To the extent that there is partial isolation, however, the culture remains distinctive. Among the Peranakan, mixed offspring of the Chinese and

[61] Gans, *The Urban Villagers, op. cit.*, Goldberg, "A Qualification of the Marginal Man Theory," *op. cit.*; and Kwan, *op. cit.*, 68–72.

[62] Broom and Kitsuse, *op. cit.*

[63] I. Steinbaum, "A Study of the Jewishness of 20 New York Families," *Yivo Annual of Jewish Social Science,* V (1950), 232–55.

the Malay, there is a strong preference for rice and pork, but these items are not consumed with chopsticks. Some items of food are imported canned from China, and special vegetables are grown in the area by Chinese farmers. Instead of tea, however, there is a decided preference for cold drinks, as among all peoples in the hot climate of Southeast Asia.[64] In ethnic colonies in the United States there are many similar survivals. Scandinavians have their gymnastic societies; Chinese have their tongs; Japanese have their fencing societies. These institutions superficially resemble those of the Old World, but they are similar in form only; none have the significance they once had.[65] Many Japanese-Americans regard themselves as Buddhists, but their beliefs would astonish Buddhists in Asia. In Japan temples are visited during the harvest season or in crisis rites; there are no congregations, hymns, Sunday schools, church buses, sermons, youth organizations, basketball leagues, nor candelabras. The Buddhist Church on the Pacific Coast is organized on the pattern of Protestant churches, and most of its members profess a religion they do not understand. Even among the more devout, there are many who do not know that there is no God in Buddhism. Their orientation toward the diety, their self-supplication before the Almighty, their beliefs about atonement for sins—all are fundamentally Christian concepts. Considerably more acculturation has occurred than members of minority groups realize, but the new patterns are used within segregated colonies.

Members of minority groups know they occupy a subordinate position in the community. However, most of them experience neither the resentment of those advocating cultural pluralism nor the desperate need for self-improvement of those advocating assimilation. Since they are familiar with the standards of the dominant group, they realize that a low estimate is placed upon them. While they may sometimes become quite sensitive about this, they do not care enough about it to participate actively in any kind of social reform. They do not take part in self-improvement campaigns, and they resent being reminded of their shortcomings by supporters of assimilation. Nor do they care enough about the preservation of the traditional values of the ethnic group to fight for autonomy.

Since they evaluate themselves at least in part in terms of standards of the dominant group, most persons of minority standing are

[64] Chen, *op. cit.* Cf. Willmott, *op. cit.*
[65] Cf. Ware, *op. cit.*

likely to feel inadequate in some ways. Such feelings are frequently discussed quite candidly among themselves. Sensitivity over their subordinate rank is also manifested in a variety of compensatory reactions. There is a tendency to magnify achievements. Great pride is taken in the accomplishments of members of the group, especially if they win recognition in the outside world. In New Zealand, for example, the Maori take pride in the wartime exploits of the Maori Battalion, in political and professional leaders who have been knighted, and in their athletic heroes.[66] Their attitude toward successful individuals, however, is ambivalent. Those who win acclaim are addressed with deference but at the same time resented, especially by those who know them personally. The successful are often accused of being "high hat," of "thinking they are too good for us." Such individuals are obliged to go out of their way to demonstrate that they are not snobbish; if they succeed in doing this, they are praised as being a "credit to the race." A sense of inadequacy is also reflected in the manner in which outsiders who take a special interest in the group are singled out as "white angels." Trivial remarks about the group by some outside writer are blown up into extravagant praise by a prominent person; anyone who says anything favorable about a minority group is acclaimed as a "well-known" figure. In forming their self-conceptions, then, such persons locate themselves in an inferior category.[67] Since many are well adjusted to life within the group, however, they do not necessarily have a low level of self-esteem.

Members of minority groups undergoing transformation are usually bilingual. In most cases the first language learned is the mother tongue of the parents, and this language continues to be used within the intimate circle of family life. But in time the language of the dominant group is learned in school and at work. In some ethnic colonies a special idiom develops. Young Mexican-Americans of the Southwest, for example, speak Pachuco, an argot borrowing many slang expressions from both Spanish and English.[68] Similar languages have developed in several other American minorities. In New Zealand the structure of the Maori language has changed; it is now more like English. The vocabulary includes a great many phonetically adapted

[66] Ausubel, op. cit., p. 116.
[67] Cf. Frazier, Black Bourgeoisie, op. cit., pp. 174-94.
[68] Barker, op. cit.

English words, and many old Maori words have been dropped from disuse. Although there is a much-admired translation of the Bible into traditional Maori, much of it is no longer understood.[69]

Those who are partially acculturated to a social world other than the one into which they were born live in two different symbolic environments and must learn to find their way in each. Their lives tend to become compartmentalized. When they are in one social world, they speak one language and act in terms of one set of values. When they are in the other social world, they must switch to another language and act in terms of a different set of standards. In his study of linguistic usage among Mexican-Americans in Tucson, Arizona, Barker found that young people spoke Spanish in intimate family circles, switched back and forth among Spanish, English, and Pachuco in informal relations with others like themselves, and spoke English in their relations with Anglo-Americans, even if the particular Anglo was known to speak fluent Spanish.[70] Similarly, the Maori spoke their own language at home, but in their contacts with Europeans they used English. Although evidence is as yet inconclusive, there are indications that bilingualism may retard intellectual development. Most bilingual children show a smaller vocabulary in each language, and even their combined vocabulary is in many cases lower than that of monolingual children. When one considers the great difficulty in mastering even one language, it is understandable that those who must learn two sometimes do not master either tongue. Many members of minority groups believe that bilingualism is responsible for their retardation and poor performance.[71] Many bilingual Mexicans in Tucson were quite shy about speaking English, for they realized that their speech was substandard. Acute consciousness of the importance of language is one of the protective devices resorted to by bilingual individuals; some become overly meticulous in speaking English, and other develop a restrained manner of speech and try to remain inconspicuous.[72]

Those who are becoming acculturated generally participate pri-

[69] Harry B. Hawthorn, *The Maori: A Study of Acculturation* (Menasha, Wis.: American Anthropological Association, 1944), pp. 17–18, 32.

[70] Barker, *op. cit.* Cf. Padilla, *op. cit.*, pp. 97–98.

[71] David P. Ausubel, *Theory and Problems of Child Development* (New York: Grune & Stratton, 1958), pp. 530–31. Cf. Sol Saporta (ed.), *Psycholinguistics* (New York: Holt, Rinehart & Winston, 1961), pp. 395–414.

[72] Bossard, *op. cit.*

marily in minority group organizations which are patterned after similar organizations of the dominant group—clubs, lodges, ladies' auxiliaries, and country clubs. These associations enable people who are busy earning a living and who might otherwise become dispersed to maintain their ties and to solve together some of the common problems that face them. Furthermore, they cushion the shock of transition by enabling them to practice recently-learned roles without exposing themselves to humiliation or to direct competition with members of the dominant group. Those who feel that they are not yet familiar enough with the customs hesitate to plunge into organizations of the larger society. Minority group organizations usually have many officers, and in some cases almost the entire membership holds some office or other within a period of about five years. They provide a permissive atmosphere for training, for the peer group reinforces the new patterns and provides sympathetic support. The caricature of the minority group "big shot" as one who is vain, pompous, and easily flattered becomes more understandable in this context. Such organizations facilitate further acculturation.[73]

Although they are becoming acculturated, enough consciousness of kind remains for most members of ethnic minorities to feel some obligation to perpetuate the group. Even those who have gone through a nationalization program feel intuitively that there is something important and worth preserving about ethnic identity. Studies reveal that a great many American Negroes who could easily "pass" into the general population do so only temporarily. When they are mistaken for white, they often continue the pretense to avoid embarrassment or trouble. Many work during the day as white in order to earn higher wages, but they return at night to segregated quarters to live as Negroes. Many very light-skinned women find that they are much in demand in the Negro social world, and they are unwilling to give up their privileged position for the uncertainty of the white man's world.[74] In 1959 citizens of the Soviet Union were asked to designate the ethnic group with which they wished to be identified. Although there were many advantages to "passing," 2,268,000 identified themselves as Jews, and 472,000 gave Yiddish as their

[73] Cf. Broom and Kitsuse, op. cit.; and Treudley, "Formal Organization and the Americanization Process," op. cit.

[74] John H. Burma, "The Measurement of Negro 'Passing'," American Journal of Sociology, LII (1946), 18–22.

mother tongue.[75] The extent to which people cling to their ethnic identity is revealed by patterns of name-changing among criminals. Criminals wish to hide their identity, but when they alter their names, they generally select a new one that designates the same ethnic category.[76]

Most members of minority groups assume that biological lineage is of some importance. Therefore, they are uncomfortable about intermarriage. Their opposition is not as vigorous nor as desperate as that of advocates of cultural pluralism, but they feel that there is something unnatural about it. Should members of their family become involved, they express disapproval. When their friends become involved, they are unhappy, although in the end most of them give their blessings. Intermarriage is not likely to become commonplace as long as a substantial proportion of a group still lives in segregated colonies.[77]

Persons characterized by dual allegiance generally have friendly but infrequent contacts with members of the dominant group. Many have become acculturated through impersonal communication channels—educational institutions or the media of mass communication. They have had few opportunities to learn through direct experience what goes on outside the minority group. At the same time most of them enjoy some kind of recognition within their group and have opportunities for pursuing their personal values within the ethnic colony. In most cases their orientation is supported by other individuals like themselves, toward whom they have developed cordial sentiments and personal obligations. Their world is largely circumscribed by the boundaries of the minority group, and they are familiar with values of the dominant group only because the group as a whole is undergoing transformation.

In families in which both parents and children have this type of orientation, inter-generational conflict is kept to a minimum. Concessions are made on both sides, and the two generations approach one another with good will. The parents accept many innovations as an inevitable part of living in a society different from the one in which they grew up, and the children accept most of the limitations

[75] Decter, op. cit.

[76] A. A. Hartman, "Criminal Aliases: A Psychological Study," Journal of Psychology, XXXII (1951), 49-56.

[77] Cf. J. E. Mayer, op. cit.

insisted upon by parents out of deference to their wishes. Thus, instead of choosing mates for their children, the parents go to the trouble of adopting stratagems to maximize the probability of mate-selection within the ethnic group. Parents who recognize and sympathize with the demands of the new generation are hailed by the young as "socially minded" or "modern," and they are condemned by other parents as "too advanced." Many imimgrants decide to settle down permanently in the host community because their children become comitted to the new way of life.

Even when a substantial portion of the members of a minority group have become acculturated and even when the dominant group is willing to accept them, segregation may not disappear. Those who advocate assimilation would welcome any opportunity to make their way into the larger society, but there are many others of minority standing who have no such desires and refuse to take advantage of opportunities, preferring to continue living with their own kind. Thus, a study of the distribution of various ethnic groups in Chicago from 1930 to 1950 shows that immigrants who have been in the city for a longer period are more acculturated but that patterns of segregation still persist.[78] To be sure, some of the ethnic minorities in Chicago have still not been accepted, but even among those that are no longer opposed, many prefer to remain in their colonies.

Summary and Conclusion

When minority groups are in the process of becoming integrated into the larger society, there is a transitional period during which several types of orientations toward ethnic identity are championed by different factions. Those who favor assimilation adopt the values of the dominant group and argue that the sooner everyone is absorbed, the more quickly their problems will be solved. Those who advocate cultural pluralism insist upon going back to the traditional values of their ethnic group, arguing that new ways can lead only to degradation and decay. Since each side believes that its most vital interests are at stake, conflict becomes intense. Most people do not commit themselves to either side, and they live by a hybrid culture

[78] Otis D. Duncan and Stanley Lieberson, "Ethnic Segregation and Assimilation," *American Journal of Sociology*, LXIV (1959), 364–74; and Gans, *The Urban Villagers, op. cit.*

that develops within the ethnic colony itself. Some persons grow into one perspective or the other, knowing only what they had learned from those around them, and they have little choice. But those who have had the opportunity to learn of more than one way of life are confronted with the necessity of choosing, and the decision depends upon the extent to which an individual believes he can pursue his personal values in one social world or the other. Once a commitment has been made, it is reinforced by his interpersonal relations with particular individuals who support or oppose the positions.

The struggle between the advocates of assimilation and of autonomous development is essentially a struggle between conservative and liberal modes of thought, and it has much in common with similar conflicts in quite different political contexts. The same kinds of charges and countercharges are made in situations in which ethnic identity is irrelevant. Whenever changes occur very quickly, there are bound to be some casualties—proud, stiff-necked men of the "old school" who "nail their colors to the mast" and die, as well as opportunists who survive at the price of living for nothing but survival. Factionalism occurs during the dissolution of any group. Because of the widely-accepted theory of the "melting pot" most Americans who profess humanitarian ideals favor assimilation. In Europe, with its long history of conquest and reconquest, the same type of people favor cultural pluralism. Paradoxically, then, the very persons who vigorously condemn the doctrine of "separate but equal" facilities for American Negroes insist upon them for European minorities. In the bitter quarrels that have developed among intellectuals, both within minority groups and outside of them, social scientists have often taken sides. Some have even devoted much time and effort to justifying one position or the other. The task of the sociologist, however, is not to take sides in political issues but to describe and explain events.

CHAPTER 19

The Formation of
New Ethnic Groups

In *Nobody Knows My Name* James Baldwin reports that he went into exile to escape the fate of being a Negro in the United States. Once in Europe, however, he was astonished to discover how much alike Americans were, be they descendants of slaves or of other immigrants. Far less perceptive members of American minority groups have made the same discovery. At home they were sensitized to differences and saw themselves as participants in special enclaves; once outside the country, however, they came into contact with people whose outlook was even more different. Their passport and money were not the only things that set them apart; they found that they had a distinct way of approaching the world. Whenever they met other Americans, they were impressed with the thousands of little things they had in common. Furthermore, they were all labelled as "Yankees" or "Gringos" and treated as such, and before long they became acutely conscious that they were a distinct type of human being—called "Americans." The frequency with which such experiences are reported is an indication of the extent to which a new ethnic group is already being formed in this land of Indians and immigrants.

The central problem of this chapter is ascertaining how people who once conceived of themselves as different become identified as members of the same ethnic group. In some cases minority groups become acculturated, assimilated, and integrated into the dominant group. In other cases a new ethnic group is formed through the combination of once-diverse units. Thus, the integration of ethnic groups involves the disappearance of one or both groups as distinct entities. It is a complex and time-consuming process that generally takes *several centuries*. During the period of transition there is a progressive decrease in social distance and a gradual redefinition of ethnic categories. Little by little the actual differences—cultural and inherited— disappear, and the descendants of once-separate peoples become incorporated into a more inclusive moral order.

The Reduction of Social Distance

As members of ethnic minorities become acculturated, they develop linguistic proficiency and acquire technical skills, and they are able to perform all kinds of tasks that had hitherto been reserved for members of the dominant group. When this happens, conventional patterns of separation become increasingly more difficult to enforce. This is especially true in urban communities, where so many contacts are impersonal and where people are not overly concerned with the pedigree of those with whom they deal. Division of labor along ethnic lines, so prominent during early phases of contact, gradually breaks down, and men are more and more selected on the basis of their ability to do the work. Patterns of residential segregation also break down, usually after a period of resistance. Especially in communities in which land is distributed through competitive bidding, affluent members of minority groups are able to outbid others for desirable places. Added wealth also means being able to influence officials to protect their new property rights. Thus, just as patterns of segregation and the division of labor initially developed through natural selection, they break down as the same processes continue— with the competitive advantages now in different hands. Even after a system of ethnic stratification has started to break down, however, the differentiation of ranks persists for some time. But the various strata become progressively less hereditary. There is more competition in terms of personal ability, and each individual has greater opportunities for advancement regardless of his ethnic identity. In the United States today, for example, it is still more difficult for a Negro to advance to a high position, but it is possible to an extent that would not have been dreamed of a century ago. Members of all other minority groups have been able to move up the social scale. Immigrants from Europe and Asia worked hard and sent their children to college, and in a single generation many worked their way into the American middle class. Upward social mobility is still more difficult for members of minority groups, but avenues are open.

As capable individuals of minority standing rise to high positions, they outrank many members of the dominant group. When such incongruities of status occur, there is at first great surprise. Initially the few who move out of the traditional tasks assigned to their ethnic category are seen as exceptions. Since members of minority groups must outperform others to advance, they are usually superior workers, and the very efficiency of their performance results in their being accepted. During the transitional period some protests may arise over persons from ethnic minorities being given too much responsibility and especially over their being given authority over women of the dominant group. Even after these protests subside, for a while a feeling persists that something is not quite right; people feel uncomfortable.[1] In time, however, they become accustomed to the arrangement. Those who have been served by efficient sales clerks or government officials of other ethnic categories are less reluctant to accept them in other contexts. This is especially true of members of the younger generation. Children who had been taught by Negro teachers, whose father had worked with immigrants, or who served as military recruits under officers of other ethnic categories are not likely to be surprised nor offended to find someone from a minority group living in the apartment next door.

Mere geographical proximity does not necessarily result in the reduction of social distance, but more frequent contacts take place. Those who are together a great deal cannot help but make some observations that contradict stereotyped conceptions, and there are

---

[1] Cf. Goode, "Theory of Role Strain," *op. cit.*; George C. Homans, *Sentiments and Activities* (New York: Free Press of Glencoe, 1962), pp. 91–102; Hughes and Hughes, *op. cit.*, pp. 162–74; and Lenski, *op. cit.*

more opportunities for breaking through the walls of ethnocentrism. A substantial body of evidence is accumulating that members of different ethnic groups who are in sustained association are more likely to alter some of their beliefs about one another.[2] In a comparative study of an integrated and a segregated housing project Deutsch and Collins found that Negroes and white people who were neighbors visited informally and helped each other. Most of the white people redefined the category of Negro in some manner; some developed more favorable conceptions, and others did not. The general direction of change, however, was positive.[3] A comparable study of Negroes in an integrated housing project showed that they too developed more positive sentiments toward white people.[4] A study of a governmental agency in Washington, D.C., showed that those who were acquainted with Negro co-workers not only had more favorable conceptions of the category but also indicated a greater willingness to associate with Negroes.[5] A partial relaxation of conventional barriers makes it easier for those who desire to establish contacts across the color line to do so. Perhaps the most important consequences of terminating residential segregation is that young children get to know one another as human beings, even when their parents still retain a polite distance from each other. Even if they subsequently pursue careers in separate social worlds, they are less likely to form stereotyped conceptions, since all their playmates had been such obvious exceptions. The process is cumulative. Frequent association tends to alter attitudes, and this in turn makes closer contacts possible. In time people fail to see any significant differences between ethnic groups and begin to wonder why distinctions have to be made at all.

A reduction of social distance is more likely to occur in situations in which members of different ethnic categories become *conscious of their interdependence*. In many cases people do not at first realize that they are mutually dependent, but once there is explicit

[2] Robin M. Williams, "Continuity and Change in Sociological Study," *American Sociological Review*, XXIII (1958), 619–33.

[3] Morton Deutsch and Mary E. Collins, *Interracial Housing* (Minneapolis: University of Minnesota Press, 1951).

[4] Ernest Works, "The Prejudice–Interaction Hypothesis from the Point of View of the Negro Minority Group," *American Journal of Sociology*, LXVII (1961), 47–52. Cf. Daniel M. Wilner *et al*, *Human Relations in Interracial Housing* (Minneapolis: University of Minnesota Press, 1955).

[5] Barbara K. MacKenzie, "The Importance of Contact in Determining Attitudes Toward Negroes," *Journal of Abnormal and Social Psychology*, XLIII (1948), 417–41.

recognition that different groups are allied in a common cause, neither side wishes to offend the other. Especially where the objective is important and the cooperation of the other is essential for success, conventional barriers that stand in the way of effective collaboration tend to be brushed aside. This does not mean, of course, that social distance is immediately dropped. In many cases members of the two groups arrive at a *modus vivendi;* they cooperate in their pursuit of common objectives without relaxing their personal reserve. Even then, however, some redefinition takes place. Members of the other ethnic category are no longer viewed as inferior or as dangerous, but as useful objects. Useful objects may not be fully respected, but they are protected against common foes. Although the relationships may still remain for the most part impersonal, they are different from what they had been, for partial identification has been established. Persons involved in such situations tend to overlook negative traits and to accentuate positive ones. Those who strive together toward common goals tend to develop a better appreciation of one another. Sharing common hopes and aspirations facilitates their being able to see each other as human beings rather than as mere instances of categories. Perhaps only a few individuals establish friendships across the color line in the beginning. What is important, however, is that such friendships are not forbidden, and the participants are not penalized for them.

Because of the impersonal character of money, economic barriers are among the first to fall. Segregated patterns usually break down first in the distribution of goods, for merchants cannot afford to antagonize potential sources of income. In the American South recognition of the purchasing power of Negroes provides a major weapon in the fight against segregation. In their study of housing in Honolulu, Ball and Yamamura found that the landlords had definite preferences along ethnic lines but were unable to follow them because of their desire for profit. More than 60 per cent of the rental units studied were operated under a preferential policy, but the market situation was such that they had to be rented on a "nondiscriminatory" basis.[6] As members of ethnic minorities become acculturated, employers hire them, for they seek the best workers available for the lowest wages. The major deterrent to hiring mem-

[6] Harry V. Ball and Douglas S. Yamamura, "Ethnic Discrimination and the Market-place," *American Sociological Review,* **XXV** (1960), 687–94.

bers of minority groups is the possibility of serious objections from other workers. After the labor force has been integrated, employers sometimes insist upon promoting personnel in terms of ability; the tendency of foremen to give preference to workers of their own ethnic group is counteracted by a company policy of striving for maximum productivity. In some instances shrewd employers realize that a labor force made up of heterogeneous groups that cannot speak the same language is not as likely to develop the same solidarity as one that is ethnically homogeneous.[7] Furthermore, businessmen engaged in similar enterprises often find it helpful to work together. Only a few are wealthy enough to send a lobbyist to the legislature, to purchase votes, or to hire hoodlums to attack labor organizers; together in an association these tasks can be accomplished. In such cases ethnic identity is of secondary importance, if relevant at all. Similarly, those engaged in the same line of work often find that they have many interests in common. As long as workers are divided on any basis, ethnic or otherwise, they can be played off one against the other. Only by joining forces in a united front can they enforce their demands against management. Many workers have difficulty in seeing this point, although once they have experienced a disastrous strike broken by the use of "scab labor" they are usually more willing to overlook ethnic differences for purposes of collective bargaining. In various industries in the South unions have accepted Negroes to protect themselves against a competing source of labor.

Social distance is frequently reduced in the face of danger. Those who face danger or privation together often forget their ethnic differences, for they are reduced to a common denominator. Conflict against a common foe often creates a sense of solidarity, for those on each side depend upon one another for victory. In no situation are men thrown closer together than in infantry combat, where numerous situations arise in which one's very life depends upon the courage and skill of his comrades. Studies reveal that definitions of ethnic categories undergo marked changes when men go under fire together. Most American soldiers in World War II were not familiar with the brilliant battle record of the 369th Infantry Regiment—the "Harlem Hell Fighters"—in 1918.[8] They therefore assumed that Negroes were

[7] Feldman, op. cit., pp. 271–73.

[8] Arthur W. Little, From Harlem to the Rhine (New York: Covici–Friede, 1936).

cowardly and undependable, and rumors of the poor performance of the 92nd Infantry Division reinforced their beliefs. When Negro platoons were incorporated into white companies on an experimental basis, therefore, there was much opposition. After going into combat together, seven divisions containing such platoons were studied, two of the divisions drawing their men predominantly from the South. The men in companies containing the experimental platoons gave overwhelming approval of the performance of Negro troops in combat; those who were not in mixed companies retained their stereotyped conceptions. The redefinitions that occurred in combat, however, did not extend into garrison duty, where difficulties arose, especially over the dating of European women.[9] During the Korean War the critical shortage of riflemen made integration necessary, and the policy of incorporating Negro troops worked so well that it subsequently became standard procedure in the U.S. Army.[10] Even in less dangerous situations men who struggle together against a common opponent tend to become closer. Members of different ethnic groups who have participated together in team sports often remain lifelong friends, for each can remember countless instances of mutual assistance.

Patterns of segregation are more readily broken in those activities in which a high value is placed upon individual ability. Thus, Tumin reports that in Guatemala the one activity in which Indians and Ladinos participated on an equal basis was the playing of the marimba, in which skill was the only consideration.[11] Dedicated artists, athletes, artisans, musicians, and writers tend to evaluate one another in terms of performance rather than conventional position. Performers in the same field have much in common, and they can appreciate one another's problems. From experience they know how much toil is involved in developing highly specialized skills. They realize just how difficult it is to do outstanding work, and they respect any man who turns in a brilliant performance. They also know that their cheering audience contains many who have no real under-

---

[9] Stouffer *et al., op. cit.,* Vol. I, pp. 587–95. Cf. Georg Simmel, *Conflict and the Web of Group–Affiliations* (Glencoe, Ill.: The Free Press, 1955), pp. 87–123; and Coser, *op. cit.*

[10] David G. Mandelbaum, *Soldier Groups and Negro Soldiers* (Berkeley: University of California Press, 1952); and Lee Nichols, *Breakthrough on the Color Front* (New York: Random House, 1954).

[11] Tumin, *Caste in a Peasant Society, op. cit.,* p. 187.

standing of their work. Sympathetic role-taking is easier among such persons, and fast friendships often develop among them long before such inter-ethnic contacts are generally approved. Initial breaks in the color line often come when an accomplished person of unquestioned stature in the dominant group accepts a promising apprentice from a minority group, trains him, sponsors him, and then fights for his right to perform. In the United States the entertainment industry has provided an important avenue of upward mobility for many individuals from underprivileged groups.[12] This is an area in which talent is of paramount importance.

Intellectuals also tend to evaluate one another in terms of ability rather than conventional rank. Scientists and scholars dedicated to the advancement of knowledge in their field appreciate the work of a man who makes important contributions, regardless of his pedigree. In ancient Rome, where learned slaves were used as tutors, doctors, and readers, close friendships developed between them and their masters. When Pliny the Younger went to his country estate, he often asked educated slaves to accompany him, for he enjoyed their conversation. Emperors from Claudius to Trajan selected advisors from among slaves, and other ministers also delegated important tasks to them. Because of numerous objections to this practice Hadrian finally established the policy of choosing imperial advisors only from members of the Equestrian Order, but many slaves continued to perform important tasks.[13] In the medical profession today doctors of various ethnic groups must work together during epidemics. They must also cooperate to maintain certain minimum standards of performance and to enforce a code of ethics. Even when a color line is strictly enforced in the rest of the community, professional men of minority groups often receive special consideration. Within the social world of each profession, however, members of different ethnic groups are sometimes assigned somewhat different roles.[14] In modern mass societies a great many intellectuals are employed in bureaucratic organizations—hospitals, universities, corporations, and governmental agencies. Bureaucracies are characterized by rationality; they are dominated by rules, procedures, and impersonality. Tasks tend to be

[12] Cf. Sidney Willhelm and Gideon Sjoberg, "The Social Characteristics of Entertainers," *Social Forces*, **XXXVII** (1958), 71–76.

[13] Jerome Carcopino, *Daily Life in Ancient Rome* (London: Rutledge, 1946), pp. 52–65.

[14] Cf. Solomon, *op. cit.*

distributed on the basis of achievement rather than status; otherwise work becomes inefficient and morale disrupted. Those who are working in bureaucracies are more likely to be promoted on the basis of ability, and members of minority groups may achieve considerable prestige.

The reduction of social distance is apparently easier among people whose social status is low. Although they learn the conventional norms that make up the color line, children more often than adults approach one another as individual human beings. In neighborhood gangs boys evaluate one another in terms of their fighting ability, courage, athletic skills, and sense of decency and fair play. As they grow older, they become more conscious of ethnic differences. In segregated areas juvenile gangs tend to identify on an ethnic basis, although in peripheral zones the gangs are often mixed.[15] Ethnic differences tend to be relatively unimportant among those engaged in contraband activities. Money-lending at illegal interest rates, smuggling and selling prohibited goods, providing sexual pleasures for money—all such enterprises bring members of different ethnic groups together. Those who are engaged in illicit activities become interdependent; they have to trust one another, for they cannot turn to the authorities to enforce violations of their agreements. Furthermore, many activities of the underworld require daring, imagination, and skill. Thus, men and women win recognition among their peers on the basis of their personal attributes. If the most skillful safecracker in an area happens to be a member of an ethnic minority, he is nonetheless acknowledged as a master craftsman. Denizens of the underworld have no accepted standing in the larger society; they are shunned by respectable people in dominant and minority groups alike. In such circles, therefore, men and women interact as human beings to a far greater extent than is possible elsewhere. Although stereotyped conceptions of ethnic groups are probably more widely held in the working classes, among the poor there tend to be fewer attempts to enforce segregation. In Puerto Rico, for example, ethnic differences do not matter among the poor, but consciousness of kind becomes more apparent as one moves up the social ladder. In public little attention is paid to skin color, but when public policy is not

---

[15] Cf. Salisbury, *op. cit.*; and Frederick M. Thrasher, *The Gang* (Chicago: University of Chicago Press, 1927).

at issue and community controls are not operative, much color consciousness is manifested in the middle and the upper classes.[16]

Persons who find themselves on the frontiers of inter-ethnic contact, those who associate with outsiders long before the practice is widespread, are generally acutely self-conscious. Members of the dominant group are careful not to offend and go out of their way to be friendly. If members of the minority group resent being called by their given names, a special effort is made to learn surnames and to use titles. Special invitations are extended to acquaintances of minority groups to attend parties at which they can meet a carefully selected circle of friends. Gifts are exchanged, and everything is done to see that such persons are made comfortable. Some women seek out men of minority groups to demonstrate that they are not "prejudiced." Some even develop pride over what they are doing, make an ostentatious display of good will, and earn the scorn of their fellows—and of members of the minority group—as "do-gooders."

Members of minority groups who find themselves in the role of the trail-blazer also become acutely conscious of their responsibilities, and informal norms arise among them to protect the chances of others who will come after them. Those who make up the vanguard believe that by exercising restraint they can break down barriers of segregation and thus make things easier for those to follow. During the decade after Jackie Robinson became the first Negro to play major league baseball, more than 50 others won berths on the various teams. In spite of their close cooperation in games with their white and Latin American teammates, most of them did not mingle off the field. Invitations extended to them by white players were usually declined, and the Negro stars formed their own circle. Because of their high salaries and fame, they became part of the elite in the Negro social world. Unwritten rules developed among them to minimize friction on the clubs, to avoid difficult problems in dealing with white players from the South, and to make desirable public appearances. Young men first breaking into a team were taken aside and given instructions so that they would not upset the arrangements inadvertently. They were taught how to dress and to behave so that they would not elicit unfavorable judgments. A number of informal

---

[16] Charles Rogler, "Some Situational Aspects of Race Relations in Puerto Rico," *Social Forces*, XXVII (1948), 72–77; and Tumin and Feldman, *op. cit.*, p. 233.

understandings arose: a Negro baseball player did not get his hair straightened; he did not criticize another Negro in front of a white player; he did not fight other Negroes in melees in which players from both benches rushed onto the field. All players realized that becoming involved with white women would lead to trouble, and the practice was strongly discouraged. An argot developed in the group, and this private slang was shared by Negroes who were still playing in the minor leagues. Thus, when one of them joked about "race" in veiled terms, all of the Negroes would laugh while the others did not know what was happening. Most of the stars became "race men," those who identify strongly with the interest of Negroes.[17]

As increasing numbers in minority groups become acculturated, numerous occasions arise for them to come into close contact with members of the dominant group. Whether or not these opportunities are pursued depends upon the individuals involved. Being in close and frequent contact over a long period of time does not necessarily result in intimate friendships. Where a color line is breaking down, it is often the persons of subordinate rank who maintain reserve. For example, studies of American Jews living in communities that are predominantly Gentile indicate that most of their closest friends are Jews. Even those who feel that they *should* make friends with some Gentiles find that they feel closer to Jews. It is easier to be with them; there is less strain in achieving a relaxed and informal relationship. They feel that they can speak more frankly when there are no outsiders present; they can not only say derogatory things about them but can also speak more candidly about themselves and their own problems.[18] Even when others no longer act differently toward them, years of differential treatment in the past and expectations built up since childhood make members of ethnic minorities defensive. But *some* of the people in daily contact do become intimate friends. Even when the elders maintain their reserve, members of the younger generation grow up among friendly individuals of other ethnic categories and have little difficulty in establishing close ties.

As individuals of different ethnic categories live together, attend school together, play together, or fight together against a common

[17] Robert Boyle, "The Private World of the Negro Ballplayer," *Sports Illustrated*, XII (March 21, 1960), 16–19, 74–84.
[18] Gans, "Park Forest," *op. cit.*; and Kramer and Leventman, *op. cit.*, pp. 104–10.

foe, increasing numbers on both sides form friendships across the color line. Friends see one another as distinct human beings, not merely as instances of categories. Once this recognition takes place, sympathetic identification becomes possible. When it is assumed that the other person is much like oneself, seeing him in an embarrassing situation elicits sympathetic reactions. As long as someone is an object with which there is no identification, his inner experiences need not be considered in dealing with him; hence, one may inadvertently humiliate him, not even realizing that he might be offended. When the person becomes a "you," however, one imputes the same feelings to him that he himself experiences in similar contexts. It is the establishment of a sense of identification that transforms relationships among men. Then, stereotyped conceptions break down, and communication becomes more efficient.

We have already noted (in Chapter 10) that the identification of another person as a human being arises from getting to know him as a unique object. Apparently this sense of being fundamentally alike arises from an appreciation of individuality. Social distance is reduced when people see one another as they actually are, when they get beneath the conventional façade of politeness; relaxation of personal reserve makes this possible. The inadequacy of popular categories becomes obvious in joint participation in a variety of transactions, for those who see one another in many different contexts have an opportunity to see several sides of each other's personalities. Appreciation of another person as a unique human being is also facilitated when people share many hours during which each is free to pursue his predilections. Another condition that facilitates the reduction of social distance is face-to-face interaction. In direct contact the participants become familiar with one another's idiosyncrasies. Furthermore, expressive movements betray all kinds of inner dispositions that one ordinarily hides from strangers. In moments of fear, anger, or joy, one reacts spontaneously and without self-consciousness and thus "gives himself away." It is in such critical moments that others gain insight into his personality.[19]

Many reformers have attempted to create good will by sponsoring fellowship programs in churches to bring people of different ethnic categories together in an atmosphere of friendship. Although

---

[19] Cf. Charles H. Cooley, "The Roots of Social Knowledge," *American Journal of Sociology*, XXXII (1926), 59–79.

such affairs have sometimes led to a transformation of beliefs, the results have often been disappointing. Since the intentions of the participants are sincere, why have they not been more successful? A church is precisely the type of setting in which a conventional façade is likely to be maintained, where everyone is polite and maintains personal reserve. The mere mixture of people on this basis can result in the reinforcement of stereotyped conceptions and even greater hostility. Unless considerable acculturation has already taken place, members of minority groups feel out of place. Their cheap clothing, their inadequate command of the language, and their poor manners make them feel too severely handicapped. At many of these meetings the participants are unequal; they are awkward gatherings at which the rich offer cakes and condescension to the poor.[20] As long as the guests act in terms of protocol, each does what he is supposed to do, and no one reveals his individuality. Thus, social distance is not reduced, and conventional beliefs about each other are reaffirmed.

The relaxation of some barriers does not result in sudden and widespread interaction of people across the color line. Close contacts generally occur first in highly institutionalized contexts—such as in classrooms or in organized athletics. For a long time only a few members of minority rank are accepted informally. But opportunities arise that did not exist before. Those who desire to contact outsiders may do so openly, providing models for others with less courage. At first only a small number establish personal relations with outsiders. Those who are involved find it increasingly difficult to think of others in terms of a rigid set of attributes, and little by little their friends and their children also learn that outsiders are not all alike. The color line breaks down first in small groups. Then, the matter becomes a subject of public discussion. Many arguments arise over the desirability of mixing. As an increasing number in minority groups become acculturated, many of the arguments of those opposing integration appear ridiculous. As more and more people alter their stereotyped conceptions, there are changes in custom and in law. A system of ethnic stratification is transformed only when the redefinition of a category of human beings enjoys consensus, not when a few individuals have changed their minds.

[20] Cf. Frazier, "Race Contacts and the Social Structure," *op. cit.*, 8; and Mannoni, *op. cit.*

The Redefinition of Ethnic Categories

As the inhabitants of a common territory become culturally more and more alike, ethnic categories undergo redefinition. The process generally requires several generations, although it can happen quickly. Kluckhohn and Strodtbeck have suggested that *the rate and the degree of integration of various ethnic minorities into American life depend upon the extent to which their values are congruent with those of the dominant group,* and in general this appears to be true.[21] A remarkable case is that of the Nisei, Americans of Japanese ancestry, whose reassessment occurred under the most unfavorable circumstances imaginable—during and soon after a war against Japan. In 1942, all persons of Japanese ancestry had been evacuated from their homes on the Pacific Coast and interned, a move that enjoyed widespread public support. Japanese were regarded as treacherous, as potential "fifth columnists" and saboteurs, and surveys reveal that American citizens were included in this category.[22] A year later a number of Nisei were released to fill critical manpower shortages, and government agencies appealed for tolerance on the ground that the enemy might retaliate against Americans who were prisoners in Japan. At the same time an attempt was made to distinguish between the loyal and the disloyal, and segregated military units were established for men willing to serve in the U.S. Army. Nisei who entered the labor market in the Midwest and the East soon won the support of their employers, some of whom openly expressed a preference for them over other workers. Along with pleas for better treatment of all ethnic minorities in a nation fighting for democratic ideals, the federal government gave widespread publicity to exploits of the 442nd Regimental Combat Team, which soon became one of the most highly decorated units in the U.S. Army. The awesome reputation won by Nisei infantrymen among American combat troops in Europe followed them home, and officials participating in ceremonies honoring these war heroes missed no opportunity to de-

---

[21] Kluckhohn and Strodtbeck, *op. cit.,* pp. 25–26. Cf. J. Lyng, *The Scandinavians in Australia, New Zealand, and the Western Pacific* (Melbourne: Melbourne University Press, 1939), pp. 149–50.

[22] Hadley Cantril and Mildred Strunk (eds.), *Public Opinion: 1935–1946* (Princeton: Princeton University Press, 1951), pp. 380–81.

nounce the injustices of the evacuation program. Job applicants were no longer turned down for their Japanese ancestry; credit and desirable housing became more readily available; and during the decade after the war the Nisei became in many walks of life a favored minority group. Although the circumstances were unusual, studies suggest that the general hypothesis applies. In their characterizations of Nisei, employers and fellow workers stressed those cultural attributes prized in the American middle class: cleanliness, politeness, intelligence, and dependability. The new stereotype of the Nisei worker included those traits that managers themselves possessed and valued in others, and Nisei were often addressed with a respect not accorded to white employees of working-class backgrounds.[23]

In most cases there is a long period of transition during which individuals vary in the extent to which they enforce barriers of segregation. When standards of conduct no longer enjoy consensus, each individual is free to pursue his personal preferences. When ethnic categories are in the process of being redefined, several types of orientations are commonly found. Some people retain the old beliefs; others declare that minority peoples are all right as long as they stay among themselves. Some persons establish friendly ties within limited contexts—in church, at work, or in classrooms—but otherwise maintain their distance.[24] Others find from a single friendship that all human beings are alike and go out seeking more contacts. Still others go out of their way to make friends with people who are different and boast of the heterogeneous origin of the population. During transitional periods meanings of ethnic categories vary, and each individual has a somewhat different conception of the units. In some cases there may be more than one conception of a category; thus, some make a distinction between a "good Jew" and a "bad Jew," retaining the stereotyped conception for the latter. Personality differences are important; some individuals are quite rigid in their manner of looking at the world and are quite insensitive to contra-

---

[23] William Caudill, "Japanese–American Personality and Acculturation," *Genetic Psychology Monographs,* **XLV** (1952), 3–102; and Alan Jacobson and Lee Rainwater, "A Study of Management Representative Evaluations of Nisei Workers," *Social Forces,* **XXXII** (1953), 35–41.

[24] Cf. R. D. Minard, "Race Relationships in the Pocahontas Coal Field," *Journal of Social Issues,* **VIII** (1952), 29–44; and Melvin L. Kohn and Robin M. Williams, "Situational Patterning in Intergroup Relations," *American Sociological Review,* **XXI** (1956), 164–74.

dictory evidence. For such persons closer contacts only confirm their suspicions and reinforce views they already had.[25]

During the transitional period there are frequent discrepancies between words and deeds. Individuals who verbally support patterns of segregation fail to enforce them in their actual encounters with members of minority groups. In the 1930's LaPiere travelled through various parts of the United States with a Chinese couple, and the three were only once refused service by innkeepers. Later, when he wrote to the places where they had stopped, asking for reservations for the Chinese, more than 90 per cent indicated that they had a policy of "nonacceptance" of Orientals.[26] On the other hand, some persons who insist that they are not prejudiced do make distinctions when they come into actual contact. Thus, in some *avant garde* circles white women who take pride in their "open-mindedness" engage in sex relations with Negro men; some of them declare that they prefer Negroes because they are more "natural" and "primitive." [27] In much of Latin America an ostentatious display is made of a public policy of "nondiscrimination." In some of these countries, however, it is customary in forming a cabinet to choose representatives of all shades of skin color, and similar quotas are assigned in less important transactions.[28] Recently the LaPiere experiment was repeated, indicating the extent to which the color line in the United States has changed. Two white women and a Negro woman went to 11 restaurants in a fashionable northeastern suburb, and they were served in all of them without incident. Subsequently a letter was sent to each of the restaurants, asking for reservations for a mixed party. When none of them replied, each was approached by telephone. Although none flatly refused, it was apparent that all were unhappy at the prospect. Some managers tried to dissuade the caller from coming to the restaurant; others insisted that they took no reservations; still others requested a personal interview to talk things over. They insisted that they themselves were not prejudiced but that their customers might object. All of them wanted to avoid the charge of

[25] Cf. Adorno *et al., op. cit.;* and Rokeach, *op. cit.*

[26] Richard T. LaPiere, "Attitudes vs. Actions," *Social Forces,* XIII (1934), 230–37; and "Type Rationalizations of Group Antipathy," *op. cit.* Cf. Brookover and Holland, *op. cit.*

[27] Cf. Eberhard and Phyllis Kronhausen, *Pornography and the Law* (New York: Ballantine Books, 1959), pp. 229–32; and Rigney and Smith, *loc. cit.*

[28] George E. Simpson, "Haiti's Social Structure," *American Sociological Review,* VI (1941), 641.

"discrimination" and feared legal action. In the end five accepted the reservation, two of them in writing.[29]

As people in different ethnic categories become more alike, the *distinctions lose their utility*. Categories of human beings, like all other popular concepts, emerge in the efforts of men to develop a meaningful orientation toward their environment. As long as members of different ethnic groups *are* different, such classifications are useful, for they enable men to approach one another with fixed expectations. Being able to anticipate what the others are likely to do, each can participate more effectively in cooperative transactions. But as people become more and more alike, stereotyped conceptions become useless; in fact, they often result in serious errors. As increasing numbers discover that their beliefs are unrealistic, they lose confidence in the scheme of classification. At first they treat their immediate associates as exceptions, but as exceptional cases multiply, they discard the category as useless. The color line rests upon a set of popular beliefs, and when an increasing proportion of the populace conclude that the old beliefs are ridiculous, conventional barriers become more difficult to enforce. One by one the laws requiring segregation are repealed. This usually happens, however, after a long period has elapsed during which most people had ceased to pay any attention to the regulations.

The various symbols of ethnic identity become less and less important, for they no longer designate significant differences among men. A Negro surgeon cannot be regarded as defective in intelligence, and one would feel silly inquiring into his preference for watermelons or disposition to fight with razors. His dark complexion indicates nothing more than the fact that some of his ancestors came from Africa, an irrelevant consideration as far as his surgical skill is concerned. In much of Latin America skin color and facial characteristics are becoming less important as status symbols. In Brazil, for example, Indians and Negroes are disappearing as distinct ethnic units. The new categories are Branco and Preto. This is not to suggest that there is no longer any awareness of skin color, for intermarriage between persons on extreme ends of the color scale is still discouraged. Darkness is still reminiscent of slave origins, but it can

---

[29] Bernard Kutner, Carol Wilkins, and Penny R. Yarrow, "Verbal Attitudes and Overt Behavior Involving Racial Prejudice," *Journal of Abnormal and Social Psychology*, XLVII (1952), 649–52.

be compensated for by other qualities. Although darker people are still concentrated in the lower classes, there is no absolute barrier to upward mobility, and many persons of unmistakable African ancestry are classified as Branco and are so treated by their associates. One popular expression is that "a rich Negro is a white man, and a poor white man is a Negro." Consciousness of ancestry still remains, but the status of a person in Brazilian society depends more up his cultural attributes. Hence, class has become the more important basis for distinctions.[30]

Names undergo transformation, and they become progressively less reliable symbols of ethnic identity. The changes are not necessarily attempts to hide ancestry; in many cases the major considerations are practical. Given names usually change first. Many immigrants to the United States were embarrassed at having a name that their co-workers could not pronounce and gave their children American names. When they did not, the children themselves adopted names of their own choice. Thus, in American schools one encounters such combinations as Peggy Chaudhuri, Sean Pellegrini, Françoise Wong, and Moses Yamaguchi. In European colonies natives who sought an education also found it convenient to adopt the naming practices of their rulers. Family names are also changed. Sometimes only the spelling is altered, or the name may be shortened for convenience. Among practices common in the United States was translating the name into English; thus, Gutjahr became Goodyear, and Morgenstern became Morningstar. Sometimes a phonetic approximation of the old name was adopted; Kukman became Cook. Or a portion of the old name was transformed phonetically; Mihajlovic became Michael. Some abbreviated or simplified their names without trying to make them sound English; thus, a long Greek name might be reduced to Pappas. People usually retain their initials, but very little else. Those in the public eye—professional entertainers in particular—have generally adopted Anglo-Saxon names; thus, reading the names of American movie stars gives one the impression that the United States is a country settled predominantly by people from the British Isles. A somewhat more accurate indication of ethnic

---

[30] Pierson, "Race Relations in Portuguese America," *op. cit.* Cf. Roger Bastide and Pierre van den Berghe, "Stereotypes, Norms, and Interracial Behavior in Sao Paulo, Brazil," *American Sociological Review,* **XXII** (1957), 689–94; and Wagley, *op. cit.*

origins is provided by the line-ups of college football teams; the immortal Knute Rockne of Notre Dame is said to have quipped, "If you can't pronounce them, they're hard to lick." But even the names on athletic programs are no longer indicative of ancestry. As intermarriage becomes widespread, names become even less reliable indices of ancestry.[31]

Members of the younger generation, who have never lived under a well-established color line, find it difficult to understand why their elders insist upon making meaningless differentiations. They know that distinctions are made, but they see them as matters of historical interest. When they encounter someone who does draw the line, they are astonished, seeing the individual as an anachronism. They find it peculiar that someone who is otherwise intelligent should feel this way. Kramer and Leventman report that many American Jews of the third generation see little difference between themselves and Gentiles other than their professed religion, and many of them wonder why their parents stress Jewish traditions and "Jewishness" as much as they do.[32] Thus, similar questions arise on both sides of a crumbling color line.

As ethnic categories are redefined or discarded, opposition to full participation by those who had once been set apart dwindles. As members of minority groups gain access to communication channels of the dominant group, their acculturation occurs at a faster rate, and those who had once been culturally distinct become even more alike. The subtlety of some of the changes and the speed with which they may occur is demonstrated by the already-cited study by Efron on the gestures of New Yorkers. The gestures used by children of Jewish and Italian immigrants differed considerably from those of their respective parental groups; furthermore, the movements of the younger people in the two groups were very similar. Members of the younger generation used fewer gesticulations generally, and the more assimilated they were the more they departed from the traditional patterns of their parents.[33] People are generally unconscious of this type of behavior; except for professional actors, few make deliberate attempts to learn bodily gestures. Yet these changes occurred in a single generation.

[31] Adamic, *op. cit.*, pp. 47–50, 128, 131–34.
[32] Kramer and Leventman, *op. cit.*, pp. 169–204.
[33] Efron, *op. cit.*

As increasing numbers become acculturated and assimilated, almost all of the distinctive traits that had once set an ethnic group apart become transformed. The only attributes to remain are those that are irrelevant to status. Food habits are usually among the last to change. This is not surprising, since dietary preferences are formed early in life. In many cases these differences assume a new significance. In the United States today it is considered fashionable to be familiar with exotic foods, and dietary differences are no longer a stigma. Just as Gypsy music and dancing have become incorporated into Spanish life, many other practices of minority groups have been adopted in other lands. When this happens, these marks no longer serve as the basis for invidious distinctions.

Thus, a *cumulative process* is set into operation, and unless organized opposition develops once-different ethnic groups become integrated. The establishment of communication channels is the key to the breakdown of minority groups and their eventual incorporation into the larger society. As once-alien peoples become acculturated, there is a relaxation of conventional barriers. This in turn facilitates further communication, which in turn makes people more alike culturally—until in the end they share common perspectives. Under such circumstances a minority group can continue to maintain its identity only if there is organized resistance—either from a powerful segment of the dominant group or from those within who insist upon separate development. There is still considerable resistance to the integration of Negroes into American life, but this appears to be weakening. The history of Jews and of Gypsies suggests that even in groups that place great emphasis upon self-perpetuation assimilation into the surrounding society is going on constantly and that the group tends to weaken whenever external hostility is absent. Jewish communities in the United States were held together at first by a common religion, then by a concern for the welfare of fellow Jews, and then by anti-Semitism. The question has been raised: if anti-Semitism declines, what will be left to hold the group together? [34]

Furthermore, with the reduction of social distance, once-different peoples tend to become physically alike. Some somatic changes occur from the adoption of a different diet. In a classic study published

[34] Oscar Handlin, "Changing Patterns in Group Life in America and Their Implications for the American Jewish Community," *Journal of Jewish Communal Service*, XXXIV (1958), 347–53.

in 1911 Boas showed that the children of immigrants differed in stature from their parents—changing in the direction of the traits of those among whom they lived.[35] A number of studies have since confirmed this finding. Although Shapiro found that Japanese immigrants to Hawaii differed from those who remained behind, he also found that those born in Hawaii were taller than their parents.[36] Since there is no evidence of genetic changes, it would appear that body form is affected by climate and diet. What is inherited genetically is not a combination of traits but the capacity to develop certain traits under given conditions. Therefore, when environmental conditions change, some somatic changes are bound to occur.[37]

Adoption of the grooming techniques and cosmetics of the dominant group also brings acculturated members of ethnic minorities more in line with standards of the larger community. In each culture certain attributes are highly valued, and all people in the area try to approximate these ideals. With the development of the media of mass communication European standards of feminine beauty have spread throughout the world. A glance at film stars of the Far East—Yu Ming of China, Netty Herrawatti of Indonesia, Yoshiko Yamaguchi of Japan, Kasma Booty of Malaya, Amalia Fuentes of the Philippines, or Supan Buranapim of Thailand—reveals that they are all beauties by Western standards. Widespread acceptance of the ideals of another culture works considerable hardship on many women in minority groups, for their physical attributes are largely limited by inheritance. Traits such as chubby legs, flat noses, protruding lips, or kinky hair cannot easily be transformed. Yet with the expenditure of considerable time and effort many women do manage to approximate what their parents would have regarded as alien standards.

In disappearing minority groups the selection of mates is based upon criteria used in the dominant group. The more successful men are likely to marry women who are considered most attractive, and

---

[35] Franz Boas, "Changes in Bodily Form of Descendants of Immigrants," *United States Immigration Commission Reports,* Vol. XXXVIII (Washington, D.C.: Government Printing Office, 1911).

[36] Harry L. Shapiro, *Migration and Environment* (London: Oxford University Press, 1939).

[37] Dobzhansky, *op. cit.,* p. 88; Bernice A. Kaplan, "Environment and Human Plasticity," *American Anthropologist,* LVI (1954), 780–800; and Marshall T. Newman, "The Application of Ecological Rules to the Racial Anthropology of the Aboriginal New World," *ibid.,* LV (1953), 311–27.

their offspring are likely to approximate more closely the appearance approved in the larger community. In Timbuctoo, women of lighter complexion were regarded as more attractive, for the Arabs, who were lighter than the others, held the highest rank.[38] Among Americans of Japanese descent some men consciously avoid women with thin eyes, short legs, and other features commonly found in Asia; thus, some women who would otherwise be eligible may never marry or reproduce. In Brazil, the more successful men tend to marry lighter women. The Preto try to "cleanse the race" by seeking out women lighter than themselves.[39] Among the Aborigines of Australia many women showed a preference for white men. After four or five generations of contact the children have gotten lighter and lighter, and many are now indistinguishable from the general population. Although some of the elders objected to "watering down" their stock, many openly favored mixture, for lightness of skin and hair enhanced the chances of attaining respectable status.[40] In time, therefore, especially in the upper classes, there is an approximation of the physical characteristics approved in the dominant group. This kind of selective reproduction, if carried on without interruption for centuries, makes once-distinct groups almost impossible to detect.

American Negroes have always made distinctions among themselves on the basis of skin color, being far more sensitive to shades of difference than white people. Disparaging remarks were constantly exchanged by lighter and darker Negroes about each other's appearance. For a long time Negroes were getting lighter on the whole because of miscegenation and preferential mating. Cultural ideals had been established through participation in a society dominated by lightly-pigmented people, and lighter women, especially those with many Caucasoid features, were much in demand. In recent years, however, the conditions favoring miscegenation—plantation life, the shortage of white women, the availability of Indians—have gone. Furthermore, Negroes are developing "race pride." Darker Negroes have long insisted that "yellow" skin is ugly, charging that light Negroes have too much white "blood" and are therefore untrustworthy.[41] It is possible, therefore, that the trend will be reversed

---

[38] Miner, *The Primitive City of Timbuctoo, op. cit.,* p. 175.
[39] Pierson, "Race Relations in Portuguese America," *op. cit.*
[40] Berndt and Berndt, *op. cit.,* pp. 65–67, 197–99, 256.
[41] Rose, *op. cit.,* pp. 63–64; Melvin Seeman, "Skin Color Values in Three All-Negro School Classes," *American Sociological Review,* **XI** (1946), 315–21; and

temporarily. Offspring will not become lighter than the lighter of their parents, and those who "pass" into the general population will marry white people so that the forsaken Negroes will not benefit from their genes.[42] Furthermore, since the differential fertility rate for Negroes is like that of other Americans, there is more reproduction in the lower classes.[43] This suggests that the overall pigmentation of the group may become somewhat darker, if the category is perpetuated.

With sustained association, then, people become alike. As the groups become more alike culturally and physically, objections to intermarriage recede. As miscegenation becomes widespread, a new physical type develops after several generations—as in the case of the Mestizo in Latin America. New physical types evolve through natural selection; although this is a biotic process, sex relations and reproduction depend upon cultural norms. Intermarriage is not a random affair; much depends upon opportunities for close contact. A study of intermarriage among the Chinese in New York in the 1930's reveals, for example, that the largest percentage of those marrying outsiders were restaurant and laundry workers.[44] Studies in New Haven reveal that even when persons from different European countries married, they tended to remain within the same religious group. Thus, the Irish, the Italians, and the Poles—all Catholics—tended to marry each other more than other ethnic groups.[45] Once intermarriage becomes an accepted practice there is a cumulative effect, for children of mixed marriages are even more likely to intermarry.[46] In fact, what constitutes intermarriage depends upon the boundaries of ethnic groups, and in a changing society these become blurred. A

Warner, Junker, and Adams, *op. cit.*

[42] William H. Kephart, "Is the American Negro Becoming Lighter?" *American Sociological Review,* XIII (1948), 437–43.

[43] Lee and Lee, *op. cit.* Cf. D. F. Roberts, "The Dynamics of Racial Intermixture in the American Negro—Some Anthropological Considerations," *American Journal of Human Genetics,* VII (1955), 361–67.

[44] Shepard Schwartz, "Mate Selection Among New York City's Chinese Males, 1931–38," *American Journal of Sociology,* LVI (1951), 562–68.

[45] Ruby J. R. Kennedy, "Single or Triple Melting Pot? Intermarriage in New Haven, 1870–1950," *ibid.,* LVIII (1952), 56–59. Cf. August B. Hollingshead, "Cultural Factors in the Selection of Marriage Mates," *American Sociological Review,* XV (1950), 619–27; and Hildegard B. Johnson, "Intermarriage Between German Pioneers and Other Nationalities in Minnesota in 1860 and 1870," *American Journal of Sociology,* LI (1946), 299–304.

[46] Jerold S. Heiss, "Premarital Characteristics of the Religiously Intermarried in an Urban Area," *American Sociological Review,* XXV (1960), 47–55.

blond American whose ancestors came from Lithuania who marries a brunette whose ancestors came from Italy may not regard their match as an *inter*marriage; they both conceive of themselves as Americans. During the latter phases of the integration of ethnic groups, then, people of diverse origins marry freely. In this manner new physical types are continually evolving, for human evolution has not ceased.[47]

The Establishment of a New Moral Order

As the inhabitants of a community become more alike, a more inclusive ethnic category gradually develops, and in time the descendants of people who had once regarded one another as fundamentally different identify as being of a kind. Ethnic categories that had once been important disappear as they lose their utility, and they are replaced by a new way of classifying human beings. The usual sequence is the acculturation of persons of subordinate rank, their assimilation to the perspective of the esteemed group, and their eventual integration through general acceptance. As the new classification becomes accepted as natural, it provides the basis for a new moral order. Unity need not rest on the presumption of common ancestry. In times past people have been united by a common religion; another basis of unity has been loyalty to a charismatic leader—Alexander the Great, Charlemagne, or Genghis Khan. In modern times people have identified with one another primarily along lines of national loyalty. Especially in time of war other differences have become secondary, and everyone has been expected to unite on this basis. This lends support to the contention of Sir Henry Maine that society was first organized on a kinship basis but with permanent settlement was transformed into a political unit on a territorial basis.

The formation and acceptance of a new classification system may be facilitated by a government program of nationalization. Laws may be passed against treating minority peoples differently from others; in some cases it may become illegal even to use an ethnic epithet. Such laws are not especially effective unless they are supported by public opinion; in the United States today, for example, most middle-class

---

[47] Cf. Theodosius Dobzhansky, *Mankind Evolving* (New Haven: Yale University Press, 1962); and Robert K. Merton, "Intermarriage and the Social Structure," *Psychiatry*, IV (1941), 361–74.

parents forbid their children's use of such epithets, even though they were quite commonplace only a generation ago. Immigration may be prohibited so that consciousness of kind within minority groups will not be further reinforced. Through a planned dispersion of minority peoples the dominant group may effect a change in cultural milieu and thus make it more difficult for minorities to maintain their solidarity. Various promotional schemes may be used to persuade members of minority groups that they are really like everyone else. A national language may be established, and all competing languages may be discouraged. Inducements may be offered to those willing to divest themselves of their old ethnic identity, such as the right to receive a free education, to establish a business or profession, or to hold public office. During the nineteenth century such measures were used by the Germans toward Poles, the Russians toward Germans, and by the Hungarians toward various minorities in the Balkans. Although attempts at nationalization in Europe and in Southeast Asia have had only limited success, they have met with popular approval in much of the Western Hemisphere, especially in Brazil and the United States. In present-day Israel Jews from many cultural backgrounds are being molded into a single ethnic group and nation.

As the trend toward integration gets under way, reformers and spokesmen for minority groups frequently join forces in a drive to abolish vestiges of the old distinctions. In the United States a number of interest groups have cooperated with minority group organizations in campaigns against the color line. The communications industry has been subjected to considerable pressure, and among the important changes that have occured since World War II has been the manner in which minority peoples are characterized. Although minority groups had received sympathetic treatment in a number of motion pictures in the past, a great many movies had tended to reaffirm ethnic stereotypes. There has been a definite change of policy. When *Island in the Sun*, released by Twentieth-Century-Fox in 1957, showed a love affair between a Negro labor organizer and a white woman, there were vehement protests in the South, but the picture was accepted without incident in the rest of the country. Since that time countless movies have been made of Americans of diverse ethnic origins in sympathetic roles, openly condemning ethnic stereotypes and depicting those who make distinctions as being unfair, vicious, or stupid. Popular movie idols have been portrayed consistently as having an understanding attitude toward different ethnic groups, while it has invariably been the villain who uses epithets and picks on innocent victims; perhaps this has been more important than the plots. At the same time national magazines as well as radio and television networks have reported news on the color line either impartially or from a standpoint slanted in favor of the national policy of desegregation. There is evidence from many sources—public opinion polls, the passage of F.E.P.C. laws, and sociological studies—that there has been a marked decline in condescending and hostile orientations toward minority groups. It appears that the younger generation of Americans has fewer objections to the intermingling of ethnic groups and somewhat more interest in meeting individuals with exotic backgrounds.

Once public opinion appears to favor integration, advocates of continued stratification are forced to assume a defensive stance. Since "prejudice" is condemned, they are no longer able to attack their foes openly without making themselves vulnerable to serious countercharges. Even those who confess privately to antagonistic feelings toward some ethnic group or other are reluctant to make such admissions in public. For a time, therefore, views that are expressed publicly may vary considerably from those that are actually held. In New Zealand, for example, the national ideology is that there is no "color bar," and political leaders often condemn "bigots" in South Africa and the United States. There is a widespread belief, however, that the chasms between Maori and Europeans cannot be bridged, and in urban areas the Maori have difficulty in getting housing. Periodically some incident brings these latent hostilities to light.[48] During the transitional period, then, there are many charges and countercharges of hypocrisy. "Race prejudice" has come under scathing attack on the American scene. There has been little public sympathy for the *apartheid* program in South Africa. Many people who would not care to eat with Negroes have supported on principle laws that prohibit the exclusion of Negroes from restaurants. As the desegregation issue came to a head many Americans were inclined to look with disgust upon the South as a backward area—an impoverished region populated by ignorant, superstitious, and immoral "hillbillies." National press coverage not only favored Negroes, but protesting Southerners

[48] Ausubel, *Maori Youth, op. cit.,* pp. 42–44, 48–50, 114–15; and Hawthorn, *op. cit.,* p. 23.

often found it difficult to get a hearing. In January, 1958, when some 350 Croatan Indians raided a Ku Klux Klan meeting in Robeson County, North Carolina, forcing the hooded members into undignified flight, national reaction was one of contemptuous laughter. Since the Indians had used firearms, they had clearly violated the law, but no one was arrested. One national magazine quipped, "Bad medicine for the Klan," and printed pictures of jubilant Indians showing off their trophies.

Political pressures are brought to bear upon those who persist in making distinctions. Once it becomes agreed that "discrimination" is wicked, politicians, clergymen, and others attack their foes vigorously—sometimes with self-righteous indignation. In the United States accusing fingers have been pointed at voluntary associations—country clubs, lodges, sororities—that do not accept members of minority groups, and officials who defend such policies have found themselves without the support of community leaders, facing spokesmen for hostile groups before an unsympathetic public. Since the desegregation troubles started in the South, institutions of higher learning there have not only lost many of their best students and professors but have found it almost impossible to recruit new faculty members from outside their own region.[49] In the European colonies in Africa expatriate clubs to which Europeans could withdraw after work were attacked by nationalists as symbols of racism. As national independence approached, Africans had to be admitted, not because the members wanted them, but because the clubs were impotent to resist.[50] In some areas the clubs closed down rather than give up their exclusiveness.

Men are not always free to act in terms of their personal desires; they are called upon to play conventional roles. Thus, a person who dislikes some ethnic group may have to speak in favor of tolerance and understanding. Executives, public officials, or professional men are under constant pressure to express publicly views that are acceptable. They meet their obligations by speaking as if these remarks were their own. Particularly if he thinks that he is saying it well, a man may begin to believe what he had originally said while enacting a

[49] Russell Middleton, "Racial Problems and the Recruitment of Academic Staff at Southern Colleges and Universities," *American Sociological Review*, XXVI (1961), 960-70.

[50] L. Proudfoot and H. S. Wilson, "The Clubs in Crisis: Race Relations in the New West Africa," *American Journal of Sociology*, LXVI (1961), 317-24.

role. Thus, participants in promotional campaigns may succeed in convincing themselves, even when they are less successful with their listeners.[51]

When favorable conceptions of ethnic categories are attributed to one's reference group, most men comply. This is revealed in a study of a neighborhood in a midwestern city in which a large number were employed in two highly unionized plants. The CIO union had a policy of "non-discrimination," and the management of both plants treated all workers alike. In the neighborhood, however, there was a property owners' association organized for the purpose of keeping Negroes out of the area. The data showed a willingness to accept Negroes in the work situation and a reluctance to have them move into the area. The more active an individual was in the union, the more likely he was to hold to the approved union view toward Negroes; the more one was involved in the neighborhood association, the more he was likely to be against having Negroes as neighbors. Many individuals appeared to be acting inconsistently, acting one way at the plant and the opposite way at home. These men were not necessarily hypocrites; in each situation they were complying with the demands of a different reference group.[52] Similarly, many English civil servants might have been personally anti-Semitic, but they did not allow their private convictions to obtrude upon the impartial administration required by their office. Thus, there was little differential treatment of Jews in England.[53] In an experiment with American college students DeFleur and Westie took those who held extreme pro-Negro and anti-Negro views and asked each to pose for a photograph with a Negro of the opposite sex. Some agreed, and others declined. Approximately one-third of the subjects acted contrary to their personal convictions, complying with what they believed to be the expectation of their peer group.[54]

When there is a displacement of reference groups, there may be a drastic change in the meaning of ethnic categories. When an individual begins to participate in a new group in which he wants to be

[51] Cf. Carl I. Hovland, Irving L. Janis, and Harold H. Kelley, *Communication and Persuasion* (New Haven: Yale University Press, 1953), pp. 215–40.

[52] Dietrich C. Reitzes, "The Role of Organizational Structures," *Journal of Social Issues*, IX (1953), 39–44.

[53] Howard Brotz, "The Position of the Jews in English Society," *Jewish Journal of Sociology*, I (1959), 99.

[54] Melvin L. DeFleur and Frank R. Westie, "Verbal Attitudes and Overt Acts," *American Sociological Review*, XXIII (1958), 667–73.

accepted, he experiences strong pressures to conform. If he finds that his new associates regard him as "prejudiced," he complies overtly with their standards. He ceases to make derogatory remarks and is careful not to offend. When he realizes that the others mingle with various categories of people as a matter of course, he begins to feel ashamed of his private convictions. Friendly contacts with members of other ethnic groups lead gradually to a change in his own orientation. Soon the category is redefined, and the old feelings subside. Imperceptibly he develops a new set of meanings that resemble those of others in his new reference group.[55] Pearlin found that changes in conceptions of Negroes took place in a Southern college for women, where the prevailing view was more favorable than what was found in most homes. Students who were least "prejudiced" were found to be those whose ties to pre-college groups were weak; 12 per cent of those willing to accept Negroes were people who had drifted away from home and had even clashed with their parents. On the other hand, 31 per cent of those who continued to reject Negroes reported no conflicts at home and maintained close ties with their parents. When asked with whom they discussed their personal problems, 80 per cent of those who accepted Negroes indicated that they went to some college group, but 45 per cent of those who rejected Negroes indicated that they took their problems home. Thus, whether or not conceptions were transformed depended upon the extent to which reference groups were displaced.[56] Recent studies show that the extent to which an individual is responsive to the demands of reference groups also depends upon his level of self-esteem. Those who are unsure of themselves are more likely to conform.[57]

After a period of sustained contact ethnic groups that were once convinced that they could never get together become so much alike that their actual differences become superficial and unimportant. This becomes especially noticeable if the community is invaded by other newcomers who are markedly different; the presence of an alien group makes the people already there conscious of how much they

[55] Cf. Daniel Glaser, "Dynamics of Ethnic Identification," *ibid.*, XXIII (1958), 31–40.

[56] Leonard I. Pearlin, "Shifting Group Attachments and Attitudes Toward Negroes," *Social Forces*, XXXIII (1954), 47–50.

[57] Cf. James E. Dittes, "Attractiveness of Group as Function of Self-Esteem and Acceptance by Group," *Journal of Abnormal and Social Psychology*, LIX (1959), 77–82.

have in common. Those who had been in minority groups no longer see themselves as being set apart in an inferior position but as an integral part of the society. They assume that they are like the others and become indignant at any kind of differential treatment. If the third party is a dangerous foe, the contrast is even greater, and this facilitates integration. Even when noticeable differences remain, anything that is likely to produce internal dissension is withdrawn from communication.[58] Explicit statements are made by leaders that genetic lineage is unimportant, and past differences are minimized. In 346 B.C., during the war against Persia, Isocrates, an Athenian educator and writer, appealed in *Panegyricus* for Greek unity; he contended that "Hellenes" no longer suggested a "race" but a mental outlook, that the term should be applied to those who shared a common culture rather than those with common "blood."[59] During World War II, in supporting the proposal that a special combat team of Japanese–Americans be formed, President Roosevelt wrote, "The principle on which this country was founded and by which it has always been governed is that Americanism is a matter of mind and heart; Americanism is not, and never was, a matter of race or ancestry."

As a new system of classifying human beings emerges, lines of demarcation are redrawn, and people conceive of themselves in different terms. Although the process of integration is not yet complete, new ethnic groups are developing throughout the Western Hemisphere. In Mexico, for example, previous ethnic distinctions have been officially abolished, and social stratification is based more on cultural traits rather than known ancestry. Actually, the physical differences shade so imperceptibly into each other that it is now impossible to draw a line in these terms; in many communities Indians have disappeared altogether. Even those who acknowledge Indian ancestry are reluctant to speak an Indian language; there are villages in which no one speaks any language but Spanish, although some admit that their parents spoke some Indian tongue.[60] Since the Portuguese who colonized Brazil mixed freely with the other ethnic groups, miscegenation

[58] Robin M. Williams, "Unity and Diversity in Modern America," *Social Forces*, XXXVI (1957), 1–8.

[59] S. Davis, *op. cit.*

[60] Roger Owen, "Marobavi: A Study of an Assimilated Group in Northern Sonora," *Anthropological Papers of the University of Arizona*, No. 3 (Tucson, 1959); and Whetten, *op. cit.*, pp. 52–53.

was widespread, and most Brazilians today are Mestizo.[61] Although they still make distinctions between the Branco and the Preto, they conceive of themselves basically as Brazilians. In the United States the first generation of each immigrant group from Europe was set apart as alien, but succeeding generations have established themselves in various parts of the American class structure. Most white Americans speak freely of their ancestry and in most social circles just what part of Europe one's forebears came from is not a matter of great importance.

Once a new category has been established, diversity of lineage tends to be overlooked. An official history is proclaimed for the whole group, and everyone adopts it as his own. Goethe once noted that history was constantly being rewritten, not so much because of the discovery of new facts but because of the changing perspectives of historians. Each new generation of scholars has somewhat different interests and becomes sensitized to different aspects of the recorded past, and their depictions are usually altered more from selection than from deliberate invention. Long-forgotten events suddenly assume new importance; new heroes emerge, and others are forgotten. This is certainly true of the collective memories of ethnic groups. In the United States it is not uncommon for a child of Chinese ancestry, writing a composition on "When Grandmother was a Little Girl," to describe the perils she faced as she crossed the prairies in a covered wagon! All American children relive the glories of their "Founding Fathers" who crossed the Atlantic Ocean on the *Mayflower*—even though most of their ancestors were at that time scattered throughout the globe. Argentines take pride in the "purity" of their European ancestry and look down upon other Latin American countries; special scorn is reserved for Brazil. Although the percentage of Mestizos in Argentina is actually quite high, heterogeneity is denied, and national history is traced back to Europe.[62] The Ngoni, a proud people in Northern Rhodesia, insist that they are more closely related to Europeans than they are to their other neighbors, whom they disdain, and their version of history justifies this contention.[63] The accepted his-

---

[61] Freyre, *op. cit.*; and Pierson, *Negroes in Brazil, op. cit.*

[62] Cf. Carl C. Taylor, *Rural Life in Argentina* (Baton Rouge: Louisiana State University Press, 1948).

[63] James A. Barnes, "The Perception of History in a Plural Society," *Human Relations*, IV (1951), 295–303.

tory of a group is important, for the members form their self-conceptions against this backdrop.

As the new category becomes widely accepted, the people regard
themselves as one of the natural divisions of mankind. Just as Americans descended from immigrants from all over Europe believe that
they are of a kind, members of ethnic groups in other parts of the
world assume that they too constitute a species—a type of human
being that has always had its present characteristics. The new arrangements therefore appear to be a part of nature and become part of a
moral order.

With the integration of ethnic groups, at least one of the old
categories disappears. Proponents of cultural pluralism view such a
possibility as a calamity, believing that a genetic strain thereby becomes extinct. This type of thinking rests on the false assumption
that mankind can be divided into a finite number of "racial" groups,
that there is an ideal prototype of each, and that there was once a
Golden Age of "race purity." Many people think of "races" as self-
contained units, each a finished product—a stable, static set of genes.
Actually, what is called a "race" is but an episode in the evolutionary
process.[64] The disappearance of an ethnic category does not mean the
death or destruction of human beings or their progeny. Ethnic groups
disappear when consciousness of kind is altered, when people change
their self-conceptions. What happens is not that a genetic strain ceases
to exist but that loyalties are realigned. What disappears is a concept
—a category with which some persons had identified. There will still
be progeny, but they will be classified in a different manner. Thus, if
Negroes are eventually integrated into American life, dark skin will
not disappear. It will cease to be important as a status symbol—just
as red hair or grey eyes are unimportant today. Many Negroid
features will persist in the American population, but those who bear
them will not be singled out for differential treatment because of
them. To underscore what was said earlier, what is commonly called
the "race problem" is essentially psychological, not genetic.

In some communities fairly consistent differences in inherited
traits between members of higher and lower classes have been
noted. In India members of the higher castes tend to be lighter in

[64] Cf. Dobzhansky, "The Genetic Nature of the Differences Among Men,"
op. cit., pp. 102–113.

complexion than those in the lower castes.[65] Although all Japanese claim to be descended from a sun goddess, studies by physical anthropologists suggest that there may be two general body types that correspond roughly with differences in class. It has also been suggested that there were similar differences between the patricians and plebeians in ancient Rome.[66] Such survivals suggest that these people were descended from different ethnic groups, that one had conquered the other but that in time they had become integrated. Although they identified as being of a kind, a larger proportion of those with attributes of the dominant group remained in the more privileged classes. Thus, slight differences that may be discernible within ethnic groups may be products of past conquests that had been forgotten.

What happened in ancient Japan, India, or Rome is shrouded in mystery, but there are other cases in which historical data are available. Excellent examples of the emergence of new ethnic groups from the integration of diverse peoples are provided by the history of England and by what is happening in Latin America today. Twice in the memory of people still living, English soldiers have been sent to the European continent to aid their French allies, and they fought and died valiantly for England. Judging from the tenacity with which the fighting occurred, one would think that human beings in this part of the world had been divided from the beginning into Englishmen, Frenchmen, and Germans. Conveniently, no one mentioned the Norman conquest of the British Isles in 1066 and the long and bitter conflict that followed between the Normans and the Saxons. Few mentioned the close ties between Germans and Saxons, although this has long been an accepted part of English history. Actually the British Isles were invaded by so many ethnic groups that it is now very difficult for scholars to trace origins.[67] This led Maine to write, "England was formerly inhabited by the English; the English today are the people who inhabit England." The process of integration is now going on in much of Latin America and can be observed. In Yucatan,

---

[65] Ghurye, *op. cit.*, pp. 46, 55, 176.

[66] Cf. Roland B. Dixon, *The Racial History of Man* (New York: Scribner's, 1923), pp. 139–51; Eugene Pittard, *Race and History*, trans. V. C. C. Collum (London: Kegan Paul, Trench, Trubner, 1926), pp. 403–10; and Shapiro, *Migration and Environment, op. cit.*

[67] Cf. Carlo Cipolla, *The Economic History of World Population* (Baltimore: Penguin Books, 1962), pp. 96–97; Otto Jesperson, *Growth and Structure of the English Language* (New York: Doubleday, 1955); and Homans, *Sentiments and Activities, op. cit.*, pp. 127–81.

Williams classified 828 people into five groups on the basis of physical traits and arranged them from most Indian to least Indian in appearance. A correlation with occupations ranked by prestige showed that those with Indian characteristics predominated in low-prestige occupations and were almost absent from high-prestige positions.[68] All these people conceive of themselves as Mexicans, but there is still a disproportionate distribution of physical types by classes.

Summary and Conclusion

People who live in the same community for a long period of time become more and more alike. They also become increasingly interdependent as their careers become intertwined in joint enterprises of all kinds. As members of minority groups become acculturated, they acquire competitive advantages, and some are able to win more desirable places in the division of labor. As increasing numbers move up the social scale there are more opportunities for contact, and personal friendships are established across the color line. This facilitates further communication, and acculturation continues at an accelerated pace. As the people become even more alike, distinctions that had once been made lose their utility and in time are discarded. With the reduction of social distance there is less objection to intermarriage, and the people become more alike physically as well. In time those who occupy a given territory identify with each other as a kind, in spite of the diversity in their ancestry. A new moral order then arises to support the revised system of classification, and the more inclusive category comes to be viewed as one of the natural divisions of mankind. With acculturation, then, ecological patterns are transformed. This facilitates communication and the establishment of intimate interpersonal ties, and this in turn results in the formation of new institutional patterns.

Because of the short-term perspective with which we generally look at the contact of peoples, reformers sometimes believe that the resolution of a given instance of conflict would mean the solution of the "race problem." Actually the disappearance of some ethnic minority as it is integrated into a larger population only means that a new ethnic group has come into existence, something that has happened

[68] George D. Williams, "Maya–Spanish Crosses in Yucatan," *Papers of the Peabody Museum of American Archaeology and Ethnology*, **XIII** (1931), No. 1.

hundreds of times in the history of mankind. But the integration of ethnic groups does not herald in the millennium. When the new group meets another ethnic group—which in turn had been formed elsewhere through the same processes—the whole cycle begins all over again. This has been one facet in the history of the human species—the incessant, recurrent processes whereby alien peoples have become integrated only to meet more foreigners.

Conclusion

CHAPTER 20

Human Nature
and Ethnic Differences

In virtually all instances of inter-ethnic contact, no matter how great the initial differences between the groups, people sooner or later become integrated into a single unit and convinced of their descent from common ancestors; the only exceptions are those few cases in which one group has been completely exterminated. The occasional groups that have managed to retain their identity in spite of numerous contacts with outsiders—as the Chinese and the Jews—are neither genetically nor culturally "pure"; there is evidence of extensive mixtures with the peoples with whom they lived. Data from anthropology, history, and genetics show that no matter how ingenious the devices to maintain separation, the long-term result has usually been integration. Policies such as *apartheid* have been attempted before and have delayed integration; when seen in historical perspective, however, they are but transitory phases in a seemingly inexorable process.

Why does contact result so frequently and regularly in the breakdown of ethnocentrism and the establishment of consciousness

glance this is contrary to expectations. Since all men
and see outsiders in unflattering ways, differentiation
ation of separate ways of life would appear to be a
ondition. Historically, however, the opposite has been
is to be accounted for? While no final answer can yet
may consider as a hypothesis a recurrent theory of
human nature.

Review: A Theory of Ethnic Stratification

We may begin with a recapitulation of the theory of ethnic
stratification presented in this book. The population in most communities is heterogeneous, the people being divided along class, religious,
or ethnic lines. The relationship between such groups varies; it may
be one of coexistence, stratification, or sustained opposition. Those
who occupy the same habitat, however, sooner or later become involved in a common web of life; in most cases they participate in a
common economic system. Ethnic stratification is one aspect of community organization; individuals are placed in a hierarchical order,
not in terms of their personal aptitudes but in terms of their supposed
ancestry. An ethnic group consists of people who conceive of themselves as being alike by virtue of common ancestry, real or fictitious,
and are so regarded by others. Where a color line develops the fate of
an individual depends upon the manner in which he is classified. The
color line is a particular type of social structure, and a theory of ethnic stratification therefore can be derived from broad sociological
generalizations about social structures.

Social structures are patterns of concerted action. In any situation *the efficiency with which concerted action can be carried out
depends upon the extent to which consensus exists among the participants.* Where there is a high degree of consensus, individual participants share common understandings as to what each is supposed to
do. Hence, each can anticipate what the others are likely to do and
can organize his own contribution to the collective product. The
overt behavior of each individual is subject to some measure of social
control in that he feels constrained to comply with the expectations
he imputes to others. Thus, ethnic stratification persists as long as people on both sides of the color line approach one another with common
expectations of how each is to act in the presence of the other. The

color line consists of a set of conventional norms. Where there is a high degree of consensus, violations of norms arouse emotional reactions; deviating acts appear immoral, perhaps even unnatural. In situations that are not adequately defined, however, individuals are more free to pursue their personal interests; where values are in short supply, competition and conflict may take place.

Consensus is built up and maintained in a communicative process; shared perspectives are shaped and reaffirmed through a succession of gestural interchanges. Thus, people who can communicate effectively are able to develop common understandings; culture is a perspective shared by members of a group. It follows that _the extent to which different individuals are able to develop consensus depends upon their participation in common communication channels_. If new communication channels are established, those who had been strangers are able to share their experiences and in time become more alike culturally. A number of theorems follow. If people in different ethnic groups who occupy similar subordinate positions communicate, they eventually develop a common culture and become alike. The extent to which members of a minority group become acculturated to the way of life of the dominant group depends upon the extent of their participation in the communication channels of their rulers. To the extent that people in service occupations develop common channels, they develop a distinct way of life, regardless of ethnic differences. Factionalism within minority groups develops from differential participation in channels serving the dominant group. To the extent that two generations of a minority group participate in different sets of communication channels, they develop different perspectives and have difficulty in understanding each other.

Inability to communicate effectively makes concerted action difficult, if not impossible. An individual who partakes in a single communication channel develops only one perspective and is ethnocentric. Ethnocentrism is the tendency to use the values of one's own group as an absolute standard for judging everyone else; an ethnocentric person is likely to misunderstand those with different cultural backgrounds. Groups that are isolated from each other have their own communication channels, and they develop separate cultures. Thus, as long as minority groups remain isolated, they retain their own way of life and remain ethnocentric. Conquered people are more likely to retain their isolation under indirect rule; those so governed are less likely to join other subjugated parties in nationalistic movements. Anything that interferes with effective communication makes concerted action more difficult. When members of diverse ethnic groups speak different languages, cooperation between them tends to be clumsy. Ethnic segregation cuts communication channels and results in the development of separate cultures. When members of different generations in an ethnic group speak different languages, they have difficulty in understanding each other, and family disorganization is a frequent result.

Efficient communication is an inverse function of social distance. Social distance refers to the extent to which individuals identify with one another, ranging from sympathetic identification, in which the other person is presumed to be just like oneself, to the conviction that he is fundamentally different in kind. Social distance varies with the type of knowledge individuals have of one another; the more personalized the knowledge, the greater the sense of identification. Anything that interferes with the acquisition of personalized knowledge prevents the lowering of social distance, and anything that facilitates acquisition of such knowledge tends to lower social distance. In intimate circles, where social distance is low, communication is easy; sentimental considerations supersede conventional obligations, and the color line tends to disappear. In formal situations, where social distance is somewhat higher, communication occurs in a customary manner; stereotyped conceptions of ethnic groups are maintained in spite of close and frequent contacts, and in many cases there are conventional norms that prevent the development of personalized knowledge, such as etiquette and segregation. In conflict situations, where social distance is at a maximum, communication between foes is almost impossible.

Patterns of concerted action persist as long as communication channels remain unchanged. Therefore, to understand changes in the color line we must focus upon changes in social distance. Social distance tends to be reduced in situations in which men are likely to see one another as individuals—when they are conscious of their interdependence, when they are faced by a common foe, or when they are in contexts in which a high value is placed on personal achievement. Social distance is also reduced among people who are culturally alike, for it is much easier for them to understand one another. As members of minority groups become acculturated, they become more like those in the dominant group and attempt to identify with them. As this happens, acculturation occurs at a faster pace. As these persons become even more alike, social distance is further reduced. Integration thus occurs through a cumulative process. When similarities between oneself and others are emphasized, consciousness of kind develops. On the other hand, when members of the same ethnic group develop incompatible interests, they are split into factions and become more and more isolated from each other. When privileged members of minority groups become acculturated, they become different from the masses, and their sense of identity is reduced. In these ways lines of demarcation between ethnic groups become blurred.

Social structures of all kinds are products of collective adjustments to extant life conditions, and the development and transformation of systems of ethnic stratification can be explained largely in these terms. An attempt is being made to account for social life in terms of response tendencies that are inherent in all living organisms. The first task of life is to live, and men continuously adjust to the succession of situations in which they find themselves. But they rarely do this alone; they must take into account the interests of those around them, and new patterns of concerted action arise as they pursue values while interacting with one another. When life conditions change, some of the old group structures break down. Consensus becomes more and more difficult to achieve, and there is a transitional period marked by trial-and-error experimentation. Misunderstandings and disagreements develop, and individual behavior becomes less subject to social control. In time new patterns of concerted action emerge that are better suited to the changed circumstances. Each color line is an accommodation to the distinctive needs that arise in a situation of contact.

If values are in short supply, individuals compete for them, and new patterns of concerted action emerge initially through natural selection. Status differentials develop as parties with competitive advantages assume positions of dominance. Competitive advantages are those characteristics that make the bearer better fitted to meet the circumstances. Although inherited capacities may sometimes enter the picture, in human beings these advantages are primarily cultural. The size of each ethnic group depends upon migration and rates of growth; hence, relative numbers in a community are set by competition and natural selection. The spatial distribution of ethnic groups also develops through competition, those with competitive advantages occupying the land they most desire. Positions occupied by different ethnic groups in the division of labor are allocated at first through competition, the group with advantages taking the most desirable work. A system of classifying human beings then develops to coincide with the distinctions being made; thus, new ethnic categories develop through a selective process, the more useful distinctions among people being perpetuated.

When competition is intensified, it is transformed into rivalry or conflict. Rivalry develops when competitors are able to identify their opponent and realize that his success will mean their own failure. They then endeavor to outdo their rival, and a contest is carried on within conventional limitations. At first rivals attempt to pursue their respective ends through politics; the maneuvers used are usually legal. When leaders become convinced that their legitimate interests cannot be pursued under the existing order, however, subversive activities begin. Lack of success in rivalry results in frustration, and one common response is aggression. As opposition is intensified, participants in disjunctive transactions become polarized into two opposing camps. Social distance between them increases, and perspectives develop separately on each side. Contrast conceptions are formed, and aggressive acts are unleashed against the foe. When there is acute awareness that success of the opponent is against one's own interest, the major objective becomes the destruction or immobilization of the enemy. In conflict, conventional norms are superseded by considerations of expediency. Although biotic factors—sheer numbers or capacity to adapt to a particular environment—may enter the picture, human beings oppose one another primarily with cultural devices. Victory generally goes to the party with competitive advantages, although these may sometimes be offset by astute leadership. Victory does not necessarily result in the complete subjugation of the losers, but there follows a period of disproportionate enjoyment of the contested values.

Patterns of concerted action initially formed through natural selection become fixed by repetition and eventually become institutionalized. Then, they are reinforced through group sanctions. Thus, the relative size of ethnic groups in a community, their spatial distribution, and their positions in the division of labor become fixed in custom; then, even individuals with the ability to violate the patterns are prevented from doing so. In a well-established society direct competition between parties of different rank is prevented by custom and law. Systems of ethnic stratification are protected by measures that perpetuate social distance, maintain relative competitive advantages, and regulate social mobility. When some of the practices prove inconvenient or painful, an ideology develops that explains and justifies them. Most ideologies arise through natural selection, through sensitivity to ideas that are more useful, and racism is one such tool. Ascendancy of the dominant group may also be protected by cooptation, in which members of minority groups who acquire competitive advantages are incorporated into the ruling group. Thus, a color line arises in competition, but it is maintained in communication.

When life conditions change again, competition is renewed. As the relative competitive strength of the parties changes, new collective adjustments take place, and social structures are transformed. As minority peoples become acculturated, they acquire competitive advantages, especially through education and economic power. The discrepancy between status and power results in demands for reform. Systems of classifying human beings may also change; as people become more and more alike culturally, old distinctions lose their utility and are dropped. A realignment of group loyalties may occur; persons who had once been different find that they have similar interests and identify; those who had been in the same group become split.

Human beings may identify with one another on the basis of a number of criteria, of which ethnic identity is but one. Once they do identify, others of their kind become important agents of social control. Each individual performs for some kind of audience; he controls his conduct to comply with the standards of those with whom he identifies. Each individual forms a self-conception, locates himself within a category, and lives up to the obligations of people in that group. If a new ethnic category is formed, it becomes a key reference group, and behavior becomes subject to its control. When members of a minority group become assimilated, they become responsive to the judgments of a new audience—the dominant group.

Consciousness of kind develops from the consistent reactions of other people. Those who occupy similar positions in a community are treated alike by others; they participate in the same communication channels, become culturally alike, and eventually identify with one another as being alike. The extent to which consciousness of kind develops among subjugated peoples varies with the consistency of their differential treatment. If persons of different ethnic minorities are treated in the same manner, they eventually recognize their common fate, and social distance is reduced among them. When subject peoples are not treated alike, as in indirect rule, they retain their sense of separate identity and remain ethnocentric. As members of ethnic minorities become acculturated, they are approached with more respect, and the more successful come to conceive of themselves as part of the larger community. As they develop a stake in the existing system, they become assimilated to it; if they are accepted, they become integrated into it. When this happens, they become subject to the social control of the larger community. Ethnic groups, then, generally do not share a common genetic strain; they are products of social interaction.

A Recurrent Theory of Human Nature

The consistency with which identity is established with the opening of communication channels implies that human beings are basically alike. When there are barriers to effective communication, they are prevented from realizing this fact; once these walls come down, they recognize their many resemblances. Biologists are generally agreed that the differences among human beings are superficial; with the exception of occasional freaks all men are born with the same number of limbs and organs, and the various biochemical processes occur in much the same manner. All the so-called "races" of mankind can interbreed, passing one of the zoological tests for delineating species. Instinctive reactions to frustration, danger, or fulfillment are the same throughout the world. Furthermore, there is no known human group without some kind of language, and all men are capable of logical reasoning, of solving problems in a rational manner.[1] Thus, the basic differences among human beings are in culture, and the barriers of segregation prevent people from getting beneath their cultural differences.

Yet a realization of the fact that men are biologically alike does not result automatically in the reduction of social distance. Men in conflict are often aware of their zoological similarities and respectful of the intellectual capacities of their foes. Yet they are convinced of

[1] Cf. Boas, *The Mind of Primitive Man, op. cit.*

being fundamentally different. Is there some other trait the detection of which lowers the walls of isolation? There are a great many theories of human nature, and one of the most plausible is a recurrent doctrine emphasizing the importance of *sentiments*. Scholars since the Scottish Moralists have pointed out that human beings throughout the world manifest the same sentiments.[2] Observation of the most exotic groups reveals much that is familiar—mothers cherishing their children, men proud of their achievements, or brothers haunted by guilt as they compete for the same prize. Strange customs often turn out to be only a cloak; the sentiments of men all over the world appear to be alike, regardless of their cultural heritage. This view of human nature seems to be implicit in the European humanistic tradition. The "truths" found in great works of literature turn out upon examination to consist of descriptions of typical experiences of a sentimental nature in recurrent contexts. Thus, men are seen not only as rational creatures but also bound to one another by sentiments. The detection of similar sentiments has much to do with the lowering of social distance.

A convenient summary of this theory can be found in Cooley's *Human Nature and the Social Order.* In speaking of sentiments Cooley was not referring to some mysterious faculty or feeling but to a *relationship* between individuals, such as love, hatred, jealousy, hero-worship, resentment, or respect. Sentiments are relationships that depend upon a capacity Cooley thought only human beings had—the ability to enter imaginatively into the inner experiences of others. Through sympathetic introspection, by imagining how another person must feel, one can anticipate his responses and relate oneself to him in given ways. For example, how can anyone become jealous without some appreciation of the inner experiences of at least two others? Is love possible without role-taking? Human nature is identifiable in terms of the typical ways in which men become involved in one another's lives.[3]

Since the concept of sentiment, as it is popularly used, lacks

[2] Adam Smith, *The Theory of Moral Sentiments* (London: George Bell & Sons, 1880). Cf. Gladys Bryson, *Man and Society: The Scottish Inquiry of the Eighteenth Century* (Princeton: Princeton University Press, 1945).

[3] Cooley, *Human Nature and the Social Order, op. cit.* Cf. Buber, *op. cit.;* Kurt Riezler, *Man: Mutable and Immutable* (Chicago: Henry Regnery, 1951); and Max Scheler, *The Nature of Sympathy,* trans. Peter Heath (New Haven: Yale University Press, 1954).

precision in meaning, it cannot be used for cross-cultural comparisons without better specification. Fortunately, an attempt has been made to define sentiments in behavioristic terms. In a much-neglected work Shand noted that when a man is in love with someone, he experiences tenderness in her presence, anxiety when she is in danger, anger when she is threatened, sorrow when she is absent, joy when she prospers or is restored to him, and gratitude toward anyone who is good to her. If a person hates someone, he has the same set of reactions under the opposite conditions.[4] Men are able to detect the manner in which one individual is related to another by observing his reactions in a variety of contexts. On the basis of a *configuration* of responses, inferences can be made. The significance of Shand's theory is shown by the manner in which people are able to detect intuitively the existence of a love relationship even when the principals deny it. By noticing the look in a person's eye when the love object is present, the irritation that arises when she is flirting with someone else, the spontaneous pleasure that arises when she gains fulfillment—an observer is able to infer that he is in love with her.

Cooley's contention was that sentiments are shaped in primary groups—those small, congenial groups in which most human beings spend their formative years. Human nature is universal because primary groups can be found everywhere. Although the structure of families vary from culture to culture, everywhere the young are brought up among people whom they know intimately. Cliques, families, neighborhood groups, and juvenile gangs can be found in all societies. Regardless of the cultural matrix in which socialization occurs, the problems encountered in adjusting to other human beings are much the same. Men everywhere develop similar curiosities about one another—their emotional reactions, their erotic preferences, peculiarities of their character. There are the same restraints and tensions, conflicting interests, cooperation to attain difficult ends, necessity of curbing aggressive tendencies, and loyalty under conditions of duress and other tests of courage. Everyone is confronted by authority figures of one sort or another and must learn to deal with them in some way. In such contexts children develop their ability to take the roles of others. They learn to respect the interests of others; they also learn to identify with them and to appreciate vicariously their pleas-

---

[4] Alexander F. Shand, *The Foundations of Character* (London: Macmillan, 1920), pp. 35–62. Cf. Shibutani, *op. cit.*, pp. 323–402.

ures and pains. Although some children remain relatively isolated, the vast majority learn to project their inner experiences to others and to sympathize with them. Thus for Cooley human nature was neither organic nor cultural; it was the product of interpersonal relations. Sentiments of people throughout the world have a similar structure because they develop in contexts that are unavoidable. They are not inborn, nor are they acquired in the same manner as conventional norms. They develop as children learn to cope with the demands of the individuals with whom they are in intimate contact.

What makes detection difficult in superficial contacts is that similar sentiments may be manifested in different ways. In the United States vanity is expressed openly in various forms of exhibitionism; those who are vain allow themselves to be seen at best advantage. In many Oriental societies, however, this would be regarded as being in bad taste, and vain men remain aloof, deriving enjoyment by imagining the admiration of others. Outsiders often believe that such individuals are modest and humble; not until they have lived among them for some time do they realize that this is not so. In spite of cultural differences in overt behavior, however, a vain man is unmistakably identified in terms of his outward self-assurance, his inner doubts about his worth, and his acute sensitivity to criticism. Vanity *is* vanity. In different societies men who fall in love make their declarations of affection in different ways—by enlisting the services of a spokesman, by performing feats of valor, by reciting poetry. Men emphasize somewhat different criteria in choosing love objects, but the relationship can be recognized in terms of selfless sacrifices in behalf of the love object, yearning for its presence and sympathetic response, and hostility against anyone who frustrates it. In spite of the diversity of culture, typical sentiments can be recognized because of similarities in the configurations of response that make up the various patterns of interpersonal relations. Human experiences, though infinitely varied, are endlessly duplicated. What men have in common arises in situations that most people know or can understand through their own experiences as human beings, things that all men learn just by living in association with others. In spite of divergencies of time, place, and culture certain experiences are apparently universal. As Cooley put it, everywhere and always men seek honor and dread ridicule, defer to public opinion, and admire courage and disdain cowardice.

People with different cultural backgrounds are able to understand one another because of their common sentiments. The detection of sentiments provides the initial crack through the walls of ethnocentrism. There is a difference between observing strange behavior from the outside and developing an appreciation of it as a participant. The recognition of another person as a human being through his sentiments makes his overt movements more understandable and predictable. External strangeness offers little difficulty once inner experiences are understood. Thus, one can read Vergil's *Aeneid* and conclude that human nature has not changed in 2,000 years; similarly, one can appreciate the novels of Dostoyevsky without knowing much about Russian culture in the nineteenth century. Sentiments enable us to get inside of others; we see the yearning of a lover for the smile of his beloved, the hopes of parents for their children, the concern of a friend for someone in danger. Such characteristics as personal integrity, courage, sense of decency and fair play are not restricted to any ethnic group, and the detection of such traits across the color line makes mutual understanding possible. It is of particular interest to note that Rudyard Kipling's famous lines about the separation of the East and West are cited the world over to show that "blood and water do not mix." Perhaps Kipling the apologist for British imperialism might have endorsed some such argument, but Kipling the insightful observer of human nature certainly did not. The entire stanza reads:

Oh, East is East, and West is West, and never the twain shall meet,
Till Earth and Sky stand presently at God's great judgment seat;
But there is neither East nor West, Border, nor Breed, nor Birth,
When two strong men stand face to face, though they come from
    the ends of the earth! [5]

From time to time situations arise in which some men are accused of being "inhuman." For example, when the mass murders in German concentration camps were disclosed after World War II, it was charged that the Nazis were "beasts." The same charge is sometimes leveled against a father who beats an infant mercilessly and against managers who place the efficiency record of their factory above all other considerations, treating their subordinates like cogs in a ma-

[5] From "The Ballad of East and West" by Rudyard Kipling. Reprinted by permission of Mrs. George Bambridge; Methuen & Co. Ltd., London; and the Macmillan Company of Canada Ltd.

chine. Sometimes a ruthless killer is found who can supply no particular motive for his deeds and admits that he gained considerable satisfaction from observing the agony of his victims as they died. As the man relates gruesome details without any manifestation of remorse, an observer experiences an eerie feeling and concludes that the animal before him is of a different breed. In many cases it is similarly difficult to identify with those who are psychotic. When people laugh at inappropriate times, cry when there is no reason for sadness, or change their sanitary napkins in public, they seem to lack some quality that marks all other human beings. No one is insisting that the employees in extermination centers, psychopathic killers, or victims of schizophrenia should not be classified as *homo sapiens*. Zoologically there is no issue; what is being charged is that these people act in ways that would be impossible for most men, once sympathetic identification is established. Those who are labelled "inhuman" are people who seem to lack sentiments.

When others are recognized as being like oneself, one feels a moral obligation to treat them with some consideration. Brutal or humiliating treatment becomes increasingly more difficult, if not impossible. The manner in which one person can mistreat another without experiencing pangs of guilt depends upon the extent to which he identifies with his victim. It is relatively easy to take the role of someone like oneself; one can readily imagine how he himself would feel if such things were done to him. Thus, identification leads to the establishment of personal claims of a moral nature.

Thus, the boundaries of a moral order are established by the range within which sentiments can be detected. Moral conduct is behavior that has no sanction other than the actor's own sense of right or wrong. Even in a totalitarian dictatorship everyone cannot be watched at all times; there can be no orderly society unless the majority of the people voluntarily inhibit proscribed impulses and conduct themselves in ways they believe to be proper. Concerted action, then, rests in large part upon the self-control of the participants. But most men are unwilling to sacrifice their gratifications without a strong sense of obligation to do so. Within a moral order men feel themselves honor-bound to meet their obligations to other men; hence, there is a sharp difference in the treatment of outsiders. Among the Tibetans studied by Ekvall robbery of a stranger was excusable if not laudable, but robbing another Tibetan was a crime the seriousness of which depended upon the position of the person against whom it was committed.[6] A sixteenth-century settler in the Dutch East Indies made the following defense of his treatment of the natives: "May not a man in Europe do what he likes with his cattle? Even so, does the master here do with his men, for everywhere, these with all that belong to them, are as much property of the master, as are the brute beasts in the Netherlands." [7] Obviously there is no identification.

Breakthroughs in the color line occur when the moral order is extended to include people who had been outsiders. MacLeod reports the experiences of a white settler in California who was participating in a massacre of Indians in the vicinity of his home. After all the adults had been killed, he came upon a group of children who were huddled together in fear. As he looked at their eyes, he could not help but notice how "cute" they were, and he was unable get himself to shoot them with his .56-caliber rifle—because it "tore them up so bad." He had to do it with his .38-caliber revolver.[8] Even in this brutal context partial identification resulted in a change of behavior. Many students of slavery have contended that Christianity killed the institution. As soon as slaves were regarded as men with souls that could be saved and not some subhuman species, they were able to establish claims on their masters. Once identification is established, mistreatment becomes difficult. Each man must live with himself even if no one else says anything; each must be able to develop a reasonably adequate level of self-esteem. He cannot conceive of himself as a decent human being while doing something that he condemns. Thus, the extension of the moral order depends upon overcoming to some extent that "certain blindness" of which William James spoke, of being able to partake vicariously in the lives of others. Once people get close enough to form intimate ties, the color line is doomed. well,

Human beings not only form sentiments toward each other but also toward themselves. A person can address himself with respect, resentment, or contempt. Vanity may be regarded as a form of hero-worship. A man's sense of personal worth is the sentiment he develops

[6] Ekvall, *op. cit.*, p. 70.
[7] K. M. Panikkar, *Asia and Western Dominance* (London: Allen & Unwin, 1953), p. 111.
[8] MacLeod, *op. cit.*, p. 487.

toward himself, and most men react sharply to anything suggesting that their esteem is being threatened. The fundamental problem in the contact of peoples is the preservation of the individual's moral worth in his own eyes. Why should a difference of status be of any importance, especially in a properous community where even members of ethnic minorities can live in comfort? Why are some people in dominant groups so upset about the misuse of status symbols, even when no one has been hurt? Why are some persons so determined to prove over and over their superiority over others? Although unfair employment practices and residential segregation are condemned by members of minority groups who seek advancement, what is resented most of all is lack of respect. It is difficult to develop self-respect if one is not respected by others. Unless men can have self-respect, they will always be discontented, no matter what else they have. Men are willing to fight and even to die for it. Without it they can neither look themselves in the face nor stand before their children without a sense of shame. Many who oppose segregation have no desire to associate with members of the dominant group; they just want to be able to live with themselves—with a sense of dignity.

This principle is recognized in the charter of the United Nations which reaffirms ". . . faith in fundamental human rights, in the dignity and worth of the human person, in the equal rights of men and women and of nations large and small. . . ." Problems of the kind discussed in this book are likely to persist until a society is established in which all human beings, regardless of status, are treated with respect.

Prospects for Inter-Ethnic Contacts

What of the future of inter-ethnic contacts? Scientific knowledge does not provide a crystal ball; it only describes regularities in nature, and forecasts in specific historical contexts—like weather forecasts—are notoriously inexact. Furthermore, the generalizations in this book cannot be regarded as established; the point of view is tentative and must remain so until the propositions have been tested. On the basis of the theory we can only hazard some guesses.

A number of momentous changes can be anticipated. With improved facilities for transportation there will probably be an increasing volume of inter-ethnic contacts. With the birth rate rising throughout the world there are likely to be intensified pressures to migrate into areas with untapped resources. The widespread application of automation is likely to lower demand for unskilled labor, and members of minority groups seem destined to fill the ranks of the unemployed in disproportionate numbers. The rising standard of living in areas undergoing industrialization will probably result in changes in the balance of political power, and those who are now in humble circumstances may entertain dreams of empire. In a world in which one finger pushing a single button could conceivably bring catastrophe to all mankind, the fostering of separation on any basis—ethnic or otherwise—would be an invitation to trouble. Yet there are a number of contexts in which tensions are likely to persist for some time. In the Middle East, for example, many Arab leaders see the founding of Israel as a part of European imperialism and have sworn a vendetta against the new country. There are several other trouble spots.

As Africa enters the industrial age, it seems likely to repeat some of the recent history of Europe. Most of the new nations are not ethnically homogeneous; they have inherited the boundaries of administrative units established by European colonial governments. Some of the people who succeed in establishing self-rule will probably become militant expansionists. Attempts to incorporate within their national boundaries all peoples even remotely related to them are likely to result in territorial claims on neighboring states. A number of ethnic groups will find themselves as underprivileged minorities in nations dominated by their traditional foes. Since rivalries among political leaders often divide people in terms of old ethnic loyalties, revolutionary uprisings and attempted secessions may be expected. But the greatest crisis is likely to come in the Union of South Africa, where even the proponents of *apartheid* appear to sense that their program is doomed to failure. So much resentment has already been generated that it has become difficult for either side to alter its course, and the foes appear headed for disaster.

It is estimated that very soon approximately half the people on earth will be Chinese. Such estimates, of course, are based on the assumption that all the offspring of Chinese now living will conceive of themselves as Chinese. Many Chinese today not only identify in terms of their old and rich cultural heritage but brood over the humiliations suffered in the hands of Europeans and Japanese. The Chinese Communist government has made it clear that it intends to reassert what it regards as the country's rightful place in world affairs, and this program includes the restoration of lost territories. Since Formosa, much of Southeast Asia, and areas in Central Asia now under Russian rule were once governed by China, this could result in serious altercations. Special problems are likely to develop in Southeast Asia, where an estimated 12 million Chinese are now living. Many have retained the Chinese way of life, and they have been persecuted for it. The resentment of the natives against the prosperous aliens in their midst has resulted in a succession of anti-Chinese riots and restrictive legislation. Since most overseas Chinese are not Communists, their ties to China are ethnic rather than ideological. They look to a powerful government in China as a protector against local persecution, and such dependency is likely to strengthen identification. The dominance of Chinese culture will probably spread, even if her political borders do not.

Another likely trouble spot is the United States, where social distance between Negroes and all other Americans will probably increase. Since World War II Negroes have developed new self-conceptions and have been insisting upon equal treatment. The long-festering hatreds have now started to explode in a series of demonstrations, riots, and bombings. As Negroes become more aggressive in their demands, resistance is likely to develop. Communication has already broken down in some communities, and many Negroes are becoming convinced that no white man can be trusted, that there can never be fair play as long as they rule. Differences in perspective make mutual understanding difficult. Negroes view the situation from the standpoint of their collective memories, which include injustices perpetrated centuries ago. But the people to whom their grievances are addressed were largely unconcerned with the color line until quite recently and are not familiar with the historical facts. Hence, they are astonished to find themselves blamed for deeds committed long before their birth by people to whom they are not directly related. Many have never mistreated Negroes and resent the charges. Europeans have long known of problems that arise when unassimilated minority groups live in their midst—sometimes resulting even in the overthrow of the government. Americans now face a similar problem. Secessionist movements such as the Black Muslims have been gaining more adherents and sympathizers, and frankly racist views are becoming more commonplace among Negroes. As these changes occur, Negro leaders are likely to become more militant; otherwise they will lose their followers.

In spite of these seemingly insurmountable difficulties the long-run prognosis for inter-ethnic contacts is the termination of strife. The development of the media of mass communication is likely to break down the walls of ethnocentrism. The increasing availability of translated novels and of foreign motion pictures and television programs should facilitate the establishment of identification, for these channels enable audiences to participate vicariously in the lives of outsiders. As they become better able to understand the lives of people whose cultures are different, they will be able to appreciate that most of their preoccupations and motives are the same. If human nature is indeed universal, more efficient communication will eventually break down ethnic barriers.

With the further development of science and education superstitious beliefs will eventually be replaced by more accurate knowledge. As the belief in "racial" differences is demonstrated to be completely unjustified, an increasing number of educated people will cease making distinctions. In spite of other differences both democratic and Communist ideologies are against invidious distinctions based on presumed ancestry. Thus, on both sides of the "Iron Curtain" official attempts will probably be made to minimize ethnic differences. In time, ethnic differentiation will be seen as a relic of the past. People of future generations will probably look upon inter-ethnic strife in the same manner that religious wars of the past are viewed today. After all, it was only a few centuries ago that Protestants and Catholics were convinced that the world was not large enough for both; only a few centuries before that Christian crusaders and Moslems felt the same way. Their descendants today live together in comparative peace.

Before such transformations take place, however, there will probably be a period characterized by conflicting loyalties—conflicts in obligations to nation, class, ideology, or ethnic group. The Chinese in Southeast Asia will have to decide whether their obligations as citizens in the countries in which they live should supersede loyalties to other Chinese. Arab and Israeli entrepreneurs may find that their interests coincide and that they each have less in common with other members of their respective ethnic groups. Should they join forces? An African Communist may find himself in a situation in which party loyalty requires his acting against the best interest of most other Africans. If so, should he continue to submit to party discipline? Many people today, even those of "liberal" persuasion, assume that ethnic loyalties should prevail and that there is something dishonest about a man who does not acknowledge what he "really" is. If ethnic identity rests upon false beliefs, however, on what rational grounds can such conduct be defended? Such questions will become more commonplace as ethnic stratification becomes less important.

In all probability, then, human beings throughout the world will eventually acknowledge that they are fundamentally alike, descended from common ancestors in the remote past, and that ethnic identity is a matter of little importance. But the passing of inter-ethnic strife will not result in a world without tension and conflict. It is difficult to imagine any complex society without social differentiation of some kind. Men will undoubtedly continue to make distinctions on *some* basis, and they will continue to compete for values in short supply. As long as they do, some of the processes described in this book will persist.

Summary and Conclusion

Human beings throughout the world are fundamentally alike. They share a common anatomical structure; they all have the ability to engage in reflective thought; and they share a pool of common sentiments. Hence, whenever social distance is reduced, individuals recognize their resemblances. The basic differences between ethnic groups are cultural, and conventional norms serve as masks to cover the similarities. Whenever men interact informally, the common human nature comes through. It would appear, then, that it is only a matter of time before a more enlightened citizenry will realize this. Then, there will be a realignment of group loyalties, and ethnic identity will become a thing of the past.

If this theory of ethnic stratification is correct, then all the sacrifices that have been made on the altar of "racial purity" have been based upon superstitious beliefs and have been in vain. The difficulties arose because people who were actually alike believed that they were different. Even casual reflection on the appalling human losses staggers the imagination. Thousands of men and women have been massacred; millions of able men have wasted their talent by being barred from tasks they could perform; intramural strife between advocates of assimilation and cultural pluralism have ended life-long friendships; children in minority groups have gone through life guilt-stricken for resenting their parents; inability to marry a lover in another ethnic group has resulted in countless cases of lifelong grief, and even suicide. One is led to wonder as Hegel did in the prolegomenon of his *Philosophy of History:* "But even regarding history as the slaughter-bench at which the happiness of peoples, the wisdom of states, and the virtue of individuals have been victimized—the question involuntarily arises—to what principle, to what final aim these enormous sacrifices have been offered." Hegel's answer was not quite satisfactory. It would appear that these deeds were but by-products of the efforts of men to live as best they could. As individuals seek a better life for themselves and those with whom they identify, they fight, cooperate, negotiate, and do things that they regret but feel are necessary. The results of these human endeavors include the formation, perpetuation, and disintegration of color lines.

Suggested Readings

The following list is neither comprehensive in its coverage nor representative of the available literature; it contains, for the most part, case studies of specific instances of inter-ethnic contact. Such concrete details will make the general principles discussed in the text more meaningful.

UNITED STATES AND CANADA

Anderson, Elin L. *We Americans: A Study of Cleavage in an American City.* Cambridge: Harvard University Press, 1937. The relative positions of the various ethnic groups in Burlington, Vermont, during the early 1930's.

Dollard, John. *Caste and Class in a Southern Town.* New York: Doubleday & Co., 1957. Patterns of accommodation between Negroes and white people in a Southern community of 75,000 during the early 1930's.

Drake, St. Clair, and Horace R. Cayton. *Black Metropolis.* New York: Harcourt, Brace, 1945. Social organization of the "Black Belt" of Chicago during the interwar years.

Frazier, E. Franklin. *The Negro Family in the United States.* Chicago: University of Chicago Press, 1939. A classic account of evolving family patterns among American Negroes from the days of slavery to the segregated communities in northern cities.

Hansen, Marcus Lee. *The Atlantic Migration, 1607–1860.* New York: Harper, 1961. A narrative of the great migration from Europe and the settlement of the United States.

Hughes, Charles C., and Jane M. *An Eskimo Village in the Modern World.* Ithaca, N.Y.: Cornell University Press, 1960. The breakdown of traditional

Eskimo culture in Gambell, Alaska, following extensive contacts with outsiders.

Key, V. O. *Southern Politics*. New York: Alfred A. Knopf, 1950. A state-by-state analysis of party politics in the South with particular attention to the significance of ethnic identity.

Kramer, Judith R., and Seymour Leventman. *Children of the Gilded Ghetto*. New Haven: Yale University Press, 1961. A comparison of the styles of life developed by three generations of American Jews.

Linton, Ralph (ed.). *Acculturation in Seven American Indian Tribes*. New York: D. Appleton-Century, 1940. A comparative study of the fate of seven Indian tribes following their contact with American settlers, revealing patterns of response and change that varied from one context to another.

Stanley, George F. G. *The Birth of Western Canada*. Toronto: University of Toronto Press, 1961. The way of life of the "half-breeds" in Western Canada and their armed rebellion against the encroachment of the Canadian pioneers.

Young, Pauline. *Pilgrims of Russian Town*. Chicago: University of Chicago Press, 1932. The settlement of Russian Molokans in Los Angeles and the breakdown of their way of life in the second generation.

CARIBBEANS AND LATIN AMERICA

Freyre, Gilberto. *The Masters and the Slaves*. New York: Alfred A. Knopf, 1946. Inter-ethnic contacts on Portuguese plantations during the early history of Brazil.

Haring, C. H. *The Spanish Empire in America*. New York: Oxford University Press, 1947. Development of Spanish colonial institutions in America from the sixteenth century to the Wars of Independence.

Henriques, Fernando. *Jamaica: Land of Wood and Water*. London: MacGibbon & Kee, 1957. The way of life that has developed in Jamaica, with special attention to consciousness of skin color.

Means, Philip A. *Fall of the Inca Empire*. New York: Charles Scribner's Sons, 1932. A history of Peru in the sixteenth century, the period of transition from Inca to Spanish rule.

Murphy, Robert F. *Headhunter's Heritage*. Berkeley: University of California Press, 1960. Changes in the economic and social structure of the Mundurucú Indians of Pará, Brazil, following their participation in the rubber industry.

Pierson, Donald. *The Negroes in Brazil*. Chicago: University of Chicago Press, 1942. Miscegenation, social status of Negroes and Mestizos, class and ethnic relations in Bahia.

Simpson, Lesley B. *The Encomienda in New Spain*. Berkeley: University of California Press, 1950. The rise and decline of a system of forced labor in Spanish Mexico.

Tumin, Melvin M. *Caste in a Peasant Society*. Princeton, N.J.: Princeton University Press, 1952. The unwritten rules governing the relations between Ladino and Indian in San Luis Jilotepeque, Guatemala.

Wagley, Charles (ed.). *Race and Class in Rural Brazil.* New York: Columbia University Press, 1952. Social class and ethnic relations in four rural communities.

Williams, Eric E. *The Negro in the Caribbean.* Washington, D.C.: Associates in Negro Folk Education, 1942. A brief survey of the economic condition and social status of Negroes in various parts of the Caribbeans.

EUROPE

Abrahams, Israel. *Jewish Life in the Middle Ages.* New York: Meridian Books, 1958. The social organization of ghetto life, with an account of variations in the status of Jews in different communities.

Banton, Michael P. *The Coloured Quarter: Negro Immigrants in an English City.* London: Jonathan Cape, 1955. Immigrants from Africa and the West Indies and their concentration in Stepney, London.

Bury, John B. *The Invasion of Europe by the Barbarians.* London: Macmillan, 1928. The gradual movement and assimilation of various Germanic and Gothic peoples to the Roman Empire from the third century, A.D.

Castro, Americo. *The Structure of Spanish History,* Edmund L. King (trans.). Princeton, N. J.: Princeton University Press, 1954. A history of Spain from the period of Roman conquest, with an extended discussion of the position of Moors and Jews.

Diller, Aubrey. *Race Mixture Among the Greeks Before Alexander.* Urbana: University of Illinois Press, 1937. The beliefs and practices of the ancient Greeks in their contacts with "barbarians."

Dubnow, Semen M. *History of the Jews in Russia and Poland,* I. Friedlaender (trans.). Philadelphia: Jewish Publication Society of America, 1920. 3 volumes. A history of Jewish settlements in Eastern Europe, Vol. III containing an account of the Kishinew massacre and other pogroms.

Kann, Robert A. *The Multi-National Empire.* 2 vols., New York: Columbia University Press, 1950. The social and political status of various ethnic minorities in the Habsburg Empire from 1848 to 1919, with an account of their nationalistic movements.

Miller, William. *The Ottoman Empire and Its Successors: 1801–1927.* Cambridge, Eng.: Cambridge University Press, 1936. A history of Turkey in the nineteenth century, with accounts of nationalistic uprisings in Greece and the Balkans.

Seton-Watson, Robert W. *A History of the Roumanians.* Cambridge, Eng.: Cambridge University Press, 1934. The preservation of ethnic identity and culture by the Rumanian people, from the period of Roman rule to World War I.

Zborowski, Mark, and Elizabeth Herzog. *Life is with People.* New York: Schocken Books, 1962. The way of life that developed in the *Shtetl,* small Jewish communities of Eastern Europe.

North Africa and the Middle East

Coon, Carleton S. *Caravan: The Story of the Middle East.* New York: Holt, 1951. The cultures of the major ethnic groups of the Middle East.

Davis, Simon. *Race Relations in Ancient Egypt.* London: Methuen, 1951. Contacts among Greeks, Egyptians, Jews, and Romans from the time of Alexander to the fall of the Roman Empire.

Hourani, Albert H. *Minorities in the Arab World.* London: Oxford University Press, 1947. A survey of the religious, linguistic, and ethnic minorities in Egypt and the Middle East.

Lerner, Daniel. *The Passing of Traditional Society.* Glencoe, Ill.: The Free Press, 1958. Breakdown of the traditional way of life in various parts of the Middle East with the development of transportation and communication facilities.

Magie, David. *Roman Rule in Asia Minor.* Vol. I, Princeton, N. J.: Princeton University Press, 1950. A history of Roman rule of the six provinces in the Middle East, from the period of conquest to the third century, A.D.

Nalbandian, Louise. *The Armenian Revolutionary Movement.* Berkeley: University of California Press, 1963. The formation of Armenian political parties, their struggles against one another and against the Turks.

Patai, Raphael. *Israel between East and West.* Philadelphia: Jewish Publication Society of America, 1953. The cultural diversity of Jewish immigrants to modern Israel and the problems arising from their inability to understand one another.

Tritton, Arthur S. *The Caliphs and Their Non-Muslim Subjects.* London: Oxford University Press, 1930. A treatise, drawn from original sources, on the treatment of Christians and Jews by Muslim rulers.

Africa

Coleman, James S. *Nigeria: Background to Nationalism.* Berkeley: University of California Press, 1958. A comprehensive case study of Nigerian nationalism and the influences of British rule upon its emergence.

Epstein, Arnold L. *Politics in an Urban African Community.* Manchester, Eng.: Manchester University Press, 1958. Urbanization and the development of a native trade union and nationalistic movement in a Northern Rhodesian industrial town.

Hellmann, Ellen. *Rooiyard: A Sociological Survey of an Urban Native Slum Yard.* Cape Town, S. A.: Oxford University Press, 1948. Detribalized natives and their illicit liquor trade in a Johannesburg slum.

Kuper, Leo, Hilstan Watts, and Ronald Davies. *Durban: A Study in Racial Ecology.* New York: Columbia University Press, 1958. A monograph on residential segregation and an official attempt to enforce *apartheid* in a South African city.

Leakey, Louis S. B. *Mau Mau and the Kikuyu.* London: Methuen, 1952. The culture of the Kikuyu, the history of their contacts with Europeans, and the background of terroristic activities.

Mayer, Philip. *Townsmen or Tribesmen.* New York: Oxford University Press, 1961. The contrast between the conservative Xhosa and those who are assimilating to the European way of life in East London, South Africa.

Mitchell, J. Clyde. *The Kalela Dance.* Manchester, Eng.: Manchester University Press, 1956. Origin, nature, and appeal of a favorite African pastime in Northern Rhodesia.

Schapera, Isaac. *Migrant Labour and Tribal Life.* London: Oxford University Press, 1947. A thorough investigation of labor migration in Bechuanaland and its repercussions on native tribal life.

Southall, Aidan W. *Alur Society: A Study in Processes and Types of Domination.* Cambridge, Eng.: W. Heffer & Sons, 1956. Structure of a primitive political state in central Africa and the relationships of the dominant Alur with other tribes.

Sundkler, Bengt G. M. *Bantu Prophets in South Africa.* London: Lutterworth Press, 1948. Religious secession and independent church movement among the natives of South Africa.

ASIA AND SOUTHEAST ASIA

Boeke, Julius H. *The Structure of Netherlands Indian Economy.* New York: Institute of Pacific Relations, 1942. Gradual replacement of the traditional village economy by the plantation system, and the subsequent transformation of social life in the Dutch East Indies.

Chen, Ta. *Emigrant Communities in South China.* New York: Institute of Pacific Relations, 1939. Chinese emigration and its effects upon the emigrants and their communities on the coast of East Kwangtung and South Fukien.

Coughlin, Richard J. *Double Identity: The Chinese in Modern Thailand.* London: Oxford University Press, 1960. A descriptive study of the life and status of the Chinese and their relationships with the Thai.

Ekvall, Robert B. *Cultural Relations on the Kansu-Tibetan Border.* Chicago: University of Chicago Press, 1939. Contrasting types of contact among four ethnic groups—the Chinese, the Chinese-speaking Moslems, the sedentary and the nomadic Tibetans—before the 1949 Communist revolution.

Jones, Francis C. *Manchuria Since 1931.* London: Royal Institute of International Affairs, 1949. The puppet state of Manchukuo under Japanese control.

Lattimore, Owen. *Inner Asia Frontiers of China.* Boston: Beacon Press, 1962. An interpretive history of China, her people, and her relationships with marginal societies.

McCully, Bruce T. *English Education and the Origins of Indian Nationalism.* New York: Columbia University Press, 1940. The introduction of English education and its contribution to the growth of nationalism in India.

Phelan, John L. *The Hispanization of the Philippines.* Madison: University of Wisconsin Press, 1959. Impact on the Philippines of the first century and a half of Spanish conquest.

Ryan, Bryce. *Caste in Modern Ceylon: The Sinhalese System in Transition.* New Brunswick, N.J.: Rutgers University Press, 1953. Castes and caste relations in Sinhalese villages and towns.

Schurz, William L. *The Manila Galleon.* New York: Dutton, 1959. The galleon trade between Manila and Acapulco from 1565 to 1815, and the Spaniards, Filipinos, Chinese, Japanese, and others involved in it.

Wertheim, Willem F. *Indonesian Society in Transition.* New York: Institute of Pacific Relations, 1959. A social history of Indonesia: as a Dutch colony, under Japanese occupation, and following the establishment of an independent state.

OCEANIA AND AUSTRALIA

Ausubel, David P. *Maori Youth.* Wellington, N.Z.: Price Milburn, 1961. An account of acculturation and disorganization among the adolescent Maori, stressing the differences between rural and urban communities.

Berndt, Ronald M. and Catherine. *From Black to White in South Australia.* Chicago: University of Chicago Press, 1952. The status of the Aborigines in South Australia—in the "outback" area, in rural communities, and in Adelaide.

Coulter, John W. *Fiji: Little India of the Pacific.* Chicago: University of Chicago Press, 1942. Fijians, East Indians, and Europeans in a Melanesian archipelago.

Lind, Andrew W. *An Island Community: Ecological Succession in Hawaii.* Chicago: University of Chicago Press, 1938. Patterns of land use and changes in occupational distribution of different ethnic groups in Hawaii.

Oliver, Douglas L. *The Pacific Islands.* Garden City, N.Y.: Doubleday, 1961. The peoples of Oceania, their contacts with different waves of aliens, and their metamorphosis.

Sutherland, Ivan L. G. (ed.). *The Maori People Today.* London: Oxford University Press, 1940. A collection of articles by qualified authors on Maori culture and the intrusion of European civilization.

Worsley, Peter. *The Trumpet Shall Sound.* London: MacGibbon & Kee, 1957. The development of the "Cargo Cult" (a nativistic millenarian movement) on various islands in Oceania as a protest against European colonization.

Yanaihara, Tadao. *Pacific Islands Under Japanese Mandate.* London: Oxford University Press, 1940. A factual report of the transformation of Japanese-administered areas in Micronesia.

Name Index

Subject

Index